INTERNATIONAL LAW AND RELIGION

THE HISTORY AND THEORY OF INTERNATIONAL LAW

General Editors

NEHAL BHUTA

Professor of Public International Law, European University Institute

ANTHONY PAGDEN

Distinguished Professor, University of California Los Angeles

BENJAMIN STRAUMANN

Alberico Gentili Senior Fellow, New York University School of Law

In the past few decades the understanding of the relationship between nations has undergone a radical transformation. The role of the traditional nation state is diminishing, along with many of the traditional vocabularies which were once used to describe what has been called, ever since Jeremy Bentham coined the phrase in 1780, 'international law'. The older boundaries between states are growing ever more fluid, new conceptions and new languages have emerged which are slowly coming to replace the image of a world of sovereign independent nation states which has dominated the study of international relations since the early nineteenth century. This redefinition of the international arena demands a new understanding of classical and contemporary questions in international and legal theory. It is the editors' conviction that the best way to achieve this is by bridging the traditional divide between international legal theory, intellectual history, and legal and political history. The aim of the series, therefore, is to provide a forum for historical studies, from classical antiquity to the twenty-first century, that are theoretically informed and for philosophical work that is historically conscious, in the hope that a new vision of the rapidly evolving international world, its past and its possible future, may emerge.

PREVIOUSLY PUBLISHED IN THIS SERIES

International Law and Empire
Historical Explorations
Edited by Martti Koskenniemi, Walter Rech, Manuel Jiménez Fonseca

The Hidden History of International Law in the Americas
Empire and Legal Networks
Juan Pablo Scarfi

System, Order, and International Law
The Early History of International Legal Thought from Machiavelli to Hegel
Edited by Stefan Kadelbach, Thomas Kleinlein, David Roth-Isigkeit

International Law and Religion

Historical and Contemporary Perspectives

Edited by
MARTTI KOSKENNIEMI
MÓNICA GARCÍA-SALMONES ROVIRA
and
PAOLO AMOROSA

OXFORD
UNIVERSITY PRESS

OXFORD
UNIVERSITY PRESS

Great Clarendon Street, Oxford, OX2 6DP,
United Kingdom

Oxford University Press is a department of the University of Oxford.
It furthers the University's objective of excellence in research, scholarship,
and education by publishing worldwide. Oxford is a registered trade mark of
Oxford University Press in the UK and in certain other countries

First Edition published in 2017

Impression: 1

Published in the United States of America by Oxford University Press
198 Madison Avenue, New York, NY 10016, United States of America

British Library Cataloguing in Publication Data
Data available

Library of Congress Control Number: 2017943887

ISBN 978–0–19–880587–8

Printed and bound by
CPI Group (UK) Ltd, Croydon, CR0 4YY

Series Editors' Preface

Religion, which only a few decades ago many believed and hoped to be slowly vanishing from the world, and especially from the world of international law and international relations, has seemingly made an unexpected, vigorous, and often violent resurgence. 'Today', as Martti Koskenniemi says, 'religion is everywhere.' Both 'religion' and 'international law', as Koskenniemi also reminds us, are capacious categories. Yet even on the most minimal description of a supernatural source of supreme authority and a transcultural, ultimately universal, rule of law, it is evident that any people, any culture that claims to possess the latter does so in part at least because it also once possessed (or in some cases still possess) a belief in the former. Gods or a god have for centuries been taken to be the ultimate source of legal authority, and our ethical premises, however much we may struggle to detach them from the will of any supposed divinity, remain heavily indebted to religious antecedents. This volume examines the degree to which religion, and theological speculation, has indeed determined the shape of modern international law since its beginnings. It is a highly innovative work covering in painstaking detail a subject which, for all its immense and obvious importance, is still relatively uncharted territory. It brings together the three great and interdependent monotheistic traditions: Judaism, Christianity (in its various forms), and Islam, and sets them up in comparison with, and sometimes in contrast to, the prevailing secularist understanding of the 'modern' conception of international law which is still believed to have come into being in the mid-seventeenth century. The volume is innovative, too, in that not only does it bring together a number of distinguished jurists and historians, it also includes writers such as Mousssa Abu Ramadan, Michele Nicoletti, and Pasquale Annicchino who approach the subject from a more theologically informed position. All the essays, despite the diversity of the positions they take, make a powerful claim that no form of international law, no conception of ultimate legal authority, can be made which, however secular it may now be, does not raise questions which were first addressed in theological (if not always religious) terms. In some modern legal systems, most obviously Islam, the distinction between theology and jurisprudence is still virtually non-existent. As Moussa Abou Ramadan explains for Muslim jurists, the key distinction between peoples, and consequently between those who had the right to exercise legal authority and those who did not, is based on a division between Muslims and non-Muslims, and between the 'peoples of the book' (primarily Jews and Christians) and the rest. The ultimate source of law is faith, not, as the Western tradition has always claimed it must be, reason. But if Christians and Jews took a less Manichean view of the sources of sovereignty, the appeal to a law of nature, which is a reflection of, if not identical with, the commands of the deity, pervades all the earlier attempts to create a truly universal code—the 'law of nations'—which could, as the great Spanish theologian Francisco de Vitoria (one of the reputed 'fathers' of International Law and discussed here by Mary M. L. Keys) insisted, also possess the force of positive law. Even Hugo Grotius, so often cast as the originator of modern international law and for so long looked upon as a sceptical companion to Thomas Hobbes was, as Janne Nijman reveals, heavily indebted to a form of Calvinist-Arminian theology; although there remains a strong case that Grotius at least tried to develop a denominationally neutral doctrine of the sources of law which made heavy use of Roman law and which distinguished between genealogical claims (the origin of reason and law lies in divine will) and claims of legal validity and obligation (recta ratio renders law both valid and obligatory).

Neither was the dependence of the concept of a global legal order upon religion limited to the earlier formative periods. The rise of modern positivist international law in the context of the European expansion into Africa and Asia in the nineteenth century was, despite its insistence upon its own secularity, heavily freighted with implicit Christian notions of virtues and obligation bound up in the idea of 'civilization'. The struggles, which have now seeped into all our lives, over the territorial rights in the Middle East are largely expressed in legal terms which depend heavily upon competing view of the various religions involved. Similarly today, the conception of 'human rights', which has led to the creation of what the Argentinian jurist Eduardo Rabossi called an ubiquitous 'human rights culture', although presented as a strictly secular concept, is in fact (as the essays in Part II of the book demonstrate) heavily indebted to Christian, in particular Catholic, understanding of natural rights—one of the main reasons why so many non-Christian peoples, particularly, but not exclusively Muslim, have been so suspicious of it.

If the long history of international law may, indeed, be viewed as struggle towards a secular and thus truly universal law, truly capable of transcending sectarian differences, a central part of that struggle can only be understood as a continuing dialogue, and conflict, with religion. The great sixteenth-century jurist Alberico Gentili's famous petard 'theologians mind your own business', and the insistence that laws could only be a matter for the lawyers, was only the beginning. The end is still not in sight. All the essays in this volume in their varying multifaceted ways will bring us closer to an understanding of how far we have come and how far we have yet to go.

Anthony Pagden
Benjamin Straumann
Nehal Bhuta
July 2017

Acknowledgements

This volume constitutes the research outcome of three years of collaboration among members of the *International Law and Religion* working group set up at the *Erik Castrén Institute of International Law and Human Rights*, University of Helsinki, in 2013. The working group was composed of an international team of researchers who held two meetings in Helsinki and Rome and numerous smaller seminars and interactions. In the course of these years, the editors of the volume have accumulated many debts in various directions. Above all, our heartfelt thanks go naturally to the authors of the chapters for putting their creativity and knowledge not only in their contributions but also in their lively interactions within the group. They made the process of producing this book an altogether enjoyable enterprise, despite the challenges of the topic. The various seminars and workshops were organized under the auspices of the research project 'Intellectual History of International Law: Empire and Religion' funded by the Academy of Finland. We are thankful for the Academy's support. The Finnish Institute in Rome hosted the workshop in the fairy-tale environment of *Villa Lante* on top of Gianicolo Hill. Walter Rech and Manuel Jiménez Fonseca from the project on 'Intellectual History of International Law' in Helsinki helped in the practical work and took active part in our exchanges.

We are grateful to the successive coordinators of the *Erik Castrén Institute of International Law* during the period of the project, Lauri Uusi-Hakala and Sanna Villikka for their support in many organizational aspects of the meetings, and in particular to Mari Taskinen who accompanied us to Rome and helped and facilitated our work at every step. Also we want to thank Maria José Belmonte Sanchez, Katri Mattila, David Scott and Johannes Kramml who helped in different stages of the copy-editing and proofing aspects of the manuscript. Rosa Carbone gave the hint of a wonderful restaurant in Piazza di Spagna, Rome, where plenty of Italian food was served at fantastic prices and contributed thus to a joyous celebration of the mysteries of science. Finally we would like to thank our families and friends for supporting us in the work with this project over the past few years.

Martti Koskenniemi,
Mónica García-Salmones Rovira,
and Paolo Amorosa
Helsinki, October 2016.

Contents

II. HUMAN RIGHTS, BETWEEN HISTORY, THE INTERNATIONAL AND RELIGION

Notes on Contributors

Paolo Amorosa is a Doctoral Candidate and a member of the research project 'Intellectual History of International Law: Religion and Empire' at the Erik Castrén Institute of International Law and Human Rights, University of Helsinki. Prior to that, he has been teaching international law and human rights at Tallinn Law School, Tallinn University of Technology. He received his LL. M. degree in Public International Law from Leiden University and worked as a research assistant at the Grotius Centre for International Legal Studies and at the Italian Embassy to the Holy See. His recent work has focused on international legal thought in the United States in the early twentieth century. He is currently working on his doctoral thesis titled *The American Project and the Politics of History: James Brown Scott and the Search for the Origins of International Law.*

Pasquale Annicchino is a Research Fellow at the Robert Schuman Centre for Advanced Studies and a Senior Research Associate at the Cambridge Institute on Religion & International Studies, Cambridge University. He has been Adjunct Professor of Law at BYU Law School (U.S.A.) and Visiting Professor at the Catholic University of Leuven (Belgium). He serves as book review editor for *Religion and Human Rights: an International Journal* and is a member of the editorial board of *Quaderni di Diritto e Politica Ecclesiastica* published by Il Mulino. His main interests include the following: legal theory, law and religion, EU law, national security law, religion and politics. Among his recent publications are: 'Esportare la Libertà Religiosa. Il Modello Americano nell'Arena Globale (Bologna, 2015); A Transatlantic Partnership for International Religious Freedom? The United States, Europe and the Challenge of Religious Persecutions', *Oxford Journal of Law and Religion*, 2016. He has been appointed by the Italian Minister of Interior as a member of the Italian Council for the relationships with Muslim communities.

Mónica García-Salmones Rovira is Adjunct Professor of International Law at the University of Helsinki, where she teaches in the area of international law and philosophy. She is also Research Fellow at the Erik Castrén Institute of International Law and Human Rights and in 2017/2018 Oskar Huttunen Visiting Fellow at Clare Hall, University of Cambridge. She is the author of *The Project of Positivism in International Law* winner of the ESIL Book Prize 2015. More recently her research has focused in the early history of international law, with a focus in the study of the conceptual, philosophical, and historical continuities between the modern international lawyers and previous theological theories.

Ofir Haivry is Vice-President of *The Herzl Institute*, Jerusalem, Israel. His research interests are in the history of political ideas, especially the sixteenth–seventeenth centuries, the Anglo-American constitutional tradition, Jewish ideas, and political Hebraism. His publications include: 'Between Reason and Imagination: Gilliam's Vision and European Nationalism' in J. Birkenstein et al (eds), *The Cinema of Terry Gilliam: It's a Mad World* (Columbia University Press, 2013) and the forthcoming *John Selden and the Western Political Tradition* (Cambridge University Press, 2017).

John D. Haskell is a Senior Lecturer in Law at the University of Manchester and a Junior Faculty member at the Harvard Law School Institute for Global Law and Policy (IGLP). His research focuses on the dynamics of organizational change and the sociology of idea production at the intersection of law, political economy, and religion. He has held visiting appointments at the University of Cambridge, Harvard Law School, the International University College of Turin, Lille Catholic University, the University of Helsinki, and the University of San Francisco.

Paul W. Kahn is Robert W. Winner Professor of Law and the Humanities, and Director of the Orville H. Schell, Jr. Center for Human Rights at Yale Law School. He earned his Ph.D. in Philosophy from Yale University and his J.D. from Yale Law School. He served as a law clerk to Justice White in the United States Supreme Court from 1980–1982. Before coming to Yale Law School in 1985, he practiced law in Washington, D.C. He teaches in the areas of constitutional law and theory, international law, cultural theory, and philosophy. He is the author of ten books, including most recently, *Political Theology: Four New Chapters on the Concept of Sovereignty; Finding Ourselves at the Movies*; and *Making the Case: The Art of the Judicial Opinion.*

Mary M. Keys is Associate Professor of Political Science at the University of Notre Dame. Her research focuses on political theory and the history of political thought, especially as they intersect with ethics, legal philosophy, and religion. She has held research fellowships and visiting scholar appointments from the National Endowment for the Humanities and at Harvard University's Government Department, the University of Chicago's Marty Center for the Advanced Study of Religion, and the Notre Dame Institute of Advanced Study. She is author of *Aquinas, Aristotle, and the Promise of the Common Good* (Cambridge 2006) and is currently at work on a book on pride, humility, and political philosophy in Augustine's *City of God.*

Martti Koskenniemi is Academy Professor of International Law at the University of Helsinki and Director of the Erik Castrén Institute of International Law and Human Rights. He was a member of the Finnish diplomatic service in 1978–1994 and of the International Law Commission (UN) in 2002–2006. He has held visiting professorships in, among other places, New York University, Columbia University, University of Cambridge, London School of Economics, and Universities of Brussels, Melbourne, Paris, Sao Paulo, and Utrecht. He is a Corresponding Fellow of the British Academy and has a doctorate h.c. from the Universities of Uppsala, Frankfurt, and McGill. His main publications include *From Apology to Utopia; The Structure of International Legal Argument* (1989/2005), *The Gentle Civilizer of Nations: The Rise and Fall of International Law 1870–1960* (2001) and *The Politics of International Law* (2011). He is currently working on a history of international legal thought from the late medieval period to the nineteenth century.

Sarah Mortimer is Student and Tutor in Modern History, Christ Church, and University Lecturer in Modern History at the University of Oxford. Her research focuses on the relationship between political and religious ideas in the early modern period; she is currently writing a book on global political thought from 1517 to 1625 for Oxford University Press. Her monograph, *Reason and Religion in the English Revolution* (2010), won the Forkosch prize for the best first book in intellectual history and she has also edited, with John Robertson, *The Intellectual Consequences of Religious Heterodoxy 1600–1750* (2012).

Michele Nicoletti is Professor of Political Philosophy at the University of Trento (Italy). Visiting fellow in Freiburg i.B., KU Leuven, Notre Dame (IN, USA), he is the scientific coordinator of national and international research projects in the field of political ethics and political theology. Editor of the academic journal *Politica e Religione. Annuario di teologia politica* and of the website 'Theopopedia. Archiving the history of theologico-political concepts', he has written on Kierkegaard, Schmitt, Hobbes, Rosmini, political theology, and international political theory.

Janne Nijman is Professor of History and Theory of International Law at the Faculty of Law of the University of Amsterdam and a senior fellow at the Amsterdam Centre for International Law (ACIL). She is the academic director of the TMC Asser Instituut in The Hague, where she leads the research program 'International and European Law as a source of Trust in a hyper-connected world.' She is an editor of the *Netherlands Yearbook of International Law* and of the *Grotiana* journal. Among her publications is the 2015 article 'Images of Grotius, or the International Rule of Law beyond Historiographical Oscillation'. She is currently engaged in a research project together with Anthony Carty on the history of European and Chinese international thought.

Elena Paris is a Doctoral Candidate and Researcher at the Law School, University of Bucharest. Her research area includes international legal theory, international law and religion, continental philosophy, cosmopolitanism, critical human rights, constitutionalism, collective security, law and development, and international economic law. She has most recently published a chapter 'Re-thinking Universalism: Post-Foundational Cosmopolitanism in a Relational Key' in a collective volume she has co-edited, *Re-grounding Cosmopolitanism. Towards a Post-foundational Cosmopolitanism* (Routledge, 2016).

Reut Y. Paz has a Ph. D. (2009) in international law/politics, and has conducted her research on the 'Jewish question' within the international legal framework at the University of Helsinki, Bar Ilan University (Israel) and at the Humboldt University in Berlin. She is the author of *A Gateway between a Distant God and a Cruel World: The Contribution of Jewish German-Speaking Scholars to International Law* (Brill, 2012) and several other publications that deal with the religious history of international law. She is currently a Senior Researcher SFB/TRR (Collaborative Research Centre), 'Dynamics of security. Types of securitization from a historic perspective', Justus-Liebig-Universität Gießen Public Law, International and European Law Faculty of Law.

Ileana Porras is the Associate Dean of Academic Affairs at the University of Miami School of Law. Professor Porras teaches international law, sustainable development, and property law. She was founding Director of the Brown International Advanced Research Institutes and has been a Visiting Professor at the Watson Institute of International Studies at Brown University, Sandra Day O'Connor College of Law at Arizona State University and Boston College Law School. Her scholarship in international law has been primarily concerned with issues of violence, colonialism, trade, the environment, and the city and sustainable development. Most recently her work has focused on the subject of scarcity, consumption, and sustainable development. Professor Porras was formerly a member of a contemplative Cistercian monastic community and has also written on Pope Francis' recent climate change Encyclical Laudato Si,' from the perspective of international law.

Moussa Abou Ramadan is Professor of Islamic Law at Strasbourg University, researching and teaching on family, contract, and international relations in Islamic law. He is responsible for the Master's degree in Islamologie, droit et gestion at Strasbourg University, and has been a Visiting Professor in various universities (EPHE, Paris-Sorbonne, IEP Lyon, Trento, Milano), and a Visiting Scholar (NYU Law School and McGill Islamic Institute).

Nahed Samour is a Post-doctoral Researcher at the Erik Castrén Institute of International Law and Human Rights, University of Helsinki/ Faculty of Law, Humboldt University Berlin, and a member of the Junior Faculty at Harvard Law School, Institute of Global Law and Policy. She works on Islamic law, public international law, constitutional law, and legal history. Amongst her articles on the Islamic history of international law are 'Is there a Role for Islamic International Law in the History of International Law?', Book Review Symposium on *The Oxford Handbook of the History of International Law*, ed. by Anne Peters/ Bardo Fassbender, *European Journal of International Law* vol. 25 (2014), and 'Modernized Islamic International Law Concepts as a Third World Approach to International Law', *Zeitschrift für ausländisches öffentliches Recht und Völkerrecht* [Heidelberger Journal of International Law] 72 (2012).

Pamela Slotte is Associate Professor in Minority Studies (tenure track) at Åbo Akademi University, an Academy of Finland Academy Research Fellow, and Senior Research Fellow at the Erik Castrén Institute of International Law and Human Rights at the University of Helsinki. She is Adjunct Professor of theological ethics with philosophy of religion at Åbo Akademi University, and Adjunct Professor of religion and law research at the University of Helsinki. She is Principal Investigator of the HERA funded project *Protestant Legacies in Nordic Law: Uses of the Past in the Construction of the Secularity of Law* (2016–19). Among her latest publications is the co-edited volume *Revisiting the Origins of Human Rights* (Cambridge University Press 2015).

Immi Tallgren is a Research Fellow at the Erik Castrén Institute of International Law and Human Rights at the University of Helsinki, and Senior Visiting Fellow at the Centre for International Studies, London School of Economics. She has previously worked for the Ministry for Foreign Affairs of Finland, the European Police Cooperation Organisation, and the European Space Agency. Her research interests and publications reach from international criminal law to history and sociology of international law, law and film, and legal anthropology.

Pia Valenzuela is currently working at the Catholic Institute, Ljubljana, Slovenia and she is doing her PhD at the Pontifical University of the Holy Cross, Rome, Italy. Prior to this, she was a Lecturer in Ethics at Universidad de los Andes, Santiago, Chile. She also worked as a Graduate Assistant of Ethics at Centro Internazionale di Studi Villa Balestra, Rome, Italy. Mag. Valenzuela received her undergraduate degree in philosophy from Universidad de los Andes, Chile, and her Master degree from University of Ljubljana, Slovenia. Besides her original publications and manuscripts, she has participated in different Philosophical Meetings and Conferences in Chile, Italy, Spain, and Slovenia. Her main research areas of interest are twofold: first, ethics and practical rationality, and more specifically normativity and intentionality; and currently, political philosophy, philosophy of law, natural law, natural rights, and ethics, practical rationality, psychology, Aristotle and Thomas Aquinas.

PRELIMINARY STUDY

International Law and Religion

No Stable Ground

Martti Koskenniemi

What an adventure the production of this volume has been! It was compiled during 2012–2016 in the context of the research project 'History of International Law: Empire and Religion', under the auspices of the Academy of Finland and University of Helsinki. As its title shows, the project consisted of two parts. One dealt with international law's complex and many-sided relationship with 'empire', another the way the forms of religiosity have interacted and continue to interact with international law. Researchers focusing on the latter item—the subject of the present volume—felt constantly that they were treading on ground that had not been much travelled, where there existed few (if any) research traditions, where controversy was rife and concerned matters that were not easily settled. In this respect, the production of this work contrasts with its sister volume, 'International Law and Empire'.[1] While the theme of international law's relationship with 'empire' seemed familiar, positions were firmly established and points of controversy honed in years of engagement at conferences and publications, no such tradition was visible with regard to 'religion'. In a word, there was no stable ground.

We were fortunate in gathering a group of scholars (most of whom did not know each other in advance, let alone having collaborated on this or any other theme) who were ready to treat each others' viewpoints with interest, sympathy, and good cheer. Many of us were able to meet twice, and to carry out extensive conversations on the topics of our papers and on how 'religion' associates with international law. It is usually expected of an introductory chapter such as this to demonstrate how the various individual pieces of research come together, ideally in a novel thesis on the volume's subject-matter. In this case, this would not only be very hard to accomplish, but would not be true to the nature of the subject where contrasting viewpoints began already from the very concepts to be related: neither 'religion' nor 'international law', it turned out, was a self-evident unit of meaning. Moreover, while some of us wrote as lawyers or historians descriptively about religion, others took

[1] Martti Koskenniemi, Walter Rech, and Manuel Fonseca, eds, *International Law and Empire* (Oxford: Oxford University Press, 2016).

their standpoint within religion, seeking to describe its encounters with that alien object, 'international law'. Legal historians are well versed in the difficulties of linking normative analyses with contextual or historicist ones so that there begins to exist a vocabulary and a set of positions from which the two items—'ought' and 'is'—can be related without reduction. With the present topic, finding a balance between narration and evaluation seemed much more difficult. There were of course the standard difficulties when experts of different disciplines—theologians, historians, lawyers—grapple towards an object that is supposed to be more or less shared among them. The conceptual frames produced different suggestions about what was central in the object, what marginal. To this was added a shared concern about not being bogged down in a clash of religious and secular vocabularies. Avoiding a blasé neutrality, the chapters of this book now rather illuminate the clash, including from critical and normative angles. As the reader will notice, the chapters adopt varied standpoints—some examine the international legal world from the perspective of a religion, others operate from the assumption that some law has 'existed' or been 'valid', and examine its encounter with the competing normativity of religion. We have tried to avoid pronouncing on the value of 'more' or 'less' intense engagement between international law and religion and instead to focus the various, often hidden forms of their alliance.

Secularism

Already some years ago, David Kennedy observed a loss of faith in the secular in the academic literatures on international law and in human sciences generally.[2] For most of the twentieth century, if the topic of international law and religion was treated at all, it was treated usually from the perspective of a self-confident secularism. As the conventional timing of the emergence of 'modern' international law at the peace of Westphalia (1648) suggests, the history of the field has been usually told as a secularizing narrative leading up to 'the coexistence of a multiplicity of states, each sovereign within its territory, equal to one another'.[3] Typical treatments of the topic have examined the past 'contribution' that Christian religion, usually some aspect of Catholicism or Protestantism, has made to law and statehood, those contributions having been purified from their 'hot' religiosity to become part of the 'cool' professionalism of global governance.[4] Central figures in this narrative have been presented as important precisely owing to the alleged ability to transcend their religious affiliation and reaching towards a 'humanity' united beyond sectarian divisions. Today, religion is everywhere, and all of this

[2] David Kennedy, 'Losing Faith in the Secular: Law, Religion and the Culture of International Governance', in *Religion and International Law*, edited by Mark Janis and Carolyn Evans (The Hague: Martinus Nijhoff, 1999), pp. 309–20.

[3] E.g. Charlotte Ku, 'Catholicism, the peace of Westphalia, and the origins of modern international law', *The European Legacy* 1 (1996): pp. 734–9.

[4] E.g. P-H. Kooijmans, 'Protestantism and the Development of International Law', *Recueil des Cours* 152 (1976/IV) 10980).

history has come to seem increasingly dubious. In Chapter 4 Janne Nijman takes a critical view of the assumption that the writings of the 'father' of international law, Hugo Grotius, were aspects of a secularizing project. Nothing could be more mistaken! The version of Arminian Christianity represented by the Protestant Grotius may have been reasonably tolerant towards variants of the Christian confession, but certainly not towards Islam or non-religion. Like most of his contemporaries, Grotius regarded his most important writings as being about Christian unity.[5] His life's project was to contribute to the reorganization of the relations between Church and State by allowing secular magistrates to intervene if public order was threatened. This did not mean turning the State into a secular institution—an impossible proposition in the thoroughly religious Dutch republic. But it did suggest that the State should seek neutrality between the opposed factions, and if need be, take command of the external administration of the Christian religion.[6] As Ofir Haivry shows, nor can Grotius' great adversary, John Selden be accredited as having supported the claims of England on large maritime areas on the basis of merely secular ideas of *ratio status.* On the contrary, Selden, whose authority in England 'was paramount on all questions relating to the sovereignty of the sea,'[7] took on much of what the Spanish theologians had written on *dominium* and as part of his Hebrew scholarship he derived natural law from God's will and the human knowledge of it from the natural faculty of intuition assisted by grace. [8]

There has been a tradition of looking for the paternity of international law further back from Grotius or Selden in the writings of the Spanish *secunda scholastica*, especially its foremost representative, the Dominican theologian and teacher Francisco de Vitoria. While twentieth century international lawyers have sometimes mistakenly labelled him 'jurist' and almost without exception treated his natural law as a kind of proto-secularizing devise enabling him to treat the Indians, though infidel, as in some respects (namely as possessors of *dominium,* or lordship) equal to the Spaniards, few have noted that his lectures were designed to teach young clerics on the management of the sacrament of penance. In this volume,

[5] See e.g. Barbara Kniepel, *Die Naturrechtslehre des Hugo Grotius als Einigungsprinzip der Christenheit, dargestellt an seiner Stellung zum Calvinism* (Kessel: Bladitsch, 1971); Hasso Hoffmann, 'Hugo Grotius', in *Staatsdenker in der frühen Neuzeit,* edited by Michael Stolleis (Munich: Beck, 1995), pp. 59–60.

[6] For a useful summary of studies and interpretations of Grotius' religious works by reference to their background in Dutch religious history, see Florian Mühlegger, *Hugo Grotius. Ein christlicher Humanist in politischen Verantwortung* (Berlin: De Gruyter, 2007), pp. 6–83 and J.P. Heeren, *Hugo Grotius as Apologist for the Christian Religion* (Leiden: Brill, 2004), esp. pp. 64–75.

[7] T. W. Fulton, *The Sovereignty of the Sea. An Historical Account of the Claims of England to the Dominion of the British Seas, and of the Evolution of Territorial Waters* (Edinburgh & London: William Blackwood and Sons, 1911), p. 20.

[8] The work in question is *De iure naturali & gentium iuxta disciplinam Ebraeorum libri septem* ('Seven Books on the Law of Nature and Nations with the Hebrew') of 1639. For the reading in the text, see J. P. Sommerville, 'John Selden, The Law of Nature, and the origins of Government', *The Historical Journal* 27 (1984): pp. 437–47 and 'Selden, Grotius and the Seventeenth-Century Intellectual Revolution in Moral and Political Theory', in *Rhetoric and Law in early Modern Europe,* edited by Victoria Kahn and Lorna Hutson (New Haven, Conn.: Yale University Press, 2001), pp. 334–9.

the theological frame of the 'Salamanca school' is taken seriously by Mary Keys, who suggests that we should even deepen our sense of the embeddedness of what Vitoria has to say about the *jus gentium* in the Christian tradition by reading him in the light of Augustine's *City of God*. Vitoria's Dominican Catholicism is then brought into a debate with Grotian Protestantism in Sarah Mortimer's contribution that shows them agreeing in an effort to bring natural law and *jus gentium* into a stable relationship with Christian duty while still wholly differing in their views about the role of the Church in administering the resulting system.

Today, not much evidence is needed to support the once controversial point that many of our most important political concepts are secularized theological concepts—at least in the sense that they have become part of vocabularies that think of themselves as 'secular'.[9] This point is used by Ileana Porras in her text on the providential approach to trade, so influential not only for the early modern writers she reviews (Vitoria, Gentili, Grotius) but also to eighteenth-century thinkers and through them, the optimistic view of commerce most of us share today in one form or another. Whose, after all is the 'invisible hand' if not God's? The issue of providence is surely one of the more obvious points of linkage between international (trade) law and religion.[10] One place where such an examination might start is Kantian teleology that situates in nature itself a tendency for peacefulness that may be discovered by the use of reason and inexorably will lead humankind into a global federation. Many international lawyers have expressly aligned themselves with Kant's cosmopolitan legalism. By this, they have also come to subscribe (at least implicitly) to Kant's view of 'religion within the limits of bare reason' where providence takes the form of reason outlining the way to an ideal future. The present is read in view of its transgression. The crucial paragraph in the famous essay from 1784 reads like a prayer international lawyers have learned to say in face of the adversities of the international world:

> Wars, tense and unremitting military preparations, and the resultant distress which every state must eventually feel with itself, even in the midst of peace—these are the means by which nature drives nations to make initially imperfect attempts, but finally, after many devastations, upheavals and even complete inner exhaustion of their powers, to take the step which reason could have suggested to them even without so many sad experiences—that of abandoning a lawless state of savagery and entering a federation of peoples [*Völkerbund*] in which every state, even the smallest, could expect its security and rights not from its own power or from its own legal judgment, but solely from this great federation (*foedus Amphictyonum*), from a united power and the law-governed decisions of a united will.[11]

[9] The classic is, of course, Carl Schmitt, *Political Theology. Four Chapters on the Concept of Sovereignty* (Chicago: University of Chicago Press, 2010).

[10] See further Martti Koskenniemi, 'The Political Theology of Trade Law: The Scholastic Contribution', in *From Bilateralism to Community Interest. Essays in Honour of Judge Bruno Simma*, edited by Ulrich Fastenrath et al. (Oxford: Oxford University Press, 2011), pp. 90–112.

[11] Immanuel Kant, 'The Idea for Universal History with a Cosmopolitan Purpose', in *Political Writings*, edited by K. Reiss (Cambridge: Cambridge University Press, 1991), Seventh Proposition, p. 47. See further, Immanuel Kant, *Religion within the Bounds of Mere Reason*, edited by A. Wood and G. Giovanni (Cambridge: Cambridge University Press, 1998).

'Faith in reason' is also a faith, as Kant (unlike many of his epigones) was ready to admit; it was not for nothing that after the critiques of pure reason and practical reason had done their work, *virtue* was left alone as the ground from which Kant would invite his readers to construct their normative worlds. The critiques not only justified 'freedom' as the highest value but also inaugurated a heavy moral responsibility in one's social relations.[12] Focus on personal qualities ('virtue') pointed both backwards into a tradition of scholastic moral theology and forwards to postmodern 'existentialism', allied by shared scepticism about the powers of secular reason. Central for the world of law and morality (at this point no longer sharply distinguished) will now become the *persona* that is ruling either as 'prince', a government member, or perhaps as the manager of some considerable private wealth. It is never enough just to apply the 'law', Aquinas and Kant would say, it must be applied in a reasonable and equitable fashion so as to attain a 'just' outcome.

The deformalization of international law by recourse to broad standards of equity, reasonableness, and 'balancing' between conflicting values that characterizes practical work across the field is also the result of a certain running-out of rules and the reason that seeks to deduce judgments from them. Practitioners are called upon to exercise contextual sensitivity, to be responsive to the call of the moment, and to adjust conflicting principles reasonably. The turn to the hermeneutics of judging is all about how to reach that moment of when, in an indeterminate environment, everything will fall into place. Moral theology and Kantian moralists discussed this predicament in terms of the virtues needed to operate power in a way that is legally—and thus both morally and theologically—responsible. It is no news that modern political and legal culture does not equip well for such work, even if it relentlessly points beyond its internal principles and rationales.[13] When Vitoria, Grotius, or indeed Kant discussed law-making or the just application of laws, they were in possession of a well-developed vocabulary of the virtues of 'justice' and 'prudence' that would assist in carrying out the tasks of government and generally conducting social relations. Justice, the virtue that regulated conduct in community with others, was defined by Aquinas the 'internal' instrument through which God pushed us towards our final end, supernatural blessedness (law being the 'external' instrument), while prudence helped to put other virtues in order and enabled the ruler to perceive the alternatives of action and choose among them. In due course, the extreme complexity of the virtue discourse ended up giving scholasticism a bad name as 'Jesuit morality' with which anything could be justified. In the absence of a formal discourse of 'virtue' in global governance today, however, the critiques of abstract reason and empiricism that form the enlightenment legacy have left legal professionals in a bind: either to espouse an openly theological

[12] I have discussed this further in 'Formalismus, Fragmentierung, Freiheit—Kantische Themen im heutigen Völkerrecht', in *Transnationale Verrechtlichung*, edited by Regina Kreide and Andreas Niederberger (Frankfurt: Campus, 2008), pp. 65–89;

[13] See especially Duncan Kennedy, *A Critique of Adjudication (fin de siècle)* (Cambridge, Mass.: Harvard University Press, 1997).

understanding of the 'ultimate ends' to which legal practice looks, or to face an existentialist predicament where the gap between what they *know* and what they *should do* appears only as a void.[14]

It is this 'gap' where religion (as well as hypocrisy, religion's dark brother) thrives in the various forms of existentialism on offer to men and women trying to operate the institutional vocabularies of modern law and governance. From law to economics, postmodernism to populism, environmentalism to developmentalism, humanitarianism to military training (and so on) professionals grapple between the formal demands of the law and the knowledge that the legal vocabularies fall short of fully dictating what is a 'right' or 'good' or 'just' thing to do. Something else is needed, and as John Haskell shows in Chapter 6, when that need is filled with religion, the result can be seen either in positive terms—religion as a source for energy, innovation, and commitment—but equally in negative terms as unreflective passion and 'bias'. The problem, as he suggests, is easiest to see in the human rights field where the Dr Jekyll/Mr Hyde structure of the debate on the roles of religion has led to a pragmatic stress on open dialogue—a position that may be hard to distinguish from an intellectually dubious refusal to engage in reflection about what interests are really being advanced under the guise of (ostensibly 'authentic') spirituality. The links between the politics of human rights and Christian moral theology are obvious but insufficiently studied. When they have been examined, attention has been directed to the tradition of assessing positive laws from the perspective of 'higher principles'. Sometimes the suggestion has been to trace all law back to God. Even natural law, as the ultimate criterion of positive lawfulness, would be unthreatening because, after all, '*Natura, id est Deus*'. But it is not necessary to look for religious influences in the law of centuries ago. As Samuel Moyn has recently shown, one of the sources of today's 'universal human rights' lies in post-war European Christian Democracy's turn to 'personalism' and the rhetoric of 'human dignity'.[15]

One large question that haunts modern jurisprudence, international as well as domestic, has to do with the justification for the use of power by humans over other humans. According to the famous statement of St Paul in Romans 13:1: 'There is no power but from God, and those that are ordained of God'. The statement has been subjected to a great many conflicting interpretations, but what it does establish beyond question is the inextricable nature of the link between divine and secular authority: in some way, the latter must be derived from the former. Medieval literature addressed the power that humans had over each other in the language of *dominium*.[16] It was assumed that this had belonged originally to God, but that

[14] Jan Klabbers is presently engaged in a large project on the role of virtue in global governance institutions. See e.g. his 'Law, Ethics and Global Governance: Accountability in Perspective', *New Zealand Journal of Public and International Law* 11 (2013): pp. 309–21.

[15] Samuel Moyn, *Christianity and Human Rights* (Princeton University Press, 2016).

[16] The literature is truly overwhelming. See especially Kurt Seelmann, *Die Lehre des Fernando Vazquez de Menchaga vom Dominium* (Cologne: Heymanns, 1979) and Marie-France Renoux-Zagamé, *Origines théologiques du concept moderne de propriété* (Genève: Droz, 1987). See also Annabel Brett, *Liberty, Rights and Nature. Individual Rights in Later Scholastic Thought* (Cambridge: Cambridge University Press, 1997), pp. 10–48; Janet Coleman, 'Property and Poverty', in *The Cambridge*

He had granted it to humans. If, however, rulers claimed the right to govern their subjects and private ownership organized humans in tall hierarchies, this was only because God had also given humans dominium in themselves—they could use their freedom to establish institutions to rule each other. Sovereignty and private property may have emerged from late medieval moral theology but continue to draw support from and remain astonishingly compatible with mainstream Christianity today.

Two basic attitudes have been taken to these institutions. For 'realists', following a line from Augustine and Hobbes, sovereignty and property have no redeeming value but exist simply to keep humans from destroying each other, and to allow the faithful to devote their lives to spiritual tasks. For other, more 'idealist' observers, following in the footsteps of Aquinas and Kant, the institutions may nevertheless be used to enable humans to act charitably towards each other and work for the security and happiness of all. The two attitudes involve rival anthropologies and views about the place of spirituality in human life. Can a secular teleology of happiness be sustained without faith? Are human institutions about corrupting spirituality or perfecting it? Both positions have their supporters and detractors.

There is of course no more central notion to international law than sovereign statehood, and no item over which the opinions of international lawyers would have been more divided. Thomas Hobbes once called the state 'Leviathan', a 'mortal God', and international jurists have often attacked him by condemning faith in statehood as idolatry, obstructing vision of the true divinity of the universal.[17] And yet, at moments of great crises—wars originating in Europe in the twentieth century, for example—even the most cosmopolitan of lawyers have sought security in a sovereign bulwark.[18] That we do not usually discuss 'property' in international law is one of the field's more important oversights. The theology of *divisio rerum* created for Europeans, and then by imperial extension to the world, a notion of the 'private realm' where material accumulation would pose a serious spiritual (as well as, of course, social) problem. But concern over poverty and inequality also remain important aspects of religious cosmopolitanism, reminding us of Christianity's complex legacy, the futility of reducing it to some single set of propositions about how society should be ruled. The story of the justification of Christian power as *dominiun iurisdictionis* or *dominium proprietatis*, is complex, and how we view those institutions depends on large assumptions about history and human nature that are hard to disentangle from assumptions we have learned to think of as religious.[19]

History of Medieval Political Thought. c. 350–c. 1450, edited by J. H. Burns (Cambridge: Cambridge University Press, 1988), pp. 611–25.

[17] Hobbes, *Leviathan*, edited by J. G. A. Gaskin (Oxford: Oxford University Press, 2008 [1651]).

[18] See e.g. Eliav Lieblich and Yoram Shachar, 'Cosmopolitanism at a Crossroads: Hersch Lauterpacht and the Israeli Declaration of Independence', *British Year Book of International law* 84 (2013): pp. 1–51.

[19] See especially Marie-France Renoux-Zagamé, *Origines théologiques du concept moderne de propriété* (Geneva: Droz, 1987).

Sovereignty

Histories of international law make much of the fall of papal and imperial universalism during European early modernity. The demise of the hierocratic view that looked at the pope as a follower of St Peter and representative of Christ on earth and the imperial theory that attributed eschatological significance to the Holy Roman Empire reconciled Christianity with statehood. 'God apportioned human laws to the human race through the emperors and kings of this world', Gratian wrote in his influential *Decretum* (*c.* 1140).[20] Even if royal jurists were never that keen on the theories of divine kingship (because that gave ultimate political authority to theologians), they did imitate the procedures of the papal chancellery and adapted the language of papal lordship to their purposes.[21] Still today, debates on the nature of sovereignty and, for instance, the division of jurisdiction between states and international institutions (such as the European Union), raise issues that early modern Christian thinkers used to debate under such expressions as *plenitudo potestatis* or the distinction between *potestas absoluta* and *potestas ordinata*, important parts of the papal ideology.[22]

The otherworldly character of debates over sovereignty is highlighted by the way they lead into apparently insoluble paradoxes: is the 'sovereignty' that produces the law itself 'outside' or 'inside' the law? If it is 'outside', then tyranny is our fate—if 'inside', well, then it is really not the highest. For if it can be articulated through law, then it becomes subordinate to that power which can authoritatively determine what 'law' says. The doctrine of papal *plenitudo potestatis* that fourteenth century Christian jurists adapted to address the highest temporal power—the power of the king or the omnipotent popular assembly—did suggest that the ruler's 'will' overrode any laws (with the partial exception of divine and natural law) or at least that there was no other authority who could judge the rightness of such supreme will. Perhaps shocked by the consequences of their logic, jurists rapidly fell back to claiming that under the Roman law principle of *Digna vox*, the ruler would nevertheless be 'honourably' bound to respect existing laws—at least in 'normal' situations where no crisis threatened the life of the nation.[23] Very little imagination is needed to see all that theological framework at play in a case such as the opinion on the *Legality of the Threat or Use of Nuclear Weapons* by the International Court of

[20] Gratian, *Treatise*, Dist. 8 Part 1 C 1 (24).

[21] See Harold J. Berman, *Law and Revolution. The Formation of the Western Legal Tradition* (Cambridge, Mass.: Harvard University Press, 1983).

[22] The basic work is still Walter Ullmann, *The Growth of Papal Government in the Middle Ages. A Study in the Ideological Relation of Clerical to Lay Power* (London: Methuen, 1962).

[23] For the relevant debates, see e.g. Dieter Wyduckel, *Princeps Legibus Solutus. Eine Untersuchung zur frühmodernen Rechts- und Staatslehre* (Berlin: Duncker & Humblot, 1979), pp. 88–94; Kenneth Pennington, *The Prince and the Law 1200–1600. Sovereignty and Rights in the Western Legal Tradition* (Berkeley: University of California Press, 1993), pp. 45–75. Also very useful is Jane Black, *Absolutism in Renaissance Milan. Plenitude of Power under the Visconti and the Sforza 1329–1535* (Oxford: Oxford University Press, 2009), pp. 8–35. See also William J. Courtenay, *Capacity and Volition. A History of the Distinction between Absolute and Ordained Power* (Pergamo: Lubrina, 1990).

Justice (ICJ) in 1996. After an examination of the various fields of law covering the use of force, humanitarian, and human rights law, the Court came to the conclusion that it could not exclude the rightness of a (limited, tactical) nuclear strike if 'the very survival of a State would be at stake'.[24] Although many liberal jurists were shocked, it is hard to see what else the Court could have said; if the law is based on the need to protect states, if states are the 'creators' of the law, then surely it cannot be so interpreted as to allow that they be destroyed. And, as with *plenitudo potestatis*, the question will always remain open as to who is to determine whether such an existential threat is at hand. Sovereignty is then never only about the nature of the power it involves but about its wielder—'*quis iudicabit*'?

This turns the debate about sovereignty from apparently rational (but actually paradoxical) analysis of the nature or criteria of legitimate use of power to the question of *trust*—to whom can we confide such awesome power over the lives of our communities? This theme, again, is today reproduced in the 'securitizing' of our societies. Early Christian political theology made the distinction between *potestas ordinata* and *potestas absoluta*, denoting thereby a contrast between the administration of Christian society in 'normal' and 'exceptional' times. The tropes of 'normal' and 'exceptional' have now penetrated deep into Western political consciousness where the depth of concerns of 'security' is no doubt enhanced by their having been triggered by professed *religious* adversaries, Islamic 'fundamentalists'. Living in a period of 'exception' (which Schmitt associated with religious miracles), citizens are invited to trust the security apparatus and to do this out of *faith* (the facts of course have to be kept secret). No doubt our acceptance of this depends on tapping on the unconscious image of existential struggle with an old religious enemy. The indecipherable iconology of security has taken the role Latin once did in religious service, a language of the sacred whose mysteries ordinary citizens are not entitled to share.

The question of 'trust' is emerging today internationally in the 'fight against impunity', the topic of Immi Tallgren's contribution. The massive rise into prominence of international criminal law relies on a powerful image of 'evil' that presupposes widely professed faith in 'humanity' represented by the judges of the International Criminal Court and the forces on which the court stands. Tallgren examines the pedigree of the religion of humanity in the world of the French enlightenment and its nineteenth century successor disciplines, economics, sociology, and humanitarianism, committed to the betterment of life, the realization of social justice, solidarity, and well-being on earth. If something about the 'religion of humanity' failed to convince in the end, as projected reforms always tended to privilege some interests or groups over others, the same phenomenon may be witnessed with regard to the controversies about the selectivity of the way in which only some (in this case African) political leaders turn out as those against whom the whole of 'humanity' is called upon to unite.

[24] ICJ, 'Legality of Threat or Use of Nuclear Weapons', Reports 1996, dispositif (266/44).

Property

But Christian power is not only the power of the sovereign, it is also the power of the owner of property against the world at large. The narrative of *divisio rerum*, a key part of the intellectual apparatus with which theologians reacted to political and socioeconomic transformations of early modernity, explained how such power was possible among human beings who, the Bible tells us, had been created free and equal. Pia Valenzuela reminds us in her chapter on Thomas Aquinas (it is astonishing how often we need to be reminded) of the way private property—and the economic system based on it—arose from the scholastic discussion of 'law' and the virtue of 'justice'. Already early canon lawyers accepted that undivided *dominium* was conceivable only in the state of innocence. After the fall, this was no longer possible: 'By divine law all things are common to all; by the enacted law, this is mine and that another's'.[25] It was then assumed by a whole tradition of Dominican theology that private property had become a necessity in a world of sinners where an economy of sharing would degenerate into endless strife and litigation. Moreover, because everyone would be more diligent with a property they own, it was useful for the State to put in place a system of private property.[26]

These private property rights were understood as *ius gentium*, just as the power of the prince was, that is, as part of the 'law of nations', and thus applicable everywhere—a fact that, among other things, prompted Spanish Dominican theologians and after them, the Spanish imperial officials, to acknowledge that the 'Indians' did have right to the things they possessed.[27] For a long time, European jurists (but also proponents of the Franco regime) used to congratulate themselves for the magnanimity and humanism of the Dominican scholars, and there is no doubt that their rejection of the theory of natural slavery was based on genuine outrage at the way the conquistadors had treated the indigenous population.[28] More recently, postcolonial scholars have pointed to the contradictory heritage involved in the treatment of the Indians by Christian natural law. From now on, this European vocabulary, and the European authorities competent to operate it, would have a base from which to set up their imperial and cultural domination over the rest of the world. [29]

[25] Gratian, *The Treatise on Laws, with the Ordinary Gloss (Decretum DD 1-20)*, translated by A. Thompson and J. Gordley (Washington, D. C.: Catholic University of America Press, 1993), Dist. 8 Part 1 C 1 (24).

[26] Aquinas, 'Summa theologiae', II-II, in *Political Writings*, edited by R. W. Dyson (Cambridge: Cambridge University Press, 2002).

[27] Francisco de Vitoria, Relection 'De Indis', in *Political Writings*, edited by A. Pagden and J. Lawrance (Cambridge: Cambridge University Press, 1991).

[28] On the Franco regime's use of the *Secunda scholastica*, see Ignacio de la Rasilla del Moral, 'The Fascist Mimesis of Spanish International Law and its Vitorian Aftermath, 1939–1953', *Journal of the History of International Law* 14 (2012): pp. 207–36.

[29] See especially Antony Anghie, *Sovereignty, Imperialism and the Development of International Law* (Cambridge: Cambridge University Press, 2003).

Of course, Christians themselves have been divided about property rights. The so-called mendicant poverty controversy in the thirteenth and early fourteenth centuries was about the effort of the members of the Franciscan order to renounce all claim of *dominium* over persons or things, enjoying only the 'factual use' of things necessary for survival. [30] Pope John XXII (1244–1334) would eventually oppose this by arguing that private property had been instituted already in the state of innocence.[31] Most, however, followed a kind of a middle view according to which although private property may have been wrongly instituted, it had become a perfectly lawful aspect of postlapsarian society. This would become the church's main position—perhaps understandably as the Church itself had become the most important landowner in Europe and the economic progress in its lands had been brought about by exchanges of private property. In order to explain how human acts could deviate from a natural law of common property in this way, the canonists ingeniously argued about the only permissive or hortatory nature ('*demonstratio*') of the original rule on common property. It did not actually *prohibit* the division of property.[32] The division was necessitated by sinfulness 'so that peace might easily be kept among men'.[33] It would be then for Aquinas to give a positive, utilitarian spin to this originally dark view: people were more diligent, the conduct of human affairs more orderly, and society more peaceful under private property.[34] Because property was not natural law but still universal—indeed, because the claim of property had to be recognized everywhere—theologians, canon lawyers, civil lawyers, and, eventually, the whole tradition of *ius naturae et gentium* came to understand it as part of the 'law of nations', a human law that deviated (but did so beneficially) from natural law.[35]

The historical narrative of private property as well as the role it occupies in international legality today resembles greatly that of sovereignty. This was no surprise for early modern Christian thinkers, who used the same word—*dominium*—for both ideas, thus highlighting that both had to do with the *power* that human beings exercised over each other as well as the need for *justifying* it in a world that simultaneously thinks of itself as one composed of subjects who are free and equal. One influential view of such justification lies in the '*labour theory*' according to

[30] For useful descriptions of the treatment of *dominium* in the Franciscan poverty dispute, see Virpi Mäkinen, *Property Rights in the Late Medieval Discussion on Franciscan Poverty* (Leuven: Peters, 2001); Annabel Brett, *Liberty, Right and Nature*, pp. 11–20; Coleman, 'Property and Poverty', pp. 629–43.

[31] In his encyclical *Quia vir reprobus*, John held that God had created Adam as owner of the world. See e.g. Andreas Thier, 'Heilsgeschichte und naturrechtliche Ordnung: Naturrecht vor und nach dem Sündenfall', in *Naturrecht in Antike und früher Neuzeit. Symposion aus Anlass des 75. Geburtstages von Klaus Luig*, edited by Matthias Armgardt and Tilman Repgen (Tübingen: Mohr Siebeck, 2014), p. 164.

[32] Ibid., pp. 158–62. For the canonists' expansive use of the permissive natural law construction, see Brian Tierney, *Liberty & Law. The Idea of Permissive Natural Law 1100–1800* (Washington, D.C.: Catholic University of America Press, 2014), pp. 15–47.

[33] John of Paris, *On Royal and Papal Power*, Ch XIII (64).

[34] Aquinas, ST II-II 66 A 2 Resp. (208).

[35] For a good introduction, see Stephen Buckle, *Natural Law and the Theory of Property. Grotius to Hume* (Oxford: Clarendon Press, 1991).

which it is labour that 'puts the difference of value on everything'.[36] Locke's argument was familiar. Humans were created with ownership of themselves, including the work of their hands. Through work something was annexed to things that entitled closing them off from use by others.

> For this 'labour', being the unquestionable property of the labourer, no man but he can have a right to what that is once joined to, at least where there is enough, and as good left for others.[37]

Locke's contribution to international law was to argue that God had given the world to humans so that humans could draw 'the greatest conveniences of life' from it.[38] This enabled him to dress colonial government in America in the language of natural rights. In the New World much land was lying unused, or used only for hunting and gathering. This was anathema for Locke. Land had been donated to humans by God and '... it cannot be supposed He meant it should always remain common and uncultivated. He gave it to the use of the industrious and rational (and labour was his title to it); not to the fancy or covetousness of the quarrelsome and contentious'.[39] By configuring English ways of agriculture—engrossing, enclosing, increasing productive capacities—as the kind of rational land-use that God had intended to accompany his donation, Locke was able to join a Puritan ethic of labour with his theory of property rights in a way that it very familiar in today's discourses of 'development', for example.[40]

The way in which religious ideas were expressed in property regimes that, again, assisted in justifying both imperial expansion and counter-imperial dissent is illustrated by Nahed Samour in Chapter 11. The narrative of how Islamic legal principles were used to justify Muslim expansion during the early period of conquest and then turned into defensive arguments at the time of European colonization reveals an important aspect about legal argumentation as a 'sword and shield'. In these manoeuvers the notions of 'sovereignty' and 'property' can be reframed in to fit the hegemonic situation as well as to defend religious values. The fact that Islamic international law is based on doctrine and precedent makes it resemble the older international law that recognized a variety of forms of territorial rule that were not classifiable as 'sovereignty'. The reality was never that simple; there was always a further question to be asked: whose 'property' did sovereignty protect, and against whom?

The most 'secular' of our political concepts—sovereignty and property—have found their sharpest articulations within a theological debate about justifying the authority human beings claim over each other. We may sometimes catch a glimpse of their pedigree when romantic imagination looks backwards (or forwards) into

[36] Locke, *Two Treatises of Government* (London: Everyman, 1984 [1698]). Second Treatise, § 40 (136).

[37] Locke, *Two Treatises*, First Treatise § 27 (130).

[38] Ibid., Second Treatise § 34 (132).

[39] Ibid., Second Treatise, § 34 (132–3).

[40] On the religious aspect of development, see especially Jennifer Beard, *The Political Economy of Desire: International Law, Development and the Nation State* (London: Routledge, 2007).

a moment where such power would be non-existent. An 'Augustinian' impulse may lurk behind our blasé acceptance of international conflict and the extreme inequality of the world, compelling us into defensiveness when confronted with 'youthful', 'dogmatic', or outright 'silly' critiques of the world we have created and whose resources we continue to deplete. In Chapter 7, Monica García-Salmones Rovira takes us to a moment before Thomasian utilitarianism, when an assessment of what we may enjoy as 'rights' was counterbalanced by the equal reality of that we were to aspire to as 'virtues'. It is not hard to see present controversies over the ideology of growth as transformations of the split in Christian thinking between rights of appropriation and virtues of care.

Eurocentrism

This reminds us that the secularizing narrative is a deeply Christian narrative that uses the trope of the 'fall' to explain the need and universality of the institutions that Christians have created. In Reut Paz's chapter on Jerusalem we view one incident where Christian missionarism expressed itself through an ostensible form of inter-nationalism as it sought to neutralize the 'Orient' into a place of religious freedom. The arrangement under the 1878 Berlin Treaty does seem astonishingly generous in this respect—though no doubt its European creators expected customers in the religious market to choose Christianity. This certainly is the suggestion behind Paolo Amorosa's analysis of United States policies in the Cuban intervention in 1898–1917 where American influences were automatically associated with the values of progress and Christianity. A fateful dialectic tends to associate intense nationalism with deeply felt internationalism; the values of my country are special because they are not only those of 'my country' but of the world at large. 'Where I rule, not imperialism but cosmopolitan freedom and progress reign.'

One thinker who was obsessed by the intensity of this dialectic was of course Carl Schmitt, and it is no wonder that in a study on international law and religion his views would be often referred to. In his contribution, Michele Nicoletti takes up the enigmatic figure of the 'Katechon'—'the restrainer'—as part of a philosophy of history that for Schmitt opened only the way of regional hegemons as an antidote to a world empire that would inaugurate the coming of the 'last days'. While the figure itself emerged from Christian eschatology, here (as elsewhere), the power of the analysis actually illuminates the very structure of geopolitics and the connected realpolitik, raising the question of the metaphysical basis on which the latter are debated and practised. Paul Kahn's contribution (Chapter 17) takes that very suggestion as its focus: is it possible to analyse the law of nations in purely internal, or systemic terms—or is it necessary (or perhaps useful) to think of it instead in view of a 'project' that different actors then either advance or seek to obstruct? In his analysis of the early practice of the US supreme court, Kahn sees both images at work and concludes in positing the tension between the two ideas—of 'system' and 'project'—in terms of the Christian ideas of theodicy. Both

Nicoletti and Kahn address the problem of how a particular agent may sometimes take on a role as guardian of the universal.

Unsurprisingly, most of the contributions to this book substitute 'Christianity' for 'religion'. Whether examined as an abstract vocabulary about political life on the globe or empirical practices among sovereigns, international law is deeply embedded in Christian dogmas, world-views, rites, and hierarchies. It would not be hard to defend the proposition that 'international law is a Christian discipline'. Its demonstration would point to its rise under a Christian ruler of Byzantium in the sixth century, its professionalization as part of the Christian academy in the eleventh and twelfth centuries, its coexistence with canon law and its cultivation by men of the secular clergy in France and Germany in the twelfth to fifteenth centuries. It would discuss how international law was adopted in the courts of Christian princes between the fifteenth and eighteenth centuries, was given its most elaborate early articulation as part of a tradition of *jus naturae et gentium* at Protestant universities, and was finally adopted as the language of 'civilization' by European imperial powers in the nineteenth century. With slight exaggeration, one could even think of international law as a *Protestant* discipline; most of the men who founded the *Institut de droit international* in 1873 were not only Protestants but active anti-Catholics.[41] Perhaps they thought that international law was needed to counterbalance the international influence of the Catholic Church. In Chapter 19, Pamela Slotte shows how the twentieth century Christian ecumenical movement, especially its practice-oriented American faction, easily aligned itself with international institutions. But she also demonstrates how voices inside the church critiqued this, reminding us that Christianity's alliance with international law may be a problem not only for international law, but for Christianity.

Writing about international law or carrying out research in international institutions is to explore a feature of European culture, deeply enmeshed in Christian moral theology. And is that a problem? Well, of course it is if the intention is to find in it some eternal essence that encloses not only European but all the world's cultures and vocabularies. This has been the heart of Christianity's missionary project. Pasquale Annicchino's contribution constitutes a useful reminder that not everything that takes the appearance of universal—LGBT rights in his case—can actually be squared with Christianity, or alternatively that what 'Christianity' is may also be deeply disputed among Christians themselves. There are and have always been 'mainstream' and 'deviant' (heretical) positions so that attributing something to 'Christian' influences may only be a starting-point of analysis: 'which Christianity do you mean?' Few issues have divided Christians in recent years as sharply as questions of sexual morality and it is certain that whatever position is taken on that matter, some 'Christians' are bound to support and others oppose it. To those wishing to read the history of international law as a history of Christian power this will of course complicate things. One usually finds Christians

[41] See my *The Gentle Civilizer of Nations. The Rise and Fall of International Law 1870–1960* (Cambridge: Cambridge University Press, 2002).

on both sides of any significant international issue. The question 'which' or 'whose Christianity?' cannot therefore be usually avoided. This becomes abundantly clear in Elena Paris' exposé of a highly interesting form of Eastern Orthodox theology for which open-endedness, relationality, and consent form the indispensable platform for engaging with universal law in, she suggests, 'a participatory, horizontal fashion'.

The relationship of international law (as befits a Christian tradition) with Islam has been hugely problematic, and continues to be so today. While an early, influential Christian political theologian, Giles of Rome, held that 'unbelievers are all unworthy of any possession, lordship, and power' ('... *infideles omni possessione et dominio et potestate qualibet sunt indigni*'),[42] the opposite view was held by the canon lawyer and later pope, Sinibaldo Fieschi (Innocent IV): 'infidels may lawfully enjoy both ownership and jurisdiction' ('... *possessiones et iurisdictiones licite sine peccato possunt esse apud infideles*'.[43] Since then the distinction between 'believers' and 'unbelievers' may have transmuted into other dichotomies ('civilized/uncivilized'; 'developed/undeveloped', 'democratic/undemocratic'), one side always described in terms of the fullness of that which the other is lacking, the very structure of the debate having a teleological structure hard (if not impossible) to separate from a providential theology. But if 'Christianity' (like 'Europe') may stand for varying positions, this is equally true of Islam. In Chapter 10, Moussa Abou Ramadan deals with the *topos* of division of the world into the opposite territories of Dar-al-Islam and Dar-al-Harb and takes us on a tour of classical 'schools' of Islamic legal doctrine, warning against 'the simplistic conception that if jurists say that they are basing their views on the Qur'an and the Sunna, this would prevent them from formulating positions that meet the social and political needs'. It is precisely such flexibility and the need of contextual judgment that emerge from Nahed Samour's analysis of the changing positions towards territorial rights in Islamic international law. It is quite important in any discussion of Christianity or Islam, to take account of the zigzag of hegemonic and counter-hegemonic positions that can associated with both.

'Religion' and *'International Law'*

Finally, any study of 'religion' and 'international law' must confront the fact that both terms are complex wholes of ideas and practices whose scope and meaning is contested by people most intimately connected to them. Even to ask the question of the 'relationship of international law and religion' is scarcely more than to gesture towards further inquiries and research agendas about how each entity should

[42] Giles of Rome, *On Ecclesiastical Power*, edited and translated by R. W. Dyson (New York: Columbia University Press, 2004), Pt. II, Ch XI (180/181).

[43] Innocent IV, *Commentaria in quinque libros decretalium* (Turin, 1581), quoted in James Muldoon, 'Extra ecclesiam non est dominium. Canonists and the Legitimacy of Secular Power, in *Canon Law, the Expansion of Europe, and World Order* (Aldershot: Ashgate, 1998), p. 573.

be best approached. 'Religion', for example, as Sudipta Kaviraj has shown, 'is actually a combination of many institutional and ideational structures', including:

> ... an intellectual system—sometimes more than one; a set of authoritative institutions—which can be many and contested; a range of social practices; a set of ritual observances.[44]

This makes the question about religion's relationship to the surrounding world immensely complicated. While lawyers have some experience in comparing the 'intellectual systems' of Christianity and international law, much less has been done in comparing the Hindu or Buddhist 'intellectual system' with anything familiar to jurists. When Western missionaries came to China with their notion of 'religion', the Chinese automatically associated 'religion' with Christianity. Confucianism could obviously not be a 'religion' (despite being treated as such by the Europeans) because it referred to a set of 'philosophical' teachings and ways of ethical behaviour and lacked anything resembling the rites celebrating a supernatural being. When does a 'system of ideas' qualify as 'religion' and when not? Should a set of desired forms of conduct or typical rituals be associated with such ideas? The matter is even more difficult if religion is thought in terms of institutions or social practices: what is the international legal status of the views by the 'Supreme Leader' of the Islamic Republic of Iran whose task, under the Iranian constitution, is to supervise all legislative, judicial and executive authority in the country? Where the 'Pope' does have a distinct (though disputed) historical role under international law, what about the heads of other religious communities? What is the religious authority of the UN Security Council?

But 'international law' is equally a complex notion—an intellectual system, a discourse, a set of practices and behavioural forms, a 'project' of world government, of 'peace and justice', and more. Jurists have also often argued that private ownership, contract, and rules of family life have an international, even universal import, that they are part of how human society 'naturally' operates. And yet, after the eighteenth century, they have *not* been read as belonging to '*public* international law'. There is now a tendency to read property, private contracts, human rights, intellectual property, insurance, transport, and a whole set of laws organizing international economic transactions as a part of a 'transnational' or 'global' law that penetrates deep into the ways of life of domestic societies, intervening in spheres that many have regarded as the legitimate purvey of 'religion'. As long as they are not property brought under the study of international law, a vital part of legal globalization—and its significance to religions—will remain obscure.[45]

I make these points only to highlight the broad expanse of ways in which 'religion' and 'international law' relate to each other, sometimes supporting, sometimes colliding against each other. Many preliminary decisions about the meaning

[44] Sudipta Kaviraj, 'On Thick and Thin of Religion: Some Critical Reflections on Secularization Theory', in *Religion and the Political Imagination*, edited by Ira Katznelson and Gareth Steadman Jones (Cambridge: Cambridge University Press, 2010), p. 339.

[45] I have advocated widening the studies of international law in my 'Expanding the Study of the History of International Law', 56 *American Journal of Legal History* (2016).

of the two entities have to be made before a study of their interaction can even start: are we interested in rites, intellectual systems, institutions, vocabularies? Inevitably, only some meeting-points can be touched upon in a book like this; the choices reflect the background of the authors—what perspective they feel confident in adopting, and what problem worthy of being examined and illuminated. We are only beginning to accept that Weber was wrong to believe that the inevitable rationalization of modern society would gradually banish religion from public life. In most spheres relevant to international law religion has a visible presence. Claims of legal significance are being made by religious entities from the Taliban to fundamental Christians, Zionists to Hindu nationalists. To deal with such claims adequately, scholars have to come to grips with the world beyond cosmopolitan rationalization. And even if we continue to value aspects of the secularization thesis (as I think we should), we must bear in mind that there is no further 'reason' that can convince us of this. Taking faith seriously is a first step in understanding the roles of 'reason' adequately, including the many ways it has failed us. In this process 'stable ground' is hardly to be expected.

Bibliography

Anghie, Antony. Sovereignty, Imperialism and the Development of International Law (Cambridge: Cambridge University Press, 2003).

Aquinas, Thomas. 'Summa theologiae', II-II. In *Political Writings*, edited by R. W. Dyson (Cambridge: Cambridge University Press, 2002).

Beard, Jennifer. The Political Economy of Desire: International Law, Development and the Nation State (London: Routledge, 2007).

Berman, Harold J. *Law and Revolution. The Formation of the Western Legal Tradition* (Cambridge, Mass.: Harvard University Press, 1983).

Black, Jane. *Absolutism in Renaissance Milan. Plenitude of Power under the Visconti and the Sforza 1329–1535* (Oxford: Oxford University Press, 2009).

Brett, Annabel. *Liberty, Right and Nature. Individual Rights in Later Scholastic Thought* (Cambridge: Cambridge University Press, 1997).

Buckle, Stephen. *Natural Law and the Theory of Property. Grotius to Hume* (Oxford: Clarendon Press, 1991).

Coleman, Janet. 'Property and Poverty'. In *The Cambridge History of Medieval Political Thought c. 350—c. 1450*, edited by J. H. Burns (Cambridge: Cambridge University Press, 1988), pp. 607–48.

Courtenay, William J. *Capacity and Volition. A History of the Distinction between Absolute and Ordained Power* (Pergamo: Lubrina, 1990).

de la Rasilla del Moral, Ignacio. 'The Fascist Mimesis of Spanish International Law and its Vitorian Aftermath, 1939–1953'. *Journal of the History of International Law* 14 (2012): pp. 207–36.

de Vitoria, Francisco. Relection 'De Indis'. In *Political Writings*, edited by A. Pagden and J. Lawrance (Cambridge: Cambridge University Press, 1991).

Fulton, T. W. *The Sovereignty of the Sea. An Historical Account of the Claims of England to the Dominion of the British Seas, and of the Evolution of Territorial Waters* (Edinburgh & London: William Blackwood and Sons, 1911).

Giles of Rome. *On Ecclesiastical Power*, edited and translated by R. W. Dyson (New York: Columbia University Press, 2004).
Gratian, *The Treatise on Laws, with the Ordinary Gloss (Decretum DD 1-20)*, translated by A. Thompson and J. Gordley (Washington, D. C.: Catholic University of America Press, 1993).
Heeren, J. P. *Hugo Grotius as Apologist for the Christian Religion* (Leiden: Brill, 2004).
Thomas Hobbes, *Leviathan*, edited by J. G. A. Gaskin (Oxford; Oxford University Press, 2008 [1651]).
Hoffmann, Hasso. 'Hugo Grotius'. In *Staatsdenker in der frühen Neuzeit*, edited by Michael Stolleis (Munich: Beck, 1995), pp. 59–60.
ICJ. 'Legality of Threat or use of Nuclear Weapons'. Reports 1996, dispositif (266/44).
Innocent IV, *Commentaria in quinque libros decretalium* (Turin, 1581), quoted in Muldoon, James. 'Extra ecclesiam non est dominium. Canonists and the Legitimacy of Secular Power'. In *Canon Law, the Expansion of Europe, and World Order* (Aldershot: Ashgate, 1998), p. 573.
John of Paris. *On Royal and Papal Power*, edited by A. P. Monahan (New York: Columbia University Press, 1974 [1302/3]).
Kant, Immanuel. 'The Idea for Universal History with a Cosmopolitan Purpose'. In *Political Writings*, edited by K. Reiss (Cambridge: Cambridge University Press, 1991), Seventh Proposition, p. 47.
Kant, Immanuel. *Religion within the Bounds of Mere Reason*, edited by A. Wood and G. Giovanni (Cambridge: Cambridge University Press, 1998).
Kaviraj, Sudipta. 'On Thick and Thin of Religion: Some Critical Reflections on Secularization Theory'. In *Religion and the Political Imagination*, edited by Ira Katznelson and Gareth Steadman Jones (Cambridge: Cambridge University Press, 2010), p. 339.
Kennedy, David. 'Losing Faith in the Secular: Law, Religion and the Culture of International Governance'. In *Religion and International Law*, edited by Mark Janis and Carolyn Evans (The Hague: Martinus Nijhoff, 1999), pp. 309–20.
Kennedy, Duncan. *A Critique of Adjudication (fin de siècle)* (Cambridge, Mass.: Harvard University Press, 1997).
Klabbers, Jan. 'Law, Ethics and Global Governance: Accountability in Perspective'. *New Zealand Journal of Public and International Law* 11 (2013): pp. 309–21.
Kniepel, Barbara. *Die Naturrechtslehre des Hugo Grotius als Einigungsprinzip der Christenheit, dargestellt an seiner Stellung zum Calvinism* (Kessel: Bladitsch, 1971).
Kooijmans, P-H. 'Protestantism and the Development of International Law'. *Recueil des Cours* 152 (1976/IV) 10980).
Koskenniemi, Martti, Walter Rech, and Manuel Fonseca. *International Law and Empire* (Oxford: Oxford University Press, 2016).
Koskenniemi, Martti. 'Expanding the Study of the History of International Law'. *American Journal of Legal History* 56 (2016).
Koskenniemi, Martti. 'Formalismus, Fragmentierung, Freiheit—Kantische Themen im heutigen Völkerrecht'. In *Transnationale Verrechtlichung*, edited by Regina Kreide & Andreas Niederberger (Frankfurt: Campus, 2008), pp. 65–89.
Koskenniemi, Martti. 'The Political Theology of Trade Law: The Scholastic Contribution'. In *From Bilateralism to Community Interest. Essays in Honour of Judge Bruno Simma*, edited by Ulrich Fastenrath et al. (Oxford: Oxford University Press, 2011), pp. 90–112.
Koskenniemi, Martti. *The Gentle Civilizer of Nations. The Rise and Fall of International Law 1870–1960* (Cambridge: Cambridge University Press, 2002).

Ku, Charlotte. 'Catholicism, the peace of Westphalia, and the origins of modern international law'. *The European Legacy* 1 (1996): pp. 734–9.

Lieblich, Eliav and Yoram Shachar. 'Cosmopolitanism at a Crossroads: Hersch Lauterpacht and the Israeli Declaration of Independence'. *British Year Book of International Law* 84 (2013): pp. 1–51.

Locke, Two Treatises of Government (London: Everyman, 1984 [1698]).

Mäkinen, Virpi. *Property Rights in the Late Medieval Discussion on Franciscan Poverty* (Leuven: Peters, 2001).

Moyn, Samuel. *Christianity and Human Rights* (Princeton: Princeton University Press, 2016).

Mühlegger, Florian. *Hugo Grotius. Ein christlicher Humanist in politischen Verantwortung* (Berlin: De Gruyter, 2007).

Pennington, Kenneth. *The Prince and the Law 1200–1600. Sovereignty and Rights in the Western Legal Tradition* (Berkeley: University of California Press, 1993).

Renoux-Zagamé, Marie-France. *Origines théologiques du concept moderne de propriété* (Genève: Droz, 1987).

Schmitt, Carl. *Political Theology. Four Essays on the Concept of Sovereignty* (Chicago: University of Chicago Press, 2010).

Seelmann, Kurt. *Die Lehre des Fernando Vazquez de Menchaga vom Dominium* (Cologne: Heymanns, 1979).

Sommerville, J. P. 'John Selden, The Law of Nature, and the origins of Government'. *The Historical Journal* 27 (1984): pp. 437–47.

Sommerville, J. P. 'Selden, Grotius and the Seventeenth-Century Intellectual Revolution in Moral and Political Theory'. In *Rhetoric and Law in early Modern Europe*, edited by Victoria Kahn and Lorna Hutson (New Haven, Conn.: Yale University Press, 2001), pp. 334–9.

Thier, Andreas. 'Heilsgeschichte und naturrechtliche Ordnung: Naturrecht vor und nach dem Sündenfall', in Matthias Armgardt & Tilman Repgen, Naturrecht in Antike und früher Neuzeit. Symposion aus Anlass des 75. Geburtstages von Klaus Luig (Tübingen: Mohr Siebeck, 2014), pp. 151–172.

Tierney, Brian. *Liberty & Law. The Idea of Permissive Natural Law 1100–1800* (Washington, DC: Catholic University of America Press, 2014), pp. 15–47.

Ullmann, Walter. *The Growth of Papal Government in the Middle Ages. A Study in the Ideological Relation of Clerical to Lay Power* (London: Methuen, 1962).

Wyduckel, Dieter. *Princeps Legibus Solutus. Eine Untersuchung zur frühmodernen Rechts- und Staatslehre* (Berlin: Duncker & Humblot, 1979).

PART I

NATURAL LAW AND *IUS GENTIUM*

1

Law, Justice, and Charity in a Divided Christendom: 1500–1625

Sarah Mortimer

All law is shaped by the values of the community that recognizes, upholds, and obeys it. In early modern Europe, those values were predominantly Christian, formed through a long process of Christian acculturation and through Christian academic traditions which had helped to create a common set of principles and assumptions. But from the 1520s, the people of Europe were divided by their shared Christian faith, as well as united by it. The Reformation would create deep rifts within Christendom, and it became increasingly clear that the fracturing of the old Church was irreversible. At the same time, the world beyond Christendom had begun to open up with the discovery of what was known as the New World. In the sixteenth century, the rules of international engagement would have to be rewritten, and the role of Christianity on the international stage became highly contested. This chapter will consider some of the implications of the Reformation for the concept of universal laws and morality. New ideas about faith, and about moral philosophy and justice were emerging, and new ways of justifying war while limiting its scope had to be found.

At the start of the sixteenth century there were few Europeans who doubted that there were laws which applied to all human beings and by which they ought to be guided. These laws were partly natural, ordained by God for the direction and flourishing of the human race, and partly consensual, developed over time through agreements between peoples. The latter set of laws was sometimes known as the *ius gentium*, or law of peoples. These laws were important, forming the basis of moral and political life. But on their own they were incomplete. They were only part of a wider ethical and spiritual framework designed to ensure human felicity in this world and the next. True Christians would not only follow the laws, but their actions would be guided by the theological virtues of faith, hope, and charity—virtues which had to be infused into them by divine grace. By 1520, however, there were very different ideas about how the international laws—of nature and of peoples—related to Christian virtues and to the Catholic Church which claimed to uphold and promote them, across the whole world. This discussion was in some ways a technical and academic one, but its impact could be felt well beyond the university halls and court chapels. The relationship between these two universal sets of norms, Christianity and the natural law, was now contested, often violently and by force of arms. In this chapter I will suggest the importance of new efforts to reimagine this relationship, especially in ways that diminished—but did not eradicate—the claims of the Church.[1]

The relationship between the Church and natural law grew more complicated after the Reformation. Protestant princes and rulers withdrew their territories from obedience to the Roman Catholic Church, and set up their own ecclesiastical establishments, but they did not deny that religion was, at least in some sense, an international concern, and not something that could be left solely to the discretion of individual rulers. From the start, the Protestants knew they would need each other's help if they were to survive for any length of time, and the creation of alliances both defensive and offensive remained crucial for the fortunes of the Protestants. Similarly, Catholics acknowledged a duty to assist the Church across national frontiers, and by 1600 the power of the papacy to intervene in political as well as religious affairs was forcefully defended—and vehemently challenged. As this suggests, the leaders of all the major churches saw their religious duty as explicitly international; the true church as they understood it extended beyond the human boundaries of nation or generation. Indeed, the claims of international, spiritual solidarity were felt so strongly that they destabilized European politics for a hundred years, prompting efforts to rein in the destructive power of religious loyalties. The result was a way of understanding the international community which, despite its violent origins, still has much to commend it. The focus of this chapter will, therefore, be the natural law and its connection to the different theologies that emerged in the early modern period. It will explore some of the ways in which new ideas about Christianity—the most powerful universal value system of the time—helped to shape international relations and concepts of international law.

Law and the Church in Early Modern Catholicism

The starting point for the most influential reflection on both law and virtue in the early modern period was the work of Thomas Aquinas. His *Summa Theologica* became the textbook for students and teachers at leading universities, notably Salamanca, and would be supplemented by the extensive commentary on the Summa provided by the great Dominican theologian, Cardinal Cajetan.[2] Although sixteenth-century commentators on the *Summa* diverged from Aquinas in many places, their use of this text gave them, at the very least, a common starting point

[1] For a modern discussion of similar issues see Anver M. Emon, Matthew Levering, and David Novak, *Natural Law: A Jewish, Christian, and Islamic Trialogue* (Oxford: Oxford University Press, 2014), esp. ch. 2.

[2] Francis Oakley, 'Christian Obedience and Authority, 1520–1550', in *The Cambridge History of Political Thought, 1450–1700*, edited by J.H. Burns (Cambridge: Cambridge University Press, 1991), pp. 153–4.

for their discussion of law. Aquinas believed that a ruler should govern in the way best suited to the common good, understood in local terms, as what was best for the particular city or territory. He gave the ruler considerable leeway and discretion, but argued that the ruler's laws would only oblige his subjects if they did not contravene the divine laws given by God to human beings. Furthermore, although the ruler could determine matters that pertained to the common good of the city here on earth, he was always subject to the Catholic Church when it came to matters of salvation. The flexibility and autonomy of particular, local human rule, founded in the law of nature, was balanced by the universal concerns of the Church, entrusted by God with responsibility for the souls of the faithful.[3] This broadly Thomist tradition also offered, therefore, a nuanced account of natural virtues, directed to life in this world, and argued that these were surpassed and fulfilled by grace, which enabled and infused the theological virtues. Cajetan developed this distinction further, and in his commentary took great care to show that virtuous actions were possible without grace, although it was impossible to perform them all the time without divine assistance. Some of the actions of pagans could even be called good, at least in a moral sense.[4] Along similar lines, Cajetan sought to separate out the various obligations of a Christian and a citizen, to show how political societies could work and could strive for the common good, even without grace or revealed religion.[5] Grace and the Christian revelation could then complete and fulfil the natural desires men had, and elevate their thoughts to the world beyond and above nature. In Cajetan's writing there is a real effort to show how the local claims of the city can be reconciled with the universal, Catholic faith.

Catholicism is a religion which makes universal claims, and international, for the power of the Church is assumed to extend across human boundaries of state and principality. Among early modern Catholics, therefore, it was widely accepted that the Papacy had some kind of spiritual jurisdiction over the faithful. But there was fierce controversy over the extent to which this spiritual power might entail the right or even the duty to intervene in the temporal affairs of individual kingdoms or states. This issue was, it is true, primarily one which concerned Christians, rather than a matter of 'international' law strictly speaking; everyone agreed that the Church had no right to the obedience of humans who had not been baptized into the faith and neither the Pope nor his agents could simply storm into pagan lands without just cause. But, as we shall see, matters on the ground were not so straightforward and the boundary between those within and without the Church's sphere of influence was a very permeable one. For, as we shall see, Catholics tended to argue that the non-Christian world was subject to a natural law which was itself

[3] On Aquinas's political thought see his *Political Writings*, edited by R. Dyson (Cambridge: Cambridge University Press, 2002). The central texts for our purposes are the questions on law in the Prima Secundae (qs 90–108) and on justice in the Secunda Secundae (especially qs 57–62).

[4] *Sancti Thomae Aquinati Opera omnia, iussu impensaque Leonis XIII* (Rome: 1882). Comments ad IaIIae Q. 109:2 'Whether a man can do or will good without grace?', vol. 7, pp. 292–4.

[5] E.g. the commentary ad. IIaIIae 47:11 (Whether the prudence that is concerned with one's own good is the same 'species' as the prudence that extends to the common good), vol. 8, pp. 359–60.

imperfect and in some sense incomplete without the Christian faith. The progress of the gospel throughout the world could be assumed and the cause of true religion promoted, even in pagan lands.

One of the most thoughtful—and well-connected—commentators on spiritual and temporal power was the Salamancan professor of theology, Francisco Vitoria.[6] Vitoria was willing to grant that 'the heathen have legitimate rulers and masters'; the unbelief of those outside Christendom does not prevent them from setting up properly constituted political authority. Moreover, even if there were no spiritual power it would still be possible to have some kind of order and authority here on earth. But this concession was limited, for he was insistent that civil authority in fact depended upon spiritual power and was subject to it, at least to some extent. The rationale for this was, for him, that 'human happiness is imperfect, and ordered towards the perfection of supernatural felicity'. Moreover, the imperfection of human happiness is universal; it is not only Christians but all human beings who desire the eternal blessedness of supernatural felicity, however dimly they apprehend it. Because this end or goal is necessarily superior to the goal of human authority, which is the common good here on earth, so must the Church be superior to the civil powers, at least in matters which concern this supernatural end. The human desire for lasting happiness brings with it an obligation to obey the Church, as the only means by which a goal can be achieved, and it follows, for Vitoria, that the duties and obligations of the Christian go beyond those of nature alone.[7] For Vitoria and Cajetan, as for their colleagues and students working with a Thomist tradition, the laws and norms of nature have their own integrity and they are essential for human life. But they are also a means to spiritual ends, and these ends ought to shape and direct human actions, even within the earthly, natural sphere.

The authority of the Church extends only to those who are baptized into it, and accept its jurisdiction, but—argued Cajetan and other Thomists—the Church can still reach into the natural sphere and order it for spiritual ends. The Church can defend Christians, even against their own rulers, and can release people from obedience to their kings if those kings apostatize or become heretical. According to Vitoria, if the people of Christendom elected an unbeliever as their ruler, then the Pope should and could depose him, even though he were a lawfully instituted sovereign. And if the people of the newly discovered Americas wanted to worship the Christian God but were commanded to practice the old idolatry instead, then Christians must protect them from rulers who were otherwise legitimate.[8] These brief examples—which could be multiplied—make clear the strength of the force

[6] For an account of Vitoria's life and work that places him in relation to wider theological traditions see *Vorlesungen (Relectiones)*, vol. I, edited by Ulrich Horst, Heinz-Gerhard Justenhoven, and Joachim Stüben (Stuttgart: W. Kohlhammer, 1995–99), pp. 16–41.

[7] Francisco de Vitoria, *Political Writings*, edited by A. Pagden (Cambridge: Cambridge University Press, 1991), quotation from p. 90. Cajetan's understanding of man's natural desire for God is explored in detail in Lawrence Feingold, *The Natural Desire to See God According to St. Thomas Aquinas and His Interpreters*, 2nd edn (Naples, FL.: Sapientia Press, 2010), esp. pp. 175–9.

[8] Vitoria, *Political Writings*, pp. 94, 286.

exerted by Christianity over the natural world. For Vitoria and those who followed him, the local, earthly city or kingdom might have its own completeness, in its own sphere, but it could not be insulated from the working of the Church. And nor should the inhabitants of any kingdom desire such a separation. Like all human beings, they have a natural desire not only for felicity in this world but also in the next, and Vitoria assumed that men and women should and will seek to join the Church.

Kings and princes could not simply be left to their own devices, but must be held within the communion of the Christian Church, at least according to the line of thinking which became increasingly powerful at Rome. The state needed to acknowledge the values beyond its reach, for the human beings who made up each state had souls and had a natural desire, however inchoate, for eternal blessedness. The leading theologians Francisco Suarez and Robert Bellarmine were both employed by the papacy to defend this line of reasoning, in Suarez's case against the views of James I of England. Suarez's argument was underpinned by a teleological vision of the universe, in which all power existed for a purpose and the lower powers served those which aimed at higher purposes. As he explained to King James, 'The temporal power is ordered to preserving the peace and moral decency of the republic ... But the ecclesiastical power is ordered to attaining eternal salvation'. Where the two conflict it was evident that the spiritual power must be superior, and where necessary the Pope could depose a heretical king. James did not accept this, of course, but he struggled to provide a coherent explanation of his own position.[9]

Christianity was not only about spiritual power, of course; the concern with infused, theological virtues was still very much present in the Catholic tradition. Chief among these virtues was charity, an umbrella term which covered all actions carried out for love of God and love of neighbour. This central virtue was one of the chief subjects of Aquinas's *Summa*, but he had treated it separately from justice and the connections between justice and charity had to be drawn out by later commentators. The central locus for such discussion was the issue of homicide and particularly of the legitimacy of killing another person in self-defence, which Aquinas had touched upon in the *Secunda Secundae*. In his commentary on this place, Cajetan offered his own, lengthy, opinion: he stressed that while it was 'of greater charity' to allow oneself to be killed so that an attacker might repent and save his soul, no one was bound to this by justice.[10] Here we see Cajetan's characteristic concern to tease out the different layers of moral obligation, and show how they might interact. The main lines of his thought were followed by Vitoria, and then by one of Vitoria's pupils, Domingo de Soto. For Soto, a person who is

[9] Francisco Suarez, *Defensio Fidei Catholicæ et apostolicæ aduersus Anglicanæ sectæ errores* (Coimbra: 1613). Quotation from III.6.12. On the controversy between Suarez and James see Charles McIlwain, ed., *The Political Works of James I, Reprinted from the Edition of 1616* (Cambridge, Mass.: Harvard University Press, 1918), Introduction.

[10] *Sancti Thomi Aquinati Opera omnia, iussu impensaque Leonis XIII*, vol. 9 (Rome: Vatican Polyglot Press, 1882), p. 75 (Ad IIaIIae Q. 64).

attacked 'has the right of defending himself: and nevertheless it is free for him to renounce such a right for the sake of charity'.[11] As Soto's account makes clear, a Christian was at liberty to follow the order of charity rather than justice, and in some circumstances this would, presumably, be meritorious. But the two must not be confused, and no one could be obliged to act in accordance with charity by their sovereign.

It is striking that the scholastics rarely drew political conclusions from their discussions of charity. Indeed, at times it can seem as though they wished to limit the implications of charity within the earthly world. The best example of this is in their treatment of war, which Aquinas had considered as a sin against charity. Vitoria and Suarez also deal with war under the heading of charity, Vitoria as part of his commentary on the Summa and Suarez in the *Opus Triplici Virtutis* (1621). But Vitoria said little about charity, and although Suarez admitted that there could be wars which were sins against charity but not against justice, he did not go into details.[12] Both focused instead on the justice of warfare, and Suarez's fellow Jesuit, Luis de Molina, even argued that war was best treated as an issue of justice rather than charity.[13] For the Catholic Thomists, therefore, the realm of natural law, justice, and civil authority was limited in two parallel ways, by the authority of the Church and by the promptings of charity. Above the universal, natural law there was a second tier of duties and obligations, relevant for human beings because they sought spiritual as well as material fulfilment.

The power of this two-tier theology, demonstrated most fully in the Jesuits' defence of the Papal deposing power, proved too much for many lay Catholics. This was especially true in France, where the lives of two successive monarchs—Henri III and Henri IV—were ended by fanatical Catholics intent on preserving the realm from heretical rulers. Though the Jesuits were quick to distance themselves from such murderous actions, the logic of Suarez's argument seemed to point in the direction of assassination and tyrannicide. When the Estates General met in 1614, four years after the death of Henri IV, they swiftly agreed that Suarez's reply to James I be burnt. The Third Estate also called for an official renunciation of the doctrine of papal deposing power, but the response from the French clergy, led by Cardinal du Perron, was uncompromising. For du Perron, Papal authority even in such high matters of state was necessary; the alternative was to allow kings and rulers unacceptably wide moral and spiritual latitude. Unchecked by the papacy,

[11] Soto, *De Iustitia et De Iure* (Lyon: 1582), p. 145 (book V Q1 a. 8). On this passage see also Annabel S. Brett, *Liberty, Right and Nature* (Cambridge: Cambridge University Press, 1997), p. 163, where a more detailed discussion is provided. For Vitoria see his *Reflection on Homicide & Commentary on Summa Theologiae IIa–IIae q. 64*, edited and translated by J. Doyle (Milwaukee: Marquette University Press, 1997).

[12] Vitoria's commentary is translated in James Scott, *Spanish Origins of International Law* (Oxford: Clarendon Press, 1934) and Suarez's disputation on war is in *Selections from Three Works* (Oxford: Clarendon Press, 1944), see esp. p. 820.

[13] For a discussion of Molina's views see Joao Manuel A. A. Fernandes, 'Luis de Molina: On War', in *A Companion to Luis de Molina*, edited by M. Kaufmann and A. Aichele (Leiden: Brill, 2013), pp. 227–56.

the king could ignore the rules of Christendom, as Protestant rulers had done, and could lead his realm down the path of moral and spiritual ruin. For James I, who replied in harsh and bitter terms to du Perron's charges, no government could be stable unless protected from Papal interference, and his position won significant sympathy in France and beyond.[14] After the 1610s, even the papacy was wary about pressing its claims too stridently, and few scholars wanted to reopen the vexed question of the relative claims of temporal and spiritual authority.

Protestantism, Resistance, and Natural Law

As the French were all too well aware, the Roman Catholic Church could provide a remedy—practical and ideological—for the excesses of a tyrannical or heretical ruler who disregarded the law of God. This particular solution, based on papal spiritual power, was not available to the Protestants, of course, and yet they still believed that rulers had a duty to obey divine law. Indeed, when Catholic princes began to clamp down hard on Protestant communities, and practised what the Protestants believed to be tyranny, theories of resistance were soon developed. Leading figures in both Lutheran and Reformed communities began to argue that such tyranny ought to be prevented, and by force if necessary.[15] In other words, the Protestants maintained that local, civil rulers had to abide by rules and norms that were given by God and were universal in their scope. They quickly found, however, that working out how the supranational laws common to all Christians could be enforced within particular kingdoms and cities presented them with a serious intellectual challenge. This section will set out briefly some of the options open to Protestants in their efforts to hold on to a concept of international universal law.

The Catholic endeavour to balance the local and the universal had relied heavily on Thomist philosophy, but the deep Protestant hostility towards Aquinas, at least in the early stages of the Reformation, ruled out this option. Indeed, Luther's opinion of the relationship between the temporal and spiritual powers was very different from that of scholastic theologians like Vitoria, for he saw the civil and spiritual realms as separate and distinct. The temporal realm was not 'ordered' towards the spiritual, and earthly virtue was not a prerequisite for the salvation of a person's soul. Instead, there were two different governments, one spiritual and one secular, which existed in parallel. Both had their distinct, separate place in the divine scheme, and secular government did not extend to matters of religion (although rulers who were also Christians ought to play their part in the Church).[16] The coherence of Luther's thought is often disputed, and not least because where his

[14] See McIlwain, *The Political Works,* Introduction; J. Michael Hayden, *France and the Estates General of 1614* (Cambridge: Cambridge University Press, 1974).

[15] On Protestant resistance theory more generally see Quentin Skinner, *The Foundations of Modern Political Thought*, vol. II (Cambridge: Cambridge University Press, 1979), part 3.

[16] W. Cargill Thompson, *The Political Thought of Martin Luther* (Brighton: Harvester Press, 1984), esp. pp. 24–35.

Catholic opponents (notably Cajetan) thought in terms of hierarchies and order, Luther preferred sharp dichotomies, often held together as paradox.[17] But his disdain for the Catholic way of thinking, with its sense of continuity between this world and the next, was unmistakable.

The Protestants did not reject one concept often associated with St Thomas: the concept of natural law. But Luther's insistence that human beings were saved by faith not good works undercut a whole Catholic tradition of discussing ethics in terms of virtues and acquired dispositions, and this had important consequences for Protestant natural law.[18] In the first systematic discussion of Lutheran theology, Melanchthon poured scorn on the concept of 'evangelical counsels', practices that were recommended rather than commanded to Christians, and which were performed most fully by the clergy and monks.[19] For him and for the Protestants who followed his ethics, the line between right and wrong action was clearly drawn, and the realm of actions which were recommended but not commanded was—in theory at least—abolished. The scope of moral philosophy was the law of nature alone, and any suggestion of an 'order of charity' was ridiculed as absurd, for salvation came through faith alone and not through efforts to live according to a higher standard of life.[20] We have seen that for Soto and Cajetan, a Christian might act for the sake of charity rather than justice, for example allowing himself to be killed rather than defending himself. Against this Catholic position, the Protestants tended to argue that the standards of divine and natural law were absolute—and that they applied across the world.

Melanchthon and his Protestant successors knew that the principles of natural law were general, and they acknowledged that cities and kingdoms could shape their own civil laws in line with those general principles. The natural law allowed for variation in local customs, and these were entirely legitimate. Similarly, when reading the Bible it was important to distinguish between the moral teaching of the natural law and the particular practices of the Israelite people. The many ceremonial and judicial rules by which they had been obliged were not part of the natural law. But while the demands of custom and local law might change, the ethical requirements of the divine, natural law would never alter. Charity and justice were united, and all people were obliged by the demands of the natural law, even though they could never fulfil them.

[17] Jared Wicks, 'Thomism between Renaissance and Reformation: The Case of Cajetan', *Archiv Für Reformationsgeschichte* 68 (1977): pp. 9–31.

[18] On Luther's understanding of virtue see Jennifer A. Herdt, *Putting on Virtue: the Legacy of the Splendid Vices* (Chicago: University of Chicago Press, 2008), ch. 6; also Servais Pinckaers, *The Sources of Christian Ethics*, translated by Mary Noble (Edinburgh: Bloomsbury Publishing, 1995), pp. 139, 282–5.

[19] From the Loci Communes in *Melanchthon and Bucer*, edited by Wilhelm Pauck (London: SCM Press, 1969), p. 57.

[20] E.g. Melanchthon, *Orations on Philosophy and Education*, edited by S. Kusakawa (Cambridge: Cambridge University Press, 1999); Dino Bellucci, 'Natural Philosophy and Ethics in Melanchthon', in *Moral Philosophy on the Threshold of Modernity*, edited by J. Kraye and R. Saarinen (Dordrecht: Kluwer Academic, 2005), pp. 235–54.

The power, and the limits, of the Protestant appeals to natural law quickly became evident, as can be seen in the writing of those English exiles who had fled from the Catholic regime of Mary Tudor. In their efforts to coax their fellow Protestants to take up arms against the Queen, they penned some of the most strident, early statements of international, natural duties applicable to all human beings. In his *Short Treatise*, perhaps the best known of these tracts, John Ponet appealed to the law of nature which 'testifieth to every mannes conscience, that it is naturall to cutte awaie an incurable member which (being suffred) would destroie the hole bodie'.[21] This law was known to the heathen and to the pagans; Ponet took care to show that it was not specifically Christian. And yet this natural law was an essential guide for all Christians, one which had not been altered or affected in any way by the coming of Christ and the redemption he brought. The natural law, for Ponet, was the one, single, universal standard for all human ethical action, by which all human beings were obliged. Any transgression of this natural law would lead to disaster and divine punishment, as the English people were currently discovering. Understood like this, the natural law was a powerful concept—so powerful that many Protestant authors were in fact quite wary of it. They tended to argue that custom, local practice, and the consent of generations were also important to political life; indeed, Protestant civil philosophy was as much concerned with the claims of utility and earthly advantages as it was with arguments from nature and natural law.[22]

It was after the massacre, on and after St Bartholomew's Day 1572, of at least five thousand French Protestants, that natural law arguments achieved real fame and notoriety. The most important tract in this regard was the *Vindiciae, Contra Tyrannos* (1579), a work written in large part to encourage foreign intervention in the affairs of France, in order to protect the Protestants. The author (whose identity remains uncertain) was deeply concerned about the direction of French policy in the 1570s, fearing that the Protestant, 'Huguenot', minority was likely to be eradicated. In these circumstances, the author argued that 'the laws of nature, of nations and civil law command us to take up arms against these tyrants' and he called upon the French people to resist and reject their king and to restore justice and true religion.[23] In the final section, he addressed himself to the princes of Europe, who ought also to assist in this noble endeavour.

It is noticeable that for the author, human beings are obliged to act in accordance with charity, for the demands of charity cannot be separated from those of justice. The final, fourth question was written to show that we must help our fellow Christians, whether they live in our own country or not, for the charity which bids us come to the aid of our spiritual brothers is itself the supreme expression of justice. The author sought to persuade the neighbouring princes that 'it is

[21] John Ponet, *A Short Treatise of Politic Power* (1556), p. [108].

[22] Annabel S. Brett, *Changes of State* (Princeton: Princeton University Press, 2011), pp. 62–7.

[23] *Vindiciae, Contra Tyrannos: or, Concerning the Legitimate Power of a Prince over the People, and of the People over a Prince,* edited by George Garnett (Cambridge: Cambridge University Press, 1994), quotation from p. 150.

much more just to defend another than oneself', because this is done out of 'pure charity' rather than anger or revenge. It is a duty which cannot be renounced and which applies to all who care about pleasing God.[24] That the ethical and religious demands of God are uniform and non-negotiable was crucial for the argument, although the author's insistence on this point was as much the product of the imperilled political situation as it was of specifically Protestant theology.

Not all Protestants agreed with this account of natural law and charity. By the late sixteenth century there were several articulate communities of Christian pacifists, men and women whose example and writings highlighted the tension between the words of Christ and the norms of this, human world. These views were found mainly among the Mennonite community in the Netherlands and in Poland among the Racovians. These groups took seriously Christ's command to 'turn the other cheek' and refused to take part in government or warfare. To them, it was clear that the charity and forgiveness demanded by Christ could not be compatible with political life as it was currently constituted. And not only did they reject the marriage of justice and charity effected by the author of the *Vindiciae*, they were even critical of Catholic accounts in which the virtue of justice was accepted as legitimate, but subordinated to the higher virtue of charity. Such counter-cultural values were seen as dangerous and threatening; few governments were willing to allow subversive beliefs like these to be expressed. But the Mennonite and Racovian position continued to present an important critique of Protestant thinking, and some of their principles would be taken up into mainstream political thought, as we shall see in the next section.[25]

Hugo Grotius: Natural Law and Christian Charity

By the 1620s, the pacifists' position seemed to some to be more persuasive than ever. The destructive potential of Christianity and of militant religious loyalties had never, perhaps, been more apparent. Not only had war broken out in Germany between the Calvinist supporters of Frederick V, Elector of the Palatinate, and the Holy Roman Emperor, Ferdinand II, but the Truce between the Spanish and the Dutch had expired and in France the Huguenots were continuing their resistance to Louis XIII with English help. All of Europe was affected, by the fighting itself or the upheaval it caused to civilian life, and ties of confessional loyalty had greatly exacerbated the conflict. Frederick's cause was upheld by the Calvinist rulers in the Empire, and by the Lutheran kings of Denmark and then Sweden; the Dutch and the German Protestants coordinated their efforts in the face of collaboration between Spanish and Austrian Habsburg; and the Stuarts' interventions in France, Spain, and the Empire were motivated, at least in part, by sympathy for their

[24] Ibid. p. 181.

[25] See George Huntston Williams, *The Radical Reformation* (London: Weidenfeld & Nicolson, 1962) and Sarah Mortimer, *Reason and Religion in the English Revolution* (Cambridge: Cambridge University Press, 2010), ch. 1.

co-religionists. All sides produced pamphlets and tracts in the hope of drumming up support for their cause, and the godliness of the wars was a prominent theme.[26]

It was in this context that one of the most influential tracts on war and international law was published—Hugo Grotius' *De Jure Belli ac Pacis* (1625). The power of Grotius' writing lay in his ability to show how Christian commitments, moral norms, and a strong conception of national sovereignty might all be combined and aligned, and the wars within Europe thereby moderated. *De Jure Belli* gained a wide readership and was certainly admired, but it is clear that many of his views were not novel. Often, he simply echoed the works of his predecessors, albeit with more style and rhetorical elegance than they had managed.[27] These predecessors were contemporary and classical; jurists and theologians; Catholics, Protestants, and pagans; and it was Grotius' achievement to have combined these different ideas into a synthesis which was distinctively his own. What I want to focus on in the last section of this chapter is the relationship between his particular version of Protestant Christianity and his understanding of natural law. For it was his heterodox theology that enabled him to show how a Christian could be true to his faith without destabilizing his local political system. Christian, supranational loyalties and commitments could be combined with citizenship, for Grotius, even where the local ruler was idolatrous or heretical. This was a matter of personal importance to him, for the Protestant Grotius had been exiled from his native Netherlands and was living in Paris, where he was unwilling to challenge the French king's campaign against the Huguenots in La Rochelle. But his views on international law were shaped by more than just expediency, and were indebted to his intense scholarship as well as his reflections on Europe's bloody confessional rivalries.

When Grotius wrote his *De Jure Belli*, he had already completed the Dutch poem that would form the basis of his most successful work, the *De Veritate Religionis Christianae* (1627)—and the relationship between these two works is important. In *De Veritate*, Grotius described Christianity as a system of ethical values which ought to appeal to all human beings. Underpinning the work is the assumption that religion must be chosen, that men and women had to make a conscious, informed decision to adopt Christianity. He argued that it was reasonable to do so, for they would be following an ethical system which they could recognize as admirable and fulfilling, and their reward would be eternal life in heaven. Conversely, because Christianity was a choice, Grotius assumed that people could live their lives here on earth without adopting it. Human life was possible without any particular religious commitments, although Grotius expected rational human

26 Ronald Asch, *The Thirty Years War: The Holy Roman Empire and Europe, 1618–1648* (Basingstoke: McMillan, 1997); for the scale and chronology of pamphlet publication see Geoffrey Parker, *The Thirty Years War* (London: Routledge & Kegan Paul, 1984), pp. 110–11.

27 On this aspect of the relationship between Grotius and previous traditions see Brian Tierney, *The Idea of Natural Rights: Studies on Natural Rights, Natural Law, and Church Law, 1150–1625* (Atlanta, Ga.: Scholars Press, 1997), ch. 13. His account is extremely valuable, but as I will argue, the conservative side of Grotius' argument should not be over emphasized.

beings to adopt some form of religious worship.[28] Similar views can also be found in *De Jure Belli*, where he argued that the principles of social life would hold even if God did not exist, while maintaining that all societies must uphold some version of natural religion.[29]

Grotius' theology was unusual in the emphasis he placed on human choice; even more striking is the absence of the Church (or any religious institution) in both *De Jure Belli* and *De Veritate*. There is no sense in either work that the Church as a community has any spiritual or temporal authority over the believer, or that the way to heaven lies through the Church. Being Christian, for Grotius, was about repentance and good works; as he explained, in a letter of 1621 to Pierre Dupuy, the gospel was 'a new teaching demanding a complete change of mind, and promising remission of sins and eternal life'.[30] Christ taught human beings a new set of ethical rules, but he had not instituted any power structure which might enforce or even encourage obedience to these rules. Grotius' views at this point were, it should be said, somewhat different from those he had expressed earlier, while still in Holland. At that time, he had believed that the magistrate should assert his authority over spiritual matters, but after his experiences in 1618–19, when a group of zealous Calvinists played an important role in his own political downfall, he became convinced of the need to separate civil authority from spiritual matters.[31] This aspect of Grotian theology helps to explain the distinction which Grotius makes between right 'strictly taken' and the laws or norms of morality and charity.[32] That distinction has long been recognized, but here I want to tease out the argument more fully and explore its implications for international law.

Announcing his intentions in *De Jure Belli*, Grotius claimed that the 'Law, which is common to many Nations or rulers of Nations' had not yet been treated of 'universally and methodically'. He proposed to offer such a systematic treatment by using two kinds of evidence, 'certain Notions, which none can deny without doing Violence to his judgement' and 'testimonies', whether of philosophers, historians, poets or orators.[33] The Bible he treated in a rather different way, however, explaining that he would use the New Testament:

> … that I may shew, what cannot be elsewhere learned, what is lawful for Christians to do; which Thing itself, I have notwithstanding, contrary to what most do, distinguished from

[28] I explore these themes in 'Grotius' *De Veritate*: Christianity and Human Nature', *Grotiana* 35 (2014): pp. 75–94.

[29] See Hugo Grotius, *The Rights of War and Peace*, vol. I, edited by Richard Tuck (Indianapolis, Ind.: Liberty Fund, 2005), p. 89 (the famous 'etiamsi daremus' clause) and vol. 2, pp. 1037–8, where Grotius argues that those who reject all religion should be punished.

[30] P. C. Molhuysen, et al., eds., *Briefwisseling van Hugo Grotius*, vol. II (Gravenhage: M. Nijhoff, 1928–2001), no. 640 p. 73. 'Evangelium, id est dogma novum resipiscentiam exactam deposcens, et promittens remissionem peccatorem et vitam aeternam'.

[31] See Harm-Jan van Dam, ed., *De Imperio Summarum Potestatum*, 2 vols (Leiden: Brill, 2001), for a modern edition of the manuscript on spiritual and civil authority which Grotius finished in 1617, a year before his arrest and subsequent sentence to lifelong imprisonment.

[32] Grotius discusses right 'strictly taken' in *The Rights of War and Peace*, vol. I, pp. 128–30.

[33] Ibid. pp. 75, 111.

the Law of Nature; as being fully assured, that in that most holy Law a greater Sanctity is enjoined us, than the meer Law of Nature in itself requires.[34]

This was a clear critique of the ethical and political theories of most of his contemporaries, especially on the Protestant side. As we have seen, Protestant writers had generally refused to countenance any distance between the moral teaching of the Bible and the natural law by which we are all obliged. Unlike these contemporaries, Grotius gave no indication that the Christian revelation was a necessary part of the natural law; natural law, for him, was directed towards the preservation of human society and not only was Grotius careful to separate it from revelation, he never suggested that nature was 'ordered' towards supernatural ends, as the Catholics held. For him, therefore, the law that applied to nations in the international arena had to be based on a law of nature that was conceptually quite distinct from Christian duties.

Throughout *De Jure Belli*, therefore, Grotius was keen to distinguish the law of nature, directed towards the preservation of the human community, from the law of Christ or of charity. The law of nature allows us to defend ourselves and our fellow men from violent death, and it also authorizes us to punish those people who violate its central principles through their disregard for human life. By the law of nature we can appropriate and use the natural world for our own benefit and for the preservation of our lives, and it grounds an understanding of justice in which human beings can own property and can defend that property, as well as their own lives. The rights we have from nature are, therefore, directed primarily at the preservation of life and secondarily at the preservation of property. Modern commentators have been keen to work out just exactly what Grotius' doctrines of property, possession and punishment are, and there is a vibrant scholarly discussion of his conception of natural right and natural sociability.[35]

The relationship between natural law and Christianity in Grotius' thought remains under-studied, however, and it needs to be understood within the context of the post-Reformation debates that I have outlined above. We have seen that Grotius understood Christianity as an ethical system, which demanded greater virtue than the law of nature alone, and his argument is dependent upon the Catholic concept of charity as a higher standard than justice. This is evident from his discussion of self-defence, where he acknowledged that, according to strict or 'expletive' justice, a person had the right to defend themselves and their property with force; if they were dishonoured they could even kill the offender.[36] But Grotius went on to say that people ought not to behave in this way, that Christians in particular ought to prefer human life to the preservation of goods. In the notes to this passage

[34] Ibid. p. 126.

[35] See e.g. Richard Tuck, *The Rights of War and Peace: Political Thought and the International Order from Grotius to Kant* (Oxford: Oxford University Press, 1999), ch. 3; James Tully, *A Discourse on Property: John Locke and His Adversaries* (Cambridge: Cambridge University Press, 1990); Martine Julia Van Ittersum, *Profit and Principle: Hugo Grotius, Natural Rights Theories and the Rise of Dutch Power in the East Indies, 1595–1615* (Leiden: Brill, 2006).

[36] Grotius, *Rights of War and Peace*, vol. II, p. 406.

he acknowledges his debt to Cajetan and Soto, whose concerns structure his own argument. [37] Later, in book III, he was even more explicit about the importance of charity. Here he allowed that by justice we might have rights to the goods of our enemies, especially in a just war, but went on to say that 'We are obliged by the Law of Charity to forbear the Prosecution of our Right [to restitution ...] since by that Law we Christians especially should set a greater Value upon the Life of a Man, than upon our Goods.' Grotius wanted to preserve the ethical rigour of Christianity, but to make it compatible with political life.[38]

Amid the wreckage of Catholic Christendom in which Grotius wrote, this was a plea for restraint and for an end to religious warfare and the confessional passions that inspired it. To be a Christian, for Grotius, was to value the life of a fellow human creature more than one's own property or even, in some cases, one's own life. Understood in this way, Christianity could never provide the rationale for offensive warfare and, since faith must be a free choice, religious persecution could never be justified. Grotius's version of Christianity made very limited claims on the natural, civil world; individual Christians were called to renounce their natural rights to restitution and self-defence but they could not force anyone else to do this. Individual states and rulers could enact religious laws, of course, but these only obliged their citizens. There was no international body to uphold or police revealed religion, although violations of natural law could and should be punished across national and territorial borders. It was natural morality, not revealed religion that was of international concern.[39]

Grotius's concern for values like charity and moderation which cannot be enforced and which are distinct from right 'strictly taken' has appealed to several modern commentators. His claim that 'sometimes our Charity to our Neighbour will not suffer us to use this rigorous Right' has led them to see in him the precursor of a 'principle of humanity' urging restraint in combat.[40] For James Turner Johnson, for example, his novelty lay in his efforts to show that all civilized nations ought to adopt the principles once associated with specifically Christian charity.[41] Certainly, it is true that Grotius has redefined charity, emphasizing that it commands us to preserve the lives, rather than the souls, of others. He tends to connect it with divine law and does not describe it as an infused theological virtue, as it was for the Thomists, nor connect it to the Church. Without the Church to uphold and promote the virtue of charity, however, and without any earthly sanctions for those who refuse to acknowledge it, the principle of charity could look rather weak and toothless. Grotius was well aware of this problem, and in trying to solve it he turned back, in later life, to the Church and to the Scriptures for support.

Because Grotius did not think that the law of charity could be enforced here on earth he was anxious to encourage his readers to adopt its principles voluntarily. In

[37] Ibid. vol. II, p. 414. [38] Ibid. vol. III, pp. 1242–3.
[39] See in particular ibid., vol. II, pp. 1024–39. [40] Ibid., vol. III pp. 1188.
[41] James Turner Johnson, 'Grotius' Use of History and Charity in the Modern Transformation of the Just War Idea' in idem, *Ethics and the Use of Force* (Farnham: Ashgate, 2011), pp. 75–86.

De Jure Belli, he was not only endeavouring to set out a clear argument, he was also seeking to persuade others of its validity. As this suggests, it is a work of rhetoric as well as theory, and Grotius' thought cannot properly be understood unless we recognize this. Just as his great Dutch predecessor, Desiderius Erasmus, had written short stories and eloquent essays in his efforts to redirect the passions of his readers, so Grotius wanted to encourage his readers to see their religion and their community through a particular lens. He appealed to examples in classical and Christian literature, showing to his readers a model of human community in which life is sacred, in the hope that they might be inspired to live by the same values. Such a community, Grotius was suggesting, need not be concerned about the souls of other people or even about the Church as an institution. The individuals within it should certainly be concerned about the teaching of Jesus, but this should not weaken their participation in the human, earthly community but instead encourage them to put the lives of their fellow men before their own. Implicit in Grotius' theology is the claim that human beings cannot be coerced to be charitable, they can only be persuaded and cajoled.

Justice strictly taken could not be, for Grotius, the only criterion for action in the international sphere; it had to be balanced by a thicker and richer set of moral commitments. These could not be enforced, but they had to be actively endorsed and upheld through the power of communal praise and blame. In his dedication to an earlier work, *Mare Liberum* (1609), he explained to his reader that God had 'assigned two judges from himself to be always present in men's affairs, whom the most happy offender cannot escape: to wit, every man's own conscience and fame, or other men's estimation of them'.[42] But societies could not be allowed to develop their own judgments without guidance, and one way of understanding the many 'testimonies' and quotations which fill the pages of the tract is as a sustained effort to shape the moral views of Grotius' readers. In chapter xxiv of book II, for example, a multitude of examples of clemency and mercy are offered to the reader—precisely because these qualities cannot be imposed. They can only be admired and imitated.

Grotius saw that establishing international order required more than arms and gunships; for him a peaceful world could best be ensured through the spread of the true Christian religion and through widespread commitment to the charitable values of Christ and the best of the ancients. He feared that the clerics around him were betraying that Christian charity, and he sought to counter the theologies which he saw as pernicious and bellicose. Indeed, he spent much of the final decades of his life working on a vast project of biblical criticism, whose purpose was to persuade his contemporaries that his reading of Christianity was the only one that could be sustained by a scholarly reading of the Scriptures.[43] At the same time, he came to see that an institutional church was necessary to bind Christians

[42] Hugo Grotius, *The Free Sea*, edited by D. Armitage (Indianapolis, Ind.: Liberty Fund, 2004), p. 7.

[43] The works of Biblical criticism were the *Annotationes in Libros Evangeliorum* (Amsterdam: Blaeu, 1641); *Annotata ad Vetus Testamentum* (Paris: Cramoisy, 1644); *Annotationum in Novum Testamentum II* and *III* (Paris: Pele, 1646–50).

together and to foster cooperation. In the 1640s he staked his own reputation and credibility on an irenic project to bring the Catholic and Protestant Churches closer together. His gamble failed, and he died in 1645 distrusted on all sides of the religious divide.[44]

In Grotius' work the connections between international law and theology are clearly drawn. His understanding of the Christian faith, shaped by both Catholic and Protestant traditions, enabled him to distinguish between the demands of justice and the ideals of the good life. He recognized that it is not sufficient simply to have a set of minimal norms that must be enforced through coercive action, though such norms are an important part of any international order. For Grotius, it was also essential to create and sustain a sense of goodness and charity that is compatible with those minimal norms, and with 'strict' justice. As he saw so clearly, strong commitments to public, institutional religion, to the salvation of others, and to the duty of the spiritual authority to intervene in the public sphere are likely to undermine international order. Conversely, if we can develop strong moral commitments that actually reinforce values shared across national boundaries and which cherish universal goods like the value of human life, then international order will be much more robust. These commitments cannot be created by force, it is only through persuasion and through the power of example that the circle of people who believe in them can be widened. Grotius' intricate analyses of Biblical texts—immensely influential at the time, but largely overlooked by modern scholars—were part of his efforts to limit war in Europe, and can properly be considered as companion volumes to *De Jure Belli.*

If international law is to encode a moral standard that is higher than the particular, positive laws of the nation state, it will only succeed if it is backed by the will of the communities to which it applies. In the sixteenth century, the Thomist vision of a natural world 'ordered' towards, and shaped by, a spiritual realm began to crumble, and early modern Europeans struggled to articulate an alternative. Grotius sought to provide a new synthesis, one which drew on elements of Catholic moral tradition but rejected Roman claims about the power of the Church and the Papacy. He hoped to show that a strong commitment to moral virtue need not be dependent upon Roman Catholicism, and that it could be combined with a pragmatic sense of the limits of human law. For Grotius, moral virtues—paradigmatically charity and moderation—were best fostered through widespread commitment to Christianity; it was, however, an increasingly secularized 'Grotian' natural law, rather than Grotian theology, which would prove most influential in the centuries after his death.

[44] For Grotius' efforts at ecclesiastical union see G. H. M. Posthumus Meyjes, 'Hugo Grotius as an Irenicist', in *The World of Hugo Grotius, (1583–1645)* (Amsterdam: Holland University Press, 1984), pp. 43–63.

Bibliography

Aquinas, Thomas. *Political Writings*, edited by R. Dyson (Cambridge: Cambridge University Press, 2002).

Asch, Ronald. *The Thirty Years War: The Holy Roman Empire and Europe, 1618–1648* (Basingstoke: Macmillan, 1997).

Bellucci, Dino. 'Natural Philosophy and Ethics in Melanchthon'. In *Moral Philosophy on the Threshold of Modernity*, edited by J. Kraye and R. Saarinen (Dordrecht: Kluwer Academic, 2005), pp. 235–54.

Brett, Annabel S. *Liberty, Right and Nature* (Cambridge: Cambridge University Press, 1997).

Brett, Annabel S. *Changes of State: Nature and the Limits of the City in Early Modern Natural Law* (Princeton: Princeton University Press, 2011).

Cajetan, Thomas. *Sancti Thomae Aquinati Opera omnia, iussu impensaque Leonis XIII.* vols 7, 9 (Rome: Vatican Polyglot Press, 1882).

Cargill Thompson, W. *The Political Thought of Martin Luther* (Brighton: Harvester Press, 1984).

van Dam, Harm-Jan, ed. *De Imperio Summarum Potestatum.* 2 vols (Leiden: Brill, 2001).

Emon, Anver M., Matthew Levering, and David Novak. *Natural Law: A Jewish, Christian, and Islamic Trialogue* (Oxford: Oxford University Press, 2014).

Feingold, Lawrence. *The Natural Desire to See God According to St. Thomas Aquinas and His Interpreters*, 2nd edn. (Naples, FL.: Sapientia Press, 2010).

Fernandes, Joao Manuel A. A. 'Luis de Molina: On War'. In *A Companion to Luis de Molina*, edited by M. Kaufmann and A. Aichele (Leiden: Brill, 2013), pp. 227–56.

Grotius, Hugo. *Annotationes in Libros Evangeliorum* (Amsterdam: Blaeu, 1641).

Grotius, Hugo. *Annotata ad Vetus Testamentum* (Paris: Cramoisy, 1644).

Grotius, Hugo. *Annotationum in Novum Testamentum*, II and III (Paris: Pele, 1646–50).

Grotius, Hugo. *The Free Sea*, edited by D. Armitage (Indianapolis, Ind.: Liberty Fund, 2004).

Grotius, Hugo. *The Rights of War and Peace.* 3 vols, edited by Richard Tuck (Indianapolis, Ind.: Liberty Fund, 2005).

Hayden, J. Michael. *France and the Estates General of 1614* (Cambridge: Cambridge University Press, 1974).

Herdt, Jennifer A. *Putting on Virtue: the Legacy of the Splendid Vices* (Chicago: University of Chicago Press, 2008).

Johnson, James Turner. 'Grotius' Use of History and Charity in the Modern Transformation of the Just War Idea'. In *Ethics and the Use of Force* (Farnham: Ashgate, 2011), pp. 75–86.

McIlwain, Charles, ed. *The Political Works of James I, Reprinted from the Edition of 1616* (Cambridge, Mass.: Harvard University Press, 1918).

Melanchthon, Philip. *Orations on Philosophy and Education*, edited by S. Kusakawa (Cambridge: Cambridge University Press, 1999).

Molhuysen, P. C., et al., eds. *Briefwisseling van Hugo Grotius*, vol. II (Gravenhage: M. Nijhoff, 1928–2001).

Mortimer, Sarah. *Reason and Religion in the English Revolution: The Challenge of Socinianism* (Cambridge: Cambridge University Press, 2010).

Mortimer, Sarah. 'Grotius' *De Veritate*: Christianity and Human Nature'. *Grotiana* 35, no. 1 (2014): pp. 75–94.

Oakley, Francis. 'Christian Obedience and Authority, 1520–1550'. In *The Cambridge History of Political Thought, 1450–1700*, edited by J. H. Burns (Cambridge: Cambridge University Press, 1991), pp. 153–4.

Parker, Geoffrey. *The Thirty Years War* (London: Routledge & Kegan Paul, 1984).
Pauck, Wilhelm, ed. *Melanchthon and Bucer* (London: SCM Press, 1969).
Pinckaers, Servais. *The Sources of Christian Ethics*, translated by Mary Noble (Edinburgh: Bloomsbury Publishing, 1995).
Ponet, John. *A Short Treatise of Politic Power* (Strassbourg: 1556).
Posthumus Meyjes, G. H. M. 'Hugo Grotius as an Irenicist'. In *The World of Hugo Grotius, (1583–1645)* (Amsterdam: Holland University Press, 1984), pp. 43–63.
Scott, James Brown. *Spanish Origins of International Law* (Oxford: Clarendon Press, 1934).
Skinner, Quentin. *The Foundations of Modern Political Thought*, vol. II (Cambridge: Cambridge University Press, 1979).
de Soto, Domingo. *De Iustitia et De Iure*, book V (Lyon: 1582).
Suarez, Francisco. *Defensio Fidei Catholicæ et Apostolicæ Aduersus Anglicanæ Sectæ Errores* (Coimbra: 1613).
Suarez, Francisco. *Selections from Three Works* (Oxford: Clarendon Press, 1944).
Tierney, Brian. *The Idea of Natural Rights: Studies on Natural Rights, Natural law, and Church Law, 1150–1625* (Atlanta, Ga.: Scholars Press, 1997).
Tuck, Richard. *The Rights of War and Peace: Political Thought and the International Order from Grotius to Kant* (Oxford: Oxford University Press, 1999).
Tully, James. *A Discourse on Property: John Locke and His Adversaries* (Cambridge: Cambridge University Press, 1990).
Van Ittersum, Martine Julia. *Profit and Principle: Hugo Grotius, Natural Rights Theories and the Rise of Dutch Power in the East Indies, 1595–1615* (Leiden: Brill, 2006).
Vindiciae, Contra Tyrannos: Or, Concerning the Legitimate Power of a Prince over the People, and of the People over a Prince, edited by George Garnett (Cambridge: Cambridge University Press, 1994).
de Vitoria, Francisco. *Political Writings*, edited by A. Pagden (Cambridge: Cambridge University Press, 1991).
de Vitoria, Francisco. *Vorlesungen (Relectiones)*, edited by Ulrich Horst, Heinz-Gerhard Justenhoven, and Joachim Stüben, vol. I (Stuttgart: W. Kohlhammer, 1995–1999).
de Vitoria, Francisco. *Reflection on Homicide & Commentary on Summa Theologiae IIa-IIae q. 64*, edited and translated by J. Doyle (Milwaukee: Marquette University Press, 1997).
Wicks, Jared. 'Thomism between Renaissance and Reformation: The Case of Cajetan'. *Archiv Für Reformationsgeschichte* 68 (1977): pp. 9–31.
Williams, George Huntston. *The Radical Reformation* (London: Weidenfeld & Nicolson, 1962).

2

Between Scylla and Charybdis

Aquinas's Political Thought and His Notion of Natural Law and *Ius Gentium*

Pia Valenzuela

Introduction

The confrontation between imperial and papal jurisdictions in the thirteenth century marks a stage in the long and turbulent history of the process of the secularization of legal institutions. In examining the evolution of the law of nations in modernity, that is, the formation and application of international legal concepts, one should not overlook their roots in the late medieval period, which could be called the pre-history of international law.

The purpose of this chapter is to show the importance of Aquinas's line of thought in this process. The chapter has two parts. First, I refer to Aquinas's political thought in the politico-theological milieu of his era, and I outline his ideas about common good, government, law, and right. Secondly, I examine Aquinas's notion of natural law and *ius gentium*. Related to *ius gentium*, I address Aquinas's notion of dominion, property rights and commerce, and slavery.

Aquinas's Political Thought

Thirteenth-century medieval Italy was a *societas christiana*,[1] though one characterized by political conflicts between the Emperor Frederick II, popes Gregory IX and Innocence IV, among others, and the northern Italian cities; all of them supporting different ideas of sovereignty and supremacy. One of the most significant

[1] In medieval times citizenship was obtained by baptism. Indeed, the society in question was a thoroughly spiritual one, since the principles that were to be fostered in society were the principles of the Christian faith. See Jacinto Choza, *Historia cultural del humanismo* (Madrid: Plaza y Valdes, S.L., 2009), p. 173; and William D. McCready, 'Papal Plenitudo Potestatis and the Source of Temporal Authority in Late Medieval Papal Hierocratic Theory', *Speculum* 48, no. 4 (October 1973): p. 661.

political doctrines developed then was the papal theocratic theory of government,[2] which, based on the superiority of the spiritual and supernatural over the temporal and natural order and power, attributed to the pope a plenitude of power in both spiritual and temporal affairs. It did not necessarily imply a claim to complete temporal sovereignty, but simply spiritual sovereignty with temporal consequences, plus temporal sovereignty in the papal territories and certain other special areas, meaning that the pope could intervene to impose peace or truces among the Christian princes, lead the management of the Crusades, and so forth.[3]

On the other hand, the Emperor Frederick II, like his father Frederick Barbarossa, attempted to unify the Holy Roman Empire by trying to regain control of the *Regnum Italicum*, which had been establishing independent governments in the Lombard cities. These cities defended their freedom against the Empire, trying to gain complete independence, even if *de iure* they had no legal support for demanding independence from the imperial power.[4]

In his attempt, the Emperor Frederick II also tried to acquire some papal territories. Popes Alexander III, Gregory IX, and Innocence IV fought to defend and secure sovereignty over the papal territories in central Italy from imperial expansionism in the north of Italy and from Sicily.

[2] The papal theocratic theory was based on different sources. First, on biblical texts, for instance, Luke 22, 38: 'See, Lord, here are two swords', which was used by theocrats to explain that the 'two swords', spiritual and temporal power, pertained to the Church, though the pope entrusted the temporal power to the prince. Giles of Rome (1243–1316) and James of Viterbo (1255–1308) used this allegory to demonstrate that ecclesiastical power was the cause of the civil power. See Castañeda, *La teocracia pontifical en las controversias sobre el Nuevo Mundo* (Mexico, UNAM Instituto de Investigaciones Historicas, Serie 'Estudios Historicos', 59, 1996), p. 226. Secondly, papal theocratic theory was argued on the basis of historical sources as the Donation of Constantine, by which the emperor conferred on Pope Sylvester I and the Roman Church extensive temporal privileges and possessions (Johann Peter Kirsch, 'Donation of Constantine', The Catholic Encyclopedia, vol. 5 (New York: Robert Appleton Company, 1909), 26 February 2014, http://www.newadvent.org/cathen/05118a.htm); and thirdly, on the letter of Pope Gelasius (494) to Emperor Anastasius on the superiority of the spiritual over temporal power. See Letter of Gelasius I (494), in *Readings in European History*, translated by J. H. Robinson (Boston: Ginn, 1905), pp. 72–3. Although the donation was a forged document, it served as an important justification of the theory until the fifteenth century. Cardinal Nicholas of Cusa (1432) was the first to demonstrate the falsity of this document. See Castañeda, *La teocracia pontifical en las controversias sobre el Nuevo Mundo*, p. 230. Early canonists interpreted the Donation not only in a political sense, but gave it a patrimonial meaning. Moreover, they maintained that what Constantine had donated to the Papacy would not be considered a donation at all, but a restitution of what belonged to the Papacy by right. See McCready, 'Papal Plenitudo Potestatis', p. 655.

[3] McCready, 'Papal Plenitudo Potestatis', pp. 654–5. At the beginning the term *plenitudo potestatis* in papal documents was used to describe the delegated power of papal legates rather than the power of the pope himself. This term acquired later the meaning of justifying theocracy. See also Castañeda, *La teocracia pontifical en las controversias sobre el Nuevo Mundo*, p. 218. By virtue of their theocracy, popes like Innocent IV and Boniface VIII attained the greatest potency of its authority, and therefore they recognized kings, or absolved their subjects from their duties of obedience; they conferred feudal possessions; they made themselves the judges of the election of the German emperors; and they deposed emperors by excommunicating them. See Maurice de Wulf, 'The Society of Nations in the Thirteenth Century', *International Journal of Ethics* 29, no. 2 (January 1919): pp. 224–5.

[4] See Quentin Skinner, *The Foundations of Modern Political Thought: Volume I: The Renaissance* (Cambridge: Cambridge University Press, 1978), pp. 5–8.

Aquinas did not refer to these conflicts; neither did he openly reject papal theocracy nor support it, because he never dealt directly with the question of the temporal power of the pope. Neither did he agree to nor reject the emperor's attempts to unify the Holy Roman Empire.

Aquinas's position between Scylla and Charybdis can be traced back to his homeland, a place between Rome and Naples, a location which posed serious political difficulty for his family because their domain lay on the border of the papal and imperial territories, forcing them to oscillate between pope and emperor, changing allegiances. As Jean-Pierre Torrell suggests, one may ask to what extent the overlapping of Thomas Aquinas the religious figure and Aquinas the member of a political family, and the reversals of alliance with pope and emperor, were the source of some of Aquinas's theories about the relationship between spiritual and temporal power.[5]

Aquinas, strongly influenced by Aristotle's political and ethical writings, wrote two strictly political works, *De regno* (*De regimine principium*) (*c.*1265) and *Commentaries on Aristotle's Politics* (1269–72), but did not complete either. Many scholars have discussed the reasons why he left them unfinished.[6] Moreover, his writings scarcely reflect political realities of his time, making almost no mention of the Papacy's political authority, and treating it with some ambiguity. Aquinas's silence about the political situation of the time could have been intentional.[7]

The most interesting hypothesis is that Aquinas did not finish *De regno* or his Commentaries on Aristotle's *Politics* for fear of the consequences for his own doctrine. As he understood that the legitimate autonomy (not absolute independence) of the temporal power from the spiritual power could lead to the political subjugation of the ecclesiastical to the imperial power, he refused to develop the doctrine of the autonomy of the temporal power more openly. Aquinas would have noted that the Emperor Frederick II was right in his claims about imperial jurisdiction

[5] See Jean-Pierre Torrell, *Saint Thomas: The Person and His Work* (Washington, D.C.: The Catholic University of America Press, 2005, 1st edn 1993). In general I follow Torrell's biography complemented with data from other authors.

[6] See Saranyana, *La filosofía medieval. Desde sus orígenes patrísticos hasta la Escolástica barroca* (Pamplona: EUNSA Colección Pensamiento filosófico medieval y renacentista, 51, 3rd edn 2011), pp. 287–9. Most of the discussions try to fix the chronology of Aquinas's *De regno* and Commentaries on Aristotle's Politics in order to explain why he didn't finish them, see for instance: James Weisheipl, *Friar Thomas d'Aquino: His Life, Thought, and Works* (Washington, D.C.: Catholic University of America Press, 1983), Fernand Bossier, 'Méthode de traduction et problèmes de chronologie', in *Guillaume de Moerbecke. Recueil d' études à l' occasion du 700 anniversaire de sa mort*, edited by Jozef Brams and Willy Vanhamel (Leuven: University Press, 1989). According to the chronology, one hypothesis is that Aquinas couldn't finish them, because of his death; another hypothesis is that if the two books are dated earlier, then it was not a problem of timing, but perhaps that Aquinas didn't feel able to deal with Aristotelian political philosophy in terms proper to the thirteenth century. See Jurgen Miethke, *Las ideas políticas en la Edad Media*, translated by Francisco Bertelloni (Buenos Aires: Biblos, 1993). Regarding the doctrinal content of Aquinas's writings, other scholars like Ignatius Theodore Eschmann ('Saint Thomas Aquinas on the Two Powers', *MS* 20 (1958): pp.177–205) doubt the authenticity of *De regno*, because it contradicts Aquinas's previous doctrine in the *Commentary on the Sentences*.

[7] John Finnis, *Aquinas: Moral, Political and Legal Theory* (Oxford: Oxford University Press, 1998), p. 6.

on northern Italian cities and the Papacy (Alexander III, Gregory IX, Innocence IV) had exceeded its power in some actions as supplying those cities with funds for their fight against the emperor. But at the same time, Aquinas understood the views of Pope Gregory IX and others, and distrusted the emperor's expansionist intentions on papal territories. Concretely, Aquinas would have disagreed with Frederick's conception of imperial lawmaking authority and attempts of centralization that derived in absolutism. He realized also that, had he followed Aristotle's political thought completely, he would have had to admit that the emperor was right in some actions against the pope, but he couldn't do that as a devout thirteen-century Dominican friar. Therefore he suspended his judgement, and left his two strictly political writings unfinished.[8]

The distinction of powers

Aquinas's ideas in his unfinished political works have to be complemented with the ideas disseminated in his other works, mainly the *Summa Theologica* (1266–73), where we find his notion of natural law, *Scriptum super libros Sententiarum* (*Commentary on the Sentences of Peter Lombard*) (1253–56), and *In decem libros Ethicorum expositio* (*Commentary on the Nicomachean Ethics*) (1271–72). Despite not dealing directly with the topic, an argument against theocratic statements about papal temporal power can be discerned in these works, for example when he asserts: 'Christ was unwilling to assume temporal government or reign'.[9]

Moreover, Aquinas draws a distinction between the domain of the temporal power and that of the spiritual power in *Scripta super libros sententiarum* II, dist. 44, q. 2, a. 3:[10]

Spiritual and secular power are both derived from the Divine power, and so secular power is subject to spiritual power insofar as this is ordered by God: that is, in those things which pertain to the salvation of the soul. In such matters, then, the spiritual power is to be obeyed before the secular. But in those things which pertain to the civil good, the secular power should be obeyed before the spiritual, according to Matthew 22:21: 'Render to Caesar the

[8] This hypothesis is defended by Josep Ignasi Saranyana. See Saranyana, *La filosofía medieval*, p. 290. According to Étienne Gilson, Thomas Aquinas was a victim of political Averroism, meaning that Aquinas admitted a double observance in political matters. On the one hand, he seems to have subscribed to the thesis of papal theocracy, but on the other hand believed that theocracy did not share the spirit of the Gospel. See Étienne Gilson, *Dante the Philosopher*, translated by David Moore (London: Sheed and Ward, 1952).

[9] *Summa Theologica* III, q. 59, a. 4 ad 1.

[10] '... quod potestas spiritualis et saecularis, utraque deducitur a potestate divina; et ideo intantum saecularis potestas est sub spirituali, inquantum est ei a Deo supposita, scilicet in his quae ad salutem animae pertinent; et ideo in his magis est obediendum potestati spirituali quam saeculari. In his autem quae ad bonum civile pertinent, est magis obediendum potestati saeculari quam spirituali, secundum illud Matth. 22: 21: reddite quae sunt Caesaris Caesari. Nisi forte potestati spirituali etiam saecularis potestas conjungatur, sicut in Papa, qui utriusque potestatis apicem tenet, scilicet spiritualis et saecularis'. I follow the translation of selections of Aquinas 's writings in *St Thomas Aquinas Political Writings*, edited and translated by R. W. Dyson (Cambridge: Cambridge University Press, 2004).

things that are Caesar's.' Unless perhaps the spiritual and secular powers are conjoined, as in the pope, who holds the summit of both powers: that is, the spiritual and the secular.

In the pope Aquinas recognizes *de facto* union of both powers—because within the papal territories near Rome the pope had secular as well as spiritual authority—and, as stated in *De regno* II, 3, he even allowed the subordination of the ends of the political society to the final end of the Church. According to Jean-Pierre Torrell, Aquinas had a dualistic conception of the connections between Church and civil society, and their mutual subordination in their respective spheres.[11] This explains the autonomy but not absolute independence of the temporal power from the spiritual power, and so of the imperial from the ecclesiastical power.

This dualistic conception about the two powers corresponds to Aquinas's distinction between the natural and supernatural order. The latter does not destroy the former, but perfects it. Aquinas is, therefore, respectful of everything natural in human beings.[12] In other words, he admits that the divine law does not supersede human law:

Now the Divine law which is the law of grace, does not do away with human law which is the law of natural reason.[13]

Aquinas's understanding and respect for everything human lead him to recognize the relative autonomy of political power (secular), because God himself respects it. God is the source of spiritual and temporal power, but he has left the organization of the 'secular' to the human being. Thus, in all that relates to the organization of political society and does not affect the domains of spiritual power (salvation of souls), there is autonomy.

Then, Aquinas's standpoint was incompatible with the appeal of secular authorities (Frederick II, Louis IX) to Christian premises to support their legal and administrative conclusions. In Aquinas's view there was no need to invoke revealed truth to support political decisions and enactments, but only natural reason, because human law is the law of natural reason. Therefore, the appeal to natural reason is the criterion to which positive legal enactments and administrative measures must conform, if they are to be appropriate law. Thus, Aquinas was really a defender and protagonist of secular power.[14]

In conclusion, if the theocratic theory was grounded on the absorption of the natural order by the supernatural order, arguing the superiority of the supernatural

[11] Torrell, *Saint Thomas: The Person and His Work*, pp. 13–14. Torrell considers that although not always easy to interpret, Aquinas's political thought is coherent, without considering *De regno* as inauthentic. James Weisheipl (*Friar Thomas D'Aquino: His Life, Thought, and Work* (N.Y.: Doubleday, 1974)) suggests that the doctrinal position reflects a personal attitude in Thomas, as he refused temporal honours or being involved in temporal affairs. See also Finnis, *Aquinas: Moral, Political and Legal Theory*, p. 324.

[12] See *Summa Theologica* I, q. 98, a. 2: 'For what is natural to man was neither acquired nor forfeited by sin.'

[13] *Summa Theologica* II–II, q. 10, a. 10.

[14] See Alasdair MacIntyre, 'Natural Law as Subversive: The Case of Aquinas', in *Ethics and Politics: Selected Essays*, vol. 2 (Cambridge/New York: Cambridge University Press, 2006).

and spiritual over the natural and temporal power, then Aquinas was not a defender of this theory, given that the distinction between the two orders was essential to his thought.[15]

On the contrary, Aquinas admired Aristotle's political thought and attempted to reconcile the teachings of Aristotle with those of the Church. Thus, the use of Aristotle's work equipped him to forge a new kind of political theory, a political theory which can be characterized as milder and more optimistic than that of Augustine precisely because it lacks Augustine's insistence on the unworthiness of this world and its ends.[16] Aquinas, on the contrary, saw no irreconcilable tension between the acquisition of present goods on earth and the achievement of eternal ones in heaven, provided that the former were directed towards the latter and the latter were not neglected in favour of the former. The interests of this world and the next could coexist.[17]

Indeed, Aquinas had a positive view of politics: government is a benevolent administration suited to the sociable nature of humankind. No one is able to provide for life sufficiently alone, thus humans need to cooperate in order to secure the benefits of a division of labour. Because there may be more than one way to achieve their ends, humans need to be guided wisely towards them just as a ship needs to be steered into harbour.[18] These are facts which have nothing to do with sin. They are simply facts of human nature which make it necessary for a community to be knit together in a collective purpose by wise leadership directed towards the common good. Therefore, political power is naturally necessary. The aim of secular government is not suppression and punishment, but the achievement of earthly wellbeing. Nor is earthly wellbeing only a matter of bodily protection and economic satisfaction. As we read in *De regno* I, 15: 'the end of human association is a virtuous life'. Therefore, an ordered and cooperative life with others in a political community should contribute to wellbeing and a virtuous life.[19]

[15] Castañeda, *La teocracia pontifical en las controversias sobre el Nuevo Mundo*, p. 107.

[16] The less optimistic tone of Augustine can be discerned from passages about dominion and the state as consequences of sin in *De civitate Dei* 19:15; *De doctrina christiana* 1:23; *Tractatus in Ioannis epistulam* 8:6–8, also from passages about his consideration of law as mere punishment, for instance, *De libero arbitrio* 1:15:32–33. See R. W. Dyson, *The Pilgrim City: Social and Political Ideas in the Writings of St Augustine of Hippo* (Woodbridge, Suffolk, UK/Rochester, N.Y.: Boydell Press, 2001), pp. 68–72.

[17] *St Thomas Aquinas Political Writings*, edited and translated by R. W. Dyson, pp. XXIV–XXV. Until the thirteenth century, the kind of political theory predominant in the Latin West was Augustine's political thought in the *City of God*: political arrangements are inseparable from the sinful condition of fallen man; government would not have come into existence at all had the Fall not occurred; earthly peace and justice are uneasy, transient, and unstable. They are pale copies of the true peace and justice laid up in heaven, which will be realized only after the end of earthly history, when the City of God enters into its inheritance of eternal bliss. See R. W. Dyson, *The Pilgrim City: Social and Political Ideas in the Writings of St Augustine of Hippo* (2001). Especially during the so-called Investiture Controversy of 1075–1122, the idea gathered momentum that the only thing which can redeem human government from being wholly sinful is the complete submission of earthly princes to the spiritual power: that is, to the guidance and censure of the Church, ruled over by the Supreme Pontiff in Rome.

[18] See *De regno* I, 1 and 15.

[19] *St Thomas Aquinas Political Writings*, edited and translated by R. W. Dyson, p. XXVI.

Common good, government, law, right

According to Aquinas, the purpose of any law is that people become just and people of virtue,[20] though it does not mean that the role of every law is to regulate the internal dispositions of its subjects, which is the purpose of divine law uniquely. It means that the law is ordained to the common good.[21] The limited common good, specific to the political community, is public good, which is distinct from the private good of individuals and of families and households. The principal elements of the common good are peace and justice.[22]

Remarkably, Aquinas limited political common good to the public good. One should ask: what is the common good in the law of nations, the good of a global, international community? Aquinas's words apply to human law in general: the principal intention of human law is to secure friendship between people. Thus, the common good in the law of nations is justice and peace, too. Without foundations in mutual love or friendship, efforts to maintain peace by laying down precepts of justice would not suffice.[23] There is a deep sense of peace related to the virtues of justice and love: peace is the 'work of justice' indirectly, in-so-far as justice removes the obstacles to peace, but it is the 'work of charity' directly, since charity, according to its very nature, causes peace.[24]

Regarding the type of government, in *De regno*, there is a clear preference for monarchy, though with restrictions,[25] while in the later *Summa Theologica* (1273) Aquinas inclined to a mixed constitution, maybe due to a more mature thought and/or also to political circumstances. By then, he could have confirmed the danger of the corruption of the monarchy by the ambition of power in some emperor's actions: for instance, when Frederick II, trying to establish a legislative absolutism by subduing the Kingdom of the Two Sicilies, and threatening to extend the system throughout Italy, named his natural son Enzio King of Sardinia, against the will of the pope who had feudal rights over the island.[26]

Aquinas stated that the two principal regimes are monarchy, where one person rules on account of his particular virtue, and aristocracy, where a few rule, again on account of their special virtue. But considering also that 'it is good that people have some share in the government',[27] he concludes that the best constitution or regime is one which consists of monarchy, aristocracy and democracy, 'well mixed'.[28] Properly, 'law' seems to be reserved in Aquinas's thought to the mixed

[20] *Summa Theologica* I–II, q.107, a. 2.

[21] Ibid., q. 90, a. 2; q. 96, a. 3. Although Aquinas did not mention, he probably disagreed with enactments of Louis IX and Frederick II that repressed all vices. See MacIntyre, 'Natural Law as Subversive: The Case of Aquinas', p. 45.

[22] *Summa Theologica* I–II q. 96, a.3; 99, a.5 ad 1. [23] Ibid., q. 99, a. 2.

[24] *Summa Theologica* II–II, q. 29, a. 3 ad 3. See Finnis, *Aquinas: Moral, Political and Legal Theory*, p. 231.

[25] *De regno* II, 22.

[26] See Castañeda, *La teocracia pontifical en las controversias sobre el Nuevo Mundo*, p. 86.

[27] *Summa Theologica* I–II, q. 105, a. 1. Aquinas derives this proposition from Aristotle. See *Politics* II, 6, and III, 5.

[28] See Nicholas Aroney, 'Subsidiarity, Federalism and the Best Constitution: Thomas Aquinas on City, Province and Empire', *Law and Philosophy* 26, no. 2 (March 2007): pp. 203–14.

government, while in other types of government there are only pronouncements of this or that other group, e.g. *plebscita, senatusconsulta.*[29]

By law in general, Aquinas understands a rule and measure of acts, whereby man is induced to act or is restrained from acting: for *lex* (law) is derived from *ligare* (to bind), because it binds one to act.[30] Specifically, human law is *ordinatio rationis,* an ordinance of reason for the common good, made by the person who has care of the community, and promulgated. It has binding force.[31]

Law is not the same as *ius*—right—but an expression of right.[32] The word *ius* has different uses. First of all, it is used to denote the just thing itself, but it also designates the art whereby what is just is known, and further denotes the place where justice is administered.[33]

According to Aquinas, the main use of right is the first one. Properly, the object of justice is called the just, which is the same as right.[34] Essentially, the right or the just is a work that is adjusted to another person according to some kind of equality.[35]

Apparently, Aquinas would not have supported the system of rights upon which modern liberal regimes are based. The right, *ius,* to which Aquinas refers, is not something that is held by individuals to use in whatever way they choose, but rather part of a right order of things, of relations between individuals or communities. Like Aristotle's *dikaion*, it is an objective right rather than a subjective one.[36]

Aquinas's Notion of Natural Law and *Ius Gentium*

Given the context of the time, and his ideas about the distinction of the two powers and orders, it is understandable Aquinas's caution to express openly his opinion in specific political issues of the moment. Notwithstanding, the essence of his political thought and his opposition to theocracy could be inferred also from his notions of natural law and *ius gentium*.

[29] *Summa Theologica* I–II, q. 95, a. 4. Aquinas's specific concern is to defend the classification of laws undertaken by Isidore in his *Etymologiae.* Among the distinctions drawn by Isidore, one of them, explains Aquinas, is to differentiate between 'laws, acts of the plebeian assembly, senatorial decrees' (*leges, plebiscita, senatusconsulta*) and the like. The various kinds of laws can be distinguished, according to the various forms of government explained by Aristotle.

[30] *Summa Theologica* I–II, q. 90, a. 1.

[31] Ibid., q. 90, a. 4.

[32] *Summa Theologica* II–II, q. 57, a. 1 ad 2.

[33] Ibid., q. 57, a. 1 ad 1.

[34] Ibid., q. 57, a. 1.

[35] Ibid., q. 57, a. 2. If it is adjusted to a person by its very nature, then it is called 'natural right'. If it is done by agreement or common consent, then it is called 'positive right'.

[36] D. DiLeo, 'Thomas Aquinas and the Overlapping Consensus', *Commonwealth: A Journal of Political Science* 13 (2007): pp. 1–21. This notwithstanding, John Finnis argues that the modern subjective notion of right can be inferred from Aquinas. General justice can be divided into the forms of particular justice. The object of particular justice is the other person's right(s) (*ius*). It follows, therefore, that one cannot respect or promote common good without respecting and promoting rights. See Finnis, *Aquinas: Moral, Political, and Legal Theory*, p. 133. Finnis quotes *Summa Theologica* II–II, q. 57 a. 1; q. 60, a. 1; q. 58, a. 7; q. 61, a.1.

Thus one of the most powerful justifications in Aquinas's thought for not supporting the theocratic theory was his notion of natural law and, derivatively, of the law of nations (*ius gentium*). To put it briefly, Aquinas's statement that civil power was derived from natural law was contrary to the theocratic theory expounded by thirteenth-century canonists.[37]

Through his notion of natural law Aquinas thus distinguished the supernatural from the natural order and defended the relative autonomy of the natural order. Aquinas also understood institutions of *ius gentium* as devised legitimately by human law.

Natural law has to do with what is just by nature and not by convention, that is, what natural reason determines as fair and good to do. Thus, by virtue of the natural law, human beings bear within themselves a knowledge of certain general principles and precepts of right and justice that are principles of just action.[38] According to Aquinas, the first of these principles is 'good is to be done and evil to be avoided'.[39] All other exceptionless precepts of the natural law are those which we recognize as indispensable in every society and in every situation for the achievement of our goods and of our final good, because they direct us towards and partially define our common good.[40]

Aquinas's account of the natural law reveals to us which are those goods that personally and in society one should pursue and defend: the preservation of human life, sexual union and procreation, education of children, peaceful coexistence in society, religious pursuit, and so forth.[41]

According to Aquinas, natural law was a reference for any other law:

> ... every human law has just so much of the nature of law, as it is derived from the law of nature. But if in any point it deflects from the law of nature, it is no longer a law but a perversion of law.[42]

Hence, to be just and fair, every law devised by human consent was to be respectful of the natural law. What does this law say about political organization?

Natural law says more about what is right for human beings to do according to their nature as individuals and persons who live with others, so in that sense also tell us about the right conditions of a just society.

Aquinas's natural law is not limited to a moral law between human being and God, but goes beyond the city as a participation of eternal law in the human being; that means a participation of God's order and government over all creatures, but specifically over human beings, because as rational beings they can know and live

[37] See Castañeda, *La teocracia pontifical en las controversias sobre el Nuevo Mundo*, p. 112.

[38] Anton-Hermann Chroust, 'The "ius gentium" in the Philosophy of Law of St. Thomas Aquinas', *Notre Dame Law Review* 17, no. 1 (1941–2): p. 22.

[39] *Summa Theologica* I–II, q. 94, a. 2.

[40] MacIntyre, 'Natural Law as Subversive: The Case of Aquinas', p. 45.

[41] Belong to the natural law 'all those things to which man has a natural inclination, are naturally apprehended by reason as being good, and consequently as objects of pursuit, and their contraries as evil, and objects of avoidance' (*Summa Theologica* I–II, q. 94, a. 2).

[42] *Summa Theologica* I–II, q. 95, a. 2.

by this order. Thus, through natural law humankind partakes of the 'lex aeterna', and properly is the name of eternal law in the human being.[43]

The provisions of natural law are too general to furnish us an immediate guide to conduct. We know that we ought to do good and avoid evil, but we do not necessarily know what is good or evil in specific circumstances, nor do we know what to do with people who do evil: what punishments should be imposed, or who should incur them.[44] Certainly, there are many matters left to human determination. This difference between our awareness of the general principles of the natural law and our need for detailed rules of behaviour creates a gap which is filled by human laws.[45]

According to Aquinas, human laws are derived from natural law, from this human capability to make laws as well as to be subject to them. As a consequence of the active participation in eternal law, practical reason allows humans to investigate what would be good for human communities.

Human law is divided into the 'law of nations' and civil law. The law of nations is even closer to natural law than is the civil law, because it is derived as a conclusion of natural law:

> ... as conclusions from premises, e.g. just buying and selling, and the like, without which people cannot live together.[46]
>
> The *ius gentium* is indeed natural to human beings in a sense, insofar as the human being is rational, because it is derived from the natural law in the manner of a conclusion not greatly remote from its first principles, which is why people agree to it so readily.[47]

First, the *ius gentium* of Aquinas emanates from the rational human faculty, which takes into consideration certain historically developed factors and their effects upon the welfare of both the individual and society as a whole.[48] Moreover, since reason dictates matters according to the right of nations, as implying a proximate

[43] According to Aquinas, 'this participation of the eternal law in the rational creature is called the natural law' (*Summa Theologica* I–II, q. 91, a. 2).

[44] See *Summa Theologica* I–II, q. 95, a. 2.

[45] *St Thomas Aquinas Political Writings*, edited and translated by R. W. Dyson, p. XXXIII.

[46] 'Nam ad ius gentium pertinent ea quae derivantur ex lege naturae sicut conclusiones ex principiis, ut iustae emptiones, venditiones, et alia huiusmodi, sine quibus homines ad invicem convivere non possent' (*Summa Theologica* I–II, q. 95, a. 4). The text continues: 'But those things which are derived from the law of nature by way of particular determination, belong to the civil law, according as each state decides on what is best for itself'. In other words, ' "civil" laws may be peculiar to a given political community and, to that extent, separated from the natural law by a longer chain of reasoning. But all human law properly so called takes its character as law from the fact that it reflects, however remotely, the general principles of the natural law' (*St Thomas Aquinas Political Writings*, edited and translated by R. W. Dyson, p. XXXIII).

[47] 'Ad primum ergo dicendum quod ius gentium est quidem aliquo modo naturale homini, secundum quod est rationalis, inquantum derivatur a lege naturali per modum conclusionis quae non est multum remota a principiis. Unde de facili in huiusmodi homines consenserunt' (*Summa Theologica* I–II, q. 95, a. 4 ad 1).

[48] A. H. Chroust and R. J. Affeldt, 'The Problem of Private Property according to St. Thomas Aquinas', *Marquette Law Review* 34, no. 3 (1950–51): p. 178. Aquinas accepts also the classification of *ius gentium* laid down by Isidore (*Etym.* v, 4, *seqq*): 'law which natural reason has set up among men'.

equality, it follows that they need no special institution, for they are instituted by natural reason itself.[49]

Aquinas's *ius gentium* has its more immediate cause of existence or validity in a common human agreement and custom, but is ultimately grounded in the natural law.[50] This closeness to natural law is precisely the reason why people can agree. Therefore, there is something in the law of nations that is not purely conventional.

As law, *ius gentium* is a principle of justice with a normative power. According to Aquinas, the force of a law depends on the extent of its justice. Now in human affairs a thing is just from being right according to the rule of reason. But the first rule of reason is the natural law.[51] Consequently every human law has just so much of the nature of law, as it is derived from the natural law.[52] *Ius gentium* has, therefore, some normative power from the natural law, but as it is also a consequence of common agreement, the force of *ius gentium* is grounded both in natural law and the human reasoning that created the institutions that flow directly from natural law. Consequently, *ius gentium* has a relative autonomy from natural law, but as to every other human law, natural law is also its reference.

To argue that the *ius gentium* is derived from natural law does not mean that its institutions will be.[53] For example, the principle that contracts should be fulfilled is not a principle of natural law *per se*. Rather it is a principle of *ius gentium*, which is nonetheless a matter of natural law.[54] Even though it is not infallible, the consensus existent between nations about certain practices such as acknowledging that contracts are binding, that legates are to be safe among enemies, and so on,[55] helps us to know which things are just by nature.[56] With his notion of *ius gentium*, Aquinas envisages a kind of positive law close to natural law that regulates relations among nations. These relations in the time of Aquinas were becoming commercial ones, which is why legal institutions surrounding sales, contracts, and property became basic issues. They are matters of positive law, but at least in their general structure were so necessary to a just social life as to be a matter of deduction from basic natural law principles and so included in the law common to all peoples, *ius gentium*.[57] This is why I will discuss property and commerce below.

Although he does not refer to it directly, Aquinas shows awareness of the situation of his era; that is, the existence of some city states, other cities that existed as parts of a realm, kingdoms, and other realms politically organized as provinces

[49] *Summa Theologica* II–II, q. 57, a. 3 ad 3.

[50] Chroust, 'The 'ius gentium' in the Philosophy of Law of St. Thomas Aquinas', p. 27.

[51] *Summa Theologica* I–II, q. 91, a. 2 ad 2. [52] Ibid., q. 95, a. 2.

[53] Following Aristotle, Aquinas understands *ius gentium* as a part of natural justice, that means is derived from natural law (*Comm.Nic.Eth.*lib. V, lectio 12, n. 1019). As we may recall, Aristotle divides political justice into natural and legal. Although Aristotle does not speak of natural law as such, he refers to it in his account of natural justice (Nic.Eth. V, 7 1134b18–1135a5).

[54] *Summa Theologica* I–II, q. 95 a. 4; II–II q. 57 a. 3.

[55] The examples are from *Comm. Nic.Eth.*lib. V, lectio 12, n. 1019.

[56] Joaquín García-Huidobro, 'La recepción de la doctrina aristotélica sobre el derecho natural en el Comentario a la Ética a Nicómaco de Tomás de Aquino', in *Filosofía y retórica del iusnaturalismo* (Mexico: Instituto de investigaciones jurídicas, 2002), pp. 95–6.

[57] See Finnis, *Aquinas: Moral, Political and Legal Theory*, p. 200.

or empires. He was aware also of the reality of peoples, nations, and regions. He was willing to regard relationships of friendship between states[58] and the widest horizons of human community, so that he envisaged treaties and other binding sources of law or right even between warring states: 'there are certain laws / rights of war (*iura bellorum*) and treaties which even between enemies, are to be kept'.[59]

Thus, Aquinas did not restrict his political views to refer to the flourishing of a concrete kingdom, but he broadened it to emphasize the element of the integral fulfilment of all persons and communities. This is the universal common good, the aim of ethics and politics. It is not merely external, but a fully practical, internal point of view, a comprehensive and extensive notion of human good[60] that includes the elements of public common good, peace, justice, and mutual love or friendship. This is the key to understanding Aquinas's account of dominium, commerce and property rights, and slavery.

Dominion, Private Property, Commerce, and Slavery

The basic issues addressed by Aquinas with reference to *ius gentium* are the questions of private property and slavery. Aquinas posits that originally, in the state of innocence, there was a universal community of property as well as the complete freedom of all people. However, by custom existing among the peoples, private property and slavery appeared as institutions. Aquinas reconciled these institutions with the precepts of natural law, explaining that they formed part of the secondary natural law, and that they were introduced for their necessity and utility in achieving the common good.[61]

Dominion

There are three types of dominion to consider: dominion over property or things, political power and authority, and slavery.

It is written that God gave humanity dominion over every creature, over all creation,[62] precisely because human beings were made in God's image. Therefore, due to their rationality, all human beings were able to have rights and exercise dominion.[63]

In a strict sense, according to Aquinas, 'all creation' encompassed all the creatures not made in God's image, the material world and irrational animals.[64] But

[58] Aquinas meant a political friendship not only between citizens of a state but also between different states, at least he interpreted Aristotle in this sense (Eth. IX.6 n.7 [1836]). See also Finnis, *Aquinas: Moral, Political and Legal Theory*, p. 114, note 54.

[59] Ibid., p. 220. The quote is from *Summa Theologica* II–II, q. 40 a. 3.

[60] See Finnis, *Aquinas: Moral, Political and Legal Theory*, pp. 103–29.

[61] Chroust, Anton-Hermann, 'The 'ius gentium' in the Philosophy of Law of St. Thomas Aquinas', *Notre Dame* Law *Review* 17, no. 1 (1941–2): pp. 22–8.

[62] *Genesis* 1:26.

[63] Castañeda, *La teocracia pontifical en las controversias sobre el Nuevo Mundo*, p. 444.

[64] *Summa Theologica* I, q. 96, a. 2.

Aquinas also referred to dominion in a wider sense, for instance the office of governing free people. This kind of dominion of one person over another person or persons would have existed originally, and was justified by the social condition of human beings, and was the source of political authority.[65]

There is still a third sense of dominion, as a mastership of one person to whom another person is subject as a slave. Aquinas explained that this kind of dominion would not have existed in the state of innocence, because such dominion necessarily implies a pain inflicted on the subject.[66]

Property rights

The topic of private property is divided into questions regarding ownership, use, and disposition. Aquinas understood the ownership of private property as a matter of positive law, concretely of *ius gentium*. Working from Aristotelian thought,[67] he distinguished between use and ownership,[68] grounding the use of property in natural law. This distinction between ownership and use is effectively absent from modern doctrines of property.

For Aquinas, private property was an institution superadded to the natural law in the *ius gentium* to achieve the common good. It was by human law that people possessed property; but that possession was justified by reference to practical considerations related to natural rights and the satisfaction of human needs. Human laws regulating property ownership were additions to, not departures from, natural law.[69] Private property was necessary and appropriate for three reasons: things held in common are usually neglected; their management tends to be confused; and they often provoke quarrels.[70] Therefore the notion of private property could work to the advantage of the whole community.[71]

What human laws conferred was a right to expropriate property from nature and manage it responsibly. They did not confer an unlimited right of acquisition and use. In fact, for Aquinas, the ultimate use of natural resources should remain fundamentally 'common',[72] because everyone had a natural right to a fair share in their consumption.[73]

How was this reservation compatible with ownership? The core of Aquinas's answer regarding the use of private property was according to the proposition that

[65] Ibid., a. 4. [66] *Summa Theologica* I, q. 96, a. 4. [67] *Politics* II, 2.

[68] Daniel Westberg, 'The Relation between Positive and Natural Law in Aquinas', *Journal of Law and Religion* XI, no. 1 (1994–95): pp.17–18.

[69] *St Thomas Aquinas Political Writings*, edited and translated by R. W. Dyson, p. XXX.

[70] *Summa Theologica* II–II q. 66, a. 2. See also *Summa Theologica* II–II q. 57, a. 3: 'there is no reason why a piece of land considered simply as such should belong to one man rather than another; but considered with respect to how best to cultivate the land and make peaceable use of it, it has a certain commensuration to be the property of one man rather than another, as the Philosopher shows at *Politics* II, 5'.

[71] *Summa Theologica* I–II q.105 a. 2 and ad 3. [72] *Summa Theologica* II–II, q. 66, a. 2.

[73] Ibid., q. 57, a. 3.

one was obliged by natural law to 'possess external things, not as one's own, but as common'.[74]

Hence he set moral limits to property rights. One can distinguish between the resources needed for the survival of an individual and his or her dependants, the resources needed for an individual to fulfil his or her responsibilities, and the resources which are superfluous (*superflua*) to these requirements. According to this distinction, Aquinas elaborated the following moral criteria:

1) everything one has is held as common in the sense that is morally available if someone has a dire need of it (to survive);
2) superfluous things are held in common, and it is a duty of justice to dispose of them for the benefit of the poor. In other words, one is entitled to as much property as needed to meet one's earthly needs comfortably. But what is held in excess of this is owed to the poor.[75]

In summary Aquinas recognized private property as something conditionally justifiable on the basis of the *ius gentium*, while at the same time he maintained that the community of all property and possessions was absolutely justified through the natural law. It was an objective justification determined by historical necessity. This justification consists in the fact he defines it as a subsequently added institution based on intelligent consideration and common human consensus.[76]

Commerce

Aquinas transcended, although never completely, the remnants of a predominant agrarian and feudalistic tradition, and the propensity towards urbanism and openness to new economic exchanges characteristic of the late Middle Ages can be detected in his work.[77] Aquinas was aware that commerce was becoming an important activity. Although not as radical as Aristotle, who alleged that commercial activity was unnecessary, unnatural, and rather low, Aquinas did issue warnings about the moral and political dangers of excessive interest in trade.[78]

According to Aquinas, commerce was an activity whereby one acquired things in order to dispose of them with profit.[79] The motives for engaging in commerce were relevant: it was usually decent to seek moderate profit for reasons such as sustaining households, helping the poor, public benefit, or supplying the needs of the country. Thus trade was reasonable (fair) for moderate rather than infinite gain, and for decent motives. Aquinas envisaged harmful consequences for a society if

[74] Ibid., q. 66, a. 2.

[75] See Finnis, *Aquinas: Moral, Political and Legal Theory*, p. 191, according to *Summa Theologica* II–II, q. 32, a. 7 ad 3; II–II, q. 66, a. 7.

[76] A. H. Chroust and R. J. Affeldt, 'The Problem of Private Property according to St. Thomas Aquinas', p. 181.

[77] Ibid., p. 179.

[78] *De regno* II, 3. According to Aristotle's Politics [V, 3: 1303a 27; VII, 6: 1327a 13-15], much engagement in trade is particularly harmful to civic customs.

[79] *Summa Theologica* II–II, q.77, a.4 ad 2.

trade was unfair: 'when the public good is despised, everyone pursues his own advantage, zeal for virtue ceases, and everyone puts profit before the honour of virtue. Hence in such a city civic life will necessarily be corrupted'.[80] Morally speaking, according to Aquinas the principle regulating fair commercial transactions was equality (equivalence) in the exchange. For example, in sales the transaction must respect equality through a mutual benefit of sellers and buyers.[81] A sound system of commercial law should respect this principle.

Dominion as political power

Dominion as political power and rule is exerted through human law, but is required by the socio–political condition of human being: 'man is by nature a social and political animal, who lives in a community (multitude)', in which 'there must be some governing power'.[82] Therefore, the origin and source of authority is natural. In other words, political power has its roots in the same natural law, though the concrete person doing the governing is determined by human law.[83] Aquinas argued that dominion in this sense would have existed even in the state of innocence, based on the social nature of the human being, and rejecting the idea that dominion was introduced as a consequence of sin.[84]

For Aquinas, subjection to a legitimate authority was not foreign to human nature, so it was in accordance with human nature to obey the commands of one's natural superiors. Christians were not excused from obeying secular power, but should obey it insofar as it was a rightful authority; when it was not, subjects were entitled to reject it and to disobey.[85]

In the context of the discord between emperors and popes in the thirteenth century, obedience to authority was not an easy matter. One could say that Aquinas was an ally of the pope in those matters that corresponded to the spiritual domain, and an ally of the emperor in secular matters, as expressed in Aquinas's formula: 'in those matters which pertain to political good (*bonum civile*), secular rather than spiritual authority is to be obeyed'.[86]

[80] *De regno* II, 3.

[81] *Summa Theologica* II–II, q. 61, a. 3; II–II, q. 77 a. 4 ad 2. A prerequisite is the right price, see Finnis, *Aquinas: Moral, Political and Legal Theory*, p. 202.

[82] *De regno* I, 1–9. Aquinas quotes the Aristotelian formula that 'man is by nature a political animal' (*Politics* 1:2; 1253 a2).

[83] Castañeda, *La teocracia pontifical en las controversias sobre el Nuevo Mundo*, p. 104.

[84] *Summa Theologica* I, q. 96, a. 4.

[85] *Summa Theologica* II–II, q. 104, a. 6. On tyranny, see *De regno* I, 7 and *Summa* II–II, q. 104, a. 6 ad 3; II–II, q. 42, a. 2 ad 3. Aquinas argued that a relatively mild tyranny ought to be tolerated and that action against the tyrant should be taken only where the harm involved in doing so would not be greater than the advantages which taking action may be expected to secure. These statements can be read in conjunction with what he says about war and violence. See *St Thomas Aquinas Political Writings*, edited and translated by R. W. Dyson, p. XXX.

[86] *Scripta super libros sententiarum* II, dist. 44, q. 3 a. 4, in *St Thomas Aquinas Political Writings*, edited and translated by R. W. Dyson.

In a *societas christiana*, Aquinas recognized the legitimacy of the temporal power based on *ius gentium*. Accordingly, even the rule of unbelievers over the faithful was legitimate provided that it was not scandalous or dangerous to the faith. Aquinas distinguished the domain of divine law and human law, of religion and politics:

> ... dominion and authority are institutions of human right, whereas the distinction between the faithful and unbelievers arises from Divine right. Now Divine right, which comes from grace, does not abolish human right, which comes from natural reason. And so the distinction between the faithful and unbelievers, considered in itself, does not abolish the dominion and authority of unbelievers over the faithful.[87]

In other words, unbelief is not in itself inconsistent with dominion, since dominion was introduced by *ius gentium*, which is a human law, whereas the distinction between believers and unbelievers was made according to divine right, which does not cancel out human right.

The purpose of human law and the purpose of divine law were different. The purpose of divine law was to lead one to eternal happiness. By contrast, the purpose of human laws was the temporal tranquillity of the state,[88] and human laws only commanded or prohibited conduct that advanced or damaged the common good. The specific common good of political communities was limited, and did not, for example, include the good of religious faith and worship, which was not, therefore, to be considered a proper subject of human laws.[89] This distinction became a grounding for the right of religious freedom.

For Aquinas, it is not actually possible to compel genuine faith and belief in those who have never received the faith, and so unbaptized subjects (Jews and heathens) should be tolerated in their rites and practices so long as they did not hinder the faith of Christ.[90]

On the other hand, heretics, apostates, and schismatics, who had at some time accepted the faith and later rejected it, were to be punished. Aquinas tried to justify this apparent inconsistency explaining that acceptance of the faith was a matter of choice, whereas keeping the faith when one has received it was a matter of obligation. Therefore heretics should be compelled to keep the faith.[91] Heresy, apostasy, and schism were considered ecclesiastical offences, acts of infidelity against

[87] 'Alio modo possumus loqui de dominio vel praelatione iam praeexistenti. Ubi considerandum est quod dominium et praelatio introducta sunt ex iure humano, distinctio autem fidelium et infidelium est ex iure divino. Ius autem divinum, quod est ex gratia, non tollit ius humanum, quod est ex naturali ratione. Et ideo distinctio fidelium et infidelium, secundum se considerata, non tollit dominium et praelationem infidelium supra fideles' (*Summa Theologica* II–II, q. 10, a. 10).

[88] *Summa Theologica* I–II, q. 98, a. 1.

[89] *Summa contra Gentiles* III, *c.*80 nn.14–15, 2559–60.

[90] *Summa Theologica* II–II, q. 10, a. 8, a.11.

[91] Ibid., q. 10, a. 8 ad 3. As MacIntyre explained, 'whenever Aquinas gives expression to this shared thirteenth-century *weltanschauung*, he does so exclusively by appeal to arguments drawn from Christian theology including canon law—arguments of a kind later to be rejected by Catholic teaching authority—and never in anyway by appeal to the natural law' (MacIntyre, 'Natural Law as Subversive: The Case of Aquinas', p. 62).

the Church, and the State cooperated with the Church to punish them as secular crimes in order to compel apostates back to the faith.

Thus, a ruler who was an apostate and not simply an unbeliever forfeited his dominion over his subjects by reason of his apostasy from the faith as soon as he was excommunicated, so that the subjects were no longer bound to obey him. The punishment of being deprived of the allegiance of his subjects was fitting, Aquinas explained, because this same allegiance might conduce to the corruption of the faith of the subjects.[92] Based on this, and not only due to the theocracy, the Church used her authority to depose apostate rulers.

This shows, however, that the relation between politics and religion was complex, due to the fact that the subjects of the State were the same members of the Church, and so the State as well as the Church had competence over them. Moreover, being a *societas christiana*, late medieval society was still united by the same faith, which is why unbelief like heresy and apostasy, threatening this unity, were also considered secular crimes.

It would not be until centuries later that the Church itself clearly enunciated that this could not be defended either in theory or in practice. The Vatican II Declaration on Religious Liberty, *Dignitatis Humanae* (1965) declared that, provided public peace and justice were respected, all persons had a right, as against political authorities, to freedom from coercion in respect of all their expressions of religious belief, consistent with Aquinas's standpoint regarding the purpose and ambit of human law and the common good.[93]

Slavery

Another basic issue of Aquinas's *ius gentium* related to dominion is the question of slavery. Liberty for all men was a matter of natural right, so slavery was not part of human nature, but was introduced by human reasoning for the practical advantages it was seen to offer.[94] The only sense in which it might be natural was if it was useful for a *servus* to be ruled by someone wiser. Aquinas allowed a place for slavery in the law of nations as natural in this second sense.[95] In other words, slavery did not arise spontaneously, but came about when reason reflected natural differences of capacity between people and calculated the consequences of one arrangement over another.[96]

[92] *Summa Theologica* II–II q. 12, a. 2.

[93] Vatican II, Declaration on Religious Liberty, *Dignitatis Humanae* (1965). This right is, however, more than the tolerance which Aquinas argues for in *Summa Theologica* II–II, q. 10, a. 11. See Finnis, *Aquinas: Moral, Political and Legal Theory*, pp. 293, 325.

[94] *Summa Theologica* I–II, q. 94, a. 5 ad 3.

[95] *Summa Theologica* II–II, q. 57, a. 3 ad 2.

[96] *St Thomas Aquinas Political Writings*, edited and translated by R. W. Dyson, p. 164. See also Héctor Zagal. 'Aquinas on Slavery: an Aristotelian Puzzle', paper presented at Congresso Tomista Internationale (Rome, Italy, 21–5 September 2003), pp. 7–8. There is no substantial but merely incidental inequality. Persons are unequal because of their education, costumes, environment and their own natural dispositions. For Aquinas, the servant has full rational capabilities, though not the same type of rationality as his master. Rationality is multiform, whether it is that of a carpenter, physician, philosopher or politician. However, these distinct types of rationality do not have the same function.

Thus, servitude is legitimated by its consequences. The relationship between servant and master is just only if it implies retribution: a wellbeing for both of the parts that constitute the relation. The fundament of this relationship is human comfort, which is the group of material, cultural, and spiritual commodities.[97]

In summary, considered absolutely, slavery was not natural (from natural right), but an institution of the right of nations, of some utility to all parties involved. By nature all people were equal and free, and no person or persons were ordered to another as an end.[98] Therefore slavery or servitude existed by positive, not natural, law and right.[99]

As a matter of positive law and positive right, slavery was limited by the requirements of morality and could not override the natural law. Thus, servants were bound to obey their masters only in matters touching on the execution of the duties of their service. They were not bound to obey their masters, nor children their parents, in matters such as getting married or remaining in the state of virginity.[100] Servants were morally and legally free to choose and practice their religion without requiring their masters' permission.[101] Moreover, servitude did not deprive slaves of other basic human rights such as not to be killed, harmed, raped, or used for any extra-marital sexual services, lied to, robbed, or cheated.[102]

Servants could be bought and sold only with respect to their service, and it was precisely in respect of this that the relationship between master and slave was one of *ius dominativum* (dominion).[103] In all other respects, the relationship between the two persons was one of justice and mutual rights.[104]

In short, Aquinas's idea of dominion and freedom was that dominion did not extend to the life and members of others, that unbelievers also have dominion over things and persons, and that freedom was of natural right while slavery was of *ius gentium*, an institution devised by human law.

The rationality of the carpenter is ordered to the production of chairs, yet not to cure any sickness; the mind of the philosopher will do to prove arguments, not to the ruling of people.

[97] Aquinas, *In Pol.*, I, 4, 47. See Héctor Zagal, 'Aquinas on Slavery: an Aristotelian Puzzle', p. 7.

[98] *Scripta super libros sententiarum* II, dist. 44 q. 1 a. 3 ad 1, in Finnis, *Aquinas: Moral, Political and Legal Theory*, p. 184.

[99] Aquinas differs from Aristotle's theory of slavery, found in *Politics*, Book I, III–VII and in *Nicomachean Ethics*, Book VII, which holds that some people are naturally slaves and others are naturally masters. Moreover, according to Héctor Zagal, 'Aquinas on Slavery: an Aristotelian Puzzle', p. 10: 'From society's point of view, there is great difference between Greek slavery and Feudal *servitudo*. The feudal *servus* is not owned by his lord. Greek slaves were. The *servus* certainly lacked liberties like free transit or willingly contracting himself to another feud, just like a basketball player cannot willingly be contracted by another team, being obligated by his previous contract. It is a good analogy, it underlines the contractual spirit of feudal servitude. The servus has, as well as obligations, certain liberties. There is no point of comparison with Greek slavery'.

[100] *Summa Theologica* II–II, q. 104, a. 5.

[101] *Scripta super libros sententiarum* IV, d. 36, in Finnis, *Aquinas: Moral, Political and Legal Theory*, p. 184.

[102] *Scripta super libros sententiarum* IV, d. 33 q. 1, a. 3 sol. 1.

[103] *Summa Theologica* II–II q. 57, a. 4 ad 1.

[104] Finnis, *Aquinas: Moral, Political and Legal Theory*, p. 185.

Final Reflections

The hesitations of Aquinas are understandable not only in the theological and political context of his era, but also because they show how religion and politics were intertwined, and consequently how hard the path was towards a just secularization; that is, a proper autonomy of temporal realities. Even if not explicitly, Aquinas however distinguished between spiritual and secular power, and claimed their relative independence.

To understand his contribution to the path towards secularization, it is necessary to distinguish between two meanings of secularization: as dechristianization (the action of removing Christian principles from the society) and as declericalization. Aquinas contributed to the secularization in its second meaning, by depriving temporal, political power of the clerical character it had in late thirteen-century Europe.

In a century in which the theocratic theory reached its height, with his notions of natural law and *ius gentium*, Aquinas defended the legitimacy of secular power, and invoked political activities as worthwhile in themselves. In this sense, Aquinas's work may be taken as a turning point in the history of political thought.

Although the law of nations flourished later, Aquinas provided the grounds for the development of doctrines on religious freedom, human natural sociability, and property rights that were used by theologians like Francisco de Vitoria (1483–1546) and Domingo de Soto (1495–1560) in their approaches regarding rights over the new world.[105]

Bibliography

AQUINAS'S WRITINGS

Commentary on Aristotle's Nicomachean Ethics, translated by C. I. Litzinger, O. P. (Notre Dame: Dumb Ox Books, 1993).

Commentary on Aristotle's Politics (*In Pol.*), translated by Richard Regan (Indianapolis: Hackett Publishing Company, 2007).

Commentary on the Sentences of Peter Lombard, translated by Ralph McInerny, Prologue by Joseph Kenny, O. P. (http://dhspriory.org/thomas/Sentences.htm).

On Kingship to the King of Cyprus (*De regno ad regem Cypri*), translated by Gerald B. Phelan, revised by I. Th. Eschmann, O. P. (Toronto: The Pontifical Institute of Mediaeval Studies, 1949).

St. Thomas Aquinas Political Writings, edited and translated by R. W. Dyson (Cambridge: Cambridge University Press, 2004).

Summa Contra Gentiles. Vol. III, translated by Vernon J. Bourke (Notre Dame: University of Notre Dame Press, 1975).

[105] See Castañeda, *La teocracia pontifical en las controversias sobre el Nuevo Mundo*, pp. 434–60, 463–88.

Summa Theologica, translated by Fathers of the English Dominican Province (2nd and Revised Edition, 1920) (Online Edition by Kevin Knight ©, 2008).

OTHER SOURCES

Alarcón, Enrique. 'Advances in our historical knowledge of Thomas Aquinas'. *Anuario Filosófico* XXXIX, no. 2 (2006): pp. 371–99.

Aroney, Nicholas. 'Subsidiarity, Federalism and the Best Constitution: Thomas Aquinas on City, Province and Empire'. *Law and Philosophy* 26, no. 2 (March 2007): pp. 161–228.

Bertelloni, Francisco. 'La teoría política medieval entre la tradición clásica y la modernidad'. In *El pensamiento político en la edad media,* edited by Pedro Roche Arnas (Madrid: Fundación Ramón Areces, 2010), pp. 17–40.

Cain, Patrick. 'Thomas Aquinas' De Regno: Political Philosophy, Theocracy, and Esoteric Writing'. *Canadian Political Science Association Annual Conference Presented* (2007), pp. 1–11.

Carlyle, A., and R. Carlyle. *A History of Medieval Political Thought in the West, vol. IV: The Theories of the Relation of the Empire and the Papacy* (New York: Barnes & Noble, 1903).

Carlyle, A., and R. Carlyle. *A History of Medieval Political Thought in the West, vol. V: The Political Theory of the Thirteenth Century* (New York: Barnes & Noble, 1909).

Castañeda Delgado, Paulino. *La teocracia pontifical en las controversias sobre el Nuevo Mundo* (Mexico, UNAM Instituto de Investigaciones Historicas, Serie 'Estudios Historicos', 59, 1996).

Choza, Jacinto. *Historia cultural del humanismo* (Madrid: Plaza y Valdes, S.L., 2009).

Chroust, Anton-Hermann. 'The 'ius gentium' in the Philosophy of Law of St. Thomas Aquinas'. *Notre Dame Law Review* 17, no. 1 (1941–42): pp. 22–8.

Chroust, A. H., and R. J. Affeldt. 'The Problem of Private Property according to St. Thomas Aquinas'. *Marquette Law Review* 34, no. 3 (1950–51): pp. 151–82.

Copleston, F. J. *A History of Philosophy. Medieval Philosophy,* vol. 2 (New York: Doubleday, 1993).

DiLeo, D. 'Thomas Aquinas and the Overlapping Consensus'. *Commonwealth: A Journal of Political Science* 13 (2007): pp. 1–21.

Dyson, R. W. *The Pilgrim City: Social and Political Ideas in the Writings of St Augustine of Hippo* (Woodbridge, Suffolk, UK/Rochester, N.Y.: Boydell Press, 2001).

Finnis, John. *Aquinas: Moral, Political and Legal Theory* (Oxford: Oxford University Press, 1998).

García-Huidobro, Joaquín. 'La recepción de la doctrina aristotélica sobre el derecho natural en el Comentario a la Ética a Nicómaco de Tomás de Aquino'. In *Filosofía y retórica del iusnaturalismo* (Mexico: Instituto de investigaciones jurídicas, 2002).

Gelasius I. Letter of Gelasius I (494). In *Readings in European History,* translated by J. H. Robinson (Boston: Ginn, 1905), pp. 72–3.

Gilson, Étienne. *Dante the Philosopher,* translated by David Moore (London: Sheed and Ward, 1952).

Gray, Phillip W. 'Political Theology and the Theology of Politics: Carl Schmitt and Medieval Christian Political Thought'. *Humanitas* 20, no. 1/2 (2007): pp. 175–200.

Hittinger, Russell. 'Natural Law and the Human City'. In *Contemporary Perspectives on Natural Law,* edited by Ana M. González (Hampshire: Ashgate Publishing Limited, 2008), pp. 29–41.

Kirsch, Johann Peter. 'Donation of Constantine'. *The Catholic Encyclopedia*, vol. 5 (New York: Robert Appleton Company, 1909). http://www.newadvent.org/cathen/05118a.htm.

Koskenniemi, Martti. 'Empire and International Law: The Real Spanish Contribution'. *University of Toronto Law Journal* 61, no. 1 (2011): pp. 1–36.

McCready, William D. 'Papal Plenitudo Potestatis and the Source of Temporal Authority in Late Medieval Papal Hierocratic Theory'. *Speculum* 48, no. 4 (October 1973): pp. 654–74.

MacIntyre, Alasdair. 'Natural Law as Subversive: The Case of Aquinas'. In *Ethics and Politics: Selected Essays*, vol. 2 (Cambridge/New York: Cambridge University Press, 2006), pp. 41–63.

Saranyana, Josep Ignasi. *La filosofía medieval. Desde sus orígenes patrísticos hasta la Escolástica barroca* (Pamplona: EUNSA Colección Pensamiento filosófico medieval y renacentista, 51, 3rd edn 2011).

Skinner, Quentin. *The Foundations of Modern Political Thought: Volume I: The Renaissance* (Cambridge: Cambridge University Press, 1978).

Torrell, Jean-Pierre. *Saint Thomas: The Person and His Work* (Washington, D.C.: The Catholic University of America Press, 2005, 1st edn 1993).

Tierney, Brian. 'A Conciliar Theory of the Thirteenth Century'. *The Catholic Historical Review* 36, no. 4 (January 1951): pp. 415–40.

Ullmann, Walter. 'Review: *Principality and Polity: Aquinas and the Rise of State Theory in the West* by Fr. Thomas Gilby'. *The English Historical Review* 73, no. 289 (October 1958): pp. 706–7.

Vitoria, Francisco de. *De indis recenter inventis*. In Obras de Francisco de Vitoria, edited by T. Urdanoz (Madrid: BAC, 1960).

Vitoria, Francisco de. *De potestate ecclesiae prior*. In Obras de Francisco de Vitoria, edited by T. Urdanoz (Madrid: BAC, 1960).

Vitoria, Francisco de. *Vitoria: Political Writings*. In *Cambridge Texts in the History of Political Thought*, edited by A. R. Pagden and J. Lawrance (Cambridge: Cambridge University Press, 1991).

Weisheipl, James. *Friar Thomas d'Aquino: His Life, Thought, and Works* (Washington, D.C.: Catholic University of America Press, 1983).

Weithman, Paul J. 'Natural Law, Property, and Redistribution'. *The Journal of Religious Ethics* 21, no. 1 (1993): pp. 165–80.

Weithman, Paul J. 'Complementarity and Equality in the Political Thought of Thomas Aquinas'. *Theological Studies* 59 (1998): pp. 277–98.

Westberg, Daniel. 'The Relation between Positive and Natural Law in Aquinas'. *Journal of Law and Religion* XI, no. 1 (1994–95): pp. 1–22.

Wulf, Maurice de. 'The Society of Nations in the Thirteenth Century'. *International Journal of Ethics* 29, no. 2 (January 1919): pp. 210–29.

Zagal, Héctor. 'Aquinas on slavery: an Aristotelian puzzle' (paper, Congresso Tomista Internationale, Rome, Italy, 21–5 September 2003).

3

Religion, Empire, and Law among Nations in *The City of God*

From the Salamanca School to Augustine, and Back Again

Mary M. Keys

Contemporary scholarship has underscored the significant role of the Salamanca School in the establishment of modern international legal norms. While disputes have questioned the extent of the School's impact, a deeper dispute probes the nature and content of the Salamanca theologians' contribution, and the salutary or deleterious character of that contribution. James Brown Scott in his path-breaking volume *The Spanish Origin of International Law: Francisco de Vitoria and his Law of Nations* claims 'that there was a Spanish school of international law in the sixteenth century, within forty years of the discovery of America; that the founder of this school was Francisco de Vitoria ... [; and that this school's legal theory] proclaims an *international community composed of all the nations, the vast majority being the small powers whose defense is righteousness, justice, and the moral standard*'.[1] Recently, Martti Koskenniemi has extended this line of analysis so as to turn it against itself, or more precisely against key aspects of the equality and equity among peoples to which the Salamancan jurists aspired. In Koskenniemi's view, the Salamanca School's 'moral standard' included a contestable theory of individual property rights that foreshadowed and so was easily assumed and extended by European Enlightenment liberalism. Koskenniemi writes:

My claim is that, by concentrating merely on what [the Salamanca theologians] say on such public law issues as territory, jurisdiction, and formal war and by ignoring those aspects of their work that deal with the universal operation of property and contract, we receive a truncated and one-sided image not only of what they were doing but of the nature of the

[1] James Brown Scott, *The Spanish Origin of International Law: Francisco de Vitoria and his Law of Nations* (Oxford: Clarendon Press, 1934), p. 9a; emphasis added. See also Georg Cavallar, *The Rights of Strangers* (Aldershot and Burlington: Ashgate, 2002), pp. 75–119; Peter Stamatov, *The Origins of Global Humanitarianism: Religion, Empires, and Advocacy* (New York and Cambridge: Cambridge University Press, 2013), pp. 24–72; and John Gladwin, review of Roger Ruston's *Human Rights and the Image of God* (2006), *Ecclesiastical Law Journal* 8, no. 39 (2006): pp. 490–1, doi:10.1017/S0956618X00006827.

legal system that was emerging at the time when they were writing and that has persisted much more powerfully as part of global history than did any formal empire.[2]

In this chapter, I contest neither Scott's nor Koskenniemi's assessment of the Salamanca School's 'real contribution'. Rather, I seek to elucidate a third contribution made by the early Salamanca theologians in their works on law and justice, a hermeneutical contribution that is modest in scope and yet sheds light on the religious and philosophic dimensions of their international ethical and legal project: their turn to Augustine of Hippo's analysis of religion, empire, and laws amongst nations in his magnum opus *The City of God* (*De civitate dei*).[3] In the eyes of the Second Scholastic's founder, Francisco de Vitoria, and his first successors, Augustine's *City of God* appeared to attribute imperial Rome's vast dominion to a form of law or right (*ius*), sanctioned or permitted by God, and accorded to the Romans on account of their superior political and moral virtues. Thus, *The City of God* became at first a stumbling block to their normative-historical critiques of both Roman and Iberian imperial expansion. In the work of Vitoria's pupils Melchior Cano and Domingo de Soto, however, this misreading began to be rectified. Soto, in particular, would undertake a more thorough rereading (*relectio*) of Augustine's classic, especially its fifth book, to reveal its argument as an ally rather than adversary of their critiques of imperial expansionism, modern as well as ancient.[4]

In this chapter, I first survey the import of and access to Augustine's *City of God* in the late Middle Ages and Renaissance. I then build on David Lupher's history and other recent scholarship to interpret and assess Augustine's place in the early Salamanca School, according special attention to the writings of Vitoria, Cano, and Soto.[5] From there I continue Soto's fruitful project of *relectio*, rereading *The*

[2] Martti Koskenniemi, 'Empire and International Law: The Real Spanish Contribution', *University of Toronto Law Journal* 63 (2011): pp. 2–3, http://www.jstor.org/stable/23018686; cf. also Antony Anghie, *Imperialism, Sovereignty and the Making of International Law* (Cambridge: Cambridge University Press, 2005).

[3] In her excellent chapter on the meanings of *ius* in the early Salamanca School, Annabel Brett does not discuss Augustine's influence on their thought, beyond noting the impact of an 'Augustinian dualism of spirit and nature' on the thought of Vitoria (Annabel S. Brett, *Liberty, Right and Nature: Individual Rights in Later Scholastic Thought* (Cambridge: Cambridge University Press, 1997), pp. 130–1). For recent interpretations of Augustine's anthropology that question this 'dualism', see Sarah Byers, 'Augustine and the Philosophers', in *Blackwell Companion to Augustine*, edited by Mark Vessey (Malden, MA and Oxford: Wiley-Blackwell, 2012), pp. 176–80, and John Cavadini, 'The Darkest Enigma: Reconsidering the Self in Augustine's Thought', *Augustinian Studies* 38, no. 1 (Spring 2007): pp. 119–32, doi:10.5840/augstudies20073817, and 'Ideology and Solidarity in Augustine's *City of God*', in *Augustine's City of God: A Critical Guide*, edited by James Wetzel (2012), pp. 93–110.

[4] David Lupher, *Romans in a New World* (Ann Arbor: University of Michigan Press, 2003), pp. 43–102. On Augustinian themes in later Salamanca school thinkers, especially Bartolomé de las Casas, see D. A. Brading, 'The Two Cities: St. Augustine and the Spanish conquest of America', *Revista Portuguesa de Filosofia*, 44, no. 1 (January–March 1988): pp. 99–126, http://www.jstor.org/stable/40338154.

[5] Parallels between ancient Roman and modern European imperialisms were perhaps the key cause of the significance of *The City of God* to the Salamancan theologian-jurists. For this reason Lupher's *Romans in a New World* constitutes the most important contemporary resource for my study here, as a foundation and interlocutor.

City of God afresh with a focus on Augustine's commentaries on right (*ius*) and law (*lex*) among nations under Rome's imperial sway. These two interpretive sections constitute the chapter's core. The *relectio* of *De civitate dei* offered here aims also to supplement recent studies of Augustine's theory of law, which tend to focus more on theoretical works, such as *On Free Choice of the Will*, than on the ground-up view of Roman imperial law and the 'international' laws of war and peace that Augustine presents in *De civitate dei*.[6] I argue that rereading Augustine's *City of God* with the themes of right and law, religion, and empire in mind deepens awareness of Augustine's alliance with the Salamanca School, even as it reveals a rift between Augustine's legal thought and Vitoria's. What is most striking in terms of alliance is what we might term the Salamancans' 'anticipatory Augustinianism': the extent to which the ethical-legal critique offered by Cano and Soto in particular is Augustinian well before Soto returns to reread in context the critical portion of book five of *The City of God*. And yet, despite Augustine's focus on justice and law in times of peace and war, and despite the considerable Ciceronian influence on his political thought, in analysing Roman law historically and ethically, Augustine never once employs the term *ius gentium*, although he does refer a handful of times to the related terms *ius pacis* and *ius belli*. In this studied avoidance, I argue, Augustine shows himself able to endorse aspects of the moral universalism and humanism of the early Salamanca theologians, traits emphasized by Scott and others, while simultaneously nodding in the direction of critical realist reservations articulated by scholars such as Koskenniemi and anticipated by Cano and Soto, especially with regard to some dimensions of the legal content and practical implications of Vitoria's jurisprudence of *ius gentium*.

Augustine's *City of God* in the Sixteenth-century European Academy

In London in 1501, a young humanist lawyer named Thomas More delivered an invited series of lectures on Augustine's *City of God*, lectures of which no record remains beyond a note that they were well attended and focused on historical and philosophical, rather than theological, themes.[7] One prominent scholar of

[6] For thoughtful studies of Augustine's legal theory, see Richard J. Dougherty, 'St. Augustine on Law—Natural, Human, and Divine' (Paper presented at the Northeastern Political Science Association annual meeting in Boston, Massachusetts, 13–15 November 2008), http://citation.allacademic.com/meta/p276721_index.html; Richard J. Dougherty, 'Law', in *The Oxford Guide to the Historical Reception of Augustine*, edited by Karla Pollmann, Willemien Otten, with Hildegund Müller, vol. 3 (Oxford: Oxford University Press, 2013), pp. 1281–3; and Anton-Hermann Chroust, 'The Fundamental Ideas in St. Augustine's Philosophy of Law', *American Journal of Jurisprudence* 18 (1973): pp. 57–79, http://scholarship.law.nd.edu/ajj/vol18/iss1/4; on Augustine on law, war, and international relations, see Richard Tuck, *The Rights of War and Peace: Political Thought and International Order from Grotius to Kant* (Oxford: Oxford University Press, 1999), pp. 55–8.

[7] Gerard B. Wegemer, *Young Thomas More and the Arts of Liberty* (Cambridge: Cambridge University Press, 2011), p. 50; and Wegemer, *Thomas More on Statesmanship* (Washington, D.C.: The Catholic University of America Press, 1996), pp. 8, 129–30; see also Michael C. Sloan, '*De civitate*

More's political philosophy has suggested that the then-recent discovery of the New World—new lands, new polities and empires, new peoples and customs—rendered this return to Augustine's classic almost unavoidable, and that reference points from *The City of God* are critical for interpreting More's *Utopia*, first published in 1516.[8] If this is so, and if assessing morally and legally the lure of European imperial expansion was also a consideration, then More had much in common not only with Spanish humanists like his friend Juan Luis Vives, but also with the 'new scholastics' of Salamanca, Francisco de Vitoria, and his successors. As J.A. Fernández Santamaria has written:

> Augustine's writings ... are works of exhortation and controversy designed to answer questions ... of his own age. These, of course, were not the same as those [of] the early sixteenth century. But the sense of crisis was common to both periods, and its effects identical in that it caused a reappraisal of the fundamental tenets which guided man, both as a Christian and as a socio-political being.[9]

Prior to the Augustinian renaissance of the fourteenth century, access to full manuscript copies of Augustine's works, including *The City of God*, varied considerably across Europe's monastic, university, and private libraries.[10] Historian E. L. Saak notes, for instance, that the Sorbonne's library in 1275, the year after Thomas Aquinas's death and the year of the earliest extant inventory of the Sorbonne's library holdings, lacked a copy of *The City of God* beyond a small volume of passages from its first book. Many monastic and private libraries possessed complete copies, however, and Saak's conclusions suggest that a scholar eager to read the work would not have had too hard a time locating it.[11] Arnoud Visser concurs, noting that even prior to 1505 'Augustine was never in short supply, but ... some parts of his oeuvre, especially the *City of God*, his commentary of the Psalms, and several exegetical treatises, were far better disseminated than others. This also applies to the famous "Augustinian revival" in the fourteenth century.'[12]

With the advent of printing in the mid-fifteenth century, access to Augustine's writings increased exponentially.

Dei', in *The Oxford Guide to the Historical Reception of Augustine*, edited by Karla Pollmann, Willemien Otten, with Hildegund Müller, vol. 1 (Oxford: Oxford University Press, 2013), p. 258.

[8] Wegemer, *Thomas More on Statesmanship*, p. 130 ff.

[9] J.A. Fernández-Santamaria, *The State, War, and Peace: Spanish Political Thought in the Renaissance, 1516–1559* (Cambridge: Cambridge University Press, 1977), pp. 129–30. See also William Bouwsma, 'The Two Faces of Humanism: Stoicism and Augustinianism in Renaissance Thought', in *Itinerarium Italicum: The Profile of the Italian Renaissance in the Mirror of Its European Transformation*, edited by Heiko A. Oberman and Thomas A. Brady, Jr. (Leiden: E. J. Brill, 1975), pp. 3–60; and Edgar H. Brookes, *The City of God and the Politics of Crisis* (London: Oxford University Press, 1960).

[10] See E. L. Saak, *Creating Augustine: Interpreting Augustine and Augustinianism in the Later Middle Ages* (Oxford: Oxford University Press, 2012), pp. 24–37. See also Alain J. Stoclet, 'Le *De civitate Dei* de saint Augustin: Sa diffusion avant 900', *Recherches Augustiniennes* 19 (1984): pp. 185–202; Charles B. Faulhaber, 'Libraries', in *Medieval Iberia: An Encyclopedia*, edited by E. Michael Gerli and Samuel G. Armistead (New York: Routledge, 2003), p. 486; and Guy Beaujouan, *Manuscrits scientifiques médiévaux de l'Université de Salamanque et de ses 'Colegios Mayores'* (Bordeaux: Féret & Fils, 1962).

[11] See Saak, *Creating Augustine*, p. 32.

[12] Arnoud S. Q. Visser, *Reading Augustine in the Reformation: The Flexibility of Intellectual Authority in Europe, 1500–1620* (Oxford: Oxford University Press, 2011), p. 17.

Before 1505, *De civitate dei* was the most frequently printed of Augustine's works, with some fifteen editions available, including French and Italian translations.[13] The years 1505–6 saw the publication by Johan Amerbach in Basel of the first Augustine *opera omnia*. Amerbach's edition of *De civitate dei* included commentaries by Dominican scholars, and Visser notes that it thus presented *De civitate* 'in the context of scholastic learning'.[14] The years 1521–2 witnessed the publication of humanist Juan Luis Vives's edition of *De civitate dei*, complete with an extensive commentary to supplement and perhaps rival scholastic readings. Erasmus soon reprinted Vives's edition of *De civitate dei* in his edition of the collected works of Augustine, published in 1528–9. Erasmus's first edition omitted Vives's commentary, apparently seeking to deflect any polemics it might provoke. He reinserted the commentary, however, in the collected works' reprints, the first of which was published in 1531–2.[15]

Thus, both the Amerbach and the Vives versions of *The City of God*, together with numerous earlier print editions and manuscript copies, were in circulation throughout Europe before the start of the great debates in Salamanca.

The City of God in the Early Salamanca School's Disputations

As the *conquista* continued and was consolidated in America, Spanish scholars increasingly turned to the history of imperial Rome in search of evidence buttressing the justice and utility of expansive rule, or indicators to caution the European monarchies in their continental and overseas ambitions. The Salamanca School's scholastic theologian-jurists first took up the debate concerning ancient Roman and contemporary European imperial rule on their own initiative, and later continued it both of their own accord and in response to a rare royal request for an examination of the nation's conduct from the vantage point of justice and right.[16] Salamanca's scholastic scholars also wrote in continuation of and in tandem with aspects of Vives's humanist essays and his commentary on *The City of God.*

The Humanist Prelude: Vives versus Sepúlveda

In 1519, Juan Luis Vives[17] published *Pompeius fugiens* (*Pompey Fleeing*), a lament in Pompey's voice for lost republican virtue and public spirit in the wake of Julius

[13] Ibid., p. 15. [14] Ibid., p. 22. [15] Ibid., pp. 26, 39–40, 141.

[16] On this topic see Dolores M. Sánchez, *El deber de consejo en el estado moderno: Las juntas 'ad hoc' en España (1471–1665)* (Madrid: Ediciones Polifemo, 1993); Luciano Pereña, *La idea de justicia en la conquista de América* (Madrid: Ediciones Polifemo, 1993); and Demetrio Ramos Perez, ed., *La ética en la conquista de América* (Madrid: Consejo Superior de Investigaciones Científicas, 1984).

[17] On Vives's life and works, see Carlos Noreña, *Juan Luis Vives* (The Hague: Martinus Nijhoff, 1970); José A. Fernández Santamaría, *Juan Luis Vives: Escepticismo y Prudencia en el Renacimiento*

Caesar. In decrying the injustice of and misery caused by this undoing of republican institutions and stoking of factional strife, and lamenting with stoic reserve his own and his family's bitter fates, Vives's Pompey calls attention to the myriad ways Rome failed to serve the cause of right on account of the injustice of leading citizens. The collective drive to expand Rome's empire, it seems, encouraged the less scrupulous among civic elites to expand their own personal *imperium*, their claims to power over others, and so stoked absolutism and inequity.[18]

Vives's persuasive plea in *Pompeius fugiens* for just political and military restraint was continued some three years later with the publication of his edition of *De civitate dei*. As David Lupher has observed:

> Fittingly enough, the same year that Vives composed this passionate rhetorical attack upon Roman imperial autocracy he began work ... on what proved to be upon its publication in 1521–2 a very widely circulated edition of Augustine's *City of God*, with a historical and philosophical commentary that extended Augustine's bitter assessment of the violence and insatiable appetite for glory of ancient Rome to the plight of a contemporary Europe 'bathed in floods of mutual blood'.[19]

Another humanist, however, a Spaniard named Juan Ginés de Sepúlveda, who had lived and worked chiefly among the scholars of Italy's Renaissance, quickly countered Vives's critique of ancient Rome and its modern imperial successors. In 1523, Sepúlveda published a dialogue entitled *De appetenda gloria dialogus, qui inscribitur Gonsalus*. The conversation among the interlocutors in *Gonsalus* endorses love of glory as a necessary and noble motive in human endeavours, certainly so in civic life. The great glory won in daring imperial expansion carried out by means of justly waged wars, *Gonsalus* contends, is a credit to contemporary Spain as it was to the Roman *res publica* and its celebrated patriots long ago. Lupher notes perceptively that Sepúlveda's case against 'those who have written books to show that glory ought to be condemned' seems to have an even larger target in view than Vives and his collaborators, among whose number were Erasmus and More. '[I]t is hard to escape the suspicion that his most formidable target here [is] none other than Augustine, whose attacks upon glory in general and Roman glory-seeking in particular had achieved renewed currency with the publication of Vives's edition [of *The City of God*] and commentary the year before.'[20]

(Salamanca: Ediciones Universidad de Salamanca, 1990); and Cathy Curtis, 'Advising Monarchs and Their Counselors: Juan Luis Vives on the Emotions, Civil Life, and International Relations', *Parergon* 28, no. 2 (2011): pp. 29–53, doi:0.1353/pgn.2011.0115.

[18] For an illuminating etymological history of the Roman concept of *imperium*, see John Richardson, 'The Meaning of imperium in the Last Century BC and the First AD', in *The Roman Foundations of the Law of Nations: Alberico Gentili and the Justice of Empire*, edited by Benedict Kingsbury and Benjamin Straumann (Oxford: Oxford University Press, 2010), pp. 21–9.

[19] Lupher, *Romans in a New World*, p. 108. D. A. Brading argues that Vives's moral vision aligns more closely to Christian stoicism than to Augustinianism (see 'The Two Cities', p. 119).

[20] Lupher, *Romans in a New World*, p. 108–9.

The City of God in the Scholastics' Reply to Sepúlveda: Vitoria, Cano, and Soto

Francisco de Vitoria

Francisco de Vitoria (*c.* 1483–1546), teacher of scholars and founder of the Spanish 'Second Scholastic' school in Salamanca, employed Augustine's *City of God* sporadically yet significantly in his legal theory and ethical-juridical assessments of the *conquista*.[21] Vitoria treated Augustine as a weighty intellectual authority, and yet his references to Augustine's *City of God* show little evidence of real personal engagement with the full work, or even with a complete book or chapter.

De civitate dei serves two main purposes in Vitoria's *De indiis* (*On the American Indians*) and *De iure belli* (On *the Law of War*). Vitoria refers to *The City of God* in the first instance to underscore what he concludes to be the fundamental or at least considerable justice of ancient Rome's imperial expansion. Vitoria's second major use of *De civitate dei* follows from and completes the first: Rome's wars of expansion were in the main just, because the Romans answered pleas for help from besieged allies, receiving dominion over conquered territories as pre-agreed 'booty' sanctioned by the 'law of war' (*ius belli*).[22]

Vitoria indeed understands Augustine as affirming Rome's just claim to mastery over most of the known world (although not over the whole world) and seeing God's will as in some sense the cause of this empire's great domain. With 'Thomas Aquinas' (not actually Aquinas, but rather Ptolemy of Lucca in *De Regimine Principum* 3.4),[23] Augustine is thought to concur that 'God delivered imperial power to the Romans on account of their justice and patriotism and excellent laws.'[24] Vitoria qualifies this conclusion, stating that God never granted a true *divine right* of rule to Rome as he had done when appointing Saul and David as kings of Israel. '[D]ivine Providence [rather] brought it about that they [the ancient Romans] should obtain universal empire by *some other right*, such as just war or some other way.'[25]

The texts of Augustine's *De civitate dei* that seem best to support this conclusion are located in its fifth book.[26] Particularly poignant is this passage from the conclusion of book five, chapter fifteen:

> [The great ancient] Romans held their own private interests in low esteem for the sake of the common good, that is, for the commonwealth [*pro … re publica*]…. [T]hey resisted avarice, took counsel for the good of their fatherland with unfettered minds; nor were they guilty of any offence against its laws, or of any unwholesome desires…. They were honored among almost all the nations; they imposed the laws of their empire on many races; and

[21] On Vitoria's work and influence, see Anthony Pagden, 'The School of Salamanca', in *The Oxford Handbook of the History of Political Philosophy*, edited by George Klosko (2011), pp. 246–57.

[22] See Vitoria, *On the American Indians*, in *Political Writings*, p. 289.

[23] Lupher, *Romans in a New World*, p. 64.

[24] Vitoria, *Political Writings*, p. 254.

[25] Ibid., emphasis added.

[26] See Lupher, *Romans in a New World*, pp. 89, 95–6.

they are glorious among almost all peoples to this day, in literature and in history. They have no cause to complain of the justice of the highest and true God ....[27]

The problem with this apparently optimistic assessment of imperial Rome, however, can easily be grasped by attentive readers of *De civitate dei* in its entirety or even simply of book five. That book aims to demonstrate the interplay of human and divine causes of Rome's imperial grandeur, indeed of the fate of any political society and regime. Book five thus opens with several chapters arguing for the compatibility of divine providence and human freedom. Given the fact of human free agency, part of the order of the cosmos God created, and given propitious circumstances, a capable and ambitious people seeking human glory chiefly by means of heroic public service and martial exploits will in fact reap this glory. Those seeking empire will most likely, sooner or later, obtain empire. This is a consequence of human freedom, permitted by God and inscribed in the order of created nature. If God does not intervene in an extraordinary way to impede such civic pride and consequent imperial expansion, as in the Biblical story of the tower of Babel, he can be understood to permit them.[28] Yet, it is wrong to conclude that Augustine thinks God is pleased with love of fame and glory as motivation for empire. Augustine explicitly argues the contrary: 'He understands the matter more truly who understands that ... love of praise is a vice.' Augustine quotes from the poet Horace to reinforce this conclusion, as accessible to honest human reason:

'Do you swell with love of human praise? There are certain remedies that will restore you to health ....' And the same author, in lyric verse, sings as follows, seeking to restrain the love of mastery: 'You will rule more widely if you can conquer greed of spirit than if you could join Lybia to far Gades, and thus make the two Carthaginian peoples serve one master.'[29]

Even apparently virtuous deeds, Augustine seeks to show, are tainted if their ultimate motivation is not truth, justice, goodness, peace, and mercy, but rather self-exaltation, personal and/or collective. Augustine observes that 'excessive' love of glory can stoke the flames of *libido dominandi*, the desire to lord it over others, falsely regarded as a good thing in itself.[30] There thus appears some link between the great self-sacrificing patriots of Roman history and lore—Marcus Regulus, Mucius, Furius Camillus, and the like—and the tyrants of later eras.[31] And so Augustine's apparently unqualified assertion that the great republican Romans were innocent of 'any unwholesome desires' must be qualified in this context.[32] They were innocent of *most* unwholesome desires, it appears, but all too often this moderation served another and perhaps still more unwholesome desire for superhuman greatness and civic domination of other peoples.

[27] Augustine, *The City of God against the Pagans*, translated and edited by R. W. Dyson, p. 216.

[28] *Genesis* 11:1–9.

[29] Horace, *Epistles*, 1.1.36 ff. and *Carmen Saeculare*, 2.2.9 ff.; cited in Augustine, *City of God* 5.13, p. 213.

[30] See Augustine, *City of God*, 6.19, p. 223.

[31] Ibid., 5.18, pp. 220–1.

[32] Ibid., 5.15.

Vitoria's second significant use of *De civitate dei* is in support of the justice of wars waged by nations to defend themselves when unjustly besieged, and to help oppressed allies, thereafter accepting *dominio* or *imperium* over conquered territories as equitable spoils, recompense for their efforts and their losses. Vitoria lists Augustine as one of several authorities who he thinks upheld the right or justice of Rome's expansion on these grounds.[33] There is, however, once again significant counterevidence in *De civitate dei*, calling into question Rome's dedication to its allies together with the preponderantly defensive motivation of Roman imperial expansion. This is so especially in chapter ten of book three.[34] The passage, full of rhetorical flourishes, twists and turns, concludes by expressing a doubt that is not and probably cannot be resolved by the historical record.

Augustine opens this passage, a commentary on the histories of the early Roman Republic written by Sallust and others, with what seems at first an unconditional affirmation of Rome's right:

> Clearly, however, the Romans did have a just defense of undertaking and waging such great wars. They were compelled to resist the savage incursions of their enemies ... as Sallust himself writes, '[E]nvy arose out of prosperity, and neighboring kings and peoples therefore undertook warfare [against Rome].... [T]he Romans, alert both at home and in the field, made haste and prepared.... Afterwards when by their valour they had repulsed the danger, they brought aid to their allies and friends.'

Nothing appears blameworthy thus far in Rome's path to empire, but Augustine does not rest content with this evidence, not even from Sallust, the historian he seems most to admire. Immediately after this passage, Augustine mentions the peace of Numa and asks how it was achieved. Was it simply that no one dared any longer to provoke war against Rome's might? Or was it more that Rome took a required respite from battle during those years and, to enable this rest, redoubled efforts at negotiating peace and cultivating friendly relations with its neighbours? And if the latter explanation is valid, even in part, could not Rome have tried such tactics earlier, with some measure of success? Might not Rome rather have rushed to war, in at least some cases, sensing opportunities to expand its *imperium*? If so, can this be called justice?

Augustine next narrates some incidents of unjust provocation of wars against their neighbours, from whom Rome seemed perfectly happy to profit by means of increased territories and numbers of subjects. Perhaps the earliest imperial expansion resulted from the abduction of the Sabine women and the armed conflict that ensued with their people; and shortly afterwards, from bloody battles provoked by the Romans against their neighbours the Albans.[35] Augustine concludes his recounting with reflections gleaned again from Sallust: 'Sallust touches in passing on this great crime' and its roots in a bygone era, when great powers began '"to

[33] See Vitoria, *Political Writings*, p. 289 (*On the American Indians*, 3.7), and p. 325 (*On the Law of War* 3.7).

[34] See Augustine, *City of God*, p. 104.

[35] See Augustine, *City of God*, 3.13–14, pp. 107–11.

deem lust for mastery sufficient reason for war, and to hold that the greatest glory belongs to the greatest empire" … Rome was conquered by this lust [for mastery] when she triumphed over Alba; and in praising her own crime, she called it glory.'[36] So much for Augustine's assessment of even the claims in human justice for Rome's increasing *imperium*!

Augustine goes on, near the close of book three, to highlight an especially egregious instance of Roman neglect of a faithful ally: the Spanish city of Saguntum, which perished in utter misery at the hands of Hannibal. It was besieged because of its alliance with Rome, and it was destroyed due to Roman indifference to its plight, or at least relative inaction on its behalf. The Saguntines, wrote Augustine, 'had no succour' outside of Rome, which never came with arms to their aid. By contrast, Augustine suggests, the Romans themselves were 'well provided with resources against Hannibal', but remained interested chiefly in 'fighting on their own behalf'.[37]

Vitoria thus seems to have exaggerated Augustine's view of the role justified protection of allies actually played in Rome's territorial acquisitions. Lupher, however, goes further, reading Vitoria to have endorsed not only the justice of Rome's conquests, but also the Spanish *conquista* on this Augustinian ethical ground, aiding the unjustly oppressed against their oppressors and reaping afterwards just spoils. Lupher bases this reading of *De indiis* and its list of possible (but not certain as applied to Spain) just causes for invasion and empire, on Vitoria's lone mention of an historical event, which occurs under the heading of 'Seventh just title, [war waged] for the sake of allies and friends'.[38] Vitoria is uncompromising that this *can* constitute a just cause of war, presuming of course that the friends and allies are suffering unjust injury and that no peaceful course of action has been omitted that could right the wrong short of bloodshed and the consequent territory annexation. Lupher seems to conclude that this 'seventh just cause' in fact justifies the Spaniards in Vitoria's eyes, because of his mention of this concrete incident: 'the Tlaxcaltecs were fighting the Mexicans [the Aztecs, their oppressors]; they made a treaty with the Spaniards that they should help them … and promised them in return whatever they might win by the laws of war'.[39] Lupher apparently understands Vitoria here to be documenting an instance of this concrete kind of injustice for which war may be waged and territory taken.

What Lupher glosses over too quickly, however, is the way Vitoria introduces this historical 'fact': '*They say that* the Tlaxcaltecs were fighting the Mexicans.'[40] Vitoria is clearly distancing his judgement from what he presents to the reader as a report, even a rumour of an event he knows *may* have happened quite otherwise

[36] Ibid., p. 111. [37] Ibid., 3.20, pp. 127–9.
[38] Vitoria, *Political Writings*, p. 289 ff.
[39] Ibid., p. 289; cf. Lupher, *Romans in a New World*, pp. 73–5.
[40] Lupher's translation; cf. Pagden's and Lawrance's, 'This is *what is said to have happened* when …' in Vitoria, *Political Writings*, p. 289; emphasis added.

than reported, and for baser motives than helping another people under unjust assault. Far from endorsing this case as claim to concrete justice, Vitoria rather judiciously suspends judgement, on account of insufficient knowledge of the case. And Vitoria again underscores this uncertainty, in his conclusion to the discussion of all potentially just causes of Spain's *conquista*, indeed to *De indiis* as a whole, in which he notes only two pages after his reference to the Tlaxcaltecs:

> *The conclusion of this whole dispute* seems to be this: that *if all these titles were inapplicable* [to Spain's expansion in the Americas], that is to say that the barbarians gave no just cause for war and did not wish to have the Spaniards as princes and so on, then the whole Indian expedition and trade would cease.[41]

Vitoria all too tersely denies the last clause's validity, but he never disputes the first premise, that it is at a minimum quite possible that *no* in-principle just cause he has listed, including that of helping allies (his 'seventh just cause'), holds up in support of Spain's conquests. It is therefore misleading to accord too much weight to Vitoria's mention of the report from America regarding the Tlaxcatlec-Spanish alliance and its aftermath, as if the Spanish Scholastic therein applied an 'Augustinian' argument conclusively in favour of imperial Spain.

In addition to these arguments, Vitoria employs other passages penned by Augustine to argue against the 'lawfulness' of human sacrifice;[42] for a definition of just war;[43] for an obligation to deal with 'every man' as truly 'your neighbour';[44] for the rightful aim of war, as peace and security;[45] and on the legitimacy for 'just men' and Christians to fight in some wars.[46] A normative reference to the practice of 'the primitive Church in times of Augustine and Jerome', supports Aquinas's and Vitoria's arguments against forced, or even voluntary but hasty, baptisms.[47] In short, one can see how Augustine's writings define critical ethical, legal, and religious norms for Vitoria's disputations, as well as provide historical exemplars for the Salamanca School's founder. That Vitoria fell short in his interpretation of Augustine's historical and rhetorical analysis of imperial Rome in *De civitate dei* reveals that his perceptive Augustinian insights vis-à-vis contemporary Iberian empire still required completion via a more nuanced, attentive reading of Augustine's complete *City of God* as it critically engaged then-contemporary imperial Rome. This task of *relectio* was accomplished by two of Vitoria's pupils and colleagues in Salamanca, Melchior Cano and Domingo de Soto.

Melchior Cano

Melchior Cano (*c*. 1509–60), who would succeed his mentor Vitoria on the latter's death to occupy the prestigious first ('morning') chair of theology at Salamanca, next took the baton in the debate concerning the *conquista*. In 1546, seven years

41 Vitoria, *Political Writings*, p. 291.
42 Ibid., p. 216.
43 Ibid., p. 270.
44 Ibid., p. 279.
45 Ibid., p. 283.
46 Ibid., pp. 297, 312.
47 Ibid., p. 345.

after Vitoria's lectures *De indiis*, Cano delivered his famed *relectio, De dominio indiorum*.[48] Cano's critique on theological, ethical, and juridical grounds went even farther in some respects, and was stated more simply and directly (one is tempted to say, even more humanely, in the sense of Ciceronian *humanitas*), than Vitoria's had been. Cano's analysis also seems at times to evince a more astute political sense, together with an ability to face facts and analogies (moral or historical) as they appear, and to resist the temptation to gild or gloss over them.

Cano employs Augustine's authority and refers to *The City of God* in several significant places in his *relectio*. As Vitoria had done before him, Cano notes with due diligence the endorsement Augustine seems to offer Roman imperial expansion in book five, and underscores the weight of Augustine's authority. Cano, however, proceeds at once to contradict the position Augustine is supposed to hold, and in more sweeping terms than Vitoria had employed. Vitoria, recall, denied that God had granted Rome a true divine right to empire, but allowed that God permitted them to rule on account of a claim of some other right, such as the right of justified war.[49] Cano, by contrast, baldly denied Rome's claims in human justice, be it by *ius naturale, civile,* or *gentium*, to most of its territorial encroachments. Without attempting to reread Augustine's fifth book to challenge the settled opinion of its sense, Cano expresses its real sense admirably in his own argument. '[We] do not deny that some provinces were captured justly, but many [including Spain] were invaded on account of avarice or ambition.'[50] As for claims that the Romans sought to help conquered peoples benefit from a better political system (*vera politeia*), at least in the case of Judea that claim fails, according to Cano: the divinely established regime outlined in the Mosaic Law outshone Rome's in its justice and goodness. Moreover, unless other peoples requested of their own accord that Rome rule them, even if Rome were to have superior laws and virtues, they would have no just claim to seize territories and rule their peoples.

Augustine and his *City of God* enter explicitly into Cano's discourse at two additional moments, both highly significant. The first is Cano's theoretical argument against the possibility and desirability of world government. With the Roman emperors' and the Holy Roman Emperor's claims to be 'Lord of the World' (*dominus mundi*) in the backdrop, Cano calls up book four of *De civitate dei* to suggest that, in principle, small or moderate-sized political communities are preferable to vast empires, which tend to be bloated by greed and are too far stretched to be effectively or fairly governed, or to constitute real *res publicae*. This point Augustine stresses near the outset and again at the centre of this book: great breadth of empire *may* at times be a necessity inspired by just defence, but even if this were so, it would be no cause to rejoice.[51] Augustine chides the Romans for idolizing the

[48] Cano's *De dominio indiorum* is reprinted in the original Latin, together with a Spanish translation, in Luciano Pereña, *Misión de España en America, 1540–1560* (Madrid: Consejo Superior de Investigaciones Científicas, 1956), pp. 90–147.

[49] See Vitoria, *Political Writings*, p. 254.

[50] Cano, *De dominio indiorum*, in Pereña, *Misión*, p. 110; my translation.

[51] See Augustine, *City of God*, 4.3, pp. 146–7, and 4.15, pp. 161–2.

glory of wide *imperium* to the point that they should have introduced these de facto Roman divinities into their Pantheon: 'Foreign Iniquity' and 'Empire'.[52]

In this regard, Cano captures Augustine's ethos well, though he does not quote directly from *De civitate dei*. Another Augustinian echo resounds in Cano's pithy reference to Alexander the Great. Early in book four of *The City of God*, just after the plea for political moderation in terms of size and ambition, Augustine tells his famous joke about the pirate and Alexander. Chapter four, merely a paragraph long, makes its point clearly in its opening line: 'Justice removed, what are kingdoms but great bands of robbers?' Augustine's witty story follows by way of illustration: A pirate is apprehended and brought to receive justice from Alexander himself. 'When the king asked what he meant by infesting the sea, the pirate defiantly replied, "The same as you do when you infest the whole world; but because I do it with a little boat I am called a robber, and because you do it with a great fleet, you are an emperor." '[53] As Augustine's pirate convicts Alexander the emperor, so Cano's Alexander convicts the Spanish *conquista*. Responding to allegations that the right under *ius gentium* to unimpeded peaceable travel and hospitality was violated by the Indians vis-à-vis the Spaniards, Cano laconically retorts: '[M]ost of all, the Spanish went there not as travellers, but as invaders, unless one should call Alexander a traveller (*peregrinus*).'[54]

In Cano's *De dominio indiorum* there are further signs of familiarity with Augustine's *De civitate dei*, especially in Cano's strong criticism of emperors' (ancient pagan and modern Christian) usurpation of the title 'Lord of the World'. Cano comments that this title, which apparently originated in Antoninus Pius's application of it to himself in the *Lex Rhodia*, reflects royal arrogance and/or others' flattery of the monarch.[55] Cano's message here echoes Augustine's caution in *The City of God* that 'many terms belonging to divine worship are, indeed, wrongly used in showing honour to human beings, whether out of an excessive humility or because of the pestilential practice of flattery'.[56] 'Lord of the World' would certainly fit this description! Perhaps most important and refreshing of all, however, is Cano's citation of Augustine to support his claim that slavery is not in accord with human nature and its natural right, for human beings are by nature free and not to be used by others primarily for their benefit.[57] Cano's ethical-legal assessment goes even farther, to clarify that slavery was introduced by human custom, not as something added to natural law by *ius civile* and *ius gentium*, though distinct from it, but precisely 'against natural right' (*contra ius naturalem*), the right or justice that by nature is owed to another member of the human race.[58] In these respects at least, most relevant to debates over the normative justification and regulation of

[52] Ibid., 4.3, p. 162. [53] Ibid., 4.4, pp. 147–8.

[54] Cano, *De dominio indiorum*, in Pereña, *Misión*, p.142, my translation; cf. Lupher, *Romans in a New World*, p. 87.

[55] See Cano, *De dominio indiorum*, in Pereña, *Misión*, p. 118, and Lupher, *Romans in a New World*, p. 92.

[56] Augustine, *City of God*, 10.4, p. 396. [57] See Ibid., 19.15, p. 943.

[58] Cano, *De dominio indiorum*, in Pereña, *Misión*, p. 102.

empire, Cano evinces an even deeper affinity to Augustine and a greater familiarity with *The City of God* than had his great mentor, Vitoria.

Domingo de Soto

The contribution of Domingo de Soto (1494–1560) to the moral and jurisprudential critique of Rome's ancient *imperium* and Spain's modern one was mammoth, as was Soto's role in continuing Vitoria's and especially Cano's reappropriation and reintroduction of the real argument of *De civitate dei* into this critical debate.

Soto was a pupil and junior colleague of Vitoria, yet he preceded his teacher in taking up the burning question of the justice of the *conquista*. Soto delivered his *Relectio de dominio* in 1535, four years prior to Vitoria's *De indiis* and a full eleven years before Cano's *De dominio indiorum*. Soto's *relectio* remains remarkable for its bold, clear denial of *any right* (*ius*) that its author can think of that could justify the Spanish invasion, conquest, and retention of rule in the Americas.[59] He rejects arguments from divine right, as well as from natural and human right: Christ commissioned his disciples to preach to the whole world, but 'not as lions but as sheep … not only without arms, but without bag, without bread, without money'.[60]

Augustine's *City of God* appears in Soto's early narrative as a hurdle to be cleared rather than a buttress of support for its claims. It was the usual text that had to be accounted for, but towards which Soto could do no more than nod and then reject by virtue of the independent argument he developed. Soto put forth his case with his trademark combination of modesty and daring:

> I do not dare to make any assertion contradicting the opinion of Augustine. … But nevertheless I do not know what right (*ius*) the Romans had to the lands they conquered. From their own historians we learn that their right was in force of arms (*ius erat in armis*), and they subjugated many unwilling nations … and one can't find where God gave them such a right.[61]

As Augustine also had done, following Cicero and Plato's Socrates before him, Soto rejected the Thrasymachean thesis that justice is the advantage of whoever has the greatest power.[62]

Soto would revisit the general question of *ius* vis-à-vis *imperium* almost two decades later in his most famous work, *De iustitia et iure* (*On Justice and Right*). By this time, he had returned to read with care Augustine's *City of God*, at least its fifth book, which was regularly trotted out as authoritative evidence proving the justice of Rome's imperial dominion. Soto's interpretation of *De civitate dei* book five, chapters twelve and fifteen seems to me unimpeachably correct when these chapters are read carefully and in their context within the work as a whole. His explication shows that the argument offered by Cano, in this case as a corrective

[59] See Domingo de Soto, *Relectio de dominio*, quoted in Lupher, *Romans in a New World*, p. 67: 'By what right, then, do we retain the overseas empire that has just been discovered. The fact is, *I* don't know (*Re vera ego nescio*).'

[60] Ibid., p. 67. [61] Ibid., p. 65. [62] See Augustine, *City of God*, 19.21, p. 950.

to Augustine's supposed assertion, is actually Augustine's own. Roman civic virtue was for the sake of Roman glory, 'and to extend their name far and wide'.[63] Augustine explicitly argues that even otherwise-noble deeds done for the goal of human glory are thereby vitiated. God does not reward vices and so can only be understood to have granted Rome its empire in the sense of *permitting* it for a time.[64] When added to Soto's earlier analysis in his *Relectio de dominio* of the testimony of Roman historians regarding Rome's bellicose annexation of unwilling peoples, an analysis that I have argued is already apparent in Augustine's *De civitate dei*, any claim Rome had over the majority of its territory appears not to have stemmed from justice.

Thanks to Soto's decision—one is tempted to say, *finally*—to reread with sufficient care Augustine's *City of God*, he and his allies could dispatch perhaps the most authoritative 'evidence' supporting the extension of European powers' *imperium* overseas that Sepúlveda and those taking his side could muster.[65] Moreover, with Soto's rereading, combined with Cano's and in the spirit of Vitoria's critical enquiry, roadblocks to a deeper understanding of Augustine's legal and political thought in *De civitate dei* were cleared for future generations of scholars.

Law amongst Nations in *The City of God*: A Brief *Relectio* with Special Attention to Religion

Near the close of his *City of God*, Augustine follows Cicero in describing the 'divinization' of Rome's founder Romulus and the spread of his cult among the peoples of the empire. '[Rome] increased and obtained a great empire; and from her position of power, as from a high place, she spread this belief among the other nations over which she held sway.... [F]ear ... compelled certain of the cities subject to Roman law (*aliquas civitates positas sub iure romano*) to worship Romulus as a god.'[66] From this passage, we grasp one of the two commonly recognized forms of laws among nations that Augustine presents to his readers in *De civitate dei: ius romanum* and *lex romana*—the law of the Roman Empire as applied to citizens, denizens, visitors, and peoples.[67] Readers also grasp from the passage just quoted the interrelation of politics, law, and religion in Rome's ancient imperialism. In some of its laws, Augustine's analysis suggests, Rome was at least as just as neighbouring polities not subject to its yoke; at times Rome approached justice more nearly; and at other times it fell terribly short of justice's real demands. So Augustine can commend Rome for not being cowed by fear of Saturn to sanction the sacrifice of children to him in its civil religion, as Carthage and other cities had done.[68] He can comment that overall, aside from the horrible suffering of Rome's wars of conquest and the

[63] Soto, *De iustitia et jure* (1967), p. 304. [64] See ibid., p. 304.
[65] For more on Soto, see Lupher, *Romans in a New World*, pp. 61–8, 93–8.
[66] Augustine, *City of God*, 22.6, pp. 1116–17. [67] See also ibid., 5.15, p. 216.
[68] ibid., 7.19, 26, pp. 290–1, 300.

denial of citizen rights to the conquered until relatively late in Rome's history, the peoples of most subjected cities and nations didn't fare worse under Roman laws than they had under their previous legislation.[69] And he can lament of Rome's ancient Voconian Law, which had forbidden any woman to inherit property, 'I do not know of any law that could be said or thought to be more unjust.'[70]

In addition to the positive and customary laws of the Rome's empire (and presumably, parallel laws of other imperial and hegemonic powers around the globe and throughout history), Augustine notes another, perhaps more genuinely international, set of norms comprised of the right or law of peace (*ius pacis*) and the right or law of war (*ius belli*). As Augustine recounts Rome's history, early in *De civitate dei*, these complementary laws seem to predate Rome's expansion and incorporation of other peoples into its empire; or, more precisely, not to be circumscribed by time in their applicability across city and national boundaries. Book two, chapter seventeen and book three, chapter thirteen together constitute a critical locus for interpreting Augustine's understanding and uses of *ius pacis* and *ius belli*.[71] The context for both discussions is the early Roman abduction, under Romulus himself, of the neighbouring Sabine women. Augustine insists that no 'right of peace' countenanced Rome's waging of war against the 'justly angered' Sabine fathers, attempting with right to recover their children; nor the annexation of the Sabines' territory, especially without allowing them to share in rule in any lasting way. Where the law of peace sanctioned no just recourse to force, no right of war may justly apply. Augustine comments that Rome implicitly acknowledged its own violation of the inter- or supra-nationally recognized norms of *ius pacis* as the Romans developed their own civil legal code: 'The Romans found it quite easy to commit the error of consecrating Romulus as a god after that iniquity; but they still did not permit any law or custom to sanction the emulation of his deeds as an abductor of women.'[72]

Although Augustine thus comments on *ius pacis* and *ius belli*, he does not refer in *The City of God* to their shared designation *ius gentium*, the 'right' or 'law of nations'. As we have noted, it is striking that Augustine nowhere in his extant writings, including *De civitate dei*, employs the Roman legal and Ciceronian political-philosophic term. Indeed, he refers to its components, *ius pacis* and *ius belli*, only a handful of times in the entire *City of God*.[73] *Ius gentium* of course represents a notoriously difficult, contested concept, in its classical as well as medieval and modern forms. Its Roman original refers to the laws of the empire pertaining to non-citizen residents and foreigners; yet Cicero and the celebrated jurists Gaius and Ulpian after him give to the term meanings and status closer to properly *international* law, in the sense that its legitimacy depended not only on Roman authority, but also and even more so on a consensus among all or most nations regarding

[69] Ibid., 5.17, p. 217. [70] Ibid., 3.21, p. 130. [71] Ibid., pp. 70–1, 107–9.
[72] Ibid., p. 70.
[73] These finding are based on word searches conducted in two online Latin-language databases containing Augustine's *opera omnia*: the Brepols Library of Latin Texts, Series A, and the Corpus Augustiniarum Gissense.

these norms; and closer also to natural right or law (*ius naturale*) itself.[74] In their articles on Cicero's *ius gentium* and its import for political and legal theory today, Thomas L. Pangle and Gary Remer concur in locating Cicero's 'law of nations' at a juncture between the particular legal codes of political societies, and the natural law applicable to and among all members of the human race, personally and in polities.[75] Given the central place of Cicero's political theory in Augustine's *De civitate dei*—consider for instance Augustine's recapitulations and critical dialogues with Cicero on providence, freedom, and citizenship, on the features of a true republic (*res publica*), and on critical concepts such as *humanitas*, honour, compassion, and the love of glory[76]—it seems unlikely that Augustine inadvertently overlooked *ius gentium* as Cicero conceived it, when it might have contributed to Augustine's own analysis of the Romans in relation to other cities and peoples.

A clue to Augustine's reasoning for passing over *ius gentium* as a central legal and moral concept may be found with the first mention of *ius belli* in *The City of God*. In book one, Augustine calls his readers' attention to the moderation of bellicose mores that Christianity appeared to have effected in the Visigoth army when it invaded Rome. While killing, plunder, and outrage were permitted the victors under the *ius belli*, Augustine notes that the sack was less brutal than it might have been, and especially that thousands of Romans received mercy because most (Arian Christian) Goths respected the right of asylum in churches.[77] And yet, Augustine notes in more than one place that this is not enough: one could do or take no more than what was permitted under *ius belli*, and still cause the disfigurement and death of one's soul, to say nothing of unjust harm to others. The principles of *ius belli* as Augustine presents it seem to represent consensus, a positive agreement among peoples regarding restraints by which they would be bound. These were in some aspects reflective of natural moral norms, and so of true *humanitas* (a Ciceronian concept Augustine embraces even while altering): ambassadors are to be respected, for instance, and treaties when not unjust are to be honoured. Yet, in other respects, *ius belli* remained unjust and inhuman: permitting the killing of non-combatants, enslaving of defeated peoples, and committing of sexual assault. Armies of nations waging war would perhaps agree to risk suffering such harm in order to be allowed to commit it when they emerged victorious, as if it were a good to do so! Committing any one of these actions, Augustine indicates throughout

74 See Peter Haggenmacher, *Grotius et la doctrine de la guerre juste* (Paris: Presses Universitaires de France, 1983), on 'Les sources romaines: la double origine du '*ius gentium*'', pp. 313–20. See also Peter Stein, *Roman Law in European History* (Cambridge and New York: Cambridge University Press, 1999), pp. 12–13; and Gary Remer, 'Ciceronian *Ius Gentium* and World Legislation', *International Organizations Law Review* 8 (2011): p. 227, doi:10.1163/157237411X601561. On natural right in *The City of God*, see Mary M. Keys, 'Augustinian Humility as Natural Right', in *Political Philosophy and Natural Right: Essays in Honor of Catherine Zuckert and Michael Zuckert*, edited by Ann Ward and Lee Ward (Notre Dame: University of Notre Dame Press, 2013), pp. 97–113.

75 Thomas L. Pangle, 'Socratic Cosmopolitanism: Cicero's Critique and Transformation of the Stoic Ideal', *Canadian Journal of Political Science* 31, no. 2 (1998): pp. 235–62, doi:10.1017/S0008423900019788; Remer, 'Ciceronian *Ius Gentium* and World Legislation'.

76 See Augustine, *City of God*, inter alia 2.20–21; 5.8–11; 5.13–14; 9.4–5; and 19.21.

77 See ibid., 1.1 ff., in particular 1.7.

De civitate dei, would suffice to kill one's deepest self, one's soul; the perpetrators of sanctioned violence thus harmed themselves even more deeply than their victims, who suffered unspeakably.

Moreover, given the realities of ancient *imperium* at war and in peace, the strongest polity and its rulers regularly had the most say in how these norms among nations were interpreted and applied: '[M]en ... wish to make even those against whom they wage war their own if they can, and to subdue them by imposing upon them *the laws of their own peace*' (*leges suae pacis imponere*).[78] This administration of *ius* was often, evidently and emphatically, not *iustum*, not just.[79] *Ius gentium* as understood by most Romans, perhaps, was thus never completely severed from Roman hegemony.[80] For nations under Rome, Augustine notes, the *ius romanum*, as adjudicated by its authorized interpreters, is the 'internationally applicable norm' with the last word in the empire's courts of law. With Augustine's trademark combination of ethical-normative and empirical-realist analysis in place, one might reasonably conclude that Augustine eschews the use of the term *ius gentium*, to indicate its ambiguity vis-à-vis religion, empire, and *humanitas*, as well as the mistake it would be to allow *ius gentium* to be the final word in any court of conscience.[81] Augustine also implies, however, that it would be just as foolish for nations or empires entirely to forget its salutary if far too limited restraints, in the form of internationally recognized rules governing relations among peoples in war and peace.

Conclusion

As Pagden and Lawrence have noted, Francisco Vitoria's 'account of *ius gentium* ... is not entirely consistent'.[82] This certainly seems the case regarding the relations of *ius gentium* to natural right or law (*ius naturale*) and to religion. On the one hand, Vitoria explains the connection of *ius gentium*, the quasi-positive law of 'the whole world, which is in a sense a commonwealth',[83] with natural law as follows: it 'either is or derives from the natural law'.[84] This close connection gives *ius gentium* great moral weight according to Vitoria: 'there are certainly many things which are clearly to be settled on the basis of the law of nations (*ius gentium*), whose derivation from natural law is manifestly sufficient to enable it to enforce binding

[78] Ibid., 19.12, pp. 934–5. [79] See again ibid., 19.21, p. 950.

[80] On this point, see also Alasdair MacIntyre, *Whose Justice? Which Rationality?* (Notre Dame: University of Notre Dame Press, 1988), p. 149.

[81] Ernest L. Fortin, in an essay I discovered only after completing this chapter, also notes Augustine's omission of *ius gentium*, and accounts for the omission in a way similar to what I have argued above: see Fortin, 'Augustine and the Problem of Modernity', in *Classical Christianity and the Political Order*, vol. 2 of *Collected Essays* (Lanham, Md.: Rowman and Littlefield, 1996), p. 148, and Michael P. Bruno's discussion in *Political Augustinianism: Modern Interpretations of Augustine's Political Thought* (Minneapolis: Fortress Press, 2014), pp. 114–16.

[82] Pagden and Lawrance, 'Introduction' to Vitoria, *Political Writings*, p. xvi.

[83] Vitoria, *Political Writings*, p. 40; cf. pp. 280–1. [84] Ibid., p. 278.

rights'.[85] Yet Vitoria also speaks in a general way of precepts of *ius gentium* that are '*not derived* from natural law'.[86] He further implies here that some of these latter precepts may not be 'for the common good of all men'.[87] So far as I have found, Vitoria offers no examples of these precepts put forth by *ius gentium*, yet outside of or against nature's law, which by definition seeks humanity's common good. So it is perplexing, to cite one instance, that Vitoria seems not to make any moral or legal distinction between the evidence and binding character of *ius gentium* precepts 'ambassadors should everywhere be inviolable,' and 'prisoners of war should be enslaved'.[88] Instead he appears to conclude that, given the 'consent of the greater part of the world' or 'the majority of men', 'all these things certainly have the force of law, even if a minority disagree'.[89]

With regard to religion and *ius gentium*, Vitoria maintains that, like *ius naturale, ius gentium* applies equally to Christians and to those who profess other religions, including 'pagan' ones. The Indians in the Americas were true owners of their lands according to *ius gentium*, argues Vitoria, and so these should no more pass to the Spaniards on account of *res nullius* than 'if they [the Indians] had discovered us'.[90] '[I]f the barbarians allowed the Spaniards to carry on their business [of commerce] in peace among them, the Spaniards could make out no more just a case for seizing their goods than they could for seizing those of other Christians.'[91] Further, Vitoria argues that persistent unbelief in Christianity, even after credible (peaceful, non-profiteering) evangelization, provides Christian nations with no legal or moral ground whatsoever for occupying the lands of others, taking their property, or usurping their civic authority.[92]

Still, on occasion Vitoria does admit the possibility of religious distinction in the application of *ius gentium*, favouring fellow Christians over others. Vitoria argues, for instance, that plundering the property of innocent civilians in war can at times be legitimate, and that this property extends also to their personal liberty:

> ... *one may lawfully enslave the innocent under just the same conditions as one may plunder them.* Freedom and slavery are counted as goods of fortune ... Hence, since our war against the [Saracens] is ... permanent because they can never sufficiently pay for the injuries and losses inflicted, it is not to be doubted that we may lawfully enslave the women and children of the Saracens.[93]

But what if the 'permanent' war were against another Christian empire or polity? Could victors rightfully enslave innocent civilians as war reparations in this sort of case? Here Vitoria appeals to *ius gentium*, but in a manner suggesting that it is really *ius gentium Christianarum*, the law of *Christian* nations. He observes, '[S]ince it seems to be accepted in the law of nations that Christians cannot enslave one another, [even in a grave and protracted just war] it is not lawful to enslave fellow-Christians.'[94]

[85] Ibid., p. 280–1; cf. p. 40. [86] Ibid., p, 281; emphasis added. [87] Ibid., p. 281.
[88] Ibid., p. 281. [89] Ibid., p. 281. [90] Ibid. p. 265. [91] Ibid., p. 284.
[92] Ibid., p. 271–2. [93] Ibid., p. 318.
[94] Ibid., p. 318; cf. p. 323, with regard to the plundering, sacking, and destruction of Christian cities.

Had Vitoria returned to read with care and reflect deeply on Augustine's *De civitate dei*, as his pupil Domingo de Soto would later do and as Melchior Cano seemed to a great extent also to have done, he might have proceeded with greater caution and a larger dose of scepticism regarding *ius gentium* as it was understood and applied also in his own 'modern' Christian context, and so have refrained from admitting religious limits to its humanizing effect on this critical issue of 'property' in persons. Augustine's *City of God*, as we have seen, stresses as a virtually universal descriptive phenomenon the impact of empire and its religion on mores and law amongst nations. That law is interpreted and applied by public authority in power, indicates that to a great extent this 'realist' principle holds: *cuius regio et religio, eius ius gentium*. Hence the elements of theoretical and empirical scepticism in the writings of Cano and Soto, even more strongly than in their teacher Vitoria's works, and their contemporary analogue in Koskenniemi's assessment of Salamanca's legal legacy.

Augustine simultaneously highlights the strengthening of just restraint and the infusion of mercy that 'true religion' (*vera religio*) ought to effect, and at least on occasion does effect in politics and international affairs.[95] Insofar as Vitoria and the other Salamanca theologian-jurists, in their interpretation and application of *ius gentium*, upheld these and other universal ethical principles, they embodied the moral-legal idealism that Scott and other contemporary scholars have noted and praised in their project. This salutary effect could not be taken as given with the spread of Christianity, however. Augustine himself implies as much, as he stresses repeatedly that no human being in this age is perfectly virtuous, and that his famous 'two cities' travel intermingled with one another through this present age.[96] These Augustinian considerations recall Aleksandr Solzhenitsyn's famous caution, that the dividing line between good and evil is not drawn across a map between nations, classes, parties, or even individuals. It travels, rather, through each nation, ancient or modern, and through each human heart.[97]

Bibliography

Anghie, Antony. *Imperialism, Sovereignty and the Making of International Law* (Cambridge: Cambridge University Press, 2005).

[95] On this topic, see Robert Dodaro's *Christ and the Just Society in the Thought of Augustine* (Cambridge and New York: Cambridge University Press, 2004). See also Michael Loriaux 'The Realists and Saint Augustine: Skepticism, Psychology, and Moral Action in International Relations Thought', *International Studies Quarterly* 36 (1992): pp. 401–20, http://www.jstor.org/stable/2600732, favourably comparing Augustine's realism and scepticism with those prominent in contemporary international relations theory.

[96] See Augustine, *City of God*, inter alia 5.14, p. 214, and 10.32, p. 448.

[97] See Daniel J. Mahoney, *Aleksandr Solzhenitsyn: The Ascent from Ideology* (Lanham, Md.: Rowman and Littlefield, 2001), pp. 105–6, for a probing discussion. See also Aleksandr Solzhenitsyn, 'Repentance and Self-Limitation in the Life of Nations', and its opening with a quotation from *City of God*, 4.4, in *The Solzhenitsyn Reader: New and Essential Writings, 1947–2005*, edited by Edward E. Ericson, Jr. and Daniel J. Mahoney (Wilmington, Del.: ISI Books, 2006), pp. 527–55.

Augustine. *De civitate Dei*. Accessed online at http://www.thelatinlibrary.com/august.html.

Augustine. *The City of God against the Pagans*, translated and edited by R. W. Dyson (Cambridge: Cambridge University Press, 1998).

Beaujouan, Guy. *Manuscrits scientifiques médiévaux de l'Université de Salamanque et de ses 'Colegios Mayores'* (Bordeaux: Féret & Fils, 1962).

Bouwsma, William. 'The Two Faces of Humanism: Stoicism and Augustinianism in Renaissance Thought'. In *Itinerarium Italicum: The Profile of the Italian Renaissance in the Mirror of Its European Transformation*, edited by Heiko A. Oberman and Thomas A. Brady, Jr. (Leiden: E. J. Brill, 1975), pp. 3–60.

Brading, D. A. 'The Two Cities: St. Augustine and the Spanish Conquest of America'. *Revista Portuguesa de Filosofia*, 44, no. 1 (January–March 1988): pp. 99–126. http://www.jstor.org/stable/40338154.

Brett, Annabel S. *Liberty, Right and Nature: Individual Rights in Later Scholastic Thought* (Cambridge: Cambridge University Press, 1997).

Brookes, Edgar H. *The City of God and the Politics of Crisis* (London: Oxford University Press, 1960).

Bruno, Michael J. S. *Political Augustinianism: Modern Interpretations of Augustine's Political Thought* (Minneapolis: Fortress Press, 2014).

Byers, Sarah. 'Augustine and the Philosophers'. In *A Companion to Augustine*, edited by Mark Vessey (Malden, Mass. and Oxford: Wiley-Blackwell, 2012), pp. 175–87.

Cavadini, John. 'The Darkest Enigma: Reconsidering the Self in Augustine's Thought'. *Augustinian Studies* 38, no. 1 (Spring 2007): pp. 119–32. doi:10.5840/augstudies20073817.

Cavadini, John. 'Ideology and Solidarity in Augustine's *City of God*'. In *Augustine's City of God: A Critical Guide*, edited by James Wetzel (Cambridge and New York: Cambridge University Press, 2012), pp. 93–110.

Cavallar, Georg. *The Rights of Strangers: Theories of International Hospitality, the Global Community, and Political Justice since Vitoria* (Aldershot and Burlington: Ashgate, 2002).

Chroust, Anton-Hermann. 'The Fundamental Ideas in St. Augustine's Philosophy of Law'. *American Journal of Jurisprudence* 18 (1973): pp. 57–79. http://scholarship.law.nd.edu/ajj/vol18/iss1/4.

Curtis, Cathy. 'Advising Monarchs and Their Counselors: Juan Luis Vives on the Emotions, Civil Life, and International Relations'. *Parergon* 28, no. 2 (July 2011): pp. 29–53. doi:0.1353/pgn.2011.0115.

Dodaro, Robert. *Christ and the Just Society in the Thought of Augustine* (Cambridge and New York: Cambridge University Press, 2004).

Dougherty, Richard J. 'Law'. *The Oxford Guide to the Historical Reception of Augustine*, edited by Karla Pollmann and Willemien Otten, with Hildegund Müller et al. Vol. 3 (Oxford: Oxford University Press, 2013), pp. 1281–3.

Dougherty, Richard J. 'St. Augustine on Law—Natural, Human, and Divine' (Paper presented at Northeastern Political Science Association annual meeting. Boston, Massachusetts, 13–15 November 2008). Accessed online http://citation.allacademic.com/meta/p276721_index.html.

Faulhaber, Charles B. 'Libraries'. In *Medieval Iberia: An Encyclopedia*, edited by E. Michael Gerli and Samuel G. Armistead (New York: Routledge, 2003), pp. 484–6.

Fernández Santamaría, José A. *Juan Luis Vives: Escepticismo y Prudencia en el Renacimiento* (Salamanca: Ediciones Universidad de Salamanca, 1990).

Fernández Santamaría, José A. *The State, War, and Peace: Spanish Political Thought in the Renaissance, 1516–1559* (Cambridge: Cambridge University Press, 1977).

Fortin, Ernest L. *Classical Christianity and the Political Order: Reflections on the Theologico-Political Problem*, edited by J. Brian Benestad. Vol. 2 of *Ernest Fortin: Collected Essays* (Lanham, Md.: Rowman and Littlefield, 1996).

Gladwin, John. Review of *Human Rights and the Image of God* (Roger Ruston, SCM Press, 2004). *Ecclesiastical Law Journal* 8, no. 39 (July 2006): pp. 490–1. doi:10.1017/S0956618X00006827.

Haggenmacher, Peter. *Grotius et la doctrine de la guerre juste* (Paris: Presses Universitaires de France, 1983).

Keys, Mary M. 'Augustinian Humility as Natural Right'. In *Political Philosophy and Natural Right: Essays in Honor of Catherine Zuckert and Michael Zuckert*, edited by Ann Ward and Lee Ward (Notre Dame: University of Notre Dame Press, 2013), pp. 97–113.

Koskenniemi, Martti. 'Empire and International Law: The Real Spanish Contribution'. *University of Toronto Law Journal* 63 (2011): pp. 1–36. http://www.jstor.org/stable/23018686.

Loriaux, Michael. 'The Realists and Saint Augustine: Skepticism, Psychology, and Moral Action in International Relations Thought'. *International Studies Quarterly* 36 (1992): pp. 401–20. http://www.jstor.org/stable/2600732.

Lupher, David A. *Romans in a New World: Classical Models in Sixteenth-Century Spanish America* (Ann Arbor: University of Michigan Press, 2003).

MacIntyre, Alasdair. *Whose Justice? Which Rationality?* (Notre Dame: University of Notre Dame Press, 1988).

Mahoney, Daniel J. *Aleksandr Solzhenitsyn: The Ascent from Ideology* (Lanham, Md.: Rowman and Littlefield, 2001).

Noreña, Carlos G. *Juan Luis Vives* (The Hague: Martinus Nijhoff, 1970).

Pagden, Anthony. 'The School of Salamanca.' In *The Oxford Handbook of the History of Political Philosophy*, edited by George Klosko (Oxford: Oxford University Press, 2011), pp. 246–57.

Pangle, Thomas L. 'Socratic Cosmopolitanism: Cicero's Critique and Transformation of the Stoic Ideal'. *Canadian Journal of Political Science* 31, no. 2 (1998): pp. 235–62. doi:10.1017/S0008423900019788.

Pereña, Luciano. *Misión de España en America, 1540–1560* (Madrid: Consejo Superior de Investigaciones Científicas, 1956).

Pereña, Luciano. *La idea de justicia en la conquista de América* (Madrid: Editorial MAPFRE, 1992).

Ramos Perez, Demetrio, ed. *La ética en la conquista de America* (Madrid: Consejo Superior de Investigaciones Científicas, 1984).

Remer, Gary. 'Ciceronian *Ius Gentium* and World Legislation'. *International Organizations Law Review* 8 (2011): pp. 225–39. doi:10.1163/157237411X601561.

Richardson, John. 'The Meaning of imperium in the Last Century BC and the First AD'. In *The Roman Foundations of the Law of Nations: Alberico Gentili and the Justice of Empire*, edited by Benedict Kingsbury and Benjamin Straumann. (Oxford: Oxford University Press, 2010), pp. 21–9.

Saak, E. L. *Creating Augustine: Interpreting Augustine and Augustinianism in the Later Middle Ages* (Oxford: Oxford University Press, 2012).

Sánchez, Dolores. *El deber de consejo en el estado moderno: Las juntas 'ad hoc' en España (1471–1665)* (Madrid: Ediciones Polifemo, 1993).

Scott, James Brown. *The Spanish Origin of International Law: Francisco de Vitoria and his Law of Nations* (Oxford: Clarendon Press, 1934).

Sloan, Michael C. '*De civitate Dei*'. In *The Oxford Guide to the Historical Reception of Augustine*, edited by Karla Pollmann and Willemien Otten, with Hildegund Müller et al. Vol. 1 (Oxford: Oxford University Press, 2013), pp. 255–61.

Solzhenitsyn, Aleksandr. *The Solzhenitsyn Reader: New and Essential Writings, 1947–2005*, edited by Edward E. Ericson, Jr. and Daniel J. Mahoney (Wilmington, Del.: ISI Books, 2006).

de Soto, Domingo. *De iustitia et iure* (Salamanca [1556]; Madrid: Instituto de Estudios Políticos, 1967).

Stamatov, Peter. *The Origins of Global Humanitarianism: Religion, Empires, and Advocacy* (New York and Cambridge: Cambridge University Press, 2013).

Stein, Peter. *Roman Law in European History* (Cambridge and New York: Cambridge University Press, 1999).

Stoclet, Alain J. 'Le *De civitate Dei* de saint Augustin: Sa diffusion avant 900 d'après les caractères externs des manuscrits antérieurs à cette date et les catalogues contemporains', *Recherches Augustiniennes* 19 (1984): pp. 185–202.

Tuck, Richard. *The Rights of War and Peace: Political Thought and International Order from Grotius to Kant* (Oxford: Oxford University Press, 1999).

Visser, Arnoud S. Q. *Reading Augustine in the Reformation: The Flexibility of Intellectual Authority in Europe, 1500–1620* (Oxford: Oxford University Press, 2011).

de Vitoria, Francisco. *Vitoria: Political Writings*, edited by Anthony Pagden and Jeremy Lawrance (Cambridge: Cambridge University Press, 1991 [1528–1539]).

Vives, Juan Luis. *Obras Completas*. Trans. Lorenzo Riber (Madrid: Aguilar, 1947–48).

Wegemer, Gerard B. *Young Thomas More and the Arts of Liberty* (Cambridge: Cambridge University Press, 2011).

Wegemer, Gerard B. *Thomas More on Statesmanship* (Washington, D.C.: The Catholic University of America Press, 1996).

4

Grotius' *Imago Dei* Anthropology

Grounding *Ius Naturae et Gentium*

Janne E. Nijman[1]

And God said, Let us make man in our image, after our likeness …
So God created man in his own image, in the image of God created he him;
male and female created he them.
And God blessed them, and God said unto them, Be fruitful, and multiply,
and replenish the earth, and subdue it:
and have dominion over the fish of the sea, and over the fowl of the air,
and over every living thing that moveth upon the earth.

Genesis I, 26–28[2]

Introduction

Etiamsi daremus… non esse Deum,[3] with these words Grotius is said to have broken the bond between God and the law of nations. Part of the standard account of the history of international legal thought is the idea that Grotius secularized natural law and therewith international law.[4] Such out of political necessity, as

[1] The author wishes to thank Harm-Jan van Dam and Marius van Leeuwen for their inspiring conversations and helpful suggestions. Thanks also to the participants to the Helsinki and Rome workshops for their comments and to the editors for their comments on an earlier version.

[2] King James Bible, 'Authorized Version', Cambridge Edition.

[3] *De Jure Belli ac Pacis, Prolegomena*, para. 11: 'What we have been saying would have a degree of validity even if we should concede that which cannot be conceded without the utmost wickedness, that *there is no God, or that the affairs of men are of no concern to Him.*' Hugo Grotius, *De Jure Belli ac Pacis Libri Tres* (1646 edition), *The Classics of International Law*, edited by James Scott, translated by Francis Kelsey (Oxford: Oxford Clarendon Press, 1925), p. 13. Hereinafter *DJBP*.

[4] Cf. e.g. Jules Basdevant, 'Hugo Grotius', in *Les Fondateurs du Droit International* (Paris: V. Giard & E. Brière, 1904), p. 233; Arthur Nussbaum, *A Concise History of the Law of Nations* (New York: Macmillan, 1947), p. 105; Joseph Kunz, 'Natural-Law Thinking in the Modern Science of International Law', *American Journal of International Law* 55 (1961): p. 951; Lassa Oppenheim, *International Law: A Treatise*, 8th edn, edited by Hersch Lauterpacht (London: Longman, 1955), p. 93; Hersch Lauterpacht, 'The Grotian Tradition in International Law', *British Yearbook of International Law* 23, no.1 (1946): p. 24; Peter Malanczuk, *Akehurst's Modern Introduction to International Law* 7th edn (New York: Routledge, 1997), pp. 15–16; Malcom Shaw, *International Law* (Cambridge: Cambridge University Press, 2008), p. 24.

only a secular international law would be able to end the religious wars waging at the time. Motivated by a pacific agenda, Grotius would have provided the law of nations with a foundation independent from religion and theology, given it a particularly 'modern' status, and put it on its course to 'autonomy' and/or 'self-sufficient normativity'.[5] Traditional historiographical claims of Hugo de Groot as the father of 'modern' international law and 'the great Emancipator'[6] or secularizer of international law have bred, however, a disregard for Grotius' theological writings in relation to his ideas on the law of nature and nations.[7] Grotius the scholar of moral, political, and legal philosophy is inseparable from Grotius the theologian.[8]

This chapter claims we should not stop at the standard account that Grotius secularized international law by grounding it on human nature, but that we rather need to dig deeper and examine the theological anthropology grounding Grotius' ideas on the law of nature and nations. With some attention for the influence of both (neo-)scepticism[9] and (neo-)stoicism[10] in analyses of Grotius' understanding of human nature and natural law, this chapter examines Grotius' ideas through the lens of the Christian theological notion of *imago Dei*—the idea that human beings are different from other animals in that they are created in 'the image and likeness of God'.

For Grotius and his contemporaries—whether scholastic or humanist scholars—the *imago Dei* doctrine provided the inevitable starting point for thinking about humanity and human nature.[11] That said, the *imago Dei* doctrine played a significant role in the background of many theological and moral philosophical controversies at the time of the Reformations. It was at the heart of debates on the moral freedom of the human will, predestination, and human participation in

[5] As mentioned in the original Research Statement.

[6] James Leger, *The 'Etiamsi Daremus' of Hugo Grotius; A Study in the Origins of International Law* (Rome: Pontificium Athenaeum Internationale, 1962), pp. 28–36, 35.

[7] Exceptions are Peter Haggenmacher, *Grotius et la doctrine de la Guerre Juste* (Paris: PUF, 1983); Oliver O'Donovan, 'The Justice of Assignment and Subjective Rights in Grotius' in *Bonds of Imperfection: Christian Politics, Past and Present,* edited by Olivier O'Donovan and Joan Lockwood O'Donovan (Grand Rapids, Mich.: W. B. Eerdmans, 2004); Christoph Stumpf, *The Grotian Theology of International Law: Hugo Grotius and the Moral Foundations of International Relations* (Berlin: Walter de Gruyter, 2006).

[8] While the standard account reserves too prominent a role for Grotius as the secularizer of international legal thought, I do not mean to argue that Grotius did not contribute to the process of European secularization at all. Cf. Mark Somos, *Secularisation and the Leiden Circle* (Leiden: Brill, 2011), pp. 5, 7–8, and 43. Even when one finds Somos' conclusions exaggerating (e.g. at 435, 384, 388, and 392), Grotius' historicizing approach to biblical texts undoubtedly contributed to Western secularization.

[9] E.g. Richard Tuck, *The Rights of War and Peace* (Oxford: Oxford University Press, 1999).

[10] E.g. Benjamin Straumann, 'Oikeiosis and Appetitus Societatis: Hugo Grotius' Ciceronian Argument for Natural Law and Just War', *Grotiana* 24/25 (2003–04): pp. 41–2; also, Hans Blom and Laurens Winkel, 'Grotius and the Stoa', Special issue of *Grotiana* 22/23 (2001–02) (Assen: Van Gorcum, 2004).

[11] E.g. Charles Trinkaus, *'In Our Image and Likeness': Humanity and Divinity in Italian Humanist Thought* (Chicago: University Press, 1970), pp. 1–2; David Cairns, *The Image of God in Man* (London: SCM Press, 1953).

salvation—issues at stake at the time. The second section relates the concept of the *imago Dei* briefly to these early seventeenth-century theological and political debates in the Dutch Republic. It moreover discusses the Arminian interpretation of the *imago Dei* along the lines of three dimensions generally set apart: ontological, teleological (the *telos* being to reach God, also through others in society), and functional (linked to the function of *dominium*).[12]

This chapter claims that the Arminian *imago Dei* anthropology is foundational to Grotius' theory of the law of nature and nations in (at least) three ways, along the lines of the three dimensions just mentioned (the third section). The three sub-sections in this section thus elaborate on the implications of *imago Dei* for the legal framework set out by Grotius. He saw God's image reflected in the natural human capacities of reason and free will, thanks to which humans are able to know natural law and justice, are able to reason, judge, and to make free choices on the basis of this knowledge. As such, they bear individual moral responsibility for their actions and the *imago Dei* underpins their natural legal personality (first sub-section). This is a—rather optimistic—conception of post-lapsarian human nature, in which the *imago Dei* has human beings live in a society and care for others (*appetitus societatis*). Grotius' conception of human nature was well-suited as a foundation for a theory of (universal) society and the law of nature and nations (second sub-section). Finally, from its creation in the image of God follows that humanity is called to represent God on earth and intrusted with the function of *dominium* (third subsection). The chapter concludes with a few remarks on how a post-sceptical reading of Grotius, through the lens of his *imago Dei* anthropology, is relevant for the future of international law thinking (fourth section).

Imago Dei at the Heart of the Calvinist-Arminian Theological and Political Disputes

Grotius' Arminianism in political context

Grotius developed his law of nature and nations in the early seventeenth century, the time of the Calvinist and Lutheran Reformations and the Catholic Counter-Reformation. The Dutch Republic revolted against Catholic Spain (*c.* 1560s–1648), consolidated itself gradually as a new and independent European state, with religious conflict however dividing society and penetrating government structures. Heated theological debates waged among Reformed Protestants on the course of the Dutch Reformed Church and the Dutch Reformation. The dispute between

[12] This distinction between ontological or substantive, teleological or relational, and functional dimensions or interpretations draws on examination of *imago Dei* conceptions in twentieth-century theological literature; see e.g. Richard Middleton, *The Liberating Image: The Imago Dei in Genesis I* (Grand Rapids: Brazos Press, 2005); Noreen L. Herzfeld, *In Our Image: Artificial Intelligence and the Human Spirit* (Minneapolis: Fortress Press, 2002); also, Cairns, *The Image of God in Man.*

the Calvinist and Arminian fractions became inextricably linked with Dutch politics.[13] Ultimately, it was as much a fight for the control of the Republic, which was ultimately won by the orthodox Calvinists, supported by Stadholder Maurits.

While Grotius tried to defer taking sides, he was unmistakably an Arminian,[14] both theologically and politically, standing in the Erasmian humanist tradition.[15] In those years of mounting tensions, Grotius wrote the *Meletius* (1611)[16] in which he aimed to 'transcen[d religious] controversy' and to (re-)unite the fighting Christians on a reduced or minimalist version of Christianity.[17] The doctrine of *imago Dei* plays a fundamental role as, what may be called, a conciliatory doctrine. Until his arrest in 1618, Grotius was among the key players of Dutch political and intellectual life.[18] He would remain faithful to the Erasmian-Arminian irenic agenda,[19] both in religious and political affairs, throughout his life. He aimed to define common ground, to stimulate toleration in case of religious diversity and disagreement and to foster fellowship as the general tissue of society, both domestic and international.[20]

[13] Jonathan Israel, *The Dutch Republic* (Oxford: Oxford University Press, 1995), p. 421 et seq. Also, Aza Goudriaan, 'The Synod of Dordt on Arminian Anthopology', in *Revisiting the Synod of Dordt (1618–1619)*, edited by Aza Goudriaan and Fred van Lieburg (Leiden/Boston: Brill, 2011), pp. 84 *et seq.*

[14] Grotius' relation with Arminian theologians was most intense and regular in his contacts with his life-long friend Uyttenbogaert, in whose house he lived while studying in Leiden. Grotius' friendship with Arminius was not intense in a personal way, but from the Eulogy he wrote we learn how much Grotius appreciated Arminius' theology, his message of toleration and the limits of human knowledge, so that peace could prevail over theological shrewdness. Henk Nellen, *Hugo de Groot: Een leven in strijd om de vrede 1583–1645* (Amsterdam: Balans, 2007), pp. 113–18.

[15] See e.g. for Grotius as Arminian theologian, the Introduction to Guillaume Posthumus Meyjes, ed., *Hugo Grotius. Meletius, sive de iis quae inter Christianos conveniunt Epistola.* Critical edition with translation, commentary and introduction (Leiden/New York: Brill, 1988); A.H. Haentjens, *Hugo de Groot als godsdienstig denker* (Amsterdam: Ploegsma, 1946), pp. 10–11; *Hugo Grotius, Theologian: Essays in Honour of G.H.M. Posthumus Meyjes*, edited by Henk J. M. Nellen and Edwin Rabbie (Leiden: Brill, 1994).

[16] Meyjes, ed., *Hugo Grotius. Meletius, sive de iis quae inter Christianos conveniunt Epistola.* Hereinafter: *Meletius.*

[17] *Meletius*, para. 1 and 6. Grotius aimed to do the same many years later in *De Veritate*. See Henk Nellen, 'Minimal Religion, Deism and Socinianism: On Grotius's Motives for Writing *De Veritate*', *Grotiana* 33 (2012): pp. 47–53.

[18] Israel, *The Dutch Republic*, p. 421 et seq. Nellen, *Hugo de Groot.*

[19] See e.g. Arminius on principles of religious liberty, 'On Reconciling Religious Dissensions among Christians (1606)', in *The works of James Arminius*, first and second vols translated by James Nichols, and third vol. by W. R. Bagnall (Auburn/Buffalo: Orton, 1853), vol 1, p. 343; the twenty-five Public Disputations are included in vol. 1 and the seventy-nine Private Disputations in vol. 2 of the 1853 edition. Cf. also Grotius in *Meletius* and *De Veritate*. See e.g. *The Truth of the Christian Religion*, pp. 17–18.

[20] Nellen, *Hugo de Groot.* Or, in the words of an irenic adagium that fits Arminius' and Grotius' agenda so well: '*Necessariis Unitas, in Non Necessariis Libertas, in Utrisque Caritas*'. See a 1634 Letter by Des Cordes to Grotius in which he refers to the adagium in De Dominis' '*De republica ecclesiastica*'. Henk Nellen, 'De Zinspreuk "in Necessariis Unitas, in Non Necessariis Libertas, in Utrisque Caritas"', *Nederlands Archief voor Kerkgeschiedenis* 79 (1999): pp. 99–106. (Translation: 'unity in necessary things; liberty in uncertain things; charity in all things.')

The *imago Dei* doctrine in the Orthodox Calvinist-Arminian theological dispute

Protestant reformers, such as Calvin and Luther, had lashed out against the Thomistic vision of human nature as taught by the Roman Catholic Church for centuries and still upheld by late-scholastics, such as Francisco de Vitoria.[21] In their view, the Thomist interpretation of *imago Dei* doctrine—the image of God consists in the capacities of reason and free will undamaged by the Fall present in human *nature*[22]—was too positive a view on human beings. Lutherans and Calvinists shared a pessimistic outlook on humanity premised predominantly on Augustinian doctrine of original sin.[23] In their view, the impact of the Fall on *imago Dei* in humanity is complete. After the Fall, human beings were 'deprived' of 'original righteousness' and their natural capacities 'totally corrupted'.[24] Their intellect and will are no longer free and oriented towards the good and just, but ruled by Satan and 'bound in slavery to sin'.[25]

Erasmus, while in many respects a reformer, argued that they 'immensely exaggerate[d]' the impact of original sin.[26] Erasmus defended the power of human reason (thanks to God's forgiveness), the moral freedom of the will, and human responsibility.[27] The influence of his undogmatic Christian humanist legacy diminished however in the early seventeenth century with the rise of orthodox Calvinism.[28] Erasmus' influence on Arminius is undisputed, even though it remains largely implicit in Arminius' own work.[29] One of Erasmus' views 'echo[ed]'[30] in Arminius' work is the view on the human person: 'a creature born

[21] Francisco de Vitoria,'On the American Indians', in *Vitoria Political Writings*, edited and introduced by Anthony Pagden and Jeremy Lawrance (Cambridge: Cambridge University Press, 1991), pp. 241–3, 247–9.

[22] Thomas Aquinas, *ST* I.95.1; I.96.1-4; IIa.100. 2.

[23] Cf. William Bouwsma, 'The Two Faces of Humanism. Stoicism and Augustinianism in Renaissance Thought', in *Itinerarium Italicum: The profile of the Italian Renaissance in the Mirror of its European Transformations*, edited by Paul Oskar Kristeller et al. (Leiden: Brill, 1975).

[24] See John Calvin, *Institutes of the Christian Religion,* vol. 1, a new translation by Henry Beveridge (Edinburgh, Calvin Translation Society, 1845), Book II Ch. II.12, pp. 313–15; Martin Luther, Sermon on the 'Two Kinds of Righteousness', para. 3: 'original righteousness lost in Adam', in *Martin Luther: Selection from his Writings*, edited and introduced by John Dillenberger (New York: Anchor Books, 1961), p. 88; Luther's 'Disputation concerning man' (1536), para. 25, in *Luther's Works*, vol. 34, edited by Lewis W. Spitz (Philadelphia: Muhlenberg Press, 1960), p. 139; Martin Luther, *The Bondage of Will*, in *Discourse of Free Will*, edited and translated by Ernst Winter (New York: Continuum, 2002), pp. 112–13.

[25] Luther, *The Bondage of Will*, p. 124; Calvin, *Institutes of the Christian Religion*, Book II, Ch. II is entitled 'man now deprived of freedom of will, and miserably enslaved.' (p. 297).

[26] Erasmus, *On Free Will*, in *Discourse of Free Will*, edited and translated by Ernst Winter (New York: Continuum, 2002), p. 63.

[27] Ibid., p. 4.

[28] Israel, *The Dutch Republic*, p. 392. See also, Keith Stanglin and Thomas McCall, *Jacob Arminius: Theologian of Grace* (Oxford: Oxford University Press, 2012), p. 44.

[29] Stanglin and McCall, *Jacob Arminius,* pp. 43–4. Erasmus is the most-well-represented Roman Catholic in Arminius' library. But due to the controversy around Erasmus, not a name to use if one has an irenic agenda. Arminius opponents recognized the obvious influence and referred to it in their accusations.

[30] Stanglin and McCall, *Jacob Arminius,* p. 44.

to peace and good will'.[31] In their turn against the pessimistic outlook of Calvinist orthodoxy on human nature,[32] the Erasmian outlook served as an inspiration to the Arminians.[33]

The Calvinist-Arminian theological controversies deeply marked Grotius' life and thought.[34] The controversies culminated in a dispute between two Leiden theology professors, Jacob Arminius (1560–1609) and Franciscus Gomarus (1563–1641) on the doctrine of predestination. The latter, who came to lead the movement against Arminius and his followers, buoyed the Calvinist Reformation in general and the doctrine of unconditional predestination in particular.

The opposition of the Heidelberg Catechisms on the points of predestination and salvation required Arminius and his followers to engage with the *imago Dei* doctrine: who is the post-lapsarian human being? In the context of the current chapter I will highlight three dimensions of the Arminian interpretation.

First, Arminius followed the Thomist line in his ontological definition of the *imago Dei* as the essential 'faculties' or intrinsic capacities of 'Understanding' (*intellectus*) or reason and 'Will' (*voluntas*), imprinted by God in human nature.[35] In the pre-lapsarian state of nature, 'holiness' and 'original righteousness' ensured human capacities of reason, love and will were directed at God, i.e. the realization of the *summum bonum*.

In the post-lapsarian world, the natural capacities of reason, love, and will may no longer be 'rightly ordered', that is, aligned automatically and completely with divine knowledge and justice.[36] This does not mean however that the *imago Dei* is lost completely, nor that the post-lapsarian human being is doomed to do evil and that sin has 'dominion' over humanity.[37] Echoing Erasmus, Arminius wrote

[31] Erasmus, *The Education of a Christian Prince*, edited by Lisa Jardine (Cambridge: Cambridge University Press, 1997), p. 103. Arminius *infra* note 36.

[32] Israel, *The Dutch Republic,* p. 392; P.H. Winkelman, *Remonstranten en katholieken in de eeuw van Hugo de Groot*, (Nijmegen: De Koepel, 1945), p. 43;

[33] Leave aside here Arminius' view on the relation between God's Grace and the human person which shows his Reformed background. See Gerrit Jan Hoenderdaal, 'Erasmus en Arminius Over de Vrede in de Kerk', in *Geschiedenis godsdienst letterkunde*, edited by Eddy Grootes and Hans den Haan (Roden: Nehalennia, 1989), pp. 63–9; see also Israel, *The Dutch Republic*; Winkelman, *Remonstranten en katholieken*; and Jozef IJsewijn, 'The Coming of Humanism to the Low Countries', in *Itinerarium Italicum: The Profile of the Italian Renaissance in the Mirror of Its European Transformations*, edited by Paul Oskar Kristeller/Thomas Brady/Heiko Oberman (Leiden: Brill, 1975).

[34] See, Stanglin and McCall, *Jacob Arminius,* pp. 104–5; see on Grotius' involvement in the controversy e.g. Nellen, *Hugo de Groot*, pp. 112 *et seq*. The Arminian-Calvinist controversies draw also on the theological debate between Pelagius and Augustine. Mathijs Lamberigts, 'Pelagius and Pelagians', in *Oxford Handbook on Early Christian Studies*, edited by Susan Ashbrook and David Hunter (Oxford: Oxford University Press, 2010), pp. 264–6. See also on accusations by Calvinists of Arminians to be Socinians and Grotius' defence of Arminians, Sarah Mortimer, 'Human and Divine Justice in the Works of Grotius and the Socinians', in *The Intellectual Consequences of Religious Heterodoxy, 1600–1750*, edited by Sarah Mortimer and John Robertson (Leiden: Brill, 2012), pp. 75–94.

[35] Arminius, *Disp. Priv.* XXVI 'On the Creation of man after the image of God', pp. 60–4.

[36] Arminius, *Disp. Priv.* XXX, p. 72, and *Disp. Priv.* XXXI, pp. 77–8.

[37] Unconditional (double) predestination was, according to Arminius, 'contrary to the nature of man, in regard to his having been created after the Divine image in the knowledge of God and righteousness—in regard to his having been created with freedom of will, and in regard to his having been created with a disposition and aptitude for the enjoyment of life eternal.' See, 'Declaration of Sentiments', *The works of James Arminius*, vol. 1, pp. 223–4. If humans are not free to sin but bound

'the will [*propendet*] has an inclination to do good'. That is not only to do good to himself, but also 'according to the mode of its nature, to universal good and to that which is the chief good; or, according to the mode of liberty, to all other [kinds of] good'.[38] For Arminius even after the Fall 'sparks of primeval wisdom remained in the intellect'.[39]

Secondly, the Arminian interpretation of the *imago Dei* has a teleological dimension.[40] The objective or *telos* of the existence of human beings, created in God's image, consists in the 'union in God' through faith and by following Christ as mediator,[41] and in the social union with other human beings, equally bearing God's image.[42]

Third, drawing on a long tradition of Christian thought the Arminian interpretation of the *imago Dei* has a functional dimension. God 'conferred' the function of *dominium* over creation upon humanity.[43] Human dominion or majesty is founded on humanity's creation in God's image, which means that in human nature resides what distinguishes humans from animals. Dominion belongs to the universal *natural* (legal) order, accordingly: Arminius 'do[es] not mean to deny that a legitimate magistracy exists among other nations than those which are Christian'.[44]

The Arminian *imago Dei* anthropology as touched upon in the context of the predestination debate thus shows 'a more optimistic view' of post-lapsarian human nature.[45] This is central to the development also of Grotius the lawyer. God has created humans not as 'tragically fated actors in a cosmic drama,'[46] but as rational, social, (morally) free, and responsible agents. Crucially, the human capacities of intellect or reason, love, and free will after the Fall have remained intact.

to sin, God created the Evil in this world and created humans for reprobation. That is cruel and therewith contrary to God's nature as supreme goodness and to human nature as the carrier of God's image. Cf. Grotius in *The Truth of the Christian Religion*, pp. 41–2.

38 Arminius, *Disp. Priv.* XXVI.v, p. 61.

39 Keith Stanglin, *Arminius on the Assurance of Salvation: The Context, Roots, and Shape of the Leiden Debate, 1603–1609* (Leiden: Brill, 2007), p. 101.

40 Stanglin and McCall, *Jacob Arminius*, pp. 118–19: The Calvinist doctrine of predestination would mean that the greater part of humanity would be created wilfully by God for reprobation and thus condemnation. Arminius rejected this view for its implications for God's nature (evil), for the *telos* of creation ('eternal perdition'), and for the *telos* of so many human beings (conformation to 'the image of Satan').

41 Arminius, *Disp. Priv.* XXXI, p. 82: 'the renewal or sanctification of sinful man after the image of God, in which is contained his adoption into a son of God…'.

42 Arminius, *Disp. Priv.* XX, p. 45. Being created as *rational* beings by nature, humans are endowed with love as 'an affection of union in God, whose objects are not only God himself and the good of justice, but also the creature, [*referens Deum,*] imitating or related to God either according to [*imaginem*] likeness, or only according to [*vestigium*] impress, and the felicity of the creature.' See also, *Disp. Pub.* XXV, p. 667: humans are 'sociable animals;' also, *Disp. Priv.* XX, p. 45; *Disp. Priv.* XXIX, p. 71; *Disp. Priv.* LXXIV, p. 177.

43 Arminius, *Disp. Priv.* XXVI, pp. 64–65.

44 Arminius, *Disp. Pub.* XXV, On Magistry, p. 669.

45 Not totally depraved of reason as the Calvinists argued. Also, Goudriaan, 'The Synod of Dordt', p. 104.

46 Stanglin and McCall, *Jacob Arminius,* p. 208.

Imago Dei as the Foundation of Grotius' Theory of *Ius Naturae et Gentium*

Who is the post-lapsarian human being on whom Hugo Grotius grounds his *Ius naturae et gentium*? As early as 1601, Grotius has Adam—just struck down in the Fall—ask: 'Who am I?'. The answer is structured by the *imago Dei* doctrine.[47] Throughout his oeuvre, Grotius writes about humans in terms of beings created in *imagine Dei*. The doctrine appears in many of his books, whether theological, political, legal or theatrical. In *DJP* and *DJBP*, *imago Dei* provides the groundwork for an anthropology of the capable, free, social and responsible human being, which is claimed to be universally valid. As such, it serves Grotius in his quest for a normative foundation for his theory of (universal) society and *Ius naturae et gentium*. Individual human nature can be the starting point of Grotius' system of universal law in both *DJP* and *DJBP*, *because* it carries God's image. Last but not least, the creation of human beings in *imagine Dei* for Grotius also grounds the functioning of humans as keepers, the establishment of human's *dominium*. Against the background of the Arminian anthropology sketched in the previous section, the present section shows that Grotius' outlook on human nature, more than being Stoic[48] or Sceptic,[49] stands in the Erasmian and Arminian tradition.

The Ontological Dimension of Grotius' *Imago Dei* Conception: The Capable, Free, Social, and Responsible Person

With the 'glorious image of [God]', the 'use of reason' and 'the liberty of will' are stamped 'deep within the human mind'.[50] Grotius, as all Christian writers from Church Father Irenaeus up to Aquinas[51] and later also Erasmus and Arminius, starts out by defining creation in the image of God in ontological terms as 'endow[ing] with a mind ["intellectual faculty" or "faculty of reason"] and free-will'.[52] The capacity of reason or judgement distinguishes humans from animals and manifests that the human being is 'a being derived from God Himself, who imprinted upon man the image of His own mind'.[53] To support this claim in *De Jure Praedae*, Grotius refers to Christian sources, such as Genesis and Aquinas),

[47] Hugo Grotius, *Adamus Exul*, line 1590: '*Quis sum?*', in *The Celestial Cycle*, edited by Watson Kirkconnell (Toronto: University of Toronto Press, 1952), pp. 192–3.

[48] Grotius' use of the many Stoic sources is not to take up himself a purely Stoic position on human nature, Stoic doctrines of fate or human passions would prevent that altogether. See *Meletius* paras 7 and 31. Rather, they are used to sustain the universality of Grotius' conception of human nature.

[49] Tuck, *The Rights of War and Peace*.

[50] Grotius, *Adamus Exul*, pp. 103, 117, 109; *Meletius*, para. 18: 'our intellectual faculty lies in the soul, the image of God'; see also, *DJBP* II.II.II.1 note 3, p. 187.

[51] Cairns, *The Image of God in Man*, p. 110.

[52] Grotius, *Defensio fidei Catholicae de satisfactione Christi*, para. 35; *Meletius*, para. 23.

[53] *DJP*, p. 24.

as well as Ancient authors such as Cicero, Seneca, and Epicharmus.[54] Grotius cites the latter, drawing on early Christian writer Clement of Alexandria, to support the universality of the claim that human reason has a divine origin: 'Man's reason from God's reason takes its being.'[55] In *DJBP*, the claim that divine reason is 'instilled in the [human] soul ... by [Gods] breath' is again supported by early Christian authors, such as Origen and Tertullian and Chrysostom, and Ancient—mostly Stoic—sources.[56] Humans are capable of moral reasoning, *because* their natural capacity to reason springs from Divine reason.

For his defence of the moral freedom of human will, Grotius, like Arminius and Erasmus, draws on early Christian authors, such as Irenaeus, Clement of Alexandra, Origen, and Tertullian, who defended human liberty and responsibility against gnostic predestinationism of their age.[57] Grotius discusses the gift of free will as a prerequisite for human virtuous conduct and divine reward.[58] Only thanks to the God-given 'deliberative power and free choice between good and bad'[59]—between receiving or resisting Grace, between justice and sin, good and evil—can one be rewarded for doing good or punished for bringing evil into this world. *DJP* refers to 'the *sovereign* attribute of reason'[60] to emphasize its liberty. With his adherence to human liberty, Grotius refuted the deterministic opposition of free will by the Stoic doctrine of fate and by the Calvinist doctrine of predestination and the post-lapsarian dominion of sin.[61]

Grotius followed indeed the Erasmian-Arminian line on the impact of the Fall on the *imago Dei*. Since divine knowledge and original righteousness are lost as punishment for the first sin, post-lapsarian humans are no longer 'in utter servitude to virtues'.[62] However, neither are they 'slaves of their vices'; their natural capacities 'are just as susceptible to the lure of sin as inclined toward virtue'.[63] Reason and free will are not destroyed yet largely intact after the first sin.[64] And so, post-lapsarian human beings are 'by nature' able to 'be or become good'.[65] With the human intellect comes 'some disposition to do good', as already visible

[54] Grotius' use of Stoic conceptions of nature, reason, or *oikeoisis* resembled the way Early Christian writers adopted these concepts into their own Christian thinking and writings.

[55] *DJP*, p. 25. Many years later, Grotius cites this line of Epicharmus again in *De Veritate* (1627–47). *The Truth of the Christian Religion*, p. 56.

[56] *DJBP*, p. 187, Grotius quotes here from Tertullian's *On the Soul*; Cf. *The Truth of the Christian Religion*, pp. 55–6.

[57] Unsurprisingly, Arminians were also accused of heretic ideas similar to Pelagianism and Socinianism by their Calvinist opponents. See n. 16 and n. 33.

[58] Cf *Meletius*. [59] *Meletius*, para. 29; *The Truth of the Christian Religion*, p. 42.

[60] *DJP*, p. 24. Emphasis added. [61] *Meletius*, para. 29.

[62] *Adamus Exul*, p. 109, also, p. 115; Cf. *Meletius*, para. 35. [63] *Meletius*, paras 35–6.

[64] In *Adamus Exul*, Grotius has God comment on the remaining *imago Dei* in post-lapsarian human beings: 'In human minds I'll cherish sparks of former light, Forerunners of salvation, cover'd by no ashes.' *Adamus Exul*, p. 123.

[65] *Meletius*, paras 29 and 30. Like Erasmus, Grotius underscores that God is Good, he knows evil but 'he actually neither wills nor does it.' Evil does 'not originat[e] in God,' that would make God less than the 'perfect goodness' He is. God's presence in us, makes us 'aim at being good ourselves.' His piety makes us seek piety, Grotius argues. Evil comes not from God, but from free choice. Without free choice, there could be neither punishment nor reward.

in children.[66] By nature the human person is 'gentle' and not 'brutelike', he may become a brute by developing 'the habit of doing wrong',[67] but he is by nature also at liberty to develop the habit of doing good. Like Erasmus and Arminius, Grotius holds that 'it is impossible for [God] who is best to create evil, ... man is in a way the image of God, namely created after the likeness of God, and indeed ... [with] an aptitude for approaching this likeness more and more closely by making an effort'.[68]

This ontological understanding carries an important epistemological implication: the image of God, consisting in the *natural* capacities of reason, free will, and sociability, and thus universally imprinted in humanity, assures that natural justice and law—that body of morality and law that is universally, eternally, and unchangeably true and valid—is cognizable to everyone.[69] Christian or non-Christian, God has provided every human person with the capacity to gain knowledge of God and the laws of the natural order He created.[70]

Consequently, being capable of knowing natural law and justice, judging right from wrong, and free to choose one's actions accordingly, post-lapsarian human beings are truly '*responsible* for their deeds'.[71] The individual (moral) responsibility—crucial for law—is thus firmly established.

Grotius thus establishes his interpretation of the *imago Dei* as the basis of an anthropology of the capable, free, social, and responsible human being on which he claims to exist '*consensus gentium*'.[72] The *imago Dei* in human nature then provides the basis for natural legal personality. Whether verbalized in Christian or natural theological terms, the imprint of the divine image in human nature means to dignify, empower and elevate the status of the post-lapsarian human being. It advances the *persona* that has natural rights and duties, it institutes the moral and legal person. In this way the natural *legal* person is constituted by, and participates in, the formation of the universal legal order.[73]

66 *DJBP*, prol. 7. 67 *DJBP*, I.I.xii.2, p. 43. 68 *Meletius*, para. 30.

69 Ibid., para. 55. At the same time, both Arminius and Grotius were cautious about human epistemological capacities, justice and (theological) truth are so hard to find that the possibility of error has to be taken into account. Cf. Grotius' observation that 'there was no one sect that had discovered all truth, nor any but what held something that was true.' *DJBP* Prol. 43. The issue of knowledge is very much related to the problems of the interpretation of Revelation, hence the agenda of Arminians and surely of Grotius to discuss revealed religious truth in terms of reasonableness. For Grotius the relationship between rationality and revelation was however largely harmonious. Thanks to his rational nature, the human person is able to understand the revealed truth. Or, the revealed truth provides 'certainty' when reason is inconclusive. *Meletius*, para. 44.

70 *Meletius*, para. 55.

71 Ibid., para. 41. Emphasis added. In *DJBP*, Grotius formulates a general responsibility for the good of society of sovereign rulers.

72 This (in origin Stoic) concept of universal agreement features in the *Meletius* para. 6; *DJP*, p. 25; *DJBP* II.XX.VL (pp. 516–18); *The Truth of the Christian Religion* Book I Sect. 16, pp. 49–83.

73 See for legal personality as rights to political participation, Janne E. Nijman, *The Concept of International Legal Personality* (The Hague: TMC Asser Press, 2004).

Teleological Dimension: *Imago Dei* as Foundation of (Universal) Society and *Ius Naturae et Gentium*

The ontological dimension of Grotius' interpretation of the *imago Dei* is the basis for the teleological dimension of his *imago Dei* conception. By nature, humans are directed towards God and their fellow human beings.[74] The natural capacities fleshed out at the ontological level of *imago Dei* interpretation—human reason, freedom, and sociability—define Grotius' conception of human nature, which then can be the foundation of his teleological theory of (universal) society and *Ius naturae et gentium*.

Approaching God, both in this life and after, is the natural *telos* of humanity and the human individual created in God's image. A true love of God entails moreover a true love of our neighbour equal bearer of God's image.[75] The social appetite is a natural capacity crucial to the teleological dimension of Grotius' *imago Dei* conception, since it directs humans to associate and to care for their fellows.[76]

Also the notion of social impulse, famously crucial for Grotius' theory of (universal) society and *Ius naturae et gentium*, thus has a clear theological basis. The ultimate *telos* is a return to God, but this runs for a significant part through relations with one's fellow human beings.

Throughout his oeuvre, Grotius instructs that with creation in God's image comes a natural love for one's fellow-human.[77] It is within this *rational* creature, the human being, that 'love for others ... known as ... 'friendliness' ... burns most brightly'.[78] The social impulse is related explicitly to the creation of human nature in the image of God. Grotius defends a Christian appreciation of human passions. Without them humans would be 'unfeeling and uncharitable'[79] and thus incapable of loving God and caring for one another.

Sharing God's image as part of their nature sets humans in a legal relationship with one another. The *imago Dei* in human beings thus underpins the natural duties of humans towards each other: 'to humanity [one] owes [natural duties of] friendship on the ground of natural kinship in the image of God'.[80] God's image in humans directs them to a life in society, including the universal society. In other words, God's image is not only constitutive of the natural legal personality of human beings but also of society. It is a natural law for humans created in God's image to seek society.

[74] In *Adamus Exul*, for example, Eve trusts fully in God's salvation and God indeed assures salvation. After the Fall, human nature still carries the image of God and through faith (ie union with God through Christ) divine likeness can be sought and the *imago Dei* fully restored.

[75] *Meletius*, para. 68; *The Truth of the Christian Religion*, p. 115–16.

[76] *Meletius*, para. 35.

[77] Ibid., para. 35, 9.

[78] *The Truth of the Christian Religion*, pp. 87, 41–2.

[79] *Meletius*, para. 31.

[80] Ibid., para. 68; also, *The Truth of the Christian Religion*, pp. 150, 125, 115–6, 117. This section is entitled 'Concerning those duties of humanity, which we owe to our Neighbour, though he has injured us.'

From the universality of the *imago Dei* in humans and their consanguinity, Grotius derives a common humanity and natural human equality. Here, he draws on a Christian version of cosmopolitan ethics, also visible with Erasmus,[81] which propagates respect for every member of humanity as equal carrier of *imago Dei*. On this basis, Grotius conceives of a universal natural ethics which amounts to the golden rule.[82] Humanity is created for society. The anthropology outlined in the previous section thus serves the development of the law of nature and nations on the basis of human nature. Thanks to the natural capacities of rationality, liberty and sociability humans are inclined to understand what is right and good as what protects and perfects (universal) society. Right reasoning stipulates what is good for society and thus what natural law and justice prescribe.

In both *DJP* and *DJBP*, Grotius develops his theory of *Ius naturae et gentium* on the basis of an *imago Dei* anthropology. Grotius' Arminian conception of *imago Dei* provides a conception of human nature that grounds primary natural law and unlocks both the primary and secondary law of nations. It underpins his theory of the *sources* of the law of nature and nations. The primary law of nature is found through right reasoning, the secondary law of nature—also called the primary law of nations—is established by universal consensus, and the secondary law of nations springs from consent to be bound to pacts (*pacta sunt servanda*). All three categories hinge on the presumption that human nature consists in reason, love, and free will.

In *DJP*, Grotius starts from what is 'truly universal' to find the normative constraints applicable to relations among nations. Its first source, the primary law of nature, comes from the Will of God: '*What God has shown to be His Will, that is law.*'[83] 'The Will of God is revealed ... above all in the very design of the Creator'—that is, for Grotius not merely in Revelation. The primary law of nature may be inferred from the Creator's design of Nature. The natural order expresses God's Will.[84] Since He willed the existence of all living beings, he created them with 'certain natural properties whereby that existence may be preserved and each part may be guided for its own good, in conformity ... with the fundamental law inherent in its origin'.[85] The principles of law inherent in the universal origin of human nature may be deduced from self-love or self-interest, which is law for all living creatures, and love of others, thanks to the natural capacities of *ratio* and *appetitus societatis* imprinted in the human mind. In the next section we will explore the substance of these natural law principles further, here it suffices to conclude that the primary law of nature is accessible through right reasoning thanks to the natural capacities of reason and love.

[81] April Carter, *Political Theory of Global Citizenship* (London: Routledge, 2001), pp. 19 et seq. Grotius' universal natural ethics is aimed at the (rational) realization of the human *telos* universally inherent in human nature as *imago Dei*.

[82] *DJP*, p. 58; *Meletius*, para. 68; *The Truth of the Christian Religion*, p. 125. In Grotius' view, 'discrimination between people' is 'an insult to nature'. Meletius, paras 3 and 69: Grotius reckons for 'the special bond' between co-religionists, 'citizens of *one* community [*unius ... civitatis*]', but underscores that the Christian 'excludes nobody from his love.'

[83] *DJP*, p. 19. [84] Ibid., p. 20. [85] Ibid., pp. 20–21.

The secondary law of nature, or primary law of nations, builds on Grotius' *imago Dei* anthropology too. His Arminian understanding of post-lapsarian human nature comes through in *DJP*: 'this rational faculty has been darkly beclouded by human vice; yet not to such a degree but that rays of the divine light are still clearly visible, manifesting themselves especially in the mutual accord of nations'.[86] In other words, thanks to the natural faculties of reason, freedom, and sociability being intact, 'universal concord' ('*consensus gentium*') among nations may arise and thus natural law and justice ascertained. While not yet phrased as in *DJBP*, Grotius seems to suggest *universal* agreement *only* emerges from *right* reasoning.[87] That is, humans are free to choose evil over good, but 'universal accord can exist only in relation to that which is good and true'.[88] Universal concord is possible only because of human *sociability*—the inclination to care for the welfare of one's fellow beings imprinted in human nature—relates humanity to the ultimate *telos*, that is the ultimate good of unity in God. That very accord is called the secondary law of nature or primary law of nations: '*What the common consent of mankind has shown to be the will of all that is law.*'[89]

Finally, the secondary law of nations also builds on Grotius' *imago Dei* anthropology. With the creation of humanity in the image of God (also called '*Logos*' or 'Word'[90]), the human person is endowed with free will and the capacity of language—the 'sacred' instrument of speech.[91]

God has given speech to man in order that human society should be more closely knit by people sharing their very thoughts. And once the licence to lie has been given it is bound to overstep all limits and to remove that which is the most important in human relations, namely mutual trust.[92]

The sacred capacity of speech is given to humans 'alone among animals', to serve 'the gratification of' reason and of the 'impelling desire for society'.[93] Without language, the rational, free and social nature of the human person could actually not exist. Language is humanity's sacred instrument of socialization—hence, its teleological dimension. Stemming from God, the sacredness of the word is then the source of the sanctity—ie binding force—of pacts.[94] It is a *sine qua non* for

86 Ibid., p. 25.

87 Grotius is here indebted to Thomas Aquinas who stipulated that for law to be law, it has to partake of right reason and thus of eternal law. Grotius draws on Aquinas' *ST* I-II, Q 93.3.

88 *DJP*, p. 25; also, *DJBP* I.I.XII.2., pp. 42–3.

89 *DJP*, p. 25.

90 *Meletius*, para. 22; *Adamus Exul*, para. 379. The capacity of speech is also essential to Ancients philosophers—Aristotle, Stoics—when they distinguish between humans and other animals.

91 *DJP*, p. 34.

92 *Meletius*, para. 83.

93 *DJBP*, prol. 7. Also, *DJBP* I.I.XII.3, p. 43, where Grotius draws on Chrysostom and Philo.

94 Similar to his words on speech, promises and trust in *De jure praedae*, Grotius states the natural command that 'promises must be kept [stringently]. [Even] to a political enemy ... a robber or a tyrant ...' Ibid., para. 84. See also, on *pacta sunt servanda*, eg *DJBP* Prol. 8 and 15 and Book II Ch. XI. Harm-Jan van Dam, *Hugo Grotius. De Imperio Summarum Potestatum Circa Sacra*. Critical edition with introduction, English translation and commentary (Leiden: Brill, 2001), pp. 693 and 249, *De imperio* 4.6.5.: 'Grotius is the first to argue at length that the rule 'pacta sunt servanda' belongs to natural law.'

the creation of obligations through the expression of one's will by a promise[95] and for nurturing a culture of truth and good faith.[96] 'From the association of reason and speech arises that binding force of a promise with which we are dealing. … [A] promise in itself confers a new right.'[97] Language being a universal gift to humanity ensures the 'sacredness of good faith'[98] sustaining the 'great society of states'.[99]

> [T]he rule of good faith is derived [from the human *liberty* to will and act]: '*What each individual has* indicated *to be his will, that is law with respect to him.*'
>
> [Such] express indication [of will], [is given] by the means which God granted to man alone for this very purpose, namely, *the medium of speech. This gift is regarded as so sacred and inviolable* an instrument for the interchange of blessings and the reciprocal intimation of human will that, in the eyes of all men, there is no more grievous disgrace than that attached to lying. *Herein lies the origin of pacts.*[100]

Thanks to the capacities of reason, free will, sociability, and speech, humans can find and create law. They have a natural law-making capacity as well as a natural capacity to be bound by law. These universal natural capacities and the natural equality of all peoples, Christian or non-Christian, advance the conclusion that treaties are binding by virtue of the natural law principle (and duty) to honour promises. The principle of *pacta sunt servanda* is a principle of universal natural law, ie the law of universal human nature, premised on human's relationship with a God handing out punishments and rewards, a bond forged by the *imago Dei*.[101] It is the basis for human volitional law, including the secondary law of nations, in both *DJP* and *DJBP*.

While in *DJP*, Grotius took a largely voluntarist approach,[102] we find more of an intellectualist stance in *DJBP*.[103] The distinction between the two should however not be exaggerated. His *imago Dei* anthropology provides the groundwork in both works.[104] In *DJBP* however Grotius argues clearly that divine volitional law and the law of nations in *stricto sensu* are subordinate to natural law. He can do this because of his *imago Dei* anthropology.

[95] *Meletius*, para. 84: there is a natural duty to 'stick faithfully to all his covenants, unless you happen to have promised something forbidden by God, which was not within your power even before you gave the promise'.

[96] See for the function of *fides* in Grotius' system of the law of nature and nations, Hans Blom, 'The Meaning of Trust: *Fides* between Self-Interest and *Appetitus Societatis*', in *The Roots of International Law/Les Fondements du Droit International*, edited by Pierre-Marie Dupuy and Vincent Chetail, (Leiden/Boston: Martinus Nijhoff, 2014).

[97] *DJBP*, III.XIX.I.3., p. 793; III.XXV.I., p. 860: the 'greater society of states' is 'sustained by good faith'; to destroy good faith is an 'impious' act.

[98] *DJBP*, III.XXV.VII., p. 862. [99] *DJBP*, III.XXV.I., p. 860.

[100] *DJP*, p. 34. Footnotes omitted emphasis added. Grotius refers to Aristotle, the Digest, and Aquinas here. Since good faith is the foundation for justice, as Grotius paraphrases Cicero, language is a prerequisite for justice and peace to exist. Similarly, in *DJBP* III.XIX on 'Good faith between enemies', Grotius emphasizes that promises even to enemies cannot be broken.

[101] *DJBP*, Prol. 15–16, pp. 14–15. [102] See text to n. 82.

[103] *DJBP*, Prol. 16, pp. 15.

[104] DJBP, Prol. 6. Grotius' reference here is to Chrysostom.

In *DJBP*, immediately after the famous words *etiamsi daremus* Grotius affirms that since human reason comes from God, it establishes and maintains the human relationship with God and his providence of this world. Hence, 'it follows that we must without exception render obedience to God as our Creator, *to Whom we owe all that we are and have*'.[105] The divine origin of rationality, liberty, and sociability explains why Grotius can put divine voluntary law at a distance in *DJBP*.[106] Natural law is laid down in Creation. It is not derived from nature as such, but from *rational* nature. Human nature as created by God in the image of God. Hence, natural law is not part of revealed but of natural truth—it is universally cognizable by human (rational and social) nature and as such its ascertainment avoids the controversies arising from the interpretation of God's Revelation:[107]

> XII. ... the law of nature of which we have spoken, comprising alike that which relates to the social life of man and that which is so called in a larger sense, proceeding as it does from *the essential traits implanted in man, can nevertheless rightly be attributed to God, because of His having willed that such traits exist in us.*[108]

Natural law proceeds from 'the essential traits implanted in man'. Thanks to God's implant, human nature is rational, free, and sociable and thus 'right' reasoning is possible and natural law ascertainable. In other words, Grotius' famous words '[t]he law of nature is a dictate of right reason'[109] are premised on the understanding of the human person created in God's image, that is, with reason, free will, and sociability. The law that is thus dictated doesn't spring from expediency but from a divinely imprinted nature. In *DJBP*, the primary law of nature and nations derives its normativity no longer directly from the Will of God, as handed down by revelation, but from universal human nature.[110] The secondary law of nations finds its origin in the will of free, sociable, and rational nations—analogue to human beings. The positive law of nations is binding thanks to the natural law principle of *pacta sunt servanda*.[111]

In short, Grotius' *imago Dei* anthropology enables him to make the move from '[l]aw [a]s the unerring mind of God' to law as derived from the human mind, which reflects the mind of God and thus is capable of knowing natural law and judging just from unjust. The normativity of the law of nature and nations draws on the divine origin of the reason God has imprinted universally in human nature, it underpins his theory of the sources and universal scope of *Ius Naturae et gentium*.[112]

[105] *DJBP*, Prol. 11; also, *Meletius* paras 84–6; *The Truth of the Christian Religion*, pp. 115–16.
[106] *DJBP*, Prol. 37, Book I.I.X.2 and I.I.XV.
[107] See n. 68 and second section of this chapter.
[108] *DJBP*, Prol. 12; emphasis added.
[109] *DJBP*, I.I.X.1., p. 38.
[110] *DJBP*, Prol. 16: 'For the very nature of man, which even if we had no lack of anything would lead us into the mutual relations of society, is the mother of the law of nature.'
[111] See text to n. 99.
[112] *DJBP*, II.XX.XLIV.

Functional Dimension: *Imago Dei* to Found and Delimit *Dominium*

For Grotius, the creation of humanity in God's image purports to the conferral of the function of *dominium* over creation to humanity. Endowed with rationality, the human being is 'master over his own actions, i.e. he who has free choice, can control other things'.[113] In *Adamus Exul*, Adam is referred to frequently as the Master or Ruler. In *DJBP*, while referring to Genesis I, Grotius states: 'Soon after the creation of the world, and a second time after the Flood, God conferred upon the human race a general right over things of a lower nature.'[114] In the natural state of integrity, public *dominium* (public authority/ jurisdiction/rulership) and private *dominium* (ownership or property) were not yet clearly set apart. Creation was given to humanity as a whole, for all to share: '[i]n consequence, each man could at once take whatever he wished for his own needs, and could consume whatever was capable of being consumed. The enjoyment of this universal right then served the purpose of private ownership.'[115] Since *dominium* is grounded on human's rational *nature*, dominion was not annulled by the first sin.[116] With the loss of original justice, however, *dominium* was no longer inherently just. With a few exceptions, 'community of property' was lost.[117] In the fallen state of nature, *dominium*—purporting to the natural order of Creation—is to be protected and guided to socially responsible use. To this Grotius' treatment of natural law and justice is geared.

In *DJP*, which aims 'to ascertain how much is owed to others and how much to oneself',[118] Grotius starts out to examine the law that governs *dominium*, that is, the law of nature and nations. Here, the *imago Dei* doctrine surfaces both to found and to delimit *dominium*.

Grotius draws the first two applicable laws from the primary law of nature: '*It shall be permissible to defend* [*one's own*] life and to shun that which threatens to prove injurious; secondly, that *It shall be permissible to acquire for oneself, and to retain, those things which are useful for life.*' These laws are based on 'the first principle of the whole natural order,' which consists in 'a true and divinely inspired self-love' (the natural impulse of self-preservation).[119] These natural laws are the basis for the natural rights to defend oneself and to acquire useful things, that is, to seize possession of things, and to consume and defend them. Hence, self-defence, the acquisition of property and the defence of ownership have a legal basis in the natural law principle of self-love and self-preservation. Immediately, however, Grotius brings up the question as to when self-love is 'just'—in his view 'excess[ive]' self-love is vicious. Here, when Grotius looks for 'just limits' on the two first laws,

113 *DJP*, p. 24; see also, *Meletius*, paras 27–28 and 30; *Adamus Exul*, pp. 103, 107, 117, 119, 139, and 148–49; *The Truth of the Christian Religion*, p. 42.

114 *DJBP*, II.II.II.1., p. 186.

115 Ibid.

116 *Adamus Exul*, p. 153.

117 *DJBP*, II.II.II.1, p. 187.

118 *DJP*, pp. 13–14, 22.

119 Ibid., p. 21 (emphasis in text).

the *imago Dei* is introduced and taken to its full legal use. For self-love to remain within the limits of justice, it needs to be kept in check. Being created in God's image, humans have a sense of moderation thanks to their rational nature that enables them to be virtuous in their self-love and pursuit of self-interest.

Being created in God's image, the human person is endowed with the natural capacity as well as the natural obligation to 'care for the welfare of others'.[120] In Grotius' view, this 'social impulse'[121] can be seen to 'burn ... most brightly' in the human being 'who is peculiarly endowed ... with the sovereign attribute of reason: that is to say, as in a being derived from God Himself, who imprinted upon man the image of His own mind.'[122] This imprint provides a profoundly social conception of human nature and a certain trust in humans to behave virtuously. The concept of a divine imprint of reason and love in human nature provides Grotius with a starting-point for his definition of natural justice.[123]

To support his refutation of natural justice as 'personal advantage' (or expediency)—a definition based fully on self-preservation or self-interest—and to argue a conception based on the care for the good of others (that is, based on the natural capacities of reason and love as fellowship) Grotius draws heavily on Lactantius. In the *Divine Institutes*, Lactantius rejects Carneades' denial of natural justice as expediency (anything else is 'folly'). Lactantius opposes Carneades with a notion of justice that has its source in knowledge of God and God's law, which humans may acquire since they are created in *imagine Dei*: thanks to the natural capacities of reason and fellowship, the human person has judgement of right and wrong.[124] Justice finds its source in human nature as rational, sociable, and generous—the *imago Dei* directs humans to seek Wisdom, God, and supreme goodness. What one is due to God, one is due to one's fellow-human because he or she is the image of God, Lactantius explains.[125] For Grotius, care for the 'good of others' is the distinctive aspect of natural justice.[126] Natural justice instructs humans to respect the body and property of others.[127]

[120] Ibid., pp. 24–8, at p. 26: 'the acceptance of this obligation might almost be termed a distinguishing characteristic of man'.

[121] Ibid., p. 28. [122] Ibid., p. 24.

[123] The *imago Dei* offers a profoundly social vision on human nature: one cares naturally for the good of others and may expect others to care for one's own good in return. In *DJP* mostly with the help of Seneca and Cicero, while in the *Meletius* more emphasis is put on the Christian appreciation of human (mutual) affections.

[124] Thanks to reason, the human person can see beyond self-interest and self-preservation, his intellect and wisdom prevent him from taking what belongs to others. Lactantius concludes section 17 to which Grotius, among others, refers with the words: 'No wise man ever aims at gain, because he has a contempt for the goods of this world; nor does he let anyone be deceived, because it is the duty of a good man to put people right when they are wrong and to bring them back in line; it is human nature to be sociable and generous. That is the unique basis for man's kinship with God.' Lactantius attributes much wisdom to Cicero and reads him as precursor to Christian wisdom yet to come. He conjoins Christian and Greek literature on man's creation which are unanimous on the distinguishing feature of reason derived from God.

[125] Anthony Bowen and Peter Garnsey, transl. and eds, *Lactantius Divine Institutes* (Liverpool: Liverpool University Press, 2003), Book 6, section 10.1, p. 349.

[126] *DJP*, p. 27. [127] Ibid., p. 21.

Consequently, Grotius may draw from the law of nature two precepts that 'complemen[t] and confin[e]' the first two laws: '*Let no one inflict injury upon his fellow.*' The other is the precept: '*Let no one seize possession of that which has been taken into the possession of another.*' These are the so-called 'law of inoffensiveness' (to render life secure) and 'the law of abstinence' (to render respect for others property).[128] Rather than to establish a law of nature and nations along humanist lines based on the universal right of self-preservation and the pursuit of self-interest,[129] Grotius grounds natural justice and law both on self-love and on the care or love of others. The latter prescribes the limits to the former. As such, the *imago Dei* in humans is for Grotius the basis of a natural law conception that both grounds ownership of property as well as its acquisition and use, but not without defining 'just limits' right away.[130]

The shared conceptual origin of ownership and liberty in the notion of *dominium* becomes visible where Grotius equates ownership of property with the God-given natural liberty of choice, or the free will:

For God created man *αυτονόμος*, 'free and *sui iuris*,' so that the actions of each individual and the use of his possessions were made subject not to another's will but to his own. Moreover, this view is sanctioned by the common consent of all nations. For what is that well-known concept, 'natural liberty,' other than the power of the individual to act in accordance with his own will? And liberty in regard to actions is equivalent to ownership in regard to property.[131]

Grounded on the free will, Grotius' theory of *dominium* builds on the late scholastics and their Thomist account of creation, human nature, and natural law.[132]

As a Thomist, Vitoria understood *dominium* to be founded on nature, not grace. In the Thomist tradition, God-given human freedom was translated into ownership over one's actions. Vitoria defined natural *dominium* as a natural right (to own or to rule), '[n]atural dominion belonged to man as a creature made in the image of God ... the likeness to God inhered in man's power of reason and this was not lost by sin'.[133] Hence, created in God's image one was capable of holding natural rights. Every human being is created in God's image—including infidels, sinners or barbarians; therefore all peoples, whether European or indigenous to the America's or the East Indies, could hold rights to own property and to rule authoritatively.[134] After all, *dominium* is established and ruled by the law of natural reason, and not divine law (of revelation). Thus all who possess natural reason hold natural rights.

Grotius the Arminian was rather comfortable with the Thomist doctrine of creation and *dominium* and the underlying conception of humanity created in

[128] Ibid., p. 27. [129] Tuck, *The Rights of War and Peace*.

[130] Subsequently, Grotius discerns natural laws on the enforcement of (compensatory) justice and punishment to protect the rights of life and property. *DJP*, p. 29: 'first, *Evil deeds must be corrected;* secondly, *Good deeds must be recompensed*'.

[131] *DJP*, p. 33. [132] Cf. Arminius, in the second section of this chapter.

[133] Brian Tierney, *The Idea of Natural Rights* (Grand Rapids, Mich.: W. B. Eerdmans 1997), p. 267; Tierney discusses Vitoria, 'On the American Indians', 1.3, pp. 243–6.

[134] Vitoria, 'On the American Indians', 1.3 and 1. Conclusion, pp. 250–1.

imagine Dei. He continued Vitoria's Thomist approach to self-dominion (*dominium sui*) of the human person as the foundation of personal liberty and dominion over things.[135] Only beings created in God's image can rule creation: reason and free will enable the human person to control herself—after the Fall, Eve is composed. More than Adam to whom she calls 'control thy senses! ... tame thy spirit, ... calm thy soul thyself! ... Grant thyself time to gain self-mastery back And shed this untamed violence by using Reason'[136]—and therewith to control creation.[137] The conception of dominion as control of the self and the world has profoundly affected the conceptualisation of human liberty: liberty starts with having dominion over oneself and becomes defined in terms of natural rights of ownership: 'liberty in regard to actions is equivalent to ownership in regard to property'[138]

An Arminian conception of free will underlies Grotius' conception of 'natural liberty': '[f]or what is that well-known concept ... other than the power of the individual to act in accordance with his own will?'[139] The analogy between individual liberty and sovereignty can be drawn legitimately, but would need to include the notion of 'just limits' rooted in the *imago Dei* doctrine of human nature.

In *DJBP* too, the natural capacity of freedom—that is power one has over oneself—is identified with the power an owner has over her property. Personal liberty, given to human beings by creation, is identified with subjective rights (*facultates*) of ownership.[140] In other words, the human person has these *facultates* by the natural design of Creation. The theological notion of the human person being created with moral liberty is conceptualized in legal terms of a person with innate legal rights which others have the duty to respect. In the post-lapsarian world, sovereignty and property rights are no longer exercised automatically in line with divine justice. Yet human beings are capable of exercising these rights legitimately and justly—that is, in conformity with natural law and justice. But the uncorrupted promotion of *summum bonum* then is a requirement.[141]

The natural subjective rights are correlated to natural duties thanks to the body of natural law and justice that founds and defines both. This delimitation is based on the (obligation to) care for the good of others,[142] which human beings have by virtue of their creation in God's image. As such, there is a sacredness to dominion, both in the form of sovereignty and in the form of ownership; it comes with 'a general *responsibility* for human society'.[143]

135 Text to note 130. 136 *Adamus Exul*, pp. 193–5.

137 Cf. *Meletius* para. 28: 'only he who is master of his own actions, i.e. he who has a free choice, can control other things. And of all creation only man and those beings we call rational spirits [angels] have this free choice.'

138 *DJP*, p. 34. 139 Ibid., pp. 33–4. 140 *DJBP*, Book I Ch. I.

141 Ibid., Book II Ch. II.

142 Martti Koskenniemi, 'International Law and the Emergence of Mercantile Capitalism: Grotius to Smith', in *The Roots of International Law/Les Fondements du Droit International*, edited by Pierre-Marie Dupuy and Vincent Chetail, (Leiden/Boston: Martinus Nijhoff, 2014), p. 6: 'There is no doubt that the natural love of human companionship and life in organised society of which Grotius speaks in *De jure belli ac pacis* was intended to counterbalance the potentially egoistic implications of his strong view on subjective rights.'

143 *DJBP*, II.XX.XLIV.i, p. 508. See also, Stumpf, *The Grotian Theology*, p. 2.

Thus, thanks to God's image imprinted in humanity, nature and natural law are two different things. Nature may not be against war, but right reason as the source that dictates natural law may very well be.[144]

Conclusion: *Imago Dei* Today—a Jurisprudence of Care and Responsibility

This chapter argues that his *imago Dei* anthropology provided Grotius with a conception of human nature crucial to the move he made to what is often understood as a modern, secular conception of the law of nature and nations. Grotius' famous *etiamsi daremus* experiment, however, never meant to disconnect humanity and human nature from the work of God in this world. Rather, Grotius depends on the relationship between God and human beings for his theory of *Ius naturae et gentium*. The principles of natural religion as well as natural law may be known through right reason, as human beings are created as *imagines Dei,* which in Grotius' interpretation means capable, free, and responsible beings. In conclusion, the ontological aspect of *imago Dei* may be said to serve as an underpinning for the natural legal personality and responsibility of humans; the teleological aspect for the sources of law doctrine; and the functional aspect of *dominium* for the legal notions property and sovereignty.

This chapter moreover has described an alternative, post-sceptic account of Grotius in that it shows how Grotius conceptualized the human impulse of self-preservation and pursuit of self-interest as delimited by a sense of natural justice not defined by utility but by care for others and the good of society. Grotius builds his legal order on human nature; and not on one defined by an immoderate, over-indulgent drive of self-preservation,[145] but rather on a much richer conception that includes rationality, liberty, and sociability and from which in turn the laws of nature and nations are derived. Thus this chapter seeks to complement the current historiography with a reading of Grotius' international legal ideas in the light of his (natural) theological anthropology of *imago Dei* and the foundational role this plays in his theory of *Ius naturae et gentium.*[146] It aims to open up our international law language to a richer and more diverse set of ideas and hopes to give some ideas for an alternative future of (the philosophy of) international law.[147] In the context of human rights theory, the *imago Dei* doctrine has indeed been

[144] *DJBP*, I.II.I.5.

[145] Richard Tuck, 'Grotius and Selden', in *Cambridge History of Political Thought, 1450–1700,* edited by J. H. Burns & Mark Goldie, (Cambridge: Cambridge University Press, 1991), pp. 499 et seq.

[146] It is not commerce and trade, capitalism, that is sacred for Grotius, both are 'introduced' by God' Providence to have men seek 'the Assistance of one another, [to] maintain and cultivate society,' which is indeed sacred. Book II. Ch. II § XIII; see Editors' abstract.

[147] Cf. Stephen Toulmin, *Cosmopolis: The Hidden Agenda of Modernity* (Chicago: University of Chicago Press, 1990), p. 2.

discussed as a possible foundation for dignity and fundamental rights inherent to all human beings.[148]

Since Grotius, legal theory has secularized further and human rights have become a dominant discourse. Grotius became reputed as one of the precursors of individualist liberalism. In this chapter I have pointed out to the account of *imago Dei* as a starting point for Grotius' anthropological foundation of the law of nature and nations. This may invite us to reconnect to a jurisprudence of care, respect, and responsibility.[149] A post-sceptical reading of Grotius' theory brings out that the *imago Dei* doctrine gave as much ground to natural duties (to respect and protect the other) as to natural rights. In Grotius' reading trade and commerce were not an end in themselves, but as a means given by God's Providence to materialize human sociability.[150] Humanity had received the right of *dominium* (whether ownership or rulership) together with the responsibility to care (for society, national and international) and preserve.

An examination of Grotius's theory through the prism of *imago Dei* invites us to recognize the Other as similar and of a common origin, and to reflect on the natural capacity of care and responsibility for the Other and society at large.[151] This chapter is not so much an argument for a theological foundation of international law; Grotius himself explicitly held his views on humanity—and ultimately on law—to be based on a universal natural truth rather than a Christian truth. Rather, this chapter proposes that reconnecting to the natural human capacity of care for the Other and society at large could redefine the international legal order to be founded in and constituted through mutual recognition, respect and responsibility.

Bibliography

Arminius, James. *The works of James Arminius*, first and second volume translated by James Nichols, and third volume by W. R. Bagnall (Auburn/Buffalo: Orton, 1853).

Basdevant, Jules. 'Hugo Grotius', in *Les Fondateurs du Droit International* (Paris: V. Giard & E. Brière, 1904).

Blom, Hans. 'The Meaning of Trust: *Fides* between Self-Interest and *Appetitus Societatis*'. In *The Roots of International Law/Les Fondements du Droit International*, edited by Pierre-Marie Dupuy and Vincent Chetail, (Leiden/Boston: Martinus Nijhoff, 2014).

Blom, Hans, and Laurens Winkel. 'Grotius and the Stoa'. Special issue of *Grotiana* 22/23 (2001–2002) (Assen: Van Gorcum, 2004).

[148] Jeremy Waldron, 'The Image of God: Rights, Reason, and Order', *New York University Public Law and Legal Theory Working Papers*, paper 10–85 (2010); see also the work of Paul Ricoeur (n 150).

[149] Anthony Carty, 'Doctrine Versus State Practice', in *The Oxford Handbook of the History of International Law*, edited by Bardo Fassbender and Anne Peters (Oxford: Oxford University Press, 2012); Anthony Carty, 'New Philosophical Foundations for International Law: From an Order of Fear to One of Respect', *Cambridge Review of International Affairs* 19, no. 2 (2006): pp. 311–30.

[150] Providence introduced Trade to foster Society, see *DJBP*, II.II.XIII.

[151] Paul Ricoeur, 'The Image of God and the Epic of Man', in *History and Truth*, translated by Charles Kelbley (Evanston: Northwestern University Press, 1965 and 2007), pp. 110–28.

Bowen, Anthony, and Peter Garnsey, transl. and eds. *Lactantius Divine Institutes* (Liverpool: Liverpool University Press, 2003).
Bouwsma, William. 'The Two Faces of Humanism: Stoicism and Augustinianism in Renaissance Thought'. In *Itinerarium Italicum: The profile of the Italian Renaissance in the Mirror of its European Transformations*, edited by Paul Oskar Kristeller et al. (Leiden: Brill, 1975).
Calvin, John. *Institutes of the Christian Religion*, vol. 1, a new translation by Henry Beveridge (Edinburgh, Calvin Translation Society, 1845).
Cairns, David. *The Image of God in Man* (London: SCM Press, 1953).
Carter, April. *Political Theory of Global Citizenship* (London: Routledge, 2001).
Carty, Anthony. 'Doctrine versus state practice'. In *The Oxford Handbook of the History of International Law,* edited by Bardo Fassbender and Anne Peters (Oxford: Oxford University Press, 2012).
Carty, Anthony. 'New Philosophical Foundations for International Law: From an Order of Fear to One of Respect'. *Cambridge Review of International Affairs* 19, no. 2 (2006): p. 311.
Erasmus. 'On Free Will'. In *Discourse on Free Will,* edited and translated by Ernst Winter (New York: Continuum, 2002).
Erasmus. *The Education of a Christian Prince*, edited by Lisa Jardine (Cambridge: Cambridge University Press, 1997).
Goudriaan, Aza. 'The Synod of Dordt on Arminian Anthopology'. In *Revisiting the Synod of Dordt (1618–1619),* edited by Aza Goudriaan and Fred van Lieburg (Leiden, Boston: Brill, 2011).
Grotius, Hugo. *Adamus Exul.* In *The Celestial Cycle,* edited by Watson Kirkconnell (Toronto: University of Toronto Press, 1952).
Grotius, Hugo. *De Jure Belli ac Pacis Libri Tres* (1646) translated by Francis Kelsey. In *The Classics of international Law*, 2nd edn, edited by James Scott (Oxford: Clarendon Press, 1925).
Grotius, Hugo. *Commentary on the Law of Prize and Booty*, edited and with an introduction by Martine Julia van Ittersum (Indianapolis: Liberty Fund, 2006). Originally published: Oxford: Clarendon Press, 1950. The Classics of International Law; no. 22 (Publications of the Carnegie Endowment for International Peace).
Grotius, Hugo. *The Truth of the Christian Religion*, edited and with an introduction by Maria Rosa Antognazza, with an English translation by John Clarke (1743) (Indianapolis: Liberty Fund, 2012).
Grotius, Hugo. *Defensio fidei Catholicae de satisfactione Christi*, edited and with an introduction and notes by Edwin Rabbie, with an English translation by Hotze Mulder, (Assen/Maastricht: Van Gorcum, 1990).
Grotius, Hugo. *Meletius, Sive De Iis quae inter Christianos Conveniunt Epistola*, critical edition with translation, commentary and introduction by Guillaume Posthumus Meyjes, (Leiden/New York: Brill, 1988).
Haentjens, A. H. *Hugo de Groot als godsdienstig denker*, (Amsterdam: Ploegsma, 1946).
Haggenmacher, Peter. *Grotius et la doctrine de la Guerre Juste* (Paris: Presses Universitaires de France, 1983).
Herzfeld, Noreen. *In Our Image: Artificial Intelligence and the Human Spirit* (Minneapolis: Fortress Press, 2002).
Hoenderdaal, Gerrit Jan. 'Erasmus en Arminius Over de Vrede in de Kerk'. In *Geschiedenis Godsdienst Letterkunde,* edited by E.K. (Eddy) Grootes and J. (Hans) den Haan (Roden: Nehalennia, 1989).
IJsewijn, Jozef. 'The Coming of Humanism to the Low Countries'. In *Itinerarium Italicum. The Profile of the Italian Renaissance in the Mirror of Its European Transformations*, edited by Paul Oskar Kristeller, Thomas Brady, and Heiko Oberman (Leiden: Brill, 1975).

Israel, Jonathan. *The Dutch Republic* (Oxford: Oxford University Press, 1995).

Koskenniemi, Martti, 'International Law and the Emergence of Mercantile Capitalism: Grotius to Smith'. In *The Roots of International Law/Les Fondements du Droit International*, edited by Pierre-Marie Dupuy and Vincent Chetail (Leiden/Boston: Martinus Nijhoff, 2014).

Kunz, Joseph. 'Natural-Law Thinking in the Modern Science of International Law'. *American Journal of International Law* 55 (1961): p. 951.

Lamberigts, Mathijs. 'Pelagius and Pelagians'. In *Oxford Handbook on Early Christian Studies*, edited by Susan Ashbrook and David Hunter (Oxford: Oxford University Press, 2010).

Lauterpacht, Hersch. 'The Grotian Tradition in International Law'. *British Yearbook of International Law* 23, no. 1 (1946): p. 1.

Leger, James. *The 'Etiamsi Daremus' of Hugo Grotius. A Study in the Origins of International Law* (Rome: Pontificium Athenaeum Internationale, 1962).

Luther, Martin. Sermon on the 'Two Kinds of Righteousness'. In *Martin Luther: Selection from his Writings*, edited and introduced by John Dillenberger (New York: Anchor Books, 1961).

Luther, Martin. 'Disputation concerning man' (1536). In *Luther's Works*, vol. 34, edited by Lewis W. Spitz (Philadelphia: Muhlenberg Press, 1960).

Luther, Martin. 'The Bondage of Will'. In *Discourse on Free Will*, edited and translated by Ernst Winter (New York: Continuum, 2002).

Malanczuk, Peter. *Akehurst's Modern Introduction to International Law*, 7th edn (New York: Routledge, 1997).

Middleton, Richard. *The Liberating Image: The Imago Dei in Genesis I* (Grand Rapids: Brazos Press, 2005).

Mortimer, Sarah. 'Human and Divine Justice in the Works of Grotius and the Socinians'. In *The Intellectual Consequences of Religious Heterodoxy, 1600–1750*, edited by Sarah Mortimer and John Robertson (Leiden: Brill, 2012).

Nellen, Henk, and Edwin en Rabbie, eds. *Hugo Grotius, Theologian: Essays in Honour of G.H.M. Posthumus Meyjes* (Leiden: Brill, 1994).

Nellen, Henk. 'De Zinspreuk 'in Necessariis Unitas, in Non Necessariis Libertas, in Utrisque Caritas''. *Nederlands Archief voor Kerkgeschiedenis* 79, no.1 (1999): p. 99.

Nellen, Henk. *Hugo de Groot. Een leven in strijd om de vrede 1583–1645* (Amsterdam: Balans, 2007).

Nellen, Henk. 'Minimal Religion, Deism and Socinianism: On Grotius's Motives for Writing De Veritate'. *Grotiana* 33 (2012): pp. 25–57.

Nijman, Janne E. *The Concept of International Legal Personality* (The Hague: TMC Asser Press, 2004).

Nussbaum, Arthur. *A Concise History of the Law of Nations* (New York: Macmillan, 1947).

O'Donovan, Olivier. 'The Justice of Assignment and Subjective Rights in Grotius'. In *Bonds of Imperfection: Christian politics, past and present*, edited by Olivier O'Donovan and Joan Lockwood O'Donovan (Grand Rapids, Mich.: W. B. Eerdmans, 2004).

Oppenheim, Lassa. *International Law: A Treatise*, 8th edn, edited by Hersch Lauterpacht (London: Longman, 1955).

Posthumus Meyjes, Guillaume, ed. *Hugo Grotius—Meletius, Sive De Iis quae inter Christianos Conveniunt Epistola*, critical edition with translation, commentary and introduction (Leiden/New York: Brill, 1988).

Ricoeur, Paul. 'The Image of God and the Epic of Man'. In *History and Truth*, translated by Charles Kelbley (Evanston: Northwestern University Press, 1965 and 2007).

Shaw, Malcom. *International Law* (Cambridge: Cambridge University Press, 2008).
Somos, Mark. *Secularisation and the Leiden Circle* (Leiden: Brill, 2011).
St. Thomas Aquinas. *Summa Theologiæ*: Latin text and English translation, introductions, notes, appendices, and glossaries, general editor Thomas Gilby (London: Blackfriars in conjunction with Eyre & Spottiswoode, London and McGraw-Hill Book Company, New York 1964–).
Stanglin, Keith. *Arminius on the Assurance of Salvation: The Context, Roots, and Shape of the Leiden Debate 1603–1609* (Leiden: Brill, 2007).
Stanglin, Keith, and Thomas McCall. *Jacob Arminius: Theologian of Grace* (Oxford: Oxford University Press, 2012).
Straumann, Benjamin. 'Oikeiosis and Appetitus Societatis. Hugo Grotius' Ciceronian Argument for Natural Law and Just War'. *Grotiana* 24/25 (2003–2004): pp. 44–66.
Stumpf, Christoph. *The Grotian Theology of International Law: Hugo Grotius and the Moral Foundations of International Relations* (Berlin: Walter de Gruyter, 2006).
Tierney, Brian. *The Idea of Natural Rights* (Grand Rapids, Mich.: W. B. Eerdmans, 1997).
Toulmin, Stephen. *Cosmopolis: The Hidden Agenda of Modernity* (Chicago: University of Chicago Press, 1990).
Trinkaus, Charles. *'In Our Image and Likeness': Humanity and Divinity in Italian Humanist Thought* (Chicago: University Press, 1970), pp. 1–2.
Tuck, Richard. 'Grotius and Selden'. In *Cambridge History of Political Thought 1450–1700*, edited by J. H. Burns and Mark Goldie (Cambridge: Cambridge University Press, 1991).
Tuck, Richard. *The Rights of War and Peace* (Oxford: Oxford University Press, 1999).
Van Dam, Harm-Jan. *Hugo Grotius, De Imperio Summarum Potestatum Circa Sacra*, critical edition with introduction, English translation and commentary (Leiden: Brill, 2001).
de Vitoria, Francisco. 'On the American Indians'. In *Vitoria: Political Writings*, edited by Anthony Pagden and Jeremy Lawrance (Cambridge: Cambridge University Press, 1991).
Waldron, Jeremy. 'The Image of God: Rights, Reason, and Order'. *New York University Public Law and Legal Theory Working Papers*, paper 246 (2010).
Winkelman, P. H. *Remonstranten en katholieken in de eeuw van Hugo de Groot* (Nijmegen: De Koepel, 1945).

5

John Selden and the Jewish Religious Fountainhead of the International Law of the Sea

Ofir Haivry

The Foundations of Modern International Maritime Law

International maritime law of the last generation has seen a dramatic rise in importance of the ideas of a formerly almost forgotten figure, John Selden (1584–1654). A prominent English legal scholar and parliamentary leader of his age, Selden also developed an unrivalled proficiency in the Hebrew traditions. This chapter will establish that these ideas have their principal source in the political Hebraism developed upon the Jewish tradition.

Modern international maritime law (IML) was born primarily out of two works, written about 400 years ago. The first was *Mare Liberum* (1609) by Hugo Grotius (1583–1645), which argued for a complete freedom of the seas, since by their nature these waters cannot be practically bound or defended; the second was Selden's *Mare Clausum* (1635), arguing for the principle and practice of dominion and ownership over tracts of sea. These two books and their authors may be regarded as co-founders of modern IML, and were regarded as such by their own generation and successive ones, which read both authors together when addressing maritime matters.[1]

Although later IML, or law of the sea, was founded on a combination of these two works, until relatively recently it tended overall far more towards Grotius, since for centuries the technological limitations of enforcing dominion over the sea meant that theory and practice restricted application of Selden's view mainly to the concept of the 'territorial waters'. Originally defined as three miles from the shore, it was eventually established as 12 miles—based on the capacity of land-based

[1] See Timothy Brook, *Mr. Selden's Map of China* (London: Bloomsbury Press, 2013), pp. 14–15, 38. See also Mónica Brito Vieira, 'Mare Liberum vs. Mare Clausum: Grotius, Freitas, and Selden's Debate on Dominion over the Seas', *Journal of the History of Ideas* 64, no. 2 (July 2003): pp. 361–77.

John Selden and the Jewish Religious Fountainhead of the International Law of the Sea. Ofir Haivry.

cannons to effectively enforce a zone of control—and remained in place until about 1985.[2]

However, in the last three decades or so, as technological advances enable the establishment of far wider areas of maritime control and ever more ambitious finds of resources lying under the sea-bed, the ideas of Selden are becoming increasingly appealing to those considering such possibilities. An intense debate over sovereign-nation control of the seas is now under way, one which is rapidly becoming more Seldenian than Grotian.

One important field in which the issue is increasingly relevant is the Exclusive Economic Zones (EEZ), extending between 200 to 350 nautical miles offshore (depending on the underwater topography), which have been established as areas in which countries are permitted to exclusively exploit natural resources, such as is happening with recent massive natural gas findings under the sea-bed of the eastern Mediterranean. There is also growing interest in establishing ownership of tracts of the Arctic Ocean up to the North Pole, principally by Russia and Canada, neither of which could make such claims of maritime sovereignty without relying on Selden's argument that it is reasonable to delineate boundaries even at sea. Amusingly, in the latter case, the argument is being put forward by the spokesmen for the Sovereign of Canada, the current heir of Charles I, to whom the *Mare Clausum* was originally dedicated.[3]

Perhaps the area where the debate is currently most contentious and belligerent, sometimes descending into downright sabre-rattling, is the China Sea, where several nations, including China, Japan, Vietnam, the Philippines, and others, are raising contesting claims to control maritime areas and the supposed mineral deposits beneath them. Even in a cursory look at reports of this debate, the explicit role of Selden's ideas is immediately evident: in *The Diplomat* of 11 July 2013, a report on the new Chinese naval theories carried the byline 'Beijing's efforts to impose a new normal on the South China Sea are more Selden than Zheng He or Grotius'; while the journal *Foreign Policy* of 16 May 2014 treating the conflict in the South China Sea, carried the byline 'This British lawyer [Selden] has been dead for 360 years. So why is he at the center of China's oil fight with Vietnam?' Thus, in the great debate now underway about the law of the sea, Selden is definitely back in vogue.[4]

[2] A good summary of the issues involved and of the practice accepted until about 1985 is Bo Johnson Theutenberg, 'Mare Clausum et Mare Liberum', *Arctic* 37, no. 4 (December 1984): pp. 481–92.

[3] A good recent treatment of the current state of IML and of Selden's role in it is T. Brook, *Mr. Selden's Map of China* (Bloomsbury Press, 2013), pp. xxii, 14–15, 36–8, 106–7, 114–20, 164–7. See also T. G. Barnes, *Shaping the Common Law: From Glanvill to Hale, 1188–1688* (Stanford: Stanford University Press, 2008), pp. 169, 253.

[4] On Selden's role in the current China Sea conflict see James R. Holmes, 'China's New Naval Theorist', *The Diplomat* (11 July 2013) byline: '*Beijing's efforts to impose a new normal on the South China Sea are more Selden than Zheng He or Grotius*'; Keith Johnson, 'Lord of the Sea', *Foreign Policy* (16 May 2014) byline 'This British lawyer has been dead for 360 years. So why is he at the center of China's oil fight with Vietnam?'; Steven Groves and Dean Cheng, 'A National Strategy for the South China Sea', *Backgrounder—The Heritage Foundation* (24 April 2014) argues: 'in a throwback to the time of John Selden's Mare Clausum, China has claimed sovereign rights to the entirety of the SCS

Customary Law against Universalist Law

Selden's *Mare Clausum* establishes its argument about dominion of the sea in the main by relying on a framework of customary laws and practices, while identifying the challenge to its thesis as coming principally from universalist theories which deny customs anything more than incidental value. Thus the tract undergirds its maritime law theory with a detailed theoretical rejection of the universalist challenge, and lays the foundations (which Selden developed in his later writings) towards building the theoretical justification for customary law.

The *Mare Clausum* had an unusually long gestation, since an earlier version had been completed by Selden in 1619, but was blocked from publication by the then Marquess of Buckingham (then also Lord Admiral of the Fleet), and it was ultimately published in a revised version only sixteen years later. This peculiar background meant the book answered universalist arguments from both the 1610s, when the case from Roman law was predominant, as well as from the mid-1630s, when the case from natural rights was becoming more prominent. Selden opposed these arguments, not only on the basis of what he regarded as their own internal contradictions, but also upon the idea that customary systems of law, such as the Jewish and the English ones, were preferable.

The first type of universalist arguments was identified by Selden as '*taken out of* Antient Lawyers' and notably raised by 'Albericus Gentilis' (Alberico Gentili) in his *Iure Belli*; the second as the opinions of 'modern Lawyers', such as 'Fernandus Vasquius' (Fernando Vazquez de Manchaca), and especially 'Hugo Grotius'. Addressing the argument from Roman law, Selden wrote:

> And here, especial care must bee taken to avoid that which som have presumed to affirm, touching those most excellent Books of *Justinian*, which make up an entire Bodie of the antient Law; *That the Law prescribed in those Books is not the Law onely of a Citie, but even of Nations and nature; and that the whole is so fitted unto nature*, that after the Empire was extinct, *though the Law was a long time buried; yet it rose again, and spread it self through all the world. And therefore that it concern's even Princes, although it was framed by* Justinian *for private persons*. As if the law natural and of Nations were to bee derived onely out of those Books.[5]

The heart of the argument that he was taking directly from Gentili's famous *De Iure Belli libri tres* (1589) was the widespread proposition that Roman law (in the form it achieved in Justinian's *Institutes*) should be identified with the law '*of Nations and nature*'—because its revival and its adoption throughout Europe,

within a "nine-dash line" that encloses the sea, encroaching on China's neighbors'. See also 'Mapping China', *The Economist* (18 January 2014).

[5] *Mare Clausum, seu De Dominio Maris* (London, 1635), book 1 chapter 24. Henceforth abbreviated as MC b1c24. The English text is from Marchamont Needham's translation, published in 1652 (while Selden was still alive) as *Of the Dominion or Ownership of the Sea*. For the circumstances of the book's composition and publication see G. J. Toomer, *John Selden: A Life in Scholarship* (Oxford: Oxford University Press, 2009), pp. 159–60.

hundreds of years after it had been long '*buried*' and the Empire 'extinct', were alleged proof of its being perfectly '*fitted unto nature*'. Selden challenged this claim unequivocally, first by disputing its factual validity, showing that many laws of states such as France and Spain, 'are not grounded at all upon the Law of *Justinian*, but have had their original from Customs quite contrarie thereto'. Secondly Selden also indicated that essentially, the customary law of these European countries was the real source of any current authority enjoyed within them by Roman laws. Selden summed up his case by remarking that:

> Other instances might bee brought, sufficiently to shew that the Law natural and of Nations is not wholly to be drawn out of such Decrees or Determinations as are found in the Books of *Justinian*; And so that what is there inserted touching a Communitie of the Sea, doth not in any wise diminish the Autoritie of the received Customs of so many ages and nations.[6]

Selden's absolute refusal to concede any intrinsic authority to Roman law (never mind identifying it with natural law), not only in the international sphere, but in any country, and particularly in England, is the most consistent theme of his works over more than four decades, recurring in one way or another in almost all of them. In his *The Historie of Tithes* (1618), written about the time he was composing the original version of *Mare Clausum*, Selden poured his aspersion on the claim 'received through lazie Ignorance' that 'the *Civill Law*; that is the old *Roman Imperiall* Law of *Iustinian*' as 'read and profest in the Universities' governs the states of Europe. He observed that this 'is so farre from Truth, that indeed no Nation in the world is governed by them'. Further he dismissed derisively those who 'can make no difference twixt the use of Laws in studie or argument (which might equally happen to the Laws of *Utopia*) and the governing autoritie of them'. Selden's recurring effort in all these cases clearly centred on denying any 'governing authoritie' to Roman law, and he based this denial on two elements: on Roman law not actually governing any particular nation, and on 'reason' not conferring by itself any political or legal 'authoritie'.[7]

Why was opposing the tradition of Roman law so important for Selden, to the point that he addressed it in much of what he wrote? It appears that at least part of the source for this hostility is connected to the danger he also detected in more modern universalist systems of law—by their tendency to destroy legitimation for particular and historical liberties, they facilitate by degrees the introduction of political despotism. This aspect is perhaps most prominent in his *Dissertatio Historica* (annexed to the 1647 printed edition of the medieval English legal commentary *Fleta*), where again and again he points to the main reason for the strong English resistance to the introduction of Roman law, being the latter's ominous absolutist political tendencies: 'absoluta principis potestate'.[8]

[6] MC b1c24. See also Martha A. Ziskind, 'John Selden: Criticism and Affirmation of the Common Law tradition', *The American Journal of Legal History* 19, no. 1 (January 1975): pp. 36–7.

[7] 'Review' annexed to John Selden, *The Historie of Tithes* (London, 1618), pp. 477–81.

[8] Reid Barbour, *Measures of the Holy Commonwealth* (Toronto: University of Toronto Press, 2003), pp. 96–7; *The Dissertation of John Selden annexed to his edition of Fleta* (1647) translated by Robert Kelham with notes (London, 1771), pp. 49–51, and also pp. 69–70.

Thus, for all their outward differences, Selden identified a strong connection between universalist arguments from Roman law and those from 'modern' natural law (or right). Moreover, he believed that often the latter were rooted on ideas, assumptions, and inferences from the former. Consequently, in *Mare Clausum*, Selden argued:

> But as the root being cut, the Tree fall's, so the Autoritie of those antient Lawyers being removed out of the way, all the determinations of the modern which are supported by it, must bee extremely weakned.[9]

Turning to address the 'modern' natural rights arguments directly, Selden began with making short shrift of Vazquez's argument, that prescription was not a binding principle in international law, by remarking that such an absurdity would simply result in the complete abrogation of 'the very intervenient Laws of Nations'—the whole of what is today called international law. Selden then went on to deal with his main target, Hugo Grotius, dissecting his views on 'a natural and perpetual Communitie of the Sea', as put forward both in the *Mare Liberum* and in his later work the *Jure Belli ac Pacis* (1625). Selden addressed inconsistencies of argumentation that he found in both of Grotius' works, pointing out the most important one for him, that since Grotius purported to identify and justify a complete system of law based solely on 'natural Right or Reason' (to Grotius synonymous), it was impossible for such a theory to then argue for naval practices as based on 'Custom' or prescription ('Right of Occupation'). As he had done in Gentili's case, on top of arguing that Grotius fails to make a convincing case from natural right only, Selden also visibly positioned Grotian natural right theory as essentially opposite to, and a negation of, customary law.[10]

Selden's efforts to defend customary law from the theories that opposed it focused on one cardinal point—the authority of law. He readily conceded that both Roman law and natural rights theories presented many valuable ideas and useful inferences, but he strenuously rejected all attempts to assert that they had any legal or political authority. Instead, he constantly upheld the authority of customary law, in England as well as in maritime international matters. Obviously, Selden's insistence that customary law was authoritative begs the question of the source for such an authority. So we turn, now, to answering this query.

[9] MC b1c26. For modern scholarship recognizing Grotius' arguments as based on a 'Roman framework', especially his (one could almost say Gentilian) extension of the Roman private right to punish to the public sphere, see B. Straumann, 'The Right to Punish as Just Cause of War in Hugo Grotius' Natural Law', *Studies in the History of Ethics* (February 2006): pp. 15–16 and note 51.

[10] For Vazquez see MC b1c26, for Grotius see MC b1c26; and see sections 11 and 16–17 of the 'Prolegomena' to Grotius' *Jure Belli* for examples of the Dutchman's attempts to blunt the dichotomy between reason (and reason-based consent) on the one hand, and tradition (and expediency) on the other hand. See also Alan Cromartie, *Sir Matthew Hale 1609–1676* (Cambridge: Cambridge University Press, 1995), pp. 39–40.

The Moral Justification for Particular Law in the Jewish Legal Tradition

All custom draws its authority from being a form of common consent, a usage to which no one has successfully objected for time out of memory. It is thus a consent that resides not in each individual, or even in a simple majority, but rather in the widespread commitment to the history and institutions of a community. Early modern advocates of customary law emphasized two of its attributes which express its basis in common consent: it is continuous and is national. To properly understand these attributes and their grounds, it is sufficient to consider the characteristics shared by the types of legal systems which traditionalists opposed, be these based on Roman law, natural right, or even divine right: they were all a-historical and universal. To the advocates of customary law, it was these very characteristics which made universalist systems of law arbitrary and tyrannical.[11]

However, while medieval thought saw no essential conflict between natural and customary law, often regarding them as two aspects of one whole, the early modern stress on abstract a priori reasoning generated a tendency to regard the two as essential opposites. Thus, defenders of custom growingly faced claims that their particularism and their denial of universalist abstract reason meant customary legal systems were intrinsically contingent, even relativist, without any sure footing in firm and universal values. Selden was aware of this challenge to the English customary common law, and devoted his career to countering it, by developing arguments that could show customary legal systems were ultimately rooted in some universal values. As early as the mid-1610s Selden had already formulated the main components of his idea that true natural law was not an abstract unchanging structure, but rather one which was for the most part in continuous change and adaptation, upon a small core of unchanging principles. He briefly outlined this view in his 'Notes' to the 1616 edition of the famous medieval tract *De Laudibus Legum Angliae* by John Fortescue. However, Selden clearly needed a far more extensive apparatus of both legal theory and practice, by which to support and articulate this outlook. A theory out of tune with so much of the intellectual fashions of the day, such as the one he was putting forward, would need, among other things, to show grounds for obligation, for identification of the immutable part of natural law, and for the benefits of customary legal system. In this quest for a more comprehensive theoretical foundation for the common law as natural law, Selden eventually found what he was looking for, in what he came to regard as by far the most successful example of a customary legal system—the Jewish legal

[11] Although Roman law of course originated in an historical and particular system, early modern proponents like Gentili posited it had transcended those origins and become a universal system. For the common lawyers' arguments against Roman law see Arthur B. Ferguson, *Clio Unbound: Perception of the Social and Cultural Past in Renaissance England* (Durham, N.C.: Duke University Press, 1979), pp. 231–32, 268–70.

tradition.[12] In seventeenth-century Europe Hebrew and non-Hebrew Jewish texts (like Maimonides) had become an important element in the intellectual battles fought about social and political issues. This was so not only in the religious sphere where such texts were most naturally employed in the conflict between Catholicism and Protestantism, but also in other fields, from issues of marriage and divorce to debates about political and legal ideas. Milton, Hobbes, Harrington, and Grotius were only some of those making use of some Jewish sources in their writings. Overall, the employment of Jewish texts had the twofold objective of better understanding the ideas and history of early Christianity (which Selden for one viewed as beginning as a 'Reformed Judaism'), as well of learning from a Jewish repository of knowledge and wisdom that was regarded as no less significant than the classical Greek and Latin ones. In Selden's case there was the added objective—for one active as he was on the legal and political English stage—of learning from what he regarded as the oldest continuous national legal tradition.

Thus within the humanist and legal discourse of the seventeenth century alongside the habitual referring to classical Greek and Roman sources, as well as modern ones like Machiavelli and Bodin, the use of the Hebrew Bible or of Hellenized Jewish sources, more or less contemporary with the birth of Christianity, like Philo and Josephus, became common practice and even regarded as mark of good learning. However, early on in his career, Selden came to engage significantly with Talmudic and post-Talmudic Jewish ideas, an approach that was far more unusual and controversial. For, such ideas, originating after the Jewish rejection of Christianity, were inherently suspect of impiety, and usually treated with circumspection or open hostility by Christian scholars. While some slight peppering of one's writings with examples of later Jewish sources would not be objected to, Selden produced a massive output dealing with Jewish texts and ideas that had no parallel, even among his contemporaries who created the 'Hebrew Republic of Letters' of the early seventeenth century.[13]

The prevalent attitude among Selden's contemporaries was of disdain towards Talmudic and post-Talmudic Jewish ideas, which were often identified negatively with the 'pharisaical' formalism of the Jews that had been rendered obsolete by the spiritual 'new law' of Christianity. The Talmudists were regarded as engaging in worthless legalistic diatribes, as too stiff-necked to recognize their own doctrinal errors, and as engaging in the useless endeavour of recording and transmitting their national legal tradition when their nation was long gone. Selden's willingness not only to treat post-biblical Jewish texts with fairness and respect, but to accord their ideas significance and even authority, was virtually unheard of. Not surprisingly,

[12] Glenn Burgess, *The Politics of the Ancient Constitution* (London: Palgrave McMillan, 1992), p. 58; Paul Christianson, 'Young John Selden and the Ancient Constitution, ca. 1610–18', *Proceedings of the American Philosophical Society* 128, no. 4 (December 1984): pp. 277–9.

[13] The early seventeenth century pan-European Hebraist discussion, which we might call a Republic of Hebrew Letters, included on top of philologists and theologians, also prominent political writers like Bodin, Sigonio, Cunaeus, Grotius, Botero, Althusius, and of course Selden. See Charles W. A. Prior, 'Hebraism and the Problem of Church and State in England, 1642–1660', *The Seventeenth Century* 28/1 (2013): p. 42.

through the years both explicit and implicit criticisms were directed against him on this account.[14]

In the earliest stages of his Jewish scholarship, Selden too articulated the widespread notions which regarded the Talmudists as mystics, full of delusional, fantastical illusions. However as early as 1618, he had become sufficiently proficient in the Jewish tradition that his attitude towards it changed decisively, to one of intellectual respect and fascination that would eventually engender a colossal effort to learn, understand, and convey the Jewish traditions, as well as to decipher its intellectual and practical implications.

Perhaps the most crucial aspect which separated Selden's attitude to the Talmudic tradition from most of his contemporaries, was that while it was largely accepted among Christian writers that the Jewish nation had long ago died with the destruction of the Temple and the exile from the land, Selden pointed out that the Jews themselves held their nation to persist even in exile and dispersion. For Selden, who regarded the mark of a nation as the common submission of a people to its law, the decisive proof of the continued existence of a Jewish nation was the fact that Jews everywhere subjected themselves to their Talmudic national law. As a result of his view, Selden had to explain what the source for the authority of Jewish traditional law over the dispersed and exiled Jewish nation was. Obviously there was no worldly authority to enforce it, so why then did the Jews submit to this law? The source of this authority, Selden found, was not in some religious hope of personal heavenly reward, but rather an expectation of an eventual future national ingathering and political restoration of the Jewish state. That is, the dispersed and exiled Jews were a nation because they adhered to the belief that eventually they or their descendants would one day return to their land and live in a Jewish state. This was how Selden explained why the Jews still clung to laws regulating the payment of tithes some 1,500 years after the destruction of the Temple:

> Yet without doubt, most of them have long since [the destruction of the second Temple] expected a third Temple; otherwise why were they so carefull to have their Laws and speciall cases of first Fruits and Tithing, so copiously deliuered in five whole *Massecheths* of their *Talmud*, or body of their Civill and Canon Law, which was, many yeers after the destruction of the second Temple, made for the direction of the dispersed of their Nation?[15]

Such preserving through the centuries of seemingly irrelevant exact historical and practical information about tithes was directed at the 'dispersed' of the Jewish nation, only because of their continuing common expectation of a future national restoration, and a 'third Temple'. The above passage is from the 'Review' to his *The Historie of Tithes* (1618), and it reflects his consistent attitude to the Jewish nation in subsequent writings. Some thirty-five years later, in the second volume of his

[14] Donald R. Kelley, *The Human Measure: Social Thought in the Western Legal Tradition* (Cambridge, Mass.: Harvard University Press, 1990), pp. 68–9, 132–3. For Pufendorf's criticism of Selden on this count see T. J. Hochstrasser, *Natural Law Theories in the Early Enlightenment* (Cambridge: Cambridge University Press, 2000), pp. 66–7.

[15] 'Review', Selden, *The Historie of Tithes,* pp. 453–5.

Synedriis (published 1653), Selden reiterated his assertion that the Jews have never given up their God-given right to their promised land, and that they expect the council of the Great Sanhedrin (and thus, their legal and political independence) to eventually be restored, regardless of their long exile and dispersion.[16]

Although Selden's Jewish learning had been constantly expanding for many years, it appears that his immersion in Jewish learning and ideas as his foremost intellectual endeavour was owed to a fortunate result of unfortunate circumstance. As a consequence of his parliamentary activities in opposition to the crown, he was imprisoned in March 1629 without charge or time limit. Initially denied access to books or writing materials, by July he was eventually allowed to receive nineteen numbered and signed sheets of paper on which to take notes, as well a small number of books which had to be individually identified. On top of a volume of works by the Hellenistic satirist Lucian of Samosata, Selden requested the massive Babylonian and Jerusalem Talmuds, comprising the main corpus of the Jewish legal tradition—in the guise of two books he had gained access to a whole library.[17] It was in these circumstances, while enjoying what he sardonically described as 'the abundant leisure of prison' (tranquillo carceris abundatimus otio) that Selden came to plan a number of works on Jewish law. Although from early 1630 the conditions of his imprisonment were gradually eased and he was successively transferred to more congenial surroundings, it was only in May 1631 that he was actually freed from imprisonment, and all constrains on his liberty formally ended only in 1635. His studies of Jewish law eventually produced a massive output, which included: *De Successionibus in Bona Defuncti, seu Jure Haereditario ad Leges Ebraeorum* (1631), *De Successione in Pontificatum Ebraeorum* (1636), *De Jure Naturali et Gentium juxta Disciplinam Ebraeorum* (1640), *De Anno Civili et Calendario Veteris Ecclesiae seu Republicae Judaicae dissertatio* (1644), *Uxor Ebraica* (1646), and the *De Synedriis et Praefecturis Juridicis Veterum Ebraeorum* (1650–55).[18]

On top of these entirely Hebraist works, several other works by Selden were significantly indebted to his mature immersion in Jewish learning: the second edition of *Titles of Honor*, published in 1631, displays a vast increase in interest and knowledge of rabbinic matters, as compared with the 1614 first edition; Even the *Table Talk*, a collection of aphorisms from his later years, posthumously published in 1689 by Richard Milward, is replete with ideas, images, and phrases that are evidently culled from Jewish sources. Significantly, the *Mare Clausum* (1635) also benefited from Selden's considerable Jewish learning, and relies on rabbinic traditions for some of its crucial premises and arguments.[19]

16 John Selden, *De Synedriis et Praefecturis Juridicis Veterum Ebraeorum,* 3 vols. (1650–1655), b2c16. See also in *Synedriis* b2c15, and discussion in Toomer, *Scholarship*, pp. 762–3.

17 See in Toomer, *Scholarship* p. 804, about the still extant note written by Selden on 4 July 1629, while in prison, to Robert Cotton, requesting the latter to borrow for him the Talmud from the library of Westminster Cathedral.

18 See in the 'Prolegomena' to the first edition of *De Successionibus in Bona Defuncti, seu Jure Haereditario ad Leges Ebraeorum* (1631) pp. i–ii. See also Toomer, *Scholarship*, pp. 447–8.

19 The second edition of *Titles of Honor* is far more in line with the biblical version of the emergence of political society, as is the *Mare Clausum*. See Toomer, *Scholarship*, p. 167. The extent of

Selden's choice of the Jewish tradition as the vehicle for his reflections was not only the result of accidental circumstances which created a period of forced and relatively isolated immersion in Jewish legal texts. All evidence points to his believing early on into his project that he had found in the Jewish legal tradition an intellectual framework fitting and justifying his own ideas and propensities. By 1640, the year he published the *Jure Naturali*, Selden had already planned and partly written his two remaining major works on Jewish law, *Uxor Ebraica* and *Synedriis*. Thus, although he studied and published Hebrew ideas and texts for another fourteen years, the *Jure Naturali* is in many ways the culmination of his Jewish learning, certainly in the theoretical sphere. Accordingly, among Selden's many works on Jewish law and tradition, the one place where he presented most directly and cohesively his own theory of law and how it resembles the Jewish one is undoubtedly the *Jure Naturali*—especially so its first book, justly defined by Toomer as the most 'philosophical' of Selden's writings.[20]

The following passage from the *Jure Naturali*, may well serve as the epitome for Selden's mature outlook on the ideas of the Jewish tradition. After pointing out that many ideas and doctrines originating in pagan sources have been accepted, after due consideration, as compatible with Christianity, he asserted:

> In just the same way, this universal Hebrew doctrine contains (in accordance with the specific character, customs, abilities, and privileges of that nation) some elements that are more or less suited to Christianity, and others that are quite a bit different. But neither should be rejected or condemned solely on that account—in fact they should be welcomed with open arms, as a means of verifying or explaining a number of ideas already established in Christian thought.

This assessment of the Jewish ideas concerning universal obligations was applied by Selden to the whole of the Jewish tradition, stressing that even ideas deemed to conflict with Christian notions and values, should at least be given a leading role in the open investigation of truth and falsehood, 'just like the ideas of other philosophers (whether barbarian, Greek or Roman) who are no less frequently at odds with Christian doctrine'.[21]

In his treatment and understanding of the Jewish legal tradition, Selden went much further than in the above passage. Describing it as 'the specific character, customs, abilities, and privileges of that nation' he explicitly deemed it a national customary law, on a par with customary laws of European nations—England included. For him the Talmud:

> ... contains the ancestral and universally accepted teachings, interpretations and decisions of the Hebrews, just as we find Roman law in the digests, the codes, the *novellae*, and the

the *Table Talk*'s reliance on Jewish learning will become evident in the new edition Professor Jason Rosenblatt is currently working on.

[20] For Selden's own theory of natural law being very much the same as what he describes as the Jewish view, see Toomer, *Scholarship*, pp. 490–3, 560.

[21] *De Jure Naturali et Gentium juxta Disciplinam Ebraeorum libri septem* (1640) book 1 chapter 2—Henceforth abbreviated as JN b1c2.

Basilica; or French law in the edicts, constitutions, collections of customs and decisions of the French; or just as the same sources in Spain constitute the Spanish law, and in England the English law.[22]

However, the Jewish legal and political tradition also possessed some peculiar features which distinguished it from others, and made it especially significant in Selden's view. The first feature was its unusually lengthy continuity, for even according to the most modest claims about the length of the Jewish tradition, it was by far the earliest recorded case of an unbroken continuous national customary law. A second and even more peculiar feature of the Jewish legal tradition was that it was explicitly based on a sacred law, the Pentateuch, one that Christianity also deemed of divine origin. The implications of this second feature were manifold, on the one hand offering a connection of customary law to divine principles and morality, on the other hand implying a possible (and problematic) conflict with Christian interpretations of that law. Selden would thread onto this path carefully, stressing repeatedly and explicitly that all his claims and conclusions were subject to the 'authority of the Holy Scriptures themselves, and of true Christianity and the values contained within it'.[23]

Selden believed that exactly because of these two unique features, its exceptionally lengthy continuity and its origin in a sacred law, the Jewish legal tradition, more than any other, had devoted great efforts over a longer time-span and in a more systematic and self-conscious manner to understanding the nature and scope of universal values, and their relationship with particular legal systems.[24]

It was in his *Jure Naturali* that Selden offered a direct, comprehensive, and explicit treatment of the issue, which is in many ways at the heart of that work. He posited that, in effect, the Jewish tradition was the only place where such a 'universal philosophy of morals' could be found since:

[N]owhere else have the precepts of a nation, or the philosophy, theology and jurisprudence it practices, fixed and defined in such detail the provisions of natural or international law, or by general agreement so clearly distinguished it from other kinds of law that it could be made distinct like a single undifferentiated body whose name and function remain always the same, in both the authority it possesses and its control of the people.

That is, the Jewish tradition had 'fixed and defined' the provisions of a universal theory of moral law, that was not merely intended to justify the Jewish law and tradition, but that effectively offered a justification for all laws and traditions, as long as they did not transgress its core moral principles. Selden thus found in the

[22] JN 'Praefatio'.

[23] JN b1c2, and see also 'Praefatio'. Selden was on various occasions accused, both directly and indirectly, of being suspiciously partial to the Jewish tradition. See Rosenblatt, *Renaissance*, pp. 220–1.

[24] See JN b1c3, on the Hebrews as the only ones who deal with a whole universal natural law clearly and distinctly because of a consistent effort and one that received common consent from all schools and groups in their society. See also John Selden, *Uxor Ebraica* (1646), b1c1, on the connection to sacred law, where Selden notes that the civil law of the Hebrews, was 'partly Sacred Law' commanded in the Torah 'and partly ancestral custom and sanctions added by those who were in charge of such matters'.

Jewish tradition not merely another living system of national customary law based on universal principles, but the very theoretical framework which could underpin every such a system. It is to this theory that we now turn.[25]

Sanctity of Contract and 7 *Noahide Precepts*—the Universal Core for All Particular Legal Systems

Before turning to the theory of law that Selden observed in the Jewish tradition, we should consider that he recognized and addressed the two principal theoretical challenges that such an approach must face, if it is to endure: on the one hand, the danger of some simplistic identification of all customary law with moral and natural law; on the other hand, the danger of a natural and moral system that, by way of its universality, would altogether jettison customary law.[26]

Selden confronted the first danger directly, by drawing from Aristotle's notion of second nature, but directing it towards whole nations rather than individuals:

> Habit quite often wears the mask of nature, and we are deceived to the point where practices adopted by nations, based solely on custom, frequently come to seem like natural and universal laws of mankind.

In other words, a customary order certainly can deceive as to its universal import, and, although as 'custom' it is necessarily adapted to a society or several societies, it might nevertheless contradict the 'law of mankind'. Implied in Selden's observation is that national law, on top of being adapted to a people, must also conform to some universal moral standards that are relevant to all 'mankind'.[27]

From this consideration, Selden proceeded to raise the question that all those who studied customary laws, whether they supported or opposed them, had to address:

> Let us grant that in ancient times there existed, and there continue to exist, some customs practiced in the same way by all the nations, or by the more familiar or civilized ones, for example in contracts, inheritance, marriage, trials, treaties, and commerce—could customs of this sort ever acquire the force of natural or universal law, and the power to obligate or permit (without which it is pointless to talk about laws at all)?[28]

Selden's answer to this question was negative. He proposed that even if one did identify some customs common to all humanity, this universal identification had nothing to do with law—because for humans, law is 'the power to obligate or permit'. Thus, even if it was found, for example, that nowhere in the world did laws and customs ever sanction marriage between two males, or that nowhere was there

[25] JN b1c3.

[26] A prominent critic of customary English law was Thomas Hobbes, who regarded Common law as totally divorced from considerations of real equity and justice. See George L. Mosse, *The Struggle for Sovereignty in England* (East Lansing: Michigan State College Press, 1950), pp. 177–8.

[27] JN b1c6. [28] JN b1c6.

human flesh offered for sale in the marketplace, how would such a realization, by itself restrain in any way a society, or even individuals within it, from overturning this seemingly universal and natural law?[29]

This consideration enabled Selden to address the second challenge facing a justification of customary law. The above quote already implied that searching for *binding* moral and legal principles by means of what we would today call comparative law research was ultimately futile. However, as we may recall, Selden went further, also explicitly connecting this realization with his additional rejection of claims made for drawing universal laws from reason:

In fact, reason sole and simple, can persuade and demonstrate, but it cannot command or obligate us to perform our duties, unless it possesses an authority superior to the one who is being commanded.[30]

Selden thus rejected both avenues upon which the 'modern' natural rights theorists like Grotius were attempting to construct a binding system of universal or natural laws—the justification of natural rights by means of reason only, and a parallel, comparative research of laws, aimed at extracting from them the principles of the natural law observed by all nations. He argued that the Jewish legal tradition had identified this fallacy, and after reviewing the arguments on both sides, he observed that:

[W]e might perhaps be justified in concluding that the Hebrews were quite right to take no account of the behavior and institutions of any, or most nations in their definition of natural law.[31]

Having thus shown to his own satisfaction how the Jewish legal tradition rejected claims for a natural or universal law founded on either unassisted reason or comparative law, Selden then proceeded to propose that the same tradition also offered a unique approach that successfully overcomes the failings of other theories and methods—one which started with the principle of authority, and defined by it what natural and national law was.

Early on in the *Jure naturali* Selden addressed this issue thus:

Before we proceed to the specific provisions of this natural law, I would like the reader to have a proper understanding of just what the Hebrews thought it was, along with the duties shared by every person, by means of a general discussion of these issues. I would also like

[29] JN b7c3. Selden refers to a Talmudic passage and Rashi's commentary on it, in which the claim is made that there are only three commandments which all the sons of Noah actually observe: they do not draw up a marriage contact for males, they do not bring the flesh of the dead to the market, they show honour to the Tora. These are public aspects of the three most abhorrent sins in the Talmudical tradition: idolatry, murder, and forbidden sexual relations. In his discussion of the passage Selden shows he clearly understands the passage's point that the nations of the world keep these commandments only in public, therefore implying they do not necessarily do so in private. See discussion in Jason Rosenblatt, *Renaissance England's Chief Rabbi: John Selden* (Oxford: Oxford University Press, 2006), pp. 240–1.

[30] JN b1c7. [31] JN b1c6.

to avoid the problems that occur whenever people try on their own to distinguish this law, this philosophy and these duties from the Mosaic, or Pentateuchal law.[32]

Selden believed the Hebrew tradition identified two essential principles, from which the whole Jewish theory of law proceeded. The first principle was an anthropological claim, to the effect that all men and societies assume there is a principle of what we may call metaphysical equity, or in his words, 'a belief that there is a God, and he deals out recompense'. Selden stressed that not only in Judaism, Christianity, and Islam, but also among the Greeks, Romans, and other pagans, there always is a deity (or many, in the pagan case) which punishes 'the violation of the duties and laws that we are bound or obliged to observe'. This equity principle enforced the keeping of obligations, which is Selden's second essential principle, in effect the fundamental natural law, or rather a meta-law, since it is the prerequisite for the existence of any coherent legal, social, and political system. To a great extent, it could be said that for Selden the keeping of obligations is the *only* natural law, in the strict sense—one that all men and societies are expected to understand and accept.[33]

Now, allowing for Selden's theory of obligation does not by itself advance us in any way towards identifying particular stipulations of universal moral principles, other than the keeping of one's obligations. Moreover, while Selden certainly thought such moral principles did exist, and indeed had been identified by the Jewish tradition, he nevertheless had to explain why these were not to be found (at least not obviously so), in the one place one would expect them to appear, that most moral and Jewish of books, the Hebrew Bible. Selden allowed that the Hebrew Bible, and especially the Pentateuch, as the oldest and most extensive record of divinely sanctioned rules, was the obvious place where one would look for stipulations of the universal law. However, as he pointed out, although also containing 'the natural or moral laws and duties that are forever binding not just for the Hebrews, but for all humanity' the Mosaic corpus nevertheless was first and foremost a body of laws given to and applicable to the Hebrews only. Simply put, the problem was one of 'separating out the natural law from an integrated code of both natural and civil legislation' in order to isolate only those laws 'that are universally binding'. This difficulty was patently proved for Selden by the failure of so many later attempts to identify the universal laws contained in the Biblical account, such as the claims of some Christians of his own time that the Decalogue was the Universal law—a claim which Selden rejected completely, regarding the Decalogue as the centrepiece of the Mosaic law, explicitly given to the Hebrew nation only.[34]

Selden explicitly refused facile equations between the biblical law, or even the Decalogue only, and the natural law, instead regarding biblical legislation

[32] JN b1c3. [33] JN b1c4. See also JN b1c8.

[34] Sir Edward Coke was among those who described the Decalogue as the basis for the 'law of God', a phrase used vaguely and supposed to have some kind of inexact relationship to the law of nature, so that it could be useful as an appeal against the king's power. See Mosse, *Struggle*, pp. 149–50.

as merely the laws divinely ordained for the Jews particularly, and as such, like every just and moral legal system, inextricably combining both universal moral principles and particular stipulations binding one nation only. He stressed the difficulties of:

> … finding the best way out of the maze, separating things that are tangled together, navigating the twists and turns that separate truth from falsehood, and drawing conclusions from the external appearances of an idea as to the foundations or principles that lie beneath—such things are very difficult to achieve, almost beyond our grasp, and within the abilities of very few mortals.

He pointed out how so many great men had failed over the years in the task of individuating the natural law. This was because these men for all their great abilities, had worked with the 'ragged scraps of overly disputed ideas' and approached the problem according to different and discording schools or disciplines, while receiving assistance neither from the theologians or the philosophers of their own school of thought, to say nothing of those trained in another doctrine. The result was that nothing even approaching to an agreement was ever reached on the issue of natural law, neither among whole nations, nor among schools of thought, indeed not even among single important thinkers—with the one exception of the legal tradition of the Jewish nation.[35]

Selden described how the Jewish tradition long held that beyond the Mosaic precepts and the teaching of the Old Testament, that were 'their special heritage', there were also in the Bible some 'precepts of law and custom, which had their beginnings before there was writing or even letters, let alone Moses', and that all men 'were obligated to observe only these precepts'. He reported that, acting on this premise, Jewish scholars and jurists had over the years laboured to individuate and describe these precepts as separate from the Mosaic law, eventually identifying them as the seven Noahide principles.[36]

Selden asserted that the unusual diligence, cohesion, and continuity (and probably, it is implied, a measure of providential assistance invited by this very industry) of the efforts by the scholars of the Jewish nation to detect and define the natural laws from within the Biblical corpus, eventually resulted in their overcoming the great obstacles before them. It was precisely through its being such a cohesive and continuous national tradition, that Jewish customary legal thought alone, had achieved a feat 'within the abilities of very few mortals'.[37]

The Jewish tradition identified this corpus of laws commanded by God 'upon the human race', and called it Mizvot bnei Noah (Selden renders the term in Hebrew characters)—'the precepts or commandments of the children or descendants of Noah,' seven basic and general rules, six of them setting out prohibitions on idolatry, blasphemy, murder, forbidden sexual relations, theft, and eating limbs from a still living animal, while the seventh commands the establishing of a judicial system. These rules were obligatory on all men, and consequently any

[35] JN b1c3. [36] JN b1c1. [37] JN b1c3.

laws contradicting them were to be regarded as void, societies contravening them beyond the pale.[38]

The Jewish theory of natural law as distinct from the Mosaic law, is a natural law consisting of two components: an 'imperative' binding universal basis comprising one primary principle of keeping obligations, as well as seven general moral precepts; upon this basis there is a 'permissive' or 'limited' structure of particular laws, by which each nation then erected its own peculiar legal system. This two-tier edifice supplied for Selden the justification for particular and national legal systems—stemming from the obvious inability of basic principles to serve by themselves as a system of law, thus requiring national laws as particular stipulations fitting circumstances and necessities. In his own time, such particular legal systems tended in many cases to be traditional ones, but this was certainly not a necessary prerequisite; particular laws were legitimate even when not traditional, as long as they did not transgress the basic obligatory principles. However, Selden did believe that traditional legal systems had an advantage over other types, an advantage that we could term as the empirical function of long-lasting systems, and one connected with the fact that only the Jewish legal system, performing traditionally over a long time, rather than any rational or even inspired individual or group, had successfully recovered the Noahide principles for all humanity. Selden did not claim the Noahide principles had been given to the Jewish nation as revelation and by it preserved since in pristine form. For the Jewish people had received as direct revelation only the law particular to their nation, the laws of Moses, within which the Noahide principles were not immediately and distinctly apparent, any more than within English or Roman law. Rather, for Selden the Noahide principles had been revealed not only to the Hebrews but to all humanity (twice, at the time of Adam and then of Noah), but since that time they had been transmitted to posterity by traditions, so that all human societies that were not totally depraved, preserved, however unaware of it, some version or remnant of the original principles. But, if this was the case, and almost every society preserved some version or remnant of the Noahide dispensation, what if any was the special advantage of the Jewish teachings on this matter? Selden allowed that the Jewish nation indeed had the benefit of an unusually large number of inspired individuals within it, but such individuals also existed in other nations, and anyway the vagaries of history meant that the activities and records of inspired men were many times disrupted. Thus, for Selden the principal advantage of Jewish tradition was another—the unusually continuous and concerted efforts of the Jewish nation, for generations upon generations, striving to uncover, record, and preserve the basic universal principles. In other words, it was first and foremost the Jewish tradition of inquiry, discussion, and preservation that had succeeded in the task in which so many others, including even some of the greatest men who ever lived, had failed—identifying and framing a coherent and accepted set of universal laws. Though certainly aided by their receiving of their own national law

[38] JN 'Praefatio'. See also JN b1c10.

by direct divine revelation, and by the unusual numbers of inspired individuals among them, it was after all, the human-inspired and practiced traditions of the Jewish nation which, uniquely long and persistent, exclusively achieved the feat of identifying the universal laws of mankind.[39]

Selden proposed that the best shot to be had at identifying universal principles was indeed those labelled by the Hebrew juridical-politic tradition as the Noahide precepts. However, in his view, this identification was not made by the Jewish tradition recording some exact revelation about these principles—that would entail accepting this and other non-biblical Jewish traditions as revelation. Rather the Jewish tradition succeeded in this task because it was such a prolonged and continuous human tradition, which nevertheless was intentionally aimed at recovering and considering traces of providential light, within an acknowledged source of revelation (the Bible). In other words, not the data, but the method and approach of the Jewish traditional learning, were the decisive elements in this success. Instructively, in describing and analysing the Noahide principles, Selden never adopted towards them an attitude of unquestionable certainty affected by many writers on such matters. Advocating the principles identified by the Hebrews instead on a combination of high credibility with desirability, his analysis always retained a probabilistic aspect.[40]

Selden's theory of the Noahide principles as universal foundations of law, meant that all particular laws were to be regarded as equally 'natural' (to be kept because of the principle of obligation) as long as they did not contravene the seven general rules. Thus, the laws of every nation were a mixture of the universal Noahide principles and their particular laws, 'mashed into an indistinguishable pulp' in which no mere human being could simply distinguish one from the other, just as was the case of the Mosaic laws to the Hebrews:

> [T]he written law was itself partly a reiteration of these [Noahide] precepts, and partly an additional set of laws—those that were particular to the Hebrews—which were added on top of them.[41]

Thus, for Selden, as long as they did not contravene the universal precepts, all national laws consisted of a core of law common to all humans, on which each nation's system of law added a superstructure of laws particular to it. The universal precepts were: the basic rule of keeping obligations, that could be described as the only law that was properly speaking natural (since all societies had to uphold it in order to exist); and the seven Noahide precepts, which Selden preferred to describe as universal rather than natural, since they obligated all men, but were not innately known.[42]

[39] JN b1c3.

[40] For the discussion of the active intellect see JN b1c9; on the Noahide principles see especially JN b1c10 and MC b1c6–7; on the advantages of Jewish tradition see JN b1c3.

[41] JN b1c3, b1c6.

[42] This theory appears in both JN and MC. See in Oleg M. Roslak, 'John Selden and the Laws of England' (PhD dissertation, Cambridge, 2000), p. 30—the translation is Roslak's.

Now, in this scheme, any law or system of laws that did not conflict with the universal principles, was clearly legitimate—however arrived at. Nevertheless, as seen above, Selden maintained that customary law was vastly preferable to other types of legal systems. He offered two reasons for this, broadly connected with what has been described as the empirical and adaptive aspects of customary law. The first had very much to do with the success of the Jewish tradition in identifying the Noahide principles, that has been already been discussed above—what can be termed as the empirical function of a long-lasting customary law. He explicitly made the connection between the 'very great esteem that that philosophy and law of the Hebrews' were deserving of, and the fact that they had survived for such a long time. Indeed, the 'philosophy or law of the Hebrews' as the only surviving part of the wisdom of the ancient east (from which the Greeks and the west had learned), was to be assumed also to be the best part of that wisdom:

> [I]t would seem that anyone who considers the matter carefully cannot, for the same reasons, help but place the highest possible value on this philosophy or law of the Hebrews as being the best part and sole survivor of a great treasure, i.e. of the sum total of the barbarian philosophies of the East.

One could even say that with this passage, and others like it, Selden in a way inverted the theological Christian notion of testimony, so that the continuing existence of the Jews, notwithstanding all their plights, does not testify to their failure to accept the new divine law, but rather to their success in keeping the old one.[43]

Selden's second argument for preferring customary law, over other systems, had to do with its adaptive function. Selden clearly assumed, throughout his works, a division of humanity into nations, and customary law as the standard legal setting for each nation. But in *Jure Naturali* he added to these assumptions, a more ambitious postulation, one to be found implied in other works by him, but best presented in this one: that national law was, to a great extent, what a nation was about. Selden treated the 'Hebrews' as a continuous entity, existing from biblical times to his own, with its particular national customary law. He pre-empted possible claims about Jewish traditions and texts being arbitrary and spurious later inventions, by pointing out the manner in which their legal corpus is constructed, as a layered structure of continuous transmission and constant debate:

> But if anyone should have his doubts as to whether the Talmud and its writers are sufficiently accurate in their discussion of these sorts of issues; whether, that is, what the Talmud hands down to us bears any resemblance at all to the laws that the ancient Hebrews knew and used, let him rest assured that the text of the Talmud as we now have it, and the other authors who commented on it, come from the time right after the destruction of the Temple and the city. On this you may consult above all the authors who carefully and painstakingly transcribed the text of the Mishna and the Gemara.

[43] JN b1c2. See also JN b1c1.

Indeed, Selden added, before doubting the reliability of the Jewish legal corpus, one should doubt Justinian's laws or the accounts about many of the early fathers of the church, relying as these do, on reports about texts from hundreds of years ago, which many times lack any outside corroboration.[44]

However, as already mentioned, there was one additional and very unusual feature about the Jewish customary law: it had developed and survived almost wholly without the usual political or even territorial attributes of nations. The Mishna, Talmud, and latter commentaries came from times in which the Hebrews did not have an independent state, most of them from when the times they had been exiled and dispersed. If the corpus of customary Jewish law, the most significant element uniting the Jews in their exile and dispersion, was to be viewed as a national one—as Selden evidently did—it then necessarily became, in itself, pretty much what made and preserved that people as a nation. In this sense, the Jewish tradition became the supreme example for those wanting to uphold the merits of adaptive customary law; for in this case, not only the law had been adapted to the nation, but at the very same time it could also be said that the nation itself had become adapted to its law, indeed to a great extent became defined by it.

A Contractual International Maritime Law

As we saw, Selden was thinking about the issue of customary law based in universal principles at least since his 'Notes' to Fortescue, and he eventually found exactly what he was looking for in the Jewish traditions, both in the more circumscribed sphere of particular Jewish law (based on the unchanging Pentateuchal laws, but interpreted through an adaptive post-biblical tradition) and in the universal one of the Jewish concept of the Noahide principles.[45]

The important point for Selden was the principle of adaptation which accounted for two vital qualities of a living law (as opposite to universalist systems of law which were abstract and unchanging): on the one hand, the inevitable changes wrought by time and circumstances; on the other hand, the continuity, which made such law into a persistent entity throughout all its changes. This combination of change and persistence became a central component of his thought, and it appears that for Selden the very authority of customary law derived to a great degree exactly from this twofold quality of its adaptive character.[46]

This intellectual framework came to fruition when Selden was working on developing his theory of international maritime law. In the *Mare Clausum*, it is the underpinning for his theory, implied by both the categories into which he divides the law (book 1, chapter 3), as well as the grounding of his treatment of divine law (both the imperative and permissive types) solely on Jewish traditions (book 1, chapter 6). In the same book, one can find Selden returning to the image of

[44] JN b1c2. [45] See Ferguson, *Clio*, pp. 132–3, 207–8.
[46] Ibid., pp. 292–3, 296–7, and 330–1.

persistence through change, when he illustrates that 'those things which naturally are thus flitting, do notwithstanding in a Civil sens remain ever the same'.[47]

Selden remained part of the natural law tradition, although he reduced its scope to a small number of precepts that admitted a very wide variety of dispensations. He succeeded in this by positing the sanctity of contract as the one supreme principle prescribed by natural law, which then was regulated upon a small core of moral principles. Thus he created a notion of a moral and natural legal framework, which nevertheless allowed by the means of contract an original and radical freedom to voluntarily order civil societies, and systems of law.[48]

Selden's theory of international maritime law, which exerts a growing influence in today's seas, is thus one of customary and consensual contracting, which while allowing for great flexibility in content and form of practical arrangements, is at the same time securely anchored in the religious and moral principles of the Jewish legal tradition.

Bibliography

Barbour, Reid. *Measures of the Holy Commonwealth* (Toronto: University of Toronto Press, 2003).

Barnes, Thomas Garden. *Shaping the Common Law: From Glanvill to Hale, 1188–1688* (Stanford: Stanford University Press, 2008).

Brito, Mónica Vieira. 'Mare Liberum vs. Mare Clausum: Grotius, Freitas, and Selden's Debate on Dominion over the Seas'. *Journal of the History of Ideas* 64, no. 2 (July 2003): pp. 361–77.

Brook, Timothy. *Mr. Selden's Map of China* (London: Bloomsbury Press, 2013).

Burgess, Glenn. *The Politics of the Ancient Constitution* (London: Palgrave McMillan, 1992).

Christianson, Paul. 'Young John Selden and the Ancient Constitution, ca. 1610–18'. *Proceedings of the American Philosophical Society* 128, no. 4 (December 1984): pp. 277–9.

Cromartie, Alan. *Sir Matthew Hale 1609–1676* (Cambridge: Cambridge University Press, 1995).

Ferguson, Arthur B. *Clio Unbound: Perception of the Social and Cultural Past in Renaissance England* (Durham, N.C.: Duke University Press, 1979).

Groves, Steven, and Dean Cheng. 'A National Strategy for the South China Sea'. *Backgrounder—The Heritage Foundation* (24 April 2014).

Hochstrasser, T. J. *Natural Law Theories in the Early Enlightenment* (Cambridge: Cambridge University Press, 2000).

Holmes, James R. 'China's New Naval Theorist'. *The Diplomat* (11 July 2013).

Johnson, Keith. 'Lord of the Sea'. *Foreign Policy* (16 May 2014).

Kelley, Donald R. *The Human Measure: Social Thought in the Western Legal Tradition* (Cambridge, Mass.: Harvard University Press, 1990).

'Mapping China'. *The Economist* (18 January 2014).

[47] MC b1c3, b1c6, and b1c21.

[48] See discussion of this aspect in Robert Zaller, *The Discourse of Legitimacy in Early Modern England* (Stanford: Stanford University Press, 2007), pp. 348–9.

Mosse, George L. *The Struggle for Sovereignty in England* (East Lansing: Michigan State College Press, 1950).

Needham, Marchamont, trans. *Of the Dominion or Ownership of the Sea* (London: 1652).

Prior, Charles W. A. 'Hebraism and the Problem of Church and State in England, 1642–1660'. *The Seventeenth Century* 28/1 (2013): pp. 37–61.

Rosenblatt, Jason. *Renaissance England's Chief Rabbi: John Selden* (Oxford: Oxford University Press, 2006).

Roslak, Oleg M. 'John Selden and the Laws of England' (PhD dissertation, Cambridge, 2000).

Selden, John. *The Historie of Tithes* (London: 1618).

Selden, John. *De Successionibus in Bona Defuncti, seu Jure Haereditario ad Leges Ebraeorum* (London: 1631).

Selden, John. *Mare Clausum, seu De Dominio Maris* (London: 1635).

Selden, John. *De Jure Naturali et Gentium juxta Disciplinam Ebraeorum libri septem* (London: 1640).

Selden, John. *Uxor Ebraica* (London: 1646).

Selden, John. *De Synedriis et Praefecturis Juridicis Veterum Ebraeorum.* 3 vols (London: 1650–1655).

Selden, John. *The Dissertation of John Selden Annexed to his Edition of Fleta* [1647], translated by Robert Kelham with notes (London: 1771).

Straumann, Benjamin. 'The Right to Punish as a Just Cause of War in Hugo Grotius' Natural Law'. *Studies in the History of Ethics* , 2/2006 (electronic journal at: http://www.historyofethics.org/): pp. 15–16 and note 51.

Theutenberg, Bo Johnson. 'Mare Clausum et Mare Liberum'. *Arctic* 37, no. 4 (December 1984): pp. 481–92.

Toomer, G. J. *John Selden: A Life in Scholarship* (Oxford: Oxford University Press, 2009) 2 vols.

Zaller, Robert. *The Discourse of Legitimacy in Early Modern England* (Stanford: Stanford University Press, 2007).

Ziskind, Martha A. 'John Selden: Criticism and Affirmation of the Common Law Tradition'. *The American Journal of Legal History* 19, no. 1 (January 1975): pp. 36–7.

PART II

HUMAN RIGHTS, BETWEEN HISTORY, THE INTERNATIONAL AND RELIGION

6

The Religion/Secularism Debate in Human Rights Literature

Constitutive Tensions between Christian, Islamic, and Secular Perspectives

John Haskell

Introduction: The Anxiety of Religion

The tension between religion and secularism within the field of human rights is a popular topic in contemporary international legal scholarship. The purpose of this chapter is to map out the argumentative logic that guides the narrative choices within the literature and highlight some difficult methodological and theoretical questions, which I believe are too often glossed over by its authors. To undertake this style of analysis is to resist the (often useful) temptation to focus on what might actually 'exist on the ground' and instead analyse how a particular literary trope (religion/secularism) functions within a disciplinary field of knowledge production (international legal scholarship). In other words, the object of this analysis is the 'legal form' of the journal article concerning international law and its target is the 'interpretive community' within academia, which in turn elicits two questions to guide this study.[1] First, how does the juxtaposition of 'religion/secularism' order the direction and disagreements between authors, and second, what does this ordering illuminate about the broader disciplinary logic?[2] This seems especially important because contrary to a significant body of scholarship that points to the Cold War and the War on Terror as seminal events in the 'turn to religion', religion has played a significant role in the development of Western international legal doctrines since its inception as a disciplinary expertise and source of policy

[1] Cf. David Kennedy, 'The Politics of the Invisible College: International Governance and the Politics of Expertise', *European Human Rights Law Review* 5 (2001): p. 463; Sahib Singh, 'Positivism and New Approaches to International Law', in *International Legal Positivism in a Post-Modern World*, edited by Jean d'Aspremont and Jörg Kammerhofer (Cambridge: Cambridge University Press, 2014).

[2] For an example of this investigation, Nathaniel Berman, 'The Sacred Conspiracy: Religion, Nationalism, and the Crisis of Internationalism', *Leiden Journal of International Law* 25, no. 1 (2012): p. 9.

knowledge.[3] Secularism and religion, in this sense, may be viewed as a productive tension within international law, not simply because it offers the possibility of general self-reflection about our disciplinary assumptions and practices (which is important), but more specifically, because it provides direct evidence of how arguments are shaped and ordered, how positions are distinguished and put into action, or even how international legal scholars construct their personalities and derive a sense of purpose or agency through the text. What is at stake here is to reveal the aesthetics within which international law is cast through a study of 'those recurrent forms that shape the creation, apprehension, and identity of law'.[4]

The study here focuses specifically on the tensions between Islam, Christianity, and liberal secularism in the context of human rights. On a theoretical level, the chapter attempts to map out the contemporary argumentative logic that shapes the available narrative choices, highlight difficulties that arise in whatever direction is privileged, and draw out some potentially questionable assumptions that often seem to guide these scholarly arguments. From a 'methodology' standpoint, the chapter seeks to foreground a series of difficulties when approaching the topic of law and religion that tend to be ignored and develops a tentative blueprint for potentially fruitful studies in the future. The dominant critique that I will develop is that international legal scholarship, when it seeks to explain or negotiate the apparent conflict between secularism and religion in relation to human rights, ultimately tends to rely on extremely parochial, if not metaphysical, arguments—what we might term, 'transcendental nonsense'—that reinforces the authority of distinctly Western liberal institutional actors.[5] Of course, to speak explicitly of theory and method in the study of international law and religion requires a certain letting go of immediate preoccupations, but my feeling here is that there is a certain rigidity or predictable rehearsal of rhetorical moves within contemporary debate around this subgenre that may require as a point of pragmatic necessity a certain stepping back and starting over at the beginning to inspect the analytical toolkits we carry with us into the field.

Modes of Argument in the Religion and Human Rights Debate

The goal in this section is to briefly outline the variety of argumentative forms deployed by legal scholars when addressing the tension between religion and

[3] It is a common assertion that religious sprung front and centre within global policy making and academic analysis in the aftermath of the Cold War—often discussed under the label, 'post-secularism'. For a general discussion of this theme, Peter Berger, ed., *The Desecularization of the World: Resurgent Religion and World Politics* (Grand Rapids, Mich.: W. B. Eerdmans, 1999).

[4] Pierre Schlag, 'The Aesthetics of American Law', *Harvard Law Review* 115, no. 4 (2012): pp. 1051, 1053.

[5] For the original discussion invoking this term 'transcendental nonsense', Felix Cohen, 'Transcendental Nonsense and the Functional Approach', *Columbia Law Review* 35, no. 6 (1935): p. 809. For a rigorous analysis of this idea closer to the context that informs our study here, Louis Althusser, *For Marx* (first published 1965, Verso 2005), pp. 87–128, 219–48.

secular human rights. At the most general level, authors tend to invest either term with positive or negative traits, that then are broken down into more specific variations, and which can lead to different conclusions. The terms of analysis, however, are relatively generalizable in that they operate similarly regardless of the specific object of analysis. To see this, we will first address how scholars discuss religion in its positive and negative attributes and then follow with a similar analysis concerning secular human rights in order to demonstrate how these differences within the literature nevertheless share a common logic.[6]

It is commonplace for the literature to posit religion (in varying degrees) as not only an important, but a positive trait, in society and international law. First, religion is located as an intrinsic source of personal and collective identity, and which is a key dynamic in the development of international legal doctrines related to human rights. Some scholars distinguish between religions, usually to assert that human rights are situated specifically within the Christian legacy. 'Christianity has functioned for the normative self-understanding of modernity as more than a mere precursor or a catalyst,' explains Habermas, 'Egalitarian universalism ... [and the value of] individual morality of conscience, human rights and democracy, is the direct heir to the Judaic ethic of justice and the Christian ethic of love. To this day, there is no alternative to it ... Everything else is just postmodern talk.'[7] Even if accepted as true, scholarship is further divided over the ramifications of this tradition within the positive approach to religion. Within one camp of scholars, the exclusively Christian origins of human rights suggests that its norms will not carry over to non-Western institutional contexts—the 'clash of civilizations' argument advanced by authors such as Huntington.[8] Here, Islam is usually associated with 'the exercise of power' and the incapacity to distinguish 'between religious and secular aspects of life', which results in Muslim country's lack of 'openness to debate, self-questioning and change'.[9] Though often identified with more conservative American-oriented perspectives and international relations scholars, the inherent distinction between a Christian heritage conducive to human rights and an Islamic tradition incompatible with many of the basic foundations for democratic life is prevalent within European legal thought, perhaps most famously

[6] For an example of this type of mapping, Duncan Kennedy, 'A Semiotics of Critique', *Cardozo Law Review* 22, no. 3–4 (2001): p. 1147.

[7] Jürgen Habermas, *A Conversation About God and the World: Time of Transitions* (first published 2001, Polity 2006), pp. 149, 150–1.

[8] Samuel Huntington, *The Clash of Civilizations and the Remaking of World Order* (New York: Simon & Schuster, 1996). Nor is this assumption about the lack of translation restricted to more conservative scholars; Charles Taylor, 'Modes of Secularism' in *Secularism and Its Critics*, edited by Rajeev Bhargava (New Delhi: Oxford University Press, 1998), pp. 35–6. For an argument that the human rights tradition originated from the Christian tradition, but is an inadequate substitute for its religious foundations, John Milbank, 'Against Human Rights: Liberty in the Western Tradition', *Oxford Journal of Law and Religion* 1, no. 1 (2012): pp. 203–34.

[9] Bernard Lewis, *Islam and the West* (New York: Oxford University Press, 1994), pp. 134–5. For a general but insightful analysis into this literature, Elizabeth Hurd, 'Political Islam and Foreign Policy in Europe and the United States', *Foreign Policy Analysis* 3, no. 4 (2007): p. 345. DOI: 10.1111/j.1743-8594.2007.00054.x.

with the contemporary jurisprudence of the European Court of Human Rights (ECHR). Noting that democratic pluralism 'has been dearly won over the centuries' within the Western European experience, the Court in *Refah Partisi* held that Shari'a is 'incompatible with the fundamental principles of democracy, as set form in the Convention', relying on the assumption that Islam was an 'invariable religion' where 'pluralism in the political sphere' and the 'evolution of public freedoms have no place'.[10]

Against this approach, other scholars argue that human rights are capable of translation into non-Christian contexts, such as Islam. For some authors, the origins of human rights are situated within the Christian tradition, but equally tap into universal concerns of humanity and hence may be readily adapted to fit other systems of belief and governance. For instance, Harold Berman locates the privileged working of the Holy Spirit in the development of Western jurisprudence (in response to Roman Catholic, Lutheran, and Calvinist teaching), but argues that it intimates a 'World Law' with the 'mission of universal community' that accommodates and brings together 'the multiple cultures of the world, guiding all races of men ... to dwell together on the face of the earth in peace and in justice'.[11] For others, human rights is not restricted to a single birthright or birthplace, but is actually embedded in all traditional religious systems. 'The principles enshrined in the Universal Declaration of Human Rights', Kofi Annan argues, 'can be found in the teaching of all the world's great cultural and religious traditions.'[12] In this variation, scholars often turn to traditional Islamic texts and practices to demonstrate the presence of the entire gamut of human rights principles, only expressed in culturally specific forms, usually concluding with an appeal for the international community to adopt a 'dialogical rather than a confrontational' attitude towards Muslim states and recognize that 'Islamic law can play a very important role in the realization of human rights'.[13] And yet, for many scholars within these styles of argument, it is not simply that human rights stems from religious origins and should hence accommodate the dynamics of religious faith, but a more profound claim that religion is the very animating spirit of law, what gives it normative force

[10] Case of *Refah Partísí (the Welfare Party) and Others v. Turkey* (2010) 37 ECtHR 42. For a discussion of the decision in a broader legal/political context within Europe, David Dyzenhaus, 'Headscarves, Extreme Speech and Democracy' <http://www.law.uwo.ca/publiclaw/PublicLaw_Documentas/Headscarves_ExtremE_Speech.pdf> accessed 12 April 2015.

[11] Harold Berman, 'World Law: An Ecumenical Christian Jurisprudence', *Fordham International Law Journal* 18 (1995): pp. 1617, 1630–2.

[12] Kofi Annan, The Secretary General, 'Universal Declaration of Human Rights Illuminates Global Pluralism and Diversity' (The Fiftieth Anniversary Year of the Universal Declaration of Human Rights, Tehran 10 December 1997) <http://www.unhchr.ch/Huricane/Huricane.nsf/60a520ce334aaa77802566100031b4bf/82ed5e4c1f33163cc125662e00352f62?OPenDocument> accessed 12 April 2015.

[13] Mashood Baderin, 'Human Rights and Islamic Law: The Myth of Discord', *European Human Rights Law Review* 2 (2005): pp. 163, 183. Occasionally, scholars push this logic further to argue that Islamic law is not only compatible but goes further to protect human dignity than what is possible within a secular human rights framework; cf. John Zinkin, 'Islam and CSR: A Study of the Compatibility between the Tenets of Islam, the UN Global Compact and the Development of Social, Human and Natural Capital', *Corporate Social Responsibility and Environmental Management* 14, no. 4 (2007): p. 206.

and communal cohesion. 'Religion gives law its spirit,' writes John Witte Jr., 'the sanctity and authority it needs to command obedience and respect ... its structural fairness, its "inner morality" ... its authority and legitimacy.'[14] It is not simply that religion can accommodate human rights, in other words, but rather that human rights is itself the product of religious values 'in the world', and as such demands its spiritual grounding to remain effective in human experience.[15]

In a related argument that religion plays a benevolent function in the development and implementation of human rights, scholars often juxtapose a religiously inspired respect for 'human dignity' against the twentieth-century horrors of European totalitarian political regimes. No longer is it simply that liberal doctrines 'free-ride' off religion and the deep normative commitments it engenders, but the frequent hostility to religious passions as 'dangerous' or 'authoritarian' obscure the crimes of modern secularism. Here, scholars, such as Michael Perry, often provide statistical accounts of 'the countless, grotesque inhumanities of the twentieth century' to demonstrate there is no necessary link between religion and violence, or conversely, between secularism and tolerance.[16] The ECHR jurisprudence, in this perspective, is not the preservation but perversion of tolerance, under the rubric of human equality and freedom authorizing a militant secularism that invokes the machinery of the state apparatuses to coerce individuals and communities to forego the tenets of their faith (e.g., Muslim women to remove their headscarves).[17] In this context, religion now functions as an important check on 'state-ism' by holding out an ethical framework that eclipses the authority of the sovereign. 'Religion defied the evil assumptions of Nazis, Fascists, and Communists alike' and preserved the belief in human dignity against 'the gulags and death camps, iconoclasm and book burnings, propaganda and mind controls'.[18] Against polemics for human rights or religion, at the expense of the other, here the point is that both phenomena are part of a shared heritage of humanity and rely upon the other to discipline its excesses, inspire new ideas, mobilize popular support, and provide sufficient answers to normative values.[19]

If religion is an intrinsic aspect of human identity that may be mobilized to buttress human dignity and reign in political excess, a substantial body of literature emphasizes that religion can also spawn dangerous passions that lead to oppressive governments and suppress basic human rights. For many scholars, though they may pay lip service to religion or argue that it may be reformed, religion is

14 John Witte Jr., 'Law and Religion: The Challenges of Christian Jurisprudence', *University of St Thomas Law Journal* 2, no. 2 (2005): p. 9.

15 Richard Falk, 'Religion and Global Governance: Harmony or Clash', *International Journal of World Peace* 19 (2002): p. 3.

16 Michael Perry, 'The Morality of Human Rights: A Nonreligious Ground?', *Emory Law Journal* 54 (2005): pp. 97, 100.

17 Kathryn Boustead, 'The French Headscarf Law before the European Court of Human Rights', *Journal of Transnational Law and Policy* 16, no. 2 (2007): pp. 167, 193.

18 John Witte Jr., 'A Dickensian Era of Religious Rights: An Update on Religious Human Rights in Global Perspective', *William and Mary Law Review* 42, no. 3 (2001): pp. 707, 769–70.

19 Heiner Bielefedt, 'Western versus Islamic Human Rights Conceptions? A Critique of Cultural Essentialism in the Discussion of Human Rights', *Political Theory* 28, no. 1 (2000): p. 90.

deeply entwined in parochial, anti-progressive tendencies. This perspective may target Christian or Islamic communities, and often differs as to what specifically is at stake (e.g., what type of violence, what or whom stands to be suppressed). When directed against Christianity, there is a long tradition within international law writing where authors expose how seemingly 'neutral' laws or political events are in fact rooted in Christian-oriented prejudices, or alternatively, how Christianity is not only a restorative but also deeply unstable drive that must be cautiously managed through a strategy of containment. Even in the interwar period, as Nathaniel Berman has demonstrated, a dominant strand of intellectual thought worried that religion, as a 'primitive' force in society, could trigger 'fierce' passions, which might infect the aspirations of Western populations like a contagious disease, and lead to the destabilization and breakdown of modern 'bourgeois' life.[20] This wariness towards religion is replete in contemporary literature condemning the encroachment of religion into the secular public sphere within domestic or regional contexts (e.g., church/state legal arguments in the United States, uneven treatment of Christian and Muslim religious practices in Europe), and equally, on the international level, often comes up as a theme within the 'war on terror' to argue that military action abroad or police actions at home are not so much about security as they are a new 'Crusade', a Christian form of jihad against 'the Other'.[21] 'The war in Iraq,' argues Antony Anghie, 'replicates many of these ancient structures of ideas ... [that assumed] the right to wage 'just war' is restricted to Christian states.'[22] The assertion that given political or legal action by Western governments is due to considerations of basic human dignity ignore how their supposed neutrality ends up consistently privileging Christian, Western populations, and often relies on traditional stereotypes of Muslims.[23] 'I must admit I am not a supporter of the Universal Declaration of Human Rights. Our history of civilization has taught us to be wary of big and noble words as the reality of our history has taught us how big words can be transformed into atrocious crimes,' writes Ismat Sayf al-Dawla, 'We must never forget either that the United Nations Organization issued the Universal Declaration of Human Rights in the same year that it recognized the Zionist state that usurped Palestine and robbed its people of every right stipulated in the Declaration.'[24] In this line of argument, within the Christian legacy itself is a drive to hegemonic practices and oppressive prejudices, which are periodically tapped into by governments at the expense of non-Christian (usually formerly colonized) populations.

[20] Nathaniel Berman, 'Modernism, Nationalism, and the Rhetoric of Reconstruction', *Yale Journal of Law and the Humanities* 2, no. 4 (1992): pp. 354–59, 363–66.

[21] For the classic argument that non-Western populations function as the constitute temptation of the 'Other' to 'Western' intellectuals and policy makers, Edward Said, *Orientalism* (first published 1978, Vintage Books, 1978).

[22] Antony Anghie, 'The War on Terror and Iraq in Historical Perspective', *Osgoode Hall Law Journal* 43, no. 1 (2005): pp. 45, 63.

[23] Mahmood Mamdani, *Good Muslim, Bad Muslim: America, the Cold War, and the Roots of Terror* (New York: Doubleday, 2005).

[24] Ismat Sayf al-Dawla, 'Islam and Human Rights: Controversy and Agreement', *Minbar al-Hiwar* 9 (1988): p. 33.

More often within the literature, however, Islam is the target of critique for scholars worried about the excesses of religiosity. As illustrated beforehand, writing within academia and the judiciary often makes the case that there is some historical or philosophical discord between human rights and (at least 'traditional') Islam. A central trope within this argument is that there is something inherently restrictive within the tradition of Islam that clashes with Western respect for human freedom. One technique often made by scholars is to link 'terrorist' acts to Islamic fundamentalism, which is typically part of a larger assumption that Islam carries a predilection to violence, especially towards non-believers. 'Islamic law enjoins Moslems to maintain a State of permanent belligerence with all non-believers,' writes Roda Mushkat, 'The Muslims are, therefore, under a legal obligation to reduce non-Muslim communities to Islamic rule in order to achieve Islam's ultimate objective, namely the enforcement of God's law (the Shari'a) over the entire world.'[25] If this sort of characterization is found predominantly among authors with conservative persuasions, a much more common technique is to focus on how Muslim states and Islamic practices restrict an individual's freedom of expression, especially in relation to gender equality and the freedom to proselytize. Pointing to reservations made by Muslim countries to international legal instruments, such as CEDAW or the UDHR, scholars such as Hilary Charlesworth and Ann Mayer focus predominantly on how Muslim governments actively suppress the self-determination of women (and other minorities), which is in turn explained as the direct result of the government's observation of Islam itself. 'Islamic governments, when pressured to observe Islam,' writes Hilary Charlesworth, 'have tended to enunciate policies that have a differential impact upon the weaker elements of society, particularly women and minorities ... Indeed, many Shari'a precepts are based on distinctions between humans—Muslims and non-Muslims, men and women.'[26] Other scholars that also see Muslim states as particular guilty of infringing individual self-determination or political radicalism differ to the extent that blame is not placed on Islam itself, but rather on extra-legal prejudices cloaked in a religious vernacular for pragmatic reasons, or alternatively, on particular interpretations of religious texts and practices, which are by no means privileged over more tolerant alternatives.[27] In this sense, the danger of religion, and particularly Islam, is not so much something fundamental to the religion itself but how it can be manipulated, consciously and unconsciously, to further all-too-human anxieties and interests.

The goal then for many scholars directly writing on the positive and negative traits of religion is to discover its authentic expressions. The difficulty, acknowledged by many scholars, is that different religious traditions and their diverse

[25] Roda Mushkat, 'Is War Ever Justifiable? A Comparative Survey', *Loyola of Los Angeles International Comparative Law Review* 9, no. 2 (1987): p. 227.

[26] Hilary Charlesworth, 'The Challenges of Human Rights Law for Religious Traditions', in *Religion and International Law*, edited by Mark Janis and Carolyn Evans (The Hague: Martinus Nijhoff Publishers, 1999), pp. 401, 411; Ann Mayer, *Islam and Human Rights: Tradition and Politics* (Boulder, Colo.: Westview, 2006).

[27] Mahmood Mamdani, 'Whither Political Islam?', *Foreign Affairs* 84, no. 1 (2005).

cultural expressions will often place varying weight on particular principles, even if agreed upon, and develop alternative vocabularies and institutional processes for implements these norms.[28] For instance, though secular human rights advocates and Muslim policy makers may both stress the importance of human dignity, they can radically differ in relation to tensions concerning communal versus individual identity or between rights and duties.[29] Likewise, the exact mode of how to advance a more just and peaceful world is often a rich terrain of disagreement: should Muslim countries be reformed by coercive tactics that enforce liberal governance structures or should it happen through more gentle internal persuasion using Islamic doctrines? Can the unequal treatment of women be squared with the human right to formal equality under the law or is this an irreconcilable difference that initiates a zero-sum game? And so forth. Whatever their particular differences, authors tend to share a common tactic of distinguishing between authentic and inauthentic modes of religious expression or justification, and peg this question to whether the given action or law contributes to the self-determination and well-being of people, however these terms might be defined.

A strikingly familiar set of analytical moves are made by scholars focusing on the virtues and dark sides of secular human rights in relation to religious systems of community and governance. First, the argument that human rights are intrinsic to human identity is repeated, often with authors depicting human rights values developing out of the distant past (e.g., Biblical sources, ancient Rome or Greece), through the gauntlet of religious and political conflicts of the early and late modern periods (usually within Western Europe), before coming into fruition and applicable to global society, usually marked by the post-Second World War codification efforts and the emergence of post-Cold War institutional apparatuses to advance human rights norms.[30] In this vein of argument, the point is not that human rights and religion may share historical or philosophical overlaps, but that human rights are distinctly privileged because they are rooted in the concrete, material reality of everyday life and function as the grounding standard upon which all claims, religious or otherwise, are to be judged. 'The human rights ideology, aiming at universality … has eschewed invoking any theistic authority … does not see human rights as integral to a cosmic order … does not derive from any sacred text,' writes Louis Henkin, 'Its sources are human, deriving from contemporary human life in human society … [that] reflects a universal contemporary moral intuition.'[31] If

[28] Duncan Kennedy, 'A Critique of Rights in Critical Legal Studies', in *Left Legalism/Left Critique*, edited by Wendy Brown and Janet Halley (North Carolina: Duke University Press, 2005), pp. 195–6.

[29] Peter Danchin, 'Suspect Symbols: Value Pluralism as a Theory of Religious Freedom in International Law', *Yale Journal of International Law* 33, no. 1 (2008): p. 1.

[30] For a description of this imagined trajectory, David Kennedy, 'Images of Religion in International Legal Theory', in *Religion and International Law*, edited by Janis and Evans (The Hague: Martinus Nijhoff Publishers, 1999), pp. 145, 146. For a critique of this perspective, John Haskell, 'Divine Immanence: The Evangelical Foundations of Modern Anglo-American Approaches to International Law', *Chinese Journal of International Law* 11, no. 3 (2012): p. 426.

[31] Louis Henkin, 'Religion, Religions and Human Rights', in *Does Human Rights Need God*, edited by Elizabeth Bucar and Barbara Barnett (Grand Rapids, Mich.: W. B. Eerdmans, 2005), pp. 146, 148.

some scholars have emphasizes that religion provide the deep foundation for the legitimacy of human rights norms, here the tables are switched: exactly because there is no ultimately agreement on whether there is a God or who that God is, the most stable foundation for any normative ordering is to be found in authentic human experience, which allows the most immediate and reliable material for developing and testing ethical intuitions. This is not to suggest that religion cannot be compatible with human rights norms—in fact, the goal is not to eradicate religion but to reform it to fit into the rubric of human rights—but rather, that human rights, as the logical conclusions derived from neutral (yet benevolent) observation, is the privileged vehicle for the ethical mooring of global governance.

Second, in a closely related argument, advocates for secular human rights also tend to provide justifications for the conceptual vocabulary and institutional implementation of the regime on the basis that it functions as a powerful check on political (and now, also religious) excesses. The background assumption here is that since religious belief requires individuals or communities that do the believing, it contains an intrinsically anthropomorphic feature, and is therefore inescapably political. Religious passion, in other words, is only another form of political passion, which itself is a subset of 'human' passion, and it is exactly the 'human' subject that human rights is specifically tailored to address and protect. Indeed, if some authors excused religious normative frameworks on the basis that its excesses and irrationalities were due to some inauthentic or extra-religious cause, secular human rights advocates posit that there is never anything but particular human (and thus, political) reasons behind any legal or religious claim and this awareness allows for more concrete appraisals of what particular dynamics are actually involved in a given series of effects: in short, secular human rights thinking cuts through religious ideology.[32] When scholars take this approach, the literature usually turns to examples of religiously oriented state laws that impose restrictive, and sometimes violent, measures on the personal freedom and material well-being of women or minority populations, which in turn usually sets the stage for an analysis of the necessity and difficulties in implementing some given set of human rights norms depending on a the particular situation under investigation. To the extent that non-religious state administrations also have a track record of human rights abuses (e.g., colonialism, fascism, the Holocaust), their prevalence is generally explained as 'aberrational' or 'quasi-religious' moments, which exactly because these moments can be depicted as moral failures, is proof of the continued viability and non-partisan nature of the secular human rights framework to identify and discipline dangerous passions, domestic or foreign.[33] Rather than sharing complicity, human rights is the reward of a mentality disciplined of its fantasies.

[32] The fact that every universal claim demands its articulation from a particular standpoint means on the one hand, that there is no scandal in revealing a specific perspective, and on the other hand, that this awareness allows for a closer study of what is 'actually going on' when a universal is posited. For a discussion of this theme, Martti Koskenniemi, 'International Law in Europe: Between Tradition and Renewal', *European Journal of International Law* 16, no. 1 (2005): pp. 113, 115.

[33] For an example of this position, Martti Koskenniemi, 'Human Rights, Politics and Love', in *The Politics of International Law* (Oxford: Hart Publishing, 2011), p. 153.

So secular human rights is intrinsic (and by extension, universal) to human experience, protects individual and collective self-determination, and reigns in political excesses—all which looks like a repeat of the claims made by legal scholars about the positive role of religion in global governance. These similarities carry over to how the literature critiques human rights ideas and practices. On the one hand, the formally equal procedural rights advanced by secular human rights are challenged as inherently unequal: either subtly encoded with Western Christian biases (e.g., the strict separation of private and public spheres, the emphasis on individual rights at the expense of communal duties) or applied hypocritically whereby victims within or the result of Western governance are depicted as unfortunate or naturalized effects of an imperfect world, rather than human rights violations perpetuated by an identifiable Western system or state actor. If cultural relativist approaches are criticized by secular human rights advocates to the extent they allow non-Western countries to cynically justify oppressive measures in the name of their cultural interpretation of religious principles, human rights norms are equally prone to being criticized as remarkably thin justifications for otherwise egregious violations of human dignity.

In this sense, secular human rights arguments are flipped around again: rather than pierce through ideology to discern the actual dynamics of history, it actually advances only another set of ideological traps that cloud the actual cultural and political aggression that is part of the human rights regime. This occurs in any number of ways. For example, secular human rights scholars tend to assume a link between the spheres of religion and politics, in that Islam (if understood even in all its particular expressions and diverse practices) is posited as a cause for some legal or political action. As Mamdani points out, what this misses is that 'contemporary fundamentalism is a modern political project' where 'Cold Warriors turned traditional institutions ... and traditional stimulants such as opium, to modern political purposes on a scale previously unimagined with devastating consequences.'[34] The idea of the Muslim serves, in other words, as a banner for political projects that are actually the responsibility and guilt of Western-oriented liberal state regimes. Often these critiques take a historical turn among authors writing in international law. The conceptual artifice and implementation of a secular liberal rule of law is deeply enmeshed in the colonial experience, and maintains its past inequalities, conceptually and materially.[35] The purpose of the narrative in this context is to analogize disparate moments, which can be linked together through historical materials (primarily key academic texts, legal instruments, archival data, and secondary literature on great power politics and the development of institutional settings), in order to reveal that the contemporary system's justifications are merely that, justifications, for what is a deeply exploitative and oppressive structure of governance, all of which disadvantages former colonized groups, such as Muslim

[34] Mahmood Mamdani, 'Good Muslim, Bad Muslim: A Political Perspective on Culture and Terrorism', *American Anthropologist* 104, no. 3 (2002): p. 766.

[35] Victor Kattan, *From Coexistence to Conquest: International Law and the Origins of the Arab-Israeli Conflict 1891–1949* (London: Pluto Press, 2009).

states and populations. Moreover, beyond any ideological difficulty, the secular human rights approach suddenly looks intellectual 'thin' to the extent that it misses the very real political factors due to its fetishization of religious phenomena.

We have come full circle. The critiques against the religious sphere are now levelled at the secular human rights regime. Here, we are confronted with a choice. On the one hand, we can invest in one particular vision at which point the literary work is to develop justifications that can sustain the practice and thought of one's camp.[36] Or, on the other hand, the scholar can become conscious of the swing within the literature between apology and utopia, and how each legal or political position carries with it a countervailing principle or exception.[37] Religion and secularism are not choices, but the rhetorical trope or paradox that generates international legal doctrines, and the goal is not to invest too heavily in one argument but to understand how they operate within the logic of the discipline.[38] In the indeterminacy of these argumentative moves, the actual mover of history is passion, which is inherently personal and often discrete. And if it is inescapable, the goal is to become self-reflective of one's particularity, to practice a rigorous hermeneutic of suspicion that is aware of its subjective limitations and that knowledge requires openness, whether it comes in the form of cultural expression, new ideas, and so forth. Among this later (and significant) camp of scholars, the literature is doing more than scholarship, it is self-consciously offering a polemic directed specifically to the discipline, or to particular institutional fields within the discipline. For them, normative validity cannot be separated from argumentative practices, and these practices are themselves rooted in extra-legal or intellectual sources. The question is how to analyse and address these passions and the almost invisible forms (e.g., interpretative assumptions, habitus) they take when influencing our reasoning. The polemic itself, therefore, is not a specific set of policy prescriptions or normative rules; it addresses the sensibility of the profession, the psychology and ritualized practices that preserve the profession and sustain the conceptual logic of its framework.[39] Between competing fantasies within the human rights regime, the role of the international lawyer is to develop an analytic set of tools that is built out of an attention to the blind spots and margins of law or political manoeuvers, of their risks and unexpected consequences, and which can encourage more active inclusion and participation in legal decision-making and exercise responsibility to others as the conditions of reason itself (discussed in terms, such as 'margin of appreciation', 'dialogical intersubjectivity', 'responsibility to others'). International legal practice becomes a reflective balancing act that is receptive and mediates competing fantasies, interests, and passions.[40] Secular human rights has

[36] Philippe Sands, *Lawless World: Making and Breaking Global Rules* (London: Penguin, 2008).

[37] Martti Koskenniemi, *From Apology to Utopia: The Structure of International Legal Argument* (first published 1989, Cambridge: Cambridge University Press, 2006).

[38] Duncan Kennedy, *A Critique of Adjudication [fin de siècle]* (Cambridge, Mass.: Harvard University Press, 1998).

[39] Pierre Bourdieu, *Outline of A Theory of Practice* (Cambridge: Cambridge University Press, 1977).

[40] Nathaniel Berman, '*Legalizing Jerusalem*, or, of Law, Fantasy, and Faith', *Catholic University Law Review* 45 (1996): p. 823.

something to contribute to religious systems and something to learn from them, and vice versa—the goal now to see this as a never-ending dialectic and to encourage more open communication and engagement that itself will council respect for others and an increased commitment to them as part of a mutual condition of existence.

Blind spots in contemporary theory and method

It is difficult not to be sympathetic with the turn to intersubjective dialogue as a possible best-of-all options strategy for engaging competing passions within global governance. There is a reflective pragmatic progressiveness to this approach, and at the same time, it remains comfortably conservative to the extent that it performs the traditional role for law: listening to the parties, balancing, counselling, mediating, and all the things one would expect from a liberal rule of law framework, now aware of its own shortcomings as a perpetual anxiety to be openly confronted. And its aversion to reified conceptions of fixed identities, interpretations, and norms all feels sufficiently concrete and grounded.

In this section, I want to suggest that this approach in fact offers a very thin analytical framework to explain the historic and contemporary dynamics of the tension between religion and secular human rights or what is actually going on in the literature. At the most general level, there is a certain progress narrative lurking here: we move from reified notions, of ideas in the clouds, of great politics and grand reasoning, to a nuanced appreciation of the complexity of experience and meaning, all which requires a concrete, interdisciplinary study of material everyday life. We move from the sky to the ground, from abstract to concrete thought, and so forth. If this were actually the case, that might be something, but what I would like to specifically develop is how its logic actually relies on a set of transcendental assumptions that only reaffirm key aspects of the very practices that it set out to undermine.

The Marginalization of Methodological Reflection

First, for all its merits in providing useful maps of the discipline's argumentative logic and seeking to inculcate sensitivity to the desires within a context without becoming partisans, there is a relatively surprising lack of reflection on methodological practice. In fact, to speak about religion and law in society poses a set of initial problems or choices for the scholar concerning what exactly to focus on, and how to go about it. The most immediate difficulty here is that we need to be able to make distinctions and potentially choose between the various regimes or terrains of everyday life that might be important in our study, and this requires we are able to sufficiently define what these categories mean (e.g., economics, law, religion, society, politics). In other words, what is the difference between religious and political conviction? Is religion a culture or something separate from culture? And so forth.

We are then almost simultaneously confronted with three additional difficulties. First, how do we analyse the dynamics within any of these fields? In speaking about economics, for instance, are we speaking about finance or industry or something in between? And pushing further, what sectors of finance or industry, and how do these sectors operate in relation to each other, and who are the actors that we will privilege in our analysis? The same might be said of religion. Are we looking at particular faiths or particular denominations? Are we focusing on its intellectual traditions or its institutional rituals or some more populist sensibility? Are we looking at in relation to how it is felt inside that faith, or how it is talked about in other settings, such as courts? The same could be said of law, are we talking about legislation or court decisions or law articles or even the background practices and sensibilities that inform our interpretation of the legal regime? More generally, what is it about the form of law as regulation that distinguishes it from other types of control, and what specific dynamics necessitated its emergence and sustains its formal character?[41]

Second, beyond the dynamics within any of these fields, we also have to ask how we study the dynamics between these fields—how they influence each other, how they are distinct, and how this more generally helps us understand the overall structure that all these fields and players exist within?[42] In looking at Christianity in America, for example, what role do ideological preferences concerning economic or political preferences shape religious trends? Or conversely, how have religious beliefs or various faith coalitions influenced debates or trends in the political arena, or in the practice and principles of law, or in our ideas about the market, or development, or society? These sorts of questions seem not only complex, but potentially endless—and importantly, require a more elaborate theoretical framework to map their engagement.

Third, if these fields must be able to be studied separately and in relation to each other, what is the relationship between these fields and the overall structure that binds them together (e.g., who determines who and how does this go on happening), and beyond this, what is the nature or character of that overall system in the first place: is it liberal, capitalist, postmodern, Western, multicultural, Christian, or all these things but then in what particular composition, or is it something else altogether? What is missing, in short, is sufficient thought to a central question at the core of a non-transcendental methodology, a type of inquiry from the sociological structuralism corner: not only must we become more attuned to the 'differentiation of functions and the relative autonomy of separate structures', but also 'how in their different places/levels and content/form exists the same cause that is the requisite and effect for the reproduction of a specific totality of unintentional

[41] China Mieville, *Between Equal Rights: A Marxist Theory of International Law* (Leiden: Brill, 2006).

[42] Louis Althusser, 'Ideology and Ideological State Apparatuses (Notes towards an Investigation)', in *Lenin and Philosophy and Other Essays* (first published 1971, New York: Monthly Review Press, 2001).

characteristic'.[43] To do so, would be to adopt a long view of history according to analytical concepts associated loosely with Marxist theory (e.g., mode of production, relations of production, interpellation, over-determination) to delineate the dynamics of the structure while paying close attention to the specific forms that allow the production and reproduction of a structure—its differentiations, relations, and reproduction—and its relationship to the conceptual vocabulary and practices of international law, all of which is fundamentally contingent in the 'big picture' and radically determined in 'everyday practice'.[44] Subjectivity is not an original state, but the name given to the result of the process that a system (in all its diversity) employs, through conscious and unconscious mediums, to forge its subjects.[45] Cultures, like corporate firms or religious communities, are not the agents of history; rather history is a process that makes subjects, and the point here is to develop an analytic that better catches when we fall into monadic or reified explanations for the dynamics of global governance over time, and more generally, 'human experience'.[46]

The Problem of the Subject

There is a further transcendental feature within the critical cosmopolitan approach, which involves the practice of self-reflection within the discipline. To explain this, I want to take a slight detour into a passage by Sartre. Sitting at a café, he notices a particular waiter serving tables. It strikes him that the waiter's movements are extremely stylized, to the point of being odd, the waiter is almost the consummate garçon. Sartre tells us in this moment, that he suddenly realized that the waiter's actions were not spontaneous, but that the waiter was playing his role deliberately, acting out the rules of the game with precision.[47] What Schlag points out, is that the passage is not actually about the waiter, but Sartre himself, and more generally, about the proper role of the intellectual or even the ideal of what counts as the standard bearer of entrance into participation and even authority.[48] This reading onto the other is what we might call in psychoanalysis 'transference', whereby we are being given a universalized way of behaving, a statement about human nature, or the proper role of the modern person.

[43] Maurice Godelier, *Perspectives in Marxist Anthropology* (Cambridge: Cambridge University Press, 1977), p. 2.

[44] This perspective is perhaps most developed among twentieth century European economic historians and theorists. Cf. Fernand Braudel, *The Structures of Everyday Life: Civilization and Capitalism, 15th–18th Century*, vol. 1 (New York: Harper and Row, 1982).

[45] For a general but interesting discussion of this theme, Susan Mark, 'False Contingency', *Current Legal Problems* 62, no. 1 (2010): p. 10.

[46] Louis Althusser, 'Remark on the Category: Process without a Subject or Goals', in Louis Althusser, *Response to John Lewis* (first published Paris: Maspero, 1973), pp. 95–9, <http://www.marx-2mao.com/Other/ESC76i.html> accessed 12 April 2015.

[47] Jean-Paul Sartre, *Essays in Existentialism* (first published 1965, Citadel, 1993), pp. 167–9.

[48] Pierre Schlag, 'The Problem of the Subject', *Texas Law Review* 69 (1991): p. 1627.

This can be analogized with ramifications to our understanding of what is happening when authors write on the topic of human rights debates concerning religion and secularism within this framework. The interpretative community and its rhetorical practices within the literature is itself now the subject of inquiry, and they may be characterized as a group upholding a certain orientation that is not necessarily about its usefulness, but the symptom of how an institutional system copes and co-opts and tames potential challenges to its reproductive needs.[49] The first thing that becomes immediately evident is that its reasoning slips into the very dilemma it sought to avoid. Assessing and mediating competing passions requires a criterion to decide authentic or good arguments from inauthentic or bad argument. This would be the case even if all possible information could be gathered and there were perfect engagement from all interests and perspectives.

In this situation, one is confronted with either falling back on some idealized form of 'reason', or alternatively, assumes that there is almost an 'invisible hand' that will take us from a situation where we have all possible information to a place where there is the implementation of a more just and peaceful global order. It is the logic of Noah, that if you build it, they will come; the logic of Adam Smith, that interaction breeds sympathy, which will lead to the best of all possible worlds. This assumption requires a leap of faith in some gentle civilizing process relying on speech acts. Nor is this transcendentalism mitigated by adopting a 'hermeneutic of suspicion' that might discipline prejudice. Other institutional frameworks may operate on a completely different basis for strategic debates and tactical calculations (e.g., deductive), and to force a foreign standard (e.g., hermeneutic of suspicion) does not simply inaugurate a competition between intellectual frameworks or ethical commitment, but constitutes a struggle for authority between camps, which bears a relation to a larger environment that is something far more theoretically complex than concepts like 'the social' or 'the individual' can explain it itself.

This is all the more troubling when situated within the historical backdrop of the interpretative community that generates the majority of international legal scholarship, and more generally, within the form of knowledge production in published law journals, monographs and textbooks. A long-standing critique of Muslims, for instance, is that Islamic law does not allow for a system of reciprocity between equal rights bearing stakeholders that is afforded by Western models of governance. This lack of reciprocity is discussed in different ways: that Islamic law is inherently violent and not prone to honouring contracts, that Islamic political structures do not allow for liberal state models that might guarantee individual property rights or free personal expression, or that Islamic law prohibits Muslim states from fully ratifying international conventions respecting the rights of minority groups, such as women, children, or members of the LGBT community.[50]

[49] Pierre Schlag, 'Law as the Continuation of God by Other Means', *California Law Review* 85 (1997): p. 427; Gunter Teubner, 'And God Laughed ... Indeterminacy, Self-Reference and Paradox in Law', *German Law Journal* 12, no. 1 (2011): pp. 376, 379.

[50] For historical studies that look at nineteenth and early twentieth century perspectives of Islam by leading international legal theorists, see H. Berman, 'World Law'; Haskell, 'Divine Immanence'.

This lack of reciprocity, however, is not in fact a display of intolerant behaviour but symptomatic of alternative institutional arrangements refusing to succumb to the particularities of Western-oriented organizational apparatuses. And yet, these judgements are quietly encoded within the processes that define which judgements and rationales are successful mobilized and shared within the interpretative community itself more often than not—namely, what conditions would be required for a Westerner to feel comfortable abroad.

Conclusion: Towards a Structuralist Jurisprudence

Talking about politics is very different from engaging power, just as following after a concrete empiricism that accurately reflects the ideas and passions of participants does not necessarily explain the dynamics by which global governance is reproduced. Focusing on the literary production of the discipline as the subject within a wider institutional setting whose results set the conditions of strategy towards certain ends, in this sense, is not a political act so much as it is an attempt to develop a less transcendental analytic for academic practice. The problem with human rights literature is that it lacks a methodological/theoretical sophistication that in turn leads to unhelpful abstractions and unwittingly reinforces the very intellectual and material conditions it sought to confront. Of course, there is a rich tradition concerning the sociology of idea production within other academic fields working through these themes—authors such as Louis Althusser, Pierre Bourdieu, James Smith, Phillip Mirowski, Charles Tilly, and so on—but this work has remained surprisingly marginal within international legal theory to date. Whatever the case, there is something rehearsed and intellectual stultifying in contemporary debates over religion and secularism that is all too humanist.[51] If this does nothing else, experimentation with a structural jurisprudence in international legal scholarship might offer something new, or at the very least, something different.

Bibliography

Althusser, Louis. *For Marx* (first published 1965, London; New York: Verso, 2005).

Althusser, Louis. 'Ideology and Ideological State Apparatuses (Notes towards an Investigation)'. In *Lenin and Philosophy and Other Essays* (first published 1971, New York: Monthly Review Press, 2001).

Althusser, Louis. 'Remark on the Category: Process without a Subject or Goals'. In *Response to John Lewis* (first published Paris: Maspero, 1973), pp. 95–9, <http://www.marx2mao.com/Other/ESC76i.html> accessed 12 April 2015.

[51] For a discussion of this feeling, Pierre Schlag, 'Spam Jurisprudence, Air Law, and the Rank Anxiety of Nothing Happening (a Report on the State of the Art)', *Georgetown Law Journal* 97, no. 1 (2009): p. 803.

Anghie, Antony. 'The War on Terror and Iraq in Historical Perspective'. *Osgoode Hall Law Journal* 43, no. 1 (2005): pp. 45, 63.

Annan, Kofi. The Secretary General. 'Universal Declaration of Human Rights Illuminates Global Pluralism and Diversity' (The Fiftieth Anniversary Year of the Universal Declaration of Human Rights, Tehran, 10 December 1997), <http://www.unhchr.ch/Huricane/Huricane.nsf/60a520ce334aaa77802566100031b4bf/82ed5e4c1f33163cc125662e00352f62?OPenDocument> accessed 12 April 2015.

d'Aspremont, Jean and Jörg Kammerhofer, eds. *International Legal Positivism in a Post-Modern World* (Cambridge: Cambridge University Press, 2014).

Baderin, Mashood. 'Human Rights and Islamic Law: The Myth of Discord'. *European Human Rights Law Review* 2 (2005): p. 163.

Berger, Peter, ed. *The Desecularization of the World: Resurgent Religion and World Politics* (Grand Rapids, Mich.: W. B. Eerdmans, 1999).

Berman, Harold. 'World Law: An Ecumenical Christian Jurisprudence'. *Fordham International Law Journal* 18 (1995): p. 1617.

Berman, Nathaniel. '*Legalizing Jerusalem*, or, of Law, Fantasy, and Faith'. *Catholic University Law Review* 45 (1996): p. 823.

Berman, Nathaniel. 'The Sacred Conspiracy: Religion, Nationalism, and the Crisis of Internationalism'. *Leiden Journal of International Law* 25, no. 1 (2012): p. 9.

Bielefedt, Heiner. 'Western versus Islamic Human Rights Conceptions? A Critique of Cultural Essentialism in the Discussion of Human Rights'. *Political Theory* 28, no. 1 (2000): p. 90.

Bourdieu, Pierre. *Outline of a Theory of Practice* (Cambridge: Cambridge University Press, 1977).

Boustead, Kathryn. 'The French Headscarf Law before the European Court of Human Rights'. *Journal of Transnational Law and Policy* 16, no. 2 (2007): p. 167.

Braudel, Fernand. *The Structures of Everyday Life: Civilization and Capitalism, 15th–18th Century*, vol. 1 (New York: Harper and Row, 1982).

Charlesworth, Hilary. 'The Challenges of Human Rights Law for Religious Traditions'. In *Religion and International Law*, edited by Mark Janis and Carolyn Evans (The Hague: Martinus Nijhoff Publishers, 1999), p. 401.

Cohen, Felix. 'Transcendental Nonsense and the Functional Approach'. *Columbia Law Review* 35, no. 6 (1935): p. 809.

Danchin, Peter. 'Suspect Symbols: Value Pluralism as a Theory of Religious Freedom in International Law'. *Yale Journal of International Law* 33, no. 1 (2008), p. 1.

al-Dawla, Ismat Sayf. 'Islam and Human Rights: Controversy and Agreement'. *Minbar al-Hiwar* 9 (1988): p. 33.

Dyzenhaus, David. 'Headscarves, Extreme Speech and Democracy'. http://www.law.uwo.ca/publiclaw/PublicLaw_Documentas/Headscarves_ExtremE_Speech.pdf. Accessed 12 April 2015.

Falk, Richard. 'Religion and Global Governance: Harmony or Clash'. *International Journal of World Peace* 19 (2002): p. 3.

Godelier, Maurice. *Perspectives in Marxist Anthropology* (Cambridge: Cambridge University Press, 1977).

Habermas, Jürgen. *A Conversation About God and the World: Time of Transitions* (first published 2001, Oxford: Polity Press, 2006).

Haskell, John. 'Divine Immanence: The Evangelical Foundations of Modern Anglo-American Approaches to International Law'. *Chinese Journal of International Law* 11, no. 3 (2012): p. 426.

Henkin, Louis. 'Religion, Religions and Human Rights'. In *Does Human Rights Need God*, edited by Elizabeth Bucar and Barbara Barnett (Grand Rapids, Mich.: W. B. Eerdmans, 2005), p. 146, 148.

Huntington, Samuel. *The Clash of Civilizations and the Remaking of World Order* (New York: Simon & Schuster, 1996).

Hurd, Elizabeth. 'Political Islam and Foreign Policy in Europe and the United States'. *Foreign Policy Analysis* 3 (2007): p. 345.

Kattan, Victor. *From Coexistence to Conquest: International Law and the Origins of the Arab-Israeli Conflict 1891–1949* (London: Pluto Press, 2009).

Kennedy, David. 'The Politics of the Invisible College: International Governance and the Politics of Expertise'. *European Human Rights Law Review* 5 (2001): p. 463.

Kennedy, David. 'Images of Religion in International Legal Theory'. In *Religion and International Law*, edited by Janis and Evans (The Hague: Martinus Nijhoff Publishers, 1999), pp. 145, 146.

Kennedy, Duncan. *A Critique of Adjudication [fin de siècle]* (Cambridge, MA: Harvard University Press, 1998).

Kennedy, Duncan. 'A Semiotics of Critique'. *Cardozo Law Review* 22, no. 3–4 (2001): p. 1147.

Kennedy, Duncan. 'A Critique of Rights in Critical Legal Studies'. In *Left Legalism/Left Critique*, edited by Wendy Brown and Janet Halley (North Carolina: Duke University Press, 2002).

Koskenniemi, Martti. *From Apology to Utopia: The Structure of International Legal Argument* (first published 1989, Cambridge: Cambridge University Press, 2006).

Koskenniemi, Martti. 'Human Rights, Politics and Love'. In *The Politics of International Law* (Oxford: Hart Publishing, 2011), p. 153.

Koskenniemi, Martti. 'International Law in Europe: Between Tradition and Renewal'. *European Journal of International Law* 16, no. 1 (2005): pp. 113, 115.

Lewis, Bernard. *Islam and the West* (New York: Oxford University Press, 1994).

Mamdani, Mahmood. *Good Muslim, Bad Muslim: America, the Cold War, and the Roots of Terror* (New York: Doubleday, 2005).

Mamdani, Mahmood. 'Good Muslim, Bad Muslim: A Political Perspective on Culture and Terrorism'. *American Anthropologist* 104, no. 3 (2002): p. 766.

Mamdani, Mahmood. 'Whither Political Islam?', *Foreign Affairs* 84, no. 1 (2005).

Mark, Susan. 'False Contingency'. *Current Legal Problems* 62, no. 1 (2010): p. 10.

Mayer, Ann. *Islam and Human Rights: Tradition and Politics* (Boulder, CO.: Westview, 2006).

Mieville, China. *Between Equal Rights: A Marxist Theory of International Law* (Leiden: Brill, 2006).

Milbank, John. 'Against Human Rights: Liberty in the Western Tradition'. *Oxford Journal of Law and Religion* 1, no. 1. (2012): pp. 203–34.

Mushkat, Roda. 'Is War Ever Justifiable? A Comparative Survey'. *Loyola of Los Angeles International and Comparative Law Journal* 9, no. 2 (1987): p. 227.

Partisis, Refah. 37 Eur. Ct. H.R. 42.

Perry, Michael. 'The Morality of Human Rights: A Nonreligious Ground?'. *Emory Law Journal* 54 (2005): p. 97.

Said, Edward. *Orientalism* (first published 1978, New York: Vintage Books, 1978).

Sands, Philippe. *Lawless World: Making and Breaking Global Rules* (London: Penguin Books, 2006).

Sartre, Jean-Paul. *Essays in Existentialism* (first published 1965, New York: Citadel, 1993).

Schlag, Pierre. 'The Aesthetics of American Law'. *Harvard Law Review* 115, no. 4 (2012): p. 1051.
Schlag, Pierre. 'Law as the Continuation of God by Other Means'. *California Law Review* 85 (1997): p. 427.
Schlag, Pierre. 'Spam Jurisprudence, Air Law, and the Rank Anxiety of Nothing Happening (a Report on the State of the Art)'. *Georgetown Law Journal* 97, no. 1 (2009): p. 803.
Schlag, Pierre. 'The Problem of the Subject'. *Texas Law Review* 69, no. 7 (1991): p. 1627.
Taylor, Charles. 'Modes of Secularism'. In *Secularism and Its Critics*, edited by Rajeev Bhargava (New Delhi: Oxford University Press, 1998), p. 35.
Teubner, Gunter. 'And God Laughed ... Indeterminacy, Self-Reference and Paradox in Law'. *German Law Journal* 12, no. 1 (2011): p. 376.
Witte, John.Jr. 'A Dickensian Era of Religious Rights: An Update on Religious Human Rights in Global Perspective'. *William and Mary Law Review* 42, no. 3 (2001): p. 707.
Witte, John.Jr . 'Law and Religion: The Challenges of Christian Jurisprudence'. *University of St Thomas Law Journal* 2, no. 2 (2005): p. 9.
Zinkin, John. 'Islam and CSR: A Study of the Compatibility between the Tenets of Islam, the UN Global Compact and the Development of Social, Human and Natural Capital'. *Corporate Social Responsibility and Environmental Management* 14, no. 4 (2007): p. 206.

7

Natural Rights in Albert the Great

Beyond Objective and Subjective Divides

Mónica García-Salmones Rovira

Introduction

Albert the Great (1200–80) frames his doctrine of *ius naturale* mainly within the famous 'On the Good' (*De bono*, 1242), which was, in his own words, soon 'widely known and commonly held' in manuscript form, but only published seven centuries later, in 1951.[1] In *De bono* Albert expounds a treatment of *ius naturale* to which he adheres for a long period—certainly, in his commentary on the *Sentences* (1243–9), where he repeatedly referred to his tract 'On Justice' from *De bono*.[2] Both works, written in sequence, are as Geyer commented intimately connected.[3] In *Super Ethica* (1250–2) similar ideas appear, but in his *Summa Theologia* there seems to be a change of approach (1268–74).[4]

[1] Bernhardus Geyer, 'Prolegomena' to Alberti Magni, *De bono*, in *Alberti Magni opera omnia*, tomus XXVIII (Monasterii westfalorum in aedibus Aschendorff, 1951), p. ix. Comprehensive works on Albert's doctrine of *ius naturale* are Jörn Müller, *Natürliche Moral und Philosophische Ethik bei Albertus Magnus* (Münster: Beiträge zur Geschichte der Philosophie und Theologie des Mittelalters, Neue Folge 59, 2001); Stanley B. Cunningham, *Reclaiming Moral Agency: The Moral Philosophy of Albert the Great* (Washington, D.C.: Catholic University of America Press, 2008). A shorter reference in Dom Odon Lottin, *Le Droit Naturel chez Saint Thomas d'Aquin et ses prédécesseurs* (Bruges: Charles Beyaert, 1931), pp. 41–8. For 'the good' as the notion underlying the entire *ouvre* of Albert, see Henryk Anzulewicz, "*Bonum*' als Schlüsselbegriff bei Albertus Magnus', in Walter Senner ed. With collaboration by Henryk Anzulewicz, Maria Burger, Ruth Meyer, Maria Nuert, Pablo C. Sicouly, Joachim Söder, Klaus-Bernward Springer, *Albertus Magnus. Zum Gedenken nach 800 Jahren: Neue Zugänge, Aspekte und Perspektiven* (Berlin: Akademie Verlag, 2001), p. 113.

[2] III Sent. D.40, a. 4 'Hic autem, qui vult, potest inducere longam quaestionem De legibus et iure naturali, quam disputavimus in tractatu De iustitia.'; IV Sent. d. 17, a.9, 'Haec tamen ut bene intelligantur, dependent a quaestionibus, quas alibi De iustia disputavimus.' A longer list of places where Albert refers to *De bono* by Geyer, 'Prolegomena', p. xi; Albert's works can be searched online in: http://albertusmagnus.uwaterloo.ca/.

[3] Bernhardus Geyer, 'Prolegomena' to Alberti Magni, *De bono*, p. xii.

[4] In the *Summa* Albert refers mainly to *lex naturale* and there is little room for the discussion on 'rights', but in *Super ethica*, there is. A chronology of Albert's writings in 'Zeittafel', Albertus-Magnus-Institut (Hg.), *Albertus Magnus und sein System der Wissenschaften*. Schlüsseltexte in Übersetzung. Lateinisch—Deutsch. Eingeleitet, übersetzt und für den Druck vorbereitet von Hannes Möhle, Henryk Anzulewicz, Maria Burger, Silvia Donati, Ruth Meyer, Martin Bredenbeck und Susana Bullido del Barrio (Münster i. W.: Aschendorff Verlag, 2011), p. 28.

For Albert, *ius naturale* is universal first and foremost, and as such is never amalgamated with particular circumstances of time or locality. Hence, the more universal the rule of common human right, the more substantially it is of natural law.

The 'universals of right', affirms Albert, employing the expression of Basilius of Caesarea (330–379), direct the actions of the human being, and in them there is no error or doubt. They supply the information to the natural rational power of judgement or synderesis, so that it understands what is to be done or not done. [5] Next, practical reason working in the form of a syllogism applies the universal of right to the particular case.[6]

Moreover, *ius naturale* is a habit. [7] In the context of thirteenth-century theology this means that human beings possess *innately* the science and the universals of right.[8] It also means that, similar to the case of the first principles of the speculative sciences such as the principle of non-contradiction (e.g. in Aristotle's *Metaphysics*, 'It is not possible that it should be simultaneously true to say that the same thing is a man and is not a man' (1006b33–4)[9]), the soul does not require any works of demonstration or conclusion to grasp the first principles of right. Human beings simply know the universals of right.[10] Thus one does not know of what is to steal with its particular words or terms, but one learns these terms. However, one *innately knows* that one ought not to steal.

How does the individual's freedom fare in all that process? In a nutshell *nature gives the habit* of *ius naturale*, but the individual has to complete it with assent and grace.[11] Unlike the case of seeing our surrounding world through the habit of vision, the habit of *ius naturale* is not complete or perfected already. One exercises one's freedom because, through the habit of *ius naturale*, we not only become human beings, but *good human beings*, something that Albert explains as follows:

But some of the habits do not belong to the notion of potency in the sense of being (*esse*), but rather in the sense of well-being (*bene esse*). That is to say that we are susceptible of

[5] 'Et vocantur universalia iuris illa dirigentia nos in opere, in quibus non est error neque dubium, in quibus naturale iudicatorium rationis vel syderesis informatum accipit, quid faciendum sit vel non faciendum', Alberti Magni, *De bono,* p. 263.23. About the synderesis in Albert see Christian Trottmann, 'La syndérèse selon Albert le Grand', in *Albertus Magnus, zum Gedenken nach 800 Jahren* (Berlin: Akademie Verlag, 2001), p. 255.

[6] Alberti Magni, *De bono*, p. 289. 18; see on this Müller, *Natürliche Moral und Philosophische Ethik bei Albertus Magnus,* pp. 235–41.

[7] 'Patet ergo ex his quod ius naturali est habitus.' Alberti Magni, *De bono,* p. 263.82.

[8] A habit is in Albert's theory that through which someone acts, as he or she wants without requiring anything extrinsic, Alberti Magni, *De homine*, ediderunt Henryk Anzulewicz et Joachim R. Söder (Monasterii Westfalorum in Aedibus Aschendorff, 2008), tomus XXVII, pars II, p. 185.53.

[9] Other examples in S. Marc Cohen, 'Aristotle on the Principle of Non-Contradiction', *Canadian Journal of Philosophy* 16 (1986): p. 359.

[10] One knows them accidentally through their names (*ex notitia terminorum*): 'ita dicimus quod est in habitu practici intellectus, qui dirigit in opere, sicut est scientia iuris, quod prima potentia est ad universalia iuris.(...) Et ideo talium principiorum notitia est inserta per naturam simpliciter, et acquiritur per accidens notitia terminorum'. Alberti Magni, *De bono,* p. 263.60.

[11] 'Ad aliud dicendum, quod natura dat quosdam habitus et complet eos, quosdam autem dat et non complet, sed complentur per assuetudinem sequentem vel per gratiam.' Alberti Magni, *De bono,* p. 264.55.

being good from nature. But the perfection of that potency happens through assent and grace, and those are not perfected by nature.[12]

All these 'seeds of right' are in the practical reason, implanted by nature and *not by opinion*. But they are in the state of potency or 'in expectation to become' and this happens freely, not automatically. Reason can judge erroneously about what is good or the will can reject the right action decreed by reason. Moreover, there is a complex chain of processes of recognition, learning, and judging by right reason and assenting by will and grace, until one acts according to right.[13]

This very brief introduction shows already that Albert's doctrine of *ius naturale* is more than a swift *ouverture* for his student Thomas Aquinas (1225–74).[14] Moreover, a second level of reading is obtained from Albert's 'On Justice', tract five of *De bono*, when Annabel Brett and Brian Tierney's invitations to consider closely the language of the sources are taken seriously.[15] In this case, such a reading leads to valuable insights about natural rights and their history. In the course of paying attention to the language that Albert employs in *De bono* three further aspects transpire from his unconventional use of concepts.

Firstly, the fact emerges that Albert is not only writing as a theologian and a legal philosopher but as a natural scientist as well. More accurately, Albert is a student of

[12] 'Quidam autem habitus non sunt de ratione potentiae quantum ad esse, sed quantum ad bene esse, quod scilicet bene esse innati sumus suscipere; sed perficere est ab assuetudine et gratia, et tales non perficit natura.' Alberti Magni, *De bono*, p. 264.63. Thus both frailty and solidity are features of Albert's doctrine of *ius naturale*.

[13] 'Ergo si ius naturale est habitus naturalis, natura dat et complet ipsum. Non autem est completus, nisi complete operetur secundum iura. Ergo omnis habens habitum illum complete operabitur vel operari potest secundum iura, quod falsum est, cum exigantur adhuc studium et doctrina.' Alberti Magni, *De bono*, p. 260.17; Müller comments that the eternal law cannot direct the operations without mediation, Müller, *Natürliche Moral und Philosophische Ethik bei Albertus Magnus*, p. 252. 'Ad primum ergo dicendum est quod facultas facilem et perfectam potestatem supponit, quae non est ita rationis et voluntatis tanquam in ipsis existat, sed tanquam inter quae, ut pate *ex praedictis*. Est enim haec facultas perfecta potestas arbitrarie eligendi decretum a ratione vel concupitum a voluntate.' Alberti Magni, *De homine*, pars II, p. 514.25; 'Et hoc modo loquuntur philosophus, Damascenus, Gregorius Nixenus, qui dicunt nos esse dominus illorum actuum qui fiunt ex libero arbitrio.' Alberti Magni, *De homine*, pars II, p. 520.76.

[14] Although usually the commonalities are stressed. So Müller, though highlighting differences and the aspects developed further by Thomas, concluded that: 'Albert prefigures in this way in his natural right and conscience doctrine central themes and positions of the Thomist model'. Müller, *Natürliche Moral und Philosophische Ethik bei Albertus Magnus*, p. 253 (translation mine). See St. Thomas Aquinas, *Summa Theologia*, v. 28, Ia2ae. 90–7, 'Law and Political Theory', Thomas Gilby O.P., translation, introduction, and notes (Cambridge: Cambridge University Press, 1966); an introduction to Thomas of Aquinas's doctrine of natural law in Michael Baur, 'Law and Natural Law', in *The Oxford Handbook of Aquinas*, edited by Brian Davies and Eleonore Stump (New York: Oxford University Press, 2012), p. 238.

[15] Brett's intention is to try to 'recover the variety of the senses of the term *ius* as employed to signify a quality or property of the individual subject in late mediaeval and renaissance scholastic discourse' Annabel S. Brett, *Liberty, Right and Nature. Individual Rights in Later Scholastic Thought* (Cambridge: Cambridge University Press, 2000) p. 7; according to Tierney: 'a historic environment is not constituted only by a play of contingent events at some particular time and place, but also by the whole tradition of thought and language that a society inherits from its past'. Brian Tierney, *The Idea of Natural Rights. Studies on Natural Rights, Natural Law, and Church Law* (Grand Rapids, Michigan/ Cambridge, Cambridgeshire: William B. Eerdmans Publishing Company, 1997), p. 6.

nature.[16] What this exactly means is difficult to articulate considering the diverse understandings of the notion of 'nature' in the history of science.[17] As a biologist, Albert is considered an innovator in that his research was founded on 'classification and experiment'.[18] This is apparent also in *De bono*, where he takes the standpoint of an observer of human nature. This attitude tends to make Albert's approach to *ius naturale* more methodological than normative.

Secondly, as a natural lawyer, Albert produces a novel treatment of *ius naturale* in three separate questions of *ius, lex*, and *iustitia* (right, law, and justice) devoting to *ius* twice as much space as that given to *lex* and *iustitia*. Albert was possibly the first to make the distinction between *ius* and *lex* in this context.[19]

Thirdly, Albert's natural rights are paradoxically subjective and objective at the same time. The argument in *De bono* is about how it is a power of the individual subject to know the objective 'universals of right'. In that sense natural rights appear to be moral qualities of the individual, as Grotius would famously later put it.[20] But in Albert's study, their relevancy lies in knowing them not in having them, a fact which is taken for granted.

My suggestion is that to view Albert as producing a *theological* discourse of natural rights is a fruitful approach for describing his threefold novel contribution to

[16] Albert as 'groundbreaker of the descriptive natural science' in Franz Pelster, 'Die ersten beiden Kapitel der Erklärung Alberts des Großen zu *De animalibus* in ihrer ursprünglichen Fassung. Nach Cod. Vat. lat. 718', *Scholastik: Vierteljahresschrift für Theologie und Philosophie* 10 (1934): p. 229. 'Hac igitur de causa etiam nostrum scientiam de animalibus sic distribuimus, ut primo dicamus omnes notas animalium diversitates in membris et generatione et cibo et moribus et aliis et postea omnium diversitatum per ordinem causas disseramus'. In this often-repeated quote Albert disclose his method founded on observation, classification, and after that, extraction of principles, the text in Pelster, p. 233; Hannes Möhle, 'Zur Methodologie der Naturwissenschaften', *Albertus Magnus und sein System der Wissenschaften. Schlüsseltexte in Übersetzung. Lateinisch—Deutsch*, Albertus-Magnus-Institut ed., Münster, introduced, translated, and edited together with H. Anzulewicz, M. Burger, S. Donati, R. Meyer, M. Bredenbeck, and S. Bullido del Barrio (Münster 2011), pp. 229–33.

[17] An insightful review of main positions, in Ludger Honnefelder, 'Natur-Verhältnisse. Natur als Gegenstand der Wissenschaften. Eine Einführung', in *Natur als Gegenstand der Wissenschaften* (München: Verlag Karl Alber Freiburg, 1992) p. 9.

[18] About Albert's innovation in developing a modern concept of natural sciences, Ludger Honnefelder, 'Albertus Magnus und die kulturelle Wende im 13. Jahrhundert—Perspektiven auf die epochale Bedeutung des großen Philosophen und Theologen', *Lectio Albertina* 13 (Münster: Aschendorff Verlag, 2012).

[19] Richard Tuck thinks that it was Gerson: '"*Ius* is a *facultas* or power appropriate to someone in accordance with the dictates of right reason. *Libertas* is a *facultas* of the reason and will towards whatever possibility is selected ... *Lex* is a practical and right reason according to which the movements and workings of things are directed towards their ordained ends." He (Gerson) was thus even able to make that distinction between *ius* and *lex* which seventeenth-century natural rights theorists thought they had invented.' Richard Tuck, *Natural Rights Theories. Their Origin and Development* (Cambridge: Cambridge University Press, 1998), p. 27; Cunningham instead claims that prior to Albert *ius* and *lex* are used interchangeably and that Albert was the first to make the distinction: Cunningham, *Reclaiming Moral Agency*, p. 216; from Lottin's classic review it seems that Cunningham's appraisal is accurate: Odon Lottin,' Le loi naturalle depuis le début du xii siècle jusqu'a saint Thomas d'Aquin', in *Psychologie et morale aux XII et XIII siecles* vol. II (Louvain: Abbaye du Mont César, 1948), pp. 71–100.

[20] The note on Grotius in the classic study on the 'subjectivism' of subjective rights, Michel Villey, 'La genèse du droit subjectif chez Guillaume d'Occam', in *Archives de Philosophie du Droit. Le droit subjectif en question,* 9 (1964): p. 97.

the wealth of theories of *ius naturale*. On the face of the increasing legal complexity inherent in the new canon law treatises of morality appearing in the early thirteenth century, such as the *Summa de casibus* by Raymund of Pennaforte and the subsequent alienation of lay men from the official knowledge of morality, Albert takes a decidedly humanist approach revolving around an individual who masters the knowledge of the principles of natural right.[21] This has been termed Albert's 'democratization' of *ius naturale*.[22] We shall see later that the question of the subject's practical knowledge of *ius naturale* is still uncertain and incomplete in *De bono*. However, the purpose of this chapter is to study Albert's novel assertion and creative development of *ius naturale* into *iura naturalia* within the ambit of theological discourse.

This reading situates Albert's *De bono* within the battle of the faculties between Theology and Canon Law, which reached its climax during the thirteenth century and continued well into the fourteenth century, after canon lawyers together with Roman law experts established an independent faculty. Theologians disdained jurists ('cavillationes et fraudes juristarum', 'dolosi legistae', and 'perversi juristae' are some of the epithets that Aquinas reserved for lawyers) and feared that the study of theology would suffer if priests devoted too much time to study law. Therefore, in solution to the question of whether the Church ought to be governed by a good lawyer or a theologian, Gottfried of Fontain concluded that the teaching of faith, morals, the conversion of life, and celebrating the sacraments were the most important tasks of the Church, for which the theologian was distinctly more qualified.[23] Although Albert himself acted often as an arbitrator—he might have even studied law in Padua before becoming a Dominican at the age of twenty-three[24]—and thus showed that he possessed the practical skills of law, he

[21] Raymund of Pennaforte, *Summa de Casibus*, is the most influential of those treatises when Albert writes *De bono*. Remarkably Raymund is only named once in the commentary to *Sentences* on the definition of confession and then as 'those who have come recently, such as Raymund', Albertus Magnus, *Super Sententiarum* (ed. Borgnet, 1893–94), Lib.IV, dist.16, art.16, p. 575b: 'Alii quidem novitii, ut Raymundus, diffinierunt sic'; on Raymund and his *Summa*, see Kenneth Pennington, 'The Decretalists 1190–1234', in *The History of Medieval Canon Law in the Classical Period 1140–1234. From Gratian to de Decretals of Pope Gregory IX*, edited by Wilfried Hartmann and Kenneth Pennington (Washington, D.C.: Catholic University of America Press, 2008), p. 211.

[22] Trottmann, 'La syndérèse selon Albert le Grand', p. 265.

[23] Aquinas's comments on the jurists and the entire discussion by Godfried in Martin Grabmann, 'Die Erörterung der Frage, ob die Kirche besser durch einen guten Juristen oder durch einen Theologen regiert werde, bei Gottfried von Fontaines (nach 1306) und Augustinus Triumphus von Ancona (1328) in *Eduard Eichmann zum 70. Geburtstag*, edited by Martin Grabmann and Karl Hofmann (Wien/F. Beck, and Zürich/ B. Götschmann, 1940), p. 1; about the sceptic critique to the sense of superiority of theologians by Ockham see Jürgen Miethke, 'Kanonistik, Ekklesiologie und politische Theorie: Die Rolle des Kirchenrechts in der politischen Theorie des Spätmittelalters' in *Proceedings of the Ninth International Congress of Medieval Canon Law*, edited by Peter Landau and Joers Mueller (Città del Vaticano: Biblioteca Apostolica Vaticana, 1997), p. 1023.

[24] Pelster gives a detailed analysis of this question that leaves open at the end whether Albert studied medicine, philosophy, or law, or studied anything at all. Exploring in the sources whether he was an artist, Pelster writes that '[T]he question can be just as well about jurists that also back then had already a school in Padua'). Albert himself only says: 'Pataviam, quae nunc Padua vocantur, in qua multo tempore viguit studium litterarum'. Franz Pelster, *Kritische Studien zum Leben und zu den Schriften Alberts des Großen* (Freiburg im Breisgau: Herder & Co. 1920), pp. 52–60; quote in p. 53.

had strong words as well against the employment of canon law in the doctrine on sacraments.[25] Brundage quotes Albert cautioning his students against the opinions of the canonists: 'They certainly say many erroneous things ... since they are men unversed in the sacred Scriptures.'[26] If one would judge this question on the basis of *De bono*, the warning was not altogether misplaced. One of Albert's main arguments in the text, on the dispensation of *ius naturale*, avoids the simplistic—though long-lasting—solution of the canon lawyers of dividing the *ius naturale* into precepts, prohibitions, and demonstrations, of which only the latter could be dispensed with, and instead develops a sophisticated theory with basis in the Scripture and other sources.[27] Albert's critical attitude extended as well towards the civil jurists, whom he considered 'call themselves *politicos* while they ignore what is the art of politics and the positive law'.[28]

Notwithstanding the critique and the somewhat understandable struggles of competences between the faculties of theology and law, Miethke points out that from the twelfth century onwards the extraordinary success of the legal experts in both defining the Church as a juridical person and the relations between people in the Church as juridical relations brought about a tendency towards juridification that was perhaps unavoidable.[29] This idea allows Miethke to reflect on the increasing impact that this had for political and theological thinking.[30] My point here is to highlight the argument that the influence of law reaches also into moral thought developed by theological speculation well beyond the field of canon law.

An interpretation of Albert seeking to make theology part of contemporary sociological and intellectual flux on moral thinking and that takes into account the factual juridification of doctrines about morality helps to situate the depth and breadth that natural right and natural rights suddenly acquired when dealt with by

[25] Grabmann, 'Die Erörterung der Frage', p. 3; for Albert as an arbitrator see, Manfred Groten, *Albertus Magnus und der Große Schied (Köln 1258)—Aristotelische Politik im Praxistest, Lectio Albertina 12* (Münster: Aschendorff Verlag, 2011).

[26] James A. Brundage, 'The Medieval Battle of the Faculties. Theologians v. Canonists', in *Liber amicorum Robert Somerville*, edited by Uta-Renate, Blumenthal, Anders Winroth, and Peter Landau (Washington, D.C.: Catholic University of America Press, 2012), p. 279.

[27] 'Chez Albert le grand, le mot (*demonstrationes*) même disparaît', Lottin, *Le droit nature chez Saint Thomas d'Aquin et ses prédécesseurs*, p. 45. Among many other canon lawyers employing the division, see *Summa in Decretum Simonis Bisinianensis* Edidit Petrus V. Aimone (Fribourg, 2007). This can be found at: http://www.unifr.ch/cdc/assets/files/summa_simonis_BAND_I%2014%2010%20 2007.pdf.

[28] 'Sophistas autem hic vocamus, non qui decipiunt locis sophisticis, sed ab imitatione sophistarum copiose ab apparente sapientia qui seipsos vocant politicos, cum nesciant quae sit ars politica aut legis positiva.' Albertus Magnus, *Ethica* (ed. Borgnet, 1891), Lib.X, tract.3, cap.3, p.639b; see also Jacques P. Krynen, 'Les légistes 'idiots politiques': Sur l'hostilité des théologiens à l'égard des juristes en France, au temps de Charles V', in *Théologie et droit dans la science politique de l'État moderne* (Rome: École française de Rome, 1991), pp. 171–2.

[29] 'Juridical argumentation and recourse to juridical argumentation were in any case in the late middle ages virtually ubiquituous'. Miethke, 'Kanonistik, Ekklesiologie und politische Theorie', pp. 1033–6; quote p. 1036 (translation mine).

[30] Thus theologians such as William of Ockham and Duns Scotus write on questions of law. Ibid. p. 1041.

the pen of a theologian. Miethke describes this disparity well. He states that canon lawyers prompted, with a single notion, volumes of literature by theologians and artists while they themselves did not engage, and showed an apparent lack of ambition in their theoretical efforts or (possibly) capacity, in the face of the masses of legal texts that they had to deal with.[31] The natural rights of Albert are integrated in a biblical tradition, a Stoic (legal) philosophy and an Aristotelian epistemology which transforms the timid attempts on *ius naturale* of the canon lawyers and the sweeping definitions of the Roman jurists into a theological concept of first relevance.[32]

In the context of a study of the history of rights theories, the main argument of this chapter is that *natural rights* enter theology by the hand of Albert the Great, never to leave that discipline in the future. This fact has been obscured by a concentration in the Aristotelian aspects of Albert's work which prevents contextual discussion.[33] Also, disregard of the theological enquiries about how humans know natural rights in the first place, in favour of analysis of the commonalities between the theological discourse on natural rights and the legal discourse—the identification of *dominium* and *ius* is the most visible example of this field of study[34]—has led to a neglect of the arguments of the theologians in their own ground.

As a philosopher, Albert is best described as a gradual discoverer of Aristotle and most of the time as an eclectic. Further, the *doctor universalis* is acutely interested in the epistemological aspect of *ius naturale*. Albert's dissatisfaction with the doctrine of *ius naturale* in *De bono* that transpires in his two later commentaries of the *Nichomachean Ethics* will not be considered here. Rather this chapter presents and explores Albert's concept of natural rights in *De bono* and thereby aims to convey complexity into the current division in scholarship between subjective natural rights and objective natural right.

[31] Miethke, 'Kanonistik, Ekklesiologie und politische Theorie', pp. 1046–8.

[32] A brief survey of theologians' doctrines of *ius naturale* prior to Albert in Cunningham, *Reclaiming Moral Agency*, pp. 209–15.

[33] Cunningham's is an insightful contribution to the discussion of Albert's doctrine of *ius naturale* but somehow categorical about the existence of a particular mind in Albert: 'Before launching directly into this part of *De bono*, the modern reader, lest he misconstrue the spirit of Albert's moral philosophy, should be forewarned about the use of the term "right" (*ius*). When Albert, or any of the medieval moralists for that matter, speaks of "natural right" (*ius naturae, ius naturale*) or "right reason" (*ius rationis*) this should not be translated into the modern sense of "individual" or "subjective right". In the thirteenth century "right" means that which *is* objectively right.' Cunningham, *Reclaiming Moral Agency: The Moral Philosophy of Albert the Great*, p. 215 (footnote omitted). Albert's Aristotelianism is of course indisputable, see e.g. Martin Grabmann, 'Der Einfluβ Alberts des Groβen auf die mittelalterliche Aristoteleserklärung', in *Gesammelte Akademie Abhandlungen* v. II, (Padeborn: Ferdinand Schöningh, 1979), pp. 1934–61.

[34] Classically so, Michel Villey: 'Le fait, capital pour l'historie du droit- que nos manuels ne signalent guère—est que le *dominium*, appelé par nous droit de propriété, devenu pour nos l'archétype et le modèle du droit subjectif, ne nous est pas présenté à Rome sous le qualificatif de droit.' Villey 'La genèse du droit subjectif', p. 106.

New Concepts for Natural Rights

In his analysis of the origin and development of natural rights theories, Richard Tuck concludes that before the threshold of the Renaissance there were three elements radiating meaning from under the surface of the concept of 'natural right': 1) the importance of naturalness, 2) the key absorption of *dominium* into *ius* that transformed the sphere of influence of an individual, spiritual and material (as property) into a sovereign realm and 3) the Gersonian theological theory about the acquisition by men of a conceptual position that could be assimilated to that of God.[35] In Albert the Great, natural rights are founded in nature, they include private property, and they belong to the 'human being who is vicar of God in the authority of power, and order of wisdom and goodness of life'.[36] And yet they can hardly be described as subjective rights in the sense that Tuck does. But neither do Albert's natural rights belong to the objective tradition exposed by Michel Villey. Villey recognized the employment in Roman texts of *jus actoris* or *jus venditoris*, for example. But he distinguished the Roman use from the faculty, advantage, or juridically protected power of the moderns.[37] What Villey saw in the authors like Hobbes, Gassendi, and Spinoza, whose precursors were in his view Scotus, Ockham, and Gerson, was a rejection of the objective natural law as articulated by the Aristotelian philosophy of metaphysics, logic and final causes. In Villey's understanding metaphysics always comes before right. Thus the change was from objective natural law, appropriate to an Aristotelian view of the world, to the subjective natural rights of the individual attuned to empiricist thinking. It was this change, according to Villey, that explained the transformation of *ius*. From being in Roman law a status, a condition of the thing within the interior of order, *ius* was transformed into an active *facultas* or power belonging to an individual. The transformation of *ius* into *facultas* brought with it a transformation of the science of law.[38]

Albert's theory does not seem to belong to any of these traditions.[39] In his Stoic reading of *ius naturale, ius*, and *iura* (rights) are not a thing or a just thing.[40] Albert's *iura* are part of moral human nature and they are about the knowing

[35] Tuck, *Natural Rights Theories*, p. 3, 20; 30.

[36] Alberti Magni, *De bono*, p. 278.1.

[37] Michel Villey, 'Suum jus cuique tribuere' in *Studi in Onori di Pietro de Francisci*, v. I, ed. Antonino Giuffré (Milan: Giuffrè, 1956), p. 364.

[38] Villey, 'Suum jus cuique tribuere', pp. 368, 371.

[39] Although I have chosen to present the perspective provided by two classic positions, Villey's and Tuck's, a recent review of the subjective-objective debate shows it being alive and kicking. Thus Mäkinen argues in a current chapter 'that the investigation of the idea of self-preservation and its meaning in the emergence of natural rights will also clarify the relationship between the objective and the subjective rights traditions'. Virpi Mäkinen, 'Duty to Self-Preservation or Right to Life? The Relation between Natural Law and Natural Rights' (1200–1600), in *Das Gesetz—The Law—La Loi*, edited by Andreas Speer and Guy Guldentops (Berlin/Boston: De Gruyter, 2014), pp. 457–70, at 459. See also Cary J. Nederman, 'Rights', in *Oxford Handbook of Medieval Philosophy*, edited by John Marenbon (2012): pp. 643–60.

[40] Referring to the fact that Albert had no access to the book on justice of Aristotle's Ethics, see Lottin: 'dans la Summa de bono, le saint docteur ne pouvait s'appuyer que sur Cicéron: mais dans son Cours sur la Morale d'Aristote, il pouvait exploiter en plus le livre V de l'èthique à Nicomaque', Lottin,'Le loi naturalle', p. 86; see also Geyer, 'Prolegomena' to Alberti Magni, *De bono*, p. xxiv.

individual subject and about particulars. The eclecticism of Albert both makes it impossible to subsume his doctrine of *ius naturale* into Villey's categories and gives one pause as to the appropriateness of describing them either as objective or subjective natural rights. Their peculiar nature is mostly expounded through Albert's language of rights.

Albert started 'On Justice' with a first question about '*ius*' in whose first article he presented Cicero's definition in *De inventione*:[41] 'From nature is right what is not born out of opinion, but is a certain power inserted in an innate manner.'[42] This is the thesis that Albert sets out to prove in the following four questions. As a consequence, the notions he employs throughout the text to refer to *ius naturale* can be divided into two groups. The first conforms to the language of a text written by a natural lawyer, and thus *ius naturale* are 'principles of right' (*principia iuris*)[43] or 'universals of right' (*universalia iuris*),[44] 'natural rights' (*naturalia iura*),[45] 'naturals' (*naturalia*),[46] or simply 'rights' (*iura*).[47] The second and more numerous set employs the language of a biologist. Accordingly, *ius naturale* is formed by 'first seeds' (*prima semina*),[48] 'seeds of right' (*semina iuris*),[49] 'first seeds of right' (*prima semina iuris*),[50] 'seedbed of the good' (*seminaria boni*),[51] 'universal seeds of right' (*semina iuris universalia*),[52] 'seedbed in the reason of human being' (*seminaria in ratione hominis*),[53] and finally 'seminal causes' (*causas seminales*).[54]

On two occasions Albert uses the second group of concepts in the manner of an analogy. Thus, 'natural rights are like the first seeds, which are the force in the plebiscites, decrees of the senate and the answers of the prudent'.[55] In the other instances the term 'seeds of right' describes the reality of what is *ius naturale*. In that sense he affirmed that 'the law, the prophets and the gospel were promulgated by the first commander God, according to the seeds of right that he who created nature had implanted in the human heart'.[56]

The concept of seed in reference to *ius naturale* serves Albert's purposes in different ways. The seed is clearly something that is in potency, and not mixed with the particular matter of what the seed will become. In this vein he proceeds to explain the third of three different modes in which the human being relates to natural law. *Ius naturale* is thus about what belongs to the advantage, utility, and provision of

[41] The first question receives the title: 'De iure et lege naturali', however the four articles deal only with *ius*, and there is in the entire article not a single mention of *lex*, which is dealt with in the second question.

[42] 'Ad primum autem subiciatur Tullii diffinitio de iure naturale in prima Rhetorica, ubi dicit sic: 'Naturae ius est, quod non opinio genuit, sed vis quaedam innata inservit'. Alberti Magni, *De bono*, p. 259.12.

[43] Alberti Magni, *De bono*, p. 275.11. [44] Ibid., p. 266.46. [45] Ibid., p. 265.41.
[46] Ibid., p. 265.41. [47] Ibid., p. 279.67. [48] Ibid., p. 265.42; 271.20.
[49] Ibid., p. 266.44. [50] Ibid., p. 266.37. [51] Ibid., p. 275.65.
[52] Ibid., p. 270.73. [53] Ibid., p. 274.89. [54] Ibid., p. 279.53.
[55] Ibid., p. 265.41; 266.37.

[56] 'Dicitur autem quandoque ius naturale id quod non humano consilio vel ratione, sed (a) primo mandatore, qui naturam condidit, secundum semina iuris, quae humano cordi inservit, promulgatum est, et sic lex et prophetiae et evangelium sunt de iure naturali.' Ibid., p. 266.44.

human being. But 'that is always in the way according to the universal seeds of right and not according to the case or a determined consultation'.[57]

However, perhaps Albert's most relevant employment of the concept of seed might be found in the notion of *causas seminales.* Albert extracts the *causas seminales* or *logoi spermatokoi,* from its creational context [58]—he refers specifically to Augustine as his source—and affirms that 'the rights (*iura*) implanted in human nature' are 'seminal reasons'. Again, that was a helpful tool for him to explain why *ius naturale* changed over time, for instance from common use to private property.[59] As the theological tradition had it originally, by *ius naturale* everything was common. And only after the fall, human beings started to greedily get hands on the common things. Hence, the right of asserting one's things ('one is to assert a claim to property') for provision of those under one's care and for the poor *became active.* At that moment nature started to use other principles than the one determining that everything was common. But both the commonality of things and private property were originally implanted in the human being, only they had appeared in different statuses of humanity. When they were needed, rights such as the right of occupation ('that which is of no one, is allowed to be occupied') were set forth.[60]

In *De bono* the question of private property is not a matter of dispute. Moreover, as Albert has it, that monks do not have anything of their own is not of *ius naturale,* nor against it. Simply, it originates by convention.[61] The issue of the 'everything is common' (*omnia sunt communia*) which he, incidentally, identifies like the canon lawyers with 'to be communicated' (*communicanda*), is a question of a past state of humanity. In case of necessity, although by natural right goods must be shared, the owner remains the *dominus* of the goods.[62] Thus the change in *ius naturale* was according to Albert's evolutionary view, a sort of efficient adaptation of nature to new moral circumstances and challenges—as mentioned above, in the present status of human beings the right that 'one is to assert a claim to property'

[57] 'et semper est in genere secundum semina iuris universalia et non secundum casus vel consulta determinata'. Ibid., p. 270.73. '[T] hat which teaches mixed with advice and comparison about particulars are civil rights (*iura civilia*), if they are sanctioned, and the distinction is not understood about them' Ibid., p. 271.34. (translation mine).

[58] Hans Meier, *Geschichte der Lehre von den Keimkräften: von der Stoa bis zum Ausgang der Patristik, nach den Quellen dargestellt* (Bonn: Peter Hansteins Verlagsbuchhandlung, 1914).

[59] 'iam patet solutio, quia secundum diversos status utriusque seminaria sunt in iure naturali'. pp. 275, 26.

[60] 'Ad alium dicendum, quod utrumque est de iure naturali et omnia esse communia et aliquid esse proprium, quia iam diximus, quod principia iuris non sunt eadem. Unde secundum statum, in quo non est rapina nec usurpatio eius quod communi usui concessum est, dictaverunt conscientia et ratio nihil esse proprium, sed in communi unicuique dimittendum, sicut etiam in commune creatum est. Sed variato statu et crescente malitia et rapina et rancore utitur natura alio principio, scilicet vindicanda esse propria ad provisionem suorum et pauperum, et ideo tunc non erit contra ius naturae habere proprium, tamen tempore necessitatis communicandum, et sic editum est ius: 'Quod enim nullius est hominis, conceditur occupanti', et huiusmodi.' Alberti Magni, *De bono*, p. 275.11.

[61] 'Sed tamen, quod religiosi non habet proprium, hoc non est de iure naturali, nec est contra ipsum, sed potius ex pacto; et hoc continentur in hoc, quod approbatione hominum hoc voventium est sancitum.' Ibid., p. 275.28.

[62] Alberti Magni, *Super Sententiarum* (ed. Borgnet, 1893–4), Lib.III, dist.33, art.3, p. 611a.

(‘*vindicanda esse propia*’) is active, and so it is that the things *nullius* can be occupied by anyone, while the general rule that everything is common was eliminated.

Furthermore, the doctrine of seminal reasons was useful to reflect on God’s direct interventions in history, apparently deviating of or dispensing with the course of established natural right. Could God operate against himself?[63] Albert’s solution for this problem is founded on a special definition of natural rights as ‘seminal causes’. In *De bono*, the *causas seminales* or *logoi spermatokoi* constituted a pair of sets of rights in the heart of human beings, a first group following the course of nature, and the second making possible that God operates in the heart of individuals beyond nature.[64] For instance, Albert described Abraham’s decision to sacrifice his innocent son not as an exception of *ius naturale*, but, firstly, as a moral case in which the end of the act determined the nature of the act, not a homicide but an act of obedience. On another level, Abraham’s obedience was not an exception of *ius naturale* but an expression of right belonging to the second pair of *iura* (rights) planted in the hearts of human being—those that enable God’s action in human’s heart. Both pairs of rights, gradually unfolded, let human nature become what it was meant to become. The first group of rights, following the course of (rational) nature, enabled human beings to evolve into a rational man, and the second group of rights allowed the work of grace and the unfolding of humanity’s redemption.

Interestingly, both types of rights (*iura*) were implanted in nature and are therefore natural rights and the second group can also be simultaneously classified as about obedience to grace. One has to assume that, in Albert’s understanding, when God created human beings the future fall and disobedience of Adam and Eve and the salvation of the human race was also present in the divine mind. In that sense God not only inserted in humanity’s heart the rights according to the status of the instituted nature, but also to its status of *natura restituta* or the status of redemption after the incarnation of Christ.[65]

[63] ‘Sed contra: Deus enim, ut supra est obiectum, non potest operari contra seipsum. Sed opus suum est id quod dictat conscientia de simpliciter malis, quia hoc inservit cordi humano. Ergo si dispensat et praecipit contrarium, operabitur contra seipsum, quod est impossibile.’ Alberti Magni, *De bono*, p. 278.82.

[64] ‘Et est simile in natura. In illa enim duplices causas seminales deus inservit, ut dicit Augustinus, scilicet quasdam, ex quibus res fiant, et quasdam, ex quibus fieri possint. Ex quibus autem fieri possint, non explicat solito cursu naturae, sed potius sua voluntate in miraculis ad significandum magnum miraculum, quod futurum erat in assumptione carnis. Et tunc non operatur contra causas seminales, quas naturae inservit, quia natura etiam istas habet, licet non sic, quod ex ipsis res fiant, sed ut ex ipsis fieri possint; ita per omnia dicimus quod *in corde humano sunt duplicia iura*, quaedam scilicet explicata ratione humana et voluntate, quae respondet rationibus illis ex quibus opera nostra fiant, quaedam autem sunt in corde iura, ex quibus ipse operetur ad ostensionem gratia redemptionis, quae non sunt, ex quibus opera nostra fiant, sed ex quibus opera sua per eum imperantem fieri possint; et ideo etiam non nisi ab eo solo possunt talia opera coniungi finibus bonis et separari a malis.’ Ibid., p. 279.59. (emphasis mine).

[65] Albert explains that Abraham’s story of obedience, and other instances prefigured the redemption: ‘Et similiter in Abraham exemplum obedientiae et figura redemptionis fuerunt fines actus.’ Alberti Magni, *De bono*, p. 279.50. See on this also, Lottin, *Le droit nature chez Saint Thomas d’Aquin et ses prédécesseurs*, p. 48.

The seeds of obedience implanted in human heart, which Albert chooses to call rights, are means for our restoration to God. Moreover, this choice of language evidences that the possibility of salvation exists within human beings thanks to natural rights. Notwithstanding, in Albert's Christian and theocentric *Weltanschauung* the salvation does not happen through our actions. The second group of rights is not there so that 'through them our works are done, but that through them, God commanding, his works are done'.[66] Hence, although a suspicion of Pelagianism might arise with regard to Albert's doctrine of natural rights in *De bono*, the theological problem is carefully avoided.[67]

Needless to say, Albert would point out in his first commentary to *Nichomachean Ethics* that Cicero's 'natural man' never existed, but his was only a manner of speaking '*ex hypothesi*'.[68]

Causas Seminales: Stoic, Augustinian, and Patristic

Probably with a view to the ample commentary devoted to his entire *ouvre*, the little attention paid to Albert's doctrine of *ius naturale* in *De bono* explains as well the general glossing over of its Stoic aspects.[69] There is no mention, let alone analysis of the concept of 'seminal reasons as natural rights' in the scholarship on Albert's *ius naturale.* [70] To be sure, Stoic and Augustinian influences are by no means an evident approach to take in the case of the *doctor universalis*. However, the large period covered by his writings (1233–75) and his curiosity and interest for every question relevant to his time,[71] among them the gradual translation of Aristotelian corpus, made Albert's work in many respects a crossroads that can lead to different paths.

More than a century ago Ehrle suggested as much when he studied the sharp division in the Dominican School of the thirteenth century between Augustinianism and Aristotelianism. The latter—more novel—started with Albert the Great, achieved maturity through the work of Thomas Aquinas, and after the Dominican's General Chapters of 1278 and 1279 became the authoritative expression for the

66 Alberti Magni, *De bono*, p. 279.70.

67 Trottman also refers to this, more generally, in Albert's articulation of the capacity by nature to grasp the first principles of action: 'Un tel principe infus par Dieu lors de la Création et qui n'est pas la grâce n'est pas sans poser quelques problèmes théologiques. On perçoit tout de suite les conséquences pélagiennes qu'on pourrait en tirer.' Trottmann, 'La synderese selon Abert le Grand', p. 272.

68 Et similiter dicendum est ad tertium de silvestribus hominibus, quod habent ordinem naturalem, si tamen ponuntur esse; non enim videtur, quod homines umquam silvestres fuerunt; Tullius autem loquitur ex hipothesi' Alberti Magni, *Super ethica*, vol. I, edited by Wilhelm Kübel (Monasterii Westfalorum in Aedibus Aschendorff, 1968–72), p. 17.1.

69 No classic study on natural rights engages with Albert's *De bono*. Richard Tuck and Brian Tierney do not even once mention Albert in their histories of natural rights; Annabel Brett mentions him in passim. Brett, *Liberty, Right and Nature*, pp. 78; 83–5.

70 Mentioning his inspiration of Cicero and employing Albert's language of *ius naturale* as seeds of right, but not dwelling upon this fact, Cunningham, *Reclaiming Moral Agency.*

71 Pelster, *Kritische Studien zum Leben und zu den Schriften Alberts des Großen*.

entire order. But, according to Ehrle, Albert the Great was also to a large extent the source of the former movement followed by the old Augustinians of the Dominican order, first in Paris, and when Paris became Thomist, in Oxford, until the decisions for the entire order of 1278 and 1279 weakened it considerably.[72]

At any rate, the recourse to *rationes seminales* was in the times of Aristotelianism a sign of positioning oneself with the old Augustinian school. Robert Kilwardby was among the Dominicans that actively opposed some of Thomas Aquinas's doctrines in what they could deviate from the old Augustinian teaching. As Archbishop of Canterbury, entrusted also with guarding over the University, he condemned in Oxford in March of 1277—only a couple of weeks after a similar condemnation in Paris—several teachings, among them Aquinas's on the unity of human being's soul and Aquinas's idea of matter without active potency. In a letter justifying his decision, Kilwardby contended with respect to the first point for a doctrine that distinguished a vegetative, sensitive, and intellectual soul in human beings and, with reference to the second, for the substantial reality of the Augustinian *rationes seminales*.[73] Kilwardby objected in the latter case that, if it would be true that there were no original potency in natural matter, then what Augustine had established on *rationes seminales* would be false, affecting directly the doctrine of simultaneous creation.[74]

The context of Augustinian *rationes seminales* was, as Kilwardby rightly pointed out, Augustine's doctrine of the simultaneous creation.[75] According to that doctrine, everything was created at the same time, matter and form. The division of creation during six days in the Bible was explained by God's care for human beings, who needed language for understanding things. The stoic-Neoplatonic teaching of the seminal reasons, however, helped Augustine to accommodate into the theory the appearance of new organisms along history without having to consider new moments of creation. Therefore, Augustine would explain, the *rationes seminales* were inserted from the beginning in all creation. Some of them

[72] Franz Ehrle, 'Der Augustinismus und der Aristotelismus in der Scholastik gegen Ende des 13. Jahrhunderts', *Archiv für Literatur und Kirchengeschichte des Mittelalters*, edited by Heinrich Deniffle and Franz Ehrle (Freiburg im Breisgau: Herdersche Verlagshandlung, 1889), pp. 605–6. More than as a simple opposition, the story of a struggle between Aristotelianism and Augustinianism in that period is told now as one far more complex process, which in a way the case of Albert exemplifies, see e.g. Steven Marrone, *The Light of Thy Countenance: Science and Knowledge of God in the 13th Century*, 2 vols (Leiden: Brill, 2001).

[73] The letter is printed at the end of Ehrle's article: 'Et rationes seminales omnium hominum sunt in primis parentibus, que per continuatam generationem per secula explicantur. Nec hoc solum est in hominibus, sed in brutis animalibus per seminalem propagationem sibi succedentibus naturaliter.' Ehrle, 'Der Augustinismus und der Aristotelismus', p. 623.

[74] 'Item, si non sunt originales potentie utcunque active in materia naturali, tunc falsum est quidquid ponit Augustinus de rationibus seminalibus sive originibus fiendorum. Item tunc falsum est, quod ponit, omnia corporalia simul esse creata in operibus conditionis, que postmodum opere nature evolvuntur per opera administrationis.' Also from Kildwardby's letter, ibid., p. 620.

[75] 'Rationes' and 'causas seminales' are interchangeble terms for Wengel; see P. Macarius Wengel, *Die Lehre von den rationes seminales bei Albert dem Großen* (Würzburg: Richard Mayr, 1937). Interestingly, Wengel's supervisor was Hans Meier, author of the still relevant *Geschichte der Lehre von den Keimkräften*. I follow Meier and Wengel in their explanation of Augustine's *rationes seminales*.

developed immediately while others would unfold only in later moments in time. For Augustine, the seminal reasons operated in the whole range of organisms guaranteeing the constancy of the species in the growing and decay of organic nature. Albert subscribes to the doctrine of the simultaneous creation. Nevertheless, as Wengel explains, the *rationes seminales* have for him a much more limited role than in Augustine.[76] His observation of the fact that there are organisms that arise from non-living matter leads Albert to divide the world of simultaneous creation into two. There are the superior animals, created by God in gendered pairs, and the other organisms, plants, and lower animals created only as *rationes seminales*. The former spread by procreation and the latter by abiogenesis or evolution from non-living matter. The seminal reasons are thus not a potential for creation of all creatures but only for the latter.[77]

Albert complains about the employment of Augustine's confusing terminology on *rationes seminales*.[78] But in his own commentary the term is also unclear, sometimes appearing that *rationes seminales* are the concept that comprehend all other causes in the world, *primordiales, obedentialis, naturales, radicales*, and *seminales*.[79] What becomes clear from his dense discussion in the commentary on the *Sentences*, however, is that for Albert *causas* or *rationes seminales* belonged, on the one hand, to the context of theological problems of demonstration of miracles and faith, yet on the other hand, Albert uses the seminal reasons in the service of an anthropological and psychological ethics to explain imperfection and deficiency in the world.

In the first case, from Albert's explanation of miracles, one gathers that in principle miracles are unrelated to the *rationes seminales*, but it can be that the miracle does not operate against nature. For instance, the fact of Aaron throwing the rod on the floor and it becoming a snake in front of the Pharaoh of Egypt did not need necessarily violate the course of nature. Only, Albert clarified, nature would do it by degrees. The rod would undergo putrefaction and after that, through the *causas seminales* a snake would be formed.[80] Similar to what he writes in *De bono*,

[76] Wengel, *Die Lehre von den rationes seminales bei Albert dem Großen*, p. 10. Although he uses the term, in the teaching of Thomas Aquinas the rationes seminales play not any more a role, so Ehrle, 'Der Augustinismus und der Aristotelismus', pp. 633–4.

[77] Wengel, *Die Lehre von den rationes seminales bei Albert dem Großen*.

[78] *Super Sententiarum* (ed. Borgnet, 1893-4), Lib.II, dist.18, art.7, p.322b/322a/ARTICULUS VII, 'SOLUTIO. Dicendum, quod Augustinus omnia ista nomina ponit absque distinctione, et multi hic multiplicem fecerunt distinctionem, nec distinctio unius concordat cum alia.'

[79] *Summa Theologiae* (ed. Borgnet, 1894–5), Pars II, tract.8, q.31, m.1, art.1, p.333 ARTICULUS II. 'De seminalibus rationibus, quot sint, et quae differentia inter eas? Deinde quaeritur, Quot sint genere, et quae differentia inter eas? Et hoc per antedicta facile est determinare.'

'Sunt enim primordiales simpliciter, quae sunt in Verbo. Et sunt originales, quae primitus inditae sunt mundo. Et sunt obedientiales, quae sunt in creatura, secundum quod per rationem debiti refertur ad Creatorem. Et sunt radicales, secundum quas elementata omnia radicantur in rationibus virtutum elementorum. Et sunt naturales, quae a principio intrinseco (quod est natura) faciunt pullulare pullulans per se, et non secundum accidens. Et sunt seminales, secundum quas secundum causam efficientem, materialem, et formalem, ex similibus in specie et forma producuntur similia. Et sunt causales, secundum quas tam ex causa supernaturali quae Deus est, quam ex causis inferioribus et naturalibus rationabiliter procedunt causata. Et sic differunt sub istis differentiis.'

[80] *Summa Theologiae* (ed. Borgnet, 1894–5), Pars I, tract.19, q.78, m.2, p.834a.

Albert sees in the *causas seminales* a sign of the wisdom of God, who inserted in all creation a power of obedience through *causas seminales.* And the Creator wants to have through them a demonstration of faith. God is not self-contradicting when from time to time, like when he asked Abraham for an act of heroic obedience, he explains directly and openly what he wants to happen.[81]

Albert might have borrowed from other early Christian theologians the employment of seminal reasons for the second case; that is, with an ethical import. In his apologetic of Christianity, Justin had adopted the seminal reasons in order to show the Romans that Christianity, and Jesus Christ himself, was in seed in every human being before his incarnation, though evidently that occurred so in a deficient manner. Paganism and Christianity were thus one for the other, the latter 'acting' in the former 'spermatically'. Justin's use of seminal reasons was analogous to the idea of the *imago dei* and his meaning was to explain deficiency.[82]

The reverse idea of deficiency appears in Albert, considering how to explain the present imperfection in the ethical actions of human beings after the fall of Adam and Eve. The inferior ethical and religious conditions of the present are thus compensated by an adaption of the *ius naturale* in human nature to postlapsarian conditions. Accordingly, nature had made efficient in the present status previously existing, but only latent, *causas seminales*, such as the *ius* of private property mentioned before.

Finally, the seminal reasons assist Albert in integrating the theological sources, in particular the Bible, with the Roman tradition of an immutable *ius naturale* inserted in nature, whose immutability Albert interprets with the historical perspective of a Christian theologian.

'Nature is Reason'

Both the *causas seminales* and the habit of natural law configure human nature but, as we have seen, they do not imply an automatic motion of nature. What is 'according to nature, and follows from the nature of man' is only considered by Albert 'in so far that man is rational'.[83]

As it was previously mentioned, in *De bono* Albert has not accessed yet the chapters on prudence and justice of *Nichomachean Ethics.* This does not bring

[81] *Super Sententiarum* (ed. Borgnet, 1893–4), Lib.IV, dist.12, art.16, p.329a 'AD ALIUD dicendum, quod ex ordinatione sapientiae divinae est, quod accidens non sit sine subjecto secundum causas seminales naturales quas prius conditor inseruit, ut dicit Augustinus: sed praeter has causas, etiam Dominus inseruit primis creatis potestatem obedientiae ad id quod Creator vellet ad fidei demonstrationem: sed in hoc sibi non contrariatur, si utraque pro tempore explicat prout voluerit, ut dicit Augustinus.'

[82] On Justine Martyr and *causas seminales* and his analogue use of *causas seminales* to the *imago dei*, Meier, *Geschichte der Lehre von den Keimkräften*, pp. 80–93.

[83] 'Ad id quod obicitur de distinctione Philosophi, concedimus de plano, quod ius naturale dicitur, quod est secundum naturam et consequens naturam hominis, inquantum homo est rationalis'. Alberti Magni, *De bono*, 271.59.

him, however, to simply follow tradition, although he is influenced by it. William of Auxerre's *Summa Aurea*, probably the most important theological treatise of *ius naturale* previous to Albert, is embedded in canon law theory and reasons of charity, and, interestingly, supported by arguments of utility.[84] In turn, Albert's almost nominalist account of natural rights as seeds of right inserted in human nature is neither typically Aristotelian nor least of all Thomist. Rather, observing human beings, Albert seems to be aiming at providing a more foundational and more natural account than those given by civilians and canon lawyers.[85]

The article 'Of which modes is spoken of natural right' in *De bono* combines a discussion of the demands of our rational nature with the overall question of the 'good', in which, after a comment on the *Glossa ordinaria*, Boethius, Isidore, Porphyrius, and Aristotle, Albert gives his own solution:

Everything that has been said so far touches a certain division which falls in the meaning of natural right. Natural right is thus nothing else than the right of reason as it is its due (*sive debitum*), in as much as nature is reason.[86]

The statement that 'nature is reason' is next divided into three modes of natural right depending on which of the two notions has more weight in it, nature or reason.

If one is to understand it as meaning more in the sense of nature, there belong to it principles of action pertaining to its consistency and health, as well as the reasoning about them, such as these things pertaining to the health of the individual, such as food, clothes, house and bed, and care to health, and procurement of medicines, and similar, that we want for us, when we reason about them; similarly what pertains to the well-being of the species, a wife, children, and love and care for them.[87]

All this ought to be done with right reason (*recta ratio*) because 'right can never establish an injustice'; thus gluttony or robbing cannot be of natural right.[88] Moreover, Albert adds the caveat that procreation, education and nutrition are common to the beasts, and only to the extent that they participate of reason—that

[84] 'sed aliqua esse propria dictat ratio naturalis quasi coacta, scit enim quod secundum statum nature, qui modo est, utilius est aliqua esse propria quam omnia esse communia.'; on the dispensation of *ius naturale*: 'Fit autem dispensation duabus causis, scilicet aut utilitate aut necessitate; et quando fit utilitate, aut fit utilitate ecclesie aut private persone.' Magistri Guillelmi Altissiodorensis, *Summa Aurea*, edited by Jean Riballier (Paris: Centre National de la Recherche Scientifique/ Roma, Editiones Collegii S. Bonaventurae ad Claras Aquas, 1986) Liber III, tomus I, tr. 18. 372, 83; 381, 7. According to Lottin, '[U]n premier mérite de Guillaume d'Auxerre est d'avoir intégré le droit naturel au sein même de la théologie'. Lottin, *Le droit nature chez Saint Thomas d'Aquin et ses prédécesseurs*, p. 33.

[85] Albert is 'a thinker anxious to exploit and adopt Aristotelian naturalism', Cunningham, *Reclaiming Moral Agency*, p. 70.

[86] Alberti Magni, *De bono*, p. 270.22.

[87] 'Si autem accipiatur ut natura, tunc ipsa erit principium operum pertinentium ad consistentiam et salute eius in quo est, et ratiocinabitur de illis, sicut sunt pertinentia saluti individui, ut cibus, vestitus, domus et lectus et dilectio sanitatis et procuratio medicinae et alia huiusmodi, quae pro nobis quaerimus ratiocinando de illis; similiter pertinentia saluti speciei, ut uxor, proles et dilectio et providentia utrorumque'. Ibid., p. 270.28.

[88] Ibid., p. 270.36.

is, to the extent that they could be acts of virtue or of vice—are they of *ius naturale*. The text constantly highlights that animals have no natural rights because human beings have them only in so far that they are rational.[89]

The second group of natural right inclines more to reason:

If it was understood more about reason than nature, then it is about those (principles) that pertain to religion and justice and the honesty of human beings in themselves and towards others, and so yet when they have something of nature and they are not completely of reason.[90]

In the third group Albert refers to the principles where there is balance of reason and nature:

The third mode of natural reason is equally reason and nature, and in this manner pertain to natural right, that which in right reason is provided for the convenience and utility of human beings such as to provide for the house, manage the family, chose the prelates 'for punishment of the bad and reward of the good', and protect what is one's own and such things, and that is always in the way according to the universal seeds of right and not according to the case or a determined consultation.[91]

Albert covers much ground with this division of the three modes of *ius naturale* and it is possibly from this article where the clearest idea transpires of what he means with 'the seeds of rights' inserted in human nature. Still, does Albert have in mind an individual right to obtain medicine, worship, protect one's belongings, or to vindicate property, or instead a series of precepts commanding one to do so? In other words, is he or is he not conceptualizing what would later be termed subjective rights? An approach towards an answer appears in the second *questio* 'On Law', where Albert defines the distinction between *ius* and *lex* as follows:

... the *lex* regards more an obligation of a command of nature, and *ius* more a reasoning about how to act by nature, and thus is apparent all the difference between natural law and natural right. Where natural right recognizes what is honest and prohibits the contrary by way of judgment, the natural law does these two by way of obligation and command through precepts and thus is exposed the difference.[92]

In the first place, the motive to act for the individual is not immediately that he or she *has* a right to food, to worship God or to protect one's goods, but mediately, because she proceeds through reasoning about the particular case to understand that this is the right or honest thing to do according to her nature. However, some action is the right thing to do because there are rights in the individual's human nature establishing that 'food and medicines are to be obtained', 'God is to be worshipped' and 'one's goods are to be protected'. In that sense the individual *has* or

[89] 'Non enim consentimus in distinctionem, quam quidam posuerunt, scilicet quod ius naturale multis modis dicatur et uno modo sit commune nobis cum brutis.' Ibid., pp. 265–6.74. Albert gives a hint in order to ascertain to what extent these activities participate of reason. One might observe the positive laws regulating them, and in all that these laws have in common, one will discover what is of *ius naturale* in them. Ibid., p. 271.15.

[90] Ibid., p. 270.60. [91] Ibid., p. 270.70. [92] Ibid., p. 285.27.

possesses a right. However, for Albert to *have* a right does not amount to an entitlement against someone else (God, nature, one's neighbour, the city). Instead, for the individual to possess a right is equivalent to having the possibility of making a judgment about *ius* in that particular case. Therefore the really relevant thing for Albert is to have that capacity to know the universals of right.

An Autonomous Power?

'From nature is right what is not born out of opinion, but is a certain power or force inserted in an innate manner.' Albert is following, in *De bono*, Cicero's definition step by step; therefore, he has to inquire as well about that power of which Cicero speaks.

The idea of right-power of action (*ius-potestas/facultas*) as 'being' in Jean Gerson brings Brett to connect him with Albert, from whom Gerson arguably received inspiration. Famously, Gerson made the claim that 'every positive being has as much right [defined as power of action] thus generally defined as it has of being, and thus of goodness'.[93] Starting the reading with Albert however, one draws the conclusion that Albert's most characteristic and striking statement is to define that innate *vis* or force called *ius naturale* as knowledge. Only in a second stage, and elaborating on his notion of intellect agent, one might indeed argue that for Albert knowledge *is* being.[94]

> If it is asked, what is that force of nature, I say that without a doubt, that force of nature is the light of the agent intellect (…) For that light (…) makes by itself, that is without proof and demonstration, to assent to first principles of the sciences and of the operations.[95]

The agent intellect is in Albert a force that illuminates and in a sense gives life to the principles of natural right embedded in human beings' practical intellect. Here Albert divides *ius naturale* into the principles of right inserted in human nature and the force, power or light of the agent intellect that makes them known to the individual.[96]

[93] Gerson quoted in Brett, *Liberty, Right and Nature,* p. 83; according to Brett this is a consequence of Albert's combination of Dyonisius with Aristotelianism and Gerson adding to this a theory of rights: 'When Gerson says that a being has as much right, defined as a power of action, as it has as being and goodness, he is appropriating Albert's peripatetic Dionysianism to the rights discourse of the fourteenth century' (p. 85).

[94] To the agent intellect 'its knowing is its being because it is always in act'. Albertus, *De homine*, pars II, p. 421.53.

[95] 'Si autem quaeritur, quae sit illa vis naturae, dico, quod absque dubio illa naturae vis est lumen intellectus agentis, cuius lumen est species specierum intelligibilium, ut probatum est in quaestionibus *De intelligibili intellectus practici et speculative.* Illud enim lumen distinctum ad species terminorum, quae sunt in principiis primis intellectus agentis et practici, facit per se, hoc est sine probatione et demonstratione, assentire principiis primis scientiarum et operationum.' Alberti Magni, *De Bono*, p. 265.58.

[96] Most usually he refers to Aristotle in the context of the agent intellect, but also to Augustine, Anaxagoras, Hermes, and others, see *Super Sententiarum* (ed. Borgnet, 1893–4), Lib.II, dist.30, art.1, p. 497b; in order to highlight the complete separation of the agent intellect from the world Albert

Albert famously developed a notion of the agent intellect drawing inspiration from Aristotle but also as a novel theoretical concept.[97] The agent intellect is a force; as he writes in the context of *ius naturale*, a power. Further, it is the individuation principle, that is to say, what makes a human being an individual. Albert also points to the fact that human beings' agent intellect is *separated* from the first source of light, that is to say God, and this is the origin of our freedom. 'This divine particle is free due to its separateness and it makes us to be lords (*dominos*) of our acts.'[98]

In this sense, Albert's agent intellect explodes Villey's dichotomy of an Aristotelian natural order of justice versus the Ockhamism of natural absolute powers.[99] The light of the agent intellect, a power, makes us at once lords of our acts and reveals us the rights of our created nature.

A combination of autonomy of the self and yet connection to the source of knowledge results from the *natural right-natural rights-agent intellect* structure.[100] Despite its power, what the agent intellect cannot achieve is to avoid error in individual's application of the natural right to the concrete case. The autonomous power of the self is not definitive because, ultimately, reason fails. This is clear when Albert indicates that human beings cannot dispense with *ius naturale*—only God can do that—but can only interpret it:

> And the cause is that interpretation is done in the application of common right to the particular case and the particular deeds, and the reason is there to do this. Reason, however, often and in many instances is deceived, but not the reason of the wise; and thus having authority, determination and interpretation or exposition is to be made according to the deliberations of the wise.[101]

refers to Anaxagoras, *De animalibus* (ed. Stadler, 1916–1920), Lib.XVI, tract.1, cap.12, p. 1096; Lib. XXII, tract.1, cap.5, p.1353. §9§.

97 According to Sellés, only Dietrich von Freiberg surpasses Albert in the manner he dwells with the agent intellect, and Dietrich employs Albert for doing so, Juan Fernando Sellés, *El intelecto agente y los filósofos. Venturas y desventuras del supremo hallazgo aristotélico sobre el hombre. I, siglos IV-a.C. –XV,* (Pamplona: Eunsa, 2012), pp. 219–38; Kurt Flasch, 'Introduction' in *Dietrich von Freiberg. Opera Omnia. T. I: Schriften zur Intellekttheorie*, edited by Burkjard Mojsisch (Hamburg: Felix Meiner Verlag, 1977).

98 'Hoc quidem modo dicendo divinam particulam, intellectus agentis divina particula est non quidem per substantiam et naturam divinam, sed secundum participationem proprietatis et virtutis, et analogiam typicae imagines ad prototypum, quod omnium est causa efficiens et formalis per aliquem modum. Haec divina particula ex separatione libera est, et facit nos esse dominos nostrorum actuum. Et ex quod divina est, formalis est ad esse et bene esse. Divinum et certissimum est hoc quod omnis causa est in nobis.' Albertus, *Ethica*, Liber I, t. 7, c. 5 (ed. Borgnet, VII, Paris, 1891); see also Paul Dominikus Hellmeier, *Anima et intellectus. Albertus Magnus und Thomas von Aquin über Seele und Intellekt des Menschen* (Beiträge zur Geschichte der Philosophie und Theologie des Mittelalters. Neue Folge, Band 75) (Münster: Aschendorff Verlag, 2011), p. 217.

99 Villey, 'Le genèse du droit subjectif chez Guillaume d'Occam'.

100 The agent intellect 'originates in God, and God is its end', Sellés, *El intelecto agente y los filósofos*, p. 239.

101 'Solutio: Dicimus ad primum, quod ius naturale numquam recipit dispensationem ab homine, sed a deo potest recipere dispensationem, et ab homine, qui vicarius dei est in auctoritate potestatis et ordine sapientiae et bonitate vitae, potest recipere interpretationem. Cuius causa est, quia interpretatio fit secundum applicationem communis iuris ad particulares casus et opera particularia, et hoc facere est rationis. Ratio autem plurium ut frequenter decipitur, sed non ratio sapientum; et ideo

Notwithstanding the nearly divine, individual-centred power of the agent intellect and the rights innate in human beings, we are confronted with the defective reason in the judgment of the particular case. In an impressive move reminiscent of the Stoics, who tend to understand true knowledge only within the reach of the few Sage, Albert concludes that it is because reason errs when enacting the good that in the application of the natural right to the particular case one must follow the deliberations of the wise.[102]

Albert's conclusion is probably also related to his understanding of creation in a hierarchy of levels. The intellect would be closer to God, less apt to err, the reason instead at a lower level. He goes so far as to state that 'man is two men: according to intellect, that is, according to his connection to God', in which 'there is nothing of the animal' in him or her, and 'according to speculative reason, according to which man is connected to time and space, and by which indeed man is also excelling among animals'.[103]

Conclusions

Subjective natural rights have been traditionally thought to be born in the early fourteenth century as a result of the poverty controversies, when *dominium* and *ius* were for the first time identified, and when human beings were placed at the same level with God in terms of sovereignty by associating *ius* with *potestas*. In both cases theologians put natural rights at the service of historically well-defined political purposes.[104] Distinctly, in these elaborations the question was about the abstract and doctrinal recognition of human beings' natural rights of *dominium* and sovereignty.

This chapter has defended the argument that half a century earlier Albert the Great developed a concept of natural rights, connecting individual human beings

habentis auctoritatem secundum consulta sapientum est determinare et interpretari vel exponere.' Alberti Magni, *De Bono*, p. 277.89.

[102] An insightful description of the role of the Sage in Stoic Ethics in Tad Brennan, *The Stoic life. Emotions, Duties, and Fate* (Clarendon Press Oxford; New York: Oxford University Press, 2005), pp. 35–47.

[103] 'Homo enim duo homines est secundum intellectum, scilicet secundum quem Deo connexus est (ut dicit Hermes Trismegitus) nihil brutale habens in seipso; et secundum rationem inquisitam secundum quam tempori et continuo conjunctus est, secundum quam quidem etiam homo est excellens bestias.' Albertus, *Ethica*, Liber X, t. 2, c. 3 (ed. Borgnet, VII, Paris, 1891). Moreover, the most characteristic feature of a human being is 'not to be a substance, or an animated substance, or a living or a sensible being, but if one wants to ask what is what makes a human being to be a human being, one would answer, that it is intellectual.' ('Est ergo talis intellectus homini proprius secundum naturam. Si enim quaeram ab aliquot, quid sit secundum esse hominis, non dicet quod substantia sit, nec quod substantia animate sit, nec quod vivum sit, nec quod sensibile sit, sed dicet quod intellectual sit.') Albertus, *Ethica*, Liber X, t. 2, c. 3 (ed. Borgnet, VII, Paris, 1891).

[104] For a description of the political uses by Ockham, see Brett, *Liberty, Right and Nature*, pp. 50–87; for the political use by Gerson see Tuck, *Natural Rights Theories*, pp. 30–1.

with God and defined as the individual's capacity of knowledge, inserted in nature, about what is good for the human being, materially, politically and morally.

A leap of thought had occurred from concreteness to abstraction between the thirteenth and the fourteenth century. The history of natural rights shifts in this manner from practice with a tendency to good, to practice without direction and the leap of thought, or the change of mentality if you wish,[105] occurs in a moment in which theologians stop counting with an external source of light (God) in order to know the rights.

But the conceptions of rights both as *dominium* and sovereignty are integrated in the comprehensive concept of natural rights of the individual exposed in this article, which is a combination of theology, morality, and law and is to be found almost a century earlier in the theological work of Albert the Great. Albert's ongoing political project seems to be a translation of the relevant social and political questions into a theological idiom, or, as Anzulewicz put it, about offering a system grounded in theology that complies with the standards of science and that is able to explain reality in a unitary manner.[106]

In this enterprise natural rights occupy a central position in the early stages of Albert's work. Natural rights are the link between the objective reality of society and the objective reality of God, a link that operates through the subjective reasoning of individuals. Natural rights are for Albert of divine origin, individual centred, founded on nature as reason, and their existence is no matter of controversy. They exist because human beings are 'vicars of God' in this world 'in the authority of power, the order of wisdom and the goodness of life'.[107] But the hopes placed on natural rights cannot be overestimated. As a subjective institution they are unable of becoming sole providers of the building blocks of society. Due to the fact that humans err as a matter of course on the particular interpretation of natural rights, in a manner that the 'vicars' seem to be unable to become autonomous, rights are not enough in order to exercise the said authority of power, the order of knowledge and the practice of the good. Therefore, for specially problematic interpretations of natural rights, individuals need to follow the advice of the experts, theologians, moralists, and jurists. We are dealing here with subjective rights with the final goal of 'acting well' (Eudaimonia) that cannot disentangle themselves from dependence on others, who would speak *objectively*, when they referred to particular goods and are exercised in a precarious status as to good and truth. Later, Albert became convinced that for living the good life individuals not only needed rights but also virtues within society. This latter point might explain Albert's posterior turn to comment twice on the *Nichomachean Ethics* and his gradual abandonment of the doctrine of individual centred natural rights. Still, Albert the Great might have been the first theologian that produced a theory of natural rights.

[105] Jacques Le Goff, 'Mentalities: A History of Ambiguities', in *Constructing the Past: Essays on Historical Methodology*, edited by Jacques Le Goff and Pierre Nora (Cambridge/New York: Cambridge University Press, 1985), p. 166.

[106] Henryk Anzulewicz, "Bonum' als Schlüsselbegriff bei Albertus Magnus', in *Albertus Magnus, Zum Gedenken nach 800 Jahren*, p. 115.

[107] Alberti Magni, *De Bono*, p. 278.2.

Bibliography

Primary Sources

Aquinas, Thomas. *Summa Theologia*, v. 28, Ia2ae. 90–7, 'Law and Political Theory', translation, introduction and notes by Thomas Gilby O. P. (Cambridge: Cambridge University Press, 1966).

Altissiodorensis, Magistri Guillelmi. *Summa Aurea*, edited by Jean Riballier (Paris: Centre National de la Recherche Scientifique/ Roma, Editiones Collegii S. Bonaventurae ad Claras Aquas, 1986).

Magni, Alberti. *De bono*. In *Alberti Magni opera omnia*, tomus XXVIII (Monasterii westfalorum in aedibus Aschendorff, 1951).

Magni, Alberti. *De homine*, ediderunt Henryk Anzulewicz et Joachim R. Söder (Monasterii Westfalorum in Aedibus Aschendorff, 2008), tomus XXVII, pars II.

Magni, Alberti. *Super ethica*, vol. I, edited by Wilhelm Kübel (Monasterii Westfalorum in Aedibus Aschendorff, 1968–1972).

Magnus, Albertus. *Super Sententiarum* (ed. Borgnet, 1893–4). http://albertusmagnus.uwaterloo.ca/.

Magnus, Albertus. *Ethica* (ed. Borgnet, 1891). http://albertusmagnus.uwaterloo.ca/.

Summa in Decretum Simonis Bisinianensis Edidit Petrus V. Aimone (Fribourg, 2007). This can be found in: http://www.unifr.ch/cdc/assets/files/summa_simonis_BAND_I%20 14%2010%202007.pdf.

Secondary Sources

Anzulewicz, Henryk. '"Bonum" als Schlüsselbegriff bei Albertus Magnus'. In *Albertus Magnus. Zum Gedenken nach 800 Jahren: Neue Zugänge, Aspekte und Perspektiven*, edited by Walter Senner. With collaboration by Henryk Anzulewicz, Maria Burger, Ruth Meyer, Maria Nuert, Pablo C. Sicouly, Joachim Söder, and Klaus-Bernward Springer (Berlin: Akademie Verlag, 2001), p. 113.

Baur, Michael. 'Law and Natural Law'. In *The Oxford Handbook of Aquinas*, edited by Brian Davies and Eleonore Stump (New York: Oxford University Press, 2012), p. 238.

Brennan, Tad. *The Stoic Life. Emotions, Duties, and Fate* (Clarendon Press Oxford; New York: Oxford University Press, 2005).

Brett, Annabel S. *Liberty, Right and Nature. Individual Rights in Later Scholastic Thought* (Cambridge: Cambridge University Press, 2000).

Brundage, James A. 'The Medieval Battle of the Faculties. Theologians v. Canonists'. In *Liber amicorum Robert Somerville*, edited by Uta-Renate, Blumenthal, Anders Winroth, and Peter Landau (Washington, D.C.: Catholic University of America Press, 2012), p. 279.

Cohen, S. Marc. 'Aristotle on the Principle of Non-Contradiction'. *Canadian Journal of Philosophy* 16 (1986): p. 359.

Cunningham, Stanley B. *Reclaiming Moral Agency: The Moral Philosophy of Albert the Great* (Washington, D.C.: Catholic University of America Press, 2008).

Ehrle, Franz. 'Der Augustinismus und der Aristotelismus in der Scholastik gegen Ende des 13. Jahrhunderts'. In *Archiv für Literatur und Kirchengeschichte des Mittelalters*, edited by Heinrich Deniffle and Franz Ehrle (Freiburg im Breisgau: Herdersche Verlagshandlung, 1889).

Flasch, Kurt. 'Introduction'. In *Dietrich von Freiberg. Opera Omnia. T. I: Schriften zur Intellekttheorie*, edited by Burkjard Mojsisch (Hamburg: Felix Meiner Verlag, 1977).

Geyer, Bernhardus. 'Prolegomena' to Alberti Magni, *De bono*, in *Alberti Magni opera omnia*, tomus XXVIII (Monasterii westfalorum in aedibus Aschendorff, 1951).

Grabmann, Martin. 'Die Erörterung der Frage, ob die Kirche besser durch einen guten Juristen oder durch einen Theologen regiert werde, bei Gottfried von Fontaines (nach 1306) und Augustinus Triumphus von Ancona (1328). In *Eduard Eichmann zum 70. Geburtstag*, edited by Martin Grabmann und Karl Hofmann (Wien: F. Beck, and Zürich: B. Götschmann, 1940), p. 1.

Grabmann, Martin. 'Der Einfluβ Alberts des Groβen auf die mittelalterliche Aristoteleserklärung'. In *Gesammelte Akademie Abhandlungen* v. II (Padeborn: Ferdinand Schöningh, 1979), pp. 1934–61.

Groten, Manfred. *Albertus Magnus und der Groſʒe Schied (Köln 1258)—Aristotelische Politik im Praxistest, Lectio Albertina 12* (Münster: Aschendorff Verlag, 2011).

Hellmeier, Paul Dominikus. *Anima et intellectus. Albertus Magnus und Thomas von Aquin über Seele und Intellekt des Menschen* (Beiträge zur Geschichte der Philosophie und Theologie des Mittelalters. Neue Folge, Band 75 (Münster: Aschendorff Verlag, 2011).

Honnefelder, Ludger. 'Natur-Verhältnisse. Natur als Gegenstand der Wissenschaften. Eine Einführung'. In *Natur als Gegenstand der Wissenschaften* (München: Verlag Karl Alber Freiburg, 1992), p. 9.

Honnefelder, Ludger. 'Albertus Magnus und die kulturelle Wende im 13. Jahrhundert—Perspektiven auf die epochale Bedeutung des großen Philosophen und Theologen'. *Lectio Albertina* 13 (Münster: Aschendorff Verlag, 2012).

Krynen, Jacques P. 'Les légistes 'idiots politiques': Sur l'hostilité des théologiens à l'égard des juristes en France, au temps de Charles V'. In *Théologie et droit dans la science politique de l'État moderne* (Rome: École française de Rome, 1991).

Lottin, Dom Odon. *Le Droit Naturel chez Saint Thomas d'Aquin et ses prédécesseurs* (Bruges: Charles Beyaert, 1931).

Lottin, Dom Odon. 'Le loi naturalle depuis le début du xii siècle jusqu'a saint Thomas d'Aquin'. In *Psichologie et Morale aux XII et XIII siecles* vol. II (Louvain: Abbaye du Mont César, 1948), pp. 71–100.

Meier, Hans. *Geschichte der Lehre von den Keimkräften: von der Stoa bis zum Ausgang der Patristik, nach den Quellen dargestellt* (Bonn: Peter Hansteins Verlagsbuchhandlung, 1914).

Miethke, Jürgen. 'Kanonistik, Ekklesiologie und politische Theorie: Die Rolle des Kirchenrechts in der politischen Theorie des Spätmittelalters'. In *Proceedings of the Ninth International Congress of Medieval Canon Law*, edited by Peter Landau and Joers Mueller (Città del Vaticano: Biblioteca Apostolica Vaticana, 1997) p. 1023.

Möhle, Hannes. 'Zur Methodologie der Naturwissenschaften'. In *Albertus Magnus und sein System der Wissenschaften. Schlüsseltexte in Übersetzung. Lateinisch—Deutsch*, Albertus-Magnus-Institut ed., Münster, introduced, translated and edited together with H. Anzulewicz, M. Burger, S. Donati, R. Meyer, M. Bredenbeck und S. Bullido del Barrio (Münster i. W.: Aschendorff Verlag, 2011), pp. 229–33.

Müller, Jörn. *Natürliche Moral und Philosophische Ethik bei Albertus Magnus* (Münster: Beiträge zur Geschichte der Philosophie und Theologie des Mittelalters, Neue Folge 59, 2001).

Pelster, Franz. *Kritische Studien zum Leben und zu den Schriften Alberts des Großen* (Freiburg im Breisgau: Herder & Co., 1920), pp. 52–60.

Pelster, Franz. 'Die ersten beiden Kapitel der Erklärung Alberts des Großen zu De animalibus in ihrer ursprünglichen Fassung. Nach Cod. Vat. lat. 718'. *Scholastik: Vierteljahresschrift für Theologie und Philosophie* 10 (1934).

Pennington, Kenneth. 'The Decretalists 1190–1234'. In *The History of Medieval Canon Law in the Classical Period 1140–1234. From Gratian to de Decretals of Pope Gregory IX*, edited by Wilfried Hartmann and Keneth Pennington (Washington, D.C.: Catholic University of America Press, 2008) p. 211.

Sellés, Juan Fernando. *El intelecto agente y los filósofos. Venturas y desventuras del supremo hallazgo aristotélico sobre el hombre.* I, siglos IV-a.C. –XV (Pamplona: Eunsa, 2012).

Tierney, Brian. *The Idea of Natural Rights. Studies on Natural Rights, Natural Law, and Church Law* (Grand Rapids, Michigan/Cambridge, Cambridgeshire: William B. Erdmans Publishing Company, 1997).

Trottmann, Christian. 'La syndérèse selon Albert le Grand'. In *Albertus Magnus, zum Gedenken nach 800 Jahren* (Berlin: Akademie Verlag, 2001), p. 255.

Tuck, Richard. *Natural Rights Theories. Their Origin and Development* (Cambridge University Press, 1998).

Villey, Michel. 'Suum jus cuique tribuere'. In *Studi in Onori di Pietro de Francisci*, v. I, edited by Antonino Giuffré (Milan: Giuffrè, 1956), p. 364.

Villey, Michel. 'La genèse du droit subjectif chez Guillaume d'Occam'. In *Archives de Philosophie du Droit. Le droit subjectif en question*, 9 (1964).

Wengel, P. Macarius. *Die Lehre von den rationes seminales bei Albert dem Großen* (Würzburg: Richard Mayr, 1937).

'Zeittafel', Albertus-Magnus-Institut (Hg.), *Albertus Magnus und sein System der Wissenschaften.* Schlüsseltexte in Übersetzung. Lateinisch—Deutsch. Eingeleitet, übersetzt und für den Druck vorbereitet von Hannes Möhle, Henryk Anzulewicz, Maria Burger, Silvia Donati, Ruth Meyer, Martin Bredenbeck und Susana Bullido del Barrio (Münster i. W.: Aschendorff Verlag, 2011).

8

The Past is Never Dead

Christian Anti-internationalism and Human Rights

Pasquale Annicchino

Introduction

Today human rights are at the core of several debates among legal scholars. They often define the boundaries of our legal argumentation, ecology, and epistemology of our normative environment. In several instances they are defined, applied, and implemented through the work of supranational institutions (for example, the United Nations [UN] or the Council of Europe). They have deep and profound roots in the classic Roman and Greek, Canon, and medieval laws and were deeply influenced by the developments within both religious and secular traditions, from Protestantism and Catholicism to secular humanism. Their definitive formulation was based on a series of key documents redacted and ratified after the Second World War, particularly during the promulgation of the Universal Declaration of Human Rights in 1948.[1] The UN played a crucial role in defining and implementing subsequent international human rights treaties. Although the 'triumph of human rights'[2] surprised several individuals immediately after the approval of the UN-sponsored Universal Declaration, it was not instantly evident that human rights will gain substantive traction within the international legal apparatus. However, Henkin argued ' … human rights is the idea of our time, the only political moral idea that has received universal acceptance'.[3] The realities of the Cold War[4] furnished regular reminders that the real subjects of the international legal arena were sovereign states and not the individuals within their borders. According to Moyn,

[1] Lynn Hunt, *Inventing Human Rights: A History* (New York: W. W. Norton & Company, 2007). On the history of the Universal Declaration of Human Rights see Mary Ann Glendon, *A World Made New: Eleanor Roosevelt and the Universal Declaration of Human Rights* (New York: Random House, 2002).

[2] This expression is used by Douzinas in Costas Douzinas, *The End of Human Rights* (Oxford: Hart Publishing, 2000), p. 1.

[3] Louis Henkin, *The Age of Rights* (New York: Columbia University Press, 1990), p. xvii.

[4] On this specific point, see M. Glen Johnson, 'The Contribution of Eleanor and Franklin Roosevelt to the Development of International Protection for Human Rights', *Human Rights Quarterly* 9, no. 1 (February 1987): pp. 19–48.

the peripheral role of human rights in international and national debates, initially, was a result of the dynamics of state sovereignty and a real cultural issue: 'The concept of human rights remained yet more peripheral in legal affairs outside the small college of international lawyers, not simply because of American Cold War imperatives, but also because of the effect of legal realism on many professors.'[5] However, it is surprising to note the shift of human rights from the periphery of the international legal discipline to its core in a relatively few years, which is a phenomenon not readily explicable by traditional theories of the customary evolution of international law.[6] A more plausible explanation centred on the various social, historical, and political variables that contributed to this sea of changes. Moreover, the emergence of human rights in the international debate is crucially linked to the history of utopianism, with the desire to improve the world and make it a better place based on our political dreams and preferences.[7] Therefore, political and legal debates on the definition of human rights policy and standards are at the centre in several states. The 'core formulation' of human rights established after the Second World War is still at the centre of the paradigm of what 'human rights' entail today.[8] In addition, a set of ontological presuppositions regarding the nature of man, the optimal political project to be pursued, and the general good for the society dwells at the core of this notion. Human rights were never taken for granted. From the first political debates, we can track historical and contemporary discussions on the lack of consensus on the notions of what constitutes every single human right, the term 'human rights' in general, and politicization and instrumentalization of human rights.[9] These conflicts are particularly acute when they involve religious groups and their theological and political positions

[5] Samuel Moyn, *The Last Utopia: Human Rights in History* (Cambridge: Belknap Press of Harvard University Press, 2012), p. 189.

[6] This point is stressed by Moyn: ' … such a theory of customary growth of norms does very little to explain the startling move of human rights from the periphery to the centre of the discipline—since it took place almost overnight …' Ibid., p. 207.

[7] Ibid., p. 225. Moyn clearly concluded his book by issuing a strong warning regarding the difficulties and problems of utopianism: 'Born in assertion of the "power of the powerless," human rights inevitably became bound up with the power of the powerful. If "human rights" stand for an exploding variety of rival political schemes, however, they still trade on the moral transcendence of politics that their original breakthrough involved. And so it may not be too late to wonder whether the concept of human rights, and the movement around it, should restrict themselves to offering minimal constraints on responsible politics, not a new form of maximal politics of their own. If human rights call to mind few core values that demand protection, they cannot be all things to people. Put another way, the last utopia cannot be a moral one. And so whether human rights deserve to define the utopianism of the future is still very far from being decided …' Ibid., p. 227.

[8] According to Mutua: 'Since World War II, the United Nations, non-governmental organizations, and scholarly writers have created a thicket of norms, processes, and institutions that purport to promote and protect human rights. Working with the so-called International Bill of Rights as their basis, the key but diverse collection of organizations and scholars has tended to agree on an irreducible human rights core …' See Makau W. Mutua, 'The Ideology of Human Rights', *Virginia Journal of International Law* 36 (1995–6): p. 593.

[9] For the right, freedom of religion, or belief, I attempted to reveal the relevance of politicization and instrumentalization at a global level: see Pasquale Annicchino, *Esportare la Libertà Religiosa. Il Modello Americano nell'Arena Globale* (Bologna: Il Mulino, 2015) now forthcoming as *Law & International Religious Freedom. The Rise and Decline of the American Model* (Abingdon: Routledge, 2017).

on moral issues.[10] In addition to previous studies, in this chapter I will first deal, in the second section, with the anthropological understanding of human rights in the contemporary era. The third section will challenge this notion with the understanding of Christian anti-internationalism, beginning with historically situating the anthropological understanding of human rights in the controversy surrounding the establishment of the League of Nations. Based on two case studies, the fourth section will include the ensuing debates and the opposition of Christian anti-internationalists towards supranational institutions and their role in shaping the human rights culture, which are still relevant in several controversies involving the implementation of human rights worldwide. The fifth section will offer some concluding remarks: I will argue that at the core of the controversy stands the competition between legal pluralism and international constitutionalism.

Human Rights and Individualism

The formulation and conception of human rights[11] not only presupposes a certain political convergence concerning fundamental values, such as their universality, despite the profound differences in political systems or culture. In addition, it, nowadays, presumes a particular underlying anthropological definition of a human being. How should the human rights bearing individual defined in anthropological terms? Roy and I have argued that this individual is traditionally perceived as a 'self' who possesses his body and thoughts and is in a contracting relationship with other free selves. Therefore, 'Possessive individualism' is most often at the core of this vision of human rights, regardless of the extension or interpretation that we attribute to this term. In this case, the social 'bind' is thus a consequence of the will or action of the self, and the centrality of the theory of the social contract in the philosophical construction of the human rights theory. This is accompanied by rejecting the conception of a holistic society and a religion where God supposedly represents the supreme norm. Therefore, the political sphere is not viewed as the expression of a transcendental power or the embodiment of a holistic society; it is rather viewed as a space ruled by law, which is in fact a set of 'rules of the game' that enables individual citizens to enjoy their rights without infringing upon those of others. Constraints are not imposed by a great 'Other' (God, the Sovereign, the 'We'); they arise from the need for rules of the game, which are established for the public good by the citizens themselves. The compatibility of the theory of human rights with religions (which posited the existence of an absolute truth and/or the will of God as the source of norms) or with cultures (which translated into an all-encompassing set of basic norms that define a holistic society, thereby

[10] For example, one of these conflicts is well represented by the clashes between supporters of same sex marriages and those who claim a wide support for the freedom of religion.

[11] This section is partially taken from Pasquale Annicchino and Olivier Roy, 'Religion, Culture and Human Rights', in *The Cultural Dimension of Human Rights*, edited by Ana Filipa Vrdoljak (Oxford: Oxford University Press, 2013), pp. 13–25. Thanks to the publisher for the authorization.

assigning places to individual human beings within the former) clearly represents a noteworthy issue regarding their generalization. Therefore, it is perceived that human rights are based on secular grounds, which is reflected by the separation of human rights theory from the original religious sources of inspiration. This change in paradigmatic terms, nowadays, creates several conflicts, particularly among the bearers of influential religious traditions, such as conservative Christians and Christian communities. Conservative Christians (though this is also true for representatives of other important religious traditions) cannot accept the privileged link between human rights and secularization and perceive their worldview as being marginalized according to the construction of fundamental rights. Gunn underlined that the Universal Declaration of Human Rights must be understood as a 'secular document'[12] notwithstanding the important role played by people with a strong religious background who drafted it.[13] However, the scepticism of some members of the Christian family may be traced back to the controversy regarding the establishment of the League of Nations. In this instance, several theological reflections shaped the political approach of conservative Christian communities to the extent that they adopted a highly sceptical perception of multilateral international organizations, international laws, and human rights.

Christian Anti-internationalism

Christian anti-internationalism is an old phenomenon. According to Ruotsila, during the controversy on the establishment of the League of Nations, two main wings of Christian fundamentalism (dispensational premillennialists[14] and conservative Calvinists) participated in the controversy by raising the arguments against international human rights and international organizations repeated today.[15] For

[12] Although several Christians played a prominent role in the drafting of the document, Gunn emphasized: 'Despite the important role played by Jacques Maritain, one of the leading theologians of the twentieth century, the document does not claim to derive any authority from any religious teaching, nor does it assert that a religious belief of any type is a prerequisite for exercising a right, nor does it presuppose that God or a divine reality underlies the statement of rights', *see* Jeremy Gunn, 'The Human Rights System', in *Christianity and Human Rights: An Introduction*, edited by John Witte Jr. and Frank S. Alexander (Cambridge: Cambridge University Press, 2010), p. 197.

[13] Samuel Moyn, *Christian Human Rights* (Philadelphia: University of Pennsylvania Press, 2015).

[14] In the Christian eschatology, pre-millennialism refers to the belief that Jesus Christ will return to the Earth and take the righteous with him back to heaven. Among the varied publications on this subject, *see* Timothy Weber, *Living in the Shadow of the Second Coming: American Premillenialism 1875–1925* (Oxford: Oxford University Press, 1979) and Ernest Sandeen, *The Roots of Fundamentalism: British and American Millenarianism, 1800–1930* (Chicago: University of Chicago Press, 1970).

[15] Ruotsila outlines how profoundly divided American Christians were on this issue: 'In each denomination, a sizable theologically and culturally conservative section disapproved the concept of modern internationalism on which the League was based and that it proposed to follow in practice': see Markku Ruotsila, *The Origins of Christian Anti-Internationalism: Conservative Evangelicals and the League of Nations* (Washington: Georgetown University Press, 2008), p. 2. Furthermore, there was an important movement of 'Christian internationalists'. For more details, see Michael G. Thompson, *For God and Globe: Christian Internationalism in the United States between the Great*

the conservative fundamentalists, the critique of the League of Nations was part of a broader theological enterprise, which opposed modern liberalism and modernist liberal theology that were linked to the final coming of the Antichrist.[16] Particularly in the wake of the First World War, the creation of the League of Nations[17] was perceived by the conservative Christians as a Satanic plan 'to convert ever more people into thinking that a secular world organization, without reference to the Christian plan of salvation, could solve all the problems that burdened the war-torn world'.[18] For some conservative Protestants, the League of Nations imposed a centralized system of social control, where individual and small communities will lose their freedom. For others, this organization was perceived to be 'controlled by mostly Catholic southern Europeans and, therefore, ultimately beholden to the Pope'.[19] The same arguments recurred during the debates concerning the Universal Declaration of Human Rights. However, several mainstream Protestant churches battled for particular human rights (particularly religious freedom) to be recognized within the text of the Declaration.[20] Conservative evangelicals were particularly active during this period because they viewed the approval of the declaration as ' … the denouement at length brought about from all that syncretist mixing of Christian and pagan faiths to which they had drawn attention at the time of the League of Nations' founding'.[21] Roosevelt's activism regarding the interventionist economic management and his dream of a global institution in the UN confirmed the deepest fears of anti-internationalist Christians: '… the United

War and the Cold War (Ithaca: Cornell University Press, 2015) and Pamela Slotte, 'Blessed are the Peacemakers': Christian Internationalism, Ecumenical Voices and the Universal Declaration of Human Rights', in *Revisiting the Origins of Human Rights*, edited by Pamela Slotte and Miia Halme-Tuomisaari (Cambridge: Cambridge University Press, 2015), pp. 293–329.

[16] Ruotsila enumerates four fundamental reasons behind the opposition of conservative Christians for the League of Nations: 'First, its adherents refused to accept that cooperation between Christians and non-Christians was legitimate. Second, they insisted that because such cooperation was not grounded in the absolute truth claims of traditional, orthodox Christianity and in them alone, it could yield neither world peace nor socioeconomic progress. This, being the case, third, Christian anti-internationalists demanded that the United States should not join any international organizations that included non-Christians. Instead, it should remain a separate Christian example to others and, when needed, a unilateral enforcer of right dealing. Fourth, these anti-internationalists maintained that all who called themselves Christians yet supported secular international organizations were in a state of apostasy', Ruotsila, *The Origins of Christian Anti-Internationalism*, p. 2.

[17] Ruotsila explains why this historical moment is of particular relevance for the study of international law: 'The creation of the League of Nations in 1919 remains one of pivotal turning points in American and world history. It marked the point of departure between a world system that had been structures around unfettered national sovereignties and merely ad hoc alliances and a new era of increasingly circumscribed sovereignty and institutionalized cooperation …' Ibid., p. 1.

[18] See Markku Ruotsila, 'American Protestantism in the League of Nations Controversy', *Church History* 72, no. 3 (2003): p. 596.

[19] Ibid., p. 599.

[20] See Samuel Moyn, 'From Communist to Muslim: European Human Rights, the Cold War, and Religious Liberty', *The South Atlantic Quarterly* 113, no. 1 (2014): pp. 63–86.

[21] Ruotsila, *The Origins of Christian Anti-Internationalism*, p. 177. For a wider and different perspective on the same historical period with a particular focus on the right to religious freedom, see Anna Su, 'Woodrow Wilson and the Origins of International Religious Freedom', *Journal of History of International Law* 15 (2013): pp. 235–67.

States was lining up with Europe in preparation for a new world dictator'.[22] The emerging role of the UN in human rights and world affairs worried dispensationalists more than others: 'They still saw liberal Christianity, political liberalism, and Soviet communism as interwoven dimensions of the gradually emerging antichristian world empire that they thought was prefigured and anticipated by the UN'.[23] For conservative anti-internationalists, the issue with supranational organizations was not only a political problem but also a religious and anthropological one. In the words of one of the leading figures within the movement, the UN was an embodiment of: '... a new humanistic culture aimed at destroying all others by means of the imperialism of world law and police ... a crusading missionary organisation ... a false and deadly faith ... an Antichristian faith'.[24]

Christian Anti-internationalism Today: Two Case Studies

Zambia and LGBT rights

An example of the recurring anti-internationalist and millenarist arguments against international human rights is offered by the current debate in several African countries regarding the protection of LGBTI (lesbain, gay, bisexual, transexual, and intersexual) rights.[25] For example, in Zambia, the visit of UN Secretary General, Ban Ki-moon, provoked an uproar when he referred to the requirement of reinforcing and developing a better system of protection of LGBTI rights.[26] Van Klinken highlighted that the dominant narrative of the reactions to Ban Ki-moon's statement was situated within the framework of millenarist Christian anti-internationalism: '(... Ban is associated with the Antichrist and the Devil, his call to recognize gay rights is interpreted as a sign of the end times, and the United Nations is considered part of a cosmic conspiracy to impose a devilish agenda on

[22] Matthew Avery Sutton, 'Why the Antichrist Matters in Politics', The *New York Times*, 25 September 2011 available at: http://www.nytimes.com/2011/09/26/opinion/why-the-antichrist-matters-in-politics.html.

[23] Ruotsila, *The Origins of Christian Anti-Internationalism*, p. 177.

[24] Ibid., p. 180. According to Samuel Moyn, another reading is possible. Particularly at the beginning, mainstream conservatives saw an opportunity of creating the international regime for the protection of human rights. He developed his argument in *Christian Human Rights* (Philadelphia: University of Pennsylvania Press, 2015). According to him: 'Christian human rights were part and parcel of a reformulation of conservatism in the name of a vision of moral constraint, not human emancipation or individual liberation. Jesus's truth had been intended to set men free, but not for the sake of their creative autonomy or the satisfaction of their preferences. This liberation was for the sake of subjugation: so that men and (perhaps especially) women could conform to God's will and moral order' (p. 10).

[25] For an introduction to the topic, see Adam J. Kretz, 'From "Kill the Gays" to "Kill the Gay Rights Movement": The Future of Homosexuality Legislation in Africa', *Northwestern University Journal of International Human Rights* 11, no. 2 (2013): pp. 207–44.

[26] President Barack Obama faced the same problem in Kenya when he urged the promoting of gay rights in that country. See Norimitsu Onishi, 'Obama Kenya Trip Sets Off Gay Rights Debate in Africa', *The New York Times*, 21 July 2015.

Zambia and Africa at large'.[27] Thus, human rights are situated within an eschatological discourse of a struggle between God and devil where the devil's role is played by the UN and international organizations. The African case is particularly interesting, because it forces us to think about our categories (legal and otherwise) of public and private, and secular and sacred, because African epistemologies[28] do not share the same approach in classification, and it is not always easy to distinguish between different plans.[29] Evident anthropological research indicates that, in post-colonial Africa, religious language and argumentation are employed to cope with modernity, globalization, and activities perceived as 'un-African', such as homosexuality: 'The issue of homosexuality, not at least because it is associated with a liberal secular western agenda imposed on Africa, becomes a battlefield where beliefs about the Devil, the Antichrist and the end times provide a powerful religious language through which people respond to this threat.'[30] Furthermore, the debate on the establishment of the League of Nations, human rights, and particularly LGBTI rights is situated within the framework of a pre-millennialist eschatology and is linked with the second coming of Christ on Earth preceded by an apocalyptic 'sign of the times'. In this scenario, the visit of Ban-Ki moon to Zambia and his focus on the need to protect the rights of LGBTI people was perceived as one of the 'signs'. The same attributions were given to the UN.[31] Within the framework of this narrative, Zambia is depicted as a Christian country, which is resisting the organized forces of international organizations that impose external values, such as human rights and LGBTI rights. The political battle also becomes 'cosmological' owing to a confrontation between good and evil in a typical millennialist fashion.[32] The

[27] *See* Adriaan S. van Klinken, 'Gay Rights, the Devil and the End Times: Public Religion and the Enchantment of the Homosexuality Debate in Zambia', *Religion* 43, no. 4 (2013): p. 519.

[28] On this topic, see Stephen Ellis and Gerrie ter Haar, 'Religion and Politics: Taking African Epistemologies Seriously', *Journal of Modern African Studies* 36, no. 2 (2007): pp. 175–201.

[29] As van Klinken highlights, African epistemologies are characterized by: ' … a holistic approach to what in the West is distinguished as 'secular' and 'sacred,' the visible and the invisible world, and thus also to religion and politics'. Supporting Casanova's theory of de-privatization of religion, he admitted that this approach is rather 'Western-centric' as ' … in Africa—as in many other parts of the world—religion has never been a private affair and has always conflated with politics and public life'… see van Klinken, 'Gay Rights, the Devil and the End Times', p. 521.

[30] Ibid., p. 522. This approach is not peculiar to Zambia, see Masijwa Ragies Gunda, *The Bible and Homosexuality in Zimbabwe: A Socio-Historical Analysis of the Political, Cultural and Christian Arguments in the Homosexual Public Debate with Special Reference to the Use of the Bible* (Bamberg: University of Bamberg Press, 2010) and Adriaan S. Van Klinken and Masijwa Ragies Gunda, 'Taking Up the Cudgels Against Gay Rights? Trends and Trajectories in African Christian Theologies on Homosexuality', *Journal of Homosexuality* 59, no. 1 (2012): pp. 114–38.

[31] 'The UN is said to be possessed by "the spirit of antichrist" and people see the devil at work through the UN and other organizations…. The reason is simple: "Justifying human wrongs as HUMAN RIGHTS is ANTI-CHRIST. UN the beast is trying to DEVOUR the Earth" … In this comment, the misinterpretation or abuse of human rights by the UN is considered evil (and is associated with the apocalyptic image of "the beast" …), a few other commenters seem to reject human rights categorically.' van Klinken, 'Gay Rights, the Devil and the End Times', p. 528.

[32] Van Klinken describes this attitude in the following terms: 'The attitude of resistance is typically millennialist, since millennialism is characterized by a strong good-evil dualism and a related "narrative of violence"… The forces of evil, that are believed to become stronger in the end times, have to be resisted by the faithful and will, eventually, be overthrown by Christ.' Ibid., p. 530.

debate is based on the same premise that surrounded the controversy regarding the establishment of the League of Nations:

> Where Ban Ki-moon represents a secular human-rights discourse, the response to his call is shaped in deeply religious discourse. People not only use religious arguments against homosexuality—for example quoting biblical passages against same-sex practices but they respond with strong emotional and violent language that reflects their millennialist view of the world.[33]

The strong resemblance between this means of arguing against a rights culture assumed to be imposed by a foreign entity and American Christian Rights discourses,[34] infused with the premillennialist tradition of opposition to international law and supranational institutions, is noteworthy. Furthermore, the debates are politically influenced by conservative evangelical religious groups; several groups from the United States view Africa as a new battlefield to wage war against an increasingly secularizing world. As Hunter stated: 'Because Africans are sensitive to neocolonialism, the conservative claim that homosexuality is part of a "Western agenda" gives African church leaders ammunition to demand greater influence and power in the affairs of the church.'[35] Because of the recurring nature of the argument, it is identifiable in the debates between African Christian churches (e.g. the recent anti-homosexuality bill approved in Uganda[36]) and in the United States, where some American bishops have employed similar language. For example, when commenting on the marriage equality legislation enacted by some US states before the decision of the US Supreme Court in the case *Obergefell v. Hodges*,[37] Archbishop John Neinstedt has argued:

[33] Ibid., p. 531.

[34] See Didi Herman, *The Antigay Agenda: Orthodox Vision and the Christian Right* (Chicago: University of Chicago Press, 1997).

[35] Nan Hunter, 'Uganda analysis: American Religious Conservatives and the Global Trade in Culture Wars', *Hunter of Justice*, 16 December 2009, available at: http://hunterofjustice.com/2009/12/uganda-analysis-american-religion-and-the-violence-of-law.html. Hunter associated the rejection of homosexuality with the African postcolonial identity: 'Denouncing homosexuality is Africa's way of claiming power over the western world. In this regard, when Africans claim that homosexuality is un-African, they are pointing to a politics of postcolonial identity'. On the influence of American conservative evangelicals on the gay rights discourse in Africa see Tim Walker, 'How Uganda was Seduced by Anti-Gay Conservative Evangelicals', The *Independent*, 14 March 2014, available at: http://www.independent.co.uk/news/world/africa/how-uganda-was-seduced-by-anti-gay-conservative-evangelicals-9193593.html and Kapya Kaoma, *Globalizing the Culture Wars: U.S. Conservatives, African Churches & Homophobia* (Somerville, MA: Political Research Associates, 2009). Kaoma also emphasized the relevance on the postcolonial African identity on this issue. For an introduction, see D. Herman, *The Antigay Agenda: Orthodox Vision and the Christian Right* and Neville Wallace Hoad, *African Intimacies: Race, Homosexuality, and Globalization* (Minneapolis: University of Minnesota Press, 2007).

[36] According to Sadgrove, Vanderbeck, Andersson, Valentine, and Ward: 'The war "for the soul of Uganda" is therefore constructed as a battle between the forces of "secularism and extreme liberalism'", and those which are advocating for a morally upright and spiritually-inclined Uganda'; see Joanna Sadgrove, et al., 'Morality Plays and Money Matters: Towards a Situated Understanding of the Politics of Homosexuality in Uganda', *The Journal of Modern African Studies* 50, no. 1 (2012): p. 114.

[37] *Obergefell v. Hodges*, U.S. Supreme Court, 576 U.S. 2015.

Today, many evil forces have set their sights on the dissolution of marriage and the debasing of family life. Sodomy, abortion, contraception, pornography, the redefinition of marriage, and the denial of objective truth are just some of the forces threatening the stability of our civilization. The source of these machinations is none other than the Father of Lies. Satan knows all too well the value that the family contributes to the fabric of a good solid society, as well as the future of God's work on earth.[38]

This personal stance towards international liberal human rights facilitates in understanding the manner in which the arguments against rights can be or are framed and how a religious epistemology can become a real political theology used to respond and react to what is perceived to be an imposition of foreign culture. However, the position of certain African Christian churches is influenced by theological factors as well as the contingent political element and strategic positioning regarding other religions on the homosexuality issue. For example, African churches and followers of other religions (Islam) present in the different countries may want to dissociate themselves from western approaches, which are perceived as more secular. The frequent association of human rights discourse with western colonial powers in several parts of Africa must be considered. Mutua recently suggested that several of these countries: ' … have not fully embraced the culture of individual rights and the antidiscrimination and equal protection norms that lie at the heart of the human rights corpus'.[39]

The Russian Orthodox Church's approach to human rights

The rights of LGBTI people represent a critical yardstick for evaluating the approach of a country towards international human rights.[40] The Russian federation cannot be considered a champion in the protection of LGBTI rights. The Russian Orthodox Church recently called for a referendum to reintroduce the criminalization of homosexuality, because for the Orthodox Church, human rights, particularly LGBTI rights, represent a western and anthropocentric embodiment.[41]

[38] John Neinstedt, 'Family as the Foundation of Culture', *Legatus Magazine*, 2 September 2013, available at: http://www.legatusmagazine.org/family-as-the-foundation-of-culture/.

[39] Makau W. Mutua, 'Is the Age of Human Rights Over?', in *The Routledge Companion to Literature and Human Rights*, edited by Sophia A. McClennen and Alexandra S. Moore (London/New York: Routledge, 2016), p. 452.

[40] For an analysis of the approach of the Russian Orthodox Church on human rights, see Alexander Agadjanian, 'Liberal Individual and Christian Culture: Russian Orthodox Teaching on Human Rights in Social Theory Perspective', *Religion State and Society* 38, no. 2 (2010): pp. 97–113.

[41] This was the original understanding by Patriarch and former Metropolitan of Smolensk and Kaliningrad Kirill, who began the debate on human rights within the Russian Orthodox Church. According to Stoeckl, at the beginning of this debate Kirill: ' … expressed the conviction that liberalism is a natural result of Western cultural development, which he outlines as follows: the Renaissance, i.e. the return to ancient paganism, triggered a chain of subsequent cultural changes through the Reformation, the Enlightenment, materialism, and atheism which finally led to the Universal Declaration of Human Rights, the ultimate codification of anthropocentrism': See Kristina Stoeckl, *The Russian Orthodox Church and Human Rights* (London/New York: Routledge, 2014), p. 43. The position of the Russian Orthodox Church on human rights is traditionally very critical of an approach that is perceived as extremely influenced by western countries.

In its recent teachings,[42] the Russian Orthodox Church stated that human rights 'cannot be superior to the values of the spiritual world'[43] because they represent a deviation from man understood as created in the image of God.[44] The critical stance of the Russian Orthodox Church regarding international human rights and supranational organizations was particularly visible in the *Lautsi* case presented at the European Court of Human Rights (ECHR) involving the mandatory display of the crucifix in Italian public schools.[45] The Russian federation and Orthodox Church sided with the Italian government defending the mandatory display to be a symbol of national cultural identity and not an implied violation of the ECHR.[46] As previously underlined,[47] the two letters sent by the leadership of the Russian Orthodox Church in the wake of this case are particularly important for analysis. With the first letter, Archbishop Hilarion of Volokolamsk, the chairman of the department of external church relations, and Tarcisio Bertone, the then Vatican's secretary of state, complained of the growing role of the ECHR[48] in addressing the European human rights controversy:

We consider this practice of the European Court of Human Rights to be an attempt to impose radical secularism everywhere despite the national experience of church-state relations. The above mentioned decision is not the only one in the practice of the Court, which has increasingly shown an anti-Christian trend. Taking into account the fact that the decisions of the European Court of Human Rights have clearly lost touch with legal and historical reality in which most of the Europeans live, while the Court itself has turned into an instrument of promoting an ultra-liberal ideology, we believe it very important that religious communities in Europe should be involved in a discussion concerning its work'.[49]

[42] See *The Russian Orthodox Church's Basic Teaching on Human Dignity, Freedom and Rights*, available at: https://mospat.ru/en/documents/dignity-freedom-rights/. For a complete chronicle and analysis on the development of the teachings of the Russian Orthodox Church on human rights, see Stoeckl, *The Russian Orthodox Church and Human Rights*.

[43] *The Russian Orthodox Church's Basic Teaching on Human Dignity, Freedom and Rights*, III, 2. The article clearly stated that human 'secular' rights must be subordinate to religious views: 'A Christian puts his faith in God and his communion with Him above his earthly life. It is inadmissible and dangerous therefore to interpret human rights as the ultimate and universal foundation of societal life to which religious views and practice should be subjected ... Not a divine institution, human rights should not come into conflict with the Divine Revelation'.

[44] This position is expressed in Section IV. 7 of the Social Doctrine: 'In the contemporary systematic understanding of civil human rights, man is treated not as the image of God, but as a self-sufficient and self-sufficing subject'.

[45] See Pasquale Annicchino, 'Winning the Battle by Losing the War: The Lautsi Case and the Holy Alliance between American Conservative Evangelicals, the Russian Orthodox Church and the Vatican to Reshape European Identity', *Religion and Human Rights* 6 (2011): pp. 213–19. For a detailed legal analysis of the case see also Frederick Mark Gedicks and Pasquale Annicchino, 'Cross, Crucifix, Culture: An Approach to the Constitutional Meaning of Confessional Symbols', *First Amendment Law Review* 13 (2014): pp. 71–139.

[46] European Convention on Human Rights.

[47] See Annicchino, 'Winning the Battle by Losing the War: the Lautsi Case'.

[48] European Court of Human Rights.

[49] See Russian Orthodox Church Official Website of the Department for External Church Relations, 'Archbishop Ilarion's Letter to Vatican Secretary of State Concerning the European Court's Decision to Ban Christian Symbols in Italian Schools', 27 November 2009, available at: https://mospat.ru/en/2009/11/27/news9297/.

During the same period, another critical letter written by Patriarch Kirill to the then Italian Prime Minister, Silvio Berlusconi, which criticized the activism of the ECHR and the pervasiveness of the human rights culture:

> The Christian heritage in Italy and other countries in Europe should not become a matter considered by European human rights institutions. Christian religious symbols present in the public space in Europe are part of the common European identity without which neither the past nor the present or the future of this continent are thinkable. The pretext of ensuring the secular nature of the state should not be used to assert an anti-religious ideology, which apparently violates peace in the community, discriminating against the religious majority in Europe which is Christian.[50]

The approach highlighted by these two documents was consistent with the recent developments within the teachings of the Russian Orthodox Church, according to which human rights are subordinate to religious teachings and should not be used as imperialistic tools by foreign governments.[51] As previously stated, this is part of an 'exceptionalist' approach towards international law, which attempts to justify the positions that normally do not comply with the international human rights regime.[52] Furthermore, the Russian Orthodox Church attempted to deal with human rights by invoking the limitations to their application, and the 'discovery' of Article 29 of the Universal Declaration on Human Rights was central to this approach, which affirmed the duties of every individual towards the community.[53] Like in the African case, this general stance on human rights adopted by the Russian Orthodox Church will be particularly influential on topics, such as

[50] *See* Russian Orthodox Church Official Website of the Department for External Church Relations, 'Patriarch Kirill supports Italian Government over European Court's decision to ban Christian symbols in schools', 26 November 2009, available at: http://www.mospat.ru/en/2009/11/26/news9194/.

[51] The extremely revealing passage of the document produced by the Russian Orthodox Church stated: 'Some civilizations ought not to impose their own way of life on other civilizations under the pretext of human rights protection. The human rights activity should not be put at the service of interests of particular countries': *The Russian Orthodox Church's Basic Teaching on Human Dignity, Freedom and Rights*, III, 4.

[52] Petkoff stresses this point in his contribution with reference to 'religious human rights bills': 'Their manifestos usually present deeper and "more cultured" human rights and appeals to reform the existing system and institutions of public international law. At the same time they also indicate a form of religious exceptionalism, which may be interpreted as a smokescreen, a way to justify non-compliance with international commitments by the states which endorse these emerging religious bill of rights', see Peter Petkoff, 'Religious Exceptionalism, Religious Rights, and Public International Law', in Malcolm D. Evans, Peter Petkoff, and Julian Rivers, *The Changing Nature of Religious Rights under International Law* (Oxford: Oxford University Press, 2015), p. 216.

[53] According to Article 29 of the Universal Declaration on Human Rights: '1) Everyone has duties to the community in which alone the free and full development of his personality is possible. 2) In the exercise of his rights and freedoms, everyone shall be subject only to such limitations as are determined by law solely for the purposes of securing due recognition and respect for the rights and freedom of others and of meeting the just requirements of morality, public order and the general welfare in a democratic society'. The centrality and the 'discovery' of Article 29 is highlighted by Kristina Stoeckl, *The Russian Orthodox Church and Human Rights*, p. 61. See also *The Russian Orthodox Church's Basic Teaching on Human Dignity, Freedom and Rights*, at III. 4: 'The acknowledgment of individual rights should be balanced with the assertion of people's responsibility before one another. The extremes of individualism and collectivism cannot promote a harmonious order in a society's life'.

LGBTI rights,[54] that are at the forefront of the global culture war today. As Stoeckl indicated: ' ... LGBT rights came to epitomize for the Church all that was threatening about human rights and that deviated from its own vision of public morality and correct human conduct'.[55] As a Patriarch, Kirill openly admitted that the issue essentially lies at the core of the epistemology of human rights and on how they are interpreted and applied:

> We have a problem of a one-sided interpretation of the idea of rights and liberties of man, an interpretation which, in our view, is dominant today especially in the theory and practice of influential international institutions. And even if European organizations refrain from exercising direct influence on the design of the Russian legal space, there remains a danger that this false perception of freedom and justice could in the future have a harmful impact on legal processes in Russia.[56]

The Russian Orthodox Church proposed to borrow a new language of rights and argumentation, which is more communitarian and less focused on individual rights (less liberal), from American neoconservative thinkers.[57] It must be noted that this approach is not limited to the Russian Orthodox Church and is part of a general trend of new counter-hegemonic 'Russian approaches to international law'.[58] Therefore, we should not be surprised when analysing this approach from a historical perspective on how international human rights were developed subsequent to the Second World War. The ties between the Russian Orthodox Church and the state have always been strong. In 1948, the Soviet Union and its satellite states abstained from signing the Universal Declaration on Human Rights. Contemporary animosity for human rights must be placed within the context of a definite historical process: 'The construction of a Russian legal tradition, the Church's denunciation of an alleged negative influence of western 'legalism' on Russia and its call for church 'resistance' has to be read against the background of the revival of conservative and nationalist ideologies inside the Church'.[59]

[54] Kristina Stoeckl highlighted the centrality of this topic for Orthodox churches: ' ... homosexuality has become one of the main topics of contestation between Orthodox churches and the liberal human rights regime as it is embodied by institutions such as the Council of Europe, the European Court of Human Rights, and the European Union with its Charter of Fundamental Rights. The rejection of LGBT rights has come to epitomize for many Orthodox churches their opposition to the liberal human rights regime': Stoeckl, *The Russian Orthodox Church and Human Rights*, p. 13.

[55] Ibid., p. 36. [56] Quoted in Stoeckl, ibid., p. 114.

[57] Ibid., p. 45. Contrary to the narrative of 'foreign imposition of values', the Russian Orthodox Church continues to find new allies in the West. As Stoeckl pointed out: ' ... the Russian Orthodox Church continues to hold true to its established role as a defender of tradition, religion, community, nation and family, but no longer sees itself as the only force pursuing this goal. Instead, it finds allies in the Catholic Church and conservative political circles in the West. At the same time the Church distances itself from liberal tendencies within contemporary Russian Society ... ' (p. 49).

[58] See Laurie Mälksoo, *Russian Approaches to International Law* (Oxford: Oxford University Press, 2015) and Maria Issaeva, 'Does 'Russian International Law' Have an International Academic Future?', *EJIL:Talk*, 21 September 2015, available at: http://www.ejiltalk.org/does-russian-international-law-have-an-international-academic-future/.

[59] Stoeckl, *The Russian Orthodox Church and Human Rights*, p. 56. On the growing role of the Russian Orthodox Church, see Christopher McCrudden, 'Human Rights, Southern Voices and "Traditional Values" at the United Nations' (University of Michigan Public Law and Legal Theory

Furthermore, this process is a part of what Petkoff[60] (building on the work of Tasioulas[61]) defined as 'religious exceptionalism in international law'. Although exceptionalism is traditionally defined as: ' … the idea that some states are not bound by the general unilateral imperative of public international law or by a particular aspect',[62] religious exceptionalism is characterized by a ' … discourse about normative pluralism within international law and religious exceptionalism seems to have in some instances the ambition of reshaping customary international law and *jus cogens*'.[63]

Conclusions

The approaches employed by several Christian conservative communities often perceived international public law and international human rights as representing a counter-narrative and a competing political project characterized by a liberal, secular, and cosmopolitan ethos. The struggle of Christian anti-internationalism is unchanged from yesterday until today;[64] it is a struggle for legal pluralism against international constitutionalism. It is a struggle between different and remote self-contained normative regimes, with one based (or perceived to be) on communitarian values, national sovereignty, and religious teachings and the other based (or perceived to be) on individual human rights, individualism, and liberal internationalism.[65] Mediation does not seem possible because both are conceived to constitute hegemonic regimes. Koskenniemi argued that these normative regimes are typical of the international law: 'Each seeks to make its special rationality govern the whole to transform its preference into the general preference, its institutions into the institutions of general jurisdiction'.[66] Despite these two regimes being based on secular human rights and religious laws and sharing different epistemological and political foundations, it is true and must be highlighted that today several religious groups are attempting to cope with the 'human rights culture' by

Research Paper Series, paper No. 419, May 2014), available at: http://papers.ssrn.com/sol3/papers.cfm?abstract_id=2474241.

60 See Petkoff, 'Religious Exceptionalism, Religious Rights, and Public International Law'.

61 John Tasioulas, 'Human Rights, Legitimacy and International Law', *American Journal of Jurisprudence* 58, no. 1 (2013): pp. 1–25.

62 Petkoff, 'Religious Exceptionalism, Religious Rights, and Public International Law', p. 212.

63 Ibid., p. 213.

64 It is commonly thought that activism in the field of human rights is a prerogative of liberal actors. Several recent studies have demonstrated that this is not the case. See Clifford Bob, *The Global Right Wing and the Clash of World Politics* (Cambridge: Cambridge University Press, 2012) and Christopher McCrudden, 'Transnational Culture Wars', *International Journal of Constitutional Law* 13, no. 2 (2015): pp. 434–62.

65 For example, in the United States, see Stephan Halper and Jonathan Clarke, *America Alone: The Neo-Conservative and the Global Order* (Cambridge: Cambridge University Press, 2004).

66 Martti Koskenniemi, 'The Fate of Public International Law: Between Technique and Politics', *The Modern Law Review* 70, no. 1 (2007): p. 23.

strategically rephrasing human rights concepts and proposing their own interpretation.[67] This is certainly true for several conservative branches of Christianity, such as the Russian Orthodox Church and several evangelical conservative communities.[68] The belief in the second coming of Christ, or the UN being the embodiment of the Antichrist, is not necessary to question and challenge the approaches undertaken in certain fields of law and on certain issues by supranational organizations. Sometimes, what is lacking is only an appropriate debate on the politics of international human rights at the political level.[69] Through this chapter, I have attempted to demonstrate a deep Christian tradition of anti-internationalism that dates back to the beginning of the first tentative cooperation on multilateral institutions at an international level and that is ongoing in today's debates on international human rights.[70] This conclusion can demonstrate an effective dissolution of boundaries between the languages of religious and legal argumentations as a recurring trend in the movement against international organizations and human rights, which has its roots deep-seated in history and should not be misunderstood as a recent phenomenon. It is a historically influenced scepticism regarding the rise of normative regimes, such as the human rights regime, which are perceived to bear a different anthropological conception of man and good in

[67] For further details on this point, see again Petkoff, 'Religious Exceptionalism, Religious Rights, and Public International Law'.

[68] *See* Joel A. Nichols, 'Evangelicals and Human Rights: The Continuing Ambivalence of Evangelical Christians' Support for Human Rights', *Journal of Law and Religion* 7 (2009): p. 629–62. Nichols also underlines the historical and anthropological scepticism of Evangelicals towards international law: 'Drawing from their Protestant heritage, evangelicals historically place theological emphasis on the sinfulness of humans. One consequence of this anthropological view is a basic lack of trust in large, international organizations (as well as, often, government in general).' According to Nichols, this is strongly grounded in an antiperfectionist view of human nature: 'To some evangelical critics, the modern human rights movement possesses a number of world-affirming tendencies that inadequately account for the human nature and sin. That is, the human rights movement is like other "utopian ideologies" and is something one should be suspicious of, for it promises more than it could possibly deliver … Moreover, some evangelical critics view it as troubling that the human rights movement seeks to impose universal views on all persons, often at the expenses of particular religious or cultural differences' (pp. 654–5).

[69] As observed, only a profound and principled debate on the role of human rights in global politics can help in the global diffusion of the real human rights culture: 'While I do not think that the human rights movement is a Western conspiracy to deepen its cultural stranglehold over the globe, I do believe that its abstraction and a-politicization obscure the political character of the norms that it seeks to universalize. As I see it, that universe is at its core and in many of its details, liberal and European. The continued reluctance to identify liberal democracy with human rights delays the reformation, reconstruction, and multiculturalization of human rights. Defining those who seek to reopen or continue the debate about the cultural nature and the raw political purposes of the human rights regime as "outsiders" or even "enemies" of the movement is the greatest obstacle to the movement to bring about true universalization.' Mutua, 'The Ideology of Human Rights', p. 653.

[70] Ruotsila, in his final findings, describes Christian anti-internationalism in the following terms: '… set of attitudes that objected to multilateral cooperation in international organizations that were multiethnic, secular, and political; that contained members from many different religious traditions; and that pretended to worldwide supranational authority … Christian anti-internationalism was a subtheme of antimodernism, because conservative evangelicals regarded the modernist embracement of the League of Nations as an aspect of apostate deviation from that divine truth that had been given once and for all': Ruotsila, 'The Origins of Christian Anti-Internationalism: Conservative Evangelicals and The League of Nations', p. 188.

a given society. These concurrent and alternative ways of understanding rights are at the core of several contemporary controversies involving the interpretation of human rights both at the national and international levels. As McCrudden stated: 'Human rights have become a central site of normative contestation over the implications of modernity, with both sides claiming to interpret human rights in the "right" way'.[71] The challenge is particularly relevant for Christians in terms of their relationship with human rights. After initial success, human rights have been associated with the advancement of secularism and individualism. This move has increased the scepticism of many Christians who have not seen the several realized promises of the human rights agenda. Moyn recently noted that for Louis Henkin, one of the founding father of human rights law, human rights 'do not provide warmth, belonging, fitting, significance, do not exclude the need for love, friendship, family, charity, sympathy, devotion, sanctity, or for expiation, atonement, forgiveness'.[72] Christian anti-internationalism reminds us of this constant struggle between human rights and constitutional pluralism shaped by religious exceptionalism.

Bibliography

Agadjanian, Alexander. 'Liberal Individual and Christian Culture: Russian Orthodox Teaching on Human Rights in Social Theory Perspective'. *Religion State and Society* 38, no. 2 (2010): pp. 97–113.

Annicchino, Pasquale. 'Winning the Battle by Losing the War: The Lautsi Case and the Holy Alliance between American Conservative Evangelicals, the Russian Orthodox Church and the Vatican to Reshape European Identity'. *Religion and Human Rights* 6 (2011): pp. 213–19.

Annicchino, Pasquale. *Esportare la Libertà Religiosa. Il Modello Americano nell'Arena Globale* (Bologna: Il Mulino, 2015).

Annicchino, Pasquale. *Law & International Religious Freedom. The Rise and Decline of the American Model* (Abingdon: Routledge, 2017, forthcoming).

Annicchino, Pasquale, and Olivier Roy. 'Religion, Culture and Human Rights'. In *The Cultural Dimension of Human Rights*, edited by Ana Filipa Vrdoljak (Oxford: Oxford University Press, 2013), pp. 13–25.

Bob, Clifford. *The Global Right Wing and the Clash of World Politics* (Cambridge: Cambridge University Press, 2012).

Douzinas, Costas. *The End of Human Rights* (Oxford: Hart Publishing, 2000).

Ellis, Stephen, and Gerrie ter Haar. 'Religion and Politics: Taking African Epistemologies Seriously'. *Journal of Modern African Studies* 36, no. 2 (2007): pp. 175–201.

Gedicks, Frederick Mark, and Pasquale Annicchino. 'Cross, Crucifix, Culture: An Approach to the Constitutional Meaning of Confessional Symbols'. *First Amendment Law Review* 13 (2014): pp. 71–139.

[71] See McCrudden, *Transnational Culture Wars*.

[72] See Louis Henkin, *The Age of Rights*, p. 186, and 'Religion and Human Rights', *Journal of Religious Ethics* 26, no. 2 (1998): p. 239, quoted in Moyn, *Christian Human Rights*, p. 180.

Glendon, Mary Ann. *A World Made New: Eleanor Roosevelt and the Universal Declaration of Human Rights* (New York: Random House, 2002).

Gunda, Masiiwa Ragies. *The Bible and Homosexuality in Zimbabwe: A Socio-Historical Analysis of the Political, Cultural and Christian Arguments in the Homosexual Public Debate with Special Reference to the Use of the Bible* (Bamberg: University of Bamberg Press, 2010).

Gunn, Jeremy. 'The Human Rights System'. In *Christianity and Human Rights: An Introduction*, edited by John WitteJr. and Frank S. Alexander (Cambridge: Cambridge University Press, 2010), pp. 193–215.

Halper, Stefan, and Jonathan Clarke. *America Alone: The Neo-Conservative and the Global Order* (Cambridge: Cambridge University Press, 2004).

Henkin, Louis. *The Age of Rights* (New York: Columbia University Press, 1990).

Henkin, Louis. 'Religion and Human Rights'. *Journal of Religious Ethics* 26, no. 2 (1998): pp. 229–39.

Herman, Didi. *The Antigay Agenda: Orthodox Vision and the Christian Right* (Chicago: University of Chicago Press, 1997).

Hoad, Neville Wallace. *African Intimacies: Race, Homosexuality, and Globalization* (Minneapolis: University of Minnesota Press, 2007).

Hunt, Lynn. *Inventing Human Rights: A History* (New York: W. W. Norton & Company, 2007).

Hunter, Nan. 'Uganda Analysis: American Religious Conservatives and the Global Trade in Culture Wars'. *Hunter of Justice*, 16 December 2009, available at: http://hunterofjustice.com/2009/12/uganda-analysis-american-religion-and-the-violence-of-law.html.

Issaeva, Maria. 'Does "Russian International Law" Have an International Academic Future?'. *EJIL: Talk*, September 21 2015, available at: http://www.ejiltalk.org/does-russian-international-law-have-an-international-academic-future/.

Johnson, M. Glen. 'The Contribution of Eleanor and Franklin Roosevelt to the Development of International Protection for Human Rights'. *Human Rights Quarterly* 9, no. 1 (February 1987): pp. 19–48.

Kaoma, Kapya. *Globalizing the Culture Wars: U.S. Conservatives, African Churches & Homophobia* (Somerville, MA: Political Research Associates, 2009).

van Klinken, Adriaan S., and Masiiwa Ragies Gunda. 'Taking Up the Cudgels Against Gay Rights? Trends and Trajectories in African Christian Theologies on Homosexuality'. *Journal of Homosexuality* 59, no. 1 (2012): pp. 114–38.

van Klinken, Adriaan S. 'Gay Rights, the Devil and the End Times: Public Religion and the Enchantment of the Homosexuality Debate in Zambia'. *Religion* 43, no. 4 (2013): pp. 519–40.

Koskenniemi, Martti. 'The Fate of Public International Law: Between Technique and Politics'. *The Modern Law Review* 70, no. 1 (2007), pp. 1–30.

Kretz, Adam J. 'From "Kill the Gays" to "Kill the Gay Rights Movement": The Future of Homosexuality Legislation in Africa'. *Northwestern University Journal of International Human Rights* 11, no. 2 (2013): pp. 207–44.

McCrudden, Christopher. *Human Rights, Southern Voices and 'Traditional Values' at the United Nations*. University of Michigan Public Law and Legal Theory Research Paper Series, paper No. 419 (May 2014), available at: http://papers.ssrn.com/sol3/papers.cfm?abstract_id=2474241.

McCrudden, Christopher. 'Transnational Culture Wars'. *International Journal of Constitutional Law* 13, no. 2 (2015): pp. 434–62.

Moyn, Samuel. 'From Communist to Muslim: European Human Rights, the Cold War, and Religious Liberty'. *The South Atlantic Quarterly* 113, no. 1 (2014): pp. 63–86.

Moyn, Samuel. *The Last Utopia: Human Rights in History* (Cambridge: Belknap Press of Harvard University Press, 2012).

Moyn, Samuel. *Christian Human Rights* (Philadelphia: University of Pennsylvania Press, 2015).

Mutua, Makau W. 'The Ideology of Human Rights'. *Virginia Journal of International Law* 36 (1995–96): p. 593.

Mutua, Makau W. 'Is the Age of Human Rights Over?'. In *The Routledge Companion to Literature and Human Rights*, edited by Sophia A. McClennen and Alexandra S. Moore (London/New York: Routledge, 2016), pp. 450–8.

Mälksoo, Lauri. *Russian Approaches to International Law* (Oxford: Oxford University Press, 2015).

Neinstedt, John. 'Family as the Foundation of Culture'. *Legatus Magazine*, 2 September 2013, available at: http://www.legatusmagazine.org/family-as-the-foundation-of-culture/.

Nichols, Joel A. 'Evangelicals and Human Rights: The Continuing Ambivalence of Evangelical Christians' Support for Human Rights'. *Journal of Law and Religion* 7 (2009): pp. 629–62.

Onishi, Norimitsu. 'Obama Kenya Trip Sets Off Gay Rights Debate in Africa'. The *New York Times*. 21 July 2015.

Petkoff, Peter. 'Religious Exceptionalism, Religious Rights, and Public International Law'. In *The Changing Nature of Religious Rights Under International Law,* edited by Malcolm D. Evans, Peter Petkoff, and Julian Rivers (Oxford: Oxford University Press, 2015), pp. 211–34.

Ruotsila, Markku. 'American Protestantism in the League of Nations Controversy'. *Church History* 72, no. 3 (2003): pp. 593–616.

Ruotsila, Markku. *The Origins of Christian Anti-Internationalism: Conservative Evangelicals and the League of Nations* (Washington: Georgetown University Press, 2008).

Russian Orthodox Church Official Website of the Department for External Church Relations, 'Archbishop Ilarion's Letter to Vatican Secretary of State Concerning the European Court's Decision to Ban Christian Symbols in Italian Schools'. 27 November 2009, available at: https://mospat.ru/en/2009/11/27/news9297/.

Russian Orthodox Church Official Website of the Department for External Church Relations, 'Patriarch Kirill supports Italian Government over European Court's Decision to Ban Christian Symbols in Schools'. 26 November 2009, available at: http://www.mospat.ru/en/2009/11/26/news9194/.

Sadgrove, Joanna, et al. 'Morality Plays and Money Matters: Towards a Situated Understanding of the Politics of Homosexuality in Uganda'. *The Journal of Modern African Studies* 50, no. 1 (2012): p. 103–29.

Sandeen, Ernest. *The Roots of Fundamentalism: British and American Millenarianism, 1800–1930* (Chicago: University of Chicago Press, 1970).

Slotte, Pamela. '"Blessed are the Peacemakers": Christian Internationalism, Ecumenical Voices and the Universal Declaration of Human Rights'. In *Revisiting the Origins of Human Rights*, edited by Pamela Slotte and Miia Halme-Tuomisaari (Cambridge: Cambridge University Press, 2015), pp. 293–329.

Stoeckl, Kristina. *The Russian Orthodox Church and Human Rights* (London/New York: Routledge, 2014).

Su, Anna. 'Woodrow Wilson and the Origins of International Religious Freedom'. *Journal of History of International Law* 15 (2013): pp. 235–67.

Sutton, Matthew Avery. 'Why the Antichrist Matters in Politics'. *The New York Times*. 25 September 2011, available at: http://www.nytimes.com/2011/09/26/opinion/why-the-antichrist-matters-in-politics.html.

Tasioulas, John. 'Human Rights, Legitimacy and International Law'. *American Journal of Jurisprudence* 58, no. 1 (2013): pp. 1–25.

The Russian Orthodox Church's Basic Teaching on Human Dignity, Freedom and Rights (2008). Available at: https://mospat.ru/en/documents/dignity-freedom-rights/.

Thompson, Michael G. *For God and Globe: Christian Internationalism in the United States between the Great War and the Cold War* (Ithaca: Cornell University Press, 2015).

Walker, Tim. 'How Uganda Was Seduced by Anti-Gay Conservative Evangelicals'. *The Independent*, 14 March 2014, available at: http://www.independent.co.uk/news/world/africa/how-uganda-was-seduced-by-anti-gay-conservative-evangelicals-9193593.html.

Weber, Timothy. *Living in the Shadow of the Second Coming: American Premillennialism 1875–1925* (Oxford: Oxford University Press, 1979).

9

Whose Justice? What Political Theology?

On Christian and Theological Approaches to Human Rights in the Twentieth and Twenty-first Centuries

Pamela Slotte

Introduction

At times there is a certain type of theology that intersects with revolutionary events. It is necessary, however, to clearly designate exactly what kind of theology we are speaking about. We must be clear here because it is equally certain that not all theologies cross revolutionary phenomena but, on the contrary, there are some theologies that cross the opposite of revolution: namely, pure ideological reproduction of Empire.[1]

This chapter explores one thesis of the group on international law and religion's research statement, which 'questions the very possibility of producing "secular law" as an aseptic product immune from religion and apart from a supposedly apolitical religious sphere. Here we follow those who have understood much of 20th century internationalism operating on the basis of a faith that has often left itself unarticulated as such.'

The chapter will not discuss things that were made sacred in the name of secularity, as the editorial statement inviting writers to contribute to this volume put it. It will, however, focus on how religiously framed matters and articles of faith were given a 'secular' reinterpretation during the first part of the twentieth century—in the name of peace and a just international order—and offer an account of the specific political theology that this reconceptualization of 'the sacred' in terms of 'the secular' expressed. In addition, the chapter will point at another political–theological counter-discourse. Whether that counter-discourse offers meaningful new spaces for emancipatory critique of the 'liberal credo' it criticizes its adversaries for too readily signing up to is the topic of another chapter.

[1] Antonio Negri in Antonio Negri and Gabriele Fadini, 'Materialism and Theology: A Conversation', *Rethinking Marxism* 20, no. 2 (2008): pp. 665–72. This article was written as part of the author's Academy of Finland Academy Research Fellow project 'Management of the Sacred—A Critical Inquiry' (2013–2018).

Whose Justice? What Political Theology? On Christian and Theological Approaches to Human Rights in the Twentieth and Twenty-first Centuries. Pamela Slotte. Published 2017 by Oxford University Press.

What is offered in the following chapter is a reading of matters of international law and religion from the perspective of theology, and on the basis of other current work on early twentieth-century Christian internationalist action for peace and a just international order, including legal order and human rights.[2] Returning to the editorial statement once more, the chapter will offer insights into religious attitudes underpinning twentieth-century internationalism and the formation of international legal concepts and institutions.

John Milbank's Critique of Human Rights

The political theologian John Milbank is regarded as one of the foremost representatives of contemporary radical orthodoxy. In his writings, he offers a foundational critique of the so-called modern liberal project—the liberal credo—and its religious roots. In the first ever issue of the Oxford Journal of Law and Religion, established in 2012, Milbank makes his case 'Against Human Rights'. His goal is, among other things, to make us aware of the distributive outcomes that human rights generate under the pretext of inalienability, absoluteness, and equality. According to Milbank these outcomes are anything but laudable. Human rights are, in fact, all about subjective entitlements, and cannot accommodate ideas about distributive justice.

What we find at the centre of human rights is a reduced notion of an isolated individual—not an individual who is shaped through her relationships with others—while being simultaneously someone unique. The last would be a reading of the person that Milbank himself favours. Instead, it is an inscrutable abstract interiority that is inviolable, while all social manifestations of the person remain subject to state will. Since if the human person is not constituted through her relationships—being an 'irreplaceable "personality"—then she is also not 'essential to the composition of any social aggregate'. Instead she becomes 'an always replaceable and disposable atom, component of an impersonal machine'.[3] Thus, paradoxically, 'the very ontological isolation ironically ensures the [individual's] substitutability, and in consequence his autonomy proves to be less of a self-defence than that provided by inherent relational dependency against the arbitrary sovereignty of God, nature or the State'.[4]

Moreover, human rights claims are infinite and can in reality lead to nothing but anarchy, ended only when authoritarian power steps in. For the rights in themselves say nothing about what they mean in practice. They are unqualified. Enter

[2] Some of the following ideas have also been elaborated in Pamela Slotte, '"Blessed are the Peacemakers:" Christian Internationalism, Ecumenical Voices and the Universal Declaration of Human Rights', in *Revisiting the Origins of Human Rights,* edited by Pamela Slotte and Miia Halme-Tuomisaari (Cambridge: Cambridge University Press, 2015), pp. 293–329.

[3] John Milbank, 'Against Human Rights: Liberty in the Western Tradition', *Oxford Journal of Law and Religion* 1, no. 1 (2012): p. 207.

[4] Ibid., p. 218.

the 'unrestricted formally-grounded power of the sovereign political power' to render operable what lies beyond the 'absolute negative liberty of the individual'—a distinction that is also ultimately in the hands of the sovereign.[5] As a result, the actual implementation of human rights involves making choices and prioritising one set of rights over another. To Milbank's mind this is an arbitrary exercise as rights are not realized against the background of the idea of a right order.

Furthermore, the space for arbitrary exercise of power is great in a society whose key components are these rights holders, as mediating bodies (organic relationships) between individuals and the 'sovereign political power' are reduced in importance. For, given the 'strictly nominalist logic of liberty'—which for Milbank underscores human rights ideology—and thus in the absence of an overarching ideal of right and notion of right order:

> ... it can appear [only] logical to conclude that all and any 'democratic' expression of collective will—whether by specific freely associating group, or by the freely associating people as a whole—violates the neutrality of the state organ, whose own absoluteness exists in order to underwrite the equal absoluteness of the inviolable will of the 'self-owning' and property-owning individual.[6]

This leaves the stage open for a capitalist economy, which according to Milbank is the political economy of human rights. Milbank thus suggests that human rights are not apolitical; nor are they a-economic.[7] The discretion at the heart of human rights discourse favours a notion of the 'just polity' that is 'explicitly based upon the primacy of individual subjective rights that will have its concomitant in the negatively free capitalist market'.[8] To quote him at length:

> [T]he more that doctrines of human rights are seen as the normative basis of all politics, then the more they covertly encourage a slide of neoliberalism towards a fully fledged totalitarian capitalism, by passing over the democratic in the name of freedom as well as efficiency—given that, without the restoration of mutualist bonds of trust, micro-organisation is the only barrier against anarchy and the violation of rights by an individual liberty appealing back through exception to the bios component of its dual bio and political foundation (as witnessed by the quotation already given from Hobbes which speaks of a pre-political right of nature).[9]

Summing up, human rights are 'an historical aberration of our genuine western identity':[10]

> Their buried foundation lies in a questionable theological voluntarism and a questionably atomising metaphysic. In either case the same logic upholds both the absolute negative liberty of the individual and the unrestricted formally-grounded power of the sovereign political power. And only the latter can render the former operable, only the latter can effectuate positively the supposedly 'natural' character of rights, whether this naturalness is taken to be 'fallen' (Ockham) or innocent (Rousseau).[11]

[5] Ibid., p. 229. [6] Ibid., p. 206. [7] Ibid., p. 230. [8] Ibid., p. 210.
[9] Ibid., p. 207. [10] Ibid., p. 209. [11] Ibid., p. 229.

Milbank's analysis of human rights has a mainly historical focus. He is a political theologian within the Christian tradition and favours another politics than that which the modern doctrine of subjective rights promotes. To him, the notion of justice accompanying the idea of subjective rights—if there really is one—is not compatible with the Christian legacy that he wishes to pick up 'for an alternative modernity'.[12]

Setting the Scene

Milbank's critical remarks regarding human rights are not totally new. The reason for taking his thoughts as a point of departure, however, is that his political theology is a counter-discourse of sorts. As regards human rights, Milbank opposes what he sees as contemporary historical revisionist accounts. These accounts are put forward by, in the main, American liberal Christians, according to whom the notion of subjective rights is compatible with the Christian faith. They stress continuity instead of rupture in the history of *ius*, and 'freedom' gains the upper hand over the notion of a right order in their thinking.[13] To return to the opening quote, by championing human rights in their theological practice, they partake in the reproduction of Empire in the form of a totalitarian capitalist order.

From here, I want to move to the year 1953, and an address offered by the Swedish diplomat Dag Hammarskjöld (1905–61) as he took up the office of Secretary General of the United Nations (UN) just after Easter. In the address, Hammarskjöld connected the Christian message of redemption (by God through Jesus Christ) with work for peace and conciliation: 'May I remind you of the great memory just celebrated by the Christian world. May I do so because of what that memory tells us of the redeeming power of true dedication to peace and goodwill to men.'[14]

Commenting on the speech was American Lutheran theologian O. Frederick Nolde (1899–1972), who by this time is the long-term Director of the Commission of the Churches on International Affairs (CCIA), a body of the World Council of Churches (WCC) that seeks to bring a Christian understanding to matters such as international law, human rights, development, peace, and disarmament.[15] Nolde is renowned as an important lobbyist for Christian organizations and the churches

[12] ibid., p, 234. [13] Ibid., pp. 209–10.

[14] Reproduced in O. Frederick Nolde, 'Human Rights in Retrospect: A Contemporary Appraisal', *The Ecumenical Review* 20, no. 4 (1968): pp. 395–403.

[15] The CCIA, which still exists, was formally established by the WCC and the International Missionary Council (IMC) in 1948. Provisionally it came into existence in 1946. The aim of CCIA was to serve the 'world-wide constituency' of these two organizations 'as a source of stimulus and knowledge in their approach to international problems, as a medium of common counsel and action, and as their organ in formulating the Christian mind on world issues and in bringing that mind effectively to bear upon such issues'. *The First Six Years 1948–1954: A Report of the Central Committee, of the World Council of Churches on the activities of the Departments and Secretariats of the Council* (Geneva: World Council of Churches, 1954), p. 92.

in the ecumenical movement during the establishment of the UN and the drafting of first the UN Charter, and later the Universal Declaration of Human Rights (UDHR). He has been particularly accredited for his efforts in connection with Article 18 of the UDHR on freedom of thought, conscience, and religion.[16]

Based on the cordial bond that he had developed with Hammarskjöld, Nolde made the following biographical remarks. As a child, Hammarskjöld entertained a friendship with the daughter of the Archbishop of Sweden, Nathan Söderblom (1866–1931). The families of Hammarskjöld and Söderblom were close and the children Dag and Brita would have breakfast first in one house and then in the other. According to Nolde, the 'Söderblom background' is important for us to appreciate the full meaning of Hammarskjöld's words and the sources on which he drew in his international work,[17] and where statements like the following can be found:

> [T]he Cross, although it is the unique factor on which Christians base their hope, should not separate those of Christian faith from other ... but should instead be that element in their lives which enables them to stretch out their hands to peoples of other creeds in the feeling of universal brotherhood which we hope one day to see reflected in a world of nations truly united.[18]

Nolde also added his own personal memory of Söderblom. In 1923, being a young fellow at the Lutheran Theological Seminary at Philadelphia, Nolde had the good fortune to meet Söderblom. He was so impressed by this encounter at a small faculty luncheon that he accompanied Söderblom when he went on to give guest lectures on comparative religions at the University of Pennsylvania.[19] Söderblom's academic field was comparative religions, and he completed his PhD at Sorbonne. He was a so-called liberal theologian—a line of thinking important in the context of this chapter.[20]

This Söderblom, whom both Hammarskjöld and Nolde remembered with such admiration and respect, has been called the father of the ecumenical movement. He was co-founder of the ecumenical Life and Work movement, which in the interwar period called on the Protestant (Lutheran, Reformed, and Anglican) Churches—as well as the Old Catholic and Orthodox Churches—to work together for peace and social reform. Throughout the First World War and beyond, Söderblom appealed

[16] See e.g. Matti Peiponen, *Ecumenical Action in World Politics: The Creation of the Commission of the Churches on International Affairs (CCIA), 1945–1949*, Schriften der Luther-Agricola-Gesellschaft 66 (Helsinki: Luther-Agricola-Society, 2012), pp. 74–80, 33, 338–9. For a thorough analysis of the formulations that found their way into Article 18 and how these connected with the political projects and personal visions of the persons involved in the work on the UDHR, see Linde Lindqvist, *Shrines and Souls: The Reinvention of Religious Liberty and the Genesis of the Universal Declaration of Human Rights* (Malmö: Boxbox, 2014).

[17] Nolde, 'Human Rights', p. 395.

[18] Hammarskjöld speaking at the Second Assembly of the WCC in Evanston 1954, as reproduced in David P. Gaines, *The World Council of Churches: A Study of Its Background and History* (Peterborough, NH: Richard R. Smith, Noone House, 1966), p. 650. Hammarskjöld thought that the churches and the UN shared a desire for peace and that the UN could be 'an instrument of faith' while at the same time not aligning itself with any particular confession. Gaines, *The World Council*, pp. 648–9.

[19] Nolde, 'Human Rights', p. 395. [20] Ibid, p. 395.

to the churches to work together for a better social order, for justice, and to support the development of international law needed for the purpose of solving international conflicts and achieving lasting peace. It was God's will that the churches help establish 'a lawful order as between states, in order that their common life may be founded "on the principles of truth, justice, and love" '.[21] In 1930, Söderblom was awarded the Nobel Peace Prize for his efforts.

Social Ethics in Liberal Protestant Clothes

Essentially, what Söderblom and others like him sought to do was to locate 'the place of global matters in ordinary Christian discipleship'.[22] Their broad focus was on so-called 'social ethical matters of modern life'; the relations between Christian faith, the Church, and society; the State, the economic, and the international order; and the contribution of Christian faith with regard to these areas.

The Life and Work movement focused on lay Christians and the work they needed to carry out in the contemporary world. Two snapshots are offered. At the first major conference of the Life and Work movement in Stockholm in 1925, which simultaneously established the organization as such, it was confirmed that the Gospel was to be applied 'to all realms of human life—industrial, social, political and international'.[23] The human being had to be defended. The soul was not to be 'subordinate to rights of property or to the mechanisms of industry'.[24] The conference reinterpreted a Christian understanding of life and vision of societal welfare in terms of public policy. Christian faith held broad relevance: 'secular' issues were seen as essentially 'religious', and social and political questions were identified as religious questions.

The meeting in Stockholm also gave its backing to the League of Nations and called on Christians to speak up for the League of Nations 'and to serve as its "Christian Soul" '.[25]

[21] Nils Karlström, 'Movements for International Friendship and Life and Work 1910–1925', in *A History of the Ecumenical Movement 1517–1948*, edited by Ruth Rouse and Stephen Charles Neill, 4th edn (Geneva: World Council of Churches, 1993 [1954]), pp. 515, 532–3. This by no means meant that everyone within the ecumenical movement—nor in the Christian churches on a whole—were outright pacifists. See e.g. Peiponen, *Ecumenical Action*, pp. 32–3.

[22] John S. Nurser, *For All Peoples and All Nations: The Ecumenical Church and Human Rights* (Washington, D.C.: Georgetown University Press, 2005), p. 71.

[23] George Kennedy Allen Bell, *The Stockholm Conference: Official Report of the Universal Christian Conference on Life and Work* (London: Oxford University Press, 1926), pp. 711ff.

[24] Ibid.

[25] Peiponen, *Ecumenical Action*, p. 43. See also e.g. Gaines, *The World Council*, pp. 49–53. Likewise, the League of Nations found almost complete support early on among leaders of liberal American Protestant churches. The FCC and its member churches, the American branch of the WA, and the so-called Church Peace Union likewise endorsed the League, considering it 'the political expression of the Kingdom of God on earth emphasised by the Social Gospel movement'. Peiponen, *Ecumenical Action*, p. 39.

It became clear through the ecumenical discussions in the early 1930s that life as a whole did concern the Church and demanded a 'total' response by faith.[26] Through the critical discussion carried out it became obvious to some that when searching for solutions to the problems confronting the societies, the gaze had to shift to the international plane. Churches had a contribution to make. The Christian message with regard to just life and peace was interpreted by many as requiring in the present day and age 'transnational institutions that might (in the concluding words of the New Testament) be "for the healing of the nations" '.[27] Talk was of, for example, 'a curative and creative United Nations', and a moral world order that would seek to realize a global ethos as articulated, among other things, through human rights.[28]

In July 1939, the Department of International Justice and Goodwill of the Federal Council of the Churches of Christ in America (FCC)—a council made up of so-called 'modernist', 'liberal' Protestants in the United States [29]—organized a meeting in Geneva in cooperation with the Provisional Committee of the WCC—into which the Life and Work movement had by now developed—and an international ecumenical organization called the World Alliance for Promoting International Friendship through the Churches (WA). The meeting on 'The Churches and the International Crisis' assembled 35 delegates from eleven countries, including a 'high-powered' American delegation which contained future U.S. Secretary of State John Foster Dulles (1888–1959). The delegates formulated a memorandum to the churches, in which the churches' task in wartime was explicated as 'the need for true Christian prayer and for preaching centred on the righteousness of the kingdom of God; the duty to maintain brotherly relations between the churches in spite of propaganda, and to work for a just and lasting peace; and the opportunities for ministering to prisoners, soldiers under arms, and the rapidly increasing number of refugees'.[30] The meeting called for recognition of essential rights to human beings, 'an international court of justice, a successor organization to the League of Nation that would have teeth, a fair system of world trade, the winding up of European colonialism and of racial discrimination, and religious liberty'. John Nurser sees 'a clear line' between the meeting in Geneva and 'the dramatic

[26] See Preface to the Conference Report, *Die Kirche und das Staatsproblem in der Gegenwart* (Genf: Forschungsabteilung des Oekumenischen Rates für Praktisches Christentum, 1934, 2nd enlarged edn 1935).

[27] Nurser, *For All Peoples,* p. 12. See also e.g. Jonas Jonson, *Gustaf Aulén: Biskop och motståndsman* (Skellefteå: Artos & Norma bokförlag, 2011), p. 198. See also Hudson, *The Ecumenical Movement,* p. 43, who remarks in a clearer fashion that a Christian social ethic was now also explicitly conceptualized as an ethic for groups rather than in traditional Protestant fashion as an ethic of individuals and inter-personal relationships, and then in naïve fashion transposed onto the international plane. This was a clear change from the initiatives of Söderblom and others at the time of the First World War and the two following decades.

[28] John S. Nurser, 'The 'Ecumenical Movement' Churches, 'Global Order,' and Human Rights: 1938–1948', *Human Rights Quarterly* 25, no. 4 (2003): pp. 841–81.

[29] For the characterization of the members of the FCC, see Peiponen, *Ecumenical Action,* p. 23.

[30] Gaines, *The World Council,* p. 173, 173 (fn 13); John Nurser, 'A Human Rights 'Soul' for a Secular World of 'Faiths': A Contradiction, or Just a Paradox?', *Political Theology* 6, no. 1 (2005): p. 53.

events of 1945 and 1948 in the life of the UN'—referring in this context also to a similar remark by Dulles.[31]

Thus matters of peace, social justice, and human rights became connected. Human rights and in particular religious liberty were a concern for the churches, and together the ecumenical bodies—including the American Joint Committee on Religious Liberty set up in 1943—pressed for adequate international provisions. Nolde became assigned specifically to this task in the time leading up to the San Francisco Conference in 1945, when the UN Charter was formulated.[32] On behalf of the WCC and the International Missionary Council (IMC), Nolde took on the same assignment when the newly established Human Rights Commission commenced its work on an International Bill of Rights and the CCIA was granted advisory status at the UN.[33] In contrast to Milbank's critique of the contemporary human rights phenomenon, the work of these ecumenical actors was clearly not void of any comprehensive understanding of justice. To phrase this differently, they did not themselves see human rights as 'empty signifiers', but rephrased in human rights language concerns of social justice, as well as spiritual freedom—and the freedom to spread the Christian gospel, of course.[34]

The 'soul' of the international system—which under the League of Nations had been identified with the input of the Christian churches and ecumenical movement—was now identified under the UN in a more 'inclusive' fashion with 'human rights'. The Christian link was, however, never far away, as the churches considered the UDHR to a great extent a result of Christian input and reflecting a Christian ethos.[35]

These efforts on the part of the ecumenical movement with regard to social and international affairs were noticed, partially as a result of their lobbying in front of the League of Nations, and later the emerging UN. To take just two anecdotes regarding the impact of the ecumenical efforts: in April 1934, Max Huber (1874–1960), the former President of the World Court at the Hague and of the International Red Cross Committee, participated in a conference in Paris organized by the Life and Work on 'The Church and the State of To-day'. Huber was struck by the optimism and enthusiasm of the meeting. Contrary to what had been the case for the more than 27 years that he had participated in 'conferences and commissions of international character—diplomatic, juridical, and scientific', he 'left without a feeling of having been disillusioned' and 'with a new confidence in the possibilities of international co-operation'.[36] The optimism that abounded

[31] *The Churches and the International Crisis (Geneva, 1939),* Report of the WCC Conference, 'The Churches and the International Crisis', held at Geneva, July 1939. WCC Archives, Box X, pp. 12 ff; Nurser, 'A Human Rights "Soul"', p. 53 (fn 5).

[32] See e.g. Nolde, *Free and Equal*, pp. 16–21.

[33] Ibid., p. 35.

[34] For the observation regarding the spreading of the Gospel, see Linde Lindkvist, 'The Politics of Article 18: Religious Liberty in the Universal Declaration of Human Rights', *Humanity* 4, no. 3 (2013): pp. 443.

[35] Nolde, *For All Peoples*, pp. 172–3; Peiponen, *Ecumenical Action*, pp. 335–6.

[36] Nils Ehrenström, 'Movements for International Friendship and Life and Work 1925–1948', in *A History of the Ecumenical Movement*, edited by Ruth Rouse and Stephen Charles Neill, 4th edn (Geneva: World Council of Churches, 1993 [1954]), p. 582.

in ecumenical circles also impressed Dulles when he attended the second major conference of the Life and Work on 'Church, Community and State' in Oxford in 1937. It stood in striking contrast with the cynicism that to his mind permeated the work of the League of Nations. As a result, he came to support the founding of the WCC into which it was decided that the Life and Work would develop in 1938.[37]

It is important to note that the ecumenical, social, and international activism during this time to a large extent took place with 'secular overtones', and was rephrased in programs of action that included suggestions that did not come across as exclusively Christian. Instead, they opened up to cooperation with organizations and actors of various kinds.

Within the ecumenical movement, there was also no unity in theological questions. Also here one took a pragmatic stance. In the attempt to unite around matters of social ethics, doctrinal diversity was often enough accepted and put aside, like in the Life and Work movement. But this did not, of course, mean that the Christian tradition did not remain a source of inspiration and authority.[38] The Stockholm meeting of the Life and Work in 1925 largely drew on visions about the Kingdom of God in the theological reflections on social action. In 1937, at the meeting of the Life and Work in Oxford, a theological shift in emphasis was recognizable to the extent that the idea of a united Church became a focal point for ecumenical efforts and reflection on the Christian contribution to international work. The situation in the German Church and the rise of totalitarianism was a great concern. The Church had to transcend distinctions of nation, class, race, and creed. The Church was universal and had to work for this unity. Moreover, it had to find out what was the specific Christian contribution to matters of conflict resolution, peace, and justice.[39]

So no matter how pre-eminently framed in 'secular' terminology, this social and international activism was embedded in the religious and theological discourse of the time. What is more, it is important here to draw attention to the shift in focus and appreciate that Christian international activism at this point in time acquired to a large degree a particular theological and social ethical framing. That Christian and ecumenical initiatives through their international action would seek to safeguard the human 'person' is unsurprising. This was the obvious way for them to take issue with, on the one hand, a libertarian modern subject and, on the other, the sort of totalitarian society (and also existentialism) that subjugated the subject to the collective—or alternatively dissolved the subject altogether. It became a natural point of connection with 'secular' protection initiatives and efforts to

[37] See e.g. Peiponen, *Ecumenical Action*, pp. 67–8.

[38] Ehrenström, 'Movements', pp. 569–70, who notes that, in consequence, the Life and Work suited better persons with a 'certain Protestant temper' whose interpretation of the Christian tradition could be seen as liberal.

[39] Peiponen, *Ecumenical Action*, p. 51; Ehrenström, 'Movements', pp. 591–2; *Oxford Conference, Official Report*, by Joseph H. Oldham (Chicago/New York: Willett, Clark & Company, 1937), pp. 20–1, 38–41, 47–8.

promote human rights, although Milbank would strongly disagree in regards to the potential that these twentieth century Christian internationalists saw in human rights.

The point that this chapter wants to make, however, is that if we truly wish to understand the theological framing and the foundations for Christian discipleship and action in the international sphere at that time, attention must also be paid to the ideas about a God that creates, redeems, and calls man (the 'person') to follow.

John Nurser has observed, moreover, that the work that ecumenical actors carried out during the creation of the UN was work that expressed a specific tradition of Christendom.[40] The Church was called to more than strict mission. Persons working in the field of international politics rephrased (and broadened) the calling in more general terms of justice—which for some constituted a troubling downgrade of the classical missionary calling in an improper way. The new view of mission was policy oriented and aimed at establishing social structures that conveyed the Christian doctrine of humanity, to paraphrase Nurser. A Christian understanding of life and vision of societal welfare was reinterpreted in terms of public policies. A democratic lifestyle stood out as desirable.[41] We encounter a vision that combined social engineering with personal Christian pilgrimage.

When interpreting the Christian message with regard to matters of peace and justice, a crucial question for champions of secular Christendom was whether what was at stake was only the transformation of personal life and relationships, or also social, economic, and political structures, and the relations between peoples. They clearly leant towards the latter. Christian faith was politically relevant. Christian faith had or should have political consequences.

There were also others for whom faith was first and foremost about individual salvation and man's relationship with God, and not about politics or the formation of society—at least no more than in a very indirect and almost incidental sense.[42] This position was socially more conservative. Christians and Christian churches

[40] Nurser, *For All Peoples*, p. 11.

[41] Ibid., pp. 16–17; Darril Hudson, *The Ecumenical Movement in World Affairs* (London: Weidenfeld and Nicolson, 1969), pp. 44–55, 63.

[42] See, e.g., Torsten Bohlin, *Den kristna gudsrikestanken—Under 1800-talet och i nutiden* (Lund: C. W. K. Gleerups förlag, 1928), pp. 205–9, 289, 329–30, for an analysis of such more individualistically framed understandings of Christian faith and its implications. Bohlin identifies two main directions in which theologians of the late-nineteenth and early-twentieth century developed their reasoning regarding the Kingdom of God and its meaning in terms of this-worldly action, which he labels universalist and individualist approaches to the notion of the Kingdom of God. Universalists agreed that the Kingdom of God not only referred to the individual and her personal relations but 'also and primary to collective societal entities, the relations of individuals to these entities as well as their relations among each other'. They put forward a 'religious-social notion of the Kingdom of God'. Bohlin, *Den kristna gudsrikestanken*, pp. 339–40 (fn 1), 416–17, 419. It is this practically oriented movement that found also an outlet in Christian internationalism in the ecumenical movement. More socially conservative interpretations of the Kingdom of God held that possible processes of transformation of society and state could indirectly attest the activity of Christians and thus give proof of the ideal of love of the Christian community. However, the notion of the Kingdom of God remained a 'purely spiritual-individualistic defined' matter. Bohlin, *Den kristna gudsrikestanken*, pp. 205–9.

could bear prophetic witness to another way of being in the world and of working for peace and justice. This too was a way to be 'political'. They should not, however, align themselves with any political ideology. The proponents of this way of thinking, often associated with Karl Barth (1886–1968), emphasized the unbridgeable gap between God and anything this-worldly and man-made—between spiritual and temporal power. Christian revelation was 'not continuous with [the] world of reason, nature, and history'.[43]

What united Christians of both camps was the assessment that a focus on nation and class should not distract from questions about truth and justice. Ideas about Christian social action with such a 'narrow' focus and scope were considered outmoded, and the accompanying theological theories and categories were regarded as at least partially inadequate in the new situation.

Yet both within and outwith the ecumenical movement people differed in how they saw Christian faith coming to have a bearing on life in community and society, and the extent to which they saw Christian faith (in the form of deduced social ethical principles) inspiring 'direct' political action or simply indirectly pointing at an alternative way of community (that resonates more with how we could read Milbank's position today). It influenced the view of how—if at all—Christians and churches should co-operate with 'man-made' organizations, like the League of Nations or the UN.[44]

Within the ecumenical movement in the first half of the twentieth century, the dividing lines were drawn largely between the more activist and pragmatic Americans and the more theologically focused and 'otherworldly' continental Europeans. The British positioned themselves somewhere in between.[45] It was predominantly American ecumenists who felt that church action in world affairs was in line with the churches' social responsibility, requiring no additional theological justification, whereas European ecumenists considered such tasks foreign to the mission of the church.[46] Importantly, especially from 1937 onwards—and within the WCC particularly up until its First Assembly in 1948[47]—ecumenical work was strongly influenced by American liberal Protestants.

[43] Peiponen, *Ecumenical Action*, pp. 49–50 (fn. 50); referring to William Richey Hogg, *Ecumenical Foundations: A History of the International Missionary Council and Its Nineteenth-Century Background* (New York: Harper & Brothers, Publishers, 1952), p. 295. See also e.g. Karl Barth, *Der Römerbrief*, 2nd edn (München: Kaiser, 1923), p. XII, Bohlin, *Den kristna gudsrikestanken*, p. 307.

[44] For the last sentence, see Peiponen, *Ecumenical Action*, p. 50. Not all Barthians, for example the first secretary general of the WCC Willem Visser't Hooft (1900–85), feared outright that the Christian revelation would be compromised through involvement in international affairs. But they clearly held that the church should preserve its integrity and that, for example, a consultative status was the way in which the churches through the CCIA could relate to the UN. Peiponen, *Ecumenical Action*, pp. 104, 123.

[45] Ehrenström, 'Movements', pp. 551, 554–5.

[46] See e.g. Peiponen, *Ecumenical Action*, p. 119.

[47] Peiponen, *Ecumenical Action*, p. 358.

Theological Framing

The turn of the gaze from the national to the international plane that took place in ecumenical circles in the context of peace and justice, firstly before the League of Nations and later the UN, had been anticipated and instigated by theologically versed individuals who conceptualized social ethical responsible action in a so-called non-pietistic sense. One important source can be found in liberal theology, not least in the form it took within American Protestantism in 'social gospel' thought.

However, these and other champions of international action within the ecumenical movement also, in turn, found their inspiration among other things in nineteenth-century continental protestant theology. More specifically, a source of inspiration was a vein of liberal theological thinking that developed in the nineteenth century and whose early leading representatives were predominantly German—above all Albrecht Ritschl (1822–89) and Adolf von Harnack (1851–1930). For these so-called 'Ritschlians', the nation still formed an important point of reference at that stage, even if there were openings pointing beyond the state.[48] Their mission was to carry out a liberal reform of the church and a social reform of society.[49] These two issues were related. In the attempt to articulate adequate answer to the societal challenges, certain theological positions were rejected and novel avenues explored.[50] The task of theology was linked to the object of religious knowledge: namely God, what was good, and the overall structure and goal of life. Ritschl refuted a theology that, in keeping with traditional confessional metaphysics, looked for realities 'beyond' the presentation of the God and Christ that could be found in Scripture and tradition. What we find here is a faith and a theology that emphasized morality and value judgements, and whose concept of knowledge was connected to these.[51]

Given the stress on faith as value judgement, it is unsurprising that Ritschl and others who followed placed emphasis on formation and vocation—in other words, discipleship. What did it mean to strive for the good and lead a just life as a servant of God and a follower of Christ? The freedom to which the Christian was delivered was a freedom that was envisioned within the framework and in relation to a life in a community (instituted by Jesus). It was not about individual freedom. Instead,

[48] It is the focus on the nation that eventually becomes a point at which German liberal protestant theology is severely criticized as, according to critics, liberal theology showed itself inept as a starting point for critique of totalitarianism. See, e.g., Arne Rasmusson, 'Historiography and Theology: Theology in the Weimar Republic and the Beginning of the Third Reich', *Kirchliche Zeitgeschichte* 20, no. 1 (2007): pp. 155–80.

[49] John E. Wilson, *Introduction to Modern Theology: Trajectories in the German Tradition* (Louisville, KY/London: Westminster John Knox Press, 2007), pp. 16–18.

[50] Helmut Thielicke, *Glauben und Denken in der Neuzeit: die großen Systeme der Theologie und Religionsphilosophie* (Tübingen: J. C. B. Mohr, 1983), p. 356.

[51] Wilson, *Introduction*, pp. 126–8; Albrecht Ritschl, *Die christliche Lehre von der Rechtfertigung und der Versöhnung*, 3 vols, 4th edn (Bonn: Adolph Marcus, 1895), vol. 3, pp. 14–25, 194, 207–9. See also Thielicke, *Glauben und Denken*, p. 357.

the Christian was delivered to freedom in the service of the world and in the world and in the personal, societal, and political contexts where he or she lived.[52]

The freedom that faith offered the individual gave hope that change was possible even in a world increasingly explained with reference to 'laws of nature' and standards set by the emerging natural sciences as to what could count as objective knowledge. Faith offered freedom and independence, offsetting a 'fusion' of man with nature and society. It countered the risk of man being reduced to simply nature or, alternatively, being conceptualized solely as a product of society.[53]

In the US, Walter Rauschenbusch (1861–1918) famously represented this line of theological thinking, which grew in influence especially after the 1890s. He was a father of the so-called social gospel movement with which, among many ecumenical dignitaries, the FCC would come to be identified, and for which it would be criticized for its supposed liberalism. Like Ritschl, Rauschenbusch disapproved of asceticism and other movements that in various respects withdrew from societal life. In view of the social crisis he urged people to abandon Christian individualism, which had 'lost sight of the great idea of the kingdom of God' and the church's 'larger mission to humanity'. Rauschenbusch identified the Kingdom of God with a truly humane society. By practicing Christian ethics, this kingdom could become a reality. Jesus was no social reformer, but Rauschenbusch found in his life the roots of a new social and political order.[54]

This type of liberal interpretation of the Christian tradition came under critique in the early twentieth century.[55] It was considered too ethically immanent, too overly optimistic about changing the world and believing humanity to be progressively developing into a humane society that could be likened to a Kingdom of God on earth. Moreover critics were, as already mentioned, wary of the ways in which Christians consequently engaged with international politics on a 'secular basis'.

Still, in the Anglo-Saxon world, liberal optimistic theology with its faith in progress kept a longer hold on the population. 'Christians bent their efforts to "hastening" the coming of the Kingdom of God. Some hailed the nascent world community, organized in the League of Nations, as a new manifestation of its glorious advance.'[56] Liberal theology and social gospel theology continued to be influential into the 1930s, at which point criticism of these ideas grew in strength.[57]

One attempt to temper the excesses was formulated by Reinhold Niebuhr (1892–1971). Niebuhr was influenced theologically, amongst other things, by

[52] Ritschl, *Die christliche Lehre*, vol. 1, p. 555; Ritschl, *Die christliche Lehre*, vol. 3, pp. 194–5; Wilson, *Introduction*, p. 128. See also Thielicke, *Glauben und Denken*, pp. 371–2; Karl Barth, *Die protestantische Theologie im 19. Jahrhundert* (Zollikon/Zürich: Evangelischer Verlag, 1947), p. 604.

[53] Ritschl, *Die christliche Lehre*, vol. 3, pp. 17, 198; Barth, *Die protestantische Theologie*, p. 604; Thielicke, *Glauben und Denken*, pp. 360–2.

[54] Walter Rauschenbusch, *Christianity and the Social Crisis* (New York: Macmillan, 1907), pp. 59–60, 71, 91, 339–40; Wilson, *Introduction*, p. 138.

[55] Cf. Wilson, *Introduction*, pp. 16–17. For a severe critique of Ritschl, see e.g., Barth, *Die protestantische Theologie*, pp. 598–605.

[56] Ehrenström, 'Movements', p. 569. [57] Ibid.

'liberal theology, including American equivalents of Ritschlianism', but also by dialectical theology and especially Emil Brunner.[58] He was sceptical of the naïve progression-optimism of liberal theologians who downplayed the sinfulness of man and overestimated the ability of human reason. Yet he still embraced the social-ethical ideals, in a so-called 'Christian realist' vein. The ideal of justice was an approximation of the Christian command for love, and could moreover be intelligent to people regardless of faith. Niebuhr, who would be involved in both the WCC and the CCIA—and supported human rights—held a realistic view of man and what could be politically accomplished in that time and age.[59]

Moreover, despite the gradual tempering of an overly optimistic attitude regarding the possibility to change temporal conditions, twentieth-century theologians and ecumenical leaders continued to share the view that one continuously needed to find ways to assert the contribution of the Christian narrative for understanding human history and agency as *history*. Over and against a mechanical understanding of the world, there was need of an inspirational vision. History had to be presented as creation by God and by man.[60] And as God's co-workers, the churches had a mission that included social responsibilities.

This was the conceptual backdrop for much of the work for peace and a just world during the early twentieth century. It is within this framework, and of course elsewhere, that we encounter the likes of Nolde and Söderblom and others in the ecumenical movement, who held religious ideas that strongly affected them, but at the same time were able to recast their agendas in a language that was reasonable and feasible in terms of public policies and international politics. They took a pragmatic attitude to their work and relied on secular, 'inclusive' arguments.[61] As Nolde notes, at the time 'freedom demands a broader base than can be offered by religion alone'.[62]

The pragmatic or 'practical' attitude featured most prominently among American liberal ecumenists. To return to Nolde,[63] for him Ritschl—maybe the most famous of the liberal theologians—was one whom he credited for his theological thought, alongside, as mentioned, the liberal theologian Söderblom. Being a professor of religious education, it is easy to see that a theology focused on formation and vocation would have had obvious appeal to Nolde.[64] The following

[58] Wilson, *Introduction*, pp. 228–9.

[59] Andrew Preston, *Sword of the Spirit, Shield of the Faith: Religion in American War and Diplomacy* (New York: Anchor Books, 2012, pp. 304–14; Peiponen, *Ecumenical Action*, p. 301; as well as e.g. Reinhold Niebuhr, *Moral Man and Immoral Society* (New York: Charles Scribner's Sons, 1960 [1932]), pp. xx–xxi.

[60] See Nurser, *For All Peoples*, p. 55 for remarks on how the discussion went at the WCC Amsterdam Assembly in 1948.

[61] Nurser, *For All Peoples*, pp. 97–8.

[62] Nolde cited in David Little, 'Foreword', in Nurser, *For All Peoples*, p. xi.

[63] As leader of the CCIA, Nolde was renowned for standing in 'the American activist tradition which always wanted "to do something" about a problem; and he did'. Darril Hudson, *The World Council of Churches in International Affairs* (Leighton Buzzard: The Faith Press, 1977), pp. 38–9.

[64] Peiponen characterizes Nolde as 'a child of liberal American Protestantism with a strong emphasis on civil commitment' which took expression in his pragmatic approach to world politics. Peiponen, *Ecumenical Action*, p. 339.

section will give a short account of Nolde's thoughts regarding working towards justice, peace, and human rights, and the religious framing he gave this work.[65] He expressed his thoughts, among other things, in a speech given in the explicitly 'religious' setting of ecumenical conversations with representatives of the Roman Catholic Church. This gives an idea of the otherwise largely concealed theological framing of his 'pragmatic' work.

The ecumenists who came together in international action held different theological positions. The following is therefore a single in-depth example of how work for peace and human rights at the level of the international community was conceptualized concretely in relation to God's redeeming and miraculous workings, at a time preceding large-scale official ecumenical human rights deliberations. The choice of Nolde is warranted as he has been credited as the key person at work for the CCIA and thus the ecumenical churches in the newly established UN.[66]

Christian Vocation and the Work for Peace and Human Rights

Reflecting in 1961 on the views that he had come to hold over the years working as a representative for the churches to the UN, Nolde concluded that he and CCIA, which he represented, viewed all humans as created in the image of God. This meant that they had equal worth and freedom, and was affirmed through the act of Christ through which God reconciled the world with Himself. Thus Nolde connected human rights both to creation and salvation. The rights were not given to men by governments, but were within men. God was their source. He recognized that Christians and non-Christians founded the rights differently, but what united all was the demand that the rights be realized.[67]

Human rights work was therefore a Christian task as well. 'Christian vocation, whatever lines it may follow, is the means through which the Christian responds to God and reflects God's purpose for him with society.' Christian vocation was centrally about action for a just society, which was a society where human rights were

[65] The analysis of Nolde's reasoning is based on his own writings, which were partly written in retrospect, but also during the turbulent years when the UN was created and the UDHR was drafted, when Nolde represented the interests of churches and ecumenical actors. I limit myself to a few central ideas.

[66] Peiponen, *Ecumenical Action*, p. 234.

[67] O. Frederick Nolde, *Free and Equal: Human Rights in Ecumenical Perspective.* With reflections on the origin of the Universal Declaration of Human Rights by Charles Habib Malik (Geneva: World Council of Churches, 1968), p. 66. See also O. Frederick Nolde, *Power for Peace: The Way of the United Nations and The Will of Christian People* (Philadelphia: Muhlenberg Press, 1946), pp. 62–3, referring also to the *Statement on Religious Liberty* by the Federal Council of the Churches of Christ in America, and the Foreign Mission Conference of North America in 1944, and O. Frederick Nolde, 'Divine Compulsion', *Ecumenical Review* 8, no. 4 (1956): p. 420. For Nolde, 'religious liberty is in one sense basic to all other human rights, especially civil rights', while simultaneously also 'inseparably related to them'. Nolde, *Free and Equal*, p. 67.

realized. This was the theological interpretation of human rights that CCIA and Nolde supported.[68] It mirrors the focus on vocation, moral action, and responsibility that was at the centre of the Ritschlian thinking Nolde considered himself indebted to,[69] and it shows how vocation in important respects is explicated in social-ethical terms.

Moreover, human rights are seen as facilitators of discipleship. Nolde conceptualized human rights not only as a task of Christians given to them by God: if men were guaranteed human rights, these rights would actually create conditions for discipleship. Nolde concluded that '[w]hile man has no claim to rights before God, the situation in human society is different. Here man's rights are based upon the gifts which God and the duties which God calls upon him to fulfill'.[70] Nolde observed that 'human rights can and ought to be recognized in society', and when they 'are recognized and observed, man is in a position more readily to fulfill his obligations to God and to his neighbor'.[71] Thus, ultimately, Nolde gave the work for human rights a religious framing.

Moreover, this work included an international component, and so international work was given a theological foundation as well. Nolde talked about 'religious liberty as a matter of international responsibility'[72]. In the same manner, he talked about work for 'a peaceful and orderly world' as the personal responsibility of every Christian.[73] Christians were not just supposed to have views about questions of central concern to the international community and the world order—they should also act to bring these views to fruition. If ecumenical bodies wanted to influence the decisions being made, they had to be present at the places and moments in time where international decisions were made. Concrete action was needed.[74] Nolde urged churches and individual Christians to support the UN: '[T]he work of the world political organization [the UN] is, or should become, relevant to rightful objectives of the Christian citizen.' According to him, their input was in fact vital.[75]

Talking at the Second Assembly of the WCC in 1954, Nolde visualized the work of his agency, the CCIA, in terms of peace, the understanding of which found its inspiration in the Christian message:

I venture to say that in this co-operative witness ... a new world peace movement is progressively developing, a movement which is rooted in the life of the churches and which seeks to express the meaning of the Christian faith for relations among nations.... It is not

[68] Nolde, *Free and Equal*, p. 66. See also Nolde, 'Divine Compulsion', p. 420, as well as e.g. Alf Tergel, *De mänskliga rättigheterna och Kyrkornas världsråd*, Tro & Tanke 1998: 5 (Uppsala: Svenska kyrkans forskningsråd, 1998), pp. 16–17.

[69] Nurser, *For All* Peoples, p. 36. Nolde's dedication to education and vocation is visible for example in his book *Power for Peace* (1946), which was structured in a way that would be useful for students who wanted to learn about the UN.

[70] Nolde, *Free and Equal*, p. 65. [71] Ibid., p. 66. [72] Ibid., p. 65.

[73] Nolde, *Power for Peace*, pp. XIV, 3, 33. See also e.g. Nolde, 'Divine Compulsion', p. 419.

[74] Nolde, *Power for Peace*, p. XI.

[75] Ibid., pp. XI, XIV. International law, e.g., should conform to Christian moral principles. Ibid., pp. 85–6.

yet, unfortunately, a popular movement but ultimately it must become so, for its success depends upon study and support by Christians in every walk of life.[76]

Coexistence was a prerequisite for peace, meaning something more than 'a world divided into compartments with an apparent commitment that both parties will respect existing geographical and ideological boundaries'. Nolde denounced compartmentalization on grounds of Christian fellowship being borderless,[77] echoing the central 1930s idea of the united church as a testimony to and vision for international fellowship.

Looking back at the first six years of the WCC in 1954, the CCIA itself noted that it had not attempted to examine and elucidate 'the theological presuppositions of the churches' witness in international affairs'. The CCIA was not equipped to carry out such a task either.[78] The influence of the pragmatist and practice-oriented attitude on part of American ecumenists, who very much initiated the creation of the CCIA, is visible in these statements.[79] Yet the CCIA did identify the following justification of its work: a Christian who has experienced the peace, righteousness, and freedom that God offers, must seek the same for his fellowmen.[80]

In conclusion, Christian faith could and should express itself in political action, including human rights work. It was in keeping with—rather than breaking from—Christian tradition. In fact, even if it did not ultimately find its way into the list in Article 18 of the UDHR of ways religion can take expression, Nolde and the WCC did repeat in the years to come that part of this religious freedom was the ability to address 'social, economic and political affairs, whether domestic or international', according to one's conscience.[81]

Concluding Discussion

To sum up, liberal theological thought, with an optimistic outlook on man and history, a progression narrative, and an attempt to mediate between theology and the epistemological demands of the positive sciences—among other things through dismissal of traditional metaphysics and a turn to 'ethics'/value judgments and 'vocation'—formed the framework within which internationalist Christian action in the early twentieth century was to a large extent grounded. As said, it was very much about lay discipleship. Salvation was deliverance to freedom of service for the world and in the world in the personal, societal, and political contexts where one lived, work on the progressive realization of a moral

[76] Reproduced in Gaines, *The World Council*, pp. 650–1.
[77] Gaines, *The World Council*, p. 651; and Nolde, 'Divine Compulsion', p. 421.
[78] *The First Six Years 1948–1954*, p. 101.
[79] See also e.g. Peiponen, *Ecumenical Action*, pp. 94–8, 119, 148–9.
[80] *The First Six Years 1948–1954*, p. 101.
[81] Nolde, *Free and Equal*, pp. 42, 67.

Kingdom of God. Eschatology was not a religious border-concept but an immanently to-be-realized socio-ethical ideal. History was presented as a creation of God and man.

This laid the ground for the optimism and vision of international work as expressive of Christian discipleship and God's vision for the world that impacted Huber and Dulles at a time when, after all, the progressive narrative had been shaken in its core. The idealistic belief in creating a world order with a moral core would soon enough be confronted and moderated by the realpolitik that impacted international relations following the Second World War. But the belief would not be lost completely.

However, as this chapter has also emphasized, within the ecumenical movement and the WCC there was no consensus on political and economic matters, nor regarding the way to bring about social reform. Darril Hudson makes clear that diverging theological positions were present already at the meeting of Life and Work in Stockholm 1925, and would 'come to life to plague the Ecumenical Movement as it found its place in international life'. Because people perceived of, for example, the relationship between the Kingdom of God and the world differently, they also differed in their views about the church and the world. Americans were denounced as naïve, non-theological, pragmatic, and activist.[82]

However, with regard to those who did favour international action, and thought that Christians could give a contribution to a new world order with a moral core—in the main, Anglo-American ecumenists—their vision of a just social order combined a liberal project of rule of law with a favourable yet not uncritical stance to capitalism. Moreover, human rights (and international law more generally) became understood as a weapon in the defence of the individual person against the totalitarian state and unlimited state power[83]—contrary to Milbank, who, as seen, does not see human rights as safeguards against totalitarian regimes (like China or Russia), but rather as their ally.

At the first General Assembly of the WCC in Amsterdam in 1948, the delegates were clearly divided on both doctrinal matters and matters of peace and war. Caution was observed in view of the East-West rivalries on the world-political scene that were also making inroads into the ecumenical discussions.[84] The 'anti-religious emphasis of the Soviet communism' was, however, a major factor behind the support for human rights of the WCC and the CCIA at the time.[85] Regarding the understanding of human rights and religious freedom, their stance coincided with the American position of the time, and the Joint Declaration on Religious Liberty adopted by the WCC at the Assembly in Amsterdam and, at a later date, by the IMC is evidence to this. But as organizations, they abstained from taking definite sides between the East and West—or capitalism and communism—even

[82] Ehrenström, 'Movements', pp. 554–5; and *Hudson, Ecumenical Movement*, p. 82.

[83] At the WCC Amsterdam Assembly in 1948, human rights and fundamental freedoms were something the delegates did agree about. Peiponen, *Ecumenical Action*, p. 292.

[84] See e.g. Peiponen, *Ecumenical Action*, pp. 284–97.

[85] Peiponen, *Ecumenical Action*, pp. 328–9.

if in particular Americans like Dulles would have wished for more. The Church should be likened with neither, and gather all Christians irrespective of national belonging.[86]

For the ecumenical actors, the freedom that human rights granted was neither unlimited nor unconditioned. In this they once more differed from Milbank. Religious liberty, for example, had to be secured in order for people to be free to seek God. The fact that the ultimate foundation of the rights lay with God—as CCIA put it, governments had to *recognize* (as oppose to *grant*) man as possessing these rights 'by virtue of his being and destiny'[87]—meant that the perception of the rights fell back on comprehensive religiously inspired ideas about the human person, about justice and just distribution, about society, and the goals of mankind. They may not have been in all respects explicitly theologically elaborated but, as seen, the framework was there, including ideas about 'right' and a transcendent moral order. Human rights were not seen—as Milbank would have it—as representations of an atomising metaphysic or authorisation of voluntarist thinking gone too far.

Yet given Milbank's severe critique, were these early 'human rights activists' naïve? Nolde, the CCIA, and other ecumenical actors quickly became aware that the UN was not functioning optimally. National interests trumped other concerns in the name of state sovereignty. Ideological conflicts hampered the work, and the veto system was abused. The UN operated 'on the frontier of international anarchy'.[88] It became evident that expectations had been unrealistic, but that there was also no clear alternative but to seek to improve and reinforce the UN.[89] Also, despite this disillusionment, human rights remained a goal of the churches. In fact, the comprehensive elaboration of the churches' understanding, beyond central notions of human dignity, human freedom, equality, and perhaps a limited number of mainly 'classical' individual rights and freedoms still lay ahead. This work got off the ground in the 1960s.[90] Still, the time period was a different

[86] Declaration on Religious Liberty, adopted by the World Council of Churches in Amsterdam and by the International Missionary Council in Oesgstgeest, the Netherlands, in September 1948, reproduced e.g. in Report of Section IV, *The Church and the International Disorder*, reproduced in *The Church and International Disorder: An Ecumenical Study Prepared under the Auspices of the World Council of Churches* (London: SCM Press LTD, 1948), pp. 229–32; Peiponen, *Ecumenical Action*, pp. 291, 345–8, 358.

[87] Nolde, *Free and Equal*, p. 38. The CCIA connected religious liberty to other rights and freedoms, considering human rights interconnected and interdependent. Nolde, *Free and Equal*, pp. 38–9. This idea of interrelatedness of human rights clearly reflects the earlier step taken by Nolde in 1944 to convince the Protestant churches he then represented (the FCC) to support 'a broad range of human rights as the path to follow in securing religious liberty'. Nurser, 'A Human Rights "Soul"', pp. 54–5.

[88] Statement of the CCIA in the report *The First Six Years*. The matter of how to relate to and view the UN was discussed at consecutive WCC Assemblies in Amsterdam 1948, Evanston 1954, and New Delhi 1961. The CCIA also produced two statements on the topic, 'Christian Look at the United Nations' (1953), and another in 1965. O. Frederick Nolde, 'Ecumenical Action in International Affairs', in *The Ecumenical Advance: A History of the Ecumenical Movement, volume 2, 1948–1968*, edited by Harold E. Fey, 3rd edn with updated bibliography (Geneva: World Council of Churches, 1970), p. 283.

[89] Nolde, 'Ecumenical Action', p. 283.

[90] See e.g. Tergel, *De mänskliga rättigheterna*, pp. 13–15, 17, who offers an account of the view taken by the WCC at the beginning of its work in 1948 and up until 1961.

one than Milbank's twenty-first century. Human rights were only one vocabulary among others and were definitely not in wide circulation. The heydays of human rights were decades away. They had not yet colonized perceptions of human life and relationships to the extent that would later become the case.

Bibliography

Barth, Karl. *Der Römerbrief*, 2nd edn (München: Kaiser, 1923).

Barth, Karl. *Die protestantische Theologie im 19. Jahrhundert* (Zollikon/Zürich: Evangelischer Verlag, 1947).

Bell, George Kennedy Allen. *The Stockholm Conference: Official Report of the Universal Christian Conference on Life and Work* (London: Oxford University Press, 1926).

Bohlin, Torsten. *Den kristna gudsrikestanken—Under 1800-talet och i nutiden* (Lund: C. W. K. Gleerups förlag, 1928).

The Church and International Disorder: An Ecumenical Study Prepared under the Auspices of the World Council of Churches. Report of Section IV (London: SCM Press LTD, 1948).

The Churches and the International Crisis. Report of the WCC Conference. Geneva, July 1939. WCC Archives, Box X, pp. 12.

Die Kirche und das Staatsproblem in der Gegenwart (Genf: Forschungsabteilung des Oekumenischen Rates für Praktisches Christentum, 1934, 2nd enlarged edition 1935).

Ehrenström, Nils. 'Movements for International Friendship and Life and Work 1925–1948'. In *A History of the Ecumenical Movement,* edited by Ruth Rouse and Stephen Neill, 4th edn (Geneva: World Council of Churches, 1993 [1954]), pp. 551, 554–5, 569–70, 582, 591–2.

The First Six Years 1948–1954: A Report of the Central Committee, of the World Council of Churches on the activities of the Departments and Secretariats of the Council (Geneva: World Council of Churches, 1954).

Gaines, David P. *The World Council of Churches: A Study of Its Background and History* (Peterborough, N. H.: Richard R. Smith, Noone House, 1966).

Hogg, William Richey. *Ecumenical Foundations: A History of the International Missionary Council and its Nineteenth-Century Background* (New York: Harper & Brothers, Publishers, 1952).

Hudson, Darril. *The Ecumenical Movement in World Affairs* (London: Weidenfeld and Nicolson, 1969).

Hudson, Darril. *The World Council of Churches in International Affairs* (Leighton Buzzard: The Faith Press, 1977).

Jonson, Jonas. *Gustaf Aulén: Biskop och motståndsman* (Skellefteå: Artos & Norma bokförlag, 2011).

Karlström, Nils. 'Movements for International Friendship and Life and Work 1910–1925'. In *A History of the Ecumenical Movement 1517–1948*, edited by Ruth Rouse and Stephen Charles Neill, 4th edn (Geneva: World Council of Churches, 1993 [1954]), pp. 515, 532–3.

Lindkvist, Linde. 'The Politics of Article 18: Religious Liberty in the Universal Declaration of Human Rights'. *Humanity* 4, no. 3 (2013): pp. 443.

Lindqvist, Linde. *Shrines and Souls: The Reinvention of Religious Liberty and the Genesis of the Universal Declaration of Human Rights* (Malmö: Boxbox, 2014).

Milbank, John. 'Against Human Rights: Liberty in the Western Tradition'. *Oxford Journal of Law and Religion* 1, no. 1 (2012): pp. 206, 207, 209–10, 218, 229, 230, 234.
Negri, Antonio, and Gabriele Fadini. 'Materialism and Theology: A Conversation'. *Rethinking Marxism* 20, no. 2 (2008): pp. 665–72.
Niebuhr, Reinhold. *Moral Man and Immoral Society* (New York: Charles Scribner's Sons, 1960 [1932]).
Nolde, O. Frederick. *Power for Peace: The Way of the United Nations and the Will of Christian People* (Philadelphia: Muhlenberg Press, 1946).
Nolde, O. Frederick. 'Divine Compulsion'. *Ecumenical Review* 8, no. 4 (1956): pp. 419, 420, 421.
Nolde, O. Frederick. *Free and Equal: Human Rights in Ecumenical Perspective, with Reflections on the Origin of the Universal Declaration of Human Rights by Charles Habib Malik* (Geneva: World Council of Churches, 1968).
Nolde, O. Frederick. 'Human Rights in Retrospect: A Contemporary Appraisal'. *The Ecumenical Review* 20, no. 4 (1968): pp. 395–403.
Nolde, O. Frederick. 'Ecumenical Action in International Affairs'. In *The Ecumenical Advance: A History of the Ecumenical Movement, Volume 2 1948–1968*, edited by Harold E. Fey, 3rd edn with updated bibliography (Geneva: World Council of Churches, 1970), p. 283.
Nurser, John S. 'The 'Ecumenical Movement' Churches, 'Global Order,' and Human Rights: 1938–1948'. *Human Rights Quarterly* 25, no. 4 (2003): pp. 841–81.
Nurser, John S. *For All Peoples and All Nations: The Ecumenical Church and Human Rights* (Washington, D.C.: Georgetown University Press, 2005).
Nurser, John. 'A Human Rights 'Soul' for a Secular World of 'Faiths': A Contradiction, or Just a Paradox?'. *Political Theology* 6, no. 1 (2005): pp. 53, 54–5.
Oldham, Joseph H. *Oxford Conference, Official Report* (Chicago/New York: Willett, Clark & Company, 1937).
Peiponen, Matti. *Ecumenical Action in World Politics: The Creation of the Commission of the Churches on International Affairs (CCIA), 1945–1949.* Schriften der Luther-Agricola-Gesellschaft 66 (Helsinki: Luther-Agricola-Society, 2012).
Preston, Andrew. *Sword of the Spirit, Shield of the Faith: Religion in American War and Diplomacy* (New York: Anchor Books, 2012).
Rasmusson, Arne. 'Historiography and Theology: Theology in the Weimar Republic and the Beginning of the Third Reich'. *Kirchliche Zeitgeschichte* 20, no. 1 (2007): pp. 155–80.
Rauschenbusch, Walter. *Christianity and the Social Crisis* (New York: Macmillan, 1907).
Ritschl, Albrecht. *Die christliche Lehre von der Rechtfertigung und der Versöhnung.* 3 vols, 4th edn (Bonn: Adolph Marcus, 1895).
Slotte, Pamela. '"Blessed are the Peacemakers": Christian Internationalism, Ecumenical Voices and the Universal Declaration of Human Rights'. In *Revisiting the Origins of Human Rights,* edited by Pamela Slotte and Miia Halme-Tuomisaari (Cambridge: Cambridge University Press, 2015), pp. 293–329.
Tergel, Alf. 'De mänskliga rättigheterna och Kyrkornas världsråd'. Tro & Tanke (Uppsala: Svenska Kyrkans Forskningsråd, 1998), p. 5.
Thielicke, Helmut. *Glauben und Denken in der Neuzeit: die großen Systeme der Theologie und Religionsphilosophie* (Tübingen: J. C. B. Mohr, 1983).
Wilson, John E. *Introduction to Modern Theology: Trajectories in the German Tradition* (Louisville, KY/London: Westminster John Knox Press, 2007).

PART III

INTERNATIONAL LAW, RELIGION, AND TERRITORY IN THE MIDDLE EAST AND THE EASTERN MEDITERRANEAN

10

Muslim Jurists' Criteria for the Division of the World into *Dar al-Harb* and *Dar al-Islam*

Moussa Abou Ramadan

Humanity has divided the world into different territories and different categories of human beings. Europe has distinguished between the civilized world and the uncivilized one. The Ottoman Empire had difficulties meeting the legal qualification of a state with equal rights.[1]

Muslim jurists focused on the legal status of the various territories relatively early on. From the beginning of Islam there had been an incredible territorial expansion and large numbers of people of different ethnicities and religions came under the control of the new Islamic entity.[2] The jurists were therefore also interested in both the different population groups and the different categories of territories. In this chapter I intend to retrace the different conceptions of the four legal schools on the issue. In their *fiqh* (jurisprudence) treaties Muslim jurists dedicated a chapter on *siyar* or jihad. Literally *siyar* refers to 'conduct', but it came to denote 'conduct during war'. The Prophet's biography, *al-sira* is also called *maghazi*, that is the history of

[1] According to Pillet, 'states are not equal to each other ... First, there is no equality of rights between civilized states and uncivilized or less civilized ones. In their dealings with the latter, the former are constantly the superior ones, responsible for the mission to bring them willy-nilly into the paths of civilization: in this capacity, they assume for themselves certain rights to management, control, and at times administration in matters those are completely unable to handle. There is a blatant inequality in status between them and the others, and that inequality is in this respect the very basis of their relations'. Antoine Pillet, *Recherches sur les droits fondamentaux des états dans l'ordre des rapports internationaux et sur la solution des conflicts qu'ils font naitre* (Paris: A. Pedone, 1899), p. 6. For the unequal relations between Europe and the Ottoman Empire, see Eliana Augusti, 'From Capitulations to Unequal Treaties: The Matter of an Extraterritorial Jurisdiction in the Ottoman Empire', *Journal of Civil Law Studies* (2011): pp. 285–308; Maurits H. van den Boogert, *The Capitulations and the Ottoman Legal Sytem: Qadis, Consuls and Beraths in the 18th Century* (Leiden/Boston: Brill, 2005). A non-egalitarian vision of humanity is given expression, for example, by Lorimer: 'As a political phenomenon, humanity in its present condition, divides itself into three concentric zones or spheres—that of civilized humanity, that of barbarous humanity, and that of savage humanity.' James Lorimer, *The Institutes of the Law of Nations: A Treatise of the Jural Relations of Separate Political Communities*, vol. 1 (Edinburgh/London: William Blackwood and Sons, 1883), p. 101.

[2] Robert Matran, *L'expansion musulmane, VII–XI siècles*, 5th edn (Paris: PUF, 1995).

Muslim Jurists' Criteria for the Division of the World into Dar al-Harb *and* Dar al-Islam. Moussa Abou Ramadan. Published 2017 by Oxford University Press.

the Prophet's wars. The first work on *siyar* was by Awza'i (d. 158/774),[3] that came to be known to us through the commentary on it by Abu Yusuf (d. 182/798).[4] The best-known book is *al-Siyar al-kabir* by Muhammad al-Shaybani (d. 189/805),[5] who was the disciple of Abu Hanifa (d. 150/767), the founder of the Hanafi school.

Territorial Categories and Distinctions between People

There were distinctions pertaining to territories and to people. The territorial category and the type of religious, ethnic, or political group involved had an influence on the applicability of legal rules. As international law is based on the key concept of sovereignty its starting point was the emergence of the state. With regard to people, the primary distinction was between Muslims and non-Muslims. Among non-Muslims, there was a distinction between believers in monotheist religions and others. The former had a privileged status giving them a right to a protection agreement, *'aqd al-dhimma*. There were also the categories of rebels (*bugha*)[6] and apostates (*murtadun*).[7] In addition, there was the category of *musta'minin*, people who had a temporary permission to reside in Muslim lands.[8] Finally, there was the possibility of a temporary peace agreement, *muwada'a*, if it served the interests of Muslims. Apart from the peace agreement, there was an obligation to fight (jihad). Several recent studies have attempted to present an apologetic view, describing jihad as defensive war.[9]

It should be noted that the sources and methods used in Islamic doctrine for international relations were not inter-state sources, but the same sources used for other legal matters, such as marriage, contracts of sale, lease, or inheritance. It was an internal law of an empire, based on the assumption that the world would be transformed into a single Muslim state and thus it did not matter what other people thought.

This law ignored the rights of other entities and was more akin to a sort of Muslim imperialism. The *fiqh* treatises of the four Sunni schools dealt with the following main issues: with regard to the nature of the obligation to jihad, it was deliberated whether it was an individual obligation of every Muslim, or a collective obligation, for which it would be sufficient that some people fulfil it, while others

[3] Founder of a Sunni school of law that disappeared in the eleventh century. On his life and work, see 'Abdil Sattar al-Shaykh, *Al-Imam al-Awza'i: Saykh al-Islam wa 'alim ahl al-sham* (88–157H) (Jadda: Dar al-Bashir, 2006).

[4] Abu Yusuf, *Al-rad 'ala siyar Awza'i* (Haydarabad: Lajnat Ihya' al-Ma'arif al-Nu'maniya, n.d.).

[5] Al-Sarakhsi, *Sharh al-siyar al-kabir* (Beirut: Dar al-Kutub al-'Ilmiyya, n.d.).

[6] See Khaled Abou El Fadl, *Rebellion and Violence in Islamic Law* (Cambridge: Cambridge University Press, 2001).

[7] See Houssame Bentabaet, 'L'apostat dans le droit musulman classique et contemporain. Définition et punition' (M.A. thesis, University of Strasbourg, 2014).

[8] 'Abdil Karim Zidan, *Ahkam al-dhimiyin wa aal-musta'minin fi dar al-islam* (Baghdad: Maktabat al-Quds, 1982).

[9] See, for example, Ahmed Al-Dawoody, *The Islamic Law of War: Justifications and Regulations* (New York: Palgrave Macmillan, 2011).

are exempted, and if so, what the conditions were that must be met; the division of the spoils of war; individuals, who may or may not be killed; the conditions for concluding a peace treaty with the non-Muslims, which means who was qualified to enter such a treaty, and its duration; the protection contract of Jews and Christians (*'aqd al-dhimma*); and the guarantees granted to non-Muslims entering Muslim lands (*musta'minun*).

It should be noted that at the international level in the Muslim world the Ottoman Empire held a predominant position among Sunnis, and the Safavid Empire among Shi'ites. In the Ottoman Empire, there was the practice of Capitulations with European countries.[10] In this chapter I deal with Islamic law, or more precisely, the legal doctrine developed by Muslim jurists over the centuries. I do not discuss the actual conventions and diplomatic practices of Muslim states.

The writings on *siyar* number in the hundreds. In every treatise on Islamic law there is a chapter dealing with the issue. In contrast, there was little development in the conception of *dar al-harb* or *dar al-Islam*. Most Muslim jurists either did not mention the issue or dealt with it in a limited manner by discussing the legal consequences of the distinction. For the present purpose, the discussion here focuses on jurists, who explicitly dealt with the issue.

In the little that has been written about international Islamic law, the division of the world is seen as a given, something unchanging. The subtleties in the criteria for that distinction are not discussed. So Majid Kuddiri writes, for example:

> The world accordingly was sharply divided into *dar al-Islam* (abode or territory of Islam) and *dar al-harb* (abode or territory of war).... The first corresponded to the territory under Muslim rule. Its inhabitants were Muslims, by birth or conversion, and the communities of the tolerated religions (the *dhimmis*) who preferred to hold fast to their own cult, at the price of paying *jizya* (poll tax). The Muslim enjoyed full rights of citizenship; the subjects of the tolerated religions enjoyed only partial rights, and submitted to Muslim rule in accordance with special charters regulating their relations with the Muslims.... The *dar al-harb* consisted of all the states and communities outside the world of Islam. Its inhabitants were often called infidels, or, better, unbelievers.[11]

In his more recently article, Bassam Tibi sees no development in the conception of the division; he writes 'I conclude that the Islamic worldview is resistant to change and that there are many obstacles to the development of an ethic of war and peace compatible with the circumstances of the modern age.'[12]

[10] van den Boogert, *The Capitulations and the Ottoman Legal System*.

[11] Majid Khadduri, *War and Peace in Islam* (Baltimore: Johns Hopkins Press, 1955), pp. 52–3.

[12] Bassam Tibi, 'War and Peace in Islam', in *Islamic Political Ethics: Civil Society, Pluralism, and Conflict*, edited by Sohail H. Hashmi (New Jersey: Princeton University Press, 2002), pp. 175–93. See also Sobhi Mahmassani, 'The Principles of International Law in the Light of Islamic Doctrine', in *Collected Courses of The Hague Academy of International Law*, vol. 117 (Leiden/Boston: Brill/Nijhoff, 1966), pp. 250–2; Mohammad Fadel, 'International Law, Regional Developments: Islam', in *Max Planck Encyclopedia of Public International Law* (2009), par. 7, at http://www.law.utoronto.ca/documents/Fadel/Max_Planck_Final.pdf (accessed 2 July 2015); Mohammad Talaat Al-Gunaimi, *The Muslim Conception of International Law and the Western Approach* (The Hague: Martinus Nijhoff, 1968), pp. 156–7; Michael Bonner, *Jihad in Islamic History: Doctrines and Practice* (Princeton and Oxford: Princeton University Press, 2006), pp. 92–3.

In contrast to those two scholars, Ahmad Al-Dawoody argues in his recent book that Islamic law does not conceive jihad as permanent war, but as a defensive war.[13] The categories of the division of the world—*dar al-harb, dar al-Islam*, and *dar al-sulh* (territory with a peace treaty)—are unchanging. There are no nuances in the jurists' arguments. In addition it is difficult, if not impossible, to know what is actually in the Qur'an and what a matter of interpretation. The attempt to establish the true interpretation of the Qur'an leads back to the works of theologians, and not the sciences.

A review of the legal literature, however, shows a much more complex and nuanced picture of the way Muslim jurists conceived the division of the world. It turns out that that the criteria are not always identical even within the same school. Some jurists gave preference to the application of Islamic regulations, and others to the safety of Muslims or to the call to prayer. Some jurists divided the world into two parts, and others into three. Finally, these criteria were assessed differently during the same time period. I proceed by analysing the four Sunni schools of law and the attitudes of various scholars in chronological order.

The Hanafi School

According to al-Dabusi (d. 430/1039),[14] for Shafiʿi the world consisted of a single territory, while for Hanafis it was divided into *dar al-Islam* and *dar al-harb*. This has legal consequences; al-Dabusi gives the example that if a Muslim or a person belonging to the People of the Book, who is protected by the Muslim state, immigrates to a Muslim state, while his spouse remains in *dar-al-harb*, their marriage is automatically dissolved according to the Hanafis, while for Shafiʿi there is no dissolution of marriage by the very fact of migration. This difference in the legal consequences stems from the fact that for Shafiʿi the world is a single territory and therefore migration does not change a person's status. Here the territory should be understood as a function of jurisdiction, since for Shafiʿi Islamic law was applicable to Muslims even outside Muslim territory.[15] Moreover, as we shall see, Shafiʿi scholars were making distinctions with regard to territory.

A survey of the other Hanafi jurists reveals that there were two basic opinions in this school regarding the criteria for distinguishing between *dar al-harb* and *dar al-Islam*. One was the opinion of the school's founder, Abu Hanifa, and the other that of his two disciples Abu Yusuf and Muhammad al-Shaybani. It is noteworthy that there are variations in the rendering of the Abu Hanifa's position by different authors. As for Muhammad al-Shaybani's position, there are variations in the same book, but pertaining to different matters.

[13] Al-Dawoody, *The Islamic Law of War*, pp. 92–102.
[14] Al-Dabusi, *Taʾsis al-nazar* (Cairo: Maktaba al-Kuliyat al-Azhariya, n. d.), p. 119.
[15] See Abou El Fadl, *Rebellion and Violence in Islamic Law*, p. 155.

According to Abu Yusuf and al-Shaybani, every territory inhabited by apostates, where there remain no Muslims nor any protected people (*dhimmis*), that is in the possession of apostates, who apply their law there, becomes *dar al-harb* (war territory) irrespective of whether it is connected to or outside *dar al-Islam*. This position was adopted by al-Tahawi (d. 321/933).[16]

He also recounts Abu Hanifa's position: a territory is only *dar al-harb* if it is adjacent to *dar al-harb*, and there is no *dar al-Islam* in between these two territories. There is no Muslim or *dhimmi*, who is safe there. If it meets these conditions it becomes *dar al-harb*, and otherwise it is *dar al-Islam*.

According to al-Sarakhsi (d. 483/1090),[17] the criteria for the distinction between *dar al-harb* and *dar al-Islam* are the following: For Abu Hanifa, he gives three conditions, of which only the first two are mentioned by al-Tihawi. For one, it is necessary that the territory is close to Turkish territory, which is territory of non-Muslims, on the condition that no *dar al-Islam* lies between that territory and *dar al-harb*. The second condition is that there is no Muslim safe there, nor any *dhimmi*. The third condition is that the laws of *shirk* (attributing 'partners' to God, polytheism) are applied there. This could be an added condition, ascribed to Abu Hanifa to give it more authority, as described by Wael Hallaq,[18] which means that it is either a mechanism of change or another version of Abu Hanifa.

For Abu Yusuf and al-Shaybani, a territory becomes *dar al-harb*, if the laws of *shirk* appear. For the territory follows the power and domination, and whenever there are laws of *shirk*, it proves that they hold the power. Thus al-Sarakhsi draws a connection between the legal system applicable to a territory and the political power, and where Islamic law is applied, there is *dar al-Islam*.

Al-Sarakhsi explains the difference between Abu Hanifa and his two disciples. Abu Hanifa requires complete submission and domination because this territory has been *dar al-Islam* and this character vanishes only with complete submission to polytheists (*mushrikun*). If it is not surrounded by *mushrikun*, there will be some Muslims in the vicinity, or a Muslim or *dhimmi* be safe, and this proves that there is no absolute subordination and domination. He distinguished between the main and the accidental aspects. The owner does not lose his property, even though there are other people living there. Thus the territory continues to be *dar al-Islam* as long as a Muslim or a *dhimmi* is living there in safety. Then al-Sarakhsi writes that this is an *asl*, a general principle, for Abu Hanifa. According to the latter, if there are traces of the principle, the principle still applies. He gives the example of alcohol: for alcohol to transform itself, all its components need to disappear, if they do not, it is not alcohol, and it is not forbidden, and thus we return to permission. Similarly in case apostates occupy a territory for an hour, for example, it does not turn into *dar al-harb*.

[16] Al-Tahawi, *Mukhtassar al-Tahawi* (Cairo: Lajanat Ihya' al-Ma'arif al-Nu'maniya, n. d.), p. 294.

[17] Al-Sarakhsi, *al-Mabsut*, vol. 10 (Beirut: Dar al-Ma'rifa, n. d.), p. 114.

[18] Wael Hallaq, *Authority, Continuity and Legal Change in Islamic Law* (New York: Cambridge University Press, 2001).

Al-Kasani (d. 587/1191) gives a similar account as al-Sarakhsi, but says that there is no divergence of opinions regarding *dar al-kufr* (territory of infidels) becoming *dar al-Islam* by the application of Islamic law.[19] The difference pertains to the transformation of *dar al-Islam* into *dar al-kufr*. Then he presents the discrepancy mentioned by al-Sarakhsi between the school's founder Abu Hanifa and his two disciples, Abu Yusuf and al-Shaybani. He states that a territory becomes *dar al-Islam* with the appearance of Islam, and *dar al-kufr* with the appearance of disbelief (*kufr*). Al-Kasani's explanation of these discrepancies is original and differs from al-Sarakhsi's presentation. He maintains that the classification of *dar al-Islam* or *dar al-kufr* is not a function of Islam or *kufr* as such, but that *dar al-Islam* means absolute safety for Muslims and the absolute fear for the infidels, while *dar al-kufr* means absolute safety for the infidels and absolute fear for Muslims. What is important for al-Kasani is safety and fear. There is no absolute safety in the proximity to *dar al-harb*. The safety of Muslims is doubtful in the proximity to *dar al-harb*.

Al-Kasani explains the difference in opinion between Abu Hanifa and his two disciples. While the two disciples hold that with the appearance of infidel laws the territory becomes *dar al-kufr* and with the appearance of Islamic law it becomes *dar al-Islam*, Abu Hanifa adds two other conditions for a territory to become *dar al-kufr*. In addition to the condition mentioned by Abu Yusuf and al-Shaybani, it is required that no Muslim or *dhimmi* is safe there and that the territory in question is near *dar al-kufr*. Abu Hanifa's differential treatment is justified by the fact that *dar al-Islam* does not turn into *dar al-kufr* by doubt, because he gives priority to Islam quoting a *Hadith*: 'Islam must have superiority and not inferiority'. The two additional conditions are both required to eliminate doubt.

The Hanafi jurist Ibn Maza al-Bukhari (d. 616/1219) refers to dominance (*ghalaba*) as a criterion.[20] If the territory is in the hands of *ahl al-harb* (enemies), it becomes *dar al-harb*. If Muslims apply their laws, it is as Abu Yusuf and al-Shaybani say; and he adds that there must be the intention to reside there permanently.

Al-Shshalabi (d. 1021/1612) defines *dar al-Islam* as a territory, in which Islamic law is applied, without mentioning the divergence between the school's founder and his two disciples.[21]

Ibn 'Abdin (d. 1252/1836) the last great Hanafi scholar recounts the views of Abu Hanifa and his two disciples as they are presented by al-Sarakhsi, and he states that if Islamic law is enforced in a territory as well as law of *ahl al-shirk* (polytheists), that territory is not *dar al-harb*.[22] Concerning the condition of

[19] Al-Kasani, *Bada'i' al-sana'i' fi tartib al-shara'i'*, vol. 9 (Beirut: Dar al-Kutub al-'Ilmiyya, 2003), pp. 518–20.

[20] Ibn Maza al-Bukhari, *al-Muhit al-burhani*, vol. 2 (Beirut: Dar al-Kutub al-'Ilmiyya, 2004), pp. 27–9, 198–9.

[21] Al-Shshalabi,hashiyat al-shshalabi 'ala *tabiyin al-haqai'iq* (Cairo: al matba 'a al-miriya, 1896), p. 253.

[22] Ibn 'Abdin, *Radd al-muhtar 'ala al-durr al-mukhtar sharh tanwir al-absar*, vol. 6 (Al-Riyad: Dar 'Alim al-Kitab, 2003), p. 288. On this scholar, see Norman Calder, 'The 'Uqud Rasm al-Mufti of Ibn 'Abdin', *Bulletin of Oriental and African Studies* 63 (2000): pp. 215–28.

proximity, he holds that there should not be *dar al-Islam* between the territory in question and *dar al-harb*. For him, the sea does not separate; and salty sea is like *dar al-harb*. Ibn 'Abdin considers that the Druze Mountain is in Lebanon and the adjacent territories are *dar al-Islam*. Then he concludes that although this territory has Druze or Christian governors and religious judges belonging to their religion, and although some of them insult Islam and Muslims, they are under the authority of Muslims, and *dar al-Islam* surrounds their territory, and the governor will apply the laws if he wants. We see that Ibn 'Abdin returns to Abu Hanifa's criterion of proximity, but also adds the ability to enforce the laws.

The Maliki School

I now turn to analysing the positions of Maliki scholars concerning their definitions of *dar al-harb* and *dar al-Islam*. The presentation is subdivided according to the main distinctive criteria chosen by these scholars, and proceeds within each category chronologically.

The call to prayer

Several Maliki jurists stipulate the call to prayer (*adhan*) as criterion for distinguishing between *dar al-Islam* and *dar al-harb*. Ibn 'Abd al-Bar from al-Andalus (d. 463/1071) sets the call to prayer as a criterion because according to him it is a sign distinguishing between *dar al-Islam* and *dar al-harb*.[23] The same holds true for the Maliki qadi 'Ayad (d. 544/1149), a judge in Granada, whose opinion is mentioned by al-Mawaq (d. 897/1492).[24]

For al-Mazari, as reported by al-Qarafi (d. 684/1285),[25] the call to prayer has two meanings; one is ceremonial, announcing that this is the territory of *dar al-Islam* and that the prayer is a collective obligation, which means that if a part of the population does fulfil the obligation, the others are exempted; and if the population does not fulfil the obligation, it will be fought. This is also the opinion of Ibn Tayib. The second meaning of the call for prayer is that it tells the time. Al-Nafrawi (d. 1120/1611) talks about the benefits of the call to prayer, in particular that it tells the time for prayer and announces that this is *dar al-Islam*.[26]

Al-Dasuqi (d. 1230/1815) goes even further; for him *dar al-Islam* does not turn into *dar al-harb* simply by conquest, but only when there are no Muslim ceremonies anymore; as long as the Muslim ceremonies are held, or at least most of them,

[23] Ibn Abd al-Bar, *al-Istisdhkar*, vol. 4 (Cairo and Aleppo: Dar al-Wa', 1993), p. 18.
[24] Al-Mawaq, *Al-Taj wa-al-iklil li mukhtasar Khalil*, vol. 2 (Dar al-Kutub al-'Ilmiyya, 1994), p. 110.
[25] Al-Qarafi, *al-Dhakhira*, vol. 2 (Beirut: Dar al-Garb al-Islami, 1994), p. 58.
[26] Al-Nafrawi, *al-Fawakihu al-dawani*, vol. 1 (Beirut: Dar al-Kutub al-'Ilmiyya, 1997), p. 265.

the territory does not become *dar al-harb*. The same opinion is expressed by Sawi (d. 1241/1826), who makes explicit reference to the French.[27]

Islamic law

Another category discussed by jurists as a condition is the implementation of Islamic law. Sahnun (d. 240/854) reports the words of Malik ibn Anas (d. 179/795), founder of the Maliki school, who determined that *dar al-harb* is a territory where the laws of the *jahiliya* (the pre-Islamic period) are applied (he probably speaks of Mecca).[28]

Al-Wansharisi (d. 914/1508) issued a long fatwa about the rules that apply to Muslims, whose territory has been occupied by Christians, and who have not emigrated, and on the sanctions that should be applied. He mentions the opinion of Ibn Rushd (Averroes), the great philosopher, who said that the obligation to emigrate is still valid and is to be applied until the last day; it is obligatory to leave the territory of *dar al-harb*, or where the laws of *shirk* are applied, in order to immigrate to *dar al-Islam*, where Islamic law is implemented.[29]

ʻIlish (d. 1299/1882), the Maliki Shaykh at al-Azhar,[30] considered the question whether it is necessary to emigrate from a territory dominated by non-Muslims, and determined that following the Qadi Ibn Rushd, *dar al-Islam* is where Islamic law is implemented, and *dar al-harb* is where the laws of *shirk* are applied.

Military power and a lack of safety for Muslims

It seems that there is also a third criterion in the Maliki School. In his gloss on *Mukhtasar Khalil*, al-Khurashi (d. 1090/1679), the first scholar given the title Shaykh al-Azhar, defines *dar al-harb* as a place where the army is encamped, even if it is within *dar al-Islam*; and a second requirement is that there is no safety for Muslims.[31] Salih al-Azhari (d. 1335/1917) holds that *dar al-harb* is a place where the enemy's army encamps, even if it is within *dar al-Islam*; and where there is no safety for Muslims.[32]

The Shafiʻi School

As we have seen, the Hanafi jurist al-Dabusi insists that the world is one *dar* according al-Shafiʻi (d. 204/820).[33] Checking the works of Shafiʻi jurists reveals

[27] Sawi, *Bulghat al-salik li akrab al-masalik*, vol. 2 (Beirut: Dar al-Kutub al-ʻIlmiyya, n. d.), p. 187.
[28] Sahnun, *Al-Mudawana al-kubra*, vol. 3 (Cairo: Matbaʻa al-Saʻada, 1905), p. 22.
[29] Al-Wansharisi, *Asna al-matajir* (Al-Zahir: Maktaba al-Thaqafa al-Diniya, 1996), p. 30.
[30] On the jurist, see Gilbert Delanoue, *Moralistes et politiques musulmans dans l'Égypte du XIX siècle (1798–1882)* (Paris: Institut français d'Archéologie Orientale du Caire, 1982), pp. 129–67.
[31] Al-Khurashi, *Sharh al-Khurashi* (Bulaq: al-Matba'a al-Kubra al-Amiriyan, 1899/1900), p. 62.
[32] Salih al-Azhari, *Al-Thamar al-dani* (n. p.: n. pub., n. d.), p. 190.
[33] Al-Dabusi, *Taʼsis al-nazar*, p. 119.

that this is not accurate since they also had a division of the world. It is likely that al-Dabusi referred to the consequences of this division. According to al-Shafi'i, the penal laws apply in *dar al-Islam* and *dar al-harb*, while according to Hanafi jurists, there are differences between the rules.

According to al-Shafi'i, a territory becomes *dar al-Islam*, if an imam enters a territory of *dar al-harb*, kills all its inhabitants or subjugates them, and there are no *mushrikun* between the territory into which the imam entered and *dar al-Islam*, or if there are *mushrikun*, they do not assist the people inhabiting the territory where the imam entered.[34]

The great jurist al-Mawardi (d. 450/1058) is known in the West for his book on government statutes, *al-Ahkam al-Sultaniya*, translated into French and English. In his discussion of emigration in his book on the issue,[35] al-Mawardi maintains that a territory may be *dar al-Islam* or *dar al-harb* according to the following conditions: (1) if he can avoid non-Muslims by isolation, propagate his religion and call to war, and if he has adopted Islam, *dar al-harb* turns for him into *dar al-Islam*; (2) if he can achieve isolation, but cannot propagate his religion or fight, this house becomes *dar al-Islam* by the fact of isolation; but if he emigrates, that territory becomes *dar al-harb*; (3) if he can avoid non-Muslims, but cannot achieve isolation nor propagate the faith nor fight, this territory does not become *dar al-Islam*, and in this case he must emigrate.

A contemporary of al-Mawardi, the Shafi'i jurist Abi Mansur 'Abdil Qahir al-Baghdadi (d. 429/1037) holds that every territory, where the Muslim faith is propagated and Islamic law is applied to *dhimmis*, and where the unlawful innovators (*ahl al-bid'a*), if there are any, do not dominate *ahl al-Sunna* (Sunnis), is *dar al-Islam*; and if these conditions are not met, it is *dar al-kufr*.[36] He also presents the view of a group called *ahl al-azariqa* (a faction of the *khawarij*/Kharijites) that divides the entire world into *dar al-shirk* and *dar al-harb*, the territory of polytheism and the territory of war, except where their (the group's) army camp is, which is *dar al-iman* (territory of faith). Abi Mansur also mentions the position of the Mu'tazila, a current in Islamic theology. For them, the world that is dominated by Sunnis is *dar al-kufr* (the territory of disbelief). Some among the Mu'tazila, he adds, consider this *dar al-fisq* (the territory of sin) and for them *fisq* has an intermediate position, that meant it is neither paradise nor hell. *Fasiq* is someone, who believes in Islam but does not follow the rules. It resembles the question whether a minor, who dies, goes to paradise or to hell. When he becomes an adult he may go either to hell or to paradise.

Ibn Hajar (d. 973/1566) defines *dar al-Islam* as a place, where the population including Muslims can live in isolation without encountering people from *dar al-harb*. Then he adds that if a house has become *dar al-Islam*, it cannot turn into *dar al-harb*, even if infidels occupy it. To support this position Ibn Hajar

[34] Al-Shafi'i, *Al-Um*, vol. 4 (Beirut: Dar al-Ma 'rifa, 1973), p. 181.

[35] Al-Mawardi, *al-Hawai al-kabir*, vol. 10 (Beirut: Dar al-Kutub al-'Ilmiyya, 1994), p. 194.

[36] Abi Mansur 'Abd al-Qahir, *Usul al-din* (Istanbul: Matba'at al-Dawla, 1928), p. 270.

invokes a Hadith that says that Islam is dominant and cannot be dominated. If one were to say that this house becomes *dar al-harb*, one would understand the matter only formally, not legally. Ibn Hajar writes that he does not think that his fellow Shafi'i jurists would tolerate that, namely that a house of Islam becomes an abode of war.[37] Ibn Hajar's words are mentioned by another prominent Shafi 'i jurist, al-Ramli (d. 1004/1596),[38] who was also called the small Shafi'i. Some later Shafi'i jurists did not accept the position of the irreversibility of *dar al-Islam*. Al-Shirwani, who finished writing his book in 1881, commented on Ibn Hajar's view, saying that his interpretation is contrary to the apparent meaning of the phrase. According to al-Shirwani, the transformation of *dar al-Islam* into *dar al-harb* is real and legal, and not only in form.[39] Another commentator, Qasim al-'Abadi (d. 992/1584) writes that Ibn Hajar's is not clear and that he must think about it.[40]

Al-Bujayrami (d. 1221/1806) provides a definition of *bilad al-Islam* (the land of Islam) by classifying it into four categories: (1) the territories that were built by Muslims, such as the cities of Baghdad and Basra; (2) territories, the inhabitants of which converted to Islam, like Medina and Yemen; (3) territories that were conquered by force, like Egypt or the area surrounding Iraq; and (4) territories that concluded a peace treaty with Muslims.[41] Al-Bujayrami's criteria for the distinctions differ from those of his predecessors. His elaboration implies that once a territory becomes part of *dar al-Islam*, it remains so forever, given that he mentions the territories by name rather than establishing abstract criteria. He reports the opinion of Khawarij jurists, whom he defines as innovators, whereby *dar al-Islam* turns into *dar al-kufr*, if grave sins (*kaba'ir*) are committed there.[42]

The Hanbali School

The Hanbali doctrine on the matter is rather confused, and there are no clear criteria. According to qadi Abi Ya'la (d. 458/1066) every house, where the laws of Islam (*ahkam al-Islam*) predominate in the absence of the laws of infidels, is *dar al-Islam*, and conversely, where the laws of the infidels predominate in the absence of the laws of Islam, there is *dar al-kufr*.[43] Then he reports the opinion of the Qadariya, also called Mu'tazila, whereby it is *dar al-fisq*,[44] if the sinners predominate; since they consider it an intermediate position. For Abi Ya'la, a person can only be a

[37] Ibn Hajar cited in al-Sharwani and Qasim al-'Abadi, *Hawashi tuhfat al-muhtaj bi-sharh al-minhaj*, vol. 9 (Cairo: Matba'a Mustafa Muhammad, n. d.), p. 269.

[38] Al-Ramli, *Nihayat al-muhtaj*, vol. 8 (Beirut: Dar al-Kutub al-'Ilmiyya, 2003), p. 82.

[39] Al-Sharwani and Qasim al-'Abadi, *Hawashi tuhfat al-minhaj*, p. 269.

[40] Ibid.

[41] Al-Bujayrami, *'Ala al-khatib*, (Beirut: Dar al-Kutub al-'Ilmiyya, 1996), vol. 3, p. 598.

[42] Ibid., vol. 5, p. 95.

[43] Abi Ya'la, *Kitab al-mu'tamad fi-usul al-din* (Beirut: Dar al-Mashreq, 1986), p. 276.

[44] Regarding the distinction between *fisq* and *kufr*: a *kafir* is someone who denies the foundations of the religion, as the existence of God or the obligation to the ritual prayer, while a *fasiq* is a person who does not deny the foundations of the religion, but does not practise the ritual prayer.

believer or an infidel. It is not possible to be neither a believer nor an infidel, and therefore also the territory can only be *dar al-kufr* or *dar al-Islam*.

Al-Ba'li (d. 709/1309) sees *dar al-harb* as a function of fighting (*qital*), distance (*al-taba'ud*), and hatred (*al-baghda'*).[45]

Shaykh al-Islam Ibn Taymiyya (d. 728/1328), an authority for today's Salafis, was asked about the status of Mardin (a city in today's Turkey), whether it is *dar al-Islam* or *dar al-harb*.[46] He replied:

> On the question of whether it is *dar al-harb* or *dar al-salam* (peace territory), it is *dar murakaba* (composite territory), there are two aspects to that territory: it is not *dar al-salam*, where Islamic laws (*ahkam al-Islam*) are applied, although its soldiers are Muslims, nor is it *dar al-harb*, where the inhabitants are infidels; but there is a third option, where a Muslim is properly treated and someone deviating from the Shari'a will be fought.

Ibn Taymiyya here introduces a third category that was not mentioned by previous jurists, nor was it taken up by his successors.

Ibn al-Qayyim (d. 751/1350), for example, states that it is the opinion of the majority of jurists that *dar al-Isalm* is a territory, where Muslims live, and where Islamic laws (*ahkam al-Islam*) are implemented. If Islamic laws are not applied, it cannot be said to be Muslim territory, even if it is close to *dar al-Islam*.[47]

Ibn Muflih al-Maqdisi (d. 763/1362) is even clearer on this issue. For him there are only two categories: if Islamic laws are implemented in a territory, it is *dar al-Islam*; if the laws of infidels (*ahkam al-kufr*) are implemented, it is *dar al-kufr*; and he adds that there is no third category. He explicitly cites the mentioned fatwa by Ibn Taymiyya, but says that he has to give preference to the opinion of the qadi, referring to Qadi Abi Ya'la, mentioned above.[48]

Ibn Muflih al-Hanbali (d. 884/1479) describes Muslim cities (*amsar al-muslimin*) as belonging to one of three categories: those built by Muslims, like Basra, Baghdad, and Wasit; those conquered by force; and those conquered peacefully. The third category is subdivided into two: (1) a peace agreement may be concluded, whereby the territory belongs to non-Muslims, and the *kharaj* tax is paid to Muslims; in this case the non-Muslims can do what they want; what apparently makes the city Muslim here is the tax payment; and (2) a peace agreement that states that the land belongs to Muslims. Here we see a different division.[49]

[45] Al-Ba'li, *al-Mutali' 'ala abwab al-muqni'* (Beirut/Damascus: al-Maktab al-Islami, 1981), p. 226.

[46] *Majmu' fatawi Sheikh al-Islam Ahmad Ibn Taymiya*, vol. 28 (Majma' al-Malik Fahd lil-Tiba'a al-Mushaf al-Sharif, 2004), pp. 240–1. For the fatwa, see Yahya Michot, *Ibn Taymiyya. Mardin: Hégire, fuite du péché et 'demeure de l'Islam'* (Paris: Librairie de l'Orient, 2004). On the fatwa and the contemporary controversies about it, see Ayoub Mazek, 'La division territoriale du monde en droit musulman (Dar al-harb et Dar al-islam) et son évolution. Critères de distinction, classification et applicabilité' (M.A. thesis, University of Strasbourg, 2014), pp. 38–50.

[47] Ibn al-Qayyim, *Ahkam ahl al-dhimma*, vol. 2 (Dammam: Ramadi lil-Nashr, 1997), p. 728.

[48] Ibn Muflih al-Maqdisi, *al-Adab al-shar'iya*, vol. 1 (Muassat al-Risala, 1999), pp. 211–12.

[49] Ibn Muflih, *al-Mubdi' sharh al-muqni'*, vol. 3 (Beirut: Dar al-Kutub al 'Ilmiyya, 1997), pp. 379–80.

At the same time another Hanbali jurist al-Mardawi (d. 885/1480) adopts the criterion of power (*hukm*), rather than laws (*ahkam*).[50] One might think that this is the same thing. He points out that some authors, who add to this the *bugha* (rebels), are innovators in religious matters (*bid ʿa*) as the *Rafida* (derogative for Shiʿites) and the Muʿtazila, which gives expression to a firmer stand against non-Sunnis.

We are now turning to the nineteenth-century Habali jurists, the Wahhabites.[51] Shaykh Hamad bin ʿAtiq (d. 1301/1883) was asked about the status of the city of al-Hasa, in the eastern part of today's Saudi Arabia, which was under Wahhabi control, then under Ottoman control, and then under the control of a rival of the Wahhabites, called Ibn Khalid. The shaykh says that if association to God leads to *shirk*, and if the prohibited is announced, and if the fundamentals of the religion are prevented, then it is *bilad al-kufr*. For him, the consequence is that it is allowed to kill the city's inhabitants and take their property as booty. He adds that the population of this region insults God and his religion, and has adopted positive laws contrary to the Qur'an and the Sunna; for him they are no longer Muslims.[52] Here we see the brand of Wahhabi ideology that legitimizes the power of the Ibn Saud family and their wars against their opponents, whereby even Muslims are turned into infidels, and their home becomes *dar al-kufr*, which authorizes war against them.[53]

Contemporary Authors

A consequence of this division is the legality and legitimacy of the war against *dar al-harb*. Even in the classical doctrine, war should not be extended to the elderly, women, and children, who are called protected persons. These specifications appear systematically in the classical treatises of the four Sunni schools. One can only fight against those, who are in a position to fight.

In the twentieth century two different trends have been developing: a dominant one that takes into account the evolution of international relations given that the Muslim world has integrated into the new UN system and that the distinction between *dar al-harb* and *dar al-Islam* thus does not make sense; and a numerically minor trend found in the more rigid interpretations of classical categories by Islamist jihadist movements.

[50] Al-Mardawi, *al-Insaf*, vol. 4 (Beirut: Dar al-Kutub al-ʿIlmiyya, 1997), p. 110.

[51] For the Wahhabites, see, for example, Muhammad Al-Atawneh, *Wahhabi Islam Facing the Challenges of Modernity: Dar al-Ifta in the Modern Saudi State* (Leiden/Boston: Brill, 2010); Nabil Mouline, *Les Clercs de l'islam. Autorité religieuse et pouvoir politique en Arabie Saoudite (XVIII–XXI siècles)* (Paris: P.U.F, 2010).

[52] Abu Yussif Midhat Bin al-Hasan al-Faraj, *Fatawi al-aʾima al-najdiya*, vol. 4 (Riyad: Maktab al-Rushd, 2007), p. 7.

[53] On the position of the Wahhabi ulema with regard to the Ottomans, see Mouline, *Les Clercs de l'islam*, pp. 104–9. See also Natana J. Delong-Bas, *Wahabi Islam: From Revival and Reform to Global Jihad* (Oxford/New York: Oxford University Press, 2004), pp. 246–7.

Integration into the UN system by contemporary Sunni jurists

Muslim jurists have integrated the contents of certain regulations of contemporary international law into classical categories. Although these divisions exist, jihad is what we would call today self-defence. One may resort to violence, if one is attacked. This is thus defensive jihad. This is the position of the great contemporary jurists, such as Shaltut, the former Shaykh of al-Azhar, Wahbe al-Zuhayli, Muhammad Abu Zahra, Ramadan al-Buti, 'Abdil Karim Zidan, and to some extent al-Qardawai, but excluding the Palestinian case. In the following I review the positions of contemporary jurists in chronological order.

'Abdil Wahab Khalaf (d. 1956), a judge and Shari'a lecturer in Egypt, gave a series of lectures to students of al-Azhar and the School of Shari'a Law in Cairo in 1924,[54] in which he holds that the call of Muslims to non-Muslims to convert to Islam is a collective duty (*fard kifaya*) of the entire Muslim community. If some Muslims fulfil that obligation, other Muslims will not fall into sin; but if no Muslim fulfils this obligation, the entire Muslim community falls into sin. He adds that the basis for the relations between Muslims and non-Muslims is a peaceful one, except in case of self-defence or if their freedom to propagate their faith peacefully is impeded. He defines *dar al-Islam* as a territory where Islamic laws are applied and Muslims live in complete safety. For him, *dar al-harb* is a territory where Muslims, the propagation of their faith, or those who propagate it are attacked. In this definition there is a link between the division of the world into two territories and the ensuing consequences. There is also a third category that he did not explicate: it is the territory of non-Muslim people, who do not attack Muslims or the propagators of their faith. It is forbidden to fight against such a territory because, according to him, there is the principle of peace, and there is no justification to deviate from that principle.

Muhammad Abu Zahra (d. 1974) taught Shari'a at the Law Faculty in Cairo; his education included a traditional Qur'an school as well as studies at the School for Shari'a Judges. Abu Zahra defines *dar al-Islam* as a state ruled by a Muslim leader, in which sovereignty and power rest with Muslims. Regarding *dar al-harb*, he traces the debate in the Hanafi school. There is an opinion whereby *dar al-harb* is a territory where Muslims do not hold power and sovereignty. According to Abu Hanifa, there are three cumulative conditions: Muslims do not hold sovereignty and power; the territory must be near *dar al-Islam* so that one can expect an attack; and that there is no Muslim and no *dhimmi*. He adds that proximity is meaningless today given that man dominates the air and also outer space, and that bombs may reach any part of the world. Therefore he assumes that if Abu Hanifa were living today, he would drop that condition. War is not a principle; and one cannot fight against a state only because it is not Muslim. He argues that in addition to the distinction between *dar al-Islam* and *dar al-harb*, there is a third category, which he calls *Dar al-'ahd*, that is, territory that concluded a peace treaty

[54] 'Abdil Wahab Khalaf, *al-Siyasa al-shar'iyya wa-nizam al-dawla al-islamiya* (Cairo: al-Matba'a al-Salafiya wa-Maktabatuha, 1931), pp. 72–5.

with Muslims. According to him, the world today is organized through the UN. The member states are obliged to the UN regulations and statutes. He says that the Qur'an makes it obligatory to meet one's commitments. Thus the entire world has turned into *dar al-'ahd*, and there is no longer a division into *dar al-harb* and *dar al-Islam*.[55]

Ramadan al-Buti (d. 2013) was a Syrian jurist with an international reputation throughout the Muslim world; he supported the Syrian regime and died in an attack in 2013.[56] He argues that during the period of *jahiliya* the faith of Islam was propagated in a *jahili* atmosphere in Mecca. The Muslims were not an independent group and had no territory of their own, where they could live their social life. They were a minority. In that period jihad was simply the propagation of their faith. With the Prophet Muhammad's emigration from Mecca to Medina, the first *dar al-Isalm* was created, and the first Muslim society. With these two elements came also political power. These three elements constituted the Muslim state. Jihad thus became war in defence of these three elements. He gives a definition of *dar al-Islam*, characterizing it as a consensus of the four Imams, the founders of the four Sunni schools. According to him, *dar al-Islam* is a territory where Muslims hold power and sovereignty, where they can present their religion and do not encounter their enemies. He also adds the implementation of Islamic law. He states that this is regardless of whether the territory in question was conquered by force or by peace treaty. The Islamic nature of the territory does not change, irrespective of whether the population is Muslim or not. The territory does not become *dar al-harb*, if the Muslims do not implement Islamic law. He criticizes thereby the view of the Islamist because according to him the transformation of a territory into *dar al-harb* entails the necessity for Muslims to emigrate from that country, but paradoxically, in his view, these Muslims are leaving their country in order to settle in Europe or the US.[57]

The Syrian alim Wahba al-Zuhayli wrote an influential thesis in the 1960s on the effect of the war in Islamic *fiqh* (jurisprudence).[58] After presenting the different positions of the jurists concerning the division of the world, he tries to explain this division giving two reasons: for one, the need to defend Muslims in an entity that is different from other entities against a common enemy; and second, the jurists' intention to provide a basis from the Shari'a for the relations of Muslims with others and for the nature of these relations, which is war. He states that no *'alim* before him had dared to say that this division has not basis either in the Qur'an or the Sunna. The division of the world should be understood like the division of the world in Roman law, for example. If we understand that war is the cause of

[55] Muhammad Abu Zahra, *Al-'Ilakat al-duwaliya fi al-islam* (Nasr City: Dar al Fikr al-'Arabi, 1995), pp. 56–60.

[56] On the Syrian ulema and the political regime, see Thomas Pierret, *Baas et Islam en Syrie* (Paris: PUF, 2011).

[57] Ramadan al-Buti, *al-Jihad fi al-islam. Kayfa nafhamuhu wa-kayfa numarisuhu* (Damascus: Dar al-Fikr al-Mu 'asir/Dar al-Fikr, 1992), pp. 74–82.

[58] Wahba al-Zuhayli, *Athar al-harb fi al-fiqh al-islami. Dirasa muqarina*, 3rd edn (Beirut: Dar al-Fikr, 1998).

this division, and if there is no war, the division is meaningless. He adopts Shafi'i's position that the world is one. Thus 'international law is in accordance with the Islamic Shari'a in holding that the world is one and that war is a transient phenomenon that exists due to animosity between two states, and that this situation will disappear with the disappearance of war'.[59]

Yussef al-Qaradawi is widely known because of his weekly appearance on *Al-Jazeera*; he is the President of the European Council of Fatwa and Research.[60] He is considered to be the most prominent religious authority for the Muslim Brotherhood. In his book on jihad, he does not agree with Wahbe al-Zahayli that the division of the world has no basis either in the Qur'an or the Sunna.[61] He mentions verse 92 of *Surat al-Nisa'* (Sura 4), which has not been used to support the division of the world. No one before him has read this verse in this sense. Muslim jurists have not used either the verse or any Hadith to support the legitimacy of the division of the world. Al-Qaradawi provides a new reading of the Qur'an. It is based directly on the sources of Islamic law. He undertakes *ijtihad*, which is an effort of interpretation directly based on the sources of Islamic law, without relying on the views of Muslim jurists. A verse exists, but that does not mean that its meaning will be understood in the same way in different periods. This is proof of the division of the world in the Qur'an. He also quotes a Hadith and the practice of the *sahaba* (companions of the Prophet). He says it is difficult to accuse the jurists of inventing the concepts of the division of the world without a basis in the Shari'a.

According to al-Qaradawi, *dar al-Islam* is a single territory even if it is composed of different regions, different languages, or even different regimes.[62] For him, ex-Soviet Muslim states in Asia are part of *dar al-Islam* as the majority of their inhabitants are Muslims, recognizing the oneness of God and that Muhammad is his messenger and Prophet. He says that they must be integrated into the Islamic organizations.[63] He criticizes the classification of Egypt as part of *dar al-harb* and categorically classifies it as part of *dar al-Islam*.[64] He asks whether the division of the world into *dar al-Islam* and *dar al-harb* remains relevant today, in the era of globalization and in a world that is no longer divided along religious lines. He says that although others may deny their religion in their lives and constitutions, this is not the case for Muslims. For him, all states referred to as Muslims or with a majority of Muslim inhabitants belong to *dar al-Islam*, even if some of them do not at all implement the Shari'a or even adhere to laicity, like Turkey. He says that one should not easily exclude these states from *dar al-Islam*.

According to al-Qaradawi, these states are Muslim:

[59] Al-Zahayli, *Athar al-harb fi al-fiqh al-islami*, pp. 192–6, citation from p. 196.

[60] See Alexandre Caeiro, 'The Power of European Fatwas: The Minority *Fiqh* Project and the Making of an Islamic Counterpublic', *International Journal of Middle East Studies* 42 (2010): pp. 435–49.

[61] Yussef al-Qaradawi, *Fiqh al-jihad. Dirasa muqarina li-ahkamihi wa-falsafatihi fi du'al qura'an wa-al-sunna*, vol. 2 (Cairo: Makatabat Wahbe, 2009), pp. 879–910.

[62] Ibid., p. 890. [63] Ibid., p. 899. [64] Ibid., p. 899.

... by their origin and also by their history. The majority of the inhabitants are Muslims, their leaders are officially Muslims. Most ceremonies of Islam and its social and religious manifestations are public, like the call to prayer, the reciting of the Qur'an, the mosques, the Friday prayers, Islamic universities, Islamic holidays, the announcement of the beginning of the month of Ramadan, the opportunity to make the pilgrimage every year, the bathing the dead, the shrouding the body, and the prayer for him etc.

He continues, saying that most of these states declare Islam as the state religion, and some also state that the Shari'a is a principal source.[65] Here al-Qaradawi is in complete disagreement with the jihadist movement, as we shall see below.

As for the rest of the world, al-Qaradawi defines it as treaty territory (*dar al-'ahd*), except for the State of Israel. But even with regard to the latter, al-Qaradawi seems ready to accept the observance of treaties signed between Israel and the Muslim states.[66] He stresses that Muslims are obliged to honour their commitments. In the end he is ready to abandon the terms *dar al-harb* and *dhimmis*.[67]

More rigid interpretations of classical categories by Islamist jihadist movements

Another trend has developed mainly in the 1960s, with Sayyid Qutb as its main ideologue. Qutb, a leader of the Egyptian Muslim Brotherhood, was imprisoned, tortured, and then executed by the Nasser regime in 1966. Tariq Ramadan has presented his ideology of violence as a deviation from Hassan al-Banna, the founder of the Muslim Brotherhood.[68]

In his book *Milestones*,[69] Qutb provides the doctrinal basis for acts of violence not only against non-Muslims but also, and perhaps especially, against Muslims, and explains that the *jahiliya* it is not a historical period of the past, but it is man's enslavement by another man. We must implement God's sovereignty on earth (*al-hakimiya*).[70] For him, the classical division of the world is irrelevant. He divides the world into *jahiliya* and Islam.[71] He does not mention any jurists. According to him, it is necessary to build a vanguard with the aim to undertake this upheaval, to apply the Shari'a and to be subjected to God. On the way, violence against non-Muslims and also Muslims is allowed.

This trend accelerated in the 1990s with al-Qaeda,[72] and in 2005 with al-Zarqawi's creation of the Islamic State in Syria and Iraq, and then with the creation

[65] Ibid., pp. 900–1. [66] Ibid., p. 907. [67] Ibid., p. 909.

[68] Tariq Ramadan, Aux sources du renouveau musulman. D'al-Afghani à Hassan al-Banna, un siècle de réformisme islamique (Paris: Bayard edition, 1998).

[69] Sayyid Qutb, *Ma'alim fi al-tariq* (Cairo: Dar al-Shuruq, 1979). On the book, see Gilles Kepel, *Le Prophète et Pharon* (Paris: La découverte, 1984).

[70] See, for example, Sayed Khatab, '"Hakimiyyah" and "Jahiliyyah" in the Thought of Sayyid Qutb', *Middle Eastern Studies* 38 (2002): pp. 145–70; William E. Shepard, 'Sayyid Qutb's Doctrine of "Jahiliyya"', *International Journal of Middle East Studies* 35 (2003): pp. 521–45.

[71] Olivier Carré, 'Le combat pour Dieu et l'État islamique chez Sayyid Qotb, l'inspirateur du radicalisme islamique actuel', *Revue française de science politique* 33 (1983): pp. 680–705, see esp. pp. 687, 691–3.

[72] For Bin Laden's view on jihad, see Delong-Bas, *Wahabi Islam*, pp. 273–8.

of the Islamic Caliphate, called in the media 'Islamic State', with the known atrocities. As for the difference between al-Qaeda and the Caliphate, the former calls for jihad now, while the caliphate calls first for the construction and strengthening of the Islamic State and then jihad with the long-term goal is to Islamize the world and to create one single territory that is *dar al-Islam*.[73]

Conclusion

Islamic law is not static; it develops, which is another refutation of the thesis of the closing of the gate of *ijtihad*. This development is not linear, but may be defined as a sort of an irregular zigzag. It develops in one direction and then some jurists adopt positions of earlier jurists.

These developments are not always linked to sacred texts such as the Qur'an and the Sunna. There is almost no concrete influence of sacred texts aside from ideological declarations; in practical terms the deduction of the rules is neither done by the classical format of *usul al-fiqh* nor in accordance with the importance of authors and texts, as some people believe.[74] For example, Ibn Hajar and al-Ramli were very important jurists of the Shafiʿi school. Normally if there is agreement between these two, later jurists would be obliged to follow their opinions. We have seen clearly that this was not the case for the issue at hand. Here we found that later Shafiʿi jurists ignored their explicit position on the definition of *dar al-Islam* and its irreversibility.

Finally we should avoid the simplistic conception that if jurists say that they are basing their views on the Qur'an and the Sunna, this would prevent them from formulating positions that meet the social and political needs. This is not the case, as we have seen, for example, when Ibn ʿAbdin determined the Druze mountain to be *dar al-Islam*; or Shaykh Ibn ʿAtiq described the Ottoman Empire in eastern Saudi Arabia as *dar al-kufr*; or Ibn Taymiyya did not hesitate to talk about Mardin as a composite territory (*dar murakaba*).

There is disagreement over the definition of *dar al-Islam* and *dar al-harb*. Different authors have laid down different criteria; we find different opinions even within the same school; and at times variations may even be found with regard to the same author and/or in the same treatise. Some jurists give preference to Islamic law, while others focus on the safety of Muslims. The majority accepts that *dar al-Islam* can be transformed into *dar al-harb*, while Ibn Hajar holds that a territory belonging to *dar al-Islam* will never lose its status. There is also divergence on the question whether the world is divided into two or three categories.

[73] Eli Alshech, 'The Doctrinal Crisis within the Salafi-Jihadi Ranks and the Emergence of Neo-Takfirism', *Islamic Law and Society* 21 (2014): pp. 419–52.
[74] Calder, 'The ʿUqud Rasm al-Mufti of Ibn ʿAbdin'.

Bibliography

'Abdin, Ibn. *Radd al-muhtar 'ala al-durr al-mukhtar sharh tanwir al-absar*, vol. 6 (Al-Riyad: Dar 'Alim al-Kitab, 2003).

Alshech, Eli. 'The Doctrinal Crisis within the Salafi-Jihadi Ranks and the Emergence of Neo-Takfirism'. *Islamic Law and Society* 21 (2014): pp. 419–52.

Al-Atawneh, Muhammad. *Wahhabi Islam Facing the Challenges of Modernity: Dar al-Ifta in the Modern Saudi State* (Leiden/Boston: Brill, 2010).

Augusti, Eliana. 'From Capitulations to Unequal Treaties: The Matter of an Extraterritorial Jurisdiction in the Ottoman Empire'. *Journal of Civil Law Studies* 4, no. 2 (2011): pp. 285–308.

al-Azhari, Salih. *Al-Thamar al-dani.*

Al-Ba'li, *al-Mutali' 'ala abwab al-muqni'* (Beirut/Damascus: al-Maktab al-Islami, 1981).

al-Bar, Ibn 'Abd. *al-Istisdhkar*, vol. 4 (Cairo and Aleppo: Dar al-Wa', 1993).

Bentabaet, Houssame. 'L'apostat dans le droit musulman classique et contemporain. Définition et punition' (M.A. thesis, University of Strasbourg, 2014).

Bonner, Michael. *Jihad in Islamic History: Doctrines and Practice* (Princeton and Oxford: Princeton University Press, 2006).

van den Boogert, Maurits H. *The Capitulations and the Ottoman Legal Sytem: Qadis, Consuls and Beraths in the 18th Century* (Leiden/Boston: Brill, 2005).

Al-Bujayrami. *'Ala al-khatib*, vol. 3 and vol. 5 (Beirut: Dar al-Kutub al-'Ilmiyya, 1996).

al-Bukhari, Ibn Maza. *al-Muhit al-burhani*, vol. 2 (Beirut: Dar al-Kutub al-'Ilmiyya, 2004).

al-Buti, Ramadan. *al-Jihad fi al-islam. Kayfa nafhamuhu wa-kayfa numarisuhu* (Damascus: Dar al-Fikr al-Mu 'asir/Dar al-Fikr, 1992).

Caeiro, Alexandre. 'The Power of European Fatwas: The Minority *Fiqh* Project and the Making of an Islamic Counterpublic'. *International Journal of Middle East Studies* 42 (2010): pp. 435–49.

Calder, Norman. 'The 'Uqud Rasm al-Mufti of Ibn 'Abdin'. *Bulletin of Oriental and African Studies* 63 (2000): pp. 215–28.

Carré, Olivier. 'Le combat pour Dieu et l'État islamique chez Sayyid Qotb, l'inspirateur du radicalisme islamique actuel'. *Revue française de science politique* 33 (1983): pp. 680–705.

Al-Dabusi. *Ta'sis al-nazar* (Cairo: Maktaba al-Kuliyat al-Azhariya, 2016).

Al-Dawoody, Ahmed. *The Islamic Law of War: Justifications and Regulations* (New York: Palgrave Macmillan, 2011).

Delanoue, Gilbert. *Moralistes et politiques musulmans dans l'Égypte du XIX siècle (1798–1882)*, vol. 1 (Paris: Institut français d'Archéologie Orientale du Caire, 1982).

Delong-Bas, Natana J. *Wahabi Islam: From Revival and Reform to Global Jihad* (Oxford/New York: Oxford University Press, 2004).

Fadel, Mohammad. 'International Law, Regional Developments: Islam'. In *Max Planck Encyclopedia of Public International Law* (2009), at http://www.law.utoronto.ca/documents/Fadel/Max_Planck_Final.pdf (accessed 2 July 2015).

El Fadl, Khaled Abou. *Rebellion and Violence in Islamic Law* (Cambridge: Cambridge University Press, 2001).

al-Faraj, Abu Yussif Midhat Bin al-Hasan. *Fatawi al-a'ima al-najdiya*, vol. 4 (Riyad: Maktab al-Rushd, 2007).

Al-Gunaimi, Mohammad Talaat. *The Muslim Conception of International Law and the Western Approach* (The Hague: Martinus Nijhoff, 1968).

Hallaq, Wael. *Authority, Continuity and Legal Change in Islamic Law* (New York: Cambridge University Press, 2001).
Al-Kasani. *Bada'i' al-sana'i' fi tartib al-shara'i'*, vol. 9 (Beirut: Dar al-Kutub al-'Ilmiyya, 2003).
Kepel, Gilles. *Le Prophète et Pharon* (Paris: La découverte, 1984).
Khadduri, Majid. *War and Peace in Islam* (Baltimore: Johns Hopkins Press, 1955).
Khalaf, 'Abdil Wahab. *al-Siyasa al-shar 'iyya wa-nizam al-dawla al-islamiya* (Cairo: al-Matba 'a al-Salafiya wa-Maktabatuha, 1931).
Khatab, Sayed. '"Hakimiyyah" and "Jahiliyyah" in the Thought of Sayyid Qutb'. *Middle Eastern Studies* 38 (2002): pp. 145–70.
Al-Khurashi. *Sharh al-Khurashi* (Bulaq: al-Matba'a al-Kubra al-Amiriyan, 1899/1900).
Lorimer, James. *The Institutes of the Law of Nations: A Treatise of the Jural Relations of Separate Political Communities*, vol. 1 (Edinburgh/London: William Blackwood and Sons, 1883).
Mahmassani, Sobhi. 'The Principles of International Law in the Light of Islamic Doctrine'. In *Collected Courses of The Hague Academy of International Law* 117 (Leiden/Boston: Brill/Nijhoff, 1966), p. 250.
Majmu' fatawi Sheikh al-Islam Ahmad Ibn Taymiya, vol. 28 (Majma' al-Malik Fahd lil-Tiba'a al-Mushaf al-Sharif, 2004).
Mansur, Abi. 'Abd al-Qahir *Usul al-din* (Istanbul: Matba'at al-Dawla, 1928).
Al-Mardawi. *al-Insaf*, vol. 4 (Beirut: Dar al-Kutub al-'Ilmiyya, 1997).
al-Maqdisi, Ibn Muflih. *al-Adab al-shar'iya*, vol. 1 (Muassat al-Risala, 1999).
Matran, Robert. *L'expansion musulmane, VII-XI siècles*, 5th edn (Paris: PUF, 1995).
Al-Mawaq. *Al-Taj wa-al-iklil li mukhtasar Khalil*, vol. 2 (Dar al-Kutub al-'Ilmiyya, 1994).
Al-Mawardi. *al-Hawai al-kabir*, vol. 10 (Beirut: Dar al-Kutub al-'Ilmiya, 1994).
Mazek, Ayoub. 'La division territoriale du monde en droit musulman (Dar al-harb et Dar al-islam) et son évolution. Critères de distinction, classification et applicabilité' (M.A. thesis, University of Strasbourg, 2014).
Michot, Yahya. *Ibn Taymiyya. Mardin: Hégire, fuite du péché et 'demeure de l'Islam'* (Paris: Librairie de l'Orient, 2004).
Mouline, Nabil. *Les Clercs de l'islam. Autorité religieuse et pouvoir politique en Arabie Saoudite (XVIII-XXI siècles)* (Paris: PUF, 2010).
Muflih, Ibn. *al-Mubdi' sharh al-muqni'*, vol. 3 (Beirut: Dar al-Kutub al- 'Ilmiyya, 1997).
Al-Nafrawi. *al-Fawakihu al-dawani*, vol. 1 (Beirut: Dar al-Kutub al-'Ilmiyya, 1997).
Pierret, Thomas. *Baas et Islam en Syrie* (Paris: PUF, 2011).
Pillet, Antoine. *Recherches sur les droits fondamentaux des états dans l'ordre des rapports internationaux et sur la solution des conflicts qu'ils font naitre* (Paris: A. Pedone, 1899).
al-Qaradawi, Yussef. *Fiqh al-jihad. Dirasa muqarina li-ahkamihi wa-falsafatihi fi du'al qura'an wa-al-sunna*, vol. 2 (Cairo: Makatabat Wahbe, 2009).
Al-Qarafi. *al-Dhakhira*, vol. 2 (Beirut: Dar al-Garb al-Islami, 1994).
al-Qayyim, Ibn. *Ahkam ahl al-dhimma*, vol. 2 (Dammam: Ramadi lil-Nashr, 1997).
Qutb, Sayyid. *Ma'alim fi al-tariq* (Cairo: Dar al-Shuruq, 1979).
Ramadan, Tariq. Aux sources du renouveau musulman. D'al-Afghani à Hassan al-Banna, un siècle de réformisme islamique (Paris: Bayard edition, 1998).
Al-Ramli. *Nihayat al-muhtaj*, vol. 8 (Beirut: Dar al-Kutub al-'Ilmiyya, 2003).
Sahnun. *Al-Mudawana al-kubra*, vol. 3 (Cairo: Matba'a al-Sa'ada, 1905).
Al-Sarakhsi. *al-Mabsut*, vol. 10 (Beirut: Dar al-Ma'rifa, n. d.).
Al-Sarakhsi, *Sharh al-siyar al-kabir* (Beirut: Dar al-Kutub al-'Ilmiyya, n. d.).
Sawi. *Bulghat al-salik li akrab al-masaik*, vol. 2 (Beirut: Dar al-Kutub al-'Ilmiyya, n. d.).
Al-Shafi'I. *Al-Um*, vol. 4 (Beirut: Dar al-Ma 'rifa, 1973).

al-Sharwani, and Qasim al-'Abadi. *Hawashi tuhfat al-muhtaj bi-sharh al-minhaj*, vol. 9 (Cairo: Matba'a Mustafa Muhammad, n. d.).

al-Shaykh, 'Abdil Sattar. *Al-Imam al-Awza'i: Saykh al-Islam wa 'alim ahl al-sham* (88–157H) (Jadda: Dar al-Bashir, 2006).

Shepard, William E. 'Sayyid Qutb's Doctrine of "Jahiliyya" '. *International Journal of Middle East Studies* 35 (2003): pp. 521–45.

al-Shshalabi, hashiyat. 'ala *tabiyin al-haqai'iq*, vol. 3 (Cairo:al matba 'a al-miriya, 1896).

Al-Tahawi. *Mukhtassar al-Tahawi* (Cairo: Lajanat Ihya' al-Ma'arif al-Nu'maniya, n. d.).

Tibi, Bassam. 'War and Peace in Islam'. In *Islamic Political Ethics: Civil Society, Pluralism, and Conflict*, edited by Sohail H. Hashmi (New Jersey: Princeton University Press, 2002), pp. 175–93.

Al-Wansharisi. *Asna al-matajir* (Al-Zahir: Maktaba al-Thaqafa al-Diniya, 1996).

Ya'la, Abi. *Kitab al-mu'tamad fi-usul al-din* (Beirut: Dar al-Mashreq, 1986).

Yusuf, Abu. *Al-rad 'ala siyar Awza'i* (Haydarabad: Lajnat Ihya' al-Ma'arif al-Nu'maniya, n. d.).

Zahra, Muhammad Abu. *Al-'Ilakat al-duwaliya fi al-islam* (Nasr City: Dar al-Fikr al-'Arabi, 1995).

Zidan, 'Abdil Karim. *Ahkam al-dhimiyin wa al-musta'minin fi dar al-islam* (Baghdad: Maktabat al-Quds, 1982).

Al-Zuhayli, Wahba. *Athar al-harb fi al-fiqh al-islami. Dirasa muqarina*, 3rd edn (Beirut: Dar al-Fikr, 1998).

11

From Imperial to Dissident

Approaches to Territory in Islamic International Law

Nahed Samour[1]

This chapter is concerned with the role of Islamic international law as a potential insight in a legal order that is simultaneously past and present, law and faith, and centre and periphery.[2] It is an attempt to assess the link between the Islamic imperial past to the Islamic dissenting present in understanding and articulating law. Despite the critique the Islamic international law tradition articulates towards modern international law, Islamic international law comes with an embedded political tradition of imperial rule that was itself hegemonic in substantial parts of the world for a long time. This purportedly universal rule is something the Islamic law tradition criticizes in today's character of the international order. It is this tension between Islamic international law as a critique of the modern international order as well as its own history of imperial rule that is my central concern here. With

[1] This work was made possible through a generous grant by the Gerda Henkel Foundation. Earlier versions of the chapter were presented at the Harvard Law School, Institute of Global Law and Policy, 'Islamic Law and Empire' conference, held in Cambridge, Mass., 1–2 June, 2015; as well as the Max Planck Institute for International Private Law and the Bucerius Law School, Hamburg, on 9 October, 2015, and the Eric Castrén Institute of International Law and Human Rights, Helsinki University at the Gerda Henkel workshop on 'Order and Contestations in Islamic International Law and Relations', 18 November, 2015. Thanks are due to the audiences of these events. I am grateful for comments by Mohammad Fadel, Faisal Chaudhry, Nada Moumtaz, Kathrin Klausing, and Salman Abu Sittah. Errors remain solely mine.

[2] 'Islamic international law' is arguably a mistranslation and possible anachronism for it does not bind states but Muslims, see e.g. Anver M. Emon, 'On Sovereignties in Islamic Legal History', *Middle East Law and Governance* 4 (2012): pp. 268–73. For a critical review of scholarship on Islamic International Law as well as Islamic international law's role in public international law, see Burgis, Michelle, 'Faith in the State? Traditions of Territoriality, International Law and the Emergence of the Modern Arab State', *Journal of the History of International Law* 11 (2009): pp. 41–48. Characterizing tendencies of scholarship on Islamic international law ranging from '1) recuperative (highlighting historical diversity in Islamic legal approaches), 2) reformist (seeking commensurability between Islamic law and contemporary international law), 3) comparative (tracing similarities, to undermine claims to Muslim civilizational backwardness) to 4) "terrorological" (setting out to reconstruct a genealogy for alleged radical groups)'. Darryl Li, 'Jihad in a World of Sovereigns: Law, Violence and Islam in the Bosnia Crisis', *Law and Social Inquiry, Journal of the American Bar Foundation* 41 (Spring 2016): pp. 3–4.

Islamic international law shifting from imperial to dissident through encounters with pre-modern and modern international law, significant changes in the field of territory, sovereignty, and population become apparent. Islamic international law is a striking example of how an international legal system that once possessed a strong imperial character has reacted to changing perceptions of threat and reinterpreted its international legal concepts to cope with infringements on its territory, jurisdiction, and faith. This historic, paradigmatic shift from a law with a formerly imperial character to law as dissent or law as resistance might explain some of the existing dissonances between Islamic international law concepts and prevailing understandings of international law. While Islamic international law concepts might have had little to no influence on international law as we know it today, it has arguably shaped dissent and resistance to international law. With this in mind, my main question is this: Can you reread the history of imperial rule with its rules, principles, and institutions that were shaped during Imperial times and still resonate today, and render this rereading into a credible and sustainable critique of today's international order? I argue that Islamic international law has shifted from imperial to dissident, and that this imperial–dissident divide is a necessary, challenging frame that might explain some of the existing dissonances within Islamic international law as well as between Islamic international law and prevailing understandings of international law.

The chapter first outlines the meaning of imperial and dissident with regard to the laws of expanding or defending territory. It then addresses the rules of territorial acquisition during the early period when the foundations for the early Islamic Empires were being laid. It shows how the laws of conquest were tightly connected to the laws of property and taxation, which had an influence on dividing conquered territory or keeping it together. Thereby it also demonstrates how the laws of charitable trusts as communal property were defined with respect to the conquering Muslims and the original inhabitants of the territory. The legal institution of charitable trusts (*waqf*) is therefore important for Islamic International Law. Through charitable trust laws, territory (and moveables) could be landlocked in perpetuity, discouraging it from being partitioned or sold and kept together for future generations. The central question of whether to distribute territory (*qasm*) or keep territory united (as *fay'*, *waqf* or else) after conquest is discussed in Islamic legal and historical literature as *qasm al- aradīn*. Two examples of the imperial mode of law of the first/seventh century are given, first that of the oasis of Khaybar (near Medina) and second the Iraqi region of Sawād. In the first incident, territory as property was divided and distributed, and in the second, territory was kept together as a charitable trust. I then shift to an interpretation of the concepts of charitable trusts and property as means of resisting colonialism and foreign domination, attempting to keep territory unified and thereby dissenting from international law at its respective time. For this dissenting mode of the law, I first portray the colonization of charitable trust territory of Algeria in the nineteenth century by France and its dire effects on Algerian society. Second, I revisit the twentieth century Palestinian example of declaring all of Palestine to be *waqf* (i.e. charitable trust, endowed, as irrevocable and perpetual territory) [3] for future Muslim generations. For this, I highlight the importance of territory to law and as well as to religion within an Islamic international law frame.

The Imperial, the Dissident

To understand the imperial is to understand a default mode of political organization throughout most of history.[4] Characteristic for an empire was that different ethnic communities fell under a common ruler, often through conquest. Capturing territory, dominating subject people, and establishing political and military supremacy is therefore essential for imperial power.[5] The origins of the empire lie in a historical development that seems almost universal in human societies,[6] that is, they are not limited to any religion, race, or culture. For the formation of any empire, the spread or exchange of information, knowledge, beliefs, and ideas as well as the exchange of economic goods by purchase or barter has been central.[7] Differently put, '[I]mperial power has usually been the rule of the road'.[8] This work addresses the foundations laid for the forming of such a default Empire through conquest.[9] The Arabic-Islamic terminology of the earliest available sources speaks not of empire or imperial but of conquest (Arabic: *fatḥ, literally opening*). The *futūh* (pl.) conquest literature became known as a genre that describes the taking

[3] *Waqf* can be both translated as a 'charitable trust', which has a public dimension and as an 'endowment', which resembles a 'will' or 'settlement' that has an additional private dimension. Gregory C. Kozlowski, *Muslim Endowments and Society in British India* (Cambridge: Cambridge University Press, 1985), pp. 1–2.

[4] John Darwin, *After Tamerlane, The Global History of Empire since 1405* (London: Allen Lane, 2007), p. 23.

[5] Ellen Meiksins Wood, *Empire of Capital* (London; New York: Verso, 2003, paperback 2005), p. xi; Dirk A. Moses, 'Empire, Colony, Genocide: Keywords and the Philosophy of History', in *Empire, Colony, Genocide. Conquest, Occupation and Subaltern Resistance in World History*, edited by Dirk A. Moses (New York; Oxford: Berghahn Books, 2008), p. 4.

[6] John Darwin, *After Tamerlane* (2007), p. 23; Empire as part of 'human history tout court', Dirk A. Moses, 'Empire, Colony, Genocide' (2008), p. 4.

[7] On the ideological and economic aspects of Empires, see John Darwin, *After Tamerlane, The Global History of Empire since 1405* (London: Allen Lane, 2007), pp. 22–3.

[8] John Darwin, *After Tamerlane, The Global History of Empire since 1405* (London: Allen Lane, 2007), p. 23. Nurdusev therefore rightly questions what was indeed specifically Islamic and what was typically imperial in analysing Islamic imperial law and power: A. Nuri Yurdusev, 'The Ottoman Attitude Toward Diplomacy', in *Ottoman Diplomacy: Conventional or Unconventional?*, edited by A. Nuri Yurdusev (New York: Palgrave Macmillan, 2004), pp. 5–35.

[9] Muslim conquests started with Prophet Muhammad's military campaigns. His example showed that armed force was going to be an acceptable aspect first in the defence of the new religion and then in its expansion. 'At the same time, diplomacy was certainly more important than military conquest in the spread of Prophet Muḥammad's influence in the Arabian peninsula. It was the network of contacts he derived from his Quraish connections rather than the sword which led people from as far away as Yemen and Oman to swear allegiance to him. Military force had ensured the survival of the Muslim community (*umma*), but in the Prophet's lifetime it was not the primary instrument in its expansion', Hugh Kennedy, *The Great Arab Conquests, How the Spread of Islam Changed the World We Live In* (London: Weidenfeld & Nicolson, 2007), p. 48.

over of territory of the Byzantine and Persian Empires.[10] The Muslim conquests in the first decade which followed the death of the Prophet Muḥammad in 11/632 were 'amongst the most remarkable and far-reaching in history'.[11] Over the course of 150 years, Muslims ruled a vast empire, covering an area ranging from Ifriqiya (modern Tunisia and Eastern parts of Algeria) and the east African coast in the West to the Indian subcontinent in the East, including Central Asia and the Caucasus, Armenia, Persia, Mesopotamia, the Ḥijāz with Mecca and Medina, the Fertile Crescent of Syria and Palestine, Egypt, and Yemen in the South and Muslim Spain (al-Andalus) in the North, as well as islands in the sea, such as Sicily, Rhodes, and Crete.[12] Parts of this territory which was taken in swift campaigns were to remain under Muslim rule right down to the present day. Not surprisingly, every rule brings resistance,[13] and so Muslim conquests also created dissent. Amongst the conquered from within the Early Islamic Empire, early dissent was articulated by Christian, Jewish, and Zoroastrian voices in the languages of Greek, Latin, Syriac, and Chinese. They span from the earliest rejections to the coming of the Arab-Muslims to the view that the new rulers are better than the old.[14] It is only much later in Europe, in the middle of the nineteenth century, the term *imperialism* became commonly used to criticize ambitions for domination and expansion.[15]

While for the longest time, Islamic legal concepts were used in an (continuously changing) imperial context, the nineteenth century in particular brought about re-interpretations of formerly imperial understandings to fit a new, that of

[10] The study of the early conquests is largely based on the great works compiled by authors of the third/ninth century and fourth/tenth centuries, like al-Baladhūrī and Ṭabarī. They have edited and republished earlier collections of accounts and transmitted the texts in the form as we know them today. Al-Baladhūrī, Aḥmad b. Yaḥyā, *Futūḥ al-Buldān* (Beirut: Dār al-Nashr, 1957); *The Origins of the Islamic State*, translated by Philipp Hitti and Francis Murgotten, 2 vols., *Columbia University Studies in History, Economics and Public Law* 68, nos. 163, 163a (New York: Columbia University Press, 1916–1924). Al-Ṭabarī, *Ta'rīkh al-rusul wa-l-mulūk*, edited by Michael Jan de Goeje et al., 15 vols (Leiden: Brill, 1879–1901); al-Ṭabarī, *The history of al-Ṭabarī*, edited by Ehsan Yar-Shater (Albany, State University of New York Press, 1985–2007). On the conquest literature, see the seminal work of Fred Donner, *The Early Islamic Conquests* (Princeton: Princeton University Press, 1981). In line with the Arabic terminology, historians of early military history use the word conquest rather than imperial/empire. See also Hugh Kennedy, *The Great Arab Conquests.*

[11] Hugh Kennedy, *The Armies of the Caliphs: Military and Society in the Early Islamic State* (London; New York: Routledge, 2001), p. 2.

[12] See the regions covered in Baladhūrī, *Futūḥ al-Buldān*. The first and last time that conquests lead to an area this vast while politically, administratively, and economically united, was when it was ruled a millennium earlier by Alexander the Great—only that the Abbasid reign over this territory lasted for several hundred years longer than Alexander's brief lifetime. Hugh Kennedy, *The Early Abbasid Caliphate*, p. 25; Dimitri Gutas, *Greek Thought, Arabic Culture: The Graeco-Arabic Translation Movement in Baghdad and early 'Abbasid society (2nd–4th/ 8th–10th century)* (London: Routledge, 1998), p. 11.

[13] Christian Daase and Nina Deitelhoff, 'Zur Rekonstruktion globaler Herrschaft aus dem Widerstand' (Working Paper 1, 2014), pp. 1–26, at p. 11, dissidenz.net/networkingpapers/wp1-2014-daase-deitelhoff.pdf.

[14] Robert Hoyland, *Seeing Islam as Others Saw It: A Survey and Evaluation of Christian, Jewish, and Zoroastrian Writings of Early Islam* (Princeton, NJ.: The Darwin Press Inc., 1997). See also 'The voice of the conquered' in Hugh Kennedy, *The Great Arab Conquests*, pp. 344–62.

[15] Moses, 'Empire, Colony, Genocide', p. 4.

a dissident mode of law. The dissident mode emerged not without creating some dissonances within the own Muslim legal tradition as well as towards the prevailing international legal order. In this sense, dissenting is meant as a disagreement with the authority of the international order. It is a dissent that comes out of violent encounters with conflicting legal orders, one that rejects, and not only opposes, the rules of the new international order, especially where they impose legally authorized forms of domination, such as colonialism and occupation.[16] Dissent, it is argued, 'does not accept the rules of order and employs unconventional forms of organization and articulation to radically critique rule'.[17] I argue that the dissent that emerged out of the Islamic legal tradition more specifically was a dissent that targeted the systematic expropriation of territory. This dissent can be read as a response to 'the arch-characteristic of European imperialism [that] was expropriation', as something qualitatively different that set the European empires apart from others, as expressed in much of the historical writings comparing empires.[18] Traditional empires differed from European empires: Traditional empires accumulated people and land, sometimes by expropriations, but largely by incorporating people and land while leaving their structure intact, relying on decentralized governance that kept power with local elites. European empires employed systematic expropriation, often for commercial ends. Therefore natives were displaced, their territorial property rights nullified on the grounds that they have not made proper use of their land.[19]

The analysis of territorial expropriation being an 'arch-characteristic' of European empires as articulated by historian John Darwin overlaps with elaborations by Wael Hallaq, scholar of Islamic law. Hallaq assessed that amongst the colonizers' most important tools in their attempts to strengthen their control over Muslim societies by undermining local property regimes, were particularly charitable trusts (*awqāf*, pl. of *waqf*), resulting in large expropriations.[20] It is against

[16] On dissent in international relations, Daase and Deitelhoff, 'Zur Rekonstruktion globaler Herrschaft aus dem Widerstand', pp. 1–26.

[17] Daase/Deitelhoff speak of opposition and dissent as *Idealtyp*, p. 12, and on opposition, unlike dissent, they state that 'opposition accepts the order of rule and employs the institutionalized forms of political participation.' Further on the distinction between opposition and dissent, Daase and Deitelhoff, 'Zur Rekonstruktion globaler Herrschaft aus dem Widerstand', pp. 11–14.

[18] Darwin, *After Tamerlane*, p. 22.

[19] Ibid. Darwin connects territorial expropriation to the expropriation of culture and identity: 'Both native peoples and slaves (by different forms of displacement) suffered the effective expropriation of their cultures and identities: they were reduced to fragments, without hope of recovering the worlds they had lost. They became peoples without a history. And where expropriation by subjugation proved insufficient, European colonizers turned to their ultimate remedies: exclusion, expulsion or liquidation.' Ibid.

[20] Because of the socially vital role of charitable trusts also as sites of learning, the demise of Muslim trusts also lead to what Hallaq controversially called the 'structural death of the Sharīʿa'. For a fuller picture of the 'structural death of Shārīʿa, see, Wael Hallaq, *Sharīʿa: Theory, Practice, Transformations* (Cambridge: Cambridge University Press, 2009), pp. 15–16; Hallaq, 'Can the Sharia be restored?', in *Islamic Law and the Challenges of Modernity*, edited by Yvonne Yazbeck Haddad and Barbara Freyer Stowasser (Walnut Creek, Calif.: Altamira, 2004), pp. 21–53.

this background, that dissent is presented here, as an attempt to formulate political alternatives to the ruling order of expropriation.[21]

Territorial Precedence and Normativity

The tension between the imperial past that aimed at hegemonic expansion and the present critiquing hegemonic expansion today can be well exemplified by the doctrines governing territory in Islamic international law.[22] Acquiring, partitioning, redistributing territory are, after all, central themes in the past and present of international law.

A mapping of the concept of territory in Islamic legal understanding, with the three central notions of *dār al-Islam* (the territory of Islam where the rule of Islamic law governed, or rather where Islam could be practised) and *dār al-ḥarb* (the territory of war or of non-Muslim rule, or rather where Islam could not be practised) as well as *dār al-ṣulḥ* (the territory of peace agreements) in mind,[23] will bring different sets of rules to the fore. Territory can refer to war over territory, territory as booty, taxation, property, population settlement, coexistence or subordination of non-Muslim communities—these are all notions reflected in the Muslim history of territorial expansion and assumption of power. On the other hand, territory also refers to protection, security, a *dār*; that is, Arabic for a home, or a homeland, living free from foreign domination—all notions reflecting, in particular, the early

[21] On dissent as formulating political alternatives, Daase and Deitelhoff, 'Zur Rekonstruktion globaler Herrschaft aus dem Widerstand', p. 12.

[22] The legal shift from offensive to defensive has also been laid out for the doctrine of jihād, see most prominently in the work of Mahmud Shaltut, *al-Da'wa al-muḥammadīyya wa-l-qitāl- fi-l-islām [Muhammad's Mission and Warfare in Islam]* (Cairo: al-Matba'a al-salafiyya, 1933) and al-Qu'rān wa'l-qitāl [*The Quran and Warfare]* (Nazareth: Matba'at al-nasr wa maktab ittiḥād al-sharq, 1948); Muhammad Abu Zahra, *al-'Alaqāt al-dawliyya fi al-islām [International Relations in Islam]* (Cairo: al-Dār al-qawmīyya li-l-tibā'a wa-l-nashr, 1964); and Wahbi Zuhayli, *al-'Alaqāt al-duwalīyya fi al-islām: muqārana bi-l-qanūn al-dawlī al-ḥadīth [International Relations in Islam: a Comparison with Modern International Law]* (Beirut: Mu'assasat al-Risāla, 1981). On Shaltut's revision of the jihād doctrine, see also Rudolph Peters, *Jihad in Classical and Modern Islam: A Reader* (Princeton, N.J.: Markus Wiener Publishers, 1996), pp. 97–8. Mohammad Fadel sees the doctrinal shift caused by the promises of the United Nations Charter (independence, self-determination, human rights) which in turn led Muslim jurists to conclude that the concept of *dār al-ḥarb* was turning obsolete, and with it the necessity for offensive jihād, Mohammad Fadel, 'International Law, Regional Developments: Islam', MPEPIL, edited by Rüdiger Wolfrum (2010), online edn, margin numbers 46–9, 52, available at http://www.mpepil.com.

[23] The Ḥanafī school of law had an explicitly territorial view, while other schools stressed the ethical connotations of a bounded territory, and focused on the tension between the formal character of a territory and the substantive quality of life that a specific territory is able to afford, see Khaled Abou El Fadl, 'Islamic Law and Muslim Minorities: The Juristic Discourse on Muslim Minorities from the Second/Eighth to the Eleventh/Seventeenth Centuries', Islamic Law and Society 1, no. 2 (1994): pp. 141–87, 159. See also Khaled Abou El Fadl, 'The Unbounded Law of God and Territorial Boundaries', in *States, Nations and Borders: The Ethics of Making Boundaries*, edited by Allen Buchanan and Margaret Moore (Cambridge: Cambridge University Press, 2003), pp. 214–27. On these Islamic categories of political-geographical units as they generate Islamic validity and normativity, see the overview by Baber Johansen, 'Territorial Concepts in Islamic Law', *The Oxford International Encyclopaedia of Legal History*, vol. 5, edited by Stanley Katz (Oxford: Oxford University Press, 2009), pp. 451–4.

Muslim community's experience with persecution and emigration from Mecca to Medina in the first/seventh century.[24] In between this comes the duty to call to the universalist message of Islam (*daʿwa*) that can come in many ways. One can already sense here that territory can stand for different, possibly even contrasting understandings, depending on historical circumstances that do not easily lend themselves to essentialist positions.

The juristic debate on how to expand the territory of Islam contained rules and principles on how to appropriate and handle territory. Conquest was only one of many ways of territorial appropriation, next to purchase, cession, or bequest.[25] Ethical, moral, and theological implications of the territory of Islam were heatedly discussed and debated. These deliberations evidence that Muslim jurists were concerned with much more than only a formally cohesive system of law but what it substantially meant to provide for a bounded entity that enabled a good Muslim life.[26] Absorbing territory through conquest, by *jihād*, was a historically important tool, but not per se considered to be violent. Conquest could occur through the enemy's capitulation by treaty or unconditional surrender (*sulḥan*) or seizing force of arms (*ʿanwatan*). Legally and practically, it was relevant if towns and provinces had been conquered peacefully or by force. If cities were taken by treaty, the population was principally granted their lives and properties (moveable and immovable) and they were only required to pay as tax that sum which had been recorded in the treaties. If they had been taken by force, on the other hand, then they had to give up their property, and taxation was much higher (because so where the costs of conquest). Non-Muslim inhabitants would have had to pay the poll tax for their protection by Muslims (*jizyā*).[27] In some accounts, there were diverging reports over how territory was conquered, or parts of the territory were conquered both by treaty *and* force (like for example Egypt, around the year 639), so that the theory of *ṣulḥ* and *ʿanwa* could have mixed elements for one and the same locality.[28]

[24] On the right or expectation of security and safety in one's homeland as pervasive theme in Islamic juristic discourse in 'Territory as a Homeland in the Qur'ān', Khaled Abou El Fadl, 'The Unbounded Law of God and Territorial Boundaries', in *States, Nations and Borders: The Ethics of Making Boundaries*, edited by Allen Buchanan and Margaret Moore (Cambridge: Cambridge University Press, 2003), pp. 214–27, 220–1.

[25] Following Shaybānī, acquisition of rights to land by the polity or an individual was treated in jurisprudence under two broad categories: (1) open land not claimed by any state or people, and (2) land in the possession of another state or people. The first category, unclaimed territory and dead or waste land (mawāt or 'adi) raised relatively few problems but was nevertheless addressed by the Quran and the jurists. The second category is further discussed in this chapter. Muhammad b. al-Hasan al-Shaybānī, *Kitāb al-Hujja ʿalā ahl al-madīna*, 4 vols. (Beirut: ʿĀlam al-Kutub, undated, reprint of the Haiderabad edition 1965–71 [1385–90]). For a brief discussion of these categories see Sohail Hashmi, 'Political Boundaries and Moral Communities: Islamic Perspectives' in *States, Nations and Borders: The Ethics of Making Boundaries*, edited by Allen Buchanan and Margaret Moore (Cambridge: Cambridge University Press, 2003), p. 199.

[26] Khaled Abou El Fadl, 'Islamic Law and Muslim Minorities: The Juristic Discourse on Muslim Minorities from the Second/Eighth to the Eleventh/Seventeenth Centuries', *Islamic Law and Society* 1, no. 2 (1994): pp. 141–87.

[27] Kennedy, *The Great Arab Conquests*, p. 19.

[28] On the origins, developments, and historical and normative debates around the *ṣulḥ* and *ʿanwa* theory, see Werner Schmucker, *Untersuchungen zu einigen wichtigen bodenrechtlichen Konsequenzen der*

The examples presented now, each with different outcomes, show not only how territory was acquired but also how territory was to be normatively categorized for the future.[29] Moreover, the cases shed light at how the conquered population and their property were treated. The importance of these territorial appropriations for the questions of property and taxation is highlighted by the fact that they were discussed not only in the books of conquests (*futuḥāt*) but also, possibly even more intensely, in the juristic literature on taxation (*kharāj*). Conquest, property, and taxation are thus constructed as important elements of Islamic international law. I chose these examples as important normative options of precedent as well as conceptionally important templates also for the modern period of dissent, to which political actors have later turned to.

Khaybar: Conquest and Division of Territory, Sometimes

In the early examples of Islamic history, some of the clashes were between Muslims and other powerful groups in Medina opposing the new Muslim rule, prominently the two Jewish tribes originally resident in Medina, the Banū Naḍīr and the Banū Qurayza. The first set of events are all related to the town of Khaybar, an oasis known for its date palm trees located around 150 km from Medina.[30] In the Islamic tradition, the story of Khaybar is much known.[31] Yet, as Khaybar was the site of forceful encounters several times, even after the Prophet's time, there is some confusion in the sources as to what happened to the landed property in some instances. Of particular importance for the course of Islamic legal history were three events that demonstrate the Prophet's action on territory.[32]

In the first event, the Banū Naḍīr tribe is reported to have instigated hostility against the Muslim community in the year 4/626. After a brief siege of their forts, they were expelled by the Muslims from Medina.[33] They took whatever they could carry of their moveable property and fled to the northern oasis of Khaybar. In this incident, the land property in Medina was claimed by the Prophet alone

islamischen Eroberungsbewegung (Bonn: Selbsverlag des Orientalischen Seminars der Universität Bonn, 1972), pp. 86–188; 88–96, here p. 90.

[29] For a legal system whose legal legitimacy has been centrally derived from a few crucial decades in the past, these intensely discussed examples determined which precedent-setting action or word would serve as the normative model for the acquisition of territory.

[30] Ibn Hishām, ʿAbd al-Mālik (d. 218/834), *Sīrat al-Nabī*, vol. 3 [The Biography of the Prophet], edited by Muḥammad Khalīl Harrās (Cairo: Maktabat al-Jumhūriyya (1971), pp. 464–72; Al-Baladhūrī, Aḥmad b. Yaḥyā, *Futūḥ al-Bulḍān* (Beirut: Dār al-Nashr, 1957), pp. 34, 39; al-Wāqidī, *Kitāb al-Maghāzī*, vol. 1, p. 375; vol. 2, p. 690; 'Khaybar', L. Veccia Vaglieri, *Encyclopaedia of Islam*, 2nd edn, vol. 4, pp. 1137–8;

[31] Ibn Hishām, ʿAbd al-Mālik (d. 218/834), *Sīrat al-Nabī* [The Biography of the Prophet], vol. 3, edited by Muḥammad Khalīl Harrās (Cairo: Maktabat al-Jumhūriyya, 1971), pp. 464–72.

[32] See also Hashmi, 'Political Boundaries and Moral Communities: Islamic Perspectives', pp. 200–1.

[33] Hostility between the Muslims and Banū Naḍīr were explained as a consequence of Banū Nādīr violating the covenant of alliance with the Muslims, and attacking Prophet Muḥammad, Balādhūri, *Futūḥ al-Buldān*, p. 18.

to dispense as he saw fit because the Banū Naḍīr capitulated without battle. The Prophet chose to distribute the booty not only to those who fought, as was the custom, but also to the poorest Meccan emigrants (*muhājirūn*) and to a few Medinan Muslims (*anṣār,* earliest followers) on the basis of their immediate need.[34] This type of land claimed in war came to be known as *fay'* from the Qur'ānic verse describing it as 'what God has bestowed (*afā'a*) on his Messenger (Qur'ān 59:6). *Fay'* became to be understood as the communal wealth of the Muslim community, in this instance by taking territory away from the losing party, and by dividing the territory to distribute it to those who fought and those who are in need.[35] The precedent lay in the Prophet's not simply dividing the spoils among the conquerors but rather managing them for the good of the community of the Faithful.

As another principle, the Prophet divided the property and implemented the rule of the one-fifth (*khums*), according to Qur'ānic prescription: 'One fifth (*khums*) goes to the Prophet, that is, the state treasury, one for the kins, one for the orphans, one for the needy, and one for the travelers' (Qur'ān 59: 7). The Qur'ān specifies that in a situation of conquest movable and immovable booty should be divided.

In a second incident, the Banū Qurayza who had remained in Medina, attempted together with the Banū Naḍīr and other Arab groups to form a confederacy to attack the Muslims. This ended dramatically for the Banū Qurayza who eventually agreed to surrender to the conditions of a Muslim arbitrator of their choosing: The men were executed and the women and children enslaved, their property divided as booty amongst the Muslims. Information on their landed property remains scarce.[36]

In a third event, in the year 7/629 the Prophet marched forth from Medina and laid siege to the forts that protected the inhabitants of Khaybar. After about a month and a half of hostilities, the Jews of Khaybar asked the Prophet for a treaty of capitulation.[37] The terms of the capitulation are in dispute. In some accounts the Prophet divided the territory into shares and divided them amongst the Muslims. In other accounts, arguably the more prevalent ones, the division of Khaybar is not mentioned and it is suggested instead that the inhabitants of Khaybar remained owners of the land even after the capitulation but had to hand over half of their dates and grain crops to the Muslim conquerors.[38]

[34] Balādhurī, *Futūḥ al-Buldān*, p. 18–21; Al-Waqīdī, Muḥammad b. 'Umar, *Kitāb al-Maghāzī*, 3 vols, edited by Marsden Jones (London: Oxford University Press, 1966), vol. 1, p. 379; Schmucker, *Bodenrechtliche Konsequenzen*, p. 47.

[35] Andrew Marsham, 'Fay'.' Encyclopaedia of Islam, THREE, edited by Kate Fleet, Gudrun Krämer, Denis Matringe, John Nawas, and Everett Rowson (Leiden: Brill Online, 2015).

[36] Ibn Isḥāq, *Sirat rasul Allah* (The Life of Muhammad), translated by Alfred Guillaume (Karachi: Oxford University Press, 1990), p. 466.

[37] Whether Khaybar was seized from Banū Nādir by capitulation or force is not unanimously answered in the early sources. According to some sources it was by treaty (*ṣulḥan*), this is why the territory was not divided, according to another, it was conquered forcefully and therefore divided into multiple shares (the numbers of the shares vary too). For an overview of the divergent views, see Schmucker, *Untersuchungen zu einigen wichtigen bodenrechtlichen Konsequenzen*, pp. 25–6.

[38] Al-Baladhūrī, *Futūḥ al-Buldān*, p. 40; Abū Yūsuf, *Kitāb al-Kharāj*, pp. 49–51; al-Ṭabarī, *Ta'rīkh al-rusul wa-al-mulūk*, vol. 3, pp.19–21; Yaḥya b. Ādam, *Kitāb al-Kharāj*, p. 38, no. 98; See

The Prophet's conquests set the precedent that both dividing landed property and expelling the population as well as keeping the territory as one and keeping the inhabitants on it, became Islamically sanctioned options of appropriating territory.

Sawād: Conquest and Keeping Territory Unified

Following the Prophet, one of his immediate successors, caliph ʿUmar b. Khaṭṭāb set the stage for another precedent that came to be important for the course of Islamic legal history. It is the case of caliph ʿUmar b. Khaṭṭāb's handling of a territory in southern Iraq between Tigris and Euphrates, known as Sawād, conquered from the Sassanids in the year 16/637. The Sawād example is arguably the most significant case for the subsequent development of acquisition of territory in Islam. At the time of Umar's decree, the vast majority of the inhabitants remained non-Muslims, although conversion had begun to occur. Despite some discrepancies in the chronology of the conquest, a dominant narrative emerged: Caliph ʿUmar declared that the territory of Sawād should be a source of revenue (*fay*ʾ) 'in trust for all Muslims, those living at that time and those to come after them, and did not distribute the land'.[39] Caliph ʿUmar did not divide the land and distribute it as war booty, he did not dispossess the inhabitants or enslave them.[40] Crucially, caliph ʿUmar left the property regime and social fabric intact, and in return ordered land tax to be paid to the treasury. In this example, the Muslims conquered the territory, but the inhabitants did not lose their property rights over the land. The Sawād lands of Iraq were left in the hands of the inhabitants of Sawād who could dispose of them.[41] In fact, by paying land tax (*kharāj*), the inhabitants proved their rights as owners of landed property. This example later served to generate that the doctrine on tax largely determined the conception of landed property.[42]

Conquest meant state control over territory through tax control, or differently put, 'Nulle Terre Sans Taxe'.[43] Significantly, it meant no expropriation of land and

also Peter G. Hennigan, *The Birth of a Legal Institution: The Formation of the Waqf in Third-Century A.H. Hanafi Legal Discourse* (Leiden: Brill, 2004), p. 117. Hashmi, 'Political Boundaries and Moral Communities: Islamic Perspectives', pp. 200–1.

[39] Qudāma, *Kitāb al-Kharāj*, p. 25.

[40] Other narratives mention that caliph ʿUmar acted so on the advice of the Prophet's cousin and later caliph ʿAlī b. Abu Ṭālib and others. Umar 'declared al-Sawād and other lands fay', Qudāma, *Kitāb Al-Kharāj*, p. 25; Abū Yūsuf, *Kitāb al-Kharāj*, p. 14. According to some traditions, Umar initially apportioned parts of Sawād to tribes that had participated in its conquest, then after two or three years requested the land to be returned.

[41] Baber Johansen, *The Islamic Law on Land Tax and Rent* (1988), p. 9; For a detailed reconstruction of the legal and historical implications of Sawād land, see Schmucker, *Untersuchungen zu einigen wichtigen bodenrechtlichen Konsequenzen*, pp. 96–133.

[42] Johansen, *The Islamic Law on Land Tax and Rent*, p. 3.

[43] Johansen aptly points out that '[w]hereas European feudalism recognized the maxim "*Nulle terre sans seigneur*", the Ḥanafite jurists adhered to the principle "*Nulle terre sans taxe*"', Johansen, *The Islamic Law on Land Tax and Rent*, p. 7, referring to Abū Yūsuf Yaʿqūb, *Kitāb al-Kharāj*, translated by E. Fagnan as *Le livre de l'impôt foncier, Librairie Orienatliste* (Paris: Paul Geuthner, 1921), p. 91: 'Je ne suis pas d'avis qu'il [the Imam] laisse une terre, sans la donner en fief car cela sert à

dispossession of the population. The caliph immobilized the revenues of the land, that is to say that he established the revenue of the Sawād territory arguably as a *waqf*, a charitable trust for future generations (Qur'ān 59:9/10).[44]

The Sawād case marked the course of Islamic legal history for three main reasons.

First, the case initiated a debate over whether to divide or keep united territory after conquest; it raised the very question of *qasm al-aradīn* (lit. division of land). Second, arguments for dividing territory could be found in pre-Islamic and Prophetic and Qur'ānic precedent. Arguments for keeping territory united made it necessary to link the concept of communal wealth (*fay'*) to charitable trust (*waqf*), expanding on the original meaning of *fay'*. The key difference between this *fay'–waqf* expansion and the Prophet's first action that was also referred to as *fay'* as related to the property of Banu Naḍīr in Medina and Khaybar, was that in the expanded version no specific shares were apportioned to individuals or tribes, nor was a fifth claimed by the state.[45] Instead, the land remained in the hands of the original owners, the inhabitants of the Sawād were to remain on their land as free tenants and owners paying (if they remained non-Muslim) the capitation tax (*jizya*) and the land tax (*kharāj*, to be paid regardless of whether they were Muslim or non-Muslim) directly to the state treasury (*bayt al-māl*).[46] The early sources generally emphasize the interest of contemporary and future (Muslim)[47] generations, referring to Qur'ānic verse 59:10 'and those who came after them' as the basis for Umar's decision. Future jurists were to keep debating whether conquered land should necessarily become *fay'* and expanded as *waqf*, or might be divided among the conquerors. But the possibility of keeping conquered territory unified was from now on an established principle in the laws of appropriating territory.

Third, the case also served as prominent example of options (*ḥiyār*) in legal reasoning. It allowed to take public interest (*maṣāliḥ al-'āmma*) into consideration for a reasoning beyond text (*ijtihād al-ra'y*). Going beyond text and precedent, without going against them, was accompanied by a fierce debate.[48] First the Prophet, and slightly later caliph 'Umar b. al-Khaṭṭāb demonstrated that they did not dogmatically follow a particular custom or rule. [49] They were willing to revise the rule and

l'accroissement de la prospèrité du pays et augmente le Kharâdj. Et c'est là à mes yeux … le but à poursuivre dans l'attribution des fiefs.'

44 See also Paul G. Forand, 'The Status of the Land and Inhabitants of the Sawad during the First Two Centuries of Islām', *Journal of the Economic and Social History of the Orient* 14, no. 1 (April, 1971), pp. 29–30.

45 Al-Mawārdi, *Al-Aḥkām al-Sultaniyya*, p. 191; Hashmi, Political Boundaries and Moral Communities: Islamic Perspectives', p. 201; Schmucker, *Untersuchungen zu einigen wichtigen bodenrechtlichen Konsequenzen*, p. 148.

46 Later systematically elaborated upon by Al-Mawārdi, *Al-Aḥkām al-Sultaniyya*, p. 191, who refered also to Shāfi'ī, see on his p. 142.

47 Schmucker argues that those to come after them ('wa'l-ladhīna jā'ū min ba'dihim…') from Qur'ān 59.10 was later extended by 'Muslim generations'. Schmucker, *Untersuchungen zu einigen wichtigen bodenrechtlichen Konsequenzen*, p. 107.

48 Covering the range of legal and historical views, see ibid. pp. 86–186.

49 Hashmi, 'Political Boundaries and Moral Communities: Islamic Perspectives', p. 201. Hashmi speaks of the Prophet only and afterwards refers to the 'improvisional approach' of 'Umar b. Al-Khaṭṭāb.

adapt to the exigency of the situation, when this promised to be beneficial, for the conquered population and the ruling powers. The examples show that there was diversity of precedent which did not lead to one doctrine of how to appropriate territory after conquest.

For future juristic debates, it is important to conclude that jurists debated *fay'* as part of *waqf*, that is, conquered land as a charitable trust that is inalienable and stands in perpetuity.[50] *Fay'* and *waqf* were fused in the normative discussions. In their famous tax treatises, Abū Yūsuf (d. 798) and Yaḥya b. Aktham (d. 857) refer to the Sawād land as irrevocable *waqf* land.[51] Clearly, the importance of linking the laws of territorial appropriation to the laws of property and taxation cannot be underestimated for the Islamic history of international law.[52] The common functionality of *fay'* and *waqf* is that territory should not be divided, and was handled synonymously with public property,[53] and the two concepts were used interchangeably[54] as legal institutions of communal property. The *fay'-waqf* concept became ground-breaking for the entire later development of economic and financial aspects of Islamic law,[55] as well as for Islamic international law.

[50] See also Schmucker, *Untersuchungen zu einigen wichtigen bodenrechtlichen Konsequenzen*, pp. 101, 141–50.

[51] Abū Yūsuf, *Kitāb al-Kharāj*, 49–51; Yaḥya b. Aktham, *Kitāb al-Kharāj*, pp. 39–42, nos. 100, 102, 104, 106–7. Some consider this a conflation between *fay'* and *waqf*: John Robert Barnes, *An Introduction to Religious Foundations in the Ottoman Empire* (Leiden: Brill, 1986), p. 10, who refers to the fact that *fay'* land cannot be transferred to private *waqf* (yet to public *waqf*). Hennigan, *The Birth of a Legal Institution*, traces no (explicit) relationship between *fay'* and *waqf*: Hennigan does not mention the *fay'* concept as related to *waqf*—other than the Muslim early sources.

[52] The link between Islamic international law (*siyār*) and taxation of landed property (*kharāj*) is also evidenced by the earliest and highly influential works on Islamic international law by Muḥammad al-Shaybānī (749/50–805), including his four volume work on *kharāj*: Muhammad b. al-Hasan al-Shaybānī, *Kitāb al-Hujja ʿalā ahl al-madīna*, 4 vols (Beirut: ʿĀlam al-Kutub, undated, reprint of the Haiderabad edn 1965–71 [1385–90]). Even in al-Shaybānī's siyār work, he discusses questions of *waqf* as a charitable trust in perpetuity that ultimately reverts to a pious cause. (*ḥabs fī sabīl Allāh*, charitable trusts made on the way to God, made in perpetuity, here specifically for *jihād*.) See Abu Dāwūd, *Sunan*, 5 vols (Beirut: Dār b. Hazm, 1997), 3:30, hadith no. 2532. The importance of linking international law and conquest to taxation and property cannot be underestimated. On al-Shaybānī's take on endowments, however without contextualization of al-Shaybānī's interest in islamic international law (*siyār*), see Norbert Oberauer, *Islamic Law and Society* 20 (2013): pp. 3–4. For important historical studies connecting the early period of conquest to taxation, see Frede Løkkegaard, *Islamic Taxation in the Classical Period with Special Reference to Circumstances in Iraq* (Copenhagen: Branner & Korch, 1950); Kosei Morimoto, *The Fiscal Administration of Egypt in the Early Islamic Period* (Kyoto: Dohosha, 1981); Jørgen Bæk Simonsen, *Studies in the Genesis and Early Development of the Caliphal Taxation System with Special References to Circumstances in the Arab Peninsula, Egypt and Palestine* (Copenhagen: Akademisk Forlag, 1988).

[53] Sanjuán, Alejandro Garciá, *Till God Inherits the Earth, Islamic Pious Endoments in al-Andalus (9–15th Centuries)* (Leiden: Brill, 2007), p. 400.

[54] Ibid.

[55] Schmucker, *Untersuchungen zu einigen wichtigen bodenrechtlichen Konsequenzen*, p. 191.

The Age of Colonialisms: Muslim Territorial Re-interpretations to Defend Territory

The European colonial era was certainly not the first time that Muslim jurists were confronted with conquest of large Muslim populations that fell under non-Muslim rule. Juristic debates entailed if Muslims were permitted to live under non-Muslim rule. Questions of safety and especially if practising a Muslim life was still possible under non-Muslim rule were heatedly discussed, with the invasion of the Mongols (1260), the Spanish Reconquista (722–1492) as well as the Napoleonic invasion of Egypt (1798) as particularly notable examples.[56] Significantly, Muslim jurists began to describe certain territories with large Muslim populations that had come under the political domination of non-Muslim powers as being part of the *dār al-Islam*, for example in Egypt following the Napoleonic invasion.[57] They did so to secure the rights of the individual Muslims in such territories against both other Muslims as well as against the foreign ruler, by declaring that any transactions conducted by the foreign ruler, such as grants of land, remained subject to the rules of Islamic law rather than that of the foreign conqueror. The effect of such a rule, of course, was to deny legitimacy to the regime of the foreign ruler.[58]

In the nineteenth century, the colonial experience also affected the view on territory of many Muslim scholars. Arguably, the destructive effects of European colonialism on the epistemic and social ecology of the Muslim legal community and on Islamic law were unparalleled.[59] A wider Muslim response to colonialism was articulated in the nineteenth century. Most prominent among them were the Afghan scholar Jamāl al-Dīn al-Afghānī (1838–97) and Arab-Egyptian Muslim legal scholars Muḥāmmad ʿAbduh (1849–1905) and Muḥammad Rashīd Riḍā (1865–1935) who all considered the colonial project an attack on the entire territory of Islam.[60] They addressed the advent of modernity with European colonialism

[56] In the course of the Mongol conquest and the Reconquista, which brought large Muslim populations under non-Muslim rule, the legal schools revised and systematized their views after the sixth/twelfth century. While their views were first largely lenient, most Mālikī scholars developed increasingly rigid positions, declaring that such Muslims were obliged to emigrate to territories that were under Muslim rule, i.e., to what they defined as *dār al-islām*. Shāfiʿīs and Ḥanafīs did not endorse this call for emigration (*hijra*), but maintained that Islam could and should continue to exist in territories that had fallen under non-Muslim rule. For the intensity of the debate and further positions, see Khaled Abou El Fadl, 'Islamic Law and Muslim Minorities: The Juristic Discourse on Muslim Minorities from the Second/Eighth to the Eleventh/Seventeenth Centuries' *Islamic Law and Society* 1, no. 2 (1994): pp. 141–87.

[57] While French occupation of Egypt after Napoleon's invasion (1798–1801) was relatively brief, it has left a lasting mark as it exposed the extent of European military superiority.

[58] Fadel, 'International Law, Regional Developments: Islam', in MPEPIL, edited by R. Wolfrum (2010), online edn, margin number 52, available at http://www.mpepil.com.

[59] Hallaq, *Sharīʿa: Theory, Practice, Transformations*.

[60] Jamāl al-Dīn Afghānī, 'Al-ḥarb al-ʿādilah wa al-ḥarb ghayr ʿādilah', in Jamāl al-Dīn al-Afghānī, *Al aʿmāl al-kāmilah [The Complete Works]*, vol. II, edited by Muḥammad ʿAmmārah (Cairo: Dār al-Kitāb al-ʿArabī, n.d.), pp. 71–9. See also Nikki R. Keddie, *An Islamic Response to Imperialism: Political and Religious Writings of Sayyid Jamāl al- Dīn al- Afghānī* (Berkeley: University of California Press, 1968); Muḥāmmad ʿAbduh, *Al-Thāʾir al-Islāmī Jamāl al-Dīn al-Afghānī* [The Islamic Revolutionary

as it affected the Muslim world. European colonizers in the Muslim world, such as the British in India, but including also the French[61] and the Dutch,[62] pursued a policy of 'demolish and replace'[63] with respect to both Islamic law and other indigenous methods of governance. Amongst the colonizers' most important tools in their attempts to solidify their control over Muslim societies, were by subverting local property regimes, particularly charitable trusts (*awqāf*), resulting in large expropriations. These systematic expropriations were arguably key in creating a dissenting mode of law with regard to territory. Concepts of landed property were now becoming focal points of colonization and resistance, most prominently in the case of Algeria in the nineteenth to twentieth century[64] and Palestine from the twentieth century onwards. Algeria was the first major conquest of an Arabic-speaking country by a European state, France,[65] and it was the first Arab country to be annexed by a European state,[66] far into the twentieth century until 1954. The conquest of Algeria in 'June 1830 set the pattern for the way in which the Arab world was to be carved up by Britain and France over the next hundred years'.[67] Also, French colonial land policy in Algeria inspired Italian colonialism of Libya, where charitable trust property was expropriated in a similar fashion.[68] The Algerian case is illuminative because territory owned as charitable trust (*waqf*, in the Maghreb synonymously called *ḥubs*) was the very target of French colonial legislation,[69] and the Algerians in return considered their *ḥubs* property a tool

Jamāl al-Dīn al-Afghānī] (Cairo: Dar al-Hilal, 1973), pp. 46–113; Muḥāmmad 'Abduh , *Al-A'māl Al-Kāmilah* [The Complete Works], introduced, and its authenticity verified, by Muhammad 'Imarah (Beirut: Dār-Al-Shurūq, 1993), vol. I., pp. 32, 55–7, 62; Rashīd Muḥammad 'Riḍā, Al-jihād fi-l Islam', *Al-Manār* 15 (Cairo, 1912): pp. 33–40. On Riḍā's critique of the West as colonizer, see Emad-ud-Din Shahin, *Through Muslim Eyes: M. Rashid Rida and the West* (Herndon, VA.: The International Institute of Islamic Thought, 1993), pp. 75–87.

61 Hallaq, *Sharī'a: Theory, Practice, Transformations*, pp. 432–42.

62 Ibid., pp. 388–95.

63 Ibid., p. 376.

64 On the effect of Afghani, Abduh, and Rida, as well as Hassan al-Banna (founder of the Egyptian Brotherhood) in Algerian Islamic resistance predominately after the First World War through the Association of Algerian Ulema, see Martin Evans and John Phillips, *Algeria, Anger of the Dispossessed* (New Haven, Conn.: Yale University Press, 2007), pp. 43–5.

65 Albert Hourani, *A History of the Arab peoples* (Cambridge, Mass.: Belknap Press of Harvard University Press, 1991), p. 263.

66 Evans and Phillips, *Algeria, Anger of the Dispossessed*, p. 1.

67 Ibid., p. 1, even if this was 'not part of a grand design for imperial expansion' at that time.

68 See Anna Maria Medici, *Waqfs of Cyrenaica and Italian Colonialism in Libya (1911–41)*, in *Held in Trust. Pious Foundations, Founders, and Beneficiarie*, edited by Pascale Ghazaleh (Cairo: AUC Press, 2011), p. 194.

69 David Powers contrasts the Algerian and the Indian experience. While the French wanted to seize land to accommodate their settlers, the British were interested (only) in keeping the land productive and in Muslims paying their taxes. Powers points out how in Algeria the Muslims remained a 'totally colonized population with virtually no political rights', while in India the British extended both the franchise and the right of representation to a limited number of natives. Muslim politicians used their rights to challenge the legislative process, and could thereby save the religious endowments as institutions in India. David S. Powers, 'Orientalism, Colonialism, and Legal History: The Attack on Muslim Family Endowments in Algeria and India', *Comparative Studies in Society and History* 31, no. 3 (July, 1989): p. 539.

in the anti-colonial resistance.[70] In the words of scholars of Algeria Evans and Philips: 'The past of Algerian history has been invoked to legitimize not just the appropriation of land by colonialism, but also the war of national liberation as well as Islamist and anti-Islamist violence.'[71] The case of Palestine is of particular interest because it is especially here that we see a new formulation of declaring all of Palestine as *waqf* territory, thereby prohibiting the land from being sold or negotiated away, and rejecting any forms of legality or legitimacy of foreign conquest. *Waqf* transformed from a landed property concept into a widely resonant anti-colonial legal metaphor. Algeria and Palestine demonstrate how Muslim societies generated reinterpreted concepts of territory to aid their survival in a world dominated by others.

Algeria: Charitable Trusts (ḥubs) under Colonial Attack

After a French military expedition to Algiers in July 1830 the French remained in Algiers and left 132 years later in 1954.[72] France initially assured other European powers that the expedition aimed at supressing piracy and slavery, and therefore served a lawful purpose according to international law.[73] The French initially called for an *occupation restreinte* (limited occupation) by which they meant the occupation of the main towns and the exercise of indirect rule over the rest of the country. However by 1840, the French adopted a policy of *total occupation*[74] and thereby both state and French expansionist early settler movement strove to control the colonization of Algerian territory.[75] Immediately following the conquest in 1830, French public law replaced Muslim laws, declaring all of the territory, including *ḥubs/waqf* as belonging to the public domain.[76] French property law began to

[70] The works of David Powers and John Ruedy are seminal in recapitulating colonial land policy regarding *ḥubs* in Algeria. Both critically revisit French colonial material. John Ruedy, *Land Policy in Colonial Algeria, The Origins of the Rural Public Domain* (Berkeley and Los Angeles: University of California Press, 1967); David S. Powers, 'Orientalism, Colonialism, and Legal History', pp. 535–71.

[71] Evans and Phillips, *Algeria, Anger of the Dispossessed*, p. 4.

[72] John Ruedy, *Land Policy in Colonial Algeria, The Origins of the Rural Public Domain* (Berkeley and Los Angeles: University of California Press, 1967), p. vii.

[73] Powers, 'Orientalism, Colonialism, and Legal History', p. 539. On how pirates were deemed outlaws in the history of international law, see e.g. Lauren Benton, *A Search for Sovereignty: Law and Geography in European Empires, 1400–1900* (Cambridge: Cambridge University Press, 2010). On slavery in the history of (Islamic) international law, see Bernard K. Freamon, 'Definitions and Conceptions of Slave Ownership in Islamic Law,' in *The Legal Understanding of Slavery: From the Historical to the Contemporary*, edited by Jean Allain (Oxford: Oxford University Press, 2012), pp. 40–60.

[74] On the legal situation of Algeria in 1830 and French annexation laws, see Mohammed Bedjaoui, *La Révolution Algérienne et le Droit* (Bruxelles: Editions de l'Association Internationale des Juristes Démocrates, 1961), pp. 18–40.

[75] Powers, 'Orientalism, Colonialism, and Legal History', p. 539.

[76] See Hallaq *Sharia: Theory, Practice, Transformations* (2009), p. 434. Crucially, Ottoman *waqf* centralization policy of Ottoman Mahmud II in 1826 can be considered a forerunner to the almost identical *ḥubs* confiscation law of the French in Algeria, see Hallaq, *Sharīʿa: Theory, Practice, Transformations*, p. 434.

replace Muslim laws controlling ownership of the land in 1844 onwards.[77] The imposition of French property law had been linked to the imposition of the *total occupation*.[78] When the Algerian Revolution started in 1854, more than 3 million hectares of agricultural lands had passed from the control of Muslim natives to the hands of European colonists.[79] To exploit the colony's important agricultural and mineral resources, France had settled increasing numbers of its civilians in the Algerian countryside.[80] They clashed almost immediately with the Muslim population over the issues of access to and control of land.[81] The Muslim resistance against French domination and expropriation was led by ʿAbd al-Qādir, who fused religion and resistance in the fight against the colonizers.[82] The French government however kept facilitating the colonists' acquisition of Algerian territory and assured them of their rights.[83]

To this end, the French endeavoured to elaborate a new system of property law that favoured the settler colonialists. One half of the land of Algeria had been landlocked as *ḥubs* (in the Maghreb use for *waqf*, French use the word *habous*).[84] Religious charitable trusts were a serious obstacle to the settlers and the French state.[85] Efforts by French settlers (*colons*) were repeatedly frustrated by the fact that much of the territory in Algeria had been designated as religious endowments and therefore could not legally be bought or sold.[86] In fact, by the beginning of the nineteenth century, one-half of the land in Algeria and one-third in Tunisia

[77] Charles-Robert Agéron, *Les Algériens musulmans et la France: 1871–1919*, vol. I (Paris: Presses Universitaires de France, 1968), pp. 67–70.

[78] Powers, 'Orientalism, Colonialism, and Legal History' p. 539.

[79] Ruedy, *Land Policy in Colonial Algeria*, p. Vii.

[80] The number of French settlers living in the Algerian countryside reportedly increased from 35,000 in 1849 to 119,000 in 1871 and to 200,000 in 1898. See Jamil M. Abun-Nasr, A *History of the Maghrib* (Cambridge; New York: Cambridge University Press, 1975), p. 268; David S., 'Orientalism, Colonialism, and Legal History', p. 540; Evans and Phillips, *Algeria, Anger of the Dispossessed*, p. 30 (for the number in 1849).

[81] Abun-Nasr, *A History of the Maghrib* (1975), pp. 260–2.

[82] Evans and Phillips, *Algeria, Anger of the Dispossessed*, p. 29. On religious resistance against French colonialism in Algeria led by ʿAbd al-Qādir, see Raphael Danziger, *Abd el-Kader and the Algerians: Resistance to the French and International Consolidation* (New York: Africana Publishing Company, 1977); Ismail al-Arabi, *Al-Muqāwama al-jazāʾirīyya that liwāʾ al-amīr ʿAbd al Qādir* (Algiers: Société Nationale d'Edition, 1982); Bruno Etienne, *Abd-el-Kader* (Paris: Hachette, 1994); Julia Clancy-Smith, *Rebel and Saint* (Oakland, CA: University of California Press, 1994). A brief account in Rudolph Peters, *Islam and Colonialism, The Doctrine of Jihad in Modern History* (The Hague: Mouton Publishers, 1979), pp. 53–62.

[83] In the words of a contemporary French writer: 'In order to have colonists, it is necessary to provide them with land, or at least to make its acquisition easy and certain. It is necessary that the buyer dealing with the natives be certain, from the day the contract is drawn up, that he will remain the definitive owner of the domain that he has acquired, and that nothing will require him to move his family and hearth elsewhere.' Andre Mameur, *La Chefa* (Paris: Librairie du Recueil Sirey, 1910), pp. 145–6; cited in Powers, 'Orientalism, Colonialism, and Legal History', p. 540.

[84] Eugène Clavel, *Droit musulman. Le waqf ou habous d'après la doctrine et la jurisprudence (rites hanafite et malékite)*, vol. 1 (Cairo: Diemer, 1986), p. 3, cited also in 'Jurist', 'Waqf', *The Muslim World* 4, no. 2 (April, 1914): p. 173.

[85] Powers, 'Orientalism, Colonialism, and Legal History', p. 540.

[86] Ibid., pp. 535–6.

reportedly had been transformed into trust land.[87] Although the French ceased to be deceived, as they grew more familiar with the system of charitable trusts, the *ḥubs* system continued to withhold large amounts of territory from the free market, thereby posing a serious, ongoing obstacle to what the French called 'economic progress'.[88]

The colonial administration endeavoured to gain control over the trust institution through a series of legislative enactments. The aim was to allow colonization of territory constituted as *ḥubs,* and to prevent territory from being constituted as *ḥubs* once more, which removes them from circulation, while allowing the colonization of the assets already constituted as *ḥubs.*[89] To crack down on the land-locked charitable trusts, the French marshalled a series of legislations, followed by campaigns to discredit the charitable trusts as institutions amongst the Algerian Muslims.[90] The *loi Warner* of 1873 decreed that all territory in Algeria was to be regulated by French law, and significantly, split up communally held land into individual lots so that it could be sold off more easily.[91] The French authorities claimed that in the long term they would benefit Algeria because it opened a way for a free-market system, but in practice it was 'an all-out land grab', and between 1871 and 1889 French settlers acquired one million hectares.[92] This policy culminated in a 'colonization of the habous [charitable trusts]'.[93] It was met by protest of Muslim legal scholars who wrote protest letters to the French government,[94] probably with little effect. The expropriation of land caused horrible living conditions for many Algerians and lead to two different economies side by side, one for the colonizers and one for the colonized.[95] The settlers 'had made the desert bloom through relentless endeavour and on this basis they felt they had a right to be in Algeria'.[96] Eventually, ʿAbd al-Qāḍir's defeat by the French and the collapse of his religious anti-colonial movement opened the road for large-scale expropriations and colonization of vast areas. [97]

Significantly, French colonial laws on landed property, particularly on charitable trusts, left their mark in different forms on the colonial powers of Italy,[98] Britain,[99]

[87] Fuad Köprülü, 'L'institution du Vakouf: Sa nature juridique et son évolution historique', *Vakiflar Dergisi* 2, no. 3 (1942): French section, p. 3; Powers, 'Orientalism, Colonialism and Legal History', p. 537.

[88] Powers, 'Orientalism, Colonialism, and Legal History', p. 540.

[89] See also the 1916 Italian documents on colonizing religious endowments in Libya, Anna Maria Medici, 'Waqfs of Cyrenaica and Italian Colonialism in Libya (1911–41)', in *Held in Trust. Pious Foundations, Founders, and Beneficiaries*, edited by Pascale Ghazaleh (Cairo: AUC Press, 2011), p. 196.

[90] On this campaign to 'conquer the mind' with the help of French orientalists, see Hallaq, *Sharīʿa: Theory, Practice, Transformations*, pp. 435–6.

[91] Hallaq, *Sharīʿa: Theory, Practice, Transformations*, p. 437; Evans and Phillips, *Algeria, Anger of the Dispossessed*, p. 34.

[92] Evans and Phillips, *Algeria, Anger of the Dispossessed* (2007), p. 34.

[93] John Ruedy, *Land Policy in Colonial Algeria. The Origins of the Rural Public Domain* (Berkeley and Los Angeles: University of California Press, 1967): pp. 67–79.

[94] Ibid., p. 67, note 1. [95] Evans and Phillips, *Algeria, Anger of the Dispossessed*, p. 38.

[96] Ibid., p. 34. [97] See Peters, *Islam and Colonialism*, p. 61.

[98] Medici, 'Waqfs of Cyrenaica and Italian Colonialism in Libya (1911–41)', pp. 194–5.

[99] Kozlowski, *Muslim Endowments and Society in British India.* On British Malaya, see Nurfadzilah Yahaya, *Courting Jurisdictions: Colonial Administration of Islamic Law Pertaining to Arabs in the British*

and the Netherlands,[100] in that they all attacked *waqf* institutions as backward, prohibiting 'economic progress'[101] and employing law to critically destruct *waqf* structure in the Muslim societies colonized by them. It is in this sense that colonial *waqf* rules had arguably become a substantial part of European international law. The example of the colonization of *ḥubs* territory in Algeria shows how *ḥubs* as inalienable territory shifted from one that previously helped sustain imperial rule of Muslims to one that was a key target of European colonialism.

Palestine: 'Palestine as an Islamic Waqf' as Response to Territorial Expropriation by Force and Law

A more recent example from Palestine demonstrates the wide resonance in the Muslim world for the approach taken to territory, in which historic precedent is reinterpreted as critique on foreign domination of territory. In Palestine, the *waqf* institution came under immense pressure under foreign domination, starting with the Ottoman centralization policy of 1826 under Mahmud II[102] and further continued by the British.[103] In 1918, while the British ruled Palestine as a Mandate, Chaim Weizmann, head of the Zionist Commission's delegation[104] to Palestine in

Straits Settlements and The Netherlands Indies, 1860–1941 (PhD dissertation, Princeton University, 2012), pp. 164–203.

100 On Netherland Indies, Yahaya, *Courting Jurisdictions*, pp. 164–203.

101 French, British, and Dutch Orientalists were 'co-founders of the field of Islamic legal studies' who helped implement colonial government policies regarding *waqf* by using the argument of waqf as impediment to 'economic process', see Hallaq, *Sharī'a: Theory, Practice, Transformations*, p. 435.

102 For an account of Ottoman *waqf* policies in the city of Jerusalem in the eighteenth and nineteenth centuries, see 'Adil Mannā', *Liwā' al-Kuds fī awāsiṭ al-'ahd al-'uthmānī: Al-Idārah wa al-mujtama' mundhu awāsiṭ al-qārn al-thāmin 'ashar ḥattā ḥamlat Muḥammad 'Alī Bāshā sanat 1831 [The District of Jerusalem in the Mid-Ottoman Period: Administration and Society, from the Mid-18th Century to the Campaign of Muhammad 'Ali Pasha in 1831]* (Beirut: Institute for Palestine Studies, 2008), on landed property and taxes see pp. 82–91; Gabriel Baer, 'The Dismemberment of Waqf in Early 19th Century Jerusalem', *Asian and African Studies* 13 (1979): pp. 220–41; Hallaq, *Sharī'a: Theory, Practice, Transformations*, p. 434. The Ottoman Land Code of 1858 included six classifications of land: mulk, mīrī, waqf, mewāt, mahlūl, and matrūka, on their significance for Palestine see Aida Asim Essaid, *Zionism and Land Tenure in Mandate Palestine* (London; New York: Routledge, 2014), pp. 59–61.

103 'Of course, emphasizing the importance of the Ottoman land legacy should not obscure the highly contested processes by which Ottoman legal and and tenurial categories of land came to be understood, or deliberately misunderstood, in the context of British colonial rule.' Martin Bunton, ed., 'Introduction', in *Land Legislation in Mandate Palestine*, vol. 1 (Cambridge: Cambridge University Press, 2009), p. vii. Seminal on British rule in Palestine, Martin Bunton, *Colonial Land Policies in Palestine, 1917–1936* (Oxford: Oxford University Press, 2007); Bunton, *Land Legislation in Mandate Palestine* ; Martin Bunton, 'Demarcating the British Colonial State: Land Settlement in the Jiftlik Villages of Sajad and Qazaza', in *New Perspectives on Property and Land in the Middle East*, edited by Roger Owen (Cambridge, MA: Harvard University Press, 2001), pp. 121–58; Yitzhak Reiter, *Islamic Endowments in Jerusalem under British Mandate* (London: Cass, 1996).

104 On the Zionist Commission and its delegation to Palestine in 1918, headed by Chaim Weizmann and its self-declared aim of preparing the grounds for a Jewish Palestine, and the opposition met by Muslim, Christian and Druze Palestinians, see Sahar Huneidi, *A Broken Trust: Sir Herbert Samuel, Zionism and the Palestinians 1920–1925* (London; New York: I.B. Tauris, 2001), pp. 29–33.

1918 (and later first president of the State of Israel in 1948) demanded from the British that the *waqf* be abandoned as the Palestinians could try to protect their property by converting it to *waqf*.[105] He understood that if considerable parts of the territory would become *waqf* territory, the Zionist Jewish project of an exclusive state would never materialize. This demand was indeed an indicative sense of how *waqf*, once again, would become a central issue of foreign domination and expropriation. In fact, the Zionist Commission has put great effort into a 'survey for identifying the lands, determining their legal status, measuring them, and staking them out, ... as strategies to establish claim to lands'.[106] In fact, Land Transfer Ordinance 1920–1921 contained that all land transactions (other than leases for a term of not more than three years) required an individual to obtain written consent of the British administration.[107] One of the reasons for requiring consent of the administration was to prevent the aggregation of large estates, as would typically be the case with *waqf* territory.[108] The consent of the administration was one of the concerns expressed by the Zionist Commission, and instigated by previous British experience in Iraq. Also, aggregating large estates would go against the British self-declared aim to promote a market in land.[109] The granting of such absolute powers to the British administration was highly criticized by the indigenous Palestinian population.[110] Palestinian landowners demanded the abolishment of British administrative consent to all land transactions and desired the '*status quo ante bellum*'.[111] As one British official enquiry noted, 'The Ordinance is objected to on religious grounds. The Sharieh Law states that 'A possessor may dispose of his dispossession as he pleases' and the Land Transfer Ordinance is in direct contradiction to this.'[112] Though this

[105] Chaim Weizmann, The *Letters and Papers of Chaim Weizmann, Letter to Foreign Under-Secretary Ronald Graham*, 13 July 1919, vol. IX, edited by Meyer Wolfe Weisgal, (London: Oxford University Press, 1973), pp. 177–81, as cited by Dov Gavish, *A Survey of Palestine under the British Mandate, 1920–1948* (London; New York: Routledge Curzon, 2005), p. 37. See also Salman Abu Sitta, *Atlas of Palestine 1948*, (London: Palestine Land Society, 2004), p. 14.

[106] Dov Gavish, *A Survey of Palestine under the British Mandate, 1920–1948*, p. 26. By 'establishing claims to land' one is to be reminded that only a relatively small proportion of Palestine, less than 10 per cent, was actually acquired by Jewish land purchasers before 1948 [the creation of the State of Israel]'. Bunton, ed., 'Introduction', in *Land Legislation in Mandate Palestine*, p. viii.

[107] Bunton, 'Demarcating the British Colonial State', pp. 123–4; On the Land Transfer Ordinance and actual land transfers between 1920–1936, Omar Khamaisi, Omar, *Von Terra zu Territorium, Die Entwicklung des Bodenrechts und der Grundeigentumsverhältnisse in Palästina vom Osmanischen Reich bis zum Staate Israel* (Zürich: Zürcher Studien zur Rechtsgeschichte, Schulthess, 2001), pp. 112–19.

[108] Paragraph 3 of the Introduction to the Law states the following reasons: 'Whereas it is necessary to make measures to prevent speculative dealings in land and to protect the present occupant'. Cited after Khamaisi, *Von Terra zu Territorium*, pp. 113. While Herbert Samuel as well as succeeding High Commissioners of Mandate Palestine are repeatedly reported to have intended to protect the Palestinian population from loss of landed property, the laws passed have nevertheless in effect facilitated expropriation of Palestinian lands for the establishment of Zionist aims. Khamaisi, *Von Terra zu Territorium*, p. 110.

[109] Bunton, 'Demarcating the British Colonial State', pp. 123–4.

[110] On British Mandate legislation on territory and Palestinian (Muslim, Christian, Druze) dissent, Khamaisi, *Von Terra zu Territorium*, pp. 108–45.

[111] Bunton, 'Demarcating the British Colonial State', p. 125.

[112] 'Land Settlement Commission's Report' CO 733/18/(611) as cited by Bunton, 'Demarcating the British Colonial State', p. 125.

land law was revised in the following year, the succeeding land laws were similar in that they kept Palestinian land rights as narrowly as possible.[113] When the state of Israel was created in 1948, *waqf* land was estimated to comprise a sixth of the country.[114] The large-scale transfer of *waqf* land, meant to be held in perpetuity, went first to British then to Israeli control through various legal mechanisms, and accelerated since the creation of the state of Israel in 1948, or *nakba* (Arabic: the catastrophe).[115] This also included the demolishing of *waqf* property, especially in and around Jerusalem.[116] The state of Israel marshalled a series of legislation that allowed Israeli authorities to confiscate *waqf* territory, to deny Muslim jurisdiction over them, with the effect of depriving the Muslim community from benefiting from the socio-economic infrastructure of the endowments.[117] To this end, Israel reformulated regulations which had been devised in 1939 by the British for wartime conditions, as the 1949 Emergency Regulations on Property of Absentees, subsequently the Absentees Property Law 1950.[118] This law was also imposed on territory and assets of *waqf*.[119] A Custodian of Absentee Property was instituted, similar to the preceding Mandate Custodian of Enemy Property by the British.[120] Property abandoned by Palestinian refugees, or even internally displaced persons,[121] passed into the control of the new Israeli administration, with the confiscation of two million *dunams* (one *dunam* equals 1000 square metres) to the Custodian, who later transferred the land to the Israeli Development Authority. Land in *waqf* ownership

[113] Bunton, 'Demarcating the British Colonial State', p. 128; Bunton cautions not to consider British colonial land policy as coherent but rather ad hoc, driven by domestic and external pressures. In 1940, The [British] High Commissioner was eventually given general powers to prohibit and regulate all transfers of land under the terms of the 1940 land transfer regulations, See Bunton, ed., 'Introduction', in *Land Legislation in Mandate Palestine*, p. x.

[114] Michael Dumper, *Islam and Israel: Muslim Religious Endowments and the Jewish State* (Washington, D.C.: Institute for Palestine Studies, 1994), p. X.

[115] Centrally on whether the British land tenure system of Mandate Palestine facilitated the land transfer from Palestinian Arabs to Zionist Jews, Aida Asim Essaid, *Zionism and Land Tenure in Mandate Palestine* (London; New York: Routledge, 2014).

[116] The Israeli authorities provoked the anger of many Muslims, in and outside of Palestine, by demolishing *waqf* property west of al-Aqsa. Included in the demolition were 130 historical homes in the Maghribi district, two mosques–including Masjid al-Buraq, named after the steed used by the Prophet Muhammad on his miʿrāj (nightjourney) and zāwiyah-schools, as well as tombs and other buildings with religious significance. Israeli authorities argued that this was done to create open space around the Wailing Wall to accommodate Jewish worshipers. The demolitions was perceived as an effort to eradicate monuments of Islamic history and civilization: Rouhi al-Khatib, *Taḥwīd madinat al-Quds (Judaizing the city of Jerusalem)* (Amman: Wizarat al-Awqaf, 1979), p. 26; Mahmud al-Abidi, *Qudsuna (Our Jerusalem)* (Cairo: Matba'atal-Jabalawi, 1972), p. 19; Muhammad Ali Abu Hamda, *Al-Masjid al-Aqsa l-mubarak wa ma yataḥaddaduhum inḥafriyyāt al-Yahūd (The blessed Aqsa mosque and the Jewish excavations that threaten it)* (Amman: M aktabata l-Risalaa l-Haditha, 1982), p. 56. Yvonne Haddad, 'Islamists and the 'Problem of Israel': The 1967 Awakening', *Middle East Journal* 46, no. 2 (Spring, 1992): pp. 276–7.

[117] Haitam Sulaiman and Robert Home, 'God is an Absentee, too: The Treatment of Wakf Land in Israel/Palestine', *Journal of Legal Pluralism* 59 (2009): p. 65. On Israeli state legislation on landed property successively excluding Palestinian ownership from 1948 to 1969 see Khamaisi, *Von Terra zu Territorium*, pp. 153–84.

[118] A detailed discussion of The Absentees Property Law from 1950, Khamaisi, *Von Terra zu Territorium*, pp. 166–71.

[119] Khamaisi, *Von Terra zu Territorium*, pp. 168, with further references.

[120] Sulaiman and Home, 'God is an Absentee, too', p. 55.

[121] Khamaisi, *Von Terra zu Territorium*, p. 167, with further references.

also passed from Muslim-Palestinian hands to the Custodian, since Israel did not distinguish between *waqf* property and other land. The Custodian of Absentee Property claimed *waqf* property stating that the Supreme Muslim Council had become an 'absentee' (most of its members becoming refugees in 1948).[122] Thus the Custodian was a conduit through which land passed to the Israeli Development Authority, and later the Israel Land Authority, in effect as a means of 'laundering' confiscated Palestinian land.[123] The Absentee Law 1950 prohibited the *sharīʿa* court from supervising *waqf* property, while the Israeli high court held, in *Habab v the Custodian over Absentee Property (58/54)* that the Custodian was neither a trustee of the properties, nor responsible for their management; and the absentee was not entitled to take legal action against the Custodian.[124]

All this was not only a question of Israeli law but, more importantly, of public international law. Crucially, Palestinians saw international law fail them twice on safeguarding their territory. First, by creating a Jewish state in 1948 on their territory against their wish through a UN-GA resolution[125] (leaving them without legal options against this resolution) and second, by international law authorizing Israel to rule the rest of Palestinian territory and people through the normative regime of occupation from 1967 onwards, leading to confiscation and annexation of territory. Both acts of international law effectively expropriated Palestinians. By the year 1988, Palestinians meanwhile saw they were made not only stateless but also almost landless. They reassessed history, went back to ʿUmar al-Khaṭṭāb's example in acquiring land, and turned concepts of acquisition of land into concepts to resist foreign domination as well as to take a dissenting position towards international law that authorized dividing Palestine against the wishes of its indigenous inhabitants,[126] and thereby expropriating them, and pressured its leadership into giving up territory. In 1988 Hamas issued its charter that says in Part Three (Strategies and Methods), clause 11:

'The Islamic Resistance Movement believes that the land of Palestine has been an Islamic Waqf throughout the generations and until the Day of Resurrection, no one can

[122] Israel took recourse to colonial legal structures as the Supreme Muslim Council was established in 1922 under British rule to manage Muslim affairs, especially *waqf* territory, Huneidi, *A Broken Trust*, p. 146.

[123] Sulaiman and Home, 'God is an Absentee, too', p. 55.

[124] Ibid.

[125] The United Nations General Assembly voted for the partition of Palestine into a Jewish and an Arab state in Resolution 181, passed on November 29, 1947. http://www.un.org/en/ga/search/view_doc.asp?symbol=A/RES/181(II).

[126] Both before and after the General Assembly passing the UN partition plan, the United Nations must have been at least insecure if the UN partition plan of Palestine was in accordance with the UN Charter. The General Assembly almost requested an advisory opinion from International Court of Justice in 1947. Only by a majority of one did a subcommittee of the General Assembly of the United Nations voted not to submit a request for an Advisory Opinion to the International Court of Justice. The question under consideration was as follows: 'Whether the United Nations, or any of its Member States, is competent to enforce or recommend the enforcement of any proposal concerning the constitution and future government of Palestine, in particular, *any plan of partition which is contrary to the wishes, or adopted without the consent of, the inhabitants of Palestine.* U.N. GAOR Ad Hoc Comm. on the Palestinian Question, Annex 25, at 300-ox, U.N. Doc. A/AC.14/3z and Add. 1 (1947).' Nabil Elaraby, 'Some Legal Implications of the 1947 Partition Plan and the 1949 Armistice Agreements', *Law and Contemporary Problems* 33, no. 1 (Winter, 1968): pp. 97–109, 101; The plan to partition Palestine met further faults and objections based on legal, moral and political grounds, as voiced during the 1930s and 1940s, see Victor Kattan, 'Palestine

renounce it or part of it, or abandon it or part of it. No Arab country nor the aggregate of all Arab countries, and no Arab King or President nor all of them in the aggregate, have that right, nor has that right any organization or the aggregate of all organizations, be they Palestinian or Arab, because Palestine is an Islamic Waqf throughout all generations and to the Day of Resurrection. Who can presume to speak for all Islamic generations to the Day of Resurrection? This is the status [of the land] in Islamic Sharī'a, and it is similar to all lands conquered by Islam by force, and made thereby Waqf lands upon their conquest, for all generations of Muslims until the Day of Resurrection. This [norm] has prevailed since the commanders of the Muslim armies completed the conquest of Syria and Iraq, and they asked the Caliph of Muslims, 'Umar Ibn al-Khattab, for his view of the conquered land, whether it should be partitioned between the troops or left in the possession of its population, or otherwise. Following discussions and consultations between the Caliph of Islam, 'Umar Ibn al-Khattab, and the Companions of the Messenger of Allah, be peace and prayer upon him, they decided that the land should remain in the hands of its owners to benefit from it and from its wealth; but the control of the land and the land itself ought to be endowed as a Waqf [in perpetuity] for all generations of Muslims until the Day of Resurrection. The ownership of the land by its owners is only one of usufruct, and this Waqf will endure as long as Heaven and earth last. Any demarche in violation of this law of Islam, with regard to Palestine, is baseless and reflects on its perpetrators.'[127]

The tension between the imperial past that aimed at hegemony and the present critiquing hegemony today is inherent in this passage. The passage refers to the rules of acquisition of land under early imperial times, and yet uses it as a dissident voice against the international legal order. The 'inherited normative'[128] comes back, and again joined *fay'and waqf* doctrines to communalize and immobilize land, once to expand land, now used as defence against a land-grab of region. This passage captures the imperial–dissident divide of Islamic International Law on questions of territory. By doing so, the clause relates to what makes *waqf* so sensitive as a legal concept, namely that a *waqf* is established in perpetuity, as an inalienable trust that is irrevocable. [129] Normatively speaking, there is no right of withdrawal in a

and International Law: An Historical Overview', in *The Palestine Question in International Law*, edited by Victor Kattan (London: British Institute of International and Comparative Law, 2008), p. xxxiii–xxxix.

[127] 'Charter of the Islamic Resistance Movement (Hamas) of Palestine', *Journal of Palestine Studies* 22, no. 4, (Summer, 1993): pp. 126–7.

[128] Martii Koskenniemi, 'Histories of International Law: Significance and Problems for a Critical View', *Temple International & Comparative Law Journal* (2013): p. 216. Writing on the inherited narratives of contemporary Public International Law and the dilemma their existence poses, Koskenniemi says, p. 224: 'The history of international law seems poised between two alternatives. Either to operate with the inherited vocabularies and seek to deal with the problems that arise from their association with dubious political causes as best one can, or to reject those vocabularies outright, and then to seek to replace them with something more congenial. Each alternative has an aspect of reductionism that makes it hard to recommend them as prima facie better or worse. Each has vital lessons to give to but also the propensity to turn into an intellectual trap, blinding adherents to history's ironies and ruptures, its counter-intuitive turns and contradictions.' This surely is applicable also to the Islamic history of International Law.

[129] Hennigan, *The Birth of an Institution*, (Leiden: Brill, 2004), p.xiii; Herbert J. Liebesny, *The Law of the Near and Middle East* (Albany: State University of New York Press, 1975), p. 226.

waqf.[130] The clause entails three dissident messages. First, this clause is an attack on the own Arab and Palestinian leadership seen as under pressure or tempted to negotiate away Palestinian territory. Second, it can also be read as a message to those immediately responsible for the foreign domination of Palestinian land, namely that their possession of Palestine is not to find acceptance by the original inhabitants and owners of the land. Third, it contains a message to the international community, namely that the joined *fay-waqf* doctrine is not only an inward-looking doctrine but the international community should not accept conquest as a means of appropriating territory *today*. Read this way, the statement is in fact not dissident, but a supportive reading of modern international law which prohibits conquest of land by force, annexation, and prolonged occupation. Dissent this way is then rather a way of manoeuvring between the 'inherited narratives' and the ideas of international law as utopia. Hamas' stance is modernist, in that it seeks to justify a present-day concern with referencing it back to the Islamic precedent, a technique that could be labelled as 'presentism'; the technique of referencing a contemporary problem back to past sources has not been used by pre-modern Muslim scholars,[131] not even in the case of the scholars of Algeria under French colonial rule. Arguably, whether Palestine has always had *waqf* status need not be judged by the strict measures of historiography that considers anachronism and presentism to be 'mortal sins' of its field.[132] However, more importantly, the 1988 clause should itself be read as a historic text. For the Cambridge school of intellectual history associated with Quentin Skinner, legal, philosophical, or political texts should not be read as sources of timeless truths or authoritative statements about fundamental concepts. In order to understand a particular statement, the historian needs to reconstruct what its author (here Hamas) was doing in making that statement, writing that text. Skinner's methodological positioning stresses the role of texts, including texts that made normative truth claims, as political interventions in particular social contexts and political power struggles.[133] Therefore, the statement is best read as an argument of international law, as an intervention in power struggles. The passage formulates dissent from international law by reverting to a reading of history that calls for disobedience to international law as formulated post-Second World War. Significantly, the passage reacts to the anachronism of the present, where the ongoing accumulation of landed property for the one is the accumulation of dispossession of the

[130] Aḥmad b. Khaṣṣāf, 'Umar (d. 874 or 875) *Aḥkām al-Awqāf* [Rules on CharitableTrusts] (Cairo: Maṭba'at Dīwān 'Umūm al-Awqāf al-Miṣrīyah, 1322, 1904), p. 248.

[131] Not even in the early third century was discourse on waqf in its relationship to other legal categories done with any reference to the past, original sources. Hennigan, *The Birth of an Institution*, p. 187.

[132] See Koskenniemi's engagement with the benefits and limits of contextualism, Koskenniemi, 'Histories of International Law', p. 227.

[133] See for example Quentin Skinner, 'Meaning and Understanding in the History of Ideas', *History and Theory* 8, no. 1 (1969): p. 3; Quentin Skinner, 'Interpretation and the Understanding of Speech Acts', in *Visions of Politics: Volume I, Regarding Method* (Cambridge: Cambridge University Press, 2002), p. 103. A nuanced reading of the meaning of anachronism for the study of international legal history, Anne Orford, 'On International Legal Method', *London Review of International Law* 1, no. 1 (2013): pp. 170–7.

other. The clause can be read as a response to the failure of post-Second World War international law to normatively protect the integrity of territory.

The case of Palestine is an example for an exegetical derivation of Islamic legal rules and institutions from an imperial distant, that re-emerged as an authoritative stance on dissenting from international law. It is an interpretation of history to fit dramatically new contexts, not only of foreign domination but of systematic, ongoing territorial expropriation.[134]

The *Palestine is waqf* theme, to what extent *waqf* territory has previously changed ownership, and importantly, what this says about land rights today, is surely disputed and reflects the question whether there is or ought to be Palestinian or Israeli ownership over territory. The narrative carries a dissident discourse within the Islamic and Arabic tradition that creates a compelling form of 'authenticity',[135] and hence 'persuasive' legitimacy, for the idea that Palestine cannot be conceded to foreign domination through conquest today, and *waqf* cannot be expropriated to destroy the Palestinian fabric. In fact, the *Palestine is waqf* narrative has since been taken up also by Palestinian groups and individuals that have a secular outlook, as well as by the Palestinian Authority, and by Islamic legal and political authorities outside of Palestine.[136] The fact that the theme of Palestine as *waqf* generated so much overwhelming resonance supports the dissident bent described here. The 'all of Palestine is *waqf*' motto mirrors a critical, albeit disillusioned, engagement with international law. Hamas thought and practice stems not solely from an historical past. It is anchored in the current reality of the dominance of an enforced system of prolonged occupation and annexation that should direct the attention of the observer to the existence and value of alternative frameworks which continue in its shadow.[137]

Conclusion

Islamic international law functions in both imperial and dissident modes. Islamic law beyond revelation largely operates as precedent-based 'jurists' law'.[138] Imperial precedent is diverse and imperial interpretations exist in books and in discourses,

[134] On why we examine inherited legal concepts today, Martti Koskenniemi aptly refers to Hans-Georg Gadamer: 'History is only present to us in light of our futurity.' Hans-Georg Gadamer, *Philosophical Hermeneutics*, edited and translated by David E. Linge (Oakland, Calif.: University of California Press, 1976), as cited in Martti Koskenniemi, 'Histories of *Philosophical Hermeneutics* International Law: Significance and Problems for a Critical View', *Temple International & Comparative Law Journal* (2013): p. 230.

[135] Hennigan recalls the voice of 'authenticity' when Muslim jurists' first legally shaped the meaning of waqf, Hennigan, *The Birth of an Institution* (2004), p. 187. This discourse was particularly necessary as questions of waqf (trust) circumvented the laws of bequests and inheritance (*'ilm al-farā'id*).

[136] Yitzhak Reiter, '"All of Palestine is holy Muslim Waqf Land": A Myth and its Roots', in *Law, Custom and Statute in the Muslim World*, edited by Ron Shaham (Leiden: Brill, 2007), pp. 173–97, 196. Reiter studies the historical status of Palestine as waqf, denying Palestine this status.

[137] Samantha May, 'God's Land: Blurring the National and the Sacred in Waqf Territory', *Politics, Religion & Ideology* 15, no. 3 (2014): pp. 421–41, 426.

[138] Joseph Schacht, *An Introduction to Islamic Law* (Oxford: Clarendon Press, 1964), pp. 5, 209. One should note that many of Schacht's views in this seminal work are now generally considered to be dated; this, however, does not apply to the characterization of Islamic law as jurists' law.

as they cannot be abolished like statute. With no ultimate Islamic legal or religious authority to give its ultimate interpretive seal, Islamic law is whatever is given authority and legitimacy to by Muslims at a given time.

For the imperial mode of law, the link and debates between conquest, property, and taxation need be revisited with a view to the rules of Islamic international law. The Qur'ān clearly specifies that movable and immovable booty should be divided among those who take part in the conquest, including territory. There is historical precedent that the Prophet acted upon this. This legal and historical legacy is one that needs to be reckoned with in the past and present of Islamic international law. However, importantly, caliph ʿUmar crucially decided to not distribute the land of Iraq among the victorious warriors, but to impose a land tax (*al-kharāj*) as a substitute, and thereby kept the land fabric intact. With this we find caliph ʿUmar giving priority to the common good over the text: the interest of future generations (*umma*) rather than the interest of some of them at that moment in time.[139] Caliph Umar's decision set off normative discussions over keeping territory united after conquest, for imperial purposes that benefitted all actors. Scripture and common good both serve as distinct precedence, and their relationship to each other merits a revisited discussion on problematic and productive dissonances and their meaning for international law.

For the dissident mode of law, the engagement with centuries-old jurisprudence with or against contemporary logics is a difficult one. Is this a 'past that is permanently present'?[140] If the dissenting voices draw their images from the past, it is in effect a 'present past'.[141]

To understand the dissident mode of Islamic International law, both the examples of Algeria and Palestine are important examples where trusts of landed property (*waqf*) were central targets of foreign rule to dispossess. Just as landed property became an important part of colonial discourse, so did Islamic international law concepts change in reaction, and turned charitable trusts into anti-colonial means. As an enduring visibility of the past, Islamic doctrines, institutions, and memories are being repeatedly contextualized and reaffirmed, and some contain aspects that work at odds to prevailing international law understandings, of the nineteenth or twentieth centuries. To reimagine the past and to reinterpret the future, the 'present past' is what creates the dissenting voices of international law.

Bibliography

al-ʿĀbidī, Maḥmūd. *Qudsunā (Our Jerusalem)* (Cairo: Maṭbaʿat al-Jabalāwī, 1972).

ʿAbduh, Muḥammad. *Al-Aʿmāl Al-Kāmilah*, vol. I [The Complete Works], introduced, and its authenticity verified, by Muhammad ʿImarah (Beirut: Dār-Al-Shurūq, 1993), pp. 32, 55–7, 62.

[139] For a discussion of caliph ʿUmar's decision for questions of modern common good, see Mohammad Abed Jabri, *Democracy, Human Rights and Law in Islamic Thought* (London: I.B. Tauris in association with the Center for Arab Unity Studies, 2009), p. 23.

[140] A similar concept of a present past is voiced by Evans and Philips: 'Time is layered upon time so that one buried layer of history seeps through to the one above ... the cumulative impact of these different layers is a past that is permanently present.' Evans and Phillips, *Algeria: Anger of the Dispossessed*, p. 25.

[141] May, 'God's Land', p. 426.

ʿAbduh, Muḥāmmad. *Al-Thāʾir al-Islāmī Jamāl al-Dīn al-Afghānī* [The Islamic Revolutionary Jamal al-Din al-Afghani] (Cairo: Dar al-Hilal, 1973), pp. 46–113.

Abou El Fadl, Khaled. 'Islamic Law and Muslim Minorities: The Juristic Discourse on Muslim Minorities from the Second/Eighth to the Eleventh/Seventeenth Centuries'. *Islamic Law and Society* 1, no. 2 (1994): pp. 141–87.

Abou El Fadl, Khaled. 'The Unbounded Law of God and Territorial Boundaries'. In *States, Nations and Borders: The Ethics of Making Boundaries*, edited by Allen Buchanan and Margaret Moore (Cambridge: Cambridge University Press, 2003), pp. 214–27.

Abu Ḥamda, Muḥammad ʿAlī. *Al-Masjid al-Aqṣā al-mubārak wa mā yataḥaddaduhum inḥafriyyāt al-Yahūd* (*The blessed Aqsa mosque and the Jewish excavations that threaten it*) (Amman: Makṭabat al-Risāla al-Ḥadītha, 1982).

Abu Sitta, Salman. *Atlas of Palestine, 1948* (London: Palestine Land Society, 2004).

Abun-Nasr, Jamil M. *A History of the Maghrib* (Cambridge and New York: Cambridge University Press, 1975).

Abu Zahra, Muhammad. *al-ʿAlaqāt al-dawliyya fi al-islam [International Relations in Islam]* (Cairo: al-Dār al-qawmīyya li-l-tibāʿa wa-l-nashr, 1964).

Aktham, Yaḥya b. *Kitāb al-Kharāj* (d. 818), [*Book of Taxes*] (al-Qāhirah: Makṭabat Dār al-Turāth, 1930).

Afghānī, Jamāl al-Dīn. Al-ḥarb al-ʿādilah wa al-ḥarb ghayr ʿādilah'. In Jamāl al-Dīn al-Afghānī, *Al aʿmāl al-kāmilah*, vol. II *[The Complete Works]*, edited by Muḥammad ʿAmmārah (Cairo: Dār al-Kitāb al-ʿArabī, n. d.), pp. 71–9.

Agéron, Charles-Robert. *Les Algériens musulmans et la France: 1871–1919*, vol. I (Paris: Presses Universitaires de France, 1968).

Al-Arabi, Ismail. *Al-Muqāwama al-jazāʾirīyya that liwāʾ al-amīr ʿAbd al Qādir* (Algiers: Société Nationale d'Edition, 1982).

Baderin, Mashood A. 'Muhammad al-Shaybānī' (749/50–805). In *The Oxford Handbook of the History of International Law*, edited by Bardo Fassbender and Anne Peters (Oxford: Oxford University Press, 2012), pp. 1081–5.

Baer, Gabriel. 'The Dismemberment of Waqf in Early 19th Century Jerusalem'. *Asian and African Studies* 13 (1979): pp. 220–41.

Al-Baladhūrī, Aḥmad b. Yaḥyā. *Futūḥ al-Buldān* (Beirut: Dār al-Nashr, 1957).

Al-Baladhūrī, Aḥmad b. Yaḥyā. *The Origins of the Islamic State*, 2 vols., translated by Philipp Hitti and Francis Murgotten, *Columbia University Studies in History, Economics and Public Law*, volume 68, nos. 163, 163a (New York: Columbia University Press, 1916–24).

Barnes, John Robert. *An Introduction to Religious Foundations in the Ottoman Empire* (Leiden, Brill, 1986).

Bedjaoui, Mohammed. *La Révolution Algérienne et le Droit* (Bruxelles: Editions de l'Association Internationale des Juristes Démocrates, 1961).

Benton, Lauren. *A Search for Sovereignty: Law and Geography in European Empires, 1400–1900* (Cambridge: Cambridge University Press, 2010).

Bunton, Martin. 'Demarcating the British Colonial State: Land Settlement in the Jiftlik Villages of Sajad and Qazaza'. In *New Perspectives on Property and Land in the Middle East*, edited by Roger Owen (Cambridge, MA: Harvard University Press, 2001), pp. 121–58.

Bunton, Martin. *Colonial Land Policies in Palestine, 1917–1936* (Oxford; New York: Oxford University Press, 2007).

Bunton, Martin, ed. 'Introduction'. In *Land Legislation in Mandate Palestine*, vol. 1 (Cambridge: Cambridge University Press, 2009), pp. vii, x.

Burgis, Michelle. 'Faith in the State? Traditions of Territoriality, International Law and the Emergence of the Modern Arab State'. *Journal of the History of International Law* 11 (2009): pp. 37–79.

Clancy-Smith, Julia. *Rebel and Saint* (Oakland, CA: University of California Press, 1994).

Clavel, Eugène. *Droit musulman. Le waqf ou habous d'après la doctrine et la jurisprudence (rites hanafite et malékite)*, vol. 1 (Cairo: Diemer, 1986).

'Charter of the Islamic Resistance Movement (Hamas) of Palestine'. *Journal of Palestine Studies* 22, no. 4 (Summer, 1993): pp. 126–7.

Daase, Christian and Deitelhoff, Nina. 'Zur Rekonstruktion globaler Herrschaft aus dem Widerstand' (Working Paper 1, 2014), pp. 1–26. dissidenz.net/networkingpapers/wp1-2014-daase-deitelhoff.pdf.

Danziger, Raphael. *Abd el-Kader and the Algerians: Resistance to the French and International Consolidation* (New York: Africana Publishing Company, 1977).

Darwin, John. *After Tamerlane, The Global History of Empire since 1405* (Allen Lane: London, 2007).

Dāwūd, Abu. *Sunan*, 5 vols. (Beirut: Dār b. Hazm, 1997).

Donner, Fred. *The Early Islamic Conquests* (Princeton: Princeton University Press, 1981).

Dumper, Michael. *Islam and Israel: Muslim Religious Endowments and the Jewish State* (Washington, D.C.: Institute for Palestine Studies, 1994).

Elaraby, Nabil. 'Some Legal Implications of the 1947 Partition Plan and the 1949 Armistice Agreements'. *Law and Contemporary Problems* 33, no. 1 (Winter, 1968): pp. 97–109.

Emon, Anver M. 'On Sovereignties in Islamic Legal History'. *Middle East Law and Governance* 4 (2012): pp. 265–305.

Essaid, Aida Asim. *Zionism and Land Tenure in Mandate Palestine* (London; New York: Routledge, 2014).

Etienne, Bruno. *Abd-el-Kader* (Paris: Hachette, 1994).

Evans, Martin and John Phillips. *Algeria, Anger of the Dispossessed* (New Haven, Conn.; London: Yale University Press, 2007).

Fadel, Mohammad. 'International Law, Regional Developments: Islam'. MPEPIL, edited by Rüdiger Wolfrum (2010), online edition, margin nos 46–49, 52. Available at <http://www.mpepil.com>.

Forand, Paul G. 'The Status of the Land and Inhabitants of the Sawad during the First Two Centuries of Islām'. *Journal of the Economic and Social History of the Orient* 14, no. 1 (April 1971): pp. 25–37.

Freamon, Bernard K. 'Definitions and Conceptions of Slave Ownership in Islamic Law'. In *The Legal Understanding of Slavery: From the Historical to the Contemporary*, edited by Jean Allain (Oxford: Oxford University Press, 2012), pp. 40–60.

Fuad Köprülü, Mehmet. 'L'institution du Vakouf: Sa nature juridique et son évolution historique'. *Vakiflar Dergisi* 2, no. 3 (1942): French section, p. 3.

Gadamer, Hans-Georg. *Philosophical Hermeneutics*, edited and translated by David E. Linge (Oakland, Calif.: University of California Press, 1976).

Gavish, Dov. *A Survey of Palestine under the British Mandate, 1920–1948* (London; New York: Routledge Curzon, 2005).

Gutas, Dimitri. *Greek Thought, Arabic Culture. The Graeco-Arabic Translation Movement in Baghdad and early ʿAbbasid society (2nd–4th/8th–10th century)* (Routledge: London, 1998).

Haddad, Yvonne. 'Islamists and the 'Problem of Israel': The 1967 Awakening'. *Middle East Journal* 46, no. 2 (Spring, 1992): pp. 266–85.

Hallaq, Wael. 'Can the Sharia be Restored?'. In *Islamic Law and the Challenges of Modernity*, edited by Yvonne Yazbeck Haddad and Barbara Freyer Stowasser (Walnut Creek, Calif.: Altamira, 2004), pp. 21–53.

Hallaq, Wael. *Sharīʿa: Theory, Practice, Transformations* (Cambridge: Cambridge University Press, 2009).

Hashmi, Sohail. 'Political Boundaries and Moral Communities: Islamic Perspectives'. In *States, Nations and Borders: The Ethics of Making Boundaries*, edited by Allen Buchanan and Margaret Moore (Cambridge: Cambridge University Press, 2003), pp. 199, 200–1.

Hennigan, Peter G. *The Birth of a Legal Institution: The Formation of the Waqf in Third-Century A.H. Hanafi Legal Discourse* (Leiden: Brill, 2004).

Ibn Hishām, 'Abd al-Mālik. *Sīrat al-Nabī*, vol. 3 [The Biography of the Prophet], edited by Muḥammad Khalīl Harrās (Cairo: Maktabat al-Jumhūriyya, 1971).

Hourani, Albert. *A History of the Arab Peoples* (Cambridge, Mass.: Belknap Press of Harvard University Press, 1991).

Hoyland, Robert. *Seeing Islam as Others Saw It: A Survey and Evaluation of Christian, Jewish, and Zoroastrian Writings of Early Islam* (Princeton, N.J.: The Darwin Press Inc., 1997).

Ibn Isḥāq, Muhammad. *Sirat rasul Allah* (*The Life of Muhammad*), translated by Alfred Guillaume (Karachi: Oxford University Press, 1990).

Huneidi, Sahar. *A Broken Trust: Sir Herbert Samuel, Zionism and the Palestinians 1920-1925* (London; New York: I.B. Tauris, 2001).

Jabri, Mohammad Abed. *Democracy, Human Rights and Law in Islamic Thought* (London: I.B. Tauris in association with the Center for Arab Unity Studies, 2009).

Johansen, Baber. *The Islamic Law on Land Tax and Rent* (London; New York: Croom Helm; New York: Methuen, 1988).

Johansen, Baber. 'Territorial Concepts in Islamic Law'. In *The Oxford International Encyclopaedia of Legal History*, vol. 5, edited by Stanley Katz (Oxford: Oxford University Press, 2009), pp. 451–4.

'JURIST', 'Waqf', *The Muslim World* 4, no. 2 (April, 1914): pp.173–8.

Kattan, Victor. 'Palestine and International Law: An Historical Overview'. In *The Palestine Question in International Law*, edited by Victor Kattan (London: British Institute of International and Comparative Law, 2008).

Keddie, Nikki R. *An Islamic Response to Imperialism: Political and Religious Writings of Sayyid Jamal ad-Din 'al-Afghani* (Berkeley: University of California Press, 1968).

Kennedy, Hugh. *The Great Arab Conquests, How the Spread of Islam Changed the World We Live In* (London: Weidenfeld & Nicolson, 2007).

Kennedy, Hugh. *The Early Abbasid Caliphate: A Political History* (London: Croom Helm; Totowa, N.J.: Barnes & Noble, 1981).

Kennedy, Hugh. *The Armies of the Caliphs: Military and Society in the Early Islamic State* (London; New York: Routledge, 2001).

Khamaisi, Omar. *Von Terra zu Territorium, Die Entwicklung des Bodenrechts und der Grundeigentumsverhältnisse in Palästina vom Osmanischen Reich bis zum Staate Israel* (Zürich: Zürcher Studien zur Rechtsgeschichte, Schulthess, 2001).

Khaṣṣāf, Aḥmad b. 'Umar (d. 874 or 875) *Aḥkām al-Awqāf* [Rules on CharitableTrusts] (Cairo: Maṭba'at Dīwān 'Umūm al-Awqāf al-Miṣrīyah, 1322, 1904).

Koskenniemi, Martti. 'Histories of International Law: Significance and Problems for a Critical View'. *Temple International and Comparative Law Journal* 27, no. 2 (2013): p. 216.

Kozlowski, Gregory C. *Muslim Endowments and Society in British India.* (Cambridge: Cambridge University Press, 1985).

Li, Darryl. 'Jihad in a World of Sovereigns: Law, Violence and Islam in the Bosnia Crisis'. *Law and Social Inquiry, Journal of the American Bar Foundation* 41 (Spring 2016): pp. 371–401.

Liebesny, Herbert J. *The Law of the Near and Middle East* (Albany: State University of New York Press, 1975).

Løkkegaard, Frede. *Islamic Taxation in the Classical Period with Special Reference to Circumstances in Iraq* (Copenhagen: Branner & Korch, 1950).
Mameur, Andre. *La Chefa* (Paris: Librairie du Recueil Sirey, 1910).
Mannā', 'Adil. *Liwā' al-Kuds fi awāsiṭ al-'ahd al-'uthmānī: Al-Idārah wa al-mujtama' mundhu awāsiṭ al-qārn al-thāmin 'ashar ḥattā ḥamlat Muḥammad 'Alī Bāshā sanat 1831 [The District of Jerusalem in the Mid-Ottoman Period: Administration and Society, from the Mid-18th Century to the Campaign of Muhammad 'Ali Pasha in 1831]* (Beirut: Institute for Palestine Studies, 2008).
Marsham, Andrew. 'Fay". Encyclopaedia of Islam, THREE. Edited by Kate Fleet, Gudrun Krämer, Denis Matringe, John Nawas, and Everett Rowson (Leiden: Brill Online, 2015).
May, Samantha. 'God's Land: Blurring the National and the Sacred in Waqf Territory'. *Politics, Religion & Ideology* 15, no. 3 (2014): pp. 421–41.
Al-Māwardī. *al-Aḥkām al-sulṭāniyya* (Constitutiones Politicae), edited by M. Enger (Bonn: Adolphus Marcus, 1853).
Medici, Anna Maria. 'Waqfs of Cyrenaica and Italian Colonialism in Libya (1911–41)'. In *Held in Trust. Pious Foundations, Founders, and Beneficiarie*, edited by Pascale Ghazaleh (Cairo: AUC Press, 2011), pp. 190–218.
Morimoto, Kosei. *The fiscal administration of Egypt in the early Islamic period* (Kyoto: Dohosha, 1981).
Moses, Dirk A. 'Empire, Colony, Genocide: Keywords and the Philosophy of History'. In *Empire, Colony, Genocide. Conquest, Occupation and Subaltern Resistance in World History*, edited by Dirk A. Moses (London; New York: Berghahn Books, 2008), p. 4.
Oberauer, Norbert. 'Early Doctrines on Waqf Revisited: The Evolution of Islamic Endowment Law in the 2nd Century AH'. *Islamic Law and Society* 20, no. 1–2 (2013): pp. 1–47.
Orford, Anne. 'On International Legal Method'. *London Review of International Law* 1, no. 1 (2013): pp. 170–7.
Peters, Rudolph. *Islam and Colonialism, The Doctrine of Jihad in Modern History* (The Hague: Mouton Publishers, 1979).
Peters, Rudolph. *Jihad in Classical and Modern Islam: A Reader* (Princeton, N.J.: Markus Wiener Publishers, 1996).
Powers, David S. 'Orientalism, Colonialism, and Legal History: The Attack on Muslim Family Endowments in Algeria and India'. *Comparative Studies in Society and History* 31, no. 3 (July, 1989): pp. 535–71.
Qudāma, Ibn Ja'far (d. 922). *Kitāb al-Kharāj* [Book of Charitable Trusts], translated by A. Ben Shemesh (Leiden: E. J. Brill, 1965).
Reiter, Yitzhak. *Islamic Endowments in Jerusalem under British Mandate* (London: Cass, 1996).
Reiter,Yitzhak. "All of Palestine is Holy Muslim Waqf Land': A Myth and its Roots'. In *Law, Custom and Statute in the Muslim World*, edited by Ron Shaham (Leiden: Brill, 2007), pp. 173–97.
Riḍā, Rashīd Muḥammad. 'Al-jihād fi-l Islam'. *Al-Manār* 15 (Cairo, 1912): pp. 33–40.
al-Khatīb, Rouḥī. *Taḥwīd madīnat al-Quds (Judaizing the city of Jerusalem)* (Amman: Wizārat al-Awqāf, 1979).
Ruedy, John. *Land Policy in Colonial Algeria: The Origins of the Rural Public Domain* (Berkeley and Los Angeles: University of California Press, 1967).
Sanjuán, Alejandro Garciá. *Till God Inherits the Earth, Islamic Pious Endowments in al-Andalus (9–15th Centuries)* (Leiden: Brill, 2007).
Schacht, Joseph. *An Introduction to Islamic Law* (Oxford: Clarendon Press, 1964).

Schmucker, Werner. *Untersuchungen zu einigen wichtigen bodenrechtlichen Konsequenzen der islamischen Eroberungsbewegung* (Bonn: Selbsverlag des Orientalischen Seminars der Universität Bonn, 1972).

Shahin, Emad-ud-Din. *Through Muslim Eyes: M. Rashid Rida and the West* (Herndon, VA.: The International Institute of Islamic Thought, 1993), pp. 75–87.

Shaltūt, Maḥmūd. *al-Daʿwa al-muḥammadīyya wa-l-qitāl fil-islām [Muhammad's Mission and Warfare in Islam]* (Cairo: al-Maṭbaʿa al-ṣalafīyya, 1933).

Shaltūt, Maḥmūd. *al-Quʾrān waʾl-qitāl [The Quran and Warfare]* (Nazareth: Maṭbaʿat al-naṣr wa makṭab ittiḥād al-sharq, 1948).

al-Shaybānī, Muḥammad b. al-Ḥasan. *Kitāb al-Hujja ʿalā ahl al-madīna*, 4 vols. (Beirut: ʿĀlam al-Kutub, undated, reprint of the Haiderabad edition 1965–71 [1385–90]).

Simonsen, Jørgen Bæk. *Studies in the Genesis and Early Development of the Caliphal Taxation System with Special References to Circumstances in the Arab Peninsula, Egypt and Palestine* (Copenhagen: Akademisk Forlag, 1988).

Skinner, Quentin. 'Meaning and Understanding in the History of Ideas'. *History and Theory* 8, no. 1 (1969): pp. 3–53.

Skinner, Quentin. 'Interpretation and the Understanding of Speech Acts'. In *Visions of Politics: Volume I, Regarding Method* (Cambridge: Cambridge University Press, 2002), pp. 103–27.

Sulaiman, Haitam and Robert Home. 'God is an Absentee, too: The Treatment of Waqf Land in Israel/Palestine'. *Journal of Legal Pluralism* 59 (2009): pp. 49–67.

al-Ṭabarī, Abū Jaʿfar Muḥammad (d. 923). *Taʾrīkh al-rusul wa-l-mulūk*, 15 vols, edited by Michael Jan de Goeje et al. (Leiden: Brill, 1879–1901).

al-Ṭabarī, Abū Jaʿfar Muḥammad (d. 923). *The History of al-Ṭabarī*, edited by Ehsan Yar-Shater (Albany: State University of New York Press, 1985–2007).

Al-Waqīdī, Muḥammad b. ʿUmar (d. 823) *Kitāb al-Maghāzī*, 3 vols, edited by Marsden Jones (London: Oxford University Press, 1966).

Weizmann, Chaim. *The Letters and Papers of Chaim Weizmann, Letter to Foreign Under-Secretary Ronald Graham*, 13 July 1919, vol. IX, edited by Weisgal, Meyer Wolfe (London: Oxford University Press, 1973).

Wood, Ellen Meiksins. *Empire of Capital* (London; New York: Verso, 2003, paperback 2005).

Yahaya, Nurfadzilah. *Courting Jurisdictions: Colonial Administration of Islamic Law Pertaining to Arabs in the British Straits Settlements and The Netherlands Indies, 1860–1941* (PhD dissertation, Princeton University, 2012), pp. 164–203.

Yurdusev, A. Nuri. 'The Ottoman Attitude Toward Diplomacy'. In *Ottoman Diplomacy: Conventional or Unconventional?*, edited by A. Nuri Yurdusev (New York: Palgrave Macmillan, 2004), pp. 5–35.

Yaʿqūb, Abū Yūsuf. *Kitāb al-Kharāj*, translated by E. Fagnan as *Le livre de l'impôt foncier* (Paris: Paul Geuthner, 1921).

Vaglieri, Laura Veccia. 'Khaybar', *Encyclopaedia of Islam*, vol.4 (2nd edn, Leiden: Brill, 1966), pp. 1137–8.

Zuhayli, Wahbi. *al-ʿAlaqāt al-duwalīyya fī al-islam: muqārana bi-l-qanūn al-dawlī al-ḥadīth [International Relations in Islam: a Comparison with Modern International Law]* (Beirut: Muʾassasat al-Risāla, 1981).

12

'If I forget thee, O Jerusalem'

Religion, International Law, and Jerusalem

Reut Yael Paz

If I forget thee, O Jerusalem, let my right hand forget her cunning.
If I do not remember thee, let my tongue cleave to the roof of my mouth;
If I prefer not Jerusalem above my chief joy.[1]

Psalms 137.5–6.1

Introduction

It took the Vatican no less than forty-five years to come to terms with the establishment of the Jewish State in Israel. And even then it was the initiation of a peace process between the Palestinians and Israelis during the Madrid Conference (1991) that prompted the Holy See to reconsider its non-existent relationship with Israel.[2] The monumental bilateral treaty entitled the Fundamental Agreement between the Holy See and the State of Israel was signed on 30 December 1993. Full diplomatic relationships followed a year later.

There are abundant reasons and possible explanations for the long postponement of the Vatican's acceptance of Israel. It is telling that most of the conventions signed by the Holy See since Vatican II were signed with European and/or Latin American countries 'where Catholicism, or at least Christianity, has had and continues to have considerable influence'.[3] It is inevitable that matters get more complicated with regards to the Holy Land due to the convoluted history between the Jews and Catholics.[4] Equally problematic were the concrete issues of the territorial

[1] In commemoration of the destruction of the Temple of Jerusalem, this is recited at Jewish weddings before a glass is broken.

[2] Marshal J. Berger, 'Jerusalem's Holy Sites in Israeli Law', in *Between Cultural Diversity and Common Heritage: Legal and Religious Perspectives on the Sacred Places in the Mediterranean*, edited by Silvio Ferrari and Andrea Benzo (Burlington, Vt.: Ashgate Publishers, 2014), pp. 119–54, 133.

[3] See more in Silvio Ferrari, 'The Holy See and Israel and the Conventions between States and the Church since the Vatican II Council', *Catholic University Law Review* 47, no. 2 (Winter, 1998): p. 385.

[4] It would be an understatement to say that the relationship of the Catholic Church to the Jewish people is long, convoluted and problematic. After all, until the 1960s the Church taught the doctrine

sovereignty, property rights, and tax exemptions of the Roman Catholic Church within the newly established Jewish State, and the latter's seizure of more Christian and Muslim properties in the Old City since 1967.

Briefly put, by the early 1990s—as the Fundamental Agreement seems to suggest—the Catholic Church had re-evaluated some of its earlier goals regarding the Holy Land and chosen for all intents and purposes to accept, even if not embrace, the Jewish State as a matter of fact. That the Holy See accepted the de facto existence of the Jewish State in the Holy Land does not however mean that it has given up on the possibility of direct Catholic control of the holy places and the Holy Land, or that it has abandoned its previous aspirations to establish a protectorate of the holy places. Neither should it mean that the Holy See surrendered its hope for the internationalization of the city that would ideally keep the holy places away from both Arab and Israeli sovereignty.[5] In fact, through the Fundamental Agreement, it both accepted the existence of the state of Israel and sustained its objectives about the Holy Land. The focus here is on *how* this was achieved. In other words, how did the Vatican manage to retain its abstract aspirations to keep a foothold in the holy places while tolerating the presence of the Jewish State there?

An understanding of how this was accomplished leads us to the double mention of the capitalized 'Status Quo' in Article 4 of the 1993 Fundamental Agreement,[6] that in turn points to the two earlier Ottoman *firmans* that had orchestrated the sharing of the Holy Land's holy places since 1757 and 1852 respectively.[7] More specifically, in 1852, after yet another attempt by the European empires to internationalize the holy places in Jerusalem, Bethlehem, and Nazareth, Sultan Abdul Mejid decided to uphold without alteration the concessions made to the Christian communities living in the area since 1757.[8] The sultan's decree of 1852 was the result of a careful examination conducted by a committee of lawyers appointed by the Porte (the central government of the Ottoman Empire) and which 'was meant to serve constantly and forever as a permanent rule'.[9] This—as the 1993

called 'Supersession' (or 'Replacement') which in brief terms claims that the 'Church is the heir to *all* promises that God made to Abraham.' (See Paul Charles Merkley, *Christian Attitudes towards the State of Israel* (Montreal: McGill University Press, 2001), p. 146. It was only in 1965, together with the Pope Paul VI Nostra Aetate proclamation, at Vatican II, that the Church relationship with non-Christian religions was revolutionized. See more in *Nostra Aetate: Origins, Promulgation, Impact on Jewish–Catholic Relations*, edited by Uri Bialer et al. (New Brunswick, N.J.: Transaction Publishers, 2007.)

[5] See Raymond Cohen, *Saving the Holy Sepulchre: How Rival Christians Came Together to Rescue their Holiest Shrine* (Oxford: Oxford University Press, 2008).

[6] See for instance Article 4 (1) in *Appendix I*.

[7] Following this lead, this chapter capitalizes Jerusalem's Status Quo as to avoid possible confusion with any other status quo.

[8] See more in Enrico Molinaro, *The Holy Places of Jerusalem in Middle East Peace Agreements: The Conflict between Global and State Identities* (Sussex: Sussex Academic Press, 2009), p. 36.

[9] 'Having defined the disputed places and investigated the conflicting claims, the *firman* determined that "all these places must be left in their present state." ... The 1852 *firman* represented a confirmation and clarification of the shared rights of the various communities in the Holy Places, demarcating which areas were under whose control and maintaining the time schedules to officiate in areas shared with more than one community.' Molinaro, *The Holy Places of Jerusalem in Middle East Peace Agreements: The Conflict between Global and State Identities*, pp. 36–7.

Fundamental Agreement substantiates—turned out to be the case for a very long time.

Although the Fundamental Agreement relies on this Status Quo for the first time in recent history, the emptiness of the very term 'Status Quo' is much as it was in the earlier versions,[10] Article LXII of the Treaty of Berlin (1878) and Article IX of the Treaty of Paris that concluded the Crimean War (1856).[11] The ensuing chapter examines some of the religious images that are at play in Article 4 (1) of the Fundamental Agreement by linking it to its predecessors. After discussing several theoretical/methodological issues, this chapter examines the different circumstances underlying the earlier treaties, which climaxed in Berlin when an Ottoman, Oriental, and predominantly Muslim Status Quo was first incorporated into the (Christian European) Law of Nations.

While the Fundamental Agreement confronts religious matters overtly, despite the fact that its main purpose was to settle property rights and tax-related issues,[12] the Berlin Treaty, in contrast, treats religious issues with more ambivalence and contradictions. This mirrors the contemporary *fin de siècle* context in which religion acted as the main identifying but also identity-giving element, while at the same time the political dangers inherent in a national identity based on religious affiliation were beginning to be understood. The idiosyncrasy of this clash only increases when we consider that the roots of the Berlin Conference go back to Article IX of the Treaty of Paris (1856) that concluded the Crimean War, which was the last European *religious* war fought in the modern era over the Holy Land. There is a clear causal relationship between the religious grounds for the Crimean War, the Treaty of Paris, and even the Treaty of San Stefano (1878) that paved the way for the Treaty of Berlin, and the integration of the abstract and (Oriental) Status Quo regime.

The leading hypothesis here is that it could not be sheer coincidence that the Berlin Conference, which paralleled the dawn of the international legal project, remains religiously ambivalent. The more openly religious content of the past is introduced into international law via the more abstract Status Quo. The contingent relationship between Christianity, Orientalism, and international law makes it equally fascinating that an Ottoman, Eastern, Oriental, and essentially Muslim Status Quo regime has been integrated internationally. While this amalgamation was the result above all of European requirements for a balance of power, it is nonetheless nothing short of an incredible historical phenomenon that such a Status Quo regime has been reaffirmed at the end of the twentieth century through the 1993 Fundamental Agreement between the Holy See and the Jewish State.

[10] As Enrico Molinaro discusses, neither the repetitive use of the term nor its capitalization intended 'to introduce any new regime or to create any norm'. Nor should the Status Quo be explained 'in relation to the legal principles that such a regime would imply, nor does the interpreter have any hint as to their specific contents or scope derived from an analysis of the Fundamental Agreement's provisions'. (Molinaro, *The Holy Places of Jerusalem in Middle East Peace Agreements: The Conflict between Global and State Identities*, p. 22.)

[11] See *Appendix II and III.*

[12] See for instance, Article 1 (2) and Article 2 (2) of the Fundamental Agreement, *Appendix I.*

On Matters of Theory and Method: Christian Missionarism and International Law

This chapter builds on a recent contribution I dedicated to the relationship between the 'supra-structures' of 'Religion, Secularism and International Law'.[13] That chapter unravels the interwoven, albeit asymmetrical relationship between these supra-structures. Religion generates everything essential in society. As *Émile* Durkheim phrases it, the very idea of society is 'the soul of religion'.[14] In its Western, European, Christian version it precedes secularism, which precedes but also pervades international law, one of secularism's many façades.[15]

Building on this earlier contribution's conclusions, I argue that secularism and international law actually orbit around Christianity's profound missionary impulse.[16] This missionary character remains disconcerting, even when the differences between Western Christianities are taken out of the equation.[17] After all, almost by the law of inertia, such missionarism is bound to maintain its movement in the direction of the non-Christian 'Other'. This remains true—albeit played out in different forms—for Christianity's secular heirs, international law included.[18] Hence, there is a clear Christian bias in international law, which is still to be reconciled, if not overcome altogether.[19]

In this chapter I take this a step further to examine how such Western Christian monotheism—through international law meets its 'Eastern' Other.[20] More specifically I ask how the problematic schism between 'East' and 'West' that Edward W.

[13] See more in Reut Yael Paz, 'Religion, Secularism and International Law,' in *The Oxford Handbook of International Legal Theory*, edited by Anne Orford and Florian Hofmann (Oxford: Oxford University Press, 2016).

[14] *Émile* Durkheim, *Elementary Forms of Religious life* (London: G Allen & Unwin, 1912), p. 314.

[15] As Martti Koskenniemi phrased it: 'Modern international law was born as liberal empires turned to formal annexation. But the ideological base lay in its religious critique of the Spanish empire.' Martti Koskenniemi, 'Empire and International Law: The real Spanish Contribution', *The University of Toronto Law Journal* 61, no. 1 (2011): pp. 1–36, 4.

[16] Christianity is a universal, inclusive and a 'sending' religion as the term missionarism itself indicates. (See more in David Marshall, *Communicating the Word: Revelation, Translation, and Interpretation in Christianity and Islam* (Georgetown, D.C.: Georgetown University Press, 2011), p. 42.

[17] See more in Reut Yael Paz, *A Gateway Between a Distant God and a Cruel World: The Contribution of Jewish German-Speaking Scholars to International Law* (Leiden: Brill Martinus Nijhoff Publishers, 2012).

[18] For more on the process of secularization see Mark Somos, *Secularisation and the Leiden Circle* (Leiden: Brill, 2011).

[19] For how this works from the School of Salamanca onwards see Paz, 'Religion, Secularism and International Law'.

[20] The construction of the Other here relies on the Freudian and Lacanian projection thesis for the relationship between the Western, European, masculine, Christian, and white to 'their Others'. (See, for instance, Franz Fanon, *Black Skin, White Masks* (New York: Grove Press 1967.) This suggests that the former people, at least since the age of Enlightenment, projected everything their culture considered unacceptable onto the latter. Once the intolerable cultural needs, desires and urges were disposed of, the superiority of the 'civilized, Western, European, white and Christian men' could be imagined to be sustained. (See more in Paz, *A Gateway Between a Distant God and a Cruel World*).

Said terms 'Orientalism' reveals itself in the very specific instance of the Status Quo that still governs the holy places in the Holy Land today.[21]

It is worth bearing in mind that given the infinite sources, methodological tools, previous studies, and possible research alternatives embodied in linking religion, international law and Jerusalem, it is almost impossible to discover much that is new.[22] The historically laden concept of Orientalism (and its dissenters) is not entirely helpful in narrowing the field of research, either. In fact, even the more specific focus on the Status Quo regime of Jerusalem's holy places is not enough of a limitation. The controversies linked to contemporary Status Quo-related matters also exceed the intention of this chapter.[23] Moreover, I avoid the explicit examination of the Jewish and/or Muslim complexities regarding the Temple Mount—one of the holiest places in the world—which has also been covered by the Status Quo since Moshe Dayan endorsed it in 1967. These complexities receive enough attention elsewhere.[24]

Bearing in mind Christianity's close affinity to international law (as a presumably secular, rational, and modern profession),[25] it remains more relevant to focus on the sites regarded as holy by the different Christian sects.[26] Because this cannot exclude intra-faith intricacies, the following paper is confined to briefly unpacking the religious images that loom over the 'internationalization' of an essentially Eastern, non-Christian, and 'Oriental' Status Quo regime through one article,

[21] Edward W. Said, *Orientalism* (London: Penguin Books, 2003).

[22] See for instance Nathaniel Berman, 'Legalizing Jerusalem or, of Law, Fantasy, and Faith', *Catholic University Law Review* 45 (1996): pp. 823–35; Henry Cattan, 'The Status of Jerusalem under International Law and United Nations Resolutions', *Journal of Palestine Studies* 10, no. 3 (1981): pp. 3–15; Chad F. Emmett, 'The Capital Cities of Jerusalem', *Geographical Review* 86, no. 2 (1996): pp. 233–58.

[23] There is plenty of research on Jerusalem's Status Quo. To mention but a few, see Cohen, *Saving the Holy Sepulchre: How Rival Christians Came Together to Rescue their Holiest Shrine*; Chad F. Emmett, 'The Status Quo Solution for Jerusalem', *Journal of Palestine Studies* 26, no. 2 (Winter, 1997): pp. 16–28; S. Shepard Jones, 'The Status of Jerusalem: Some National and International Aspects', *Law and Contemporary Problems* 33, no. 1, *The Middle East Crisis: Test of International Law* (Winter, 1968): pp. 169–82; and Enrico Molinaro, *The Holy Places of Jerusalem in Middle East Peace Agreements: The Conflict between Global and State Identities* (Sussex: Sussex Academic Press, 2009).

[24] See for instance Meron Benvenisti, *City of Stone: The Hidden History of Jerusalem*, (California: University of California Press, 1996).

[25] As discussed in more detail below, here I follow Martti Koskenniemi's argument, which states that the establishment of modern international law as a profession occurred after the creation of international legal associations and institutions during the last third of the nineteenth century (For the whole argument see Martti Koskenniemi, *The Gentle Civilizer of Nations* (Cambridge: Cambridge University Press, 2001)).

[26] At least since Saladin's time, the keys to the Church of the Holy Sepulchre have been kept by a Muslim family, the Nusseibehs, in order to avoid excessive brawling over but also in the church. While such Muslim custodianship was and still is essential to contain Christianities' struggles over the ownership of holiness in the Old City, these struggles by the different strands of Christianity both go beyond and deeper into the church per se. For instance, the Greeks argued with the Armenians over the division of the Virgin's Tomb; the Armenians struggled with the Syriac Jacobites over the cemetery of Mount Zion; the Orthodox fought with the Catholic over the ownership of the St Nicodemus Chapel in the church; while the Armenians competed with the Orthodox over the ownership of the churches east of the main entrance staircases; and the Copts disputed with the Ethiopians over ownership of the rooftop monasteries (Simon Sebag Montefiore, *Jerusalem* (London: Phoenix, 2012), pp. 315, 509).

Article LXII of the Berlin Treaty (1878) that then reappears, inter alia, in the Fundamental Agreement (1993).

In order to understand the dramatic aspect behind such incorporation I construct a historical paradigm through a two-fold axis (see Figure 12.1). The first axis links what could very loosely be defined the *West* together with the 'its' opposite, the Ottoman, Oriental, and Muslim *East*. The second axis links mid-nineteenth century European (Bismarck-led) *Realpolitik* and/or principle of balance of power (that includes the Berlin Conference in 1878) together with the principle of Status Quo.[27]

More concretely, the purpose here is to recognize the historical link between the Eastern Status Quo meticulously spelled out in Article LXII of the Berlin Treaty on the one hand, and on the other, the nineteenth-century imperial internationalism rooted in the profoundly fragile European balance of power that relied on avoiding another imperial war in the West. The suggestion below is two-fold: First, Otto von Bismarck's success in unifying Germany—by disrupting Europe—was later sustained through a foreign policy that established a relatively peaceful balance in Western Europe. Second, the 'butterfly-effect' consequence of this was the preservation of the holy places' Status Quo, but also the Occidental/Oriental schism that is part and parcel of Jerusalem's presence today.[28]

The holistic picture I wish to portray focuses on the Holy Land's holy places: spaces that form a perfect meridian through which both the East/West

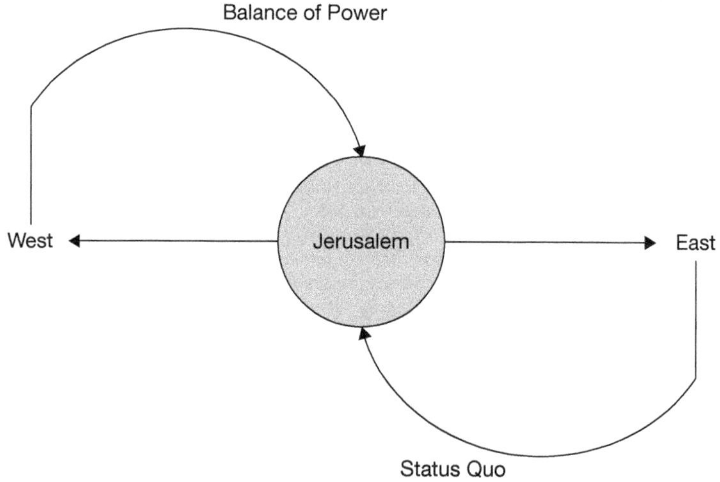

Fig. 12.1 Balance of Power and Status Quo

[27] Note that in Figure 12.1 Jerusalem stands as an abridged version of the Holy Land's holy places.

[28] According to Eric Hobsbawm, Bismarck 'remained undisputed world champion at the game of multilateral diplomatic chess for almost twenty years after 1871, [when he] devoted himself exclusively, and successfully, to maintaining peace between the powers'. (Eric Hobsbawm, *The Age of Empire: 1875–1914* (London: Weidenfeld & Nicolson, 1987)), p. 312.

axis and the Status Quo/Balance of Power axis meet. Other aspects are necessarily at play here as different and important parts that sustain the powerful relationship between the East/West and Status Quo/Balance of Power axes: the differences between the three Abrahamic religions; Orientalism that ultimately encroaches on the geneses of the pseudo-neutral term of international law; the Concert of Europe; and even the Crimean War. The history of the Status Quo can hardly be told in a linear, clear-cut, or orderly fashion, even if organized along such geometrical axes. Thus, although the narrative below starts with the historical context of the Western Balance of Power and moves to that of the Eastern Status Quo, it only underlines several important fragments that exemplify the complexities that remain central to the holy places in the Holy Land today.

Western 'Concerted' Balance of Power Meets Eastern Status Quo

The space in question here fluctuates from the 'Occident' to the 'Orient', where the remnants of the Napoleonic Wars were experienced differently. The period under scrutiny is the second part of the nineteenth century. The question on everyone's minds (especially imperial European minds) was how to inhibit the social unrest that caused the French Revolution and still lurked beneath Europe's surface.[29] The solution was thought to lie in widening and internationalizing the world in general and the East more specifically.

But the meaning of this internationalism remained an exclusively Western, imperial, and European question. The conservatives sought closer imperial networking that would restore the European balance of power necessary for the survival of the existing dynasties,[30] while the liberals hoped to change that which 'had been a sovereign's club' into 'a family of independent nations'.[31] Eventually, the conservatives took the lead and formed the European Concert. This was essentially the first union 'of the European great powers, founded on their shared willingness to engage in systematic consultation and cooperation'.[32] This does not mean

[29] It is of course impossible (and unnecessary) to define Europe here. It suffices to keep in mind the somewhat vague conceptualization of what it was understood to be Europe at the end of the nineteenth century: Europe is the physical and spiritual space that can be traced back to Greece and Rome. It was consolidated at Westphalia and then extended to other spheres of influence. In international legal terms prevalent in the nineteenth century, Europe consisted of a few Christian nations mainly in Europe and in America that made up a family of advanced nations with particular habits and ideas (See further Koskenniemi, *The Gentle Civilizer of Nations*, p. 49).

[30] As Edward Keene phrases it: 'The conservatives were quite happy with the notion that international society should take an interest in how domestic societies and political systems were organized; they had an illiberal view of what the outcome of that process should be.' (Edward Keene, *International Political Thought: An Historical Introduction* (Cambridge: Polity Press, 2005), p. 172).

[31] Adam Watson, *The Evolution of International Society* (New York: Routledge, 1992), p. 245.

[32] Watson, *The Evolution of International Society*, p. 173. Importantly, alongside the Concert securing the balance of power—or rather suppressing revolutionary and nationalist movements—was the Holy Alliance or Dreikaiserbund of 1873 in which Otto von Bismarck attempted to revive the traditional cooperation between Russia, Austria, and Prussia from 1815–54. And the Dual Alliance

that the liberal critique evaporated. Instead, a certain 'marriage of convenience' between the liberals and the conservatives developed. This marriage guaranteed an ever-growing gap between imperial Europe—where the Concert maintained its fragile balance of power—and everywhere else that was granted, whether they wanted it or not, the liberal notion of self-determination. This opened the non-European Other to both nationalism and international agendas.

In effect, by founding the Concert of Europe, the four powers—Austria, Prussia, the United Kingdom, and Russia—only augmented their importance. Swiftly, the Concert became the first exclusive club of sovereign powers. Significantly, the geo-political shift in ex-Napoleonic Europe from the 'centre' (France and Austria) to its 'margins' (Britain and Russia) heightened the importance of the expansion to the East, which was now being further appropriated through the materiality of texts, languages, and civilization.[33] Thus, from being a geographical location adjacent to Europe, the Orient conveniently became the Near East, and later, from the American perspective, the Middle East. After all, it was most useful that from a Western European perspective there is always another, more distant East for the West to find. In its wake came the consequent oppressive imperial regulations necessary to ensure that the Orient, the Levant and the 'East' by and large fitted this picture.[34]

Here Edward Said's notion of Orientalism is enlightening, even if some of the justified critique of his approach is kept in mind.[35] By now, Said's argument—that Orientalism as a complete governing structure was dictated by the European hegemons—is scarcely in dispute. Accordingly, European supremacy works through a two-fold construction: First, the Orient remained 'the place of Europe's greatest and richest and oldest colonies, the source of its civilization and languages, its cultural contestant, and one of its deepest and most recurring images of the Other'. Second, Orientalism is something that 'can be discussed and analysed as the corporate institution for dealing with the Orient—dealing with it by making statements about it, settling it, ruling over it. This way, Orientalism as a Western

(1879) originally between Austria and Germany that intended to keep Austria from further provocation of Russia, was extended later to include Italy in the Triple Alliance (1882) that included Italy. (See more in Stephen J. Lee, *Imperial Germany 1871–1918* (New York: Routledge, 2005), pp. 37–8). For more on the European Concert, see Martin Schultz, *Normen und Praxis: Das Europäische Konzert der Großmächte als Sicherheit, 1815–1860* (Munich: Oldenburg Wissenschaftsverlag, 2009).)

[33] The almost obsessive need to cement the power relationship between the Orient and Occident was made more obvious with Russia's systematic expansion of its Trans-Caspian Railroad, which encompassed Samarkand and Bokhara in 1868; the focus of Britain's foreign policy on the region following the Treaty of Chanak (1806); and Napoleon's hope of intercepting Britain's Oriental Empire in Egypt at the beginning of the nineteenth century. Said, *Orientalism*, pp. 17, 77–9.

[34] Ibid., p. 191.

[35] According to Ibn Warraq, it is problematic to accept Said's claim as it takes away any agency whatsoever from Europe's oriental Others. For more on the inherent complexities in assuming that the 'Orient East' passively accepted the heavily biased colonialist attitudes, racism, and political exploitation for over two millennia see Ibn Warraq, *Defending the West: A Critique of Edward Said's Orientalism* (Amherst, N.Y.: Prometheus Books, 2007).

style for dominating and restructuring sustains authority over the Orient.'[36] From our perspective it is significant to acknowledge how both Orientalism and international law, or in its original name the Law of European Nations, were interchangeably sought in order to Orientalize (through a Westernizing pretext) the rest of world.

The East as an international (missionary and/or legal) career

It is essential to note that exchanges between Orientalism and international law are inherent to both projects. According to Jean Allain, the nexus between the Orientalist thesis and international law is easily 'found in the use of "facts" propagated by Orientalists which allowed for the great divide to emerge in international law between "civilized nations" and "backward territories"'.[37] This is perfectly exemplified by the scholarship of John Westlake (1828–1913). Together with the other ten founding members of the first institute of international law, the Institut de Droit International (1874), Westlake appropriates 'the juridical conscience of the civilized world'.[38] Later he argues in *Chapters on Principles of International Law* (1894) 'that regions of the earth designated as "uncivilized" ... ought to be annexed or occupied by advanced powers'.[39]

Benjamin Disraeli was the first to note in his renowned novel *Tancred* (1847) that 'the East is a career'. While ostensibly this is still the case, during the second half of the nineteenth century, university faculties opened oriental and international legal studies faculties with a fully developed curriculum across Europe. Fortunately, the exchanges between both projects (and careers) receive sufficient attention elsewhere.[40] What remains interesting and relevant here is how both these essentially imperial projects dialectically interacted with European Christianities in order to cement the Western 'civilization' across the globe.

As mentioned above, the missionary nature of Christianity was inherited by its succeeding supra-structures: imperialism, Orientalism, and international law. Edward Said formulates this with much precision when he argues that what was

[36] Elsewhere Said adds that 'Orientalism is not an airy European fantasy about the Orient, but a created body of theory and practice in which, for many generations there has been a considerable material investment.' Said, *Orientalism*, pp. 1, 3, 6.

[37] Jean Allain, 'Orientalism and International Law: The Middle East as the Underclass of the International Legal Order', *Leiden Journal of International Law* 17 (2004): pp. 391–404.

[38] See more in Koskenniemi, *The Gentle Civilizer of Nations*, pp. 113–24.

[39] See Said's discussion of this in *Orientalism*, pp. 217–19.

[40] Be it through Edward Said's methodological approach or the 'New Historiography' movement in Israel (see for instance Benny Morris, 'The New Historiography: Israel and its Past', in *1948 and After: Israel and the Palestinians* (Oxford: Clarendon Press, 1994). But most importantly the contemporary post-colonial international legal research, also known as Third World Approaches to International Law (TWAIL). Apart from the previously mentioned article by Jean Allain, 'Orientalism and International Law', see for instance Karin Mickleson, 'Rhetoric and Rage: Third World Voices in International Legal Discourse', *Wisconsin International Law Journal* 16 (1998): pp. 361–2; Nathaniel Berman, 'The Grotius Lecture Series', *American University International Law Review* 14 (1999): pp. 1516–69; and Antony Anghie, 'Finding the Peripheries: Sovereignty and Colonialism in the Nineteenth-Century International Law', *Harvard International Law Journal* 40 (1999): pp. 1–80.

perceived to be religion's 'existential paradigms' was 'reconstituted, redeployed, redistributed' in modern secularism.[41] In fact, Said's entire thesis is structured on the argument that

> Essential aspects of modern Orientalist theory and praxis (from which present-day Orientalism derives) can be understood, not as a sudden access of objective knowledge about the Orient, but as a set of structures inherited from the past, secularized, redisposed, and re-formed by such disciplines as philology, which in turn were naturalized, and laicized substitutes for (or versions of) Christian supernaturalism.[42]

This reached a new peak when it was argued that the Crimean 'World War' began when several European powers came to rescue 'their' corresponding Christian communities in the Holy Land. But just as this religious aspect looms in this war's background, so does its Easternness: lest we forget, in Russian historiography the Crimean War is referred to as 'the Eastern War'.[43] Arguably, it was only after Russia lost to an alliance made of Britain together with France, the Ottoman Empire, and Sardinia—in the bloodiest war to date—that it was understood that the Christian religious issues should be forced into the closet.

The Concert of Europe and its East (a.k.a. Crimea and the Holy Land)

Clearly, the Eastern and/or the Crimean War prompted new worries. The force of modern-day technology (and the medical failures that then forced the professionalization of modern nursing of the wounded à la Florence Nightingale) hardly escaped anyone.[44] Neither could its relationship to religion and/or the East. Cardinal John Henry Newman (1801–90)—one of the leading religious figures of the nineteenth century—made, for instance, a specific reference in 1853 to Oriental Islam to justify Britain's intervention in the Crimean War, although this had very little to do with Islam itself.[45]

The uncomfortable aspect that Cardinal Newman—an Evangelical priest of the Church of England who later converted into the Roman Catholic Church—wished to ignore, was that Christianity was fragmented to begin with.[46] Such fragmentation was made too visible by the inability of the diverging Christianities to agree over issues of the custodial rights of the holy place.[47]

[41] Said, *Orientalism*, p.121. [42] Ibid., p.122.

[43] See more in Candan Badem, *'The' Ottoman Crimean War: (1853–1856)* (Leiden: Kroninklijke Brill, 2010), p. 3.

[44] Ibid., p. 3.

[45] John Henry Newman's book *The Turks in their Relation to Europe* (London: 1853) is mentioned by Said, *Orientalism*, on p. 153.

[46] See more in George Herring, *What was the Oxford Movement?* (London: Continuum, 2002).

[47] The general reference here is to the Church of the Nativity and several other significant early Christian sites in Jerusalem and its vicinity. More specifically, however, the matter revolved around the pseudo-trivial question of whether 'Latin or Greek clergy would possess the key to the Great Church of Bethlehem and which of them would have priority of holding services in the Church of the Holy Sepulchre.' Candan Badem, *'The' Ottoman Crimean War: (1853–1856)* (2010), p. 64.

After all, Christianity's universal/missionary agenda makes any internal conflicts and ruptures more difficult to accept and/or explicate on philosophical and/religious grounds. Adding Orientalism and Islam, the predominant religion of the East, to the equation became a handy 'solution'.[48] This way the differences within European Christianities got a new and larger perspective, which helped in sustaining a certain level of peace within the European context.

In actuality, the Ottomans—after centuries of experience—had actually sustained their Christian populations in the Holy Land mostly peacefully. This changed only when the local Christian communities begin to mirror the socio-political destabilization of Europe's balance of power, together with the nineteenth-century Oriental agenda.[49] Such parallelism meant that it got harder and harder for the Ottoman bureaucracy to satisfy all of its Christian subjects.

Irrespective of the religious issues, the real burning issue was—as spelled out in the Treaty of Paris (1856) that concluded the Crimean War—the need to reduce Russia's imperial power in the Black Sea.[50] This in turn meant the need to ensure that the Ottomans kept their Empire's gates open to the Europeans. Ergo, 'the Ottoman Empire became an area in which "the Concert of Europe" was working out its manoeuvres to preserve the balance of power'.[51]

This is not to imply that the Concert followed a clear strategy in its dealing with its Orientalist-constructed Other, the Ottoman Muslims. But a clear strategy was redundant. It was enough to remain within the guidelines set by the Oriental and/or the European Law of Nations, which provided the necessary flexibility and all-inclusiveness required. Such an 'approach' enabled the rapid transformation of the Ottoman Empire, known until recently as 'the terror of the world', into the 'sick man of Europe' that needed to be healed by the big powers.[52] Its price—the official acceptance of the Ottoman Empire as an equal member to the Concert of

[48] Islam's universalism/missionarism made these interactions more complex because it resembles that of Christianity's. The existence of its diverging *Da'wa* movements proves that its missionary agenda exists although not in the institutionally organized form in which missionarism is present in most Western Christianities. In the words of Bassam Tibi, 'The *Da'wa* call to Islam, like Christian evangelism, is supposed to be peaceful. But if the peoples to whom Muslims bring the message of Islam do not submit to it voluntarily ("Islam" means "submission to God"), Muslims are entitled to use force in defending the *Da'wa* against the resistance of the unbelievers.' Bassam Tibi, *Fundamentalism: Political Islam and the New World Order* (California: University of California Press, 1998), p. 55. See more also in *Travellers in Faith: Studies of Tagblighi Jama'at as a Transnational Islamic Movement for Faith Renewal*, edited by Muhammad Khalid Masud (Leiden: Brill, 2000).

[49] See more in Badem, *'The' Ottoman Crimean War: (1853–1856)*, pp. 64–6.

[50] Significantly, 'the Crimean War was the only occasion between 1815 and 1914 when Britain sent a military expedition to Europe to fight another great power ...' See more in *The Cambridge Historical Encyclopedia of Great Britain and Ireland*, edited by Christopher Haigh (Cambridge: Cambridge University Press, 2000), p. 266.

[51] Malcolm D. Evans, *Religious Liberty and International Law in Europe* (Cambridge: Cambridge University Press, 1997), p. 68.

[52] Indeed 'it was during this time that the image of the Ottoman Empire gradually descended from being perceived as "the terror of the world" to being "the sick man of Europe"'. (Aslı Çırakman, *From the 'Terror of the World' to the 'Sick Man of Europe': European Images of Ottoman Empire from the 16th century to the 19th* (New York: Peter Lang Publishing 2005), p. 1).

Europe—was made affordable by the legal flexibility of the Concert itself. It did not, as discussed further below, entitle the Ottomans to substantial equality.

The Ottoman East enters the West through the Holy Land

It is essential to pause here to appreciate the domino effect that started with the Crimean War and concluded with Article VII of the Treaty of Paris, which 'declares the Sublime Porte admitted to participate in the advantages of the Public Law and System (Concert) of Europe'.[53] The message is loud and clear: The Ottoman Empire's help in containing the Russian aggressor during the Crimean War is rewarded with an entry ticket to the sovereign equal Concert of Europe 'club', and all that it entails. Thus, by opening the Concert of Europe to the Ottoman Empire, the Treaty of Paris unsealed the legal language reserved for the European Christian nations just wide enough to include its Muslim Other. This barely implied equal participation. In fact, it is as if the Concert *almost* forgave the Ottomans their Islam, Orientalism, Eastern Otherness, and/or 'in-between' chair in the European geopolitical map.[54]

Article VII of the Treaty of Paris admitted the Ottomans into the European Concert. It needs to be read together with Article IX of the Treaty in order to understand an important condition for the Ottoman entry to the Concert of Europe that remains mostly forgotten: namely the sultan's commitment to the protection of religious freedom and racial discrimination, in particular towards 'the Christian populations of his Empire'.[55] The full article reads as follows:

> His Imperial Majesty the Sultan, having, in his constant solicitude for the welfare of his subjects, issued a Firman which, while ameliorating their conditions without distinction of religion or race, records his generous intentions towards the Christian populations of his Empire, and wishing to give a further proof of his sentiments in that respect, has resolved to communicate to the Contracting Parties the said Firman emanating from his sovereign will. The Contracting Parties recognize the high value of this communication. It is clearly understood that it cannot, in any case, give to the said powers the right to interfere, either collectively or separately, in the relations of His Majesty the Sultan with his subjects, nor in the internal administration of his Empire.

While it may be argued that Article IX is almost a requirement given that the Crimean War was officially sparked by religious conflicts, the interest here lies in how it singles out the Christian subjects under the Sultan's rule. Not only does the Treaty of Paris ignore all other religious minorities that composed the multi-cultural mosaic of the Empire by referring only to Christianity, it also overlooks the need to impose the principle of religious freedom equally on all signatories' parties. All

[53] For the full Article VII reads as follows: see the full Treaty of Paris in *Appendix II*.

[54] Heinz Duchhardt, 'From Westphalia to the Revolutionary Era', in *Peace Treaties and International Law in European History: From the Late Middle Ages to World War One*, edited by Randall Lesaffer (Cambridge: Cambridge University Press, 2004), p. 50.

[55] See more Evans, *Religious Liberty and International Law in Europe*, pp. 68–71.

other national and/or religious minorities in the East and/or West are mentioned only as the background for the Christian population. Furthermore, the Treaty of Paris does not unpack the divergent claims of the different Christianities—claims which were responsible for the strife that supposedly sparked the Crimean War.[56]

Once Article IX is viewed as complimentary to Article VII, it is clear that the acceptance of the Ottoman Empire as a member of the Concert of Europe depended on a binary circumstance: Whereas it was essential that the Ottoman 'terror of the world' was weakened, it was equally beneficial that the 'sick man in Europe' could nonetheless help the 'real' Western powers sort out their imperial issues in the face of another threat from the East. Russia, although predominantly Christian, European, and a member of the Concert since its birth, was cast as another Eastern Other when convenient.[57] This proves the flexible hierarchical relationship between Eastern and Western Christianities just as it shows how Western powers resorted to the technique of 'divide and conquer' for the 'elastic' East. Arguably such a strategy still maintains both Eastern regions, the Crimea and the Holy Land, that are somewhat linked in their contemporary instabilities. However, the bottom line here is that the acceptance of the Ottoman Muslim Empire into the Concert of Europe was preconditioned by the sultan's commitment to the religious freedom of the Christian populations. This substantiates the inequity of the religious question of both the East and West.

Unpacking these and similar religious biases, discrepancies and hypocrisies that are attached to the Paris Treaty—the document that actually sought to secure both religious freedoms and imperial inclusion—has immense implications. Such dialectics essentially personify the way both Orientalism and international law as Western European civilizing projects have cemented a specifically Christian but also Western bias even when their doors were quasi-opened to their Others.

Despite all efforts, neither the religious nor the 'Eastern Question' were resolved in Paris. Escalations in the East, arguably also caused by the Western need to divide and conquer its constructed East, led to the Russo-Turkish Wars and were readdressed in the San Stefano Treaty (1878). This treaty changed very little. Although, as A. J. P. Taylor argues: 'If the treaty of San Stefano had been maintained, both the Ottoman Empire and Austria-Hungary might have survived to the present day.'[58] Perhaps the San Stefano Treaty was more promising than its predecessor, the Treaty of Paris (1856), because it remained silent on minority issues? Be that as it may, in 1878 Otto von Bismarck seized the opportunity to introduce himself as the 'honest broker' coming to rescue imperial Europe from 'the Eastern Question'.[59] He was determined to do whatever it took to avoid any unanticipated

[56] Note that the only reference that is made to any difference within Christianity is the plural form that is used: 'Christian populations'.

[57] For more on Russia's religious history in relationship to Europe and/or Asia, see Ernst Benz, *The Eastern Orthodox Church: Its Thought and Life* (USA: Rowohld Taschenbuch Verlag, 2009).

[58] See A. J. P. Taylor, *The Struggle for Mastery in Europe 1914–1918* (Oxford: Oxford University Press, 1954), p. 253.

[59] See exact quote in Edgar Feuchtwanger, *Bismarck: A Political History* (New York: Routledge, 2014), p. 202.

developments—above all another Balkan conflict—that might threaten Europe's balance of powers.[60]

In retrospect, Bismarck failed with the East just as he would in the subsequent and more famous conference in Berlin that regulated the Scramble for Africa (1884–85). Despite the similarities between these two conferences, as Eric D. Weitz argues, historians 'almost never consider the two Berlin meetings together. Diplomatic histories of Europe refer to the Berlin West Africa Conference only in passing, if at all. Historians of Africa almost never discuss the Berlin Congress. Studies in international legal history reproduce this division.'[61] Arguably, it was not until the First World War that the imperial powers realized the inherent limitations in maintaining the European balance of power by outsourcing conflicts elsewhere,[62] but despite this, Article LXII of the Treaty of Berlin has clearly been a success. Not only does this Status Quo stay more or less intact today, it has also borrowed and integrated an originally Eastern regime into the Christian Law of Nations.

The Integration of the Status Quo from the East by the West

The detail above necessarily sets the stage for the second last sentence of the three paragraphs that compose Article LXII of the Berlin Congress, which reads as follows:

> The Sublime Porte having expressed the intention to maintain the principle of religious liberty, and give it the widest scope, the Contracting Parties take note of this spontaneous declaration. In no part of the Ottoman Empire shall difference of religion be alleged against any person as a ground for exclusion or incapacity in matters relating to the enjoyment of civil or political rights, admission to public employments, functions, and honors, or the exercise of the various professions and industries, in any locality whatsoever. The freedom and outward exercise of all forms of worship shall be assured to all, and no hindrance shall be offered either to the hierarchical organization of the different communions, or to their relations with their spiritual chiefs.
>
> Ecclesiastics, pilgrims, and monks of all nationalities traveling in Turkey in Europe, or in Turkey in Asia, shall enjoy the same rights, advantages, and privileges.
>
> The right of official protection by the Diplomatic and Consular Agents of the Powers in Turkey is recognized both as regards the above-mentioned persons and their religious, charitable, and other establishments in the Holy Places and elsewhere. The rights possessed by

[60] The so-called 'big powers' were convinced of his sincerity, partly due to his famous statement—that the Balkans 'were not worth the healthy bones of a single Pomeranian musketeer'. (Edgar Feuchtwanger, *Bismarck: A Political History* (2014), p.198).

[61] See more in Eric D. Weitz, 'From the Vienna to the Paris System: International Politics and the Entangled Histories of Human Rights, Forced Deportations and Civilizing Missions', *The American Historical Review* 113, no. 5 (December 2008): pp. 1313–43, 1319.

[62] In fact, it was the fears of the 'war in sight' instigated by 'the oriental crisis of 1875–1878 that eventually provided a fuse for the future explosion' of the first Great War in 1914 (See more in Imaneul Geiss, *German Foreign Policy 1871–1914* (London: Routledge Press, 1976), p. 32).

France are expressly reserved, **and it is well understood that no alterations can be made in the *status quo* in the Holy Places.** The monks of Mount Athos, of whatever country they may be natives, shall be maintained in their former possessions and advantages, and shall enjoy, without any exception, complete equality of rights and prerogatives.[63]

At first glance, this is a beautifully written article, particularly if one remains oblivious to the article's historical context. It is 'A chorus of affirmation for the principle of religious freedom' by the six signatories, the United Kingdom, Austria-Hungary, France, Italy, Russia, and the Ottoman Empire.[64] Such precise religious, civil, and political freedoms and economic rights are the embodiment of nineteenth-century liberal hopes and dreams.

It is strategically helpful that the formulation remains rather neutral (i.e., the Contracting Parties 'take note' of the 'spontaneous declaration' by the Ottomans). This ensures the intactness of the sovereign equality of the contracting parties. It also diverts attention from the one-sidedness of Article LXII. After all, while the focus here is the 'spontaneous declaration' by the Ottoman Empire, which almost suddenly commits itself to protect and uphold the human rights of all of its national minorities, such a commitment was hardly the common practice of the other contracting parties.

Or, in the words of William Gladstone:

It is ... a little amusing to observe with what edifying zeal all the great States of Europe united to force religious liberty upon those new-fledged bantlings of politics, on their very first light of day; and yet these great States have hardly in any case learnt ... to adopt it at home.[65]

Because this partiality may suggest the Treaty's inadequacy and a general insincerity on the part of the contracting parties,[66] it was crucial that the Ottomans were going through their own independent process of reorganization, the Tanzimat period of Westernization (1839–1876).[67] These reforms are monumental particularly with reference to religion because it was since 1839 that the subjects of Sultan

[63] Emphasis added. See the Treaty of Berlin (1878) in *Appendix III*.

[64] Carole Finke, *Defending the Rights of Others: The Great Powers, the Jews, and International Minority Protection 1878–1938* (Cambridge: Cambridge University Press, 2004), p. 28.

[65] William Ewart Gladstone, The Berlin Treaty and the Anglo-Turkish Convention (1878, revised version of speech in the House of Commons, 30 July 1878. Quoted in Evans, *Religious Liberty and International Law in Europe*, p. 73).

[66] For more on the big powers lacking interest to sustain an enforceable agreement see Finke, *Defending the Rights of Others*, p. 8.

[67] In general the intention of the Tanzimat (which is often divided into two parts from 1839–56 and 1856–76) was to bring the Ottoman Empire form of government closer to European-style structures. It is often compared with the French Revolution mainly because of the era but also because it too attempted to eliminate the landholding class and the corrupt pashas. However, the Ottoman changes came from the top and were encouraged and closely monitored by British, who viewed them very positively, given the clear economic stakes involved. Just these stakes and also more general geographic dominance by the United Kingdom was not seen so positively by the Russians and Austrians (See more in details in *The Ottoman Empire and the World-Economy*, edited by Huri Islamogu-Inan (Cambridge: Cambridge University Press, 2004).

Abdülmecid—Muslim and non-Muslim alike—became instantaneously equal before the law.[68]

These reforms intended 'to satisfy European demands for the protection of the Christian communities and to inculcate a notion of national and secular subjecthood'. But the Tanzimat's agenda[69] could hardly be reconciled with the region's demographics and traditional relationships between majorities and minorities.[70] Neither was it easy to accommodate the 'new laws' of the Tanzimat with the age-old local customs that the Ottomans pledged to uphold, particularly because such customs and also identities 'were at once private and public, communal and national, elite and subaltern, modern and traditional'.[71]

The consequence was not only unprecedented confusion, it soon—as the 1860s Druze-Maronite conflict illustrates—turned extremely violent. As Ussama Samir Makdisi terms it:

> On its own terrain, Europeans, Ottomans, and locals were locked in a war over the meaning and direction of the *Tanzimat* which itself several overlapping discourses, of religious equality, Islamic tradition, political legitimacy, past glory, and present sovereignty, all framed implicitly by Europe-dominated modernity.[72]

From a Western perspective, it nonetheless made perfect sense that the Ottomans, who first became 'the sick man of Europe', now aspired to recover by establishing a more ambitious version of European-style form of government. It was a plus that this includes 'a spontaneous' declaration of their dedication to religious, political and economic freedoms and rights even if those remained an abstract aspiration for imperial Europe itself.

European inter-nationalism versus Ottoman international imperialism

Clearly, much is left to be desired when it comes to the concisely mentioned and negatively described Status Quo. All that we are left with is that 'it is well understood that no alterations can be made in the *Status Quo* in the Holy Places'. Considering the first sentences of Article LXII—' *the Sublime Porte having expressed the intention to maintain the principle of religious liberty* … '—one can assume that the objective of the Status Quo is related to the religious practices of different believers, of whatever nationality, ethnicity and/or specific role. However, the lack of any legal and/or political description of the Status Quo remains both enchanting and challenging, particularly because of all the differences that are mentioned in Article LXII (i.e., Sublime Port, Ottoman Empire, ecclesiastics, pilgrims, and monks of *all nationalities,* Turkey, Europe, Holy Places, France, and Mount Athos). Nowhere is it explained what this Status Quo means. Where does it come from? How is it to be

[68] Ussama Samir Makdisi, *The Culture of Sectarianism: Community, History, and Violence in Nineteenth-Century Ottoman Lebanon* (Berkeley: University of California Press, 2000), p. 3.
[69] Ibid., p. 3 and 57. [70] Ibid., 57. [71] Ibid., p. 60. [72] Ibid., 57.

recognized and/or appropriated? By whom? Furthermore, given the reference to *all nationalities*, what could this mean from an international legal perspective today? In contrast, what did it mean when international law openly conceded its origins as the Christian European Law of Nations?

These questions only become harder to answer when we consider that the term 'status quo' poses a consistent difficulty in international law. Susanne Wasum-Rainer—in her attempt to define the 'status quo' for *The Max Planck Encyclopedia of Public International Law*—argues that: 'In many cases where the term [status quo] is used, it refers to a purely factual and political state of affairs, not a legal one ...' while claiming however that 'one can talk of international law—of its nature as a decentralized normative order with no single fount—as having a status quo "orientation" '.[73] While this remains a troublesome approach to positive international law, it is hardly surprising that political realists embrace it. Hans J. Morgenthau (1904–80), one of the founding fathers of the realist school in the twentieth century, believed that the principle of status quo is more efficient in limiting the powers of the state than international law (and/or international morality for that matter).[74] Interestingly, the similarities between the status quo principle and that of the balance of power—that, as discussed above, were contingent to one another during the nineteenth century—do not escape Morgenthau. For Morgenthau both principles are vital to the international realist,[75] even though both notions expose international law's 'Achilles's heels'.[76]

This professional Achilles heel only enhances the importance of the Status Quo that still describes the prevailing modus operandi in the Holy Land, in its religious, legal and/or political sense, at least since the seventeenth century. Even Wasum-Rainer singles out this Status Quo. In her words, the Holy Land's Status Quo 'describes the preservation of the situation created by the Ottoman decrees of 1757 and 1852, and confirmed in Art. LXII of the Berlin Treaty of 13 July 1878 ("and it is well understood that no alterations can be made in the Holy Places"; Berlin Congress [1878])'.[77] Ostensibly, the term Status Quo 'has had the special technical meaning of the normative regime or set of binding arrangements concerning possession, usage, and ceremony at the holy places'[78] since at least 1878. At best, the Status Quo allows the different communities to sustain their religious worship

[73] Susanne Wasum-Rainer, 'Status Quo', in *Max Planck Encyclopedia of Public International Law* (Oxford: Oxford University Press, 2013). Available at http://opil.ouplaw.com.

[74] See more in Hans J. Morgenthau, *Politics among Nation: The Struggle for Power and Peace* (New York: Alfred A. Knopf, 1960).

[75] Ibid.

[76] The reference here is to what Martti Koskenniemi calls international law's insoluble 'ascending/descending' liberal dyad structured between theory and practice, concreteness and normativity, law and politics, and so on. (See more in Martti Koskenniemi, *From Apology to Utopia: The Structure of International Legal Argument* (Cambridge: Cambridge University Press, 2005), pp. 46–7.)

[77] Koskenniemi, *From Apology to Utopia.*

[78] Cohen, *Saving the Holy Sepulchre*, p. 8.

peacefully. At worst, contentious issues were said to fall '"under the Status Quo" and no change was permitted'.[79]

Whatever the 'original' flaws of the Status Quo,[80] it seems to have been within the interest of both local and global communities to strictly maintain it.[81] It is, in other words, impossible to exaggerate the importance of this regime's success, its imperfections included. Not only is Article LXII borrowed from the Ottoman Empire, which was essentially non-Christian and had an only partially modernized legal system,[82] it also manages to do something that remains contested and complex to this day. In fact, today even the very classification of a holy place has no generally recognized definition; although the United Nations made a list of holy places, it remains non-binding.[83] As Winnifred Fallers Sullivan terms it: 'in order to enforce laws guaranteeing religious freedom you must first have religion.... Defining religion is very difficult, particularly at the beginning of the twenty-first century'.[84]

Conclusion: The Unforgettable Jerusalem

The Status Quo, as mentioned in Article LXII of the Treaty of Berlin and/or its more recent mention in Article 4 (1) of the Fundamental Agreement between the Holy See and Israel (1993), demonstrates a specific presence from an almost forgotten past. This past links *the* city of God to a once powerful and Muslim Empire that becomes the newest member of a European 'Western' union with all its deficiencies (e.g., Christianites, Orientalism, international law, and nineteenth century *Realpolitik*).

The Status Quo originated in a nineteenth century international legal treaty (which otherwise had mostly expired)—survived the fall of its Ottoman 'founders' through the British Mandate (1923–48) and the Jordanian Rule (1948–67), and is still used by the Israeli government. Its persistence remains a historical riddle with many alternative answers. It would be an Orientalist prejudice to discard this history by claiming that the Ottomans succeeded in this, inter alia, because the East is and always was more emotional, passionate, sentimental, zealous, warm, and

[79] Change was permitted only if the communities involved reached an amicable agreement. Ibid., p. 9.

[80] Inter alia, the most blatant loophole in the Status Quo regime is the absence of a satisfactory way to manage the necessary repairs/renovations of the holy places. Ibid., p. 11.

[81] In 1909 Father Ferdinando Diotallevi wrote in his memorandum that 'since the sixteenth century there had been 'almost continual war there' and only the firm maintenance of the Status Quo had kept the peace'. (Ferdinando Diotallevi quoted in Cohen, *Saving the Holy Sepulchre*, p. 16.)

[82] For more on legal borrowing see for instance Alan Watson, 'Legal Transplants and European Private Law', *Electronic Journal of Comparative Law* 4.4 (2000): http://www.ejcl.org/44/art44-2.html.

[83] See more in *Whither Jerusalem?: Proposals and Positions Concerning the Future of Jerusalem*, edited by Moshe Hirsch, Deborah Housen-Couriel, and Ruth Lapidot (The Hague: Martinus Nijhoff, 1995), p. 157.

[84] Winnifred Fallers Sullivan, *The Impossibility of Religious Freedom* (Princeton: Princeton University Press, 2005), pp. 1–2.

altogether more religious than the rational, sensible, objective, scientific, progressive, cold, and enlightened West.

Instead, the Eastern and non-Christian Ottomans accomplished much through the Status Quo mainly because of their realist approach, which was in its turn based on considerable experience as an international and multicultural Empire. Furthermore, the Ottoman Empire—particularly during the nineteenth century—was predisposed to accommodate Western demands. Such demands, as the Crimean example shows, were not necessarily religious per se. The Ottoman readiness to make such concessions and Western adjustments (i.e., Tanzimat) was not only due to its diminishing power; it was also because it was 'made' to understand itself as the foreign and Eastern Other that is doomed to live in the confines of an eternal tension that Orhan Pamuk formulates as 'Why am I the way I am?'[85] This meant that the Ottomans were made to wait by the gate before the West, Europe, and consequently also international law. The Ottoman Empire's rationalism struck a more balanced and human balance of power for its subjects because but also in spite of these experiences, which encapsulated diversity rather than the idealized national/religious homogeneity alternative promoted in Christian Europe.

After the explosive costs of the Crimean War, which was less about religion and more about the need to reduce Russia's imperial power in the Black Sea, it was clear—particularly because of Bismarck's foreign policy approach—that any mention of religious grounds ought to be excluded. Moreover, the Eastern crisis clarified the way that the balance of power at home depended on a certain Status Quo in the East, and, vice versa, that an Eastern Status Quo depended on a Western balance of power. Such mutual dependency was now verbalized through Christianity's 'other means'—namely Orientalism and international law. The specific Status Quo 'offered' by the Ottomans corresponded well to local religious issues and was smoothly integrated. Not only did it help the balance of power in the West, it demanded relatively little from Western powers. Whether it was entirely coincidental that the needs of the West were simply 'found' in the East remains an open question.

There is a big discrepancy between the success of this Status Quo, which is linked to Western nineteenth century *Realpolitik* enshrined in international law with all its potentialities and limitations, and the shortcomings of twentieth and even twenty-first century attempts to internationalize Jerusalem. As Nathaniel Berman argues, Jerusalem is the perfect example of the inadequacies, weaknesses, and debatable nature of such internationalization to begin with.[86] The

[85] Orhan Pamuk, *The White Castle*, translated by Victoria Holbrook (Manchester: Carcanet Press, 1990).

[86] Significantly Nathaniel Berman's article was written in 1996, shortly after the assassination of Yitzhak Rabin, which arguably shattered all previous hopes for a peaceful settlement of Jerusalem, but he correctly points out that it was Resolution 181 (II), 1947, that 'followed in a long tradition and has remained a model for international legal plans for nationalist conflicts. One can draw a direct chain of influence and evolution from the 1878 Treaty of Berlin for the settlements of nationalist conflicts in the Balkans, to the 1923 Geneva Convention for Upper Silesia for the settlement of a German-Polish territorial dispute, to the 1947 Palestine Partition Resolution, to the Dayton Agreement on

1993 Fundamental Agreement between the Jewish State of Israel and the Vatican exemplifies this perfectly. As discussed, the Fundamental Agreement cannot be read as implying that the Holy See has given up its aspiration to control, or at the very least internationalize, the holy places in the Holy Land.[87] Neither should it be forgotten that the Israeli Knesset has yet to ratify the Agreement altogether![88] Eloquently, Article 4 (1) of the Agreement secures Israel's de facto 'commitment to maintain and respect the Status Quo in the Christian Holy Places' and 'guarantee of the freedom of Catholic worship' on the one hand, while on the other it simultaneously safeguards the Vatican's concrete needs and allows the Church to sustain its future, hypothetical aspirations for more control over the sites.

To sum up, if one of the main achievements of Jerusalem's Status Quo was, as Raymond Cohen argues, 'to remove the holy places from the scope of international conflict and so prevent a repetition of the diplomatic crisis that preceded the Crimean War (1853–1856),'[89] then the fact that it is still in use is revolutionary. In contrast to today's overbearing idealistic international law, the Status Quo captures both the realistic need for and the guidelines necessary to a continuing and functioning governance of a holy city that in any case exists twice already—in heaven and on Earth.[90]

The real elegance of the Status Quo stems from its legal imperfection, because it accomplishes such an incredible undertaking with so little. It does not define what the Status Quo actually means or to which religious communities it refers to; no specific references to ownership/possession are made; in fact, there is no mention to the city of Jerusalem or even the Holy Land. Significantly, the required legal knowledge here is almost taken for granted. Somewhat biblically, it is assumed that when it comes to Jerusalem, it is as if the Abrahamic religions simply know 'that which has been is that which will be'.[91] Arguably, it is for this reason that the Status Quo—together with endless other aspects—helps enshrine our inability but also our unwillingness to forget the City of God.

Bosnia.' (See more in Nathaniel Berman, 'Legalizing Jerusalem or, of Law, Fantasy, and Faith', *Catholic University Law Review* 45 (1996): pp. 825–6.)

[87] Nathaniel Berman's argument explicates that this type of internationalism, like the others, attempts to 'participate in two other characteristic international fantasies: the universality and rationality of international authority … (These) 'may take many forms; the 'universality' of any particular form, its claim to stand above the partisan fray, must be justified in substantive terms'. (Nathaniel Berman, 'Legalizing Jerusalem or, of Law, Fantasy, and Faith', p. 826.)

[88] See for instance Lisa Palmieri-Billig, 'Vatican upset at non-finalized agreement with Israel', The *Jerusalem Post*, 12 December 2007. Available at http://www.jpost.com/Israel/Vatican-upset-at-non-finalized-agreement-with-Israel.

[89] Cohen, *Saving the Holy Sepulchre*', p. 9.

[90] Montefiore, *Jerusalem: The Biography*, p. xxvi.

[91] Ecclesiastes 1:9. This is very similar to Romans 4:18, which refers to Abraham as he 'Who against hope believed in hope, that he might become the father of many nations, according to was spoken, So shall your descendants be.'

Epilogue

Be it the Status Quo's Eastern 'birth' and/or its Western adoption, one ought to mention another explanation for this unprecedented success: namely its ability to mirror and accommodate the tension intrinsic to monotheism itself. Although the above article mostly focuses on the religious images looming in the background of the interaction between Western Christian balance of power and the Eastern Status Quo, it shows how such an interface facilitates the 'ancestral relationship' between the three monotheistic religions in the smallest place provided to it in the Holy Land.

Similarly to most biblical families, the monotheistic family—composed of Judaism, Christianity, and Islam, upon their oversized religious loyalties, subsects, and ethnic groupings—is destined to share the need for parental love and God's singularity just as it needs to share the same space. Just as Jacob fought Esau to receive the first-born birthright/blessing from Isaac, so do the monotheistic religions struggle for God's individual love. Such a construct of mutual commitment between God and his monotheistic believer is as serious as the 'sibling competition' that ensues. The tension here originates from the fact that both the commitment and the competition are contingent to the existence of a singular God but also the monotheistic family. After all, without Esau, Isaac's blessing of Jacob would be less prestigious. So without any Other-yet-insider observers and/or competitors the monotheistic idea would lose much of the centrality of God but also of the importance of the traditional/hierarchical social/family structure.

Arguably, it is less difficult to accept the existence of minor differences between sibling religious communities, than the need to share God's love and his holy places. It remains impossible to overemphasize the radicalism behind the Oneness of God—or Jerusalem.[92] It is here that the most significant of monotheism's psycho-historical consequences takes its shape.

The worship of a one parental and paternal God means that humanity, at least its masculine part, is 'entitled' to act in a Godly manner. The contingent hierarchical schism this created has, among other things, formed the relationship between God/humanity, man/woman but also true and false religions. In other words, man's self-entitlement transformed the world on so many levels but also *into* so many levels.

[92] At the heart of monotheism stands the believer who worships a single God. The monotheistic believer acquires much freedom but also responsibilities from the notion of a 'detached deity' that watches over the cosmos. (See more in William Scott Green, 'Approaching Distinctiveness', in *Monotheism & Ethics: Historical and Contemporary Intersections Among Judaism, Christianity and Islam*, edited by Tzvi Langermann (Leiden: Brill, 2011), pp. 25–45, 40.)

The need to create hierarchies is exactly where the importance of the differences, however minor, between the monotheistic religions grows. As Sigmund Freud argues of the narcissism of small differences, 'minor' differences are not really small. The minor differences that can be detected in the different monotheistic faiths describe 'communities with adjoining territories, and related to each other in other ways as well, who are engaged in constant feuds and ridiculing each other'.[93] One can share much, in other words, without necessarily having more acceptance or understanding. As the monotheistic family shows, it is actually the other way around.[94] As Pierre Bourdieu, who took Freud's point further, explains: 'Social identity lies in difference, and difference is asserted against what is closest, which represents the greatest threat.'[95]

The real radicalism and energizing agendas inherent to the monotheistic 'way-of-thinking' is therefore the initiation of a competitive relationship between the monotheistic religions: A struggle that almost instantly turned into a deadly clash about 'who are the real chosen people?'[96] While this explains why international law that originated from Christian secularism is inter alia criticized for its attempt to subjugate, civilize, and Westernize the non-Christian Other, it also explains the intransigent attempts by the different monotheistic religions to take possession of 'their' holy places in Jerusalem.[97]

Whatever its imperfections, the awe-inspiring quality of the originally Ottoman Status Quo lies in its ability to permit the diverging monotheistic family members to exist side-by-side while each sustains its individuality. This works more or less well as long as each of the monotheistic religions worships the singularity of a paternal God differently. This difference can only be maintained through a challenging discourse with one another about the centrality of a shared abstract God. That this works in the God's small and very concrete holy places, is as close as humanity can get to love a singular divinity. Evidently, such love is 'not a victory march, it is a cold and it is a broken Hallelujah'.[98]

[93] Sigmund Freud, *Civilization, Society and Religion* (London: Penguin, 1991), p. 131.

[94] Freud's 'softer' approach that eventually turns ambivalent develops further in the hands of Georg Simmel, Emile Durkheim, Claude Levi-Straus, Pierre Bourdieu, and others who have continued this line of thought to explain why 'violent confrontations usually take place in close circles, that is, within the limits of the tribe, between neighbours, friends or relatives—in short, between people who share many social and cultural features'. (See more in Anton Blok, 'The Narcissism of Minor Differences', *European Journal of Social Theory* 1, no. 1 (1998): pp. 33–56, 37.)

[95] Pierre Bourdieu, *Distinction: A Social Critique of the Judgment of Taste* (Harvard: Harvard University Press, 1984), p. 479.

[96] See more on this in Reuven Firestone, *Who are the Real Chosen People? The Meaning of Chosenness in Judaism, Christianity and Islam* (Woodstock, Vt.: SkyLight Publishing, 2008).

[97] Indeed the presence of God's Oneness—even if only in the form of a universal 'metaphysical fixed idea'—is traceable in both Orientalism and international law (For more on the universal 'metaphysical fixed idea' as the core of both monotheism and international law see Reut Yael Paz, *A Gateway between a Distant God and a Cruel World: The Contribution of Jewish German-Speaking Scholars to International Law* (2012), p. 24.)

[98] Leonard Cohen, 'Hallelujah', Originally released in his album *Various Positions*, 1984. Text available at http://www.songtexte.com/songtext/leonard-cohen/hallelujah-7bdb72c0.html.

APPENDIX I

Convention: Inter Apostolicam Sedem Atque Israelis Statum

Fundamental Agreement between the Holy See and the State of Israel[99]

Signed in Jerusalem, this thirtieth day of the month of December, in the year 1993, which corresponds to the sixteenth day of the month of Tevet, in the year 5754.

Preamble

The Holy See and the State of Israel,

Mindful of the singular character and universal significance of the Holy Land;

Aware of the unique nature of the relationship between the Catholic Church and the Jewish people, and of the historic process of reconciliation and growth in mutual understanding and friendship between Catholics and Jews;

Having decided on 29 July 1992 to establish a 'Bilateral Permanent Working Commission', in order to study and define together issues of common interest, and in view of normalizing their relations;

Recognizing that the work of the aforementioned Commission has produced sufficient material for a first and Fundamental Agreement;

Realizing that such Agreement will provide a sound and lasting basis for the continued development of their present and future relations and for the furtherance of the Commission's task,

Agree upon the following Articles:

Article 1

§ 1. The State of Israel, recalling its Declaration of Independence, affirms its continuing commitment to uphold and observe the human right to freedom of religion and conscience, as set forth in the Universal Declaration of Human Rights and in other international instruments to which it is a party.

§ 2. The Holy See, recalling the Declaration on Religious Freedom of the Second Vatican Ecumenical Council, *Dignitatis humanae*, affirms the Catholic Church's commitment to uphold the human right to freedom of religion and conscience, as set forth in the Universal Declaration of Hu-man Rights and in other international instruments to which it is a party. The Holy See wishes to affirm as well the Catholic Church's respect for other religions and their followers as solemnly stated

[99] See the 'Fundamental Agreement', *A.A.S.*, vol. LXXXVI (1994), n. 9, pp. 716–28. Also available at http://www.vatican.va/roman_curia/secretariat_state/archivio/documents/rc_seg-st_19931230_santa-sede-israele_en.html.

by the Second Vatican Ecumenical Council in its Declaration on the Relation of the Church to Non-Christian Religions, *Nostra aetate*.

Article 2

§ 1. The Holy See and the State of Israel are committed to appropriate cooperation in combatting all forms of antisemitism and all kinds of racism and of religious intolerance, and in promoting mutual understanding among nations, tolerance among communities and respect for human life and dignity.

§ 2. The Holy See takes this occasion to reiterate its condemnation of hatred, persecution and all other manifestations of antisemitism directed against the Jewish people and individual Jews anywhere, at any time and by anyone. In particular, the Holy See deplores attacks on Jews and desecration of Jewish synagogues and cemeteries, acts which offend the memory of the victims of the Holocaust, especially when they occur in the same places which witnessed it.

Article 3

§ 1. The Holy See and the State of Israel recognize that both are free in the exercise of their respective rights and powers, and commit themselves to respect this principle in their mutual relations and in their cooperation for the good of the people.

§ 2. The State of Israel recognizes the right of the Catholic Church to carry out its religious, moral, educational and charitable functions, and to have its own institutions, and to train, appoint and deploy its own personnel in the said institutions or for the said functions to these ends. The Church recognizes the right of the State to carry out its functions, such as promoting and protecting the welfare and the safety of the people. Both the State and the Church recognize the need for dialogue and cooperation in such matters as by their nature call for it.

§ 3. Concerning Catholic legal personality at canon law the Holy See and the State of Israel will negotiate on giving it full effect in Israeli law, following a report from a joint subcommission of experts.

Article 4

§ 1. The State of Israel affirms its continuing commitment to maintain and respect the 'Status quo' in the Christian Holy Places to which it applies and the respective rights of the Christian communities thereunder. The Holy See affirms the Catholic Church's continuing commitment to respect the aforementioned 'Status quo' and the said rights.

§ 2. The above shall apply notwithstanding an interpretation to the contrary of any Article in this Fundamental Agreement.

§ 3. The State of Israel agrees with the Holy See on the obligation of continuing respect for and protection of the character proper to Catholic sacred places, such as churches, monasteries, convents, cemeteries and their like.

§ 4. The State of Israel agrees with the Holy See on the continuing guarantee of the freedom of Catholic worship.

Article 5

§ 1. The Holy See and the State of Israel recognize that both have an interest in favouring Christian pilgrimages to the Holy Land. Whenever the need for coordination arises, the proper agencies of the Church and of the State will consult and cooperate as required.

§ 2. The State of Israel and the Holy See express the hope that such pilgrimages will provide an occasion for better understanding between the pilgrims and the people and religions in Israel.

Article 6

The Holy See and the State of Israel jointly reaffirm the right of the Catholic Church to establish, maintain and direct schools and institutes of study at all levels; this right being exercised in harmony with the rights of the State in the field of education.

Article 7

The Holy See and the State of Israel recognize a common interest in promoting and encouraging cultural exchanges between Catholic institutions worldwide, and educational, cultural and research institutions in Israel, and in facilitating access to manuscripts, historical documents and similar source materials, in conformity with applicable laws and regulations.

Article 8

The State of Israel recognizes that the right of the Catholic Church to freedom of expression in the carrying out of its functions is exercised also through the Church's own communications media; this right being exercised in harmony with the rights of the State in the field of communications media.

Article 9

The Holy See and the State of Israel jointly reaffirm the right of the Catholic Church to carry out its charitable functions through its health care and social welfare institutions; this right being exercised in harmony with the rights of the State in this field.

Article 10

§ 1. The Holy See and the State of Israel jointly reaffirm the right of the Catholic Church to property.

§ 2. Without prejudice to rights relied upon by the Parties:

a) The Holy See and the State of Israel will negotiate in good faith a comprehensive agreement, containing solutions acceptable to both Parties, on unclear, unsettled and disputed issues, concerning property, economic and fiscal matters relating to the Catholic Church generally, or to specific Catholic Communities or institutions.

b) For the purpose of the said negotiations, the Permanent Bilateral Working Commission will appoint one or more bilateral subcommissions of experts to study the issues and make proposals.

c) The Parties intend to commence the aforementioned negotiations within three months of entry into force of the present Agreement, and aim to reach agreement within two years from the beginning of the negotiations.

d) During the period of these negotiations, actions incompatible with these commitments shall be avoided.

Article 11

§ 1. The Holy See and the State of Israel declare their respective commitment to the promotion of the peaceful resolution of conflicts among States and nations, excluding violence and terror from international life.

§ 2. The Holy See, while maintaining in every case the right to exercise its moral and spiritual teaching-office, deems it opportune to recall that, owing to its own character, it is solemnly committed to remaining a stranger to all merely temporal conflicts, which principle applies specifically to disputed territories and unsettled borders.

Article 12

The Holy See and the State of Israel will continue to negotiate in good faith in pursuance of the Agenda agreed upon in Jerusalem, on 15 July 1992, and confirmed at the Vatican, on 29 July 1992; likewise on issues arising from Articles of the present Agreement, as well as on other issues bilaterally agreed upon as objects of negotiation.

Article 13

§ 1. In this Agreement the Parties use these terms in the following sense:

a) 'The Catholic Church' and 'the Church'—including, *inter alia*, its Communities and institutions;

b) 'Communities' of the Catholic Church—meaning the Catholic religious entities considered by the Holy See as Churches *sui iuris* and by the State of Israel as Recognized Religious Communities;

c) 'The State of Israel' and 'the State'—including, *inter alia*, its authorities established by law.

§ 2. Notwithstanding the validity of this Agreement as between the Parties, and without detracting from the generality of any applicable rule of law with reference to treaties, the Parties agree that this Agreement does not prejudice rights and obligations arising from existing treaties between either Party and a State or States, which are known and in fact available to both Parties at the time of the signature of this Agreement.

Article 14

§ 1. Upon signature of the present Fundamental Agreement and in preparation for the establishment of full diplomatic relations, the Holy See and the State of Israel exchange Special Representatives, whose rank and privileges are specified in an Additional Protocol.

§ 2. Following the entry into force and immediately upon the beginning of the implementation of the present Fundamental Agreement, the Holy See and the State of Israel will establish full diplomatic relations at the level of Apostolic Nunciature, on the part of the Holy See, and Embassy, on the part of the State of Israel.

Article 15

This Agreement shall enter into force on the date of the latter notification of ratification by a Party.

Done in two original copies in the English and Hebrew languages, both texts being equally authentic. In case of divergency, the English text shall prevail.

ADDITIONAL PROTOCOL

1. In relation to Art. 14 § 1 of the Fundamental Agreement, signed by the Holy See and the State of Israel, the 'Special Representatives' shall have, respectively, the personal rank of Apostolic Nuncio and Ambassador.
2. These Special Representatives shall enjoy all the rights, privileges and immunities granted to Heads of Diplomatic Missions under international law and common usage, on the basis of reciprocity.
3. The Special Representative of the State of Israel to the Holy See, while residing in Italy, shall enjoy all the rights, privileges and immunities defined by Art. 12 of the Treaty of 1929 between the Holy See and Italy, regarding Envoys of Foreign Governments to the Holy See residing in Italy. The rights, privileges and immunities extended to the personnel of a Diplomatic Mission shall likewise be granted to the personnel of the Israeli Special Representative's Mission. According to an established custom, neither the Special Representative, nor the official members of his Mission, can at the same time be members of Israel's Diplomatic Mission to Italy.

4. The Special Representative of the Holy See to the State of Israel may at the same time exercise other representative functions of the Holy See and be accredited to other States. He and the personnel of his Mission shall enjoy all the rights, privileges and immunities granted by Israel to Diplomatic Agents and Missions.
5. The names, rank and functions of the Special Representatives will appear, in an appropriate way, in the official lists of Foreign Missions accredited to each Party.

APPENDIX II

Treaty of Paris

Peace Treaty between Great Britain, France, the Ottoman Empire, Sardinia and Russia March 30, 1856.[100]

Article I

From the day of the exchange of the Ratifications of the present Treaty there shall be Peace and Friendship between Her Majesty the Queen of the United Kingdom of Great Britain and Ireland, His Majesty the Emperor of the French, His Majesty the King of Sardinia, His Imperial Majesty the Sultan, on the one part, and His Majesty the Emperor of All the Russias, on the other part; as well as between their heirs and successors, their respective dominions and subjects, in perpetuity.

Article II

Peace being happily re-established between their said Majesties, the Territories conquered or occupied by their armies during the War shall be reciprocally evacuated. Special arrangements shall regulate the mode of the Evacuation, which shall be as prompt as possible.

Article III

His Majesty the Emperor of All the Russias engages to restore to His Majesty the Sultan the Town and Citadel of Kars, as well as the other parts of the Ottoman Territory of which the Russian troops are in possession.

Article IV

Their Majesties the Queen of the United Kingdom of Great Britain and Ireland, the Emperor of the French, the King of Sardinia, and the Sultan, engage to restore to His

[100] See Treaty of Paris, The Crimean Crisis, http://www.amitm.com/thecon/lesson5.html.

Majesty the Emperor of All the Russias, the Towns and Ports of Sebastopol, Balaklava, Kamiesch, Eupatoria, Kertch, Jenikale, Kinburn, as well as all other Territories occupied by the Allied Troops.

Article V

Their Majesties the Queen of the United Kingdom of Great Britain and Ireland, the Emperor of the French, the Emperor of All the Russias, the King of Sardinia, and the Sultan, grant a full and entire Amnesty to those of their subjects who may have been compromised by any participation whatsoever in the events of the War in favour of the cause of the enemy.

It is expressly understood that such Amnesty shall extend to the subjects of each of the Belligerent Parties who may have continued, during the War, to be employed in the service of one of the other Belligerents.

Article VI

Prisoners of War shall be immediately given up on either side.

Article VII

Her Majesty the Queen of the United Kingdom of Great Britain and Ireland, His Majesty the Emperor of Austria, His Majesty the Emperor of the French, His Majesty the King of Prussia, His Majesty the Emperor of All the Russias, and His Majesty the King of Sardinia, declare the Sublime Porte admitted to participate in the advantages of the Public Law and System (Concert) of Europe. Their Majesties engage, each on his part, to respect the Independence and the Territorial Integrity of the Ottoman Empire; Guarantee in common the strict observance of that engagement; and will, in consequence, consider any act tending to its violation as a question of general interest.

Article VIII

If there should arise between the Sublime Porte and one or more of the other Signing Powers, any misunderstanding which might endanger the maintenance of their relations, the Sublime Porte, and each of such Powers, before having recourse to the use of force, shall afford the other Contracting Parties the opportunity of preventing such an extremity by means of their Mediation.

Article IX

His Imperial Majesty the Sultan having, in his constant solicitude for the welfare of his subjects, issued a Firman, which, while ameliorating their condition without distinction of

Religion or of Race, records his generous intentions towards the Christian population of his Empire, and wishing to give a further proof of his sentiments in that respect, has resolved to communicate to the Contracting Parties the said Firman, emanating spontaneously from his Sovereign will.

The Contracting Powers recognise the high value of this communication. It is clearly understood that it cannot, in any case, give to the said Powers the right to interfere, either collectively or separately, in the relations of His Majesty the Sultan with his subjects, nor in the Internal Administration of his Empire.

Article X

The Convention of 13th of July, 1841, which maintains the ancient rule of the Ottoman Empire relative to the Closing of the Straits of the Bosphorus and of Dardanelles, has been revised by common consent.

The Act concluded for that purpose, and in conformity with that principle, between the High Contracting Parties, is and remains annexed to the present Treaty, and shall have the same force and validity as if it formed an integral part thereof.

Article XI

The Black Sea is Neutralised; its Waters and its Ports, thrown to the Mercantile Marine of every Nation, are formally and in perpetuity interdicted to the Flag of War, either of the Powers possessing its Coasts, or of any other Power, with the exceptions mentioned in Articles XIV and XIX of the present Treaty.

Article XII

Free from any impediment, the Commerce in the Ports and Waters of the Black Sea shall be subject only to Regulations of Health, Customs, and Police, framed in a spirit favourable to the development of Commercial transactions.

In order to afford to the Commercial and Maritime interests of every Nation the security which is desired, Russia and the Sublime Porte will admit Consuls into their Ports situated upon the Coast of the Black Sea, in conformity with the principles of International Law.

Article XIII

The Black Sea being neutralised according to the terms of Article XI, the maintenance or establishment upon its Coast of Military-Maritime Arsenals becomes alike unnecessary and purposeless- in consequence, His Majesty the Emperor of All the Russias, and His Imperial Majesty the Sultan, engage not to establish or to maintain upon that Coast any Military-Maritime Arsenal.

Article XIV

Their Majesties the Emperor of All the Russias and the Sultan having concluded a Convention for the purpose of settling the Force and the Number of Light Vessels, necessary for the service of their Coasts, which they reserve to themselves to maintain in the Black Sea, that Convention is annexed to the present Treaty, and shall have the same force and validity as if it formed an integral part thereof. It cannot be either annulled or modified without the assent of the Powers signing the present Treaty.

Article XV

The Act of the Congress of Vienna, having established the principles intended to regulate the Navigation of Rivers which separate or traverse different States, the Contracting Powers stipulate among themselves that those principles shall in future be equally applied to the Danube and its Mouths. They declare that its arrangement henceforth forms a part of the Public Law of Europe, and take it under their Guarantee.

The Navigation of the Danube cannot be subjected to any impediment or charge not expressly provided for by the Stipulations contained in the following Articles: in consequence, there shall not be levied any Toll founded solely upon the fact of the Navigation of the River, nor any Duty upon the Goods which may be on board of Vessels. The Regulations of Police and of Quarantine to be established for the safety of the States separated or traversed by that River, shall be so framed as to facilitate, as much as possible, the passage of Vessels. With the exception of such Regulations, no obstacle whatever shall be opposed to Free Navigation.

Article XVI

With a view to carry out the arrangements of the preceding Article, a Commission, in which Great Britain, Austria, France, Prussia, Russia, Sardinia, and Turkey, shall each be represented by one delegate, shall be charged to designate and to cause to be executed the Works necessary below Isatcba, to clear the Mouths of the Danube, as well as the neighbouring parts of the Sea, from the sands and other impediments which obstruct them, in order to put that part of the River and the said parts of the Sea in the best possible state for Navigation.

In order to cover the Expenses of such Works, as well as of the establishments intended to secure and to facilitate the Navigation at the Mouths of the Danube, fixed Duties, of a suitable rate, settled by the Commission by a majority of votes, may be levied, on the express condition that, in this respect as in every other, the Flags of all Nations shall be treated on the footing of perfect equality.

Article XVII

A Commission shall be established, and shall be composed of delegates of Austria, Bavaria, the Sublime Porte, and Wurtemberg (one for each of those Powers), to whom shall be added

Commissioners from the Three Danubian Principalities, whose nomination Shall have been approved by the Porte. This Commission, which shall be permanent: 1. Shall prepare Regulations of Navigation and River Police; 2. Shall remove the impediments, of whatever nature they may be, which still prevent the application to the Danube of the Arrangements of the Treaty of Vienna- 3. Shall order and cause to be executed the necessary Works throughout the whole course of the River; and 4. Shall, after the dissolution of the European Commission, see to maintaining the Mouths of the Danube and the neighbouring parts of the Sea in a navigable state.

Article XVIII

It is understood that the European Commission shall have completed its task, and that the River Commission shall have finished the Works described in the preceding Article, under Nos. I and 2, within the period of two years. The signing Powers assembled in Conference having been informed of that fact, shall, after having placed it on record, pronounce the Dissolution of the European Commission, and from that time the permanent River Commission shall enjoy the same powers as those with which the European Commission shall have until then been invested.

Article XIX

In order to insure the execution of the Regulations which shall have been established by common agreement, in conformity with the principles above declared, each of the Contracting Powers shall have the right to station, at all times, Two Light Vessels at the Mouths of the Danube.

Article XX

In exchange for the Towns, Ports, and Territories enumerated in Article IV of the present Treaty, and in order more fully to secure the Freedom of the Navigation of the Danube, His Majesty the Emperor of All the Russias consents to the rectification of his Frontier in Bessarabia.

The new Frontier shall begin from the Black Sea, one kilometre to the east of the Lake Bourna Sola, shall run perpendicularly to the Ackerman Road, shall follow that road to the Val de Trajan, pass to the south of Bolgrad, ascend the course of the River Yalpuck to the Height of Saratsika, and terminate at Katamori on the Pruth. Above that point the old Frontier between the Two Empires shall not undergo any modification.

Delegates of the Contracting Powers shall fix, in its details, the Line of the new Frontier.

Article XXI

The Territory ceded by Russia shall be Annexed to the Principality of Moldavia, under the Suzerainty of the Sublime Porte.

The Inhabitants of that Territory shall enjoy the Rights and Privileges secured to the Principalities; and during the space of 3 years, they shall be permitted to transfer their domicile elsewhere, disposing freely of their Property.

Article XXII

The Principalities of Wallachia and Moldavia shall continue to enjoy under the Suzerainty of the Porte, and under the Guarantee of the Contracting Powers, the Privileges and Immunities of which they are in possession. No exclusive Protection shall be exercised over them by any of the guaranteeing Powers.

There shall be no separate right of interference in their Internal Affairs.

Article XXIII

The Sublime Porte engages to preserve to the said Principalities an Independent and National Administration, as well as full liberty of Worship, of Legislation, of Commerce, and of Navigation.

The Laws and Statutes at present in force shall be revised. In order to establish a complete agreement in regard to such revision, a Special Commission, as to the composition of which the High Contracting Powers will come to an understanding among themselves, shall assemble, without delay, at Bucharest, together with a Commissioner of the Sublime Porte.

The business of this Commission shall be to investigate the present state of the Principalities, and to propose bases for their future organization.

Article XXIV

His Majesty the Sultan promises to convoke immediately in each of the two Provinces a Divan ad hoc, composed in such a manner as to represent most closely the interests of all classes of society. These Divans shall be called upon to express the wishes of the people in regard to the definitive organization of the Principalities.

An Instruction from the Congress shall regulate the relations between the Commission and these Divans.

Article XXV

Taking into consideration the opinion expressed by the two Divans, the Commission shall transmit, without delay, to the present seat of the Conferences, the result of its own labours.

The Final Agreement with the Suzerain Power shall be recorded in a Convention to be concluded at Paris between the High Contracting Parties; and a hatti-sché rif, in conformity with the stipulations of the Convention, shall constitute definitively the organization of those Provinces, placed thenceforward under the Collective Guarantee of all the signing Powers.

Article XXVI

It is agreed that there shall be in the Principalities a National Armed Force, organized with the view to maintain the security of the interior, and to ensure that of the Frontiers. No impediment shall be opposed to the extraordinary measures of defence which, by agreement with the Sublime Porte, they may be called upon to take in order to repel any external aggression.

Article XXVII

If the Internal tranquillity of the Principalities should be menaced or compromised, the Sublime Porte shall come to an understanding with the other Contracting Powers in regard to the measures to be taken for maintaining or re-establishing legal order.

No armed Intervention can take place without previous agreement between those Powers.

Article XXVIII

The Principality of Servia shall continue to hold of the Sublime Porte, in conformity with the Imperial Hats which fix and determine its Rights and Immunities, placed henceforward under the Collective Guarantee of the Contracting Powers.

In consequence, the said Principality shall preserve its Independent and National Administration, as well as full Liberty of Worship, of Legislation, of Commerce, and of Navigation.

Article XXIX

The right of garrison of the Sublime Porte, as stipulated by anterior regulations, is maintained. No armed Intervention can take place in Servia without previous agreement between the High Contracting Powers.

Article XXX

His Majesty the Emperor of All the Russias and His Majesty the Sultan maintain in its Integrity the state of their possessions in Asia such as it legally existed before the rupture.

In order to prevent all local dispute the Line of Frontier shall be verified, and, if necessary, rectified, without any prejudice as regards Territory being sustained by either Party.

For this purpose a Mixed Commission, composed of two Russian Commissioners, two Ottoman Commissioners, one English Commissioner, and one French Commissioner, shall be sent to the spot immediately after the re-establishment of diplomatic relations between the Court of Russia and the Sublime Porte. Its labours shall be completed within the period of 8 months after the exchange of the Ratifications of the present Treaty.

Article XXXI

The Territories occupied during the War by the troops of their Majesties the Queen of the United Kingdom of Great Britain and Ireland, the Emperor of Austria, the Emperor of the French, and the King of Sardinia, according to the terms of the Conventions signed at Constantinople on the 12th of March, 1854, between Great Britain, France, and the Sublime Porte; on the 14th of June of the same year, between Austria and the Sublime Porte and on the 15th of March, 1855, between Sardinia and the Sublime Porte; shall be evacuated as soon as possible after the exchange of the Ratifications of the present Treaty.

The periods and the means of execution shall form the object of an arrangement between the Sublime Porte and the Powers whose troops have occupied its Territory.

Article XXXII

Until the Treaties or Conventions which existed before the War between the Belligerent Powers have been either renewed or replaced by new Acts, Commerce of importation or of exportation shall take place reciprocally on the footing of the regulations in force before the War; and in all other matters their subjects shall be respectively treated upon the footing of the Most Favoured Nation.

Article XXXIII

The Convention concluded this day between their Majesties the Queen of the United Kingdom of Great Britain and Ireland, the Emperor of the French, on the one part, and His Majesty the Emperor of All the Russias on the other part, respecting the Aland Islands, is and remains annexed to the present Treaty, and shall have the same force and validity as if it formed a part thereof

Article XXXIV

The present Treaty shall be ratified, and the Ratifications shall be exchanged at Paris in the space of 4 weeks, or sooner if possible.

In witness whereof the respective Plenipotentiaries have signed the same, and have affixed thereto the Seal of their Arms. Done at Paris, the 30th day of the month of March, in the year 1856.

APPENDIX III

The Treaty of Berlin

Treaty Between Great Britain, Austria-Hungary, France, Germany, Italy, Russia and Turkey.

July 13, 1878.[101]

Article I

Bulgaria is constituted an autonomous and tributary Principality under the suzerainty of His Imperial Majesty the Sultan. It will have a Christian government and a national militia.

[101] See Modern History Sourcebook: The Treaty of Berlin, 1878 Excerpts on the Balkans, Fordham University: The Jesuit University New York, available at http://www.fordham.edu/halsall/mod/1878berlin.asp.

Article XXIII

The Sublime Porte undertakes scrupulously to apply in the Island of Crete the Organic Law of 1868 with such modifications as may be considered equitable. Similar laws adapted to local requirements, excepting as regards the exemption from taxation granted to Crete, shall also be introduced into the other parts of Turkey in Europe for which no special organization has been provided by the present treaty. The Sublime Porte shall depute special commissions, in which the native element shall be largely represented, to settle the details of the new laws in each province. The schemes of organization resulting from these labors shall be submitted for examination to the Sublime Porte, which, before promulgating the Acts for putting them into force, shall consult the European Commission instituted for Easter Roumelia.

Article XXV

The provinces of Bosnia and Herzegovina shall be occupied and administered by Austria-Hungary. The government of Austria-Hungary, not desiring to undertake the administration of the Sanjak of Novi-Pazar [modern Kosovo Province], which extends between Serbia and Montenegro in a South-Easterly direction to the other side of Mitrovitza, the Ottoman administration will continue to exercise its functions there. Nevertheless, in order to assure the maintenance of the new political state of affairs, as well as freedom and security of communications, Austria-Hungary reserves the right of keeping garrisons and having military and commercial roads in the whole of this part of the ancient vilayet of Bosnia. To this end the governments of Austria-Hungary and Turkey reserve to themselves to come to an understanding on the details.

Article XXVI

The independence of Montenegro is recognized by the Sublime Porte and by all those of the High Contracting Parties who had not hitherto admitted it.

Article XXXIV

The High Contracting Parties recognize the independence of the Principality of Serbia, subject to the conditions set forth in the following Article.

Article XXXV

In Serbia the difference of religious creeds and confessions shall not be alleged against any person as a ground for exclusion or incapacity in matters relating to the enjoyment of civil or political rights, admission to public employments, functions, and honors, or the exercise of the various professions and industries, in any locality whatsoever. The freedom and outward exercise of all forms of worship shall be assured to all persons belonging to Serbia, as well as to foreigners, and no hindrance shall be offered either to the hierarchical organization of the different communions, or to their relations with their spiritual chiefs.

Article XLIII

The High Contracting Parties recognize the independence of Romania, subject to the conditions set forth in the two following Articles.

Article XLIV

In Romania the difference of religious creeds and confessions shall not be alleged against any person as a ground for exclusion or incapacity in matters relating to the enjoyment of civil or political rights, admission to public employments, functions, and honors, or the exercise of the various professions and industries, in any locality whatsoever. The freedom and outward exercise of all forms of worship shall be assured to all persons belonging to Romania, as well as to foreigners, and no hindrance shall be offered either to the hierarchical organization of the different communions, or to their relations with their spiritual chiefs. The subjects and citizens of all the Powers, traders or others, shall be treated in Romania without distinction of creed, on a footing of perfect equality.

Article XLV

The Principality of Romania restores to His Majesty the Emperor of Russia that portion of the Bessarabian territory detached from Russia by the Treaty of Paris of 1856, bounded on the West by the mid-channel of the Pruth [River], and on the South by the mid-channel of the Kilia Branch and the Stary-Stamboul mouth [now the modern state of Moldova].

Article LVIII

The Sublime Porte cedes to the Russian Empire in Asia the territories of Ardahan, Kars, and Batum [modern Armenia and Georgia, with a bit of Northeastern Turkey], together with the latter port.

Article LIX

His Majesty the Emperor of Russia declares that it is his intention to constitute Batum a free port, essentially commercial.

Article LXII

The Sublime Porte having expressed the intention to maintain the principle of religious liberty, and give it the widest scope, the Contracting Parties take note of this spontaneous declaration. In no part of the Ottoman Empire shall difference of religion be alleged against any person as a ground for exclusion or incapacity in matters relating to the enjoyment of civil or political rights, admission to public employments, functions, and honors, or the exercise of the various professions and industries, in any locality whatsoever. The freedom and outward exercise of all forms of worship shall be assured to all, and no hindrance shall be offered either to the hierarchical organization of the different communions, or to their relations with their spiritual chiefs.

Ecclesiastics, pilgrims, and monks of all nationalities traveling in Turkey in Europe, or in Turkey in Asia, shall enjoy the same rights, advantages, and privileges.

The right of official protection by the Diplomatic and Consular Agents of the Powers in Turkey is recognized both as regards the above-mentioned persons and their religious, charitable, and other establishments in the Holy Places and elsewhere. The rights possessed by France are expressly reserved, and it is well understood that no alterations can be made in the *status quo* in the Holy Places. The monks of Mount Athos, of whatever country they may be natives, shall be maintained in their former possessions and advantages, and shall enjoy, without any exception, complete equality of rights and prerogatives.

Bibliography

'The Fundamental Agreement'. *A.A.S.* vol. LXXXVI, no. 9 (1994): p. 716. http://www.vatican.va/roman_curia/secretariat_state/archivio/documents/rc_seg-st_19931230_santa-sede-israele_en.htm.

Abua Ramadan, Moussa. 'The Haram el Shariff in Jerusalem: An Israeli Law Perspective'. In *Between Cultural Diversity and Common Heritage: Legal and Religious Perspectives on Sacred Place of the Mediterranean*, edited by Silvio Ferrari and Andrea Benzo (Burlington, Vt.: Ashgate Publishers, 2014).

Allain, Jean. 'Orientalism and International Law: The Middle East as the Underclass of the International Legal Order'. *Leiden Journal of International Law* 17 (2004): p. 391.

Anghie, Antony. 'Finding the Peripheries: Sovereignty and Colonialism in the Nineteenth-Century International Law'. *Harvard International Law Journal* 40 (1999): p. 1.

Assmann, Jan. *The Price of Monotheism*, translated by Robert Savage (Stanford, Calif.: Stanford University Press, 2009).

Badem, Candan. *'The' Ottoman Crimean War: (1853–1856)* (Leiden: Kroninklijke Brill, 2010).

Benvenisti, Meron. *City of Stone: The Hidden History of Jerusalem* (Berkeley: University of California Press, 1996).

Benz, Ernst. *The Eastern Orthodox Church: Its Thought and Life* (USA: Rowohld Taschenbuch Verlag, 2009).

Berger, Marshal J. 'Jerusalem's Holy Sites in Israeli Law'. In *Between Cultural Diversity and Common Heritage: Legal and Religious Perspectives on the Sacred Places in the Mediterranean*, edited by Silvio Ferrari and Andrea Benzo (Burlington, VT: Ashgate Publishers, 2014).

Berman, Nathaniel. 'Legalizing Jerusalem or, of Law, Fantasy, and Faith'. *Catholic University Law Review* 45 (1996): p. 823.

Berman, Nathaniel. 'The Grotius Lecture Series'. *American University International Law Review* 14 (1999): p. 1516.

Bialer, Uri, et al. ed. *Nostra Aetate: Origins, Promulgation, Impact on Jewish–Catholic Relations* (New Brunswick, NJ: Transaction Publishers, 2007).

Blok, Anton. 'The Narcissism of Minor Differences'. *European Journal of Social Theory* 1, no. 1 (1998): p. 33.

Bourdieu, Pierre. *Distinction: A Social Critique of the Judgment of Taste* (Harvard: Harvard University Press, 1984).

Cattan, Henry. 'The Status of Jerusalem under International Law and United Nations Resolutions'. *Journal of Palestine Studies* 10, no. 3 (1981): p. 3.

Çırakman, Aslı. *From the 'Terror of the World' to the 'Sick Man of Europe': European Images of Ottoman Empire from the 16th century to the 19th* (New York: Peter Lang Publishing 2005).

Cohen, Leonard. 'Hallelujah'. In *Various Positions* (1984). http://www.songtexte.com/songtext/leonard-cohen/hallelujah-7bdb72c0.html.

Cohen, Raymond. *Saving the Holy Sepulchre: How Rival Christians Came Together to Rescue their Holiest Shrine* (Oxford: Oxford University Press, 2008).

Dawson, Christopher. *Progress and Religion: A Historical Inquiry* (London/New York: Sheed and Ward, 1929).

Duchhardt, Heinz. 'From Westphalia to the Revolutionary Era'. In *Peace Treaties and International Law in European History: From the Late Middle Ages to World War One*, edited by Randall Lesaffer (Cambridge: Cambridge University Press, 2004).

Durkheim, *Émile. Elementary Forms of Religious life* (London: G Allen & Unwin, 1912).

Emmett, Chad F. 'The Status Quo Solution for Jerusalem'. *Journal of Palestine Studies* 26, no. 2 (1997): p. 16.

Emmett, Chad F. 'The Capital Cities of Jerusalem'. *Geographical Review* 86, no. 2 (1996): p. 233.

Evans, Malcolm D. *Religious Liberty and International Law in Europe* (Cambridge: Cambridge University Press, 1997).

Fanon, Franz. *Black Skin, White Masks* (New York: Grove Press, 1967).

Ferrari, Silvio. 'The Fundamental Agreement between the Holy See and Israel and the Conventions between States and the Church since the Vatican II Council'. *Catholic University Law Review* 47, no. 2 (1998): p. 385.

Feuchtwanger, Edgar. *Bismarck: A Political History* (New York: Routledge, 2014).

Finke, Carole. *Defending the Rights of Others: The Great Powers, the Jews, and International Minority Protection 1878–1938* (Cambridge: Cambridge University Press, 2004).

Firestone, Reuven. *Who are the Real Chosen People? The Meaning of Chosenness in Judaism, Christianity and Islam* (Woodstock, Vt.: SkyLight Paths Publishing, 2008).

Freud, Sigmund. *Civilization, Society and Religion* (London: Penguin, 1991).

Geiss, Imaneul. *German Foreign Policy 1871–1914* (London: Routledge Press, 1976).

Green, William Scott. 'Approaching Distinctiveness'. In *Monotheism & Ethics: Historical and Contemporary Intersections among Judaism, Christianity and Islam*, edited by Tzvi Langermann (Leiden: Brill, 2011).

Haigh, Christopher, ed. *The Cambridge Historical Encyclopedia of Great Britain and Ireland* (Cambridge: Cambridge University Press, 2000).

Herring, George. *What was the Oxford Movement?* (London: Continuum, 2002).

Hirsch, Moshe, Deborah Housen-Couriel, and Ruth Lapidot eds. *Whither Jerusalem?: Proposals and Positions Concerning the Future of Jerusalem* (The Hague: Martinus Nijhoff, 1995).

Hobsbawm, Eric. *The Age of Empire: 1875–1914* (London: Weidenfeld & Nicolson, 1987).

Islamogu-Inan, Huri. *The Ottoman Empire and the World-Economy* (Cambridge: Cambridge University Press, 2004).

Jones, S. Shepard. 'The Status of Jerusalem: Some National and International Aspects'. *Law and Contemporary Problems* 33, no. 1 (1968): p. 169.

Kafka, Franz. *Before the Law.* http://www.kafka-online.info/before-the-law.html.

Keene, Edward. *International Political Thought: An Historical Introduction* (Cambridge: Polity Press, 2005).

Kennedy, Duncan. 'Three Globalisations of Law and Legal Thought: 1850–2000'. In *The New Law and Economic Development. A Critical Appraisal, edited by* D. Trubek and A. Santos (New York: Cambridge University Press, 2006).

Koskenniemi, Martti. 'Between Empire and Legal Formalism'. Speech in Recife, Brazil (2003). http://www.helsinki.fi/eci/Publications/MRecife.pdf.

Koskenniemi, Martti. 'Empire and International Law: The real Spanish Contribution'. *The University of Toronto Law Journal* 61, no. 1 (2011): p. 1.

Koskenniemi, Martti. *From Apology to Utopia. The Structure of International Legal Argument* (Cambridge: Cambridge University Press, 2005).

Koskenniemi, Martti. *The Gentle Civilizer of Nations* (Cambridge: Cambridge University Press, 2001).

Koskenniemi, Martti. 'Histories of International Law: Dealing with Eurocentricism'. *Rechtsgeschichte: Zeitschrift des Max-Planck-Instituts für europäische Rechtsgeschichte* 19 (2011): p. 152.

Lee, Stephen J. *Imperial Germany 1871–1918* (New York: Routledge, 2005).

Makdisi, Ussama Samir. *The Culture of Sectarianism: Community, History, and Violence in Nineteenth-Century Ottoman Lebanon* (Berkeley: University of California Press, 2000), p. 3.

Maritain, Jacques. 'Lettre à la Conference du *Seelisberg*'. In *The Holocaust and the Christian World*, edited by Carol Rittner et al. (USA: Continuum, 2000).

Marshall, David. *Communicating the Word: Revelation, Translation, and Interpretation in Christianity and Islam* (Georgetown, DC: Georgetown University Press, 2011).

Masud, Muhammad Khalid, ed. *Travellers in Faith: Studies of Tagblighi Jama'at as a Transnational Islamic Movement for Faith Renewal* (Leiden: Brill, 2000).

Merkley, Paul Charles. *Christian Attitudes towards the State of Israel* (Montreal: McGill University Press, 2001).

Mickleson, Karin. 'Rhetoric and Rage: Third World Voices in International Legal Discourse'. *Wisconsin International Law Journal* 16 (1998): p. 361.

Modern History Sourcebook: The Treaty of Berlin, 1878 Excerpts on the Balkans. Fordham University: the Jesuit University New York. http://www.fordham.edu/halsall/mod/1878berlin.asp.

Molinaro, Enrico. *The Holy Places of Jerusalem in Middle East Peace Agreements: The Conflict between Global and State Identities* (Sussex: Sussex Academic Press, 2009).

Montefiore, Simon Sebag. *Jerusalem* (London: Phoenix, 2012).

Morgenthau, Hans J. *Politics among Nations: The Struggle for Power and Peace* (New York: Alfred A. Knopf, 1960).

Morris, Benny. 'The New Historiography: Israel and its Past'. In *1948 and After: Israel and the Palestinians* (Oxford: Clarendon Press, 1994).

Palmieri-Billig, Lisa. 'Vatican upset at non-finalized agreement with Israel'. The *Jerusalem Post* (12 December 2007). http://www.jpost.com/Israel/Vatican-upset-at-non-finalized-agreement-with-Israel.

Pamuk, Orhan. *The White Castle*, translated by Victoria Holbrook (Manchester: Carcanet Press, 1990).

Paz, Reut Yael. 'Religion, Secularism and International Law'. In *Oxford Handbook of International Legal Theory*, edited by Anne Orford and Florian Hofmann (Oxford: Oxford University Press, 2016).

Paz, Reut Yael. *A Gateway between a Distant God and a Cruel World:* The Contribution of Jewish German-Speaking Scholars to International Law (Leiden: Brill Martinus Nijhoff Publishers, 2012).

Said, Edward W. *Orientalism* (London: Penguin Books, 2003).

Schultz, Martin. *Normen und Praxis: Das Europäische Konzert der Großmächte als Sicherheit, 1815–1860* (Munich: Oldenburg Wissenschaftsverlag, 2009).

Somos, Mark. *Secularisation and the Leiden Circle* (Leiden: Brill, 2011).

Sullivan, Winnifred Fallers. *The Impossibility of Religious Freedom* (Princeton: Princeton University Press, 2005).

Taylor, A. J. P. *The Struggle for Mastery in Europe 1914–1918* (Oxford: Oxford University Press, 1954).

Tibi, Bassam. *Fundamentalism: Political Islam and the New World Order* (California: University of California Press, 1998).

Wade, Robert Plumer. *An enquiry into the foundation and history of the law of nations in Europe, from the time of the Greeks and Romans, to the age of Grotius* (1795). https://archive.org/stream/enquiryintofound12ward#page/n43/mode/2up/search/christianity.

Warraq, Ibn. *Defending the West: A Critique of Edward Said's Orientalism* (Amherst, N.Y.: Prometheus Books, 2007).

Wasum-Rainer, Susanne. 'Status Quo'. In *Max Planck Encyclopedia of Public International Law* (Oxford: Oxford University Press, 2013). http://opil.ouplaw.com.

Watson, Adam. *The Evolution of International Society* (New York: Routledge, 1992).

Weitz, Eric D. 'From the Vienna to the Paris System: International Politics and the Entangled Histories of Human Rights, Forced Deportations and Civilizing Missions'. *The American Historical Review* 113, no. 5 (2008): p. 1313.

PART IV

POLITICAL THEOLOGY AND INTERNATIONAL LEGAL THEORY

13

The Doctrine of the Providential Function of Commerce in International Law

Idealizing Trade

Ileana M. Porras

Introduction

The focus of this chapter is the doctrine of the providential function of commerce[1] in the work of Francisco de Vitoria (*c.* 1492–1546), Alberico Gentili (1552–1608), and Hugo Grotius (1583–1645). Comprised of a set of inherited but vague assumptions and ideas about the providential origin and function of international trade, this doctrine and its elements, neither explicitly religious nor yet economic, nonetheless provided all three primitive legal scholars[2] with a useful perspective from which to construct an optimistic vision of international commerce. Introduced into the international legal canon through their work, the doctrine had a decisive and lasting influence, giving shape to international law's predominantly favourable opinion of the practice of international trade, even as the doctrine itself, never fully theorized, was largely forgotten. The puzzle at the back of my inquiry concerns the persistence of the optimistic view of commerce in international law. Why, despite almost five centuries of contrary examples, has the vision of international commerce as beneficent and productive of international friendship proved so compelling? The answer, I suggest, lies in the interplay between two factors. First, and most obvious, is the fact that while the doctrine is not in origin a religious doctrine, its elements and its narrative logic carried an

[1] The doctrine, whose full expression economist Jacob Viner traces back to the Pagan Libanius in the fourth century, consists of the combination of two sub-ideas: '(1) providence favors trade between peoples as a means of promoting the universal brotherhood of man; (2) to give economic incentives to people to trade with each other providence has given to their respective territories different products.' *See* Jacob Viner, *The Role of Divine Providence in the Social Order: An Essay in Intellectual History* (Philadelphia: American Philosophical Society, 1972).

[2] The term is used by David Kennedy to refer to the corpus of European international legal scholarship produced prior to the 1648 Peace of Westphalia, a date which many modern legal historians consider as marking the birth of their discipline. *See* David Kennedy, 'Primitive Legal Scholarship', *Harvard International Law Journal* 27, no. 1 (1986): pp. 1–5.

unmistakable religious sensibility that became indissolubly associated with international trade. Viewed through the prism of the providentialist doctrine of commerce, the practice of international trade came to be understood not merely as an economic activity among others, but as one responding to a divine mandate in pursuit of religious ends. But the doctrine's true efficacy, I argue, lies in a more subtle internal effect. In essence, the doctrine, which holds at its core an act of exchange among distant peoples, allowed its adherents to idealize international trade by blurring the distinction between the act of commercial exchange and that of gift-exchange. In this manner, international exchange came to be portrayed as an act of friendship and community recognition, rather than a cold commercial act between strangers.

Elsewhere, I have analysed Vitoria's and Grotius' use of the doctrine of the providential function of commerce in the context of elaborating a right to engage in commerce, a right that in their work served to justify war and conquest.[3] In this chapter, I turn my attention to the religious dimensions implicated in their use of the doctrine, and begin an exploration of how their use of the doctrine intersected with the nascent science of economics and economic thinking about trade. My aim is to take seriously the claim that these primitive legal scholars were not simply engaged in a project of whitewashing violence and exploitation, but were instead, seeking to articulate an ethically informed and religiously grounded philosophy of international relations, which at the same time would provide a normatively positive perspective on the new commercial practices that had emerged in Christian Europe starting in the sixteenth century. In other words, I approach the works of Vitoria, Gentili, and Grotius as those of highly educated scholars, each steeped in a particular religious tradition, with deeply held and sincere religious convictions, whose faith governed their life and practice. Indeed, none of the three was merely a passive receiver of religious doctrine. Instead, each intervened in current religious and doctrinal debates and produced works that were both educational and persuasive in nature on religious topics. At the same time, each scholar was a sophisticated contributor to contemporaneous debates concerning the new commercial practices and was sensitive to the relevance of international commerce to the economic development and political stability of their sovereigns and their nations. Thus, the question I am seeking to address is how the providentialist doctrine and its elements functioned within their analysis and how it came to fit both their religious purpose and their political objectives.

The chapter is composed of three parts: first, I address the subject of international commerce as it emerges in the work of the primitive legal scholars and highlight the negative attitudes towards commerce, merchants and profit still prevalent in sixteenth century Christian Europe in order to emphasize the unfavourable

[3] For a discussion of the role played by the right to commerce and the providentialist doctrine in Francisco de Vitoria's *De Indis* and Hugo Grotius' *De Iure Praedae, see* Ileana M. Porras, 'Constructing International Law in the East Indian Seas: Property, Sovereignty, Commerce and War in Hugo Grotius' De Iure Praedae—The Law of Prize and Booty, or "On How to Distinguish Merchants from Pirates"', *Brooklyn Journal of International Law* 31, no. 741 (2006): p. 756 et seq.

context against which the providentialist view of commerce was adopted; second, I map out some key elements of the optimistic doctrine of the providential function of commerce adopted and deployed by Vitoria, Gentili, and Grotius; and third, I focus on the act of exchange, which lies at the heart of the providentialist doctrine, and explore the distinction between two categories of exchange: gift-exchange and commercial exchange, and argue that Vitoria and the others ascribe positive normative power to international commerce by blurring the distinction between gift and trade.

Usury, Greed, and Commercial Practices—Merchants in the Economy of Salvation

None of the primitive legal scholars, whose work was to influence the development of modern international law, set out specifically to address the subject of international commerce. On the contrary, the ostensible subject of authors as diverse as Francisco de Vitoria, Alberico Gentili, and Hugo Grotius was first and foremost the law of war. Each sought to provide an authoritative account of the conditions necessary for just or legitimate war, and to map out the rightful limits of the possible effects or consequences of just war. Indeed, it was in this context that each author grappled with a conception of sovereignty and developed a theory of rights, for according to the fourth century Augustinian theological tradition theorized by Thomas Aquinas in the thirteenth century,[4] just war could only be waged by a true sovereign in defence of or as punishment for a violation of rights. Nonetheless, in the midst of their doctrinal ruminations concerning war and justice, international commerce emerged as a decisive subject as each scholar recognized a right to engage in international commerce, founded either in natural law or a universally applicable *ius gentium*.[5]

In their work, interference with the right to engage in international commerce was deemed a significant injury,[6] and within their respective systems, it thus served as a justification for war, the taking of prize and booty, territorial conquest, and even the deposition of rightful sovereigns. Reflecting the aspirations and anxieties of their particular context, Vitoria, Gentili, and Grotius evinced a preoccupation

[4] In Aquinas' formulation, the three necessary conditions for 'just war' include: sovereign authority, just cause, and right intention. See St. Thomas Aquinas, *Summa Theologica*, translated by Fathers of the English Dominican Province (New York: Benziger Bros., 1947), pt. 2, question 40, art. 1.

[5] For the argument that commerce was nonetheless at the heart of Hugo Grotius' early work *De Iure Praedae*, written *circa* 1604, *see* Porras, 'Constructing International Law', p. 756 et seq.

[6] For instance, according to Gentili: 'One who takes away [the privilege to engage in international commerce] inflicts a *wound* on human society.' (Emphasis added). Alberico Gentili, *De Jure Belli Libri Tres* (Reproduction of the 1612 edition, with a translation by John C. Rolfe (Oxford: Classics of International Law, 1933) (1598), Book 1, chapter XIX at p. 88. Grotius goes even further, stating that those who take away the right to engage in commerce 'violate nature herself'. H. Grotius, *The Free Sea,* edited by David Armitage (Indianapolis, Ind.: Liberty Fund, 2004), [hereinafter Grotius, *Mare Liberum*] chapter I at 11.

with the economic impact of international commerce. Each was keenly aware of the riches or profit that their sovereigns and countrymen stood to gain from the new flows of 'goods' to Europe from distant places.[7] With the twin sciences of economics and political economy barely in their infancy, each man nonetheless intuited that the future relative greatness of their nations within Europe depended to some no small extent on their ability to secure a share of the long-distance seaborne trade with peoples and lands beyond Christian Europe. To embrace the practice of international commerce, however, these authors had to reimagine trade in a positive light in order to circumvent the predominantly negative attitude towards commerce, merchants, profit, and money still widespread in Christian Europe in the sixteenth and seventeenth centuries.

Throughout the long Middle Ages,[8] the practice of commerce was tainted because of its association with usury, or lending at interest, a practice severely condemned by the Church as a mortal sin 'against nature'.[9] In popular lore and as told by Catholic preachers, Purgatory was the common abode of the souls of avaricious, usurious, and fraudulent merchants whose repentance came late in the day, and whose eventual passage to Heaven depended on spouses and heirs fulfilling their obligation to make restitution and 'pay back' the ill-gotten gains. In addition, merchants were viewed with suspicion because, at a time when travel was not common, theirs was an itinerant lifestyle. Merchants were deemed foreigners (or at least suspected of being influenced by foreign ideas and practices) and thought to be contaminated by their involvement with the city, the hubs of commerce, feared by the non-urban population as dens of iniquity, criminality, and corruption.

[7] For instance, at the conclusion of his important lecture on the subject of the Spanish conquest of the New World, Vitoria notes with concern that, if there were no just cause for war against the Indians, '*the whole Indian expedition and trade would cease*, to the great loss of the Spaniards. And this in turn would mean a huge loss to the royal exchequer, which would be intolerable.' Francisco de Vitoria, 'On the American Indians', in *Francisco de Vitoria, Political Writings*, edited by Anthony Pagden and Jeremy Lawrance (Cambridge: Cambridge University Press, 1991), pp. 231–92 at 291. [hereinafter Vitoria, *De Indis*]. Grotius, for his part, begins his youthful tract *De Iure Praedae* arguing for the right of Dutch privateers to take a Portuguese Carrack in the East Indies as prize by stressing the extent to which Dutch fortunes depended on international commerce: '[T]he wealth of our state is chiefly if not entirely sustained [by it].' Hugo Grotius, *Commentary on the Law of Prize and Booty*, edited by M. J. van Ittersum (Indianapolis: Liberty Fund, 2006), p. 10. [hereinafter Grotius, *De Iure Praedae*]. For a discussion of Grotius' preoccupation with commerce and his presentation of the virtuous profit-seeking Dutch *see* Porras, 'Constructing International Law', p. 756 et seq.

[8] I use the term the 'long Middle Ages' to allude to the work of Jacques Le Goff, who argued against a traditional periodization that assumes a radical break between the Middle Ages and the Renaissance in the sixteenth century, insisting instead on the continuities and discontinuities throughout the period. *See* Jacques le Goff, *Time, Work, and Culture in the Middle Ages*, translated by Arthur Goldhammer (Chicago: University of Chicago Press, 1980); *See also* Jacques le Goff, *Un Long Moyen Âge* (Paris: Tallandier, 2004).

[9] For a lively account of the Catholic Church's long-standing condemnation of usury and its increasing preoccupation with the practice, starting in the twelfth century, as the money economy became more prevalent in Europe, *see Jacques Le Goff, Your Money or Your Life: Economy and Religion in the Middle Ages*, translated by Patricia Ranum (New York: Zone Books, 1990), p. 23 et seq. Famously, in his Divine Comedy, Dante Alighieri (1265–1321) placed usurers in the lower depths of hell; see *Dante: The Divine Comedy, Vol. I:* Inferno, translated by Mark Musa (Harmondsworth: Penguin Books, 1984), *XI: 94–111 and XVII.*

In the sixteenth century, the Catholic Church and Protestants of every stripe continued to condemn the practice of usury,[10] but by and large their interpretations had become more nuanced. Both interest and profit, for instance, so long as they were reasonable (rather than predatory), were deemed justifiable by reference to labour expended and the risks taken. In response to the new monetary and commercial practices of the age, theologians of the Salamanca school in the sixteenth century, of which Vitoria was a prominent member, drew careful ethical distinctions between permissible practices such as lending for profit as a form of capital investment or the provision of risk insurance, and usurious forms of lending on interest.[11] This nuanced anti-usury approach came to be widely accepted and was still the dominant perspective on usury in the early seventeenth century. Grotius, for instance, devotes a chapter to it in his 1625 treatise *De Jure Belli ac Pacis* (on the Rights of War).[12] Merchants, however, remained a morally suspect class, still under the cloud of classical opprobrium: men engaged in a base and loathsome profession, according to the influential Greek and Roman sources Aristotle[13] and Cicero.[14] Even as commerce became widespread and merchants more numerous,

[10] While major Protestant reformers such as Martin Luther and John Calvin rejected the canon law on usury, they took a narrow view of acceptable interest payments, and shared a strong negative view of usurers and their practices. John Calvin made an important exception for a limited interest on certain types of commercial loans, but prohibited the charging of interest on 'charitable' loans. Many of their followers retained the stricter views on usury and the opprobrium against usurers remained culturally relevant up through the industrial revolution. See R. H. *Tawney, Religion and the Rise of Capitalism* (London: John Murray, 1926). For a recent re-evaluation of the Protestant perspective on usury, *see* John Munro, 'Usury, Calvinism and Credit in Protestant England: From the Sixteenth Century to the Industrial Revolution', in *Religion and Religious Institutions in the European Economy 1000–1800* (Firenze: Firenze University Press, 2012), pp. 155–84. According to Munro, in the sixteenth and early seventeenth centuries followers of Calvin and Luther were more hostile to usury than were contemporary Catholics (p. 168).

[11] There is a growing literature on the variety of approaches taken by the Salamanca School's authors to the new economic and business practices that emerged in the sixteenth and early seventeenth centuries. See e.g. Domenec Mele, 'Early Business Ethics in Spain: The Salamanca School (1526–1614)', *Journal of Business Ethics* 22, no. 3 (1999): pp. 175–89; see also Louis Baeck, 'Spanish Economic Thought: The school of Salamanca and the *arbitristas*', *History of Political Economy* 20, no. 3 (1988): pp. 381–408; and Juan Manuel Eligido, 'The Just Price: Three Insights from the Salamanca School', *Journal of Business Ethics* 90, no. 1 (2009): pp. 29–46. The topic of the relationship between Vitoria's careful analysis of business practices, commutative justice, and the sacrament of confession, is addressed in Martti Koskenniemi, 'Empire and International Law: The Real Spanish Contribution', *University Toronto Law Journal* 61, no. 1 (2011): p. 18.

[12] Grotius, *De Jure Belli ac Pacis*, vol. II., chapter XII, pp. 753–60.

[13] Aristotle drew a distinction between barter (household management) necessary for self-sufficiency and exchange for moneymaking (commerce). The first was in accordance with nature, the second he deemed contrary to nature. See *Thomas Aquinas, Commentary on Aristotle's Politics*, translated by Richard J. Regan (Indianapolis: Hackett Publishing Company, 2007), Book I, chapters 7–9 on Moneymaking. Aquinas cited to Aristotle's text approvingly in his own *Summa Theologiae* (1266–73), concluding 'It follows that trade in itself has a certain quality of baseness since it does not of its own nature involve an honorable or necessary end.' *Summa Theologiae*, Second Part of Part II Q.77.4. Fraud. *St. Thomas Aquinas on Politics and Ethics*, translated and edited by Paul E. Sigmund (New York: Norton, 1988), p. 73.

[14] Cicero's *De Officiis* (44 BCE) (a.k.a. On Obligations) was widely read and proved highly influential throughout the Middle Ages and into the Renaissance. See *Cicero, On Obligations*, translated and introduced by P. G. Walsh (Oxford: Oxford University Press, 2001), XXXIV et seq. For Cicero's trenchant view of money-makers and small scale merchants, see Book I (150) at p. 50; however,

especially in the urban centres of Europe, and despite a growing recognition of the importance of their role, observers continued to assume that merchants, driven by culpable self-interest, would, if given the opportunity, inevitably cross over the fine line and engage in usury, fraud, and theft, all considered offenses against justice. Merchants, in the theological economy, were in perpetual risk of falling into the sin of avarice.

Embracing the Doctrine of the Providential Function of Commerce

In a move that would prove of great significance to the future of international law, in the course of articulating their theories of war and justice, rather than propagate the commonplace negative view of merchants and commerce, Vitoria, Gentili, and Grotius each in turn endorsed an optimistic set of assumptions and attitudes about international commerce. While each of the three scholars embraced international commerce as a positive force, Francisco de Vitoria, a Catholic Dominican priest and theologian teaching at Salamanca in the second quarter of the sixteenth century and thus the earliest of the three, was the most cautious. In *De Indis,* his seminal 1539 *relectio* analysing the just and unjust 'titles' for the Spanish conquest of the New World, he put into question the most common contemporaneous justifications for the Spanish territorial conquest of the New World. The great violence and culpable greed of the Spanish conquistadors in the Indies were not unknown to him, and these troubled him. 'When we hear subsequently of bloody massacres and of innocent individuals pillaged of their possessions and dominions, there are grounds for doubting the justice of what has been done.'[15] Nonetheless, in *De Indis* Vitoria articulated a right to engage in trade, which he anchored in a right to travel that he found in 'the law of nations (*ius gentium*), which either is or derives from natural law'[16] and in the concomitant right of strangers to be received with hospitality when arriving on foreign shores.[17] Underlying the right to travel and the right of foreigners to be received hospitably, lay various principles that spoke to a common human origin, an original endowment of the undivided common ownership of the Earth and all its goods to all mankind, and a duty to love one's neighbour and not do him harm (so long as he neither does nor intends evil or harm):

> Amongst all nations it is considered inhuman to treat strangers and travelers badly without some special cause, humane and dutiful to behave hospitably to strangers. This would not be the case if travellers were doing something evil by visiting foreign nations. Second, in

Cicero makes a qualified exception for large scale traders who travel the world transporting commodities, supposing that their profession is not altogether dishonourable, so long as there is no dishonesty involved and on condition that once they have made their profits, they return to the land and settle in estates. Book I (151) at p. 51.

[15] Vitoria, *De Indis,* p. 238. [16] Ibid., p. 278. [17] Ibid., pp. 278–84.

the beginning of the world, when all things were held in common, everyone was allowed to visit and travel through any land he wished. This right was clearly not taken away by the division of property (*diuisio rerum*); it was never the intention of nations to prevent men's free mutual intercourse with one another by this division. ... The Spaniards are the barbarians' neighbors ... and [they] are obliged to love their neighbors as themselves.... The Spaniards may lawfully trade among the barbarians, so long as they do no harm to their homeland.[18]

The overarching framework on which Vitoria built his analysis in support of the rights to travel and dwell, to be received with hospitality and to trade, he labelled in a somewhat tentative way 'natural partnership and communication' (*primus titulus potest vocari naturalis societatis et communicationis*).[19] Vitoria considered both natural partnership and communication, not as rights in themselves, but as describing the proper and necessary condition of human existence. The rights to travel and dwell, the right to be treated hospitably and the right to trade were deemed necessary to sustain this natural human condition. In light of the fact that in *De Indis* he was addressing the question of the proper relationship between Catholic Spain and the non-Christian peoples of the New World (barbarians), Vitoria was attentive to the need to find a legal foundation that was not based solely on Christian revelation or theology. His purpose was to develop arguments that did not depend on faith alone. For this reason, despite the fact that *De Indis* was a lecture presented at a school of theology to co-religionists, it is remarkably light on scriptural or Patristic references or citations. Nonetheless, Vitoria's starting point was a traditional Christian anthropology and teleology: human beings were created in the image of God and endowed with reason and their end was to return to God (to love God). Because of their common origin and God-given reason, all human beings and all peoples, regardless of apparent differences, shared identical criteria of justice. In order to encompass both Christians and non-Christians, Vitoria turned to the principles of natural law and the Roman law of nations (*ius gentium),* for these principles, he believed, could be derived without recourse to faith by any human being applying the natural light of reason with which they were endowed. Christian anthropology supplied another important dimension that supported Vitoria's search for principles that could support the condition of natural partnership and communication. Because the same God created all men, all were related by kinship, regardless of their apparent differences. 'Every living creature loveth his like' and 'amity (*amicitia*) between men is part of natural law.'[20] Vitoria located the same notion, albeit in slightly different form, in classical sources: 'nature has decreed a certain kinship between all men' (Digest I.1.3) and 'man is not a 'wolf to his fellow man,' as Ovid says, but a fellow'.[21] The universal kinship alluded to

[18] Ibid., pp. 278–9.

[19] 'The first title *may be called* natural partnership and communication.' (emphasis added) ibid., p. 278. It should be noted that despite commentators' references to the contrary, Vitoria never uses the term '*ius communicationis*'. It is thus by no means clear that he considered there to be a universal 'right' to communication, any more than he was arguing for a 'right' to natural partnership.

[20] Ibid., p. 279. [21] Ibid., p. 279.

by Vitoria was a thin, rather than a thick kinship, but it was sufficient to underpin the human condition of natural partnership and communication that he asserted in *De Indis*.

The challenge of articulating the proper relationship that should govern interactions between New World Indians and Spaniards lay not only in overcoming the sense of difference brought about by diversity of culture, practices or belief, but also in addressing the practical implications of the geographic distance that separated the two. Given the distances at play, a central concern was how to ensure the safety of travellers once they set out on their perilous journeys. Fortunately for Vitoria, the duty of hospitality to strangers was found not only in Judeo-Christian sources, but was common to classical Greek and Roman sources. This was sufficient for Vitoria to render it a universal duty. The duty of hospitality assumes the presence of a traveller, for it is owed to the stranger who arrives in an alien land where his status as a foreigner makes him automatically suspect as presenting a hostile danger. Absent the duty of hospitality, the travelling stranger risks being met with hostility and violence. For the right to travel to be freely exercised, the right to be received with hospitality must be recognized. In this sense, the two are indissoluble. The right to travel and the duty of hospitality are here understood as natural rights that serve as the necessary condition for the possibility of human intercourse or exchange in support of natural partnership and communication. Stressing that it is a 'law of nature to welcome strangers' and applying the New Testament parable of the Good Samaritan (Luke 10: 29–37), Vitoria concludes that the Indians are obliged to love the Spaniards (the strangers who are also their neighbours) as themselves.[22] In this way, the duty of hospitality to strangers is transformed into a duty of love (*caritas*) to neighbours. While the classical sources relied on by Vitoria to support a duty of hospitality to strangers were not addressed to the specific circumstance of merchants engaged in trade, in Vitoria's day commerce was the primary motivation for long distance seaborne travel. Furthermore, the etymological connection in Latin between the terms for commerce, communication, community, and common, all derived from the Latin root *committo* meaning to unite, join, connect, or bring together, supported the suggestion that commerce was an activity that united or brought together peoples and created community. As we will see below, a strong version of this idea became a key element within the doctrine of the providential function of commerce subsequently adopted by Gentili and Grotius.

When considering the long distance seaborne trade, Vitoria imagined commerce as an act involving the voluntary exchange of surpluses of goods, '[the Indians] may import the commodities which they lack, and export the gold, silver, or other things they have in abundance';[23] or alternatively, as an act of appropriation by the foreign traveller of common goods that had remained common, and

[22] Ibid., p. 279.

[23] Ibid., p. 279. '[T]he barbarians have a surplus of many things which the Spaniards might exchange for things which they lack. Likewise they have many possessions which they regard as uninhabited, which are open to anyone who wishes to occupy.' Ibid., p. 291.

therefore available, even after the division of property because of their inexhaustible character:

> if there are any things among the barbarians that are held in common both by their own people and by strangers, it is not lawful for the barbarians to prohibit the Spaniards from sharing and enjoying them ... Secondly, in the law of nations (*ius gentium*) a thing which does not belong to anyone (*res nullius*) becomes the property of the first taker ... ; therefore, if gold in the ground, or pearls in the sea or anything else in the rivers has not been appropriated, they will belong by the law of nations to the first taker, just like the little fishes of the sea.[24]

In either case, in Vitoria's presentation, the 'goods' acquired by the Spaniards and placed into the stream of commerce were pictured as not needed by the Indians. Trade, the exchange of goods (surpluses) or their appropriation by the traveller from a common source, could not be conceived as constituting a loss to the Indians. At the same time they provided a great benefit to both parties in the case of exchange of goods or, to one of them, in the case of appropriation. For Vitoria, then, the right to engage in trade, derivative from the right to travel and the right to hospitality, was understood as a right to engage in an activity that harmed no one, but could render great benefits. For this reason, interference by the Indian rulers with the Spaniards' right to trade was considered by Vitoria to be a significant injury sufficient to justify war: '[I]f the barbarians deny the Spaniards what is theirs by the law of nations, they commit an offence against them. Hence if war is necessary to obtain their rights (*ius suum*), they may lawfully go to war.'[25]

The powerful argument in favour of a right to engage in trade sketched out by Francisco de Vitoria in the context of the Spanish conquest of the Indies was picked up and elaborated by both Alberico Gentili and Hugo Grotius to address somewhat different circumstances. Vitoria, in *De Indis* had touched on many key themes central to the doctrine of the providential function of commerce, but in his work the doctrine's details were not fully articulated. While his endorsement of international commerce did not stretch to the assertion that international trade was willed by God, such a conclusion could easily be deduced from his argument in favour of the right to trade. Gentili and Grotius, on the other hand, in their work fully embraced the doctrine of the providentialist function of commerce.

The doctrine of the providential function of commerce, as described by economist Jacob Viner, obscure in origin and never fully theorized, was transmitted through classical texts that were familiar to the primitive legal scholars.[26] Briefly stated, the providentialist doctrine of commerce holds that international commerce (particularly the seaborne trade) is an activity willed by a benevolent Providence (God/Nature). In the aftermath of a fallen world, the objective of Providence is to bring separated peoples back together in friendship. God's chosen tool to achieve this objective is international commerce, imagined here as the reciprocal voluntary exchange of goods between separated peoples. But to move men to act and

[24] Ibid., p. 280. [25] Ibid., p. 282.
[26] See *Viner, The Role of Divine Providence*, pp. 36–42.

overcome an assumed unwillingness, God's design incorporates a painful edge. Indeed, according to the doctrine, the providential design depends on the co-production, and geographical separation, of need (scarcity) and the means to fulfil it (plenty).[27] From this perspective, the possibility of a people's self-sufficiency worked against the providential design. A self-sufficient people would remain comfortably at home. The key was that peoples should need or depend in some way on one another. In order to drive peoples in search of one another, Providence had distributed scarcity and its counterbalancing abundance across the globe. In this Providentialist vision, international commerce was simply a necessary exchange of correlating abundances to offset scarcities. Since international commerce was the means for both peoples involved in an act of exchange to address their own scarcity, while providing an outlet for their surplus, commerce would promote sociability and friendship. Commerce would be the means of peoples helping each other, in the course of pursuing their own good,[28] thereby creating goodwill and international friendship.

Alberico Gentili, an Italian Protestant exile teaching at Oxford, was England's first significant contributor to the law of nations. In his seminal text *De Iure Belli* (on the laws of war) (1588) he provides the first full-blown modern rendition of the providentialist doctrine of commerce.[29] All the elements later mentioned by Viner are present and used to support a natural right to engage in trade.[30] Building on Vitoria, Gentili presents commerce as both a manifestation and an effect of human sociability. Gentili begins by arguing against the Greek position of 'antipathy' that there is a natural enmity between men due to their diversity. Rather he argues, 'we are by nature all akin' and he insists 'men are not foes to one another by nature'.[31] War in other words does not have a natural cause, but is always the result of human dissension, which disrupts the natural kinship of society. He contrasts war and commerce as two forms of human relations: 'With the Saracens (who are Turks) we have irreconcilable war. With other foreign peoples we have

[27] For a discussion of the role of the concept of scarcity in international law *see* Ileana Porras, 'Binge Development in the Age of Fear: Scarcity, Consumption, Inequality and the Environmental Crisis', in *International Law and Its Discontents: Confronting Crises*, edited by Barbara Stark (Cambridge: Cambridge University Press, 2015).

[28] This is not the same as Adam Smith's 'invisible hand' argument, which holds that economic man's pursuit of private self-interest has an unintended positive effect on general welfare. *See* Adam Smith, *Wealth of Nations* (1776). Yet in a way, the Providentialist function of commerce can be read as a precursor of it.

[29] The subject of commerce is addressed primarily in Book 1, Chapter XIX 'Of Natural Reasons for Making War'. Gentili, *De Jure Belli Libri Tres*, pp. 86–90. It is in this context that Gentili sketches out the doctrine of the providentialist function of commerce since in his analysis interference with the natural right to engage in commerce will become the first legitimate justification for war.

[30] *Viner, The Role of Divine Providence*, p. 32. While Gentili, like Vitoria uses the natural right to engage in trade to serve as a justification for war, Gentili, *De Jure Belli Libri Tres*, p. 90, he is careful to make a distinction between what we would today call legitimate regulation of commerce and a total ban. Only the latter, according to Gentili could give rise to a just cause for war: '[C]ommerce cannot be said to be prohibited as soon as some phase of it is forbidden, but only when all trade is prohibited.' *De Jure Belli Libri Tres*, p. 89.

[31] Gentili, *De Jure Belli Libri Tres*, Book 1, chapter XII, 'Whether there are Natural Causes for Making War', pp. 54 and 55.

commercial relations, but certainly not war.'[32] In a work devoted to the subject of war, he nonetheless emphasizes the overarching moral foundation of international relations by citing a series of classical sources to support the claim that 'the whole world is one body'.[33] Like Vitoria before him, Gentili emphasizes the bonds of kinship, love, kindliness, and fellowship.[34] Citing to classical sources, rather than to scripture, Gentili expounds on our common origin and our shared abode. 'Now you have heard that the whole world is one body, that all men are members of that body, that the world is their home, and that it forms a state. Listen to these words again for they are beautiful.'[35] Citing Cicero and Augustine, Gentili acknowledges that there are different degrees or strength of kinship ties, but his primary purpose is to assert a universal fellowship, which he then characterizes as a bond of love '[a] law of nature constrains us to universal charity (*caritas*)' not just towards our own people but towards foreigners, and this he expands into a universal duty to render mutual aid to one another 'we are bound by a natural law … to aid one another' (in opposition to the simple obligation not to do harm).[36] Gentili thus establishes the moral foundation for international relations based on universal kinship and a duty to render aid not only to our own people but also to strangers. He picks up the theme again when he turns to the subject of commerce in Book 1, chapter XIX. Indeed, Gentili inscribes commerce as a necessary facet of human society stating that those who take away the privileges of intercourse and commerce inflict a wound on human society.[37] The long classical quotation that Gentili relies on to do much of the work setting forth the providential function of commerce includes the idea that distribution of plenty and scarcity was necessary because if goods were evenly distributed to all equally 'the reasons for loving one another would readily be destroyed; for it is through this inequality that we ask and give in turn without ceasing'. In this image, we see that love, the glue of human society, is constructed by a continuous process of asking, taking, and giving in turn.[38] The image of the power of reciprocal exchange driven by mutual need is so compelling that Gentili associates it with the notion of universal harmony and completeness. Citing Philo he states: 'All things need one another because of mutual service and their interchange makes the completeness of the universe.'[39]

Hugo Grotius, a Dutch Protestant of Arminian tendencies,[40] best known today for his tract *De Mare Liberum* (The Free Sea) (1609) and his late work *De Iure Belli ac Pacis* (The Rights of War and Peace) (1625) was also a lay theologian whose

[32] Ibid., Book 1, chapter XII at 56.
[33] Ibid., Book 1, chapter XV, 'Of Defense for the Sake of Honor' p. 67.
[34] Ibid., Book 1, chapter XV, p. 67.
[35] Ibid., Book 1, chapter XV, p. 67.
[36] Ibid., Book 1, chapter XV, p. 68.
[37] Ibid., Book 1, chapter XIX, p. 88.
[38] See n. 59 and the accompanying text in this chapter for a discussion of the tripartite structure of 'giving, receiving, and returning' in Marcel Mauss, *The Gift: The Form and Reason for Exchange in Archaic Societies*, translated by W. D. Halls (London: Routledge, 1990) pp. 13–14; and pp. 39–44.
[39] Gentili, *De Jure Belli Libri Tres*, p. 89.
[40] Grotius who was also accused of being a Remonstrant never specifically admitted to being an Arminian, but it is evident that he was not sympathetic to the strict Calvinism that was politically dominant in the Netherlands in his lifetime.

apologetic text *De Veritate Christiana* (On the Truth of the Christian Religion) was widely read and reprinted during his lifetime.[41] Grotius first addressed the topic of commerce in his early, unpublished legal brief *De Iure Praedae* (On the Law of Prize and Booty) (c. 1603). In this text, which was the original context for *Mare Liberum*, Grotius develops a full-blown account of the doctrine of the providential function of commerce. In *De Iure Belli ac Pacis* the subject of commerce is treated less extensively but the providential function of commerce still emerges recognizably.[42] It is not possible to provide a comprehensive account of Grotius' three versions of the providential function of commerce in this chapter but suffice it to say that all of the familiar themes already touched on by Vitoria and Gentili are at play. Indeed, Grotius uses many of the same classical citations used by Gentili to emphasize the trope of scarcity and plenty that drives the providential design of commerce.[43] Unlike Vitoria, but like Gentili, in *De Jure Belli ac Pacis* and in *Mare Liberum* Grotius does not anchor the right to trade in a duty of hospitality. Rather, Grotius begins by asserting a right to trade from which he then derives the 'most sacred law of hospitality'.[44] Like Gentili, Grotius associates the duty of hospitality with the strong claims he first makes regarding common property and the retained right of access.[45] It is possible that the difference between the two approaches is due simply to the fact that for Gentili and Grotius, the primary concern was not whether foreign peoples (e.g. the Indians) had a duty of hospitality to Europeans, but rather whether competing Europeans could legitimately interfere with the exercise of others' right to trade with willing partners. In that respect, the continued reference to the duty of hospitality in Gentili and Grotius appears as a curious yet perhaps instructive vestige from the earlier Vitorian text. In *De Indis,* Vitoria had charged the Indians with a failure to extend hospitality, which he deemed an offense against love. Gentili and Grotius may not have needed the duty of hospitality to anchor a right to engage in trade, but this duty still offered a useful set of ready associations to friendship and love that they could and did put to the service of supporting the right to commerce. By the time he came to write *De Jure Belli ac Pacis,* Grotius no longer makes reference to the duty of hospitality whereas he gives considerable scope to the associated principles of common ownership and common access, which he links strongly to the assertion of an original common origin of mankind bound together by love. Thus, while the duty of hospitality has dropped out, nonetheless, the glue of love and kinship is retained on behalf of the argument in favour of commerce. Grotius paints the story of natural society and kinship founded on a common origin in God in all three of

[41] For an excellent analysis of this text and its reception *see* J. P. Heering, *Hugo Grotius as Apologist for the Christian Religion: A Study of His Work De Veritate Religionis Christianae, 1640* (Leiden and Boston: Brill, 2004).

[42] Grotius addresses the subject of commerce in Book II, which is devoted to a discussion of the just causes for war. See Grotius, *De Jure Belli ac Pacis*, Book II, chapter 2, p. 444.

[43] For a more extensive discussion of this point see Ileana Porras, 'Appropriating Nature: Commerce, Property, and the Commodification of Nature in the Law of Nations', *Leiden Journal of International Law* 27, no. 3 (2014): pp. 652–4.

[44] Grotius, *Mare Liberum*, p. 11.

[45] Ibid., p. 12.

his major legal works. In the preface to *Mare Liberum*, for instance, he tells a story of a God who created a diverse mankind 'but would have them of one kind and to be contained under one name; and gave moreover the same beginning and the like composition of members, countenances turned each to other and speech also, and other instruments of imparting, that all might understand there was a natural society and kindred between them'.[46] In *De Jure Belli ac Pacis* Grotius provides his most elaborate account of the common origin of mankind and weaves into it the familiar justification for common property and common access, but in this late work its primary purpose is to serve as a starting point for the long exploration of the origin of the institution of private property. Nonetheless, in both instances in which he discusses commerce in *De Jure Belli ac Pacis*, Grotius, following the logic of the providential function of commerce that he has already adopted elsewhere, presents it under the light of friendship.[47]

Building on Vitoria's favourable attitude towards international commerce and embracing the providentialist doctrine of commerce, Gentili and Grotius transmuted international commerce from the vulgar domain of moneymaking and profit to the elevated plane of divinely inspired instrument of social ordering. They did so despite the inconvenient fact that the actual practice of long-distance seaborne trade with non-European peoples was well known to be associated with conquest, plunder, exploitation, and other forms of coercion, violence, and fraud. Even though the international commerce they were concerned with did not resemble the ideal of reciprocal, consensual, and mutually beneficial exchange of surpluses imagined by the doctrine, the primitive legal scholars chose to present commerce as the virtuous face of international relations. In their work, international commerce was contrasted with war. War produced enmity, whereas commerce encouraged friendship. By means of the providentialist doctrine, international trade became embedded in international law as a virtuous and presumptively necessary mechanism to promote friendship and peace among separated peoples. By the eighteenth century, the idea that international commerce could generate peace had become commonplace and was accompanied by the conviction that commerce had a gentle civilizing function.[48] As is well known, the apotheosis of the idea that universal peace could be achieved through international trade found expression in Immanuel Kant's late eighteenth-century essays,[49] and continues to shape much of

[46] Grotius, *Mare Liberum*, Prefatory Letter at 5.

[47] Grotius, *De Jure Belli ac Pacis*, pp. 443, 450.

[48] Both ideas were, for instance, expressed by Montesquieu in his L'Esprit des Lois (1748). *See* Baron de Montesquieu, L'Esprit des Lois, XX.

[49] *See* in particular Immanuel Kant, 'Idea for a Universal History with a Cosmopolitan Purpose' (1784), 'Perpetual Peace: A Philosophical Sketch' (1795), p. 93; and 'The Metaphysics of Morals' (1797), in *Political Writings*, edited by Hans Reiss, 2nd edn (Cambridge: Cambridge University Press, 1991); For a discussion of Immanuel Kant's use of the doctrine of the providential function of commerce, see Ileana M. Porras, 'Liberal Cosmopolitanism or Cosmopolitan Liberalism? Notes from International Law', in *Parochialism, Cosmopolitanism, and the Foundations of International Law*, edited by Mortimer Sellers (Cambridge: Cambridge University Press, 2011).

the discourse on trade today. Despite much evidence to the contrary, the faith in international commerce as the promoter of peace persists.

The fact that Vitoria, Gentili, and Grotius, despite their sectarian differences, endorsed the doctrine of the providential function of commerce might seem to suggest that it is in some sense a Christian doctrine beyond denominational rivalry. However, there is no easy correspondence between any particular Christian theological tradition and the doctrine or its elements. While it entered the international law canon through the works of self-consciously Christian authors, the providentialist doctrine of commerce is not per se a religious doctrine, nor is it required by any version of Christianity. Indeed, what is striking in the elaboration of the doctrine in the works of Vitoria, Gentili, and Grotius is the near total absence of scriptural references and the paucity of allusion to other Christian sources (whether Patristic, canonical, or theological). This stands in stark contrast to the frequency with which they associate the doctrine and its elements with classical texts. Nonetheless, it must be remembered that in early modern Europe, the Roman and Greek classics were read through Christian lenses and indeed were most familiar through Christian interpretations.[50] The classic texts used by the primitive legal scholars were cited either because they provided examples of historical events or, to the extent that they were referenced for their normative authority, because they were thought to be consistent with Christianity or to support Christian doctrines.[51] They were never presented as posing a challenge to the religious assumptions of the age. Thus, whatever their references, we can assume these scholars believed the doctrine to be congruent with their faith, and that their propositions would be convincing to their co-religionist audiences. Vitoria, Gentili, and Grotius were significant innovators. All three were keenly aware of the novelty of the questions they were addressing and the context in which they lived, and they approached their task creatively making use of the tools at their disposal. The practice of international commerce that they sought to promote was still under suspicion. As international trade became vital to competing European nations, stories of violence, injustice, piracy, and greed abounded. The doctrine of the providential function of commerce the primitive legal scholars adapted from classic sources provided them with a unique and rich opportunity to transform the image of international commerce for its vocabulary of fellowship, love, and friendship served to imaginatively transmute international commerce from the

[50] The tradition of integrating and appropriating certain classical authors and texts into the Christian intellectual patrimony began as early as the fourth century with Augustine. Perhaps the most remarkable and influential instance of Christian appropriation of the classics was that effected by Aquinas, whose interpretation of Aristotle's Politics, based on a Latin translation from the second half of the thirteenth century, became the standard. *See* Thomas Aquinas, *Commentary on Aristotle's Politics*, translated by R.J. Regan (Indianapolis: Hackett Publishing Company, 2007).

[51] But see David J. Bederman, 'Reception of the Classical Tradition in International Law: Grotius' *De Jure Belli ac Pacis*', *Emory Law Review* 10, no. 1 (1996): pp. 1–49 stating that the Classics were used by Grotius not as sources of legal or normative authority but to provide examples of state behaviour. Bederman also points out that Grotius in *De Jure Belli ac Pacis*, unlike his earlier work, uses few citations to the canonists probably because of the strict official Dutch censorship. (p. 4).

calculating realm of commercial exchange to the community-building realm of gift-exchange.

The Act of Exchange: Between Gift and Commercial Exchange

The act of exchange lies at the core of the doctrine. My argument is that by drawing on a web of existing associations and conflations between the notions of exchange, mutuality, reciprocity, love, and friendship, available to them from a common grammar of Christian theology and anthropology, inflected by Classical sources, the primitive legal scholars fashioned a novel and compelling vision of a universal community bound in love through voluntary reciprocal acts of commercial exchange. The practice of international trade was not new in sixteenth-century Europe. There was a busy and flourishing intra-European trade even before the age of discovery, and the Mediterranean trade with the Muslim world, in hiatus during the early Middle Ages, had re-emerged as an important engine of economic growth by the fourteenth century. Europeans, in other words, were not unfamiliar with the idea and practice of trade with foreigners, or commercial exchange with peoples from foreign nations. Nonetheless, it is important to note that the modern doctrine of the providential function of commerce was elaborated in the context of the encounter of Europeans with the peoples of the New World and other far distant places. As I have emphasized elsewhere, the doctrine served as a means to justify conquest and violent appropriation.[52] Here, however, I wish to put temporary brackets on this aspect of the doctrine and instead delve into the doctrine's notion of exchange and the play the primitive legal scholars made with it.

One of the striking effects of adopting the providentialist frame to discuss international commerce is that the act of exchange at the heart of the encounter between distant peoples is permanently removed from the domain of ordinary everyday life and elevated to the plane of sacred history. In other words, in accordance with Christian teleological understanding the act of exchange becomes part of the story of God's plan of salvation for humanity.[53] If international commerce is part of a providential design to bring a separated humanity back to friendship, then those engaged in commerce are participating in God's plan and doing God's work. The act of exchange itself appears transmuted from the realm of the profane to the realm of the sacred. It is also performative in that it promises an instance of real (post Babel) communication between diverse peoples who, in the moment of exchange, recognize their need for one another and open up in friendship and love to one another. Within the frame of the doctrine, the international act of exchange

[52] See Porras, *Appropriating Nature*.

[53] For an interesting reading arguing that *De Indis* is essentially a text in support of a Christian missionary objective and that Vitoria's right to trade is simply a vehicle for this higher purpose in the service of a Christian eschatology, *see* Johannes Thumfart, 'On Grotius's *Mare Liberum* and Vitoria's *De Indis*, Following Agamben and Schmitt', *Grotiana* 30, no. 1 (2009): p. 84.

no longer has to answer to the concerns of what we may call the ordinary market transaction.

When addressing the new economic and financial practices that emerged in the sixteenth century, the scholars of the School of Salamanca focused considerable attention on questions of justice in business practices such as fair price, fair interest, and fair wages.[54] Deviations from the just price were considered sinful and required restitution. Broadly speaking, everyday commercial exchange was understood to be regulated by the law of equivalences. The preoccupation was that an exchange should not enrich one party to the detriment of another. Reciprocity in exchange was the objective. There was no obligation to enter into a commercial transaction. Thus commercial exchange required parties to enter into transactions freely. One of the obligations parties to an act of commercial exchange willingly undertook was to act with reciprocity or mutual justice towards each other. Such parties must have sufficient knowledge of the value of that which was being exchanged and the goods must be as represented. Nonetheless, as commentators have pointed out, it would be a mistake to assume that these authors had a simplistic understanding of value or of real world business practices. On the contrary, they had a sophisticated understanding of the fluctuation of value based on context and circumstance and were well aware that not all commercial transactions could be said to be voluntary. Vitoria, for instance, wrote at length on the principles that should be kept in mind when deciding on the just price.[55] Among these was that absent fraud or deceit, if a buyer of luxuries (as opposed to necessaries) pays more than their value, there is no harm.[56] On the other hand, Vitoria was clear that even apparently voluntary transactions if they are motivated in part by fear, necessity, or violence could not be considered truly voluntary.[57]

Reciprocity was, as we have seen, also a central element within the doctrine of the providential function of commerce, though the reciprocity at play is not reciprocity of value. Reciprocity in the doctrine is not specifically addressed as an obligation of equivalence. Indeed, when addressing international commerce (and finding a right to engage in trade) none of the primitive legal scholars seems worried about the difficulty of establishing just price or fair value. Further, none of them are explicit about what goods exactly are to be 'exchanged'. According to Vitoria, for instance, the Indians are free to exchange their plentiful gold and silver for something they lack.[58] But, what goods exactly do the Spaniards have plenty of that are scarce in the New World? How are gold and silver as commodities to be valued? What is the proper equivalence? Vitoria, who in his economic writing shows a

[54] On the Salamancan School see references at n. 11 in this chapter. See also Juan Antonio Widow, 'The Economic Teachings of the Spanish Scholastics', in *Hispanic Philosophy in the Age of Discovery*, edited by Kevin White (Washington, D.C.: Catholic University of America Press, 1997), pp. 130–44.

[55] Vitoria, *Commentarios a la II–II, q. 77 a. 1*, quoted in Widow, 'The Economic Teachings', p. 138.

[56] Ibid. [57] Ibid.

[58] *See* Vitoria, *De Indis*, p. 279. At times Vitoria seems to suggest that gold and pearls, like fish, are simply laying unclaimed in common rivers, common property available to the first taker, e.g. at p. 291, but at others he refers to gold and silver as 'goods' that the Indians may choose to exchange.

clear understanding of price and value, nonetheless seems unconcerned that what he is dealing with may be an unjust bargain, in which the Indians are not receiving a just price or fair value. Since the providentialist doctrine is premised on the divine objective of bringing the diverse and dispersed human family back together in love and friendship, the providentialist act of exchange is treated as though it were an act of perfect communication. The radical difficulty of real communication in the circumstances of the encounter with far distant peoples, of conveying accurate information and knowledge, of comprehending desire or voluntariness are entirely absent from the providentialist analysis. There is no sense in which the primitive legal scholars, when viewing international commerce through the lens of the providentialist doctrine, could imagine an actual commercial exchange or business encounter. They did not envision a business deal, characterized by bargain and negotiation, the coming to agreement, the setting of conditions, the determination of equivalent values and the setting of a just price. The providentialist function of commerce did not require a contract.

How are we to understand this lacuna? How could theorists as sophisticated as Vitoria, Gentili, and Grotius fail to recognize the irreconcilable gap between the idealized image of commerce painted by the providentialist doctrine (with its perfect act of communication–exchange) and real-life international commerce (with its messy and unreliable communication and the ever-present risk of unfair dealing). I think we can safely reject the idea that they were misled or misguided and believed that actual international trade resembled that depicted by the providentialist doctrine. The easiest solution may be to argue that they used the providentialist doctrine as a metaphor of sorts. The solution I would like to propose is somewhat different. As stated at the outset, my view is that these authors used the providentialist doctrine to defend against and counter an anti-commerce, anti-merchant narrative still prevalent in their age. The positive spin on commerce provided by the doctrine had two sources, one more evident than the other. The first, more obvious reason is that the doctrine suggests that God has himself taken an interest in commerce (and brought it into being to fulfil his purpose). But, if they found it so compelling it was also because it spoke to a strain of thinking about exchange that, at the risk of applying modern distinctions to the past, I will characterize as that between gift-exchange and commercial exchange.

Our modern understanding of the function of gift-exchange comes largely from Marcel Mauss' ethnographical *Essai sur le Don* (The Gift) (1950).[59] Mauss' insight was that in certain 'archaic' societies, the form of exchange that he labelled 'the gift' functioned at a symbolic as well as a practical level and served primarily as a means of constituting and strengthening community, even if in some cases the objects exchanged also provided a use value. While Mauss' focus was on primitive societies with highly ritualized and orchestrated systems of gift circulation, his insight is a reminder that the act of exchange need not always be understood as a cold commercial transaction. The modern tendency has been to emphasize the gift as a

[59] *Mauss, The Gift.*

one-way street, a gratuitous donation that, by definition, does not expect or anticipate return. From this perspective the gift would escape the logic of reciprocity. But, of course, this description of the gift has never quite fit the bill. Without needing to go as far as Mauss' unending cycle of giving, receiving and returning, which builds and maintains the community, we are familiar with the notion that there is no such thing as a free gift. The gift, even freely given, always supposes a return. And the appropriate return should be in some sense equivalent. In other words, the gift, like the act of commercial exchange, is governed by the notion of reciprocity.[60] Nonetheless, gift-exchange is different in nature than commercial exchange, the main difference being that the gift is always first and foremost about relationship. Good gift giving builds amicable relationships and strengthens them. Reciprocity in gift giving does not require a quantifiable equivalence, rather it is a reciprocity of love or kinship whose purpose is to maintain mutual obligation. In gift giving there can be no final fulfilment of obligation, no final accounting. To remain productive, the gift-exchange must always retain a surplus of obligation. If it could be 're-paid' then it would be transmuted and enter the world of commercial exchange. The surplus at the heart of the gift is love.

Long before Mauss, some of the classical authors relied on by Vitoria, Gentili, and Grotius, including Cicero (106–43 BCE),[61] Seneca (4 BCE–65 CE),[62] and Horace (65–8 BCE),[63] wrote about gifts and the act of giving, about the character of the giver and that of the receiver and the obligation of return.[64] At the heart of their accounts was the claim that gift-exchange was an act of love and friendship. It was also an act of recognition of the other. Even in the guise of patronage, gift giving was about building relationships and patronage worked because of the expectation of return. But, at the same time both the giving, the receiving, and the return were to be free voluntary acts in order to count as such. For the classic authors, the

[60] Karl Polanyi's important essay on the Embedded Economy reminds us that in pre-capitalist societies, elements of exchange are embedded in non-economic institutions such as marriage, kinship, associations, and so forth. Even in capitalist societies vestiges of the embedded economy persist and colour acts of exchange and our social institutions. See Karl Polanyi, *Primitive, Archaic, and Modern Economies: Essays of Karl Polanyi*, edited by George Dalton (Garden City, New York: Anchor Books, 1968).

[61] See especially Book I of Cicero, *De Officiis* (On Obligations) (*c*.46–44 BCE). Cicero's Stoic ethics in *De Officiis* was introduced to the Christian West by the writings of influential Patristic authors such as Lactantius (*c*. 240–320) and Ambrose (339–97). Thomas Aquinas cited Cicero's *De Officiis* extensively in his *Summa Theologiae*, the work that was the starting point for Vitoria's theological reflections. Erasmus (*c*.1466–1536) who published his own edition of *De Officiis* (in 1501) was a Ciceronian scholar as was Lutheran reformer Philip Melanchthon (1497–1560), who greatly influenced Hugo Grotius. For the influence of Cicero's work on Christian authors *see Cicero, On Obligations*, translation and introduction by P. G. Walsh (Oxford: Oxford University Press, 2001), introduction at xxxiv–xliv.

[62] *Seneca, On Benefits* (*De Beneficiis*) (*c*. 56–64), translated by Miriam Griffin and Brad Inwood (Chicago: University of Chicago Press, 2011).

[63] On Horace's writing on gift and patronage *see* Phoebe Lowell Bowditch, *Horace and the Gift Economy of Patronage* (Berkeley: University of California Press, 2001).

[64] 'Therefore we should follow nature as our guide in this sense of making available shared benefits by exchange of our obligations, by giving and receiving, and in this way binding the community and its individuals closely together by our skills, our efforts and our talents.' *Cicero, On Obligations*, p. 10. See also the section on munificence and generosity, pp.17–22.

value of the gift was non-quantifiable in that it could not be discharged. The gift as opposed to the commercial exchange carried with it a surplus that meant that it could never be fully liquidated. Instead, the gift created a debt of love or friendship that demanded a continuation of relationship.

As we have seen, the writings of Vitoria, Gentili, and Grotius that surround the subject of commerce are characterized by frequent references to love, friendship, kinship, and community formation. Whatever they envisaged in terms of the possibility of an actual universal society of mankind, it is clear that these scholars shared a belief in the common origin of mankind. The doctrine of the providential function of commerce was suggestive of a teleological objective of a return in harmony to God that fit well with their religious convictions. The act of exchange at the heart of the doctrine did not give rise to anxiety about just price and fair dealing and the inadequacy of communication because it was closer to the ideal of the gift-exchange than to that of an act of commercial exchange. While gift-exchange like the act of commercial exchange was governed by an ethic of reciprocity, the reciprocity of the gift was as much a reciprocity of love as a reciprocity of value. At a time when the real-world practices of international trade were characterized by violence and conflict and when concern with the greed and avarice of merchants was growing, the providential function of commerce and the vestigial associations of the gift-exchange provided an alternative and optimistic vision for trade. The act of exchange in international trade could be blurred and thereby portrayed as both commercial exchange and as gift. Viewed from the perspective of the gift, the act of exchange became elevated to an act of friendship and love and mutual benefit. International exchange was made possible because of the common origin of mankind and, by reinforcing the reciprocity of friendship and love through the power of exchange that was coloured by the surplus value of the gift it worked towards building the new global community. By propagation of this line of reasoning, international trade and the merchants involved in it became respectable.

Conclusion

In the works of the primitive legal scholars, beginning with Vitoria, exchange in international commerce is presented primarily in the register of gift, hospitality, and friendship (all freely given) and therefore productive of community and peace rather than in the register of commercial exchange with its requirements of valuation, equivalence, competition, and what we have come to know as arms-length transactions. Regardless of the concrete reality of the long distance seaborne trade with which their works are concerned, characterized by exploitation and violence, the primitive legal scholars present the end of international commerce as mutual assistance, friendship, and peace, and thus congruent with the Christian God's desire for a universal human community based on love of neighbour. In other words, in the work of Vitoria and the others, international commerce is transmuted from the realm of the morally questionable commercial exchange of merchants (which is not intended to create friendship and community) by its association with gift-exchange—and it is this that gives rise to the idea that international commerce is a force for good. At the same time, this positive and optimistic idea of commerce ultimately contributes to the redemption of merchants as a class.

Bibliography

Alighieri, Dante. *The Divine Comedy, Vol. I: Inferno*, translated by Mark Musa (Harmondsworth: Penguin Books, 1984).

Aquinas, St. Thomas. *Summa Theologica*, translated by Fathers of the English Dominican Province (New York: Benziger Bros., 1947).

Aquinas, St. Thomas. *St. Thomas Aquinas on Politics and Ethics*, translated and edited by Paul E. Sigmund (New York: Norton, 1988).

Aquinas, St. Thomas. *Commentary on Aristotle's Politics*, translated by Richard J. Regan (Indianapolis: Hackett Publishing Company, 2007).

Baeck, Louis. 'Spanish Economic Thought: The School of Salamanca and the *Arbitristas*'. *History of Political Economy* 20, no. 3 (1988): pp. 381–408.

Bederman, David J. 'Reception of the Classical Tradition in International Law: Grotius' *De Jure Belli ac Pacis*'. *Emory Law Review* 10, no. 1 (1996): pp. 1–49.

Bowditch, Phebe Lowell. *Horace and the Gift Economy of Patronage* (Berkeley: University of California Press, 2001).

Cicero, Marcus Tullius. *On Obligations*, translation and introduction by P. G. Walsh (Oxford: Oxford University Press, 2001).

Eligido, Juan Manuel. 'The Just Price: Three Insights from the Salamanca School'. *Journal of Business Ethics* 90, no. 1 (2009): pp. 29–46.

Gentili, Alberico. *De Jure Belli Libri Tres* (Reproduction of the 1612 edition, with a translation by John C. Rolfe, Oxford: Classics of International Law, 1933) (1598).

Le Goff, Jacques. *Time, Work, and Culture in the Middle Ages*, translated by Arthur Goldhammer (Chicago: University of Chicago Press, 1980).

Le Goff, Jacques. *Your Money or Your Life: Economy and Religion in the Middle Ages*, translated by Patricia Ranum (New York: Zone Books, 1990).

Le Goff, Jacques. *Un long Moyen Âge* (Paris: Tallandier, 2004).

Grotius, Hugo. *The Free Sea,* edited by David Armitage (Indianapolis, Ind.: Liberty Fund, 2004).

Grotius, Hugo. *Commentary on the Law of Prize and Booty*, edited by M. J. van Ittersum (Indianapolis: Liberty Fund, 2006), p. 10.

Grotius, Hugo. *De Iure Belli ac Pacis,* Vol. II. (The Rights of War and Peace) (1625), Chapter XII, at pp. 753–60.

Heering, J. P. *Hugo Grotius as Apologist for the Christian Religion: A Study of His Work De Veritate Religionis Christianae, 1640* (Leiden and Boston: Brill, 2004).

Kant, Immanuel. *Political Writings*, edited by Hans Reiss, 2nd edn (Cambridge: Cambridge University Press, 1991).

Kennedy, David. 'Primitive Legal Scholarship'. *Harvard International Law Journal* 27, no. 1 (1986): pp. 1–5.

Koskenniemi, Martti. 'Empire and International Law: The Real Spanish Contribution'. *University Toronto Law Journal* 61, no. 1 (2011): pp. 1–36.

Mauss, Marcel. *The Gift: The Form and Reason for Exchange in Archaic Societies*, translated by W. D. Halls (London: Routledge, 1990).

Mele, Domenec. 'Early Business Ethics in Spain: The Salamanca School (1526–1614)'. *Journal of Business Ethics* 22, no. 3 (1999): pp. 175–89.

Montesquieu, Charles–Louis de Secondat. *L'Esprit des Lois* (1748).

Munro, John. 'Usury, Calvinism and Credit in Protestant England: From the Sixteenth Century to the Industrial Revolution'. In *Religion and Religious Institutions in the European Economy 1000–1800* (Firenze: Firenze University Press, 2012), pp. 155–84.

Polanyi, Karl. *Primitive, Archaic, and Modern Economies: Essays of Karl Polanyi*, edited by George Dalton (Garden City, N.Y.: Anchor Books, 1968).

Porras, Ileana M. 'Constructing International Law in the East Indian Seas: Property, Sovereignty, Commerce and War in Hugo Grotius' De Iure Praedae—The Law of Prize and Booty, or "On How to Distinguish Merchants from Pirates"'. *Brooklyn Journal of International Law* 31, no. 741 (2006): p. 756 et seq.

Porras, Ileana M. 'Liberal Cosmopolitanism or Cosmopolitan Liberalism? Notes from International Law'. In *Parochialism, Cosmopolitanism, and the Foundations of International Law*, edited by Mortimer Sellers (Cambridge: Cambridge University Press, 2011).

Porras, Ileana M. 'Appropriating Nature: Commerce, Property, and the Commodification of Nature in the Law of Nations'. *Leiden Journal of International Law* 27, no. 3 (2014): pp. 641–60.

Porras, Ileana M. 'Binge Development in the Age of Fear: Scarcity, Consumption, Inequality and the Environmental Crisis'. In *International Law and Its Discontents: Confronting Crises*, edited by Barbara Stark (Cambridge: Cambridge University Press, 2015).

Seneca, Lucius Annaeus. *On Benefits* (*De Beneficiis*) (*c.* 56–64), translated by Miriam Griffin and Brad Inwood (Chicago: University of Chicago Press, 2011).

Smith, Adam. *Wealth of Nations* (1776), edited by Andrew Skinner (London: Penguin Books, 1999).

Tawney, R. H. *Religion and the Rise of Capitalism* (London: John Murray, 1926).

Thumfart, Johannes. 'On Grotius's *Mare Liberum* and Vitoria's *De Indis*, Following Agamben and Schmitt'. *Grotiana* 30, no. 1 (2009): pp. 65–87.

Viner, Jacob. *The Role of Providence in the Social Order: An Essay in Intellectual History* (Philadelphia: American Philosophical Society, 1972).

de Vitoria, Francisco. 'On the American Indians'. In *Francisco de Vitoria, Political Writings*, edited by Anthony Pagden and Jeremy Lawrance (Cambridge: Cambridge University Press, 1991), pp. 231–92.

Widow, Juan Antonio. 'The Economic Teachings of the Spanish Scholastics'. In *Hispanic Philosophy in the Age of Discovery*, edited by Kevin White (Washington, D.C.: Catholic University of America Press, 1997), pp. 130–44.

14

The Faith in Humanity and International Criminal Law

Immi Tallgren[1]

Introduction

'There is an idea that we absolutely have to get used to ... humanity is left on this earth to its own devices and can only count on itself to direct its own destiny',[2] urged Emile Durkheim a century ago. Nevertheless, there is a cosmic loneliness in the idea of 'humanity' all on its own charged with directing its destiny, against all odds and hazards. The efforts to find guidance and create some stable structure in the declared absence of divinities take many forms. Fears for the survival and health of human societies and the human species may be local, but the responses today are often presented as beyond the national, be it regional, international, or global. Internationalism and humanitarianism, international law and institutions, and the human rights ideology are, for many, contributing to preventing and alleviating disasters, threats, and fears, carrying a universal promise of protection of humans and 'humanity'.[3]

My chapter participates in this research project by reflecting on the potential transformation of international law into a new kind of religiousness, 'internationalism operating on the basis of faith that has often left itself unarticulated as such' but has 'made sacred the laws of nations and the task of the judges'.[4] In academic commentary today, it is not uncommon to address international law in terms of

[1] I would like to thank warmly the conveners of the research project 'International Law and Religion' at the Erik Castrén Institute and the editors of the volume, as well as all friends and colleagues who have commented on the draft in its various forms. I am grateful for the research funding Emil Aaltonen Foundation provided during the early phase of this research.

[2] Emile Durkheim, contribution to discussion in F. Abauzit et al., 'Les Sentiments religieux à l'heure actuelle' (Paris: Vrin, 1919), translated and reprinted in J. Redding and W. S. F. Pickering, eds., *Durkheim on Religion* (London; Boston: Routledge and Kegan Paul, 1975), p. 187.

[3] See, for example, Ruti G. Teitel, *Humanity's Law* (Oxford: Oxford University Press, 2011), see preface and pp. 3–4; Antônio Augusto Cançado Trindade, *International Law for Humankind: Towards a New Jus Gentium* (The Netherlands: Martinus Nijhoff Publishers, 2010). On representations of human suffering as a key to these dynamics, see, for example, Richard Ashby Wilson and Richard D. Brown, eds, *Humanitarianism and Suffering* (New York: Cambridge University Press, 2009).

[4] The research statement of the Working Group on International Law and Religion.

religiousness, attributing to it religion-like roles or calling its adherents believers or priests.[5] Much of the attention has focused on human rights, a belief in which is considered at least as 'a kind of world-wide secular religion'.[6] I have myself referred to 'belief' and 'religiousness' in discussing international criminal law and its institutional practice by the International Criminal Court (ICC) and the ad hoc international criminal tribunals, as well as the ways in which they are represented in (international) political fora, civil society, academia, and media.[7] In those fora, international criminal law and its institutional practice at times appear to call for a faith in law, as a token for the collective desires of 'humanity's' progress towards a better future when faced with violence and 'evil' that is addressed as international criminality. For those having the faith, the law and its institutional practice manifest consensual moral boundaries, those boundaries being translated into universally applicable policies supposedly beneficial for all human beings, thereby building a moral community of 'humanity', if not immediately then at least in the future. The faith in 'humanity' and its law is—or some residual components of it—celebrated in a cult of criminal justice with its distinct rituals, symbols, and mythologies.[8]

This chapter takes issue with the transcendental reference in 'humanity' by situating it within the broader discussions on religion, the non-deist religions in particular.[9] In the search for further continuities and breaks, I propose here to put today's

[5] For a discussion on this, see, for example, David Kennedy, 'Losing Faith in the Secular: Law, Religion, and the Culture of International Governance', in *Religion and International Law*, edited by Mark Janis and Carolyn Evans (The Hague; Boston: Martinus Nijhoff Publishers, 1999), pp. 309–20. In a historical perspective, Nathaniel Berman, '"The Sacred Conspiracy": Religion, Nationalism, and the Crisis of Internationalism', *Leiden Journal of International Law* 25, no. 1 (2012): pp. 9–54; John Haskell, 'Divine Immanence: The Evangelical Foundations of Modern Anglo-American Approaches to International Law', *Chinese Journal of International Law* 11, no. 3 (2012): pp. 429–67.

[6] Elie Wiesel, 'A Tribute to Human Rights', in *The Universal Declaration of Human Rights: Fifty Years and Beyond*, edited by Danieli Yael et al. (Amityville, N.Y.: Baywood, 2009), p. 3. For a virulent critique of Wiesel, see Michael Ignatieff, *Human Rights as Politics and Idolatry* (Princeton: Princeton University Press, 2003). See also, for example, Elizabeth M. Bucar and Barbra Barnett, eds, *Does Human Rights Need God?* (Grand Rapids, Mich.: W. B. Eerdmans, 2005); Helle Porsdam, ed., *Civil Religion, Human Rights and International Relations* (Cheltenham: Edward Elgar, 2012). Susan Marks evokes 'a contemporary *cliché*' on human rights as 'a secular religion: an object of faith, a basis for hope and a code of morality we can all accept, whatever other systems of belief we may cherish or reject'. 'Human Rights in Disastrous Times', in *The Cambridge Companion to International Law*, edited by James Crawford and Martti Koskenniemi (Cambridge: Cambridge University Press, 2012), pp. 309–26, 313–14.

[7] See, for example, Immi Tallgren, 'The Sensibility and Sense of International Criminal Law', *European Journal of International Law* 13, no. 3 (2002): pp. 561–95.

[8] For discussion, see, for example, Edwin Bikundo, *International Criminal Law: Using or Abusing Legality?* (Farnham: Ashgate, 2014), in particular pp. 15–45; Kamari M. Clarke, *Fictions of Justice* (Cambridge; New York: Cambridge University Press, 2009). See also Audra Mitchell, *International Intervention in a Secular Age: Re-enchanting Humanity?* (London: Routledge, 2014).

[9] I will not focus on the pair of words 'civil religion' that has either a fairly recent, primarily North American context of understanding following Robert Bellah's much-discussed article of 1967, or figures in eighteenth- and nineteenth-century European thought, associated primarily to Jean-Jacques Rousseau or John Stuart Mill. See Robert Bellah, 'Civil Religion in America', *Journal of the American Academy of Arts and Sciences* 96, no. 1 (Winter, 1967): pp. 1–21; Jean-Jacques Rousseau, *Du contrat social* (Paris: Garnier-Flammarion, 1966 [1762]); John Stuart Mill, 'The Utility of Religion', in *Three Essays on Religion* (Amherst: Prometheus, 1998 [1874]).

discussions on religiousness of international law in front of an alternative mirror in the work of three French thinkers: Henri Saint-Simon (1760–1825), Auguste Comte (1798–1857) and Emile Durkheim (1858–1917). In their distinct historical and intellectual landscapes, they also believed that the intertwined evolution of 'new' moral rules and internationalism were to accompany and guide a general economical, political, and social progress of the human communities or 'humanity' towards greater happiness, both individually and collectively. The period from Saint-Simon's first publication in 1802 to Durkheim's death in 1917, encompassing in between them Comte's prolific career, is a major part of international law's 'rise'.[10] The period could be characterized by the contradictory aftermath of the French revolution in the turmoil of reforms and conservatism, the increasing role of science and technology and the decreasing role of religion; industrialization and its social effects; the emergence of utilitarianism; romanticism and the birth of historiography, and many other features.[11] Saint-Simon, Comte and Durkheim could all, in broad terms, be described as enthusiastic towards the advances of science, technology, economy, and commerce, and the related changes in societies. However, they also shared a fundamental anxiety: should utilitarian logics become exclusive in the absence of religions, any apparent progress could end up being used for negative ends. The unity of societies was at risk. A dissolution of 'humanity' in the egoist materialism constituted 'la grande hérésie' haunting the modern world, to quote Comte.[12] The key question for the three thinkers was: in the conditions of industrialism and division of labour, what binds societies together, to replace the role earlier held by religion? Whereas they celebrated some aspects of individualism and democratic government, they also saw dangers in them, here in the words of Durkheim: 'Political liberty is a means, not an end.... If those who handle this weapon do not know how to use it in fruitful battles, they will not be slow in turning it against themselves.'[13]

To counter such scenarios, they emphasized how spiritual, religious, and moral dimensions consisting of commonly held beliefs transmitted from generation to generation remain essential for the health of societies. All three were interested in what these commonly held beliefs are or should be, and each developed ideas of secular religiousness. Their focus was thus not on the French ideas of their times

[10] For this period of time in the history of international law, see, Martti Koskenniemi, *The Gentle Civilizer of Nations: The Rise and Fall of International Law 1870–1960* (Cambridge: Cambridge University Press, 2002), pp. 266–352. See also Wilhelm G. Grewe, *The Epochs of International Law* (Berlin; New York: Walter de Gruyter, 2000), pp. 422–4, 438–542.

[11] For a poetic description of the nineteenth century, see, for example, Juliette Grange, *La philosophie d'Auguste Comte: science, politique, religion* (Paris: PUF, 1996), pp. 5–7.

[12] Auguste Comte, *Système de politique positive ou traité de sociologie instituant la religion de l'Humanité, I* (Paris: Libraire positiviste, Georges Crès et Cie, 1851–54), p. 641. Similar anxieties were expressed earlier by Rousseau, followed by Tocqueville and Mill, see Ronald Beiner, *Civil Religion* (New York: Cambridge University Press, 2011), pp. 261–2.

[13] Emile Durkheim, 'L'Individualisme et les intellectuels', in *Revue Bleue* 4e série, X, (1898): pp. 7–13, 10; translated by S. and J. Lukes, *Political Studies*, XVII (1969), pp. 19–30, reprinted in W. S. F. Pickering, *Durkheim on Religion* (London and Boston: Routledge & K. Paul, 1975), pp. 59–73, at p. 70.

in the sense of strict separation of the religious and the political, but rather on the design of a secular civil religion that mobilizes the affects and beliefs for the benefit of society and of 'humanity'. My reading of Saint-Simon, Comte, and Durkheim highlights themes or elements that were common and central to all of them: The progress of humans and their communities occurs both by natural or 'biological' (Comte) evolution of human capacities, competencies and their communities, and by increasing cooperation, individually and collectively. Solidarity, sociability, or social sentiment are evoked often and forcefully. The three thinkers speak in general, universalizing terms, be it of humanity or the individual. They tend to attribute human beings with a natural instinct of sociability, sharing, and caring. They focus on the protection of individuals, human communities, and human life in general, faced with continuous existential dangers. The renouncement of war as a means of politics, and the desuetude of militarism as a way to organize societies or international relations is an important part of that. In Comte's work particularly, this protection and pacification also take the form of concern for the cultural and historical achievements and monuments of humanity and the call for common limits and precaution in exploiting the Earth's resources. Saint-Simon and Comte, in particular, share the conviction that international (primarily figured as European) cooperation and integration is both beneficial and unavoidable. International institutions and rules are seen as a way of achieving the goals uniting human beings and nations as they follow their instincts of sociability and solidarity. Simultaneously, they act as a safeguard against the destructive potential present in humans themselves. In this exercise, an avant-garde role is given to European industrial states; a certain type of society and economic organization becomes the model and measuring unit of common human progress.

Presented in these broad lines, the parallels of their ideas with today's internationalism and the objectives of international law strike one as obvious, both in the scope of ambitions and in the limitations of their realization.[14] Yet their work is clearly just a tiny and random path amongst many others. What to make out of such comparisons and what methodological temptations or concerns are at stake? As Samuel Moyn puts it, 'the past is not simply a mirror for our own self-regard'.[15] The reader may rightly be wary of what looks like cutting a random path of micro-history of ideas as the picturesque setting of a macro-historical paradigm change: the rational replacement of providence and eternal life in paradise by progress, welfare, and justice equated with humanitarian love. It may even look as if the hints in the direction that international law and human rights law today occupy roles and functions of symbolic reference and mediation that in

[14] Some of the continuities of ideas are evoked in commentaries. Saint-Simon is typically mentioned in the context of first ideas for European economic integration and institutional developments, aside from l'abbé de Saint-Pierre and his ideas on confederation in Europe, see Juliette Grange, *Saint-Simon (1760–1825)* (Paris: Ellipses, 2005), pp. 47–51. See also Koskenniemi, *The Gentle Civilizer of Nations*, pp. 266–352, on French 'solidarism' and international law.

[15] Samuel Moyn, *Human Rights and the Uses of History* (London; Brooklyn, NY: Verso, 2014), p. xii. See also George Rodrigo Bandeira Galindo, 'Force Field: On History and Theory of International Law', *Rechtsgeschicte* 20 (2012): pp. 86–103.

the past used to be accomplished by religion, are aimed as a demonstration of a 'truth' that nothing can really be secular, after all. My intentions lie elsewhere, however. In terms of today's renewed research interest in 'political theology', I suggest that Saint-Simon, Comte, and Durkheim are particularly stimulating intellectual figures—often neglected or caricatured.[16] Each in his individual context was reacting creatively to what they saw as a crisis of societies and of religions, drawing new borders for the domains of politics (the political) and theology.[17] Their idea—and others', such as Rousseau, of course—was to acknowledge the indispensable role of religion at the core of not only the social and moral but also the political collectivity, even up to the point of disowning the individual and her belief or its absence.[18] At the same time, their emphasis on giving a sense and a direction to time, structured as a gradual human progress, is part of the story of how history became understood as universal, as a history of humanity. It is clear that their objectives as well as the inventions they offered for societal questions figure in many other parts of the different genealogies of international law, both before and after them: in theology, political science, philosophy, or economics. What matters here is how they presented their visionary products: working in the key moments of secularization, they insisted on picturing them as *religions*, underlining this by creating dogmas, symbolism, and ritual practices that evoked the traditional religions, in particular Christianity. Yet they declared the transcendental divinities dead. By that move the human individual, human communities, or humanity were further elevated yet declared 'positive', victorious over any superstition. In that sense, their religions aimed to capture the best of two worlds: secular and religious, rational and affective.

At the first sight, that modern and 'reasonable' appearance of their religions may render them appealing as sympathetic cousins of international law, free from the pejorative connotations of irrationality and mysticism. However, what difference does it make to see ideas, beliefs, faith, or commitment as religious or as something else, such as politics or ideology? I will return to this dilemma and to today's international law in my conclusions, focusing in particular on international criminal law and its institutional practice that are, to quote Frédéric Megret, 'for many international lawyers ... the ultimate test of global justice, a unique hope of

[16] For example, Beiner's rich *Civil Religion* is silent on Saint-Simon and Durkheim and mentions Comte only in passing, in relation to Mill.

[17] On the current heterogeneous understanding of what 'political theology' is, see, for example, Hent de Vries, 'Introduction', in *Political Theologies*, edited by Hent de Vries and Lawrence E. Sullivan (New York: Fordham University Press, 2006), pp. 25–7; Graham Hammill and Julia Reinhard Lupton, 'Introduction', in *Political Theology and Early Modernity*, edited by Graham Hammill and Julia Reinhard Lupton (Chicago; London: The University of Chicago Press, 2012), pp. 1–7; Elisabeth Phillips, *Political Theology—A Guide for the Perplexed* (London; New York: T&T Clark, 2012).

[18] See, for example, Karl Löwith's disapproving comments on Auguste Comte's 'neglect of individual destiny', Karl Löwith, *Meaning of History* (Chicago; London: The University of Chicago Press, 1949), p. 89; for claims on Durkheim denying human creativity and agency, see Steven Lukes and Andrew Scull, 'Introduction', in *Durkheim and the Law*, edited by Steven Lukes and Andrew Scull (Great Britain: Billing and Sons Ltd, 1983).

redemption for the international legal order'.[19] To ground my conclusions, I will first discuss those parts of the work by Saint-Simon, Comte, and Durkheim that I find most relevant with regard to the questions evoked. My treatment is necessarily fragmentary and reductive. How they are presented here should not lead the reader to the mistaken impression that Saint-Simon, Comte, and Durkheim could or should be reduced to a harmonious trio behind a chronological evolution of a few key ideas—that would both flatten the richness and multiple influences of their individual work and disguise the major discontinuities and conflicts in their thinking.[20]

Henri Saint-Simon

A philosopher, economist, and forerunner sociologist, Henri Saint-Simon is associated with various ideas or developments: the scientific positivism that his assistant Auguste Comte later made famous under his own name, the historical method developed by Saint-Simon's pupil Augustin Thierry, (utopian) socialism and Marxism, international industrialism, the early seeds of European integration, and so forth.[21] My interest here is in how Saint-Simon develops his vision of an improved society with social and economic well-being for all, in a manner that intertwines the roles his new religion, of industrialism, and increasing international cooperation and unity.

Saint-Simon was an adept at historical determinism, with a focus on physiological parallels. He believed that he could 'embrasser dans une seule conception tous les termes de la série des progrès de l'esprit humain, et cela d'une manière

[19] Frédéric Megret, 'International Criminal Justice: A Critical Research Agenda', in *Critical Approaches to International Criminal Law*, edited by Christine Schwöbel (Abingdon: Routledge, 2014), p. 43.

[20] The latter have been analysed in detail in a number of commentaries. On Saint-Simon and Comte, see, for example, Grange, *Saint-Simon*; Christian Laval, *L'ambition sociologique* (Paris: Editions La Decouverte & Syros, 2002). On Durkheim and Comte, see, for example, Albin W. Gouldner, 'Introduction', in Emile Durkheim, *Socialism and Saint-Simon* (Ohio: The Antioch Press, 1958). On Saint-Simon's influence on Durkheim, see Steven Lukes, *Emile Durkheim: His Life and Work—a Historical and Critical Study* (Stanford, California: Stanford University Press, 1973); Roger Cotterell, *Emile Durkheim: Law in a Moral Domain* (Edinburgh: Edinburgh University Press, 1999).

[21] See, for example, Pierre Musso, *Saint-Simon et Saint-Simonisme* (Paris: PUF, 1999); Pierre Ansart, *Saint-Simon* (Paris: PUF, 1969); Grange, *Saint-Simon*; Laval, L'*ambition sociologique*, p. 36–82. Marx in his writing appears both recognizant and critical of Saint-Simon, and particularly critical of his followers, the Saint-Simoniens. See, for example, Karl Marx and Friedrich Engels, *Utopisme et communauté de l'avenir* (Paris: François Maspero, 1976.); Karl Marx, *The Capital*, Volume III, pp. 431–4, https://www.marxists.org/archive/marx/works/download/pdf/Capital-Volume-III.pdf; see also Emile Durkheim, *Socialism and Saint-Simon*. On historicism: crediting Saint-Simon with the idea that with the correct theory, humanity would be able to intervene in creating its own future, Keith Taylor found this 'sufficiently original to justify the view of Saint-Simon as one of the founders of modern historicism'. Keith Taylor, *The Political Ideas of the Utopian Socialists* (Great Britain: Frank Cass and Company Limited, 1982). In the following, unless otherwise indicated, the references to Saint-Simon's work are to *Oeuvres complètes*, vols I–IV, edited by Juliette Grange, Pierre Musso, Philippe Régnier, and Frank Yonnet (Paris: PUF, 2012).

piquante, en établissant une comparaison entre le développement moral de l'intelligence générale et celui de l'intelligence individuelle'.[22] His vision of the twelve phases of humanity that situates them analogically in relationship with the development of a human being[23] is interesting for my argument here in several aspects. From 'primitive' to the feudal and the military society Saint-Simon described a childhood and puberty during which the organs necessary for the adult life of society gradually develop. A young child is concerned foremost with eating. Instead of producing, working, or fabricating, his primary occupation is to seize tasty food.[24] The same holds true for primitive societies, where the lowest scale consists of individuals whose intelligence and memory 'n'etait guère plus étendue que celle du castor ou de l'éléphant'.[25] To prevent puerile behaviour, repressive authorities in society are necessary up to the point when the child matures and gradually becomes reasonable. Saint-Simon sees a parallel to this evolution taking place in societies. Only when a human society reaches the age of majority, it can truly focus on producing, in a reasonable and peaceful manner, instead of instinctively merely satisfying its needs.[26] In the childhood of a society, humans are ignorant, passionate in their reactions, and prone to all sorts of disorders and disturbances. The minority has to be organized militarily to keep the majority under control. The use of force is necessary to keep society together. 'Ainsi jusqu'à présent le principales forces de la société ont été employées à se maintenir en société, et les travaux ayant pour objet l'amélioration du bien-être moral et physique des nations n'ont pu et n'ont dû être considérés que comme des travaux accessoires.'[27] From the Middle Ages, a new principle of unification of society, taking shape with industrialization, entered into conflict with the ancient society. The broadening scope of education, employment, and an increasing desire for a peaceful life progressively make police forces, permanent armies, and spies redundant. The repressive and military components of the state were gradually transformed into administrating productive work. When societies turn adult, the moment is ripe to take conscience of the real telos of humans: no longer the domination of men over men but the collective exploitation of nature. Repression is no longer necessary. Secular happiness is at hand. The greatest achievement of this evolutionary march of civilization is precisely this: governed humans will manage to replace the principle of divine justice with that of the well-being of societies. This twelfth phase of evolution was, at the moment Saint-Simon was writing, to appear in the future:

[22] Saint-Simon, *Mémoire sur la science de l'homme*, Oeuvres completes, II, p. 1135. See also Saint-Simon, *De l'organisation sociale*, Oeuvres complètes, IV.

[23] Saint-Simon, *Mémoire sur la science*, pp. 1129–59. Saint-Simon's presentation of civilization period by period was inspired by Nicolas de Condorcet's famous *Esquisse d'un tableau historique des progrès de l'eprit humain* (1794–95). Bibliothèque de Philosophie (Paris: Boivin, 1933). Before Condorcet, Turgot presented his *Tableau philosophique des progrès successifs de l'esprit humain* at Sorbonne in 1750.

[24] Saint-Simon, *Mémoire sur la science*, p. 1135.

[25] Ibid., p. 1130.

[26] See Laval, *L'ambition sociologique*, pp. 68–70, based on Saint-Simon, *De l'organisation sociale*.

[27] Saint-Simon, *De l'organisation sociale*, p. 3078.

Le système général de nos connaissances sera réorganisé. Son organisation sera basée sur la croyance que l'univers est régi par une seule loi immuable. Tous le systèmes d'application, tels que les systèmes de religion, de politique, de morale, de législation civile, seront mis en accord avec le nouveau système de nos connaissances.[28]

How did Saint-Simon envisage this evolution taking place? The common thread throughout was the influence of ideas, in particular moral and religious ideas. At the heart of this was, to quote Durkheim's commentary *Socialism and Saint-Simon*, the 'sentiment of universal unity,'[29] the two aspects of which are 'the idea of God and the idea of the fundamental law'.[30] Saint-Simon's ideas grew increasingly visionary and political toward the end of his life. In *Nouveau Christianisme*[31] he claimed a totally fresh start both for society and religion. *J'accuse!*, Saint-Simon repeated incessantly, accusing Catholics, in particular the Pope, the clergy, and Jesuits of being dangerous heretics. Protestants and Martin Luther were not much better valued.[32] To remedy the alarming dissociation of economic progress and social cohesion—not only had the human species made no moral progress since Jesus Christ, it had retrograded—a new social morality for the new era had to be created, Saint-Simon argued.[33] This moral had to be 'positive', in the sense of being contemporary to the age of science and industry, and widely shared. What were its components? The key was industrial progress, bringing maximum happiness to maximum people, echoing contemporary utilitarian ideas that were central to Saint-Simon in particular in his early writings.[34] Nevertheless, mobilizing the affective and sentimental in human beings was the particular aim of Saint-Simon's new moral, thereby in his view strengthening sociability and solidarity. Even if this new industrial morality had to abandon previous theological representations, Saint-Simon underlined its continuity with Christianity. Pacification of men by the belief in a single God and fraternal love were the dogmas of Christianity that Saint-Simon valued most.[35] In his new religion, they were to receive universal application, thereby supporting humans in their efforts to economic and technological progress globally, in particular for the poor.

The exact relationship of Saint-Simon's religion ('new Christianity')—that Durkheim qualified, as 'a doctrine of philanthropy having a pantheistic conception of the universe as its basis'[36]—to Christian religions remains ambiguous. The clearest differences appear to be its 'positive' and temporal character, its earthliness, the impersonality of the god figure, as well as the primary role given to morality, at the expense of creed, dogma, and clergy.[37] This does not mean Saint-Simon did

[28] Saint-Simon, *Mémoire sur la science*, p. 1153.
[29] Durkheim, *Socialism*, p. 186.
[30] Ibid., p. 184.
[31] First published in 1825, Saint-Simon, *Nouveau Christianisme, Oeuvres complètes*, vol. IV.
[32] Ibid., pp. 3196–222.
[33] Ibid., pp. 3222–4. See also Laval, *Ambition*, p. 74.
[34] Saint-Simon, *L'Industrie*. See also Grange, *Saint-Simon*, pp. 41–7.
[35] See Saint-Simon, *L'Industrie*, Oeuvres complètes II, pp. 1575–6 and Saint-Simon, *Catéchisme des industriels*, Oeuvres complètes IV, p. 2974.
[36] Durkheim, *Socialism*, p. 193.
[37] Saint-Simon, *Nouveau Christianisme*, pp. 3191–2.

not envisage a cult. Throughout his career Saint-Simon emphasized how society needed a sentimental and aesthetic cement that could be expressed in ceremonies and art. This spiritual component needed its specific organs. The first of them was the 'academy of sentiments', the purpose of which was to codify and perfect the sentiments useful for cohesion and social efficacy.[38] The organs foreseen for the direction of intellectual production comprised artists and moralists tasked with generating presentations and pieces of arts that touched the affective. The various activities of cult had the purpose of making human beings feel their common existence.

For my reading here, the key message from Saint-Simon is the linkage of internationalism and economic development. In Durkheim's opinion, considering how little the phenomena was otherwise accorded attention in his time, it was Saint-Simon who 'prophesied the International'.[39] Saint-Simon believed that '[t]he great moral movement which should make society pass from the modified despotic regime to one most advantageous to the majority of society' is necessarily 'common to the most enlightened peoples'.[40] Internationalism was essential in allowing nations to enter the stage of industrialism, for a people could disarm only if its neighbours, likewise, renounced militarism. Saint-Simon also saw a still deeper reason for internationalism. It lay in 'a kind of political solidarity;' invisible bonds binding together nations at the same level of civilization that were, for Saint-Simon, manifest in the example of the Holy Alliance.[41] He envisaged an exit from feudal and military rule and a redirection towards an ideal of an international (European) concord or understanding by industry and an industrial spirit, integrating those who were 'united by the general interests of production, by the need they all have for security in work and liberty in exchange. The producers of all countries are therefore essentially friends'.[42] Saint-Simon called for an international (European) organization that would contribute to establishing, in each particular society, the industrial system. The organization was not destined to remain forever restricted to the European continent. It would gradually embrace all humanity, since 'the industrial regime will be the ultimate organization of the humankind'.[43] The future would see the formation of a society that included all men. It would undertake the systematic exploitation of the earth, the territorial property of human kind.[44] However, as Durkheim pointed out, this was 'but a dream which is dear to him and which, from time to time, crosses his mind—but which he does not conceive as realizable for the present'.[45]

[38] Saint-Simon, *Catéchisme des industriels*, pp. 2988–91.
[39] Durkheim, *Socialism*, pp. 174–5.
[40] Saint-Simon, *Système industriel*, V, p. 80, referred to by Durkheim, *Socialism*, p. 170.
[41] Saint-Simon, *Système industriel*, VI, pp. 99–100, referred to by Durkheim, *Socialism*, p. 170.
[42] Saint-Simon, *Système industriel*, III, p. 47, referred to by Durkheim, *Socialism*, p. 172.
[43] Saint-Simon, *Système Industriel*, Oeuvres complètes III, p. 2421.
[44] Saint-Simon, *Nouveau*, pp. 3190, 3194.
[45] Durkheim, *Socialism*, p. 175.

Auguste Comte

Comte started his professional life as an assistant of Saint-Simon who was an ever-present influence on his thinking.[46] Often credited as the 'founder of positivism' and one of the 'fathers of sociology', Comte produced a voluminous and opaque oeuvre. His areas of interest ranged from philosophy to politics, religion, social sciences, and, in particular, the role of scientific progress for the future of humanity. Several commentators see the oeuvre of Comte as divided into two parts: The first focusing on establishing a 'history of the intelligence of the objective world,' while the second part is Comte's sociology of the sentiment of sociability, culminating in the invention of the 'religion of Humanity'.[47]

My attention focuses on how Comte advocated unity, human and social, in particular the sense of coherence of shared human history that lay at the foundation of his religion. How did he articulate the fact that 'united' humanity had to be directed by the Europeans—and with such a heavy hand? Comte's method to understand history was based on an evolutionary model of law of three ages.[48] 'L'esprit human', which John Stuart Mill—Comte's close support and correspondent for a few years[49]—interpreted to refer to 'every distinct class of human conceptions,'[50] passes through three successive stages: theological (divided into fetishism, polytheism, and monotheism), metaphysical, and positive.[51] By positivism Comte meant the acceptance by humans that it was impossible to acquire absolute notions concerning the origins and destiny of the universe or phenomena. Invariable laws governed all phenomena, with which no volitions, either natural or supernatural, interfere. By combining reasoning and observation in the progress of science, these laws could be discovered.[52] The turn to positivism was, for Comte, the terminal moment in human history.

[46] Several commentators have pointed out how Comte failed to adequately recognize this; see Laval, *Ambition*, p. 86 and fn. 3. Löwith, *Meaning*, pp. 91–2: 'There is little in Comte's ideas that cannot be traced back to either Saint-Simon, Condorcet, or Turgot.' For biographical accounts of Comte, see, for example, Mary Pickering, *Auguste Comte: An Intellectual Biography*, vols 1–3 (Cambridge; New York: Cambridge University Press, 1993, 2009); Henri Gouhier, *La vie d'Auguste Comte* (Paris: Gallimard, 1931).

[47] John Stuart Mill, Comte's close correspondent in his early career, considered the second part 'false and misleading'; see John Stuart Mill, *Auguste Comte and Positivism* (London: Trübner, 1866), p. 5. Mill's *Three Essays on Religion* (1874) later faced similar reactions, see Beiner, *Civil Religion*, p. 268–75. On the division of Comte's work, see also Raymond Aron, *Les étapes de la pensée sociologique* (Paris: Gallimard, 1967), pp. 79–80; Laval, *Ambition*, pp. 122–4.

[48] The idea of the three ages was first presented in Comte, *Opuscules* and developed in *Cours de philosophie positive, I*, reprinted in Auguste Comte, *Philosophie des sciences*, edited by Juliette Grange (Paris: Gallimard, 1996), pp. 52–6.

[49] Their correspondence is published as *Lettres inédites de John Stuart Mill à Auguste Comte* (Paris: Alcan, 1899).

[50] Mill, *Auguste Comte*.

[51] Comte, *Troisieme opuscule: Considérations philosophiques sur les sciences et les savants* (1825), http://classiques.uqac.ca/classiques/Comte_auguste/la_science_sociale_extraits/1_opuscules_philo_soc/opuscules_philo_sociale.pdf (last visited 8 June 2015).

[52] *Cours de philosophie positive, I*, reprinted in Comte, *Philosophie des sciences*, pp. 52–6. For analysis, see, for example, Mill, *Auguste Comte*; Aron, *Les étapes*, pp. 81–3.

For Comte, the history of Europe absorbed in itself the history of the human species. He saw industrial society—the society of Western Europe—as the exemplar for the rest of humanity, in particular in how to acquire prosperity and power. The telos of the united human history was the development and blossoming of human nature, progressing from generation to generation. Comte was satisfied that his historical method added the key idea of solidarity between human generations to the general ideas of solidarity between social classes.[53] Humanity was defined primarily by its intellectual and moral nature, by the capacity to accumulate cultural and material treasures. 'La grande sociéte mondiale' was constituted of micro-societies of families, towns, and 'nationalités libres et durables' that were compact societies—'petites Humanités'—gradually replacing modern states too large to unite people, and humanity.[54]

Faced with the irreversibility of individualization, Comte sought something that could nevertheless represent humanity as a whole, supported by institutions, constituting a 'force spécialement destinée à y ramener aux vues et aux sentiments d'ensemble des agents qui tendent toujours à s'en écarter'.[55] He believed that the sentiments of sociability of humans were not only an essential factor of morality but also a constitutive part of the human species.[56] Comte did not think highly of individual human rights or legal regulation, in general. The broad lines of historical development demonstrated, for him, how egoism was to regress owing to the biological evolution of the instinct of sympathy and the blooming of the positive spirit. Progress for Comte was not essentially economic, but moral, sentimental, and intellectual.[57] It was manifest in the development of universal love and altruism, in an orientation towards a collective happiness.[58] This progress culminated in the 'religion of Humanity'.

In Comte's view, a religion was necessary because of the chaos of varying and contrasting interests, both at the individual and societal level. Only a powerful sentiment towards an external object that intelligence recognised as transcending rivalling and conflicting tendencies could create an accord. Psychological and physical health required the recognition of a superior authority capable of imposing firm rules for private and collective conduct.[59] That is why the problem posed by 'la désuétude de Dieu' had to be solved. The new religion of Humanity 'irrevocably eliminated the conception of God'[60] and advantageously replaced the 'insufficient

[53] Comte positions his focus on history in contrast to 'sectes rénovatrices' whose 'esprit anti-historique suppose toujours une société sans ancêtres', Auguste Comte, *Discours sur l'ensemble du positivisme* [1848] (Paris: Flammarion, 1998), p. 193.

[54] See Grange, *La philosophie*, pp. 296, 319–24.

[55] Comte, *Catéchisme positiviste* (1825), p. 205.

[56] See, Comte, *Discours*, p. 245. See also Pierre Arnaud, *La sociologie de Comte* (Paris: PUF, 1969), pp. 132–3.

[57] See Comte, *Discours*, pp. 235–300. On the concept of progress in Comte's work in general, see Löwith, *Meaning*, pp. 67–91.

[58] Comte, *Discours*, pp. 352–4.

[59] Auguste Comte, *Systeme de politique positive, II* (Paris: Libraire positiviste, Georges Crès et Cie, 1851–54), p. 8.

[60] Comte, *Discours*, p. 353.

fiction of Christ'.[61] Comte was very critical of Christianity, and Protestantism in particular. He accused it of having favoured modern egoism, to the detriment of collective orientation. Here Comte departed from Saint-Simon. The Christian love for your brother valued highly by Saint-Simon was, for Comte, just a roundabout way for an individual to guarantee her own salvation by good deeds, by obeying obligations and commands.[62] Christians were preoccupied with themselves, they did not truly care for the fate of others, Comte argued. In contrast, the Comtean 'religion of Humanity' offered collective salvation, by unifying dispersed humans, and promoting a unique centre that embraced 'la raison, l'imagination et le sentiment'.[63]

Comte emphasized how humanity needed dogmas, rites, and myths that were explicitly religious but positivist, and secular. He described them as 'mèta-religieux', based on a moral cognisance of the historic role of religions and the general history of civilization.[64] Their task was to condense the social sentiment, the spirit of being together.[65] This was also served by the 'new fetishism' of the religion of Humanity: the new god 'le Grand-Etre' ('the Supreme Being'); the fetish of world and space called 'Grand Milieu'; and that of the Earth called 'Grand Fetish'. [66] Comte's Supreme Being possessed a double quality. It figured as an objective being outside each individual, as a reality with its own laws. It was also the cultural or symbolic organism to which each individual aspired to adhere by his accomplishments.[67] Comte's religion also involved a cult and organization inspired by the Catholic one.[68]

Like Saint-Simon, Comte aspired to combine altruism with social and economical cooperation in a new manner. Whereas previous religions called for contemplation and inactivity, the religion of Humanity pushed to actively realize the good.[69] In this spirit, it also set limits of conduct on the political and economic spheres, military contest, excessive individualism, destructive exploitation of nature, or spoiling of the human patrimony. The religion of Humanity encouraged participation and universal cooperation by considering 'les hommes non comme autant d'êtres séparés, mais comme les divers organes d'un seul Grand-Etre'.[70] But were *all* human beings equal organs of the Supreme Being? Comte was writing at the juncture of the dissolution of the colonial empires constituted in the sixteenth to

[61] Comte, *Système de politique positive, I*, p. 411. [62] Comte, *Discours*, pp. 182–3.

[63] Ibid., p. 356. [64] See Grange, *La philosophie*, p. 18.

[65] See analysis by Laval, *Ambition*, p. 134.

[66] See Grange, *La philosophie*, pp. 358–68 who offers analysis and multiple references to Comte's treatment of these figures that I am not able to address in detail. See also, Andrew Wernick, *Auguste Comte and the Religion of Humanity: The Post-theistic Program of French Social Theory* (Cambridge; New York: Cambridge University Press, 2001).

[67] Comte, *Système de politique positive, II*, p. 68.

[68] Mill qualified Comte's religion as 'une forme de catholicisme sans christianisme', Grange, *La philosophie*, p. 18. For a comparison with Durkheim's religion, see W. S. F. Pickering, *Durkheim's Sociology of Religion* (Cambridge: James Clarke & Co, 2009), pp. 483–7. On Comte's emphasis on a private cult rather than a public one, see Grange, *La philosophie*, pp. 401–13.

[69] Comte, *Discours*, p. 386.

[70] Ibid., p. 387. See also analysis by Laval, *Ambition*, p. 137.

eighteenth centuries and the creation of the empires of the nineteenth century. His thoughts on race, universality, and international governance appear ambivalent to today's reader.[71] Comte envisaged how in the future 'les cinq cents sociocraties partielles du globe régénéré composent la république universelle, après un concours toujours libre'.[72] The 'Comité positif occidental' was to be European first, but get enlarged progressively to other continents and institutes as a global 'pouvoir spirituel' and, in the course of two centuries, an international society.[73] Comte however did not foresee society as a way of political organization but as a contract of morality and of faith.[74] In his critique of past colonialism, Comte argued that it had rendered evident the radical failure of the politics of systematically destroying human races, in the powerlessness to assimilate them.[75] Thereby it had demonstrated that progress was meant to gradually concern the whole of humanity. By stimulating the importance of the military and the risk of war, the colonial expansion tragically contrasted Comte's schemas of evolution according to which war in the developed industrial societies, 'elite of humanity,'[76] became an anachronism. Regretting humanity's 'inevitable primitive tendency', Comte nevertheless continued to see as its 'final destination, not less irresistible, an essentially industrial life'.[77] Comte looked forward to further institutional developments in Europe to rectify the 'provisory default of any systematic organisation of international relations,' celebrating 'our industrial and pacific instinct' that was constantly striving towards 'the fundamental rest of the civilized world'.[78] Comte had a strong emphasis on unity of human history, dear to evolutionists in general. As Raymond Aron critically points out, Comte, even if also known as the creator of scientific positivism, advocated thinking that could be seen as reminiscent of providentialism: the inevitable course of history is advancing on its line of evolution that is fixed either by religion or by the nature of humans.[79] In Comte's religion of humanity, the trans-generational continuity played a key role. The dead, the living, and those who will be born form together, in the relations between them, the cyclical humanity. Comte laid much weight on the ideas of intergenerational fidelity and gifts between generations, of the dead to current and future generations and *vice versa*, as well as the call to make generations feel both the weight and the honour of those gifts.[80] The goal of

[71] For comments on this, see Löwith, *Meaning*, p. 232.

[72] Comte, *Système de politique positive ou traité de sociologie instituant la religion de l'Humanité*, IV, edited by Carilian-Goeury Mathias and V. Dalmont, 5th edn (Paris: Siege de la Société Positiviste, 1929 [1851–54]), p. 355.

[73] Comte, *Système de politique positive*, p. 392.

[74] See Grange, *Philosophie*, p. 322.

[75] Auguste Comte, *Cours de philosophie positive, Œuvres VI* (Paris: Les Editions Anthropos, 1968), p. 68.

[76] Ibid., p. 239. See also Raymond Aron, *La société industrielle et la guerre* (Paris: Plon, 1959).

[77] Comte, *Cours de philosophie positive*, p. 375.

[78] Ibid. Aron is critical of this excessive optimism: Comte 'a devalorisé les conflits idéologiques dont on vécu les sociétes européennes et dont tant de millions de gens sont morts'. Aron, *Les étapes*, p. 95.

[79] Aron, *Les étapes*, p. 97, 103. See also Löwith, *Meaning*, pp. 71–4.

[80] The continuity of the maxim 'rendre à autrui ce que l'on a recu' from Saint-Simon to Comte to Durkheim and Mauss, see Laval, *Ambition*, p. 137.

human action was, in Comte's view, the subjective immortality in the memory of the posteriority.[81]

Since Comte's time, 'progress' has become, for many, a word 'entangled with a history of racism and Eurocentric self-congratulations'.[82] Yet the idea of universal progress by law and institutional legal practices remains the underlying premise of much international law thinking.[83] Intergenerational transfer is also a central element of international law and the epistemic community of international lawyers. Not only in celebratory speeches or festschrifts but also in law journal articles and commentaries, the 'international criminal justice system' is accorded a status above historicity, breaking free from the contingent, temporally, and socially situated character of currently held beliefs and values, of today's random institutions and practices.[84] It is a gift that past generations hand to future ones. For Comte, the subjective trans-generational element figured at the source of all transcendence, but until the emergence of the 'religion of Humanity' it had been travestied in the theory of immortality of souls promoted by previous theologies.[85]

Emile Durkheim

In contrast, Emile Durkheim saw value in the antithesis of body and soul, the immortal soul being 'useful in rendering intelligible the continuity of the collective life'.[86] The protecting ancestors were, for Durkheim, to be interpreted amongst other external projections of the individual soul, representing 'an outside power, superior to us, which gives us our law and judges us, but which also aids and sustains us'.[87] Durkheim was the first professor of sociology in the world, at Sorbonne University, and an important public figure in France.[88] His major publications include *The Division of Labour in Society, Suicide, The Rules of Sociological*

[81] Comte, *Système de politique positive, IV*, p. 35.

[82] Bruce Robbins, *Feeling Global: Internationalism in Distress* (New York; London: New York University Press, 1999), p. 123.

[83] For analysis, see, for example, Thomas Skouteris, *The Notion of Progress in International Law Discourse* (The Hague: T.M.C. Asser Press, 2010); Nathaniel Berman, 'In the Wake of Empire', *American University International Law Review* 14 (1999): p. 1515.

[84] See, for example, M. Cherif Bassiouni's speech in the ceremony for the opening of signature of the Rome Treaty, in Bassiouni, *The Statute of the International Criminal Court: A Documentary History* (Ardsley, NY: Transnational Publishers, Inc., 1998), at xxi; Claus Kreß, 'Towards a Truly Universal Invisible College of International Criminal Lawyers', *FICHL Occasional Paper Series*, no. 4 (2014), https://www.legal-tools.org/doc/82bf10/ (last visited 15 April 2015).

[85] See Comte, *Discours*, pp. 371–2.

[86] Emile Durkheim, *Les Formes élémentaires de la vie religieuse* (1912), references here to the translation *The Elementary Forms of the Religious Life*,7th edn (London: Allen & Unwin, 1971), p. 269.

[87] Durkheim, *The Elementary*, p. 280.

[88] For biographical accounts, see M. Fournier, *Émile Durkheim 1858–1917* (Paris: Fayard, 2007); Steven Lukes, *Emile Durkheim: His Life and Work—a Historical and Critical Study* (London: Allen Lane the Penguin Press, 1973). See also Jeffrey C. Alexander and Philip Smith, 'Introduction: the new Durkheim', in *The Cambridge Companion to Durkheim*, edited by Jeffrey C. Alexander and Philip Smith (Cambridge: Cambridge University Press, 2005).

Method, several publications on education, as well as on religion, most famously *The Elementary Forms of Religious Life*.[89] Durkheim also broadly addressed the historical evolution of law, 'the origins of law' as he called it, and defended his central methodological view of law as an index of social solidarity. Of the three thinkers discussed, only Durkheim explicitly focused on questions of crime and punishment.[90] Not that he was interested in utilitarian criminological theories, fashionable in his time. Instead, he gave crime and criminal law a special social role in his general evolutionary theories on society, the intertwined causalities of the division of labour in society, social solidarity, and common morality. Durkheim is not known for having directly worked on international criminal law, but appeared sensitive to the underlying ideas of accountability for and in armed conflict.[91] My analysis will focus on his ideas on social solidarity and criminal law, in particular how collective expressions of affects relate to morality and law.

Durkheim and his closest colleagues were preoccupied with the religious origins of all social phenomena, including criminal law.[92] But what was religion for Durkheim? His definition of it as 'a system of ideas by means of which individuals represent to themselves the society of which they are members, and the obscure but intimate relations which they have with it' was indebted, on Durkheim's own account, to Robertson Smith and his school, as well as 'the ethnographers of England and America'.[93] Smith's view of religion as 'a relation of all the members of a community to the power that has the good of the community at heart'[94] was adopted by Durkheim, as well as the conviction that 'religion did not exist for the saving of souls but for the preservation and welfare of society'.[95] Durkheim's sociology of religion differed in focus from that of his contemporary, Max Weber (1864–1920). Each of them acknowledged both the central force of religion in societies in general and the declining role of traditional religions in modern societies. Yet they presented differing interpretations for the consequences of this. Weber addressed rationalization, intellectualization, and the growing importance accorded to sciences as disenchantment with the world and emphasized the legal-rational foundations of authority and the role of bureaucratic governance in modernity. [96]

[89] For a bibliography of Durkheim, see Lukes, *Emile Durkheim*, pp. 561–90.

[90] Dispersed in several pieces of work not dealing primarily with criminal law, see, for example, *The Division of Labour in Society* (New York: Macmillan, 1984, re-edited New York: The Free Press, 1997); *Moral Education* (New York: The Free Press of Glencoe, 1961); 'Two Laws on Penal Evolution', reprinted in *Economy and Society* 2, no. 3 (August 1973): pp. 285–308; *Individualism*.

[91] As suggested by biographical accounts, Durkheim's public positions on WWI, and the last orientations of his research. I am touching upon this in Immi Tallgren, 'The Durkheimian Spell of International Criminal Law?', in *Revue interdisciplinaire d'études juridiques* 71 (2013): pp. 157–89.

[92] See Paul Huvelin, 'Magie et droit individuel', *L'Année sociologique*, (1905–06); Marcel Mauss, *La religion et les origines du droit pénal d'après un livre récent*, Oeuvres, 2. Representations collectives et diversité des civilisations (Paris: Les editions de minuit, 1968), pp. 651–98.

[93] Durkheim, 'Deploige, Simon, Le conflit de la morale et de la sociologie', *L'Année sociologique* XII (1913): pp. 326–8, at p. 326. For analysis, see Lukes, *Emile Durkheim*, pp. 237–44, 450–84. Lukes highlights also the influence of Fustel de Coulanges, p. 450, fn 1.

[94] Robertson Smith, *Lectures on the Religion of the Semites* (Edinburgh: 1889; 3rd edn, London: 1927), p. 55. Quoted by Lukes, *Emile Durkheim*, p. 450.

[95] Smith, *Lectures*, p. 32.

[96] Max Weber, *Theory of Social and Economic Organization* (New York: Free Press, 1947).

In contrast, Durkheim turned to developing ideas where both society and the individual acquire a religious character, as discussed in the following.

In *The Division of Labour* (first published in 1893), Durkheim presented an evolutionary theory where social solidarity is gradually transformed from mechanical to organic due to changes in the division of work in society and other factors, in particular a greater role for science. These societal developments lead towards a regression of traditional religions or religiousness. However, a foundation of underlying moral principles that meet with consensus in society remained crucially important, even in modernity. The repressive law was a partial reflection of the conscience collective, the 'totality of beliefs and sentiments common to the average members of a society,' internalized by its members.[97] Durkheim pictured crime as a violation of collective sentiments and punishment as an expression of them: 'Crime disturbs those feelings which in any one type of society are to be found in every healthy consciousness.'[98] The main function of punishment was not prevention but maintaining cohesion intact. Crime and punishment contribute to social integration, in so far as crime elicits punishment which in turn reaffirms and reinforces collective beliefs and sentiments and thereby social solidarity.[99] Whereas crimes of different types exist, what mattered was the reaction that they provoked: 'they strike the moral consciousness of nations in the same way and universally produce the same consequence'.[100]

In *Division*, Durkheim pictured an evolution where the progress of division of labour diminished the collective sentiments and thereby the need for repression, replaced by restitutive law. One could perhaps see Saint-Simon's influence here. But in '*L'Individualisme et les intellectuels*' (1898) Durkheim turned to argue that individualism and distributive justice involved not the abandonment but the transformation of collective beliefs and sentiments, whose need for penal expression and reinforcement survived. Punishment was protecting moral values even in a secular modern society of organic solidarity, and nourishing itself from the expressions of reprove.[101] In '*L'Individualisme et les intellectuels*', Durkheim took the defence of individualism targeted in the public campaign against the defenders of Dreyfus. To counter the accusations of the 'egoistic cult of the self', Durkheim emphasized how for both Kant and Rousseau, referred to by Durkheim as the *spiritualistes*, 'the only ways of acting that are moral are those which are fitting for all men equally, ... implied in the notion of man in general'.[102] In Durkheim's reading, this ideal surpassed the limit of utilitarian ends so greatly that those holding the ideal experienced it as marked with a religious character. He considered the human person

[97] Durkheim, *The Division*, pp. 38–9. [98] Ibid., p. 34. [99] Ibid., pp. 60–3.

[100] Ibid., p. 31.

[101] Durkheim, *Individualism*. For commentaries, see, for example, Roger Cotterell, *Emile Durkheim: Law in a Moral Domain* (Edinburgh: Edinburgh University Press, 1999); Lukes and Scull, *Durkheim*, pp. 15–19; Jeffrey C. Alexander and Philip Smith, 'Introduction: the new Durkheim', in *The Cambridge Companion to Durkheim*, edited by Jeffrey C. Alexander and Philip Smith (Cambridge: Cambridge University Press, 2005).

[102] Durkheim, *Individualism*, p. 61.

as sacred ... It has something of that transcendental majesty which the churches of all times have given to their Gods. It is conceived as being invested with that mysterious property which creates an empty space around holy objects, which keeps them away from profane contacts and which draws them away from ordinary life.[103]

Once the confusions clarified between individualism and utilitarianism, the 'religion of humanity whose rational expression is the individualist morality'[104] appeared. Durkheim argued that religion essentially was 'nothing else than a system of collective beliefs and practices that have a special authority'. Symbols and rites, or temples and priests were only superficial aspects. Durkheim attributed the evolution towards his new religion to two factors. Territorially extended societies caused plasticity and instability of traditions and practices, and the advancing division of labour made men's minds differ in a growing manner. Once particular religious rites and prejudices disappeared,

there remains nothing that men may love and honour in common, apart from the man itself. This is why man has become a god for man, and it is why he can no longer turn to other gods without being untrue to himself. And just as each of us embodies something of humanity, so each individual mind has within itself something of the divine, and thereby finds itself marked by a characteristic which renders it sacred and inviolable to others.[105]

From the religiousness vested in the human person it followed that '[w]hoever makes an attempt on a man's life, on a man's liberty, on a man's honour inspires us with a feeling of horror.'[106] Violations could not occur without eroding the sentiments they violated. As these sentiments were all that individuals still had in common, they could not weaken without disturbing the cohesion of society: 'A religion which tolerates acts of sacrilege abdicates any sway over men's minds.'[107] Durkheim here appears partly to meld his previous ideas on criminal law into his religion, as part of his move from functionalism towards a more symbolic understanding of society.[108] Expressions of reproof were simultaneously representations of the Durkheimian secular religion.

Durkheim later abandoned explicit analysis of the religion of individual, society or humanity, but elements of the combination of individualism, rationalism and collective sentiments towards society and humanity appear scattered in Durkheim's later writings.[109] In *The Elementary Forms*, a study on the religiousness of Australian aboriginals but to which Durkheim himself gave a more general bearing, he emphasized how all societies generate belief-systems which hold certain beings and activities as sacred. Among modern forms of this were 'the sacred character' accorded to 'princes, nobles, and political leaders', the belief in progress and the commitment to free inquiry, which is itself 'untouchable, that is to say ... sacred'.[110] For Durkheim, there was something 'eternal in religion which is

[103] Ibid., p. 62. [104] Ibid., p. 67. [105] Ibid., p. 67. [106] Ibid., p. 62.
[107] Ibid., p. 69. [108] See, for example, Alexander and Smith, 'Introduction'.
[109] See, for example, Pickering, *Durkheim's Sociology*, pp. 503–21; Lukes, *Emile*; Camille Tarot, *De Durkheim à Mauss, l'invention du symbolique* (Paris: Editions la Découverte/M.A.U.S.S., 1999), p. 213.
[110] Durkheim, *The Elementary*, p. 213.

destined to survive all the particular symbols in which religious thought has successively enveloped itself'; no society could exist without 'the need of upholding and reaffirming at regular intervals the collective sentiments and the collective ideas which make its unity and its personality'.[111] Durkheim was convinced that 'a society has all that is necessary to arouse the sensation of the divine in minds'.[112] Society was exercising moral authority and required obedience, while at the same time exercising a stimulating influence towards what was good and benevolent.[113] Durkheim evoked the possibly of *faux semblante*: the commitment and admiration felt for the society and its moral norms could be 'so closely related to the religious sentiment that many people have confounded the two'. The moral power conferred by public opinion and that with which sacred beings, objects or institutions were invested were 'at bottom of a single origin and made up of the same elements'.[114] Societies were constantly creating sacred out of the ordinary, be it by sacralizing founding texts or deifying leaders.[115]

As Beth van Schaack observes, 'many ICL cases proceed as though a transcendent law exists that has yet to be reduced to positive law but that can be discovered and invoked in criminal proceedings'.[116] Durkheim's work has recently served as an inspiration for the analysis of suggestions that international criminal law condenses how moral values and beliefs of a global community are present in international law and guide its application.[117] They are no longer expressed, as in the early days of international criminal law, in terms of 'values which are immutable and eternal' in the light of the 'Christian-Judaic absolutes of good and evil,' or as a result of the 'universal brotherhood under the fatherhood of God'.[118] Even in their more neutral appearance, such as the 'principle of humanity which has recently taken centre stage in international law debates,'[119] international criminal law and its institutions appear as the most visible and powerful incarnations of this, symbolizing 'morality' and 'justice'—and thereby, also 'love'[120]—in international law.

111 Ibid., p. 427. 112 Ibid., p. 206. 113 Ibid., pp. 211, 212.

114 Ibid., p. 213.

115 I am not able here to discuss this in comparison to Weber's ideas on charisma as extraordinary power and grace ascribed to certain individuals and institutions, see Weber, *Theory*, nor more recent elaborations, see, for example, Edward Shils, *The Constitution of Society* (Chicago: University of Chicago Press, 1982). See also Clifford Geertz, 'Centers, Kings and Charisma: Reflections on the Symbolics of Power', in *Local Knowledge: Further Essays in Interpretative Anthropology* (New York: Basic Books, 1983); David Kertzer, *Ritual, Politics, and Power* (New Haven, CT; London: Yale University Press, 1988).

116 Beth van Schaak, 'Crimen sine lege: Judicial Lawmaking at the Intersection of Law and Morals', *Georgetown Law Journal* 97 (2008–09): p. 157.

117 See Salif Nimage, 'An International Conscience Collective?', *International Criminal Law Review* 7 (2007): pp. 561–619. For a more reserved view, see Roger Cotterrell, 'The Concept of Crime and Transnational Networks of Community', in *Globalisation, Criminal Law and Criminal Justice*, edited by V. Mitsilegas, P. Alldridge, and L. Cheliotis (Oxford: Hart, 2015).

118 Joseph B. Keenan and Brendan F. Brown, *Crimes Against International Law* (Washington, Public Affairs Press, 1950), pp. vi, vii, and 72, referred to by Nimage, 'An International Conscience'.

119 Isabel Feichtner, 'Realizing Utopia through the Practice of International Law', *European Journal of International Law* 23 (2012): p. 1143, at 1154. See also Teitel, *Humanity's Law*.

120 See Jean-Luc Nancy, 'Church, State, Resistance', in *Political Theologies*, edited by Hent de Vries and Lawrence E. Sullivan (New York: Fordham University Press, 2006), pp. 111–12.

In such a reading, international criminal trials figure amongst the ways of revivifying 'the most essential elements of the collective consciousness', so that an international community 'periodically renews the sentiment which it has of itself and of its unity'.[121] The international trials, relayed globally by way of outreach activities and media, may aspire to functions Durkheim accorded to religious practices: 'representing or imprinting [the past] more deeply in the mind'.[122] When 'a society is going through circumstances which sadden, perplex or irritate it,'[123] religiousness is representing society in the sense of expressing these social realities.

Conclusions

Saint-Simon's, Comte's, and Durkheim's religions of humanity and international law all present features of a system of communication of ideas and sentiments; they involve specifying and regulating social relationships by expressive means. In their different ways, they strive to create a sense of shared history where humans can learn from their experiences and evolve constructively. Also shared is how communicating ideas and sentiments and regulating social relationships require effort. Think of, for example, how Auguste Comte emphasized the role of civic education in spreading the religion of humanity. He developed elaborate dogmas and symbols of humanity, as well as a flag and temples of humanity for commemoration. International law and its institutional practice create and evoke dogmas and symbols manifest in the traditions of assembly, procedure, language, and attire, or in the memorabilia and forums of commemorating moments of institutional creation, law-making, or famous trials or crimes. In international institutions' communication, outreach and media policies have an important role. Fetishism or not, great care is put on the material dimension of institutional presence, as, for example, demonstrated by the new International Criminal Court (ICC) headquarters. The ICC building complex under construction in The Hague is intended to convey 'the eminence and authority of the ICC, while at the same time relating it on a human scale', making 'visible to anyone and everyone' that the ICC has 'become a cornerstone of international justice and the modern global civilization by making known to the remotest corners of the world that the most serious crimes do not go unpunished anymore'.[124]

Just as Durkheim identified the 'recreative and aesthetic element' of religions, comparing rites to 'dramatic representations',[125] Comte foresaw 'free missionaries who would preach everywhere the universal doctrine'.[126] Would Saint-Simon have

[121] Durkheim, *The Elementary*, p. 375. [122] Ibid., pp. 376, 378.

[123] Ibid., p. 419.

[124] Statement by H.E. Ambassador Markus Börlin, Vice-President of the Assembly of States Parties, 16 April 2013 http://www.icccpi.int/en_menus/icc/press%20and%20media/press%20releases/Documents/pr898/Groundbreaking-Ceremony-ASP-Vice-President-Statement.pdf (last consulted 14 April 2015).

[125] Durkheim, *The Elementary*, pp. 379–83.

[126] Comte, *Système de politique positive* I, p. 387.

let international lawyers enter his 'academy of sentiments', indispensable in secular societies? David Luban recently has suggested that 'moral learning' by international criminal law becomes 'common property of humankind' in which positive complementarity and outreach activities are supposedly 'helping to devolve norms to local institutions'.[127] Is it not such sympathetic thoughts towards the local that, by making palpable the distance that characterizes how international law relates to everyday lives, accentuate its resemblance with religion in terms of faith in its positive potential to bring about changes, if not miracles? Just as 'the *world of religious things* is a partially imaginary world,' therefore lending 'itself more readily to the free creations of the mind,'[128] the fact that international law addresses issues that are vast and cumbersome to comprehend may render it easier to believe—even in 'things' that would seem absurd in closer circles, nationally or amongst people known personally.

It is in particular the symbolism of condemning and punishing disgraced national leaders and their era that may take dramatic features as a culmination of the eschatological anticipation of a future salvation, as if correcting the (totalitarian, nationalistic) past in a judgement by international judges-priests. At the same time, it may appear as a neutral way for an international community to become conscious of itself and to assure the continuation of this consciousness, sociological characteristics that Durkheim accorded to religion.[129] The mechanisms of international law contribute to forming an international authority, be it moral or political, with contingent direction and programme. For Durkheim, an individual believer feels within him more force, to endure the trials of existence or to conquer them. In current times, could one see international law as part of the fragile but sympathetic symbolic structures by which an individual manages to rise 'above the miseries of the world, ... above his condition as a mere man'?[130] If not yet then in the future, international law would stand for the chance that the believer will finally be saved from evil, under whatever form he conceives the evil. After all, 'the first article in every creed is salvation by faith'.[131]

But the mirror is splintered. As the utopian aspirations of current international law and its institutional practice figure, to quote Antonio Cassese, 'gradually [to] transform world society into a really international community endowed with paramount communal values and at least a modicum of community institutions so that public or collective concerns may prevail over private interests'.[132] Cassese's language on common values, collective concerns, and institutions based on values echoes Saint-Simon, Comte, and Durkheim. Yet the ambition today is elsewhere. More than the international economic institutions or development agencies, immersed in their complicity or perceived inefficacy, it is human rights and the

[127] David Luban, 'After the Honeymoon', *Journal of International Criminal Justice* 11 (2013): p. 512.
[128] Durkheim, *The Elementary*, p. 381 (italics added).
[129] Ibid., p. 231.
[130] Ibid., p. 416.
[131] Durkheim, *The Elementary*, p. 416.
[132] Antonio Cassese, 'Introduction', in *Realizing Utopia: The Future of International Law*, edited by Antonio Cassese (Oxford: Oxford University Press, 2012), p. xx.

international criminal jurisdictions—sending 'real persons to real prisons'[133] in Leila Nadya Sadat's jubilatory passage—that incarnate the most emblematic parts of today's international law. In contrast, societies at the highest stages of evolution in Saint-Simon's chronicle of human progress step-by-step no longer needed criminal law and the repressive administrations that go with it. Instead, energies were to be collectively directed towards the finality of ameliorating 'as promptly and as completely as possible the moral and physical existence of the most numerous class',[134] the poor. Saint-Simon's religion of humanity focused on common moral ideas inspired by utilitarianism but with the strong social emphasis and concern which also inspired Marx and Engels. In his dream of future, progress at the age of maturity of human societies meant concrete well-being, spiritually and materially, not the possibility to condemn crimes or rights violations in order to express values for a better future.

Does anyone playing with the idea of international law as a 'religion of humanity' thus face the risk that a closer look reveals the famous opium in the valley of tears of human suffering, the illusion necessary to make the world seem to stand upright, although it is upside down?[135] The apparent paradox is accentuated by unequal conditions of socio-economic, political, and military power and the firm grip 'civilized humanity'[136] continues to hold on international law. One may dream of the ICC as an 'embodiment of ... a sovereigntyless conscience of humanity',[137] yet its jurisdictional architecture rests on the presumption of protection of a sovereign state's might over its territory, nationals, and interests. Just as the ad hoc tribunals, the ICC was established only for situations where the state having jurisdiction is not respecting 'the duty of every State to exercise its criminal jurisdiction over those responsible for international crimes'.[138] The reasons for the 'unwillingness or inability of the State genuinely to prosecute'[139] can relate to a multitude of circumstances. The policy of 'positive complementarity' aims at 'developing national legal systems' of the weaker, typically post-colonial societies. [140] The critique of this

[133] Leila Nadya Sadat, *The International Criminal Court and the Transformation of International Law: Justice for the New Millennium* (Ardsley, N.Y.: Transnational Publishers, 2002), p. 8.

[134] Saint-Simon, *Nouveau Christianisme*, p. 3185.

[135] Karl Marx, *Introduction to a Contribution to the Critique of Hegel's Philosophy of Rights*, [1843–4], in *Collected Works*, vol. 3 (New York: Lawrence & Wishart, 1979).

[136] Martti Koskenniemi, *From Apology to Utopia*, p. 946. Compare to Arnulf Becker Lorca, 'Eurocentrism in the History of International Law', in *The Oxford Handbook of the History of International Law*, edited by Bardo Fassbender and Anne Peters (Oxford: Oxford University Press, 2012); Liliana Obregón, 'The Civilized and the Uncivilized', in *The Oxford Handbook of the History of International Law* (Oxford: Oxford University Press, 2012).

[137] Bruce Rosenstock, 'Against Sovereign Impunity: The Political Theology of the International Criminal Court', in *After Secular Law*, edited by Winnifred Fallers Sullivan et al. (Stanford: Stanford Law Books, 2011).

[138] Rome Statute of the International Criminal Court 91 July 2002), preamble.

[139] Rome Statute, Article 17, see also Article 20.

[140] The term is used by the Prosecutor's Office (http://www.icc-cpi.int/NR/rdonlyres/66A8DCDC-3650-4514-AA62-D229D1128F65/281506/OTPProsecutorialStrategy20092013.pdf), the Assembly of States Parties and NGOs. For analysis, see Benson Olugbuo, 'Positive Complementarity and the Fight Against Impunity in Africa', in *Prosecuting International Crimes in Africa*, edited by Chacha Murungu and Japhet Biegon (Pretoria: PULP, 2011); Hitomi Takemura, 'A Critical Analysis

setting as 'neo-colonial' has valid points, while at the same time such claims are instrumentalized in national and international power struggles.[141]

Saint-Simon's narrative of the evolution of humanity has familiar features: the childlike barbaric early humans that need constraints to evolve into producers of economic well-being is reminiscent of how indigenous peoples were represented by international lawyers and politicians in times of conquests and colonialism. Past caricatures aside, how to explain that repression today is still considered more necessary in some societies, 'naturally' prone to conflict and violence?[142] Or that the understanding of violence as crime has a hierarchical ladder? How else to explain why technologically sophisticated violence—drone attacks being its most emblematic example today—does not feature in the focus of international criminal repression? Or large-scale economic, social, environmental crimes, part of which is 'slow violence', to use a term Rob Nixon coined in the context of the environment for 'violence that occurs gradually and out of sight, a violence of delayed destruction that is dispersed across time and space, an attritional violence that is typically not viewed as violence at all'[143]? A distinctively Durkheimian tone of sociological experiments with primitive societies—'since the facts there are simpler, the relations between them are more apparent'[144]—lingers around the testing of dogmas of accountability, such as 'no peace without justice',[145] that are not necessarily in use in the Global North.

The language and institutions of international criminal justice have in this manner taken a central place in the futurist, teleological, or eschatological streams of international law, right on the spot occupied some decades earlier by the development discourse that ran out of power. But focusing on individual criminal responsibility is not necessarily forwarding Saint-Simon's objective of creating a paradise of well-being and progress on Earth for people living right now, not in the future nor in heaven. In any case, the material or social benefits of international criminal

of Positive Complementarity', in *Criminal Law between War and Peace*, edited by Stefano Manacorda and Adán Nieto (Cuenca: Ed. de la Universidad de Castilla-La Mancha, 2009); Morten Bergsmo, Olympia Bekou, and Annika Jones, 'Complementarity After Kampala: Capacity Building and the ICC's Legal Tools', *Goettingen Journal of International Law* 2 (2010): pp. 791–811.

141 See, for example, Ifeonu Eberechi, 'Rounding Up the Usual Suspects: Exclusion, Selectivity, and Impunity in the Enforcement of International Criminal Justice and the African Union's Emerging Resistance', *African Journal of Legal Studies* 4, no. 1 (2011): p. 51; Nicholas Waddell and Phil Clark, eds, *Courting Conflict? Justice, Peace and the ICC in Africa* (London: Royal African Society, 2008); Dire Tladi, 'The African Union and the International Criminal Court: The Battle for the Soul of International Law', *South African Yearbook of International Law* 34 (2009): p. 57. For a recent analysis of the discourse, see Anne-Charlotte Martineau, 'La justice pénale internationale, l'Afrique et le refoulé colonial', *Champ pénal*, vol. XIII (2016). https://champpenal.revues.org/9300.

142 For discussion on this, see Frédéric Mégret, 'Cour pénale internationale et néocolonialism: au-delà des évidences', *Études internationales* 45, no. 1 (2014): pp. 27–50.

143 Rob Nixon, *Slow Violence and the Environmentalism of the Poor* (Cambridge, MA; London: Harvard University Press, 2011).

144 Durkheim, *The Elementary*, p. 7.

145 See, for example, Adam Branch, Keynote address delivered at 'The Politics of Peace and Justice' (Panel Discussion, International Criminal Court Review Conference, Kampala, Uganda, 3 June 2010).

norms or procedures have yet to be documented, both in general and in the societies concerned. The experience of victims and victimized communities is particularly challenging to research, and the jury is still out on the pros and cons of retributive versus restitutive justice—which should in any case not be viewed as mutually exclusive. The ambitions of the ICC Trust Fund for Victims, for example, to use the meagre funds available towards 'transformative reparations' in the territories where ICC jurisdiction is exercised, 'with a view to eliminating the pre-existing structural inequalities that have led to or encouraged the violence',[146] remain isolated but telling rhetorical interventions symptomatic of the interventionist and omnipotent hubris of the international actors, at great distance from local ownership and agency, as well as democratic government.[147]

Saint-Simon's, Comte's, and Durkheim's ideas of progress were radically different from the progress aspired to by international law today. Ultimately, the difference culminates on what constitutes progress and who has access to the means to create progress. International criminal law and its institutions are arguably installed in the systemic conditions of capitalism, as part of a neo-liberal agenda.[148] Saint-Simon's friendship of 'producers of all countries'[149] may have turned into today's 'transnational capitalist class'[150] with a reduced agenda. In Saint-Simon's, Comte's, or Durkheim's visions for a better future, capitalism was not invariably malignant: the early phases of modern capitalism also symbolized human progress by commerce, industry, science, and technology. Durkheim, in particular, expected these changes to contribute to an organic division of work in societies bound together by social solidarity. My analysis has highlighted how this socio-liberal optimistic strain of heritage in international law today appears transformed into promises of progress by international norms-creation and institutional practice. Yet in the absence of global solidarity based on a consensual division of work,[151] international law's current flagship—international criminal law and its institutional practice—may strike one as less related to palpable well-being in the countries or regions directly

[146] Observations on Reparations in Response to the Scheduling Order of 14 March 2012, Lubanga (ICC-01/04-01/06-2872), Trials Chamber I, April 2012, § 77.

[147] For discussion, see Carolyn Hoyle and Leila Ullrich, 'New Court, New Justice?', *Journal of International Criminal Justice* 12 (2014): pp. 681–703. For a detailed analysis of the legal framework, see Conor McCarthy, *Reparations and Victim Support in the International Criminal Court* (Cambridge: Cambridge University Press, 2012).

[148] See, for example, Grietje Baars, 'Making ICL History: On the need to move beyond pre-fab critiques of ICL', in *Critical Approaches to International Criminal Law*, edited by Christine Schwöbel, (Abingdon: Routledge, 2014); Tor Krever, 'International Criminal Law: an Ideology Critique', *Leiden Journal of International Law* 26 (2013): pp. 701–23. See also China Miéville, *Between Equal Rights: A Marxist Theory of International Law* (Netherlands: Brill, 2005); B.S. Chimni, 'International Institutions Today: An Imperial Global State in the Making', *European Journal of International Law* 15 (2004): pp. 1–37.

[149] See Saint-Simon, *Système industriel*, III, p. 47, referred to by Durkheim, *Socialism*, p. 172.

[150] See Robinson and Harris, 'Towards a Global Ruling Class? Globalization and the Transnational Capitalist Class', *Science and Society* 64 (2000): pp. 11–54.

[151] Applying Durkheim's *Division of Labour* to today's discourse on globalization, see Paul Hirsch, Peer C. Fiss, and Amanda Hoel-Green, 'A Durkheimian Approach to Globalization', in *Oxford Handbook of Sociology and Organisational Studies*, edited by Paul S. Adler (Oxford: Oxford University Press, 2008).

concerned by the criminality it addresses than to desires for order and stability outside them. The evident problem is that the different 'stages of human development' are not gliding smoothly towards the future along the linear trajectories envisaged by evolutionary theorists and international law; they are concomitant, confronting each other in conflict, domination, subordination, or extermination. The same goes for the national and international sovereignties, their interests and their political, military, religious, or cultural agendas. Picturing these struggles and violence in the conditions of post-colonial instability and inequality as 'international crimes' subject to individual criminal responsibility, in accordance with criminological theories on attaining societal objectives by punishment—developed in the socio-economic conditions of the eighteenth-, nineteenth-, and twentieth-century Christian societies in Western Europe[152] and recently imported into the international politics as a powerful instrument to express shared values—requires a congregation of dogmas, mythologies, and credulity that would make many well-known histories of miracles pale in comparison.

The foregoing suggestions flag the need for alternative frames of analysis of international law in order to redirect the focus from the eventual temptation of religiousness, old or new. The visions of Saint-Simon, Comte, and Durkheim were admirably ambitious in their orientation towards social, palpable justice, and solidary well-being. Yet Auguste Comte's deadline, the two centuries, has not been sufficient to create a moral community that is truly universal. Reading the UNDP Human Development Report 2014, there is no ambivalence on whether Saint-Simon's twelfth phase of development of humanity has been reached.[153] A dissolution of 'humanity' in the egoist materialism, Comte's 'grande hérésie',[154] may strike one as a more adequate description. In contrast, the sweet scent of a powerful universal morality of 'humanity' currently imparted to international law, a secular surrogate religion, leans to the familiar European originalism in a hegemonic redescription of how international law and its institutions came about. A focus on religiousness as a discourse is a further choice of a point of view inwards, to 'our' beliefs and faith in setting up and dominating legal constructs and bureaucratic structures of institutional justice. With that move, the risk is that outward looking and critical research questions will remain in the margins. Who dares to inquire, for instance, how far international criminal law and its institutional practice today are one of the key mechanisms through which ideas about (political, social, cultural, racial) inferiority, subordination, or abject are constructed in international relations? Whereas international law can and also should be about justice, it is not carved in stone in the temples of 'humanity' nor whispered from behind the clouds by 'our' ancestors. Or else the risk is getting ruled out the politics of international

[152] On the limits of criminology and on its Eurocentric or imperial tendencies, and on the possibilities of a renewal, see, for example, Biko Agozino, *Counter-Colonial Criminology: A Critique of Imperialist Reason* (London: Pluto, 2003); Wayne Morrison, *Criminology, Civilisation and the New World Order* (Abingdon: Routledge Cavendish, 2006).

[153] http://hdr.undp.org/sites/default/files/hdr14-report-en-1.pdf.

[154] Auguste Comte, *Système de politique positive*, I, p. 641.

law that have social justice and solidarity as its objectives, including a broader and more just entitlement to economic welfare aspired by Saint-Simon, Comte, and Durkheim. Declining to address today's international law and its mediatized ceremonies of naming the crime and punishment as an incarnation of a fashionable retro faith has consequences for what is articulated and how, thereby becoming visible, open to critique, and change.

Bibliography

Abauzit, F. et al. 'Les Sentiments religieux à l'heure actuelle' (Paris: Vrin, 1919), translated and reprinted in *Durkheim on Religion*, J. Redding and W. S. F. Pickering, eds (London; Boston: Routledge and Kegan Paul, 1975), p. 187.

Agozino, Biko. *Counter-Colonial Criminology: A Critique of Imperialist Reason* (London: Pluto, 2003).

Alexander, Jeffrey C., and Philip Smith. 'Introduction: the new Durkheim'. In *The Cambridge Companion to Durkheim*, edited by Jeffrey C. Alexander and Philip Smith (Cambridge: Cambridge University Press, 2005).

Ansart, Pierre. *Saint-Simon* (Paris: PUF, 1969).

Arnaud, Pierre. *La sociologie de Comte* (Paris: PUF, 1969).

Aron, Raymond. *La société industrielle et la guerre* (Paris: Plon, 1959).

Aron, Raymond. *Les étapes de la pensée sociologique* (Paris: Gallimard, 1967).

Baars, Grietje. 'Making ICL History: On the Need to Move beyond Pre-fab Critiques of ICL'. In *Critical Approaches to International Criminal Law*, edited by Christine Schwöbel (Abingdon: Routledge, 2014).

Bandeira Galindo, George Rodrigo. 'Force Field: On History and Theory of International Law'. *Rechtsgeschicte* 20 (2012): pp. 86–103.

Bassiouni, M. Cherif, ed. *The Statute of the International Criminal Court: A Documentary History* (Ardsley, N.Y.: Transnational Publishers, Inc., 1998).

Beiner, Ronald. *Civil Religion* (New York: Cambridge University Press, 2011).

Bellah, Robert. 'Civil Religion in America'. *Journal of the American Academy of Arts and Sciences* 96, no. 1 (Winter, 1967): pp. 1–21.

Bergsmo, Morten, Olympia Bekou, and Annika Jones. 'Complementarity After Kampala: Capacity Building and the ICC's Legal Tools'. *Goettingen Journal of International Law* 2 (2010): pp. 791–811.

Berman, Nathaniel. 'In the Wake of Empire'. *American University International Law Review* 14 (1999): p. 1515.

Berman, Nathaniel. '"The Sacred Conspiracy": Religion, Nationalism, and the Crisis of Internationalism'. *Leiden Journal of International Law* 25, no. 1 (2012): pp. 9–54.

Bikundo, Edwin. *International Criminal Law: Using or Abusing Legality?* (Farnham: Ashgate, 2014).

Branch, Adam. 'The Politics of Peace and Justice' (Keynote address, Panel Discussion, International Criminal Court Review Conference, Kampala, Uganda, 3 June 2010).

Bucar, Elizabeth M., and Barbra Barnett, eds. *Does Human Rights Need God?* (Grand Rapids, Mich.: W. B. Eerdmans, 2005).

Cançado Trindade, Antônio Augusto. *International Law for Humankind: Towards a New Jus Gentium* (The Netherlands: Martinus Nijhoff Publishers, 2010).

Cassese, Antonio. 'Introduction'. In *Realizing Utopia: The Future of International Law*, edited by Antonio Cassese (Oxford: Oxford University Press, 2012), p. xx.

Chimni, B. S. 'International Institutions Today: An Imperial Global State in the Making'. *European Journal of International Law* 15 (2004): pp. 1–37.

Clarke, Kamari M. *Fictions of Justice* (Cambridge; New York: Cambridge University Press, 2009).

Comte, Auguste. *Troisieme opuscule: Considérations philosophiques sur les sciences et les savants* (1825). http://classiques.uqac.ca/classiques/Comte_auguste/la_science_sociale_extraits/1_opuscules_philo_soc/opuscules_philo_sociale.pdf (last visited 8 June 2015).

Comte, Auguste. *Système de politique positive ou traité de sociologie instituant la religion de l'Humanité*, vols I–II (Paris: Libraire positiviste, Georges Crès et Cie, 1851–54).

Comte, Auguste. *Système de politique positive ou traité de sociologie instituant la religion de l'Humanité*, vol. IV, edited by Mathias, Carilian-Goeury and V. Dalmont, 5th edn (Paris: Siege de la Société Positiviste, 1929 [1851–54]).

Comte, Auguste. *Cours de philosophie positive, Œuvres VI* (Paris: Les Editions Anthropos, 1968).

Comte, Auguste. *Philosophie des sciences*, edited by Juliette Grange (Paris: Gallimard, 1996).

Comte, Auguste. *Discours sur l'ensemble du positivisme* [1848] (Paris: Flammarion, 1998).

de Condorcet, Nicolas. *Esquisse d'un tableau historique des progrès de l'eprit humain* (1794–95). Bibliothèque de Philosophie (Paris: Boivin, 1933).

Cotterell, Roger. *Emile Durkheim: Law in a Moral Domain* (Edinburgh: Edinburgh University Press, 1999).

Cotterell, Roger. 'The Concept of Crime and Transnational Networks of Community'. In *Globalisation, Criminal Law and Criminal Justice*, edited by V. Mitsilegas, P. Alldridge, and L. Cheliotis (Oxford: Hart, 2015).

Durkheim, Emile. 'Deploige, Simon, Le conflit de la morale et de la sociologie'. *L'Année sociologique* XII (1913): pp. 326–8.

Durkheim, Emile. *Socialism and Saint-Simon* (Ohio: The Antioch Press, 1958).

Durkheim, Emile. *Moral Education* (New York: The Free Press of Glencoe, 1961).

Durkheim, Emile. *The Elementary Forms of the Religious Life*, 7th edn (London: Allen & Unwin, 1971).

Durkheim, Emile. 'Two Laws on Penal Evolution'. *Economy and Society* 2, no. 3 (August 1973): pp. 285–308.

Durkheim, Emile. 'L'Individualisme et les intellectuels'. In *Revue Bleue* 4e série, X (1898), pp. 7–13, 10; translated by S. Lukes and J. Lukes, *Political Studies*, XVII (1969), pp. 19–30, reprinted in W. S. F. Pickering, *Durkheim on Religion* (London; Boston: Routledge & K. Paul, 1975).

Durkheim, Emile. *The Division of Labour in Society* (New York: Macmillan, 1984, re-edited New York: The Free Press, 1997).

Eberechi, Ifeonu. 'Rounding Up the Usual Suspects: Exclusion, Selectivity, and Impunity in the Enforcement of International Criminal Justice and the African Union's Emerging Resistance'. *African Journal of Legal Studies* 4, no. 1 (2011): p. 51.

Feichtner, Isabel. 'Realizing Utopia through the Practice of International Law'. *European Journal of International Law* 23 (2012): pp. 1143, 1154.

Fournier, M. *Émile Durkheim 1858–1917* (Paris: Fayard, 2007).

Geertz, Clifford. 'Centers, Kings and Charisma: Reflections on the Symbolics of Power'. In *Local Knowledge: Further Essays in Interpretative Anthropology* (New York: Basic Books, 1983).

Gouhier, Henri. *La vie d'Auguste Comte* (Paris: Gallimard, 1931).

Gouldner, Albin W. 'Introduction'. In Emile Durkheim, *Socialism and Saint-Simon* (Ohio: The Antioch Press, 1958).

Grange, Juliette. *La philosophie d'Auguste Comte: science, politique, religion* (Paris: PUF, 1996).
Grange, Juliette. *Saint-Simon (1760–1825)* (Paris: Ellipses, 2005).
Grewe, Wilhelm G. *The Epochs of International Law* (Berlin; New York: Walter de Gruyter, 2000).
Hammill, Graham, and Julia Reinhard Lupton. 'Introduction'. In *Political Theology and Early Modernity,* edited by Graham Hammill and Julia Reinhard Lupton (Chicago; London: The University of Chicago Press, 2012), pp. 1–7.
Haskell, John. 'Divine Immanence: The Evangelical Foundations of Modern Anglo-American Approaches to International Law'. *Chinese Journal of International Law* 11, no. 3 (2012): pp. 429–67.
Hirsch, Paul, Peer C. Fiss, and Amanda Hoel-Green. 'A Durkheimian Approach to Globalization'. In *Oxford Handbook of Sociology and Organisational Studies,* edited by Paul S. Adler (Oxford: Oxford University Press, 2008).
Hoyle, Carolyn, and Leila Ullrich. 'New Court, New Justice?'. *Journal of International Criminal Justice* 12 (2014): pp. 681–703.
Human Development Report 2014. Available at: http://hdr.undp.org/sites/default/files/hdr14-report-en-1.pdf.
Huvelin, Paul. 'Magie et droit individuel'. *L'Année sociologique* (1905–06).
Ignatieff, Michael. *Human Rights as Politics and Idolatry* (Princeton: Princeton University Press, 2003).
Keenan, Joseph B., and Brendan F. Brown. *Crimes Against International Law* (Washington, Public Affairs Press, 1950).
Kennedy, David. 'Losing Faith in the Secular: Law, Religion, and the Culture of International Governance'. In *Religion and International Law,* edited by Mark Janis and Carolyn Evans (The Hague; Boston: Martinus Nijhoff Publishers, 1999), pp. 309–20.
Kertzer, David. *Ritual, Politics, and Power* (New Haven; London: Yale University Press, 1988).
Koskenniemi, Martti. *The Gentle Civilizer of Nations: The Rise and Fall of International Law 1870–1960* (Cambridge: Cambridge University Press, 2002).
Kreß, Claus. 'Towards a Truly Universal Invisible College of International Criminal Lawyers'. *FICHL Occasional Paper Series* No. 4 (2014). https://www.legal-tools.org/doc/82bf10/ (last visited 15 April 2015).
Krever, Tor. 'International Criminal Law: An Ideology Critique'. *Leiden Journal of International Law* 26 (2013): pp. 701–23.
Laval, Christian. *L'ambition sociologique* (Paris: Editions La Decouverte & Syros, 2002).
Lettres inédites de John Stuart Mill à Auguste Comte (Paris: Alcan, 1899).
Lorca, Arnulf Becker. 'Eurocentrism in the History of International Law'. In *The Oxford Handbook of the History of International Law,* edited by Bardo Fassbender and Anne Peters (Oxford: Oxford University Press, 2012).
Luban, David. 'After the Honeymoon'. *Journal of International Criminal Justice* 11 (2013): pp. 505–15.
Lukes, Steven. *Emile Durkheim: His Life and Work—a Historical and Critical Study* (London: Allen Lane the Penguin Press; Stanford, CA: Stanford University Press, 1973).
Lukes, Steven, and Andrew Scull. 'Introduction'. In *Durkheim and the Law,* edited by Steven Lukes and Andrew Scull (Great Britain: Billing and Sons Ltd, 1983).
Löwith, Karl. *Meaning of History* (Chicago; London: The University of Chicago Press, 1949).
Marks, Susan. 'Human Rights in Disastrous Times'. In *The Cambridge Companion to International Law,* edited by James Crawford and Martti Koskenniemi (Cambridge: Cambridge University Press, 2012), pp. 309–26, 313–14.

Martineau, Anne-Charlotte. 'La justice pénale internationale, l'Afrique et le refoulé colonial'. *Champ pénal*, vol. XIII (2016). https://champpenal.revues.org/9300

Marx, Karl. *The Capital*, Volume III. pp. 431–34. https://www.marxists.org/archive/marx/works/download/pdf/Capital-Volume-III.pdf.

Marx, Karl, and Friedrich Engels. *Utopisme et communauté de l'avenir* (Paris: François Maspero, 1976).

Marx, Karl. 'Introduction to a Contribution to the Critique of Hegel's Philosophy of Rights, [1843–44]'. In *Collected Works*, vol. 3 (New York: Lawrence & Wishart, 1979).

Mauss, Marcel. *La religion et les origines du droit pénal d'après un livre récent.* Oeuvres, 2. Representations collectives et diversité des civilisations (Paris: Les editions de minuit, 1968).

McCarthy, Conor. *Reparations and Victim Support in the International Criminal Court* (Cambridge: Cambridge University Press, 2012).

Mégret, Frédéric. 'Cour pénale internationale et néocolonialism: au-delà des évidences'. *Études internationales* 45, no. 1 (2014): pp. 27–50.

Mégret, Frédéric. 'International Criminal Justice: A Critical Research Agenda'. In *Critical Approaches to International Criminal Law*, edited by Christine Schwöbel (Abingdon: Routledge, 2014), pp. 17, 43.

Miéville, China. *Between Equal Rights: A Marxist Theory of International Law* (Netherlands: Brill, 2005).

Mill, John Stuart. *Auguste Comte and Positivism* (London: Trübner, 1866).

Mill, John Stuart. *The Utility of Religion*. In *Three Essays on Religion* (Amherst: Prometheus, 1998 [1874]).

Mitchell, Audra. *International Intervention in a Secular Age: Re-enchanting Humanity?* (London: Routledge, 2014).

Morrison, Wayne. *Criminology, Civilisation and the New World Order* (Abingdon: Routledge Cavendish, 2006).

Moyn, Samuel. *Human Rights and the Uses of History* (London; Brooklyn, N.Y.: Verso, 2014).

Musso, Pierre. *Saint-Simon et Saint-Simonisme* (Paris: PUF, 1999).

Nancy, Jean-Luc. 'Church, State, Resistance'. In *Political Theologies*, edited by Hent de Vries and Lawrence E. Sullivan (New York: Fordham University Press, 2006).

Nimage, Salif. 'An International Conscience Collective?'. *International Criminal Law Review* 7 (2007): pp. 561–619.

Nixon, Rob. *Slow Violence and the Environmentalism of the Poor* (Cambridge, Mass.; London: Harvard University Press, 2011).

Obregón, Liliana. 'The Civilized and the Uncivilized'. In *The Oxford Handbook of the History of International Law* (Oxford: Oxford University Press, 2012).

Observations on Reparations in Response to the Scheduling Order of 14 March 2012, Lubanga (ICC-01/04-01/06-2872), Trials Chamber I, April 2012, § 77.

Olugbuo, Benson. 'Positive Complementarity and the Fight Against Impunity in Africa'. In *Prosecuting International Crimes in Africa*, edited by Chacha Murungu and Japhet Biegon (Pretoria: PULP, 2011).

Phillips, Elisabeth. *Political Theology—A Guide for the Perplexed* (London; New York: T&T Clark, 2012).

Pickering, Mary. *Auguste Comte: An Intellectual Biography*, vols 1–3 (Cambridge: New York: Cambridge University Press, 1993, 2009).

Pickering, W. S. F. *Durkheim's Sociology of Religion* (Cambridge: James Clarke & Co, 2009).

Porsdam, Helle, ed. *Civil Religion, Human Rights and International Relations* (Cheltenham: Edward Elgar, 2012).

Robbins, Bruce. *Feeling Global: Internationalism in Distress* (New York; London: New York University Press, 1999).

Robinson, William I. and Jerry Harris. 'Towards a Global Ruling Class? Globalization and the Transnational Capitalist Class'. *Science and Society* 64 (2000): pp. 11–54.

Rosenstock, Bruce. 'Against Sovereign Impunity: The Political Theology of the International Criminal Court'. In *After Secular Law*, edited by Winnifred Fallers Sullivan et al. (Stanford: Stanford Law Books, 2011).

Rousseau, Jean-Jacques. *Du contrat social* (Paris: Garnier-Flammarion, 1966 [1762]).

Sadat, Leila Nadya. *The International Criminal Court and the Transformation of International Law: Justice for the New Millennium* (Ardsley, N.Y.: Transnational Publishers, 2002).

Saint-Simon, Henri. *Oeuvres complètes*, vols I–IV, edited by Juliette Grange, Pierre Musso, Philippe Régnier, and Frank Yonnet (Paris: PUF, 2012).

van Schaak, Beth. 'Crimen sine lege: Judicial Lawmaking at the Intersection of Law and Morals'. *Georgetown Law Journal* 97 (2008–09): p. 157.

Shils, Edward. *The Constitution of Society* (Chicago: University of Chicago Press, 1982).

Skouteris, Thomas. *The Notion of Progress in International Law Discourse* (The Hague: T.M.C. Asser Press, 2010).

Smith, Robertson. *Lectures on the Religion of the Semites* (Edinburgh: 1889; 3rd edn London: 1927).

Statement by H.E. Ambassador Markus Börlin, Vice-President of the Assembly of States Parties, 16 April 2013. Available at: http://www.icccpi.int/en_menus/icc/press%20and%20media/press%20releases/Documents/pr898/Groundbreaking-Ceremony-ASP-Vice-President-Statement.pdf (last consulted 14 April 2015).

Takemura, Hitomi. 'A Critical Analysis of Positive Complementarity'. In *Criminal Law between War and Peace*, edited by Stefano Manacorda and Adán Nieto (Cuenca: Ed. de la Universidad de Castilla-La Mancha, 2009).

Tallgren, Immi. 'The Sensibility and Sense of International Criminal Law'. *European Journal of International Law* 13, no. 3 (2002): pp. 561–95.

Tallgren, Immi. 'The Durkheimian Spell of International Criminal Law?'. In *Revue interdisciplinaire d'études juridiques* 71 (2013): pp. 157–189.

Tarot, Camille. *De Durkheim à Mauss, l'invention du symbolique* (Paris: Editions la Découverte/M.A.U.S.S., 1999).

Taylor, Keith. *The Political Ideas of the Utopian Socialists* (Great Britain: Frank Cass and Company Limited, 1982).

Teitel, Ruti G. *Humanity's Law* (Oxford: Oxford University Press, 2011).

Tladi, Dire. 'The African Union and the International Criminal Court: The Battle for the Soul of International Law'. *South African Yearbook of International Law* 34 (2009): p. 57.

de Vries, Hent. 'Introduction'. In *Political Theologies*, edited by Hent de Vries and Lawrence E. Sullivan (New York: Fordham University Press, 2006), pp. 25–7.

Waddell, Nicholas and Phil Clark, eds. *Courting Conflict? Justice, Peace and the ICC in Africa* (London: Royal African society, 2008).

Weber, Max. *Theory of Social and Economic Organization* (New York: Free Press, 1947).

Wernick, Andrew. *Auguste Comte and the Religion of Humanity: The Post-theistic Program of French Social Theory* (Cambridge; New York: Cambridge University Press, 2001).

Wiesel, Elie. 'A Tribute to Human Rights'. In *The Universal Declaration of Human Rights: Fifty Years and Beyond*, edited by Danieli Yael et al. (Amityville, N.Y.: Baywood, 2009), p. 3.

Wilson, Richard Ashby, and Richard D. Brown, eds. *Humanitarianism and Suffering* (New York: Cambridge University Press, 2009).

15

Religion and Empire

Carl Schmitt's *Katechon* between International Relations and the Philosophy of History

Michele Nicoletti

(English translation by Rachel Murphy)

Eschatology and History in Schmitt's Thought from *c.* 1910 to the 1930s

Schmitt's reflections on international affairs are found more often in his literary essays than in the juridical works of his first years.[1] It is in these essays that we most clearly sense Schmitt's connection to the spirit of the time and particularly to the rapidly multiplying contemporary ideas about eschatology and the end of history.

In a piece he wrote in 1916 on the poem *Nordlicht* by Theodor Däubler, many of the themes that Schmitt goes on to develop over the years already appear. The contemporary spirit of the time is, according to Schmitt, dominated by a philosophy of history which is at root a 'faith in human progress', in the rationality of man, in his innate goodness, and ability to transform and transcend himself. And this applies not only to the currents of Enlightenment and positivist thought but also to Hegelian historicism: 'The panlogism of the Swabian Hegel is, at bottom, no more than faith, faith in human thought, in the rationality of all being, in the intrinsic goodness of nature; faith in humanity, in its history and its development'.[2]

Schmitt contrasts this faith in progress as a human endeavour with Däubler's work, in which the culmination of the development of the human spirit—absolute consciousness, the 'visio Dei'—when time and history end and the earth is illuminated forever, is not achieved by man, but is a gift from God.[3] Men can try to build

[1] See Michele Nicoletti, 'Die Ursprünge von Carl Schmitts "Politische Theologie"', in *Complexio Oppositorum. Über Carl Schmitt*, edited by Helmut Quaritsch (Berlin: Duncker & Humblot, 1988), pp. 109–28.

[2] Carl Schmitt, *Theodor Däublers "Nordlicht". Drei Studien über die Elemente, den Geist und die Aktualität des Werkes* (München: Georg Müller, 1916), p. 55.

[3] Ibid., p. 60.

a 'final' kingdom, in which God and his Providence are substituted by planning, but this attempt is destined to fail: man's fulfilment will come about by Grace, that is, through Divine action: 'The reign of the spirit is not a future state, it is a *regnum gratiae* [reign of grace]'.[4]

This is the basis of his criticism of contemporary civilization. Our age—according to Schmitt—is 'mechanistic', capitalistic, relativist, an age of commerce, technology, bureaucracy. It is the age in which enterprise has been elevated as the means to achieve every end, and it is precisely this domination of the end by the means which crushes the individual, who is no longer able to control anything. Men have become poor devils who don't believe in anything. They are interested in everything and marvel at nothing. They understand everything, given that their experts record everything in history, nature, and their very souls. They are connoisseurs of men, psychologists and sociologists who end up writing sociologies of sociology.[5] The unfortunates of our time are the children of this spirit in Schmitt's analysis: they want heaven on earth, a heaven produced by commerce and industry, made of cars and bathroom fixtures and not by a loving, gracious God:

The most important, most basic, things had already been secularized. Law had become power, beauty good taste, Christianity a pacifist organization. People's souls were overwhelmed by a general transformation and falsification of values. A lofty distinction between the useful and the detrimental has taken the place of that between good and bad.[6]

In this description of the current era, as the era of ever increasing worldliness, the Antichrist also appears, emerging here for the first time and destined to leave its mark on much of Schmitt's later thought. The fulfilment of the prophecy of the Antichrist, in Schmitt's analysis, will not be a dramatic, violent, and blood-soaked event, but rather inviting—even tempting—and all the more dangerous for that. The Antichrist appears as an upright man, according to the description in the Pseudo-Efrem quoted by Schmitt: 'He will be deceptively peaceful with everybody, will not aspire to any role nor prefer one person to another, will be loving towards everyone and calm in everything, will refuse any gift and be gentle with his neighbours so that men will glorify him: "This is a righteous man"', his mysterious power—the author comments—lies in his similarity to God.[7] The Antichrist subjugates nature and heralds an age of security and planning, he satisfies all needs—not just the material—and knows how to reduce all truths to absurdity; speaking brilliantly of religious, artistic, and philosophical questions, he leaves out not a single saint, or sin, not even Christ on the cross. Nobody who follows, or even draws near to him, can retain their faith; his disciples are sceptics and come to believe that everything that exists or occurs in the world is due to human endeavour:

The fairy-tale effect is certainly irrefutable: huge cities, clean, luxurious steamboats; the prison of the soul has become a holiday resort ... Anyone who understood what the moral

[4] Ibid., p. 61. [5] Ibid., p. 64. [6] Ibid., p. 65.

[7] ibid., p. 66. The sentence is taken from the *Sermo de fine mundi* from the Latin Efrem which Schmitt probably used in C.P. Caspari's edition, *Briefe, Abhandlungen und Predigten aus der zwei letzten Jahrhunderten des kirchlichen Alterthums und dem Anfang des Mittelalters* (Christiania: 1890).

significance of the time was, while simultaneously knowing himself to be a child of his time, could only become a dualist.[8]

Facing this era in which all distinctions are erased and dissolve into the mean of 'functionality', those who do not want to throw themselves into society's race towards planning and production end up feeling excluded from the doings of the world and questioning the very meaning of their existence:

An intelligent contemporary critic [Rathenau?] identified the conflict between machinery and the soul: but knew the reality of life so well that the poor soul was abandoned to its impotence. Only one thing remained: to say, as does the gnostic Marcion, that the world is undoubtedly the devil's work, and, in it, absence of spirit will always triumph over spirit. Here is the root of angst: the universe may be doomed to failure and the desire for something good and right may lack meaning or purpose; God may be defenceless, powerless; the whole history of the world a ditty which any foolish child could play on a tuneless instrument; the world hopelessly undone ... Nothing more can be done for us and, to save our souls at least, we must try to escape from this prison. An eschatological terror had overwhelmed many people even before the atrocities of the war became a reality.[9]

This passage is a rather significant testimony to the sense of disorientation and crisis that characterized Europe in the early years of the twentieth century, a crisis of meaning which lay behind the literature and philosophy of the existentialists and which it is no surprise to find corresponding with Schmitt's formative years. It is also noteworthy that in this general state of disorientation war was seen as a further atrocity and most definitely not as a liberating act, as some warlike strands of thought imagined it would be.

Schmitt's perspective, however, does not seem to be that of gnosticism,[10] nor does he counterpose an Eastern-style contemplative spiritualism—characterized by passivity and withdrawal from the world and expressed in the rejection of violence typical of the fatalistic—to this machine-dominated age: 'They did not want to use the force which is a necessary part of the conquest of the kingdom of heaven.'[11] Instead, he wants to show the West another form of rationality, different from the scientific, instrumentalist one and thus more similar to a historical, Hegelian-style reason; and another sort of action, different to the economic and technological and therefore with the potential to revitalize juridic and political activity.

[8] Schmitt, *Nordlicht*, pp. 67–8. This interpretation of the Antichrist recalls to some extent that of Benson, see Robert H. Benson, *The Lord of the World* (London: 1907), in which the Antichrist is identified with the secular and humanist naturalism which sweetly worms its way into human lives and pleases men.

[9] Schmitt, *Nordlicht*, p. 68.

[10] Interpretations of Carl Schmitt's thought as a form of gnosticism can be found in: Ellen Kennedy, 'Politischer Expressionismus' in *Complexio Oppositorum*, edited by Helmuth Quaritsch (Berlin: Duncker & Humblot, 1987), pp. 233–65; Jürgen Manemann, *Carl Schmitt und die Politische Theologie. Politischer Anti-Monotheismus* (Münster: Aschendorff-Verlag, 2002). My arguments against those interpretations in: Michele Nicoletti, 'Sul concetto di "teologia politica" in Carl Schmitt', in *Il dio mortale: teologie politiche tra antico e contemporaneo*, edited by Paolo Bettiolo and Giovanni Filoramo (Brescia: Morcelliana, 2002), p. 327–48.

[11] Schmitt, *Nordlicht*, p. 76.

As can be seen, we have here, *in nuce,* many of the key elements of Schmitt's outlook: the predominance of a philosophy of history as faith in progress (which, in his writing after the Second World War will be seen as an ideology common to East and West[12]), the triumph of technology as the end of history, the condemnation of the spiritualistic and gnostic critique (the abandonment of the world to Satan), and the theology of incarnation (Kierkegaard) as an alternative to Hegel's monism and to dualism.

This outline of the theology of history, based on a dialectic between sin and redemption which demands incarnation and struggle against evil, but knows that in the end it can only win through the power of grace, also appears, if only in passing, in the 1923 *Römischer Katholizismus*, where Dostoevsky's dualism between justice and power is criticized and Schmitt claims a close connection between the theology of incarnation, centred on the person of Christ, and the theology of glory, that is, the reign of Christ over all things. The solution of this dialectic is not to refuse to act in history or to turn to earthly powers, but to accept the inherent impurity of earthly existence and to choose to live this dialectic in time in order to prevent creation falling into the hands of evil.[13]

Schmitt's reflections on history are more fully expressed in *Das Zeitalter der Neutralisierungen und der Entpolitisierungen* (1929), where his criticism of technology arises from an analysis based in the philosophy of history and in eschatology.

According to Schmitt the emergence of faith in technology horrified the representatives of traditional civilization who screamed and shouted about the death of the spirit and the domination of machinery and materialism: the observations of Troeltsch, Weber, Rathenau, and of Spengler, Scheler, and Ziegler bear witness to the anguish provoked by the rise of technology and, at the same time, the powerlessness of the spirit when faced with this ascent. But the reaction to the emergence of the power of technology ought to be more than the lament—however noble and elevated—of the spirit which feels itself to be threatened and in decline. Faith in technology is still 'faith'; however badly placed, it is still an expression of the spirit:

> The spirit of technicity, which has led to the mass belief in an anti-religious activism, is still spirit; perhaps an evil and demonic spirit, but not one which can be dismissed as mechanistic and attributed to technology. It is perhaps something gruesome, but not itself technical and mechanical. It is the belief in an activistic metaphysics—the belief in unlimited power and the domination of man over nature, even over human nature; the belief in the unlimited 'receding of natural boundaries', in the unlimited possibilities for change and prosperity. Such a belief can be called fantastic and satanic, but not simply dead, spiritless, or mechanized soullessness.[14]

Today's culture risks being reduced to mere complaint, to nostalgia, to a rejection of the present. Schmitt condemns this anti-modernist attitude which derives

[12] See, in particular, the text *La Unidad del Mundo* which is quoted below.

[13] See Carl Schmitt, *Römischer Katholizismus und politiche Form* (Hellerau: Jakob Hegner, 1923; München: Theatiner, 1925), p. 44.

[14] Carl Schmitt, *Der Begriff des Politischen: Mit einer Rede über das Zeitalter der Neutralisierungen und Entpolitisierungen* (München-Leipzig; Duncker u. Humblot, 1932; Berlin: Duncker u. Humblot, 1963), p. 93; English translation by George Schwab, *The Age of Neutralization and Depoliticization*, in Carl Schmitt, *The Concept of the Political* (Chicago: University of Chicago Press, 1996), p. 94.

from a lack of understanding of history and culture and from the fear of the intellectual establishment that they are going to lose their power: it is, in other words, a rearguard battle.

The loss of ground suffered by faith in spiritual values to faith in material values and technology should not necessarily be seen as a lasting defeat, as decline, decadence, death. The life of the spirit is not opposed by death in the shape of technology, but by a faith in the secular spirit. We must not complain, or shut ourselves away in the defence of our own positions, but take up the challenge posed by the present. From this perspective the difficulty in which spiritual values find themselves does not necessarily represent the defeat of the spirit. On the contrary. A tough situation provides an experience which tempers the spirit, renewing it and restoring its energy and creativity:

> All new and great impulses, every revolution and reformation, every new elite originates from asceticism and voluntary or involuntary poverty (poverty meaning above all the renunciation of the security of the *status quo*). Original Christianity and all serious reforms within Christianity—the Benedictine, Cluniac, and Franciscan renewals, the Baptists, and the Puritans—every genuine rebirth seeking to return to some original principle, every genuine *ritornar al principio*, every return to pure, uncorrupted nature appears as cultural or social nothingness to the comfort and ease of the existing *status quo*.[15]

The rebirth of a European culture is thus entrusted to an 'ascesis', a process of purification through which the culture abandons the historical form it has taken on—and all that encrusted it—and regains its original integrity, expressing itself in new ways and clearly identifying the spiritual order (or chaos) that needs to be combatted. The spirit succeeds in producing new forms by opposing, not that which is not spirit, but that which is also spirit; creative opposition is not that of life against death, but of certain forms of life against others:

> A grouping which sees on the one side only spirit and life and on the other only death and mechanism signifies nothing more than a renunciation of the struggle and amounts to nothing more than a romantic lament. For life struggles not with death, spirit not with spiritlessness; spirit struggles with spirit, life with life, and out of the power of an integral understanding of this arises the order of human things. *Ab integro nascitur ordo* [Order arises from integrity].[16]

Important elements of Schmitt's vision of history appear in these pages. The theme of the '*ritornar al principio* [return to the origin]' should not be read as proof of a pessimistic conception of history, seen unambiguously as a 'fall', as the decomposition of the primordial substance. Schmitt is neither nostalgic for the past nor an anti-modernist. His attitude is, in fact, positive, expressed in the invitation to welcome every era as a challenge to the human spirit in order that it can manifest its creative potential. The process of secularization is seen not as a gradual loss of meaning, but as a progressive manifestation of the varied forms of the human spirit. History thus appears as an open, creative process, in which the spirit obtains

[15] Schmitt, *Begriff*. [16] Schmitt, *Begriff*, p. 96.

new strength to respond to the challenges of the present through a continual '*ritornar al principio*'. So Schmitt continues to take the perspective that '*ab integro nascitur ordo*', since *integritas* is unquestionably necessary for the creation of order, if only as the *integritas* of a will which makes conscious decisions[17]. Reference to a primordial order, to an ideal of order, appears to be inescapable.

This vision of history retains the idea of the challenge represented by evil, by chaos—possibly camouflaged beneath the spoils of the mass society—to which the spirit is called upon to respond, but does not support the sense of a forthcoming 'end' of history in which a strand of western thought seemed to indulge. His concern seems rather to be to avoid the risk that the dominant key of the culture be that of complaint rather than of struggle, and Schmitt conceives this struggle as not between spirit and matter, but between different spiritual forms: between the different orders upon which the historical juxtapositions of friend and enemy are based.

Katechon in the Work of Carl Schmitt

The figure of the *katechon* appears in Schmitt's reflections within this context of the philosophy and theology of history. *Katechon* is a Greek word[18] which means 'who (or that which) restrains'. It is used in the Second Letter to the Thessalonians, where the author describes the coming of the Antichrist at the end of time. The *katechon* is a force which checks the dominance of the 'mystery of iniquity', 'a power which restrains':

> Let no one deceive you in any way. For unless the apostasy comes first and the lawless one is revealed, the one doomed to perdition, who opposes and exalts himself above every so-called god and object of worship, so as to seat himself in the temple of God, claiming that he is a god—do you not recall that while I was still with you I told you these things? And now you know what is restraining, that he may be revealed in his time. For the mystery of lawlessness is already at work. But the one who restrains is to do so only for the present, until he is removed from the scene (2 Thess 2, 3–7).

The use of the word *katechon* in Carl Schmitt's writings has been analysed and interpreted by many scholars, in numerous studies.[19] Although our knowledge of his work is not yet complete—Schmitt's bequest includes material which has

[17] See Hans Freyer, 'Positionen und Begriffe', *Deutsche Rechtswissenschaft* 5 (1940): p. 266.

[18] See Paul Metzger, *Katechon: II Thess 1–12 im Horizont apokaliptischen Denkens* (Berlin: Walter De Gruyter, 2005).

[19] See Emanuele Castrucci, *La forma e la decisione* (Milano: Giuffrè, 1985); Michele Nicoletti, *Trascendenza e potere. La teologia politica di Carl Schmitt* (Brescia: Morcelliana, 1990); Lutz Berthold, 'Wer hält zur Zeit der Satan auf?—Zur Selbstglossierung Carl Schmitts', *Leviathan* 21, no. 2 (1993): pp. 285–99; Günther Meuter, *Der Katechon: Zu Carl Schmitts fundamentalistischer Kritik der* Zeit (Berlin: Duncker & Humblot, 1994); Felix Großheutschi, *Carl Schmitt und die Lehre vom Katechon* (Berlin: Duncker & Humblot, 1996); Wolfgang Schuller, '"Dennoch die Schwerter halten" Der katéchon Carl Schmitts', in *Geschichte-Tradition-Reflexion. Festschrift für Martin Hengel zum 70. Geburtstag*, edited by Hubert Cancik, Hermann Lichtenberger, and Peter Schäfer, Bd. II, *Griechische und Römische*

still not been transcribed—most references to the subject can be said to have been broadly identified and can be retraced, as now follows.

Although Carl Schmitt says, in a letter to Pierre Linn written on the 11th of January 1948, and published in the *Glossarium*, that he developed his theory of the *katechon* in 1932 ('Vous connaissez ma théorie du κατέχων, elle date de 1932'[20]), the term only appears explicitly in his work from 1942 onwards. We can suppose that Schmitt was inspired to tackle this theme by his conversations with Erik Peterson[21] and in his discussions with other theologians, including Karl Eschweiler.

The term *katechon* first appears in an article published in the magazine 'Das Reich' on the 19th of April 1942, the subject of which is the role of the United States in the ongoing world war.[22] The very title of the article ('Beschleuniger wider Willen') draws our attention to the functions of the political powers as either 'accelerators' or 'restrainers' of historical processes. Schmitt analyses the particular case of the United States of America and its role within international politics, a subject which he goes on to deal with in detail in *Der Nomos der Erde* (1950). According to Schmitt the USA would have functioned as an 'accelerator' of the historical process of the dissolution of the European international order during the nineteenth century if it had not abandoned its isolationist policy when it intervened first in the First World War and then in the Second, in order to carry out the role—previously played by the British Empire—of defender of the universalist model of free trade. And so it found itself functioning not as an 'accelerator' but as a 'delayer'. It is this profound internal contradiction which, in Schmitt's opinion, renders the United States incapable of leading the way towards a 'new order' for the world. Its actions on the international stage can do no more than export the 'chaos' which characterizes it. It is in this context that the reference to the ancient term *katechon* appears: 'Historians and philosophers of history should analyse and distinguish the various figures and models of those who have slowed the rhythm of history and of those who have accelerated it. In Late Antiquity and the Middle Ages men believed in a mysterious restraining force—for which they used the Greek term *katechon*—thought to have halted the occurrence of

Religion, edited by Hubert Cancik (Tübingen: Mohr, 1996), pp. 389–408; Carlo Galli, *Genealogia della politica* (Bologna: Il Mulino, 1996); Alfons Motschenbacher, *Katéchon oder Großinquisitor? Eine Studie zu Inhalt und Struktur der politischen Theologie Carl Schmitts* (Marburg: Tectum Verlag, 2000); Martti Koskenniemi, *The Gentle Civilizer of Nations: The Rise and Fall of International law 1879–1960* (Cambridge: Cambridge University Press, 2001); Théodore Paleologue, *Sous l'oeil du grand inquisiteur: Carl Schmitt et l'héritage de la théologie politique* (Paris: Cerf, 2004); Massimo Maraviglia, *La penultima Guerra. Il "katéchon" nella dottrina dell'ordine politico di Carl Schmitt* (Milano: LED, 2006).

[20] Carl Schmitt, *Glossarium: Aufzeichnungen der Jahre 1947–1951* (Berlin: Duncker & Humblot, 1991), p. 80 (11.1.1948). A new edition, with additional texts dated as late as 1957, is being brought out by the same publishers. As we will see, in a subsequent letter to Hans Blumenberg dated 1974 Schmitt says that he started work on the subject of the *katechon* in 1936.

[21] According to Karlfried Gründer, during a discussion at a seminar organized by Speyer: see Helmuth Quaritsch (ed.), *Complexio Oppositorum* (Berlin: Duncker & Humblot, 1988), p. 230.

[22] Carl Schmitt, 'Beschleuniger wider Willen oder: Problematik der westlichen Hemisphäre', *Das Reich* (19.4.1942), now in Carl Schmitt, *Staat, Großraum, Nomos. Arbeiten aus den Jahren 1916–1969*, edited by Günther Maschke (Berlin: Duncker & Humblot, 1995), pp. 431–6.

the Apocalyptic ending of time, the hour of which had almost come. Tertullian, and others, saw this restraining force in the late Roman Empire of their time, its existence having 'restrained' the eon and postponed the end. Medieval Europe had to return to this belief and many of the fundamental processes in medieval history can only be understood with reference to it. In a different, although similar, sense, Hegel—the last great systematic German philosopher—was also considered to have been a delayer and restrainer of the process aiming towards the achievement of total atheism. But both the delaying and restraining forces can also assume a specific and symbolic form in many historical and political figures. The existence alone of the old Emperor Franz Joseph seemed, again and again, to delay the end of the decrepit Hapsburg Empire, and there was more to the then widespread idea that Austria would never collapse as long as the ruler lived than foolish superstition. After the First World War, in 1918, the Czech president, Masaryk, took on the role of delayer, although to a commensurately lesser extent. In Poland, Marshall Pilsudski became a kind of *katechon*. These examples probably demonstrate adequately the political and historical meaning of the function of the 'delayer'.[23] In this passage, as has been noted,[24] the concept of *katechon* is still ambiguous: on the one hand it acts to preserve the existing order, and has a neutral, almost negative, value; on the other, in its more specific meaning as a force which holds off a threat from a negative power standing in opposition to God (the Antichrist) or to his worship (philosophical or political atheism), it has a positive value.

A second pair of references to the figure of the *katechon* appears, again in 1942, in the book *Land und Meer*,[25] in which Schmitt interprets the history of civilization as the product of a continual struggle between land and maritime powers, the first linked to the solid, stable reality of law, the second to the uncertain realities of trade. Among the latter, the main characters are again Britain and the United States of America. On the subject of struggles between land and maritime powers, Schmitt recalls the conflict between the Western empire and the Byzantines, mentioning how the latter, as a maritime power, were able to achieve what the empire of Charles the Great failed to do, as a land power:

> It acted as a rampart, a *katechon*, as it is called in Greek. However weak, it held several centuries against the onslaughts of Islam, preventing the Arabs from conquering the whole of Italy. In its absence, Italy would have become part of the Moslem world, like Northern Africa, and all of the Ancient and Christian civilization would have been destroyed.[26]

The second reference to *katechon* is linked to Franz Grillparzer's depiction of Rudolph of Hapsburg in his tragedy *Ein Bruderzwist in Habsburg*. According to Schmitt the tragedy reveals how the emperor 'Rudolph II was not an active hero,

[23] Ibid., p. 436. [24] See Maraviglia, *La penultima guerra*, p. 208.

[25] Carl Schmitt, *Land und Meer: Eine weltgeschichtliche Betrachtung* (Leipzig: Reclam, 1942; Köln-Lövenich: Hohenheim, 1981), p. 19; English translation by Simona Draghici, *Land and Sea* (Washington, D.C.: Plutarch Press, 1997), p. 8.

[26] Schmitt, *Land und Meer*, p. 19; English translation p. 8.

but rather a brake, a delaying factor. He was something of a *katechon*.'[27] In this case, too, the term embraces a variety of situations, from the containing of an external enemy who bears a different religion, to the delaying of the dissolution of a social and political order, but in both cases the function of the *katechon* now appears to have a more obviously positive connotation.

A third series of references to the figure of the *katechon* appears in Schmitt's diaries kept between 1947 and 1957, which were published after his death in 1991, in a volume entitled *Glossarium*.[28] The term appears in thirteen fragments written between '47 and '57 and, as before, Schmitt refers to the biblical passage (2 Thessalonians 2.6–7), to its reception in both the ancient world and the Middle Ages, to the historical figures who have been 'restrainers'; however here he also emphasizes the importance of this subject in the context of a Christian theology of history.

The first three fragments deal with the relationship between *katechon* and the Christian theology of history. The first is:

With regard to the κατέχων: I believe in the κατέχων; it is for me the only way in which to understand history as a Christian and to make sense of it. The mysterious Pauline doctrine is no more mysterious than Christian existence, but, likewise, it is no less so. Someone with no concrete knowledge of the κατέχων cannot understand the passage. Haimo von Halberstadt reaches a deep understanding of the κατέχων and, as a source on the κατέχων, is much more precise than this. (Migne, vol. 117, col. 779). Today's theologians no longer have this knowledge and do not, deep down, even want it. To tell the truth, I wanted to find out from you: who is today's κατέχων? It certainly isn't Churchill or John Foster Dulles. The question is more important than that about Jünger's head forester. It must be possible to point to a κατέχων for each era of the last 1,948 years. The post has never been empty, or we wouldn't still exist. Every great medieval Christian emperor fully believed himself to be the κατέχων, and so indeed he was. It is quite impossible to write a history of the Middle Ages without perceiving and understanding this key fact. There are temporary, transitory and incomplete repositories of this charge. I am sure that as soon as the concept has been sufficiently clarified we will be able to agree on many of the actual names, up to the present day. Donoso Cortés failed theologically because this concept remained alien to him.[29]

This criticism of Donoso is repeated in the second fragment:

Poor Donoso, the only fitting theological concept for his political theory would have been that of the κατέχων, but he loses himself in the labyrinthine doctrine of relative and absolute natural law. There is a very simple explanation for the hopeless cry of Charles Péguy, who regrets never having had any success with the Catholics. Maybe the Jesuits were the κατέχων. But since 1814? The restoration of the κατέχων?.[30]

The third fragment in which the concept of *katechon* appears is the abovementioned letter to Pierre Linn, written in French, where Schmitt writes:

[27] Ibid., p. 80; English translation p. 43. [28] See Schmitt, *Glossarium*.
[29] Ibid., (19.12.1947), p. 63. [30] Ibid., (27.12.1947), p. 70.

We are still—as were the 14th and 17th centuries—in the Christian eon, still in agony, and every essential event is just a question of Kat-echon, of 'he who restrains', 'qui tenet nunc' (2Thess. 2:6–7). You know my theory of the κατέχων, which dates back to 1932. I think that in every century there is a concrete bearer of this force, it is just a question of finding him or it. I will avoid speaking of this to theologians, since I know the deplorable fate of the great, unfortunate Donoso Cortés. It is omnipresent, hidden behind the veil of history.[31]

Other fragments refer to contemporary historical figures who may or may not have played the part of a *katechon,* including Masaryk, Schmitt himself, and Churchill. The first:

Masaryk the father was a genuine European *katechon;* the *katechon* of western liberal democracy. Masaryk the father operated with admirable historical awareness—infinitely superior to that demonstrated at the time by German politicians, philosophers and historians—and he made a very prudent choice in favour of the West. '[32]

And the second:

Now I am more than Thomas Masaryk.[33] …

That which he [Toynbee] calls Western Europe (Germany is excluded) is a bourgeoisie in social conditions like those of the German bourgeoisie in 1919: a halfway stage between capitalistic prosperity and the pauperization of the underprivileged among the Asiatic peoples. Germany belongs fully to the underprivileged. According to Toynbee its only option is to adopt Russian communism. Here is the Spengler of the second post-war period, just as Churchill became the Clémenceau of the second world war; *no* κατέχων.[34]

The third group of fragments contained in the *Glossarium* examines the relationship between the functions of *katechon* and institutions, particularly the medieval Roman empire and the Catholic Church. It is the concept of the *katechon* which establishes the legitimacy of these institutions' historical actions ('the Christian empire of the medieval emperors was legitimate in so far as it was a κατέχων, in accordance with 2 *Thess.,* 6–7'[35]), but Schmitt emphasizes that this legitimacy is, nevertheless, 'limited':

The *katéchon* can be identified by the fact that it does not strive for this world unity, but instead overthrows the imperial crown. The heredity of the imperial throne is naive, but this inheritance is in accordance with the tradition of dynastic power; cannot a dynasty also be a *katéchon*?.[36]

This historicity and conditionality also touches the institution of the Catholic Church, which has been criticized on precisely these grounds by those who consider all historical elements to be impure:

The Roman church is an historical reality; idealistically it is *eo ipso* evil action. It is a κατέχων, which is undoubtedly the worst of criminals. From an idealistic perspective

[31] Ibid., (11.1.1948, *Letter to Pierre Linn*), p. 80. [32] Ibid., (13.3.1948), p. 113.

[33] Ibid., (25.3.1948), p. 118. The actual term *katechon* does not appear in these fragments, but there is an implicit reference in the figure of Masaryk.

[34] Ibid., (9.4.1948), pp. 124–5. The word 'underprivileged' is originally in English.

[35] Ibid., (23.5.1948), p. 153. [36] Ibid., (16.6.1948), p. 165.

all historical actions are evil; in idealistic terms: right [*Recht*] = tort [*Unrecht*] = position [*Setzung*] = arbitrary act [*Willkür*]. Here is what they call tragedy! Sohm's thesis is not only valid for canonical law.[37]

Here the subject of the institutional and juridical nature of the Catholic Church dealt with by Schmitt in his *Die Sichtbarkeit der Kirche* (1917) and *Römischer Katholizismus* (1923) is again taken up, centred on a debate with the position of Rudolf Sohm. Moreover, it is important to note that the association of *katechon* with the Roman Church, as heir to the Roman empire, was already a theme in medieval interpretations of the concept.[38]

Another fragment takes up this theme of limitation and likens *katechon*—resistance to chaos—to the dynamics of contemporary society, in which chaos is represented by the masses and the government which claims to rule this chaos is represented by absolute planning: 'The κατέχων is deprivation, hunger, need and powerlessness. Those who do not govern, who are the people, are these. Everything else is the mass and subject to planning. The wonderful force of non-oppositional negation, the social state of law, historiography.'[39]

And lastly, an important reference to the decline of the role of the *katechon* as modernity was born and state began to replace empire:

Important to Hobbes and in Cromwell's time: the informed surrender of the κατέχων tradition of the Roman empire (even in Vitoria there is no longer any trace of it!). No third Rome (like in Moscow)! No succession: even though in France there is, until Napoleon I. Empire, Caesarism. Hobbes sees the Roman Church, in any case, as the phantom perched on the tomb of the *imperium romanum*. Criticism of the *imperium romanum* in Bacon and Hobbes: it was not in fact universal, it was not *orbis* [of the whole world].[40]

In diary entries from the 1950s we find three other references. The first (17.2.1953) describes Hegel as a *katechon*, considering him to be the 'last Christian' who tried to maintain the history of the world within the Christian eon, slowing down the progress of nihilism and of modern atheism. The second, more significant, dated 16.4.55, in which—for the first time—even modern statehood in its function as a neutralizer of internal conflicts performs a *katechontic* function:

When all distinctions (like those between state and society, politics and economics) and all incompatibilities dissolve, then actually all that remains is the distinction between friend and enemy. The internal regulation [*Ordnung*] of the state is then the neutralizing of the primary latent distinction between these last, through secondary differentiations. The neutral state as *katechon*.

In the third (10.8.57), he rejects the idea that Switzerland, a neutral state, can be considered a *Katechon*.

[37] Ibid., (4.7.1949), p. 253.

[38] Großheutschi, *Carl Schmitt und die Lehre vom Katechon*, p. 54, refers to the passage from St. Thomas Aquinas in this regard ('the empire did not collapse, but was transformed from temporal to spiritual'); see also Maraviglia, *La penultima guerra*, p. 194.

[39] Schmitt, *Glossarium* (25.9.1949), p. 272.

[40] Ibid., (1.10.1949), p. 273.

A fourth piece of writing which contains a reference to the figure of the *katechon* is *Ex Captivitate Salus,* published in 1950.[41] Here *katechon* is associated with another important figure in Schmitt's thought, that of the 'Christian Epimetheus'[42]—invented by the poet Konrad Weiss in 1933[43] to contrast the 'Pagan Prometheus'—which Schmitt uses to explain his own behaviour in relation to the Nazi regime. The references to the *katechon* are found in a paragraph on Tocqueville:

[Tocqueville] did not become that which, more than anyone else, he seemed destined to be: a Christian Epimetheus. His failing was the fact that he lacked an account of salvation which could protect his historical idea of Europe from despair. Without the idea of a *katéchon*, Europe was lost. Tocqueville did not recognise any *katéchon.* Instead, he sought intelligent compromises.[44]

Schmitt also refers to the *katechon*—reflecting on the philosophy of history—in his review of Karl Löwith's *Meaning in History*; here there is a clear reference to the idea we find in Schmitt's early writings: the expectation of an imminent end risks depriving all of history of meaning, and it causes an eschatological paralysis. That's why we need a mediation, what Schmitt defines as 'a bridge', between the end of history and the present time. A bridge which can avoid this paralysis and give meaning to human action in history. This bridge is the conception of a force, which delays the end and suppresses the evil one. This is the *kat-echon*:

The vivid expectation of an imminent end seems to take away the meaning from all of history, and it causes an eschatological paralysis for which there are many historical examples. And yet there is the possibility of a bridge. For this we have astonishing examples in the history of the medieval empire. The bridge consists in the conception of a force, which defers the end and suppresses the evil one. This is the *kat-echon* of the mysterious passage of Paul's second letter to the Thessalonians. The medieval empire of the German rulers understood itself historically as the *kat-echon.* Luther still understood it in these terms, whereas Calvin takes a significant turn by no longer taking the empire but rather the preaching of God's words as the *kat-echon.* The conception of restraining [haltender] and deferring [aufhaltender] forces and powers can in some form probably be demonstrated to be active for every great historian. Nietzsche furiously identified Hegel and the sixth sense of the Germans, i.e., the historical sense, as the great deferrer on the way to expressed atheism. In Hans Freyer's recently published *World History of Europe* (II, 6_6, 9_5), restraining forces appear as *katechontic* forces. Of course we have to be careful not to transform this term into a generalized designation of simply conservative or reactionary tendencies. We must not

[41] Carl Schmitt, *Ex Captivitate Salus. Erfahrungen der Zeit 1945/1947* (Köln: Greven Verlag, 1950).

[42] Epimetheus, Prometheus' brother, 'realised too late' the damage he had done in opening Pandora's box.

[43] See Konrad Weiß, *Der deutsche christliche Epimetheus*, in *Der christliche Epimetheus*, s.i.l. / Edwin Runge, 1933. On the relationship between Schmitt and Weiß, see Stefan Nienhaus, *Carl Schmitt tra poeti e letterati*, in Carl Schmitt, *Aurora boreale*, edited by Valeria Bazzicalupo (Napoli: ESI, 1995), pp. 5–48. Weiß's teleological attempt to mitigate Schmitt's decisionism by evoking the figure of Mary, mother of God, is interesting. For an interpretation of connections between Maria and the *katechon*, see Maraviglia's stimulating commentary, cit., p. 251.

[44] Schmitt, *Ex Captivitate*, p. 31.

use it to add, along with the concept of restrainer and deferrer, a couple of exemplars to Dilthey's typological collection of historicism. The original historical force of the figure of a *kat-echon,* however, remains and is capable of overcoming the otherwise occurring eschatological paralysis.[45]

Der Nomos der Erde, Carl Schmitt's synthesis of his analyses of the history of international law, was also published in 1950. In his historical reconstruction of the Middle Ages the term *katechon* appears in the title of a chapter on the 'Christian *Reich* as restrainer (*katechon*)'. According to Schmitt, the medieval *Reich* was well aware that:

... this Christian empire was not eternal. It always had its own end and that of the present eon in view. Nevertheless, it was capable of being a historical power. The decisive historical concept of this continuity was that of the restrainer: katechon. 'Empire' in this sense meant the historical power to *restrain* the appearance of the Antichrist and the end of the present eon; it was a power that withholds (*qui tenet*), as the Apostle Paul said in his Second Letter to the Thessalonians.... The empire of the Christian Middle Ages lasted only as long as the idea of the *katechon* was alive. I do not believe that any historical concept other than *katechon* would have been possible for the original Christian faith. The belief that a restrainer holds back the end of the world provides the only bridge between the notion of an eschatological paralysis of all human events and a tremendous historical monolith like that of the Christian empire of the Germanic kings.[46]

In *La Unidad del Mundo*, written in 1951, Schmitt returns to the theme, with the same references to the Christian conception of history and the medieval empire:

There are yet other possible Christian conceptions of history. There is the doctrine of St. Paul the Apostle on man and the strength which redeem the power of evil and of the Antichrist, so delaying the beginning of the final catastrophe. This is the doctrine on that which St. Paul calls, in Greek, the *katechon*, namely the belief that entire centuries of medieval Christian history and its idea of empire are based on the conviction that the significance of the empire of a Christian ruler is precisely that of being a *katechon*. Great medieval emperors, like Otto the Great and Frederick Barbarossa, saw the historical essence of their imperial dignity to be their struggle, as *katechon*, against the Antichrist and his allies, thus postponing the end of time.[47]

The term appears again in a piece of writing dedicated to Hans Freyer on his seventieth birthday,[48] called *Die andere Hegel-Linie.* In his book *Weltgeschichte Europas*[49] Freyer interprets the function of the *katechon* dialectically: that which

[45] Carl Schmitt, 'Drei Stufen historischer Sinngebung', *Universitas* 5 (1950): pp. 927–31, here pp. 929–30; translated by Mario Wenning under the title *Three Possibilities for a Christian Conception of History.*

[46] Carl Schmitt, *Der Nomos der Erde im Völkerrecht des Jus Publicum Europaeum* (Köln: Greven, 1950; Berlin: Duncker u. Humblot, 1974); English translation by G. Ulmen, *The Nomos of the Earth in the International Law of the Jus Publicum Europaeum* (New York: Telos Press, 2006), p. 245.

[47] Carl Schmitt, 'La Unidad del mundo', *Anales de la Universidad de Murcia* IX (1950–51): pp. 353–4. The passage does not appear in Wolfgang Schuller's anthology.

[48] Carl Schmitt, 'Die andere Hegel-Linie. Hans Freyer zum 70. Geburtstag', *Christ und Welt* (25.7.1957).

[49] (Wiesbaden: Dieterich, 1948).

stands against the advance of an external danger not only saves whatever it is defending, but actually causes it to evolve towards a higher state. The Byzantine Empire, for example, not only resisted the Arab invasions but also evolved internally: converting the Slavs to Christianity and thus integrating them within European society. The Catholic Church—and then the German Empire—also evolved through their conflicts with the Roman Empire. And so Schmitt moves beyond a merely conservative interpretation of the concept of *katechon*:

In an outburst of rage Nietzsche declared: Hegel is the great delayer on Germany's path towards atheism. All the accelerators of this journey will unite against a man like Hans Freyer, who speaks in his books of the *Katéchon* in the Second Letter to the Thessalonians. This is the force which restrains the power of evil for a certain time and opposes the worst accelerators on the path to the fall into the abyss. All that which, since the 19th century, has been defined as conservative or proclaims itself to be such, is overtaken and sidelined by this concept of the restrainer, which we find in Freyer's *Weltgeschichte*.[50]

The term is found once again, similarly nuanced, in a 1958 note on a text written in 1943–44 about the situation of European public law. Here again the term *katechon* is applied to cultural figures like Hegel and Savigny:

Savigny and Hegel had an historical sense, that sixth sense, as Nietzsche defined it, furious because it *delays* the Germans on their path to open atheism ... Both were true restrainers, *katechon* in the actual meaning of the word, restrainers of the voluntary and involuntary accelerators on the path of integral functionalisation ... I just hold to be important the reference to the fact that the two adversaries are both *katechon*. It is risky, today, to speak in this way.[51]

And finally, the last mentions are found in the *Politische Theologie II* (1970) and are linked to the two authors about whom the book was written: Eusebius of Caesarea and the theologian Erik Peterson. In the two passages we find the two interpretations of the *katechon,* which can, in a certain sense, be said to differentiate the two men's political theologies. On the one hand Eusebius' 'political' interpretation which sees the role of a political power in the *katèchon*, the Roman empire in this case: "It would be interesting to learn more about Eusebius' attitude and, in particular, more about his view on the Roman Empire as the restrainer of the antichrist, the *Kat-Echon* [= *katechon*, 'restrainer'] in Paul's letter (2 Thessalonians 2.6)'.[52] On the other hand we have the 'theological' interpretation of Peterson, who considers the *katechon* to be a religious category, associating it with the Jewish people's lack of faith: "We know what Peterson, the learned philologist and exegete, thought about the *Kat-Echon*: the unbelief of the Jews, their continued refusal, until

[50] Carl Schmitt, 'Die andere Hegel-Linie. Hans Freyer zum 70. Geburtstag'.

[51] Carl Schmitt, *Die Lage der europäischen Rechtswissenschaft* [1950] in *Verfassungsrechtliche Aufsätze aus den Jahren 1924–1954. Materialien zu einer Verfassungslehre* (Berlin: Duncker & Humblot, 1958, 1985), pp. 386–429, here pp. 428–9.

[52] Carl Schmitt, *Politische Theologie II. Die Legende der Erledigung jeder politischen Theologie* (Berlin: Duncker & Humblot, 1970), p. 81; English translation by Michael Hoelzl and Graham Ward, *Political Theology II: The Myth of the Closure of Any Political Theology* (Cambridge: Polity Press, 2008), p. 92.

the present day, to become Christians withholds the end of the Christian aeon'.[53] In this text—the culmination of Schmitt's politico-theological reflection—the interpretation of the *katechon* undoubtedly becomes the distinguishing feature of the interpretation of political theology: on the one hand, the persistence of the role of the 'political' in the final moments of history—the *katechon* as a delaying force which thus gives meaning to the actions of Christianity in history; on the other hand, the last judgement as the moment when faith alone is at stake and scepticism and witness to the truth stand in stark confrontation: here time is delayed for the sole purpose of allowing possible conversions.

Apart from some mentions in, still unedited, material in the *Nachlass*, Schmitt's last references to the *katechon* appear in a few letters written in the 1970s and 1980s. There are two letters to Hans Blumenberg, from 1974 and 1975, for example. In the first Schmitt emphasizes his continued interest in the subject and states unequivocally that *katechon* is the 'core question' in his political theology: 'For more than 40 years I have been collecting material on the problem of *katéchon* or *katechon* (2 Thess. 2,6); I am searching for a human ear which will listen to and understand this question—for me the key question of (my) political theology.'[54] In the second Schmitt tells a personal anecdote and then traces a link between the *Second letter to the Thessalonians* and the *Book of Habakkuk*:

> The subject of 'katéchon' will kill me. I've been working on it since 1936; in 'Nomos der Erde' it is even found in the analytical index. In the month of May 1952, Bishop Bender at the last minute prohibited the taking place of a conference which I wanted to hold on the subject in Herrenhalb, when I had already appeared before the guests. Since then, my material has become even vaster. It is based on the verses 2 Thessalonians 2:2,6 and Habakkuk 2:2,3.[55]

There is another reference in a letter from 1980 in which Schmitt reiterates that he has been collecting material on the subject for the last fifty years and says that official Christian theology is avoiding the problem and dispelling the risk of world imperialism. He says that official Christian theology is avoiding the problem and dispelling the risk of world imperialism by evoking its delay, as Dilthey might have done, due to a 'conservative' revolution.

It can thus be seen that, if we treat the *Glossarium* as a single work, the figure of the *katechon* appears explicitly in seven of Schmitt's texts. There are references to the function of the *katechon* in other texts: to the 'restraining' and 'delaying' of the manifestation of the mystery of wickedness,[56] but without explicit mention of the *katechon*. And lastly, there are the references in Schmitt's letters and private notes.

[53] Schmitt, *Politische Theologie*, p. 92.

[54] Carl Schmitt and Hans Blumenberg (20. October 1974), in Hans Blumenberg—Carl Schmitt, *Briefwechsel 1971–1978*, edited by Alexander Schmitz and Marcel Lepper (Frankfurt a. M.: Suhrkamp, 2007), p. 120.

[55] Schmitt and Blumenberg, p. 138. Notes on a history of the *Katechon* dated 1974–75 in which there are references to the biblical passages, the Patristic interpretations, and then to the people and doctrines already mentioned in the collection of quotations which we examined above, found in Schmitt's *Nachlass*.

[56] Wolfgang Schuller, *Dennoch die Schwerter halten.*

When these references are viewed as a whole, two aspects in particular stand out. The first regards their timings: although Schmitt says that he discovered the term in 1932 (unless he mistakenly wrote '1932' when he meant '1942'), the time frame in which they appear is from 1942 to 1970 (after this there are only a few mentions in letters and private notes), with the majority dating between 1947 to 1950. The second aspect regards the two contexts in which the references are found: in Schmitt's writing on international studies (international politics, geopolitics, international law), and in his work on the philosophy and theology of history. If we take the two above areas to be closely connected, as the great internationalist thinkers like Kant and Hegel have taught us to do, the references can be seen to be fairly tightly clustered in terms of context, as well as of time. In fact, with the outbreak of the Second World War and a renewed focus on international relations, Carl Schmitt's reflections turn again to the theology and philosophy of history. He is trying to overcome the current crisis of *Jus Publicum Europaeum*—characterized by the balance between the modern European states—by moving towards a pluralist order made up of 'Großräume', that is, geopolitical entities which are sufficiently internally homogeneous and led by a hegemonic power. This is the context in which Schmitt takes up the concept of the *Reich* to overtake the modern form of the *Staat*; it is also the backdrop against which the concept of *katechon* appears in his writings of the 1940s and 1950s.

The *Katechon* between Philosophy of History and International Relations

It can be clearly demonstrated that Schmitt's interpretation of the *katechon* within the philosophy and theology of history is not unambiguous. On the one hand, it is undoubtedly linked to the medieval and Patristic tradition which identifies the 'power which restrains' as a political institution—the Empire, first Roman and then medieval. On the other hand, Schmitt holds that a similar role can be played by individual politicians or intellectuals. The Pauline double use (masculine and neuter)—'he who restrains' and 'that which restrains'—of the term *katechon* is thus maintained.

In the second place: when Schmitt refers the function of *katechon* to a political institution, he is usually referring to an empire: first the Roman, then the Byzantine, and then the German, heir to the Roman Empire. In one instance the Roman Church is the *katechon*, but, as we know, it too was considered by Schmitt to have inherited Roman law and to have a special link to the idea of the Holy Roman Empire. When he mentions individual powers (like Britain or the United States), they are treated as actors on the international stage rather than as political institutions. The modern state—the political institution which, for Schmitt, is the incarnation *par excellence* of the political order, that is, of the order created by sovereign decision in the face of the chaos of civil wars—is only once explicitly linked to the figure of the *katechon*. It does not therefore seem tenable to say that for

Schmitt the concept of *katechon* functions to provide a theological foundation for the state, which, in his thought, as we have noted, is an 'historical concept', not an eternal one, related to the form of political unity which emerged from the dissolution of the medieval *res publica christiana* and characterizing the modern political order until its crisis in the late nineteenth–early twentieth century.[57]

While on the one hand the theme of the *katechon* draws attention to the role of institutions in the restraint of evil, on the other it opens up the question of the relationship between political institutions and the historico-temporal dimension. The era in which the political institution was considered to be a *katechon* is above all the medieval, a period profoundly open to eschatology. The form, which corresponds to this temporality open to eschatology, is the *Sacrum Imperium,* the *Reich*, or *regnum*, a *dynamic* figure which refers, by analogy, to the 'kingdom to come'. From this perspective the holder of political power can consider himself to be a *katechon,* a figure which simultaneously restrains the 'mystery of anomie' and announces the coming of the kingdom of heaven, making room for it in the world. In contrast, the era of modern statehood is the era of temporality which thwarts the intrusion of eschatology in history, blocking time through the machinery of the State: a *static* figure which saves a *status* from the corruption of time and places the kingdom of heaven outside history. The figure of the *katechon* re-emerges, in fact, when statehood is in crisis and the eschatological perspective again intrudes upon history.

This intrusion of eschatology into history produces two contrasting behaviours: either historical 'paralysis'—inaction, the condemnation of all historical acts as impure and useless; or the sacralization of history itself, as if simply historical becoming, understood as progressive, could alone lead mankind to salvation. It is the latter perspective of the philosophy of history which, according to Schmitt, plays a role in the new political theology, from the first half of the nineteenth century onwards,[58] but its consequences are dramatic because its logic is that of annihilation: that which belongs to the past is destined to end and is therefore valueless, while that which declares itself to be part of the future claims absolute value. The philosophy of history thus becomes the creator of absolute worldly powers.

The figure of the *katechon*, as 'he who restrains and delays' symbolizes opposition to all the philosophies of history of absolute progress; the historical future will not necessarily be a reign of happiness, it may be the reign of the Antichrist. The earthly paradise which the philosophy of history announces is in fact the complete negation of transcendence and therefore coincides with the reign of the Antichrist, and it is no accident that this reign appears to us not as dramatic and frightening, but as alluring. The *katechon* again takes on the character of a theologico–political figure in the age of immanence, after the end of the modern age, and plays its role of opposing the coming of an artificial paradise and reaffirming a transcendence

[57] This is Giorgio Agamben's thesis.

[58] See Carl Schmitt, *Donoso Cortés in gesamteuropäischer Interpretation* (Köln: Greven, 1950). On this, see the analyses of Karl Löwith, *Weltgeschichte und Heilsgeschehen. Die theologische Voraussetzungen der Geschichtsphilosophie* (Stuttgart: Kohlhammer, 1953), and of Eric Voegelin, *The New Science of Politics* (Chicago: Chicago University Press, 1952).

which is incarnated within—not extraneous to—history. This is why it is necessary to find a 'bridge' between history and eschatology in order to avoid either radical immanentization or paralysis, as Schmitt repeats on a number of occasions. This seems to echo the need for 'mediation' which Schmitt sometimes pondered in his early writing.[59] This 'bridge' cannot be 'natural law'—as Schmitt makes explicit in his criticism of Donoso Cortes—for his static nature and for his rootedness in a metaphysical context which cannot be accessed by contemporary reason. It is impossible, in this regard, to avoid imagining an implicit criticism of those who in the years immediately after the Second World War believed it was possible to use natural law to build a new 'bridge' between Christian theology and history.

The centrality of the second important area in which *katechon* operates, that of international relations, is revealed by the fact that the predominant political function of *katechon* seems to be the restraining, not so much of the enemy within a political unit, as of the enemy without. When the *katechon* is alluded to as opposing disintegration from within, this appears to be more of a social or cultural nature, rather than overtly political.

In this case, too, periodization is important. The figure of the *katechon* appears to be linked to eras other than that of statehood, that is, of the *Jus Publicum Europaeum*. As Schmitt says in *Der Nomos der Erde, katechon* is typical of the medieval order; he then disinters the concept when considering a new international order to follow the crisis of modern statehood. From this perspective it seems to embody the figure of opposition to monist universalism—which can be interpreted theologically as the mark of the reign of the Antichrist, who alone can reduce the earth to a single kingdom—and can thus be seen as the defender of pluralism. This pluralism is not represented by the East–West dualism, which Schmitt considers false, since both powers—the United States and the USSR—are expressions of a single philosophy of history, that of the unstoppable, dehumanizing progress of technology. Viewed thus, only Europe can defend pluralism and therefore function as a *katechon*: Europe is the guardian of the tradition of jurisprudence which is the 'bridge' between theology and technology and, moreover, the instrument with which to shape an order in which a plurality of individuals recognize each other's equal sovereign dignity.

Bibliography

Blumenberg, Hans, and Carl Schmitt. *Briefwechsel 1971–1978*, edited by Alexander Schmitz and Marcel Lepper (Frankfurt a. M.: Suhrkamp, 2007).

Castrucci, Emanuele. *La forma e la decisione* (Milano: Giuffrè, 1985).

Freyer, Hans. 'Positionen und Begriffe'. *Deutsche Rechtswissenschaft* 5 (1940): p. 266.

Freyer, Hans. *Weltgeschichte Europas* (Wiesbaden: Dieterich, 1948).

Galli, Carlo. *Genealogia della politica* (Bologna: Il Mulino, 1996).

[59] I would refer the reader here to the first two chapters of my *Trascendenza e potere*.

Großheutschi, Felix. *Carl Schmitt und die Lehre vom Katechon* (Berlin: Duncker & Humblot, 1996).
Kennedy, Ellen. 'Politischer Expressionismus'. In *Complexio Oppositorum*, edited by Helmuth Quaritsch (Berlin: Duncker & Humblot, 1987), pp. 233–65.
Koskenniemi, Martti. *The Gentle Civilizer of Nations: The Rise and Fall of International law 1879–1960* (Cambridge: Cambridge University Press, 2001).
Löwith, Karl. *Weltgeschichte und Heilsgeschehen. Die theologische Voraussetzungen der Geschichtsphilosophie* (Stuttgart: Kohlhammer, 1953).
Lutz, Berthold. 'Wer hält zur Zeit der Satan auf?—Zur Selbstglossierung Carl Schmitts'. *Leviathan* 21, no. 2 (1993): pp. 285–99.
Manemann, Jürgen. *Carl Schmitt und die Politische Theologie: Politischer Anti-Monotheismus* (Münster: Aschendorff-Verlag, 2002).
Maraviglia, Massimo. *La penultima Guerra. Il 'katéchon' nella dottrina dell'ordine politico di Carl Schmitt* (Milano: LED, 2006).
Metzger, Paul. *Katechon: II Thess 1–12 im Horizont apokaliptischen Denkens* (Berlin: Walter De Gruyter, 2005).
Meuter, Günther. *Der Katechon: Zu Carl Schmitts fundamentalistischer Kritik der Zeit* (Berlin: Duncker & Humblot, 1994).
Motschenbacher, Alfons. *Katéchon oder Großinquisitor? Eine Studie zu Inhalt und Struktur der politischen Theologie Carl Schmitts* (Marburg: Tectum Verlag, 2000).
Nicoletti, Michele. 'Die Ursprünge von Carl Schmitts "Politische Theologie" '. In *Complexio Oppositorum. Über Carl Schmitt*, edited by Helmut Quaritsch (Berlin: Duncker & Humblot, 1988).
Nicoletti, Michele. *Trascendenza e potere: La teologia politica di Carl Schmitt* (Brescia: Morcelliana, 1990).
Nicoletti, Michele. 'Sul concetto di "teologia politica" in Carl Schmitt'. In *Il dio mortale: teologie politiche tra antico e contemporaneo*, edited by Paolo Bettiolo and Giovanni Filoramo (Brescia: Morcelliana, 2002), p. 327–48.
Nienhaus, Stefan. *Carl Schmitt tra poeti e letterati*. In Carl Schmitt, *Aurora boreale*, edited by Valeria Bazzicalupo (Napoli: ESI, 1995), pp. 5–48.
Paleologue, Théodore. *Sous l'oeil du grand inquisiteur: Carl Schmitt et l'héritage de la théologie politique* (Paris: Cerf, 2004).
Quaritsch, Helmuth, ed. *Complexio Oppositorum* (Berlin: Duncker & Humblot, 1988).
Schmitt, Carl. *Theodor Däublers 'Nordlicht': Drei Studien über die Elemente, den Geist und die Aktualität des Werkes* (München: Georg Müller, 1916).
Schmitt, Carl. *Römischer Katholizismus und politiche Form* (Hellerau: Jakob Hegner, 1923; München: Theatiner, 1925).
Schmitt, Carl. *Der Begriff des Politischen. Mit einer Rede über das Zeitalter der Neutralisierungen und Entpolitisierungen* (München-Leipzig; Duncker u. Humblot, 1932; Berlin: Duncker u. Humblot, 1963), p. 93; English Translation by George Schwab, *The Age of Neutralization and Depoliticization*. In Schmitt, Carl. *The Concept of the Political* (Chicago: University of Chicago Press, 1996).
Schmitt, Carl. 'Beschleuniger wider Willen oder: Problematik der westlichen Hemisphäre'. *Das Reich* (19.4.1942), now in Schmitt, Carl. *Staat, Großraum, Nomos. Arbeiten aus den Jahren 1916–1969*, edited by Günther Maschke (Berlin: Duncker & Humblot, 1995), pp. 431–6.
Schmitt, Carl. *Land und Meer. Eine weltgeschichtliche Betrachtung* (Leipzig: Reclam 1942; Köln-Lövenich: Hohenheim, 1981), p. 19; English Translation by Simona Draghici, *Land and Sea* (Washington, D.C.: Plutarch Press, 1997).

Schmitt, Carl. *Ex Captivitate Salus. Erfahrungen der Zeit 1945/1947* (Köln: Greven Verlag, 1950).
Schmitt, Carl. *Donoso Cortés in gesamteuropäischer Interpretation* (Köln: Greven, 1950).
Schmitt, Carl. 'Drei Stufen historischer Sinngebung'. *Universitas* 5 (1950): pp. 927–31, here pp. 929–30; translated by Mario Wenning under the title *Three Possibilities for a Christian Conception of History*.
Schmitt, Carl. *Der Nomos der Erde im Völkerrecht des Jus Publicum Europaeum* (Köln: Greven, 1950; Berlin: Duncker u. Humblot, 1974); English translation by G. Ulmen, *The Nomos of the Earth in the International Law of the Jus Publicum Europaeum* (New York: Telos Press, 2006).
Schmitt, Carl. 'La unidad del mundo'. *Anales de la Universidad de Murcia* IX (1950–51): pp. 343–55.
Schmitt, Carl. 'Die andere Hegel-Linie. Hans Freyer zum 70. Geburtstag'. *Christ und Welt* (25.7.1957).
Schmitt, Carl. *Die Lage der europäischen Rechtswissenschaft* [1950]. In *Verfassungsrechtliche Aufsätze aus den Jahren 1924–1954. Materialien zu einer Verfassungslehre* (Berlin: Duncker & Humblot, 1958, 1985), pp. 386–429.
Schmitt, Carl. *Politische Theologie II. Die Legende der Erledigung jeder politischen Theologie* (Berlin: Duncker & Humblot, 1970), p. 81; English translation by Michael Hoelzl and Graham Ward, *Political Theology II: The Myth of the Closure of Any Political Theology* (Cambridge: Polity Press, 2008), p. 92.
Schmitt, Carl. *Glossarium: Aufzeichnungen der Jahre 1947–1951* (Berlin: Duncker & Humblot, 1991).
Schuller, Wolfgang. "Dennoch die Schwerter halten' Der katéchon Carl Schmitts'. In *Geschichte-Tradition-Reflexion: Festschrift für Martin Hengel zum 70. Geburtstag*, edited by Hubert Cancik, Hermann Lichtenberger, Peter Schäfer, Bd. II, *Griechische und Römische Religion*, edited by Hubert Cancik (Tübingen: Mohr, 1996), pp. 389–408.
Voegelin, Eric. *The New Science of Politics* (Chicago: Chicago University Press, 1952).
Weiß, Konrad. *Der deutsche christliche Epimetheus*. In *Der christliche Epimetheus* (s.i.l.: Edwin Runge, 1933).

16

International Law-making and Metaphysical Foundations of Universality

Retrieving an Alternative Metaphysics

Elena Paris

Universality and certainty are pervasive themes in contemporary theory concerning international interaction. The deliberative quality of international law, understood at Westphalia as a legal order amongst members of a political community equally entitled to political standing,[1] is constantly trumped by invocation of foundational certitudes resulting from the objectivity of reason or natural order, but also by invocation of the sovereign self-assertion of particular regimes. These are all ways of ushering away consent from international law-making. It appears that, in the space of international law, knowledge—either scientific but also ethical—seems to be promoted as given certainty, and thus becomes automatically coercive, even though it is formed in an autonomous way, completely outside the idea of participation in knowledge-formation.

I am concerned in this chapter with the way the universal is formed and expressed in international law, and with locating the origins of its oppressive operation. My suggestion is that one might find a useful key for this analysis in the critique of foundationalism. It can help discern—and challenge—the specific articulations of thought that prompt us to imagine the universal as something already *a priori* established, that we should merely acknowledge and endow with legal authority, with the effect of submitting to it the spontaneous unfolding of life.

I challenge this foundational approach resting on the idea that the social is grounded in principles that transcend politics and society, like divine will, or iron laws of nature, the human condition, irrefutable necessities of the laws of the market, all of which stand immune to political revision. I avoid, however, the anti-foundationalist temptation also: the idea of the social world being entirely of an

[1] As described, for instance, by Martti Koskenniemi, 'What is International Law For?', in *The Politics of International Law* (Oxford: Hart Publishing, 2011), p. 243.

ungrounded nature.[2] And while still concerned with the dimension of grounding, I look beyond the Kantian search for a moral ground in *factum rationis*,[3] in search of a solution to overcome both relativism and absolutism and allow democratic participation in international law-making.

My aim is twofold: initially, I seek to unpack the practice of universalizing claims formulated in international law, by tracing the theological roots of such foundational universalisms in Western Christianity. In so doing, I challenge the standard narrative about secularization[4] and build upon one of the observations this volume is structured around, namely regarding the tendency to make sacred the laws of nations and the tasks of judges and that 'the history of international law in modernity partly consists in several attempts at reconceptualising faith into a juristic and rationalist form'. I suggest that faith itself has been conceived, at a specific point in time, into a juristic and rationalist form to the detriment of the spiritual, and this facilitated the appropriation of its argumentative structures for various secular purposes, with the result of depriving faith of the critical potential it has in relation to the secular. From this perspective, we can observe how the universal manifests itself in the secular realm, and we can understand it as established by a tradition that is known by the name of Western metaphysics.[5]

But, I subsequently make a daring suggestion, namely that this is not necessarily the only way of doing metaphysics, nor the only message faith could send about the possibilities of law and of the political. Hence, I advance the proposition that theology could be a source of inspiration for pointing to a direction of transformation of the way we conceive the universal inherent in secular international law.[6] In so doing, while drawing on the criticism of Western metaphysics and Enlightenment rationality formulated by authors like Nietzsche and Heidegger, I inquire what a non-Western Christian theology can contribute to this debate. An engagement with this perspective is, I suggest, worth exploring because Orthodox theology draws on a body of thought that flourished centuries before the Enlightenment and presents a different rationality which thus appears capable of offering fresh insights on the theme of the oppressiveness of the universal. And, despite its historical location, I also suggest that this line of thought is not to be dismissed as merely

[2] For an exposition of anti-foundationalism as merely a negative version of foundationalism, see Oliver Marchart, *Post-Foundational Political Thought: Political Difference in Nancy, Lefort, Badiou and Laclau*, (Edinburgh: Edinburgh University Press, 2007), p. 12.

[3] As examples of such grounding in international law, see, for instance, Jurgen Habermas, 'The Crisis of the European Union in the Light of a Constitutionalisation of International Law', *European Journal of International Law* 23, no. 2 (2012): p. 335, or, in international law, Martti Koskenniemi, 'Constitutionalism as Mindset: Reflections on Kantian Themes About International Law and Globalization', *Theoretical Inquiries In Law* 8 (2007): p. 9.

[4] See Adrian Pabst, 'Rival Modernities: Theological Theorisations of International Society', in *Medieval Foundations of International Relations*, edited by William Bain (Routledge, 2017) for a bibliography on the standard narrative for secularity.

[5] As problematized by authors like Nietzsche, Heidegger, J. Derrida, or Jean-Luc Marion.

[6] For an understanding of post-secularity as an endeavour of re-thinking, by the secular, of 'the place that the non-secular has in relationship to it', see Manuel Sumares, 'Post-Secularity, Orthodoxy and the *Theosis* Factor: Blondel and St. Gregory Palamas', *Revista Portuguesa de Filosofia* 67 (2011): pp. 81, 81–2.

a pre-modern response to modernity. It can, in fact, be interpreted from within the modern condition, because it develops themes of concern for modern thought.

Along the lines of this understanding, I address the following questions: how can we insist on the universally valid and still preserve individual freedom and political agency of all involved in international interactions? How should international law operate to achieve this goal and come to terms with this tension? What has religion to say about these themes, and what does Christian theology in a non-Western tradition bring that is new and useful to the discussion?

I look at a set of relevant theological confrontations within Christianity to discern what critique against foundationalism can be derived from Eastern Christianity, how this critique supports post-modernity's stance, and also what it has to say about its limits. I hope, in this way, to also fill a lack of an account of the relevance of theological debates within Christianity in relation to the contemporary international order.[7]

I propose that this alternative theology, which presents a different space and temporality from the perspective in which international law originated and developed (modern Western European thought), has the resources to inspire a movement of 'putting politics back in international politics',[8] as well as re-imagine the political capacity of the subject. In this paradigm, the critique of scientific certitudes and universalism is expressed in the concept of *apophaticism* as epistemological attitude, according to which truth is not exhausted in its formulation and knowledge is socially verified. This attitude marks a crucial difference between Western and Eastern metaphysics: one a world of spiritual and scientific certitudes; the other a world of hesitation and doubts,[9] with the advantage of being unpropitious for erecting foundational assurances for political power.[10] It determines many other differences between the two traditions, including a difference at the level of the degree of participation in law-formation. I mean to present the physiognomy of law that results from this model as a possible alternative source of inspiration for the contemporary preoccupation of international legal scholars with what the

[7] The only similar accounts that I am aware of, with valuable insights in fields closer to international law, are those of Marinos Diamantides (constitutional law), and, in international relations and political theory John Milbank and Adrian Pabst, from the 'Radical Orthodoxy' movement.

[8] Citing David Kennedy's essay 'Putting the Politics Back in International Politics', *The Finnish Yearbook of International Law* IX (1998): p. 17.

[9] Hélène Ahrweiler, *L'Idéologie Politique de l'Empire Byzantin* (Paris: Presses Universitaires de France, 1975), p. 147.

[10] In this respect, Marinos Diamantides documents the existence of a 'legitimacy deficit' at the very foundation of the political presence of the Byzantine *basileus*, producing the consciousness of the 'inherent vacuity and precariousness of the political ...'. This is contrasted to the Occidental self-confidence with roots located by this author in medieval natural theology that created a 'deficient immanence', a sense of absolute secular power, through the concept of an unlimited but immanent power without *telos*, which in law translates into neutral cognitive or normative certainties. Marinos Diamantides, 'Constitutional Theory and its Limits—Reflections on Comparative Political Theologies', *Law, Culture and the Humanities* 11, no. 1 (2012): pp. 4, 27, doi: 10.1177/1743872112437683.

function of international law could be: a non-foundational way of law-making, relying on participation, and in which the ethical is not legal-normative but the acknowledgement of man's freedom from any pre-set model.

In so doing, I take Christos Yannaras' guidance into the works of the Greek fathers of the Church from the second into the fifteenth century, whose works shaped the faith and ethos of Eastern Christianity. Christos Yannaras (b. 1935) is a Greek philosopher and theologian, considered to be one of the most important contemporary Orthodox thinkers,[11] but whose writings are little known to the Western public, perhaps also due to the scarcity of translations, not available until recently, from the original Greek. Yannaras develops an alternative reading of history in the wake of Heidegger's critique of Western metaphysics. His contention is that Christianity in the West lapsed early on into legalism under the influence of the Roman legal spirit introduced in theology by Augustine,[12] hence the ensuing moralism and intellectualism. He further asserts that there is a genuine biblical theology of the revelation, alternative to the denounced Western metaphysics, which shows the signs of a different, non-foundational metaphysics, and which is to be found in the Christian tradition of thought developed in the Eastern Roman Empire through the writings of the Greek fathers of the Church. This tradition, Yannaras reveals, was long lost from the consciousness of the Western historian of thought, which:

> has been accustomed to date the end of Greek philosophy to AD 529, that is, to the year in which the last Neoplatonic school of Athens was formally closed by order of the Emperor Justinian. The centuries that followed this closure—the entire period of Greek cultural life within the borders of the Eastern Roman Empire—Western historiography has regarded as philosophically 'dead.' And it has been accustomed to identify the resumption of philosophical developments with the appearance of Scholasticism, to which it attributed the only historical continuation of ancient Greek philosophy. It was only toward the end of the nineteenth century ... that some Europeans began to discover that ... the Greek Empire of the Christian East ... had some texts to offer that might be of philosophical interest.[13]

The Schism in Phylosophy, one of Yannaras' early writings, is dedicated to filling this gap, to the retrieval of the philosophical contribution of the Greek fathers of the Church. In this respect, particularly relevant to the discussion about the metaphysical origins of foundationalism, Yannaras points out that the specific synthesis created through the encounter between ancient Greek thought and Christian revelation managed to dislocate and overcome elements of foundationalism in classical Greek ontology, and to place it in history by insisting on the experience of personal relation with the incarnate God.[14] Contrastingly, Western Christianity, affected by rationalism and absolutism, preserved the influence of neoplatonism apparent,

[11] Andrew Louth, 'Some Recent Works by Christos Yannaras in Translation', *Modern Theology* 25, no. 2 (2009): p. 329.

[12] Christos Yannaras, *The Schism in Philosophy*, translated by Norman Russell (Brookline, Massachusetts: Holy Cross Orthodox Press, 2015), esp. pp. 91–5, 148.

[13] Ibid., p. 198. [14] Ibid., p. 196.

for instance, in the image of God as utter being, pure act, or pure form. In this light, Yannaras' effort throughout his work is to propose an ontological argument which is freed from its Kantian bias (not subjected to the operation of laws, nor determined by laws[15]), and, in epistemology, an apophatic attitude to knowledge which relies on a relational ontology.

I see in Yannaras' critical engagement with Western philosophy a resemblance to the post-modern response to the totalitarian potential of the modern political project, with which it shares the starting point in the rejection of classical metaphysics. But it seems to me that Yannaras brings, through his own route, a viewpoint which challenges in several ways the limits of many directions of critique of liberalism formulated within Western secular thought (like left-liberalism, communitarianism, or post-modernism). As a brief illustration, post-modernity now recognizes that thinking in terms of substance is dubious, having reached this conclusion *against* the prevailing metaphysical view of the world.[16] In international law this idea is basically expressed in the theory of law's indeterminacy, most systematically formulated by Martti Koskenniemi.[17] Yannaras shares with post-modernity the insistence on the ontological and semantic indeterminacy, and points out that Eastern Christianity offers a theological approach that *supports* such findings reached in the realm of the secular. And he goes beyond the point where the post-modern critique stops (usually in agonism[18]), and proposes meaningful ways in which we may deal with the ascertainment of the lack of ultimate foundations of the political society without suggesting any sharp closure. Yannaras proposes that there is a *telos*, a foundation of the social, but it is one that resists a theologico-political formulation. This *telos* is to be found in man's paradoxical condition of freedom and relatedness (most fully developed in his *Relational Ontology*[19]), and in apophaticism as corresponding epistemological attitude. One can find in his writings, I claim, theological support for alternatives to essentialism, and for a dialogical (international) law-making.

In the first part of this chapter, I delineate the field of the enquiry with a sketch of the contemporary operation of the universal in various structures of global governance, to further proceed with presenting Yannaras' critique of the theological and intellectual origins of the universal and foundational certitudes inhabiting the project of international law. I subsequently describe the coordinates of the alternative

[15] 'Here [philosophy] should prove its purity as self-sustainer of its own laws, not as a herald of those that an implanted sense or who knows what tutelary nature whispers to it'. Immanuel Kant, *Groundwork for the Metaphysics of Morals*, edited and translated by Allen W. Wood (New Haven and London: Yale University Press, 2002), p. 43.

[16] Along these lines, '[Christianity's] historical significance ... lies ... in the fact that since the beginning of and throughout the modern age it has continued to be that *against which* the new freedom ... must be distinguished'. Martin Heidegger, *Nietzsche*, vol. 4, 'Nihilism', translated by Frank A. Capuzzi, edited by David Farell Krell (San Francisco: Harper, 1996), p. 99.

[17] Martti Koskenniemi, *From Apology to Utopia. The Structure of International Legal Argument* (Cambridge: Cambridge University Press, 2005).

[18] Chantal Mouffe, *Agonistics: Thinking the World Politically* (London/New York: Verso, 2013).

[19] Christos Yannaras, *Relational Ontology*, translated by Norman Russell (Brookline: Holy Cross Orthodox Press, 2011).

metaphysics resulting from Yannaras' thought, which would allow us to conceive and use the universal always implicit in international law without lapsing into absolutism, totalitarianism or hegemony, in a vocabulary that is different from that of natural law, and also outside Kantianism. Finally, I discuss the consequences of this resulting post-foundational approach to the universal for international law-making, showing that the polarity between consent and authority/law's normativity might be overcome by the practice of the social verification of knowledge.

Modes of the Universal in Global Structures of Governance

There are several ways in which foundational certitudes operate in contemporary structures of governance—they can be discerned in the invocation of objectivity of reason or natural order, but also in the sovereign self assertion of particular regimes.

Thus, one way the universal operates can be seen in foundational propositions of the market, relying on abstract principles advanced by economic theories. Such propositions trump away political debate and consent, as can be observed in the manner in which solutions were designed to the sovereign debt crisis across Europe. The 2015 confrontation between the Syriza Government in Greece and EU technocracy gave a sense of the balance of power between the technocratic apparatus and the possibility of inclusive participation by the 'demos' in decision-making. Despite the Greek people having clearly stated by referendum and on the streets of Athens that they objected to austerity, this radical democratic performance remained irrelevant and impotent in confrontation with the reason and wisdom of the Eurogroup.[20] Similarly, international law is being resorted to as a helper in curtailing the usual forms of democratic law-making within the EU. It ends up prescribing the financial behaviour of domestic public authorities, along the lines of a principle of budgetary discipline, the 'obviousness' of which functions as powerful rhetoric to inhibit substantial debates in domestic parliaments.[21] Here, as in other instances, international law lends its formal authority to a specific universalist mode of discourse which increasingly defines the common sense way we understand the world, and discourages the attempt to think critically about what it is that makes this universal mandatory. International law is made to operate as tool for the hegemony of a specific universalist mode of discourse and as a foundation for public policies worldwide. It also accompanies all the features brought about by a specific ideology of governance, grounded in ideas of efficiency and rationality of administration, together with the habit of technical knowledge and

[20] A paternalistic attitude very suggestively deconstructed in Martti Koskenniemi, 'Declaratory Legislation. Towards a Genealogy of Neoliberal Legalism', in *International Law-Making: Essays in Honor of Jan Klabbers*, edited by Rain Liivoja and Jarna Petman (New York: Routledge, 2014), esp. at pp. 17–18.

[21] The Treaty on Stability, Coordination and Governance in the Economic and Monetary Union (TSCG or the Fiscal Compact) (Brussels, 2 March 2012), which was concluded as an international treaty among twenty-five EU Member States, although, by the substance, it could have taken the form of ordinary EU legislation.

expert neutrality. Law, thus obtained, replaces politics and solidifies the tendency towards political neutrality.

Another manifestation of foundational certitudes appears with constitutionalism. The project of 'new' cosmopolitanism, as David Harvey calls it,[22] implies again a heavy reliance on law to bring the universal as a regulative principle in the global order. The 'new' cosmopolitans are 'new', according to Harvey, in comparison to classical liberalism, which used law against the parochialism of nation states to express universality, hence escaping political contestation of its basic propositions. Classical liberals deemed these propositions to be universal and inclusive due to their abstract generalizations about human nature.[23] There is a whole tradition in international law, especially in anti-colonial writing, that reveals the oppressiveness and exclusionary operation of the universal by classical international law. Such writings show how the universalization of international law through either natural law or positivism means taking consensualism away by application of a series of techniques that deny voice to actors on the periphery, the 'others' of European states.[24]

The 'new cosmopolitanism', as compared to the 'old', focuses on the international rule of law and institutional blueprints for global governance[25] and is particularly legalistic in nature. For instance, in his 'juridico-philosophical' type of proposals,[26] Jurgen Habermas pleads for the increasing constitutionalization of international law,[27] which amounts to the increasing juridification of world order. Law is derived from moral and normative foundations, grounded in reason, with the consequence of displacing politics, since power relations are to be appeased through the Kantian solution of rational deliberations, and political disagreement through legal procedure.

The most visible manifestation in international law of the 'new cosmopolitanism' is the work on 'constitutionalization' of international law.[28] Constitutionalization

[22] David Harvey, *Cosmopolitanism and the Geographies of Freedom* (New York: Columbia University Press, 2009), pp. 77–98.

[23] Ibid., p. 77.

[24] See: Michael Hardt and Antonio Negri, *Empire* (Cambridge, Mass.: Harvard University Press, 2000); Anthony Angie, *Imperialism, Sovereignty and the Making of International Law* (Cambridge: Cambridge University Press, 2004); Uday Singh Mehta, *Liberalism and Empire: A Study in Nineteenth Century British Liberal Thought* (Chicago: University of Chicago Press, 1999).

[25] Daniele Archibugi and David Held, eds, *Cosmopolitan Democracy: An Agenda for a New World Order* (Cambridge: Polity, 1995); Daniele Archibugi, ed., *Debating Cosmopolitics* (London: Verso, 2003); Richard Falk, *Law in an Emerging Global Village: A Post-Westphalian Perspective* (Ardsley: Transnational Publishers, 1998).

[26] Michel Foucault, 'Society Must Be Defended', *Lectures at the Collège de France 1975–1976* (London: Allen Lane/Penguin, 2003).

[27] Jürgen Habermas, *The Postnational Constellation: Political Essays* (Cambridge: Polity, 2001); 'The Constitutionalization of International Law and the Legitimation Problems of a Constitution for World Society', *Constellations* 15, no. 4 (2008), pp. 444–55.

[28] Erika de Wet, 'The Emergence of International and Regional Value Systems as a Manifestation of the Emerging International Constitutional Order', *Leiden Journal of International Law* 19 (2006): p. 611; Armin von Bogdandy, Sergio Dellavalle, 'Universalism and Particularism as Paradigms of International Law', IILJ Working Paper no. 3 (2008) (History and Theory of International Law Series); Pierre Dupuy, 'L'Unité de l'ordre juridique international. Cours général de droit international public', *Recueil des Cours de l'Académie de Droit International* 297 (2002), etc.

entails a departure from the horizontal character of international law established at Westphalia. Certain values are to ensure the hierarchical prevalence of international law,[29] just like domestic constitutional law, while, at once, insulating international law from the capricious desires and volitional weaknesses of law-makers. The universal they propose is obtained by abstracting general values placed in imperative hierarchies like *ius cogens* and obligations *erga omnes*, but also general principles of law, and usually the liberal catalogue of rights,[30] which, importantly, exists somehow independent of consent.[31]

The new cosmopolitan project seems to deepen the erosion of participatory democracy. Neo-liberalism's appeal to the obviousness of economic and technical solutions[32] is doubled by the new cosmopolitanism's assumption that adequate models of democracy have already been perfected in the West (like democracy, free market, and the rule of law) and the only problem is to extend these models across jurisdictions.[33] The language of rights also deepens, in fact, the curtailment of the democratic public realm, and accentuates the shift towards an unaccountable and non-participatory jurisdictional and executive power.

Finally, pluralism completes the scene of foundational certitudes in international law. It sets itself against constitutionalism's totalizing narrative, but the challenge it produces tends to target only the centralized monopoly of the foundational propositions of the latter. Foundationalism itself is not contested, it is perpetuated in each particular regime's claim for special relevance which takes the form of a hegemonic claim, one that aims 'to make their partial view ... appear as the total view, their preferences seem like the universal preference'.[34] And since there is no meta-rule to distinguish the true universal from the fake, the peril of instrumentalism looms large. Dialogue and participation on the international scene is additionally vitiated by the adversarial styles of interaction within the larger context employed by various coexisting specialized regimes and legal orders.[35] Very much like nation states, they formulate competing claims for jurisdictional supremacy, acting in a solipsistic manner,[36] absorbed in self-assertion, denying horizontal

[29] Bardo Fassbender, 'The United Nations Charter as a Constitution of the International Community', *Columbia Journal of Transnational Law* 36 (1998): p. 530.

[30] Erika de Wet and André Nollkaemper, 'Review of the Security Council by National Courts', *German Yearbook of International Law* 45 (2002): pp. 166–202.

[31] For a critical view of the project of constitutionalization of international law from the perspective of law-making, see Jan Klabbers, 'Setting the Scene' and 'Law-making and Constitutionalism', in *The Constitutionalization of International Law*, edited by Jan Klabbers, Anne Peters, and Geir Ulfstein (Oxford: Oxford University Press, 2009); see also Jan Klabbers, 'Constitutionalism Lite?', *International Organisations Law Review* 1 (2004): p. 31.

[32] Harvey, *Cosmopolitan Geographies*, pp. 51–76.

[33] See, for instance, William P. Alford, 'Exporting the Pursuit of Happiness', *Harvard Law Review* 113 (2000): p. 1677.

[34] Martti Koskenniemi, 'International Law and Hegemony: A Reconfiguration', *Cambridge Review of International Affairs* 17 (2004): p. 197.

[35] A. Fischer-Lescano and Gunter Teubner, 'Regime-Collisions: The Vain Search for Legal Unity in the Fragmentation of Global Law', *Michigan Journal of International Law* 25 (2004): p. 999.

[36] A certain normative proposition of pluralism advances the premise that we are to conceptualize domestic courts as bound by the political community to which their legal order is associated, to a particular *demos*. The relationship with the outside world is placed on different premises than the intense

interaction with whichever actor would have different normative preferences, and rejecting relations with the overall frame of general international law that provides the larger context in which they are situated. Recent examples of such interaction, which refuses dialogue, the possibility of mutual learning, and may 'pathologize communication',[37] comes to contradict the appeasing conclusion of the report on fragmentation by the International Law Commission that there is no threat to the unity and cohesion of international law: all special legal regimes stay inside general international law.[38]

This description is to illustrate how the universal operates in the ethos of technical specialization, cosmopolitanism, or pluralism, by ushering away participation in constituting international life with its norms.

Theologies of Jurisprudence

Theological roots of the certainty of knowledge

The culture of expert knowledge in global governance has the effect of ushering away participation in law formation, because its claims are posited to be objective, grounded in empirical or logical necessities.[39] For instance, the Fiscal Compact, an international treaty concluded between twenty-five EU Member States, prescribes, under the sanction of refusing financial assistance through the European

relationality of the legal reasoning to be practiced at internal, domestic level, where the interpreter of the law, like the architect evoked by Heidegger, should identify the '*genius loci*', the spirit of the place (the legal order) in which the legal decision is taking place (Miguel Poiares Maduro, 'In Search of a Meaning and not in Search of the Meaning: Judicial Review and the Constitution in Times of Pluralism', *Wisconsin Law Review* 2 (2013): pp. 541, 561). Interaction with the external, international legal order or other domestic or specific orders is even named by a separate concept 'external pluralism': it is an agonistic struggle for each court to maximize the integrity of their legal order and to promote externally the normative preferences of their legal order; the purpose is to minimize to the extent possible potential jurisdictional conflicts, but this for the sake of their own domestic jurisdictional effectiveness. Particular actors (domestic or regional courts) are not to be committed to the integrity and coherence of the larger legal order (the international). The international legal order's pretence of an 'order of orders' is contested in this particularist vision, and no international political community is acknowledged to exist. Miguel Poiares Maduro, 'Courts and Pluralism: Essay on a Theory of Judicial Adjudication in the Context of Legal and Constitutional Pluralism', in *Ruling the World? Constitutionalism, International Law and Global Governance*, edited by Jeffrey L. Dunoff and Joel P. Trachtman (Cambridge: Cambridge University Press, 2009), pp. 373–5. But this pluralistic vision is exposed to the same doubt raised as regards the Heideggerian spirit—that it could lead to exclusionary attitude toward what is exterior to it (Harvey, *Cosmopolitan Geographies*, p. 81).

[37] Neil Walker, 'Idea of Constitutional Pluralism', *Modern Law Review* 65 (2002): pp. 317, 357. Examples of such style of communication might be the decisions of the European Court of Justice in the Joined Cases C-402 & 415/05P, *Kadi & Al Barakaat Int'l Found. v. Council & Comm'n*, 2008 E.CR 1-6351, or *Mox Plant* case ECJ, Case C-459/03, Judgment of 30 May 2006.

[38] *Fragmentation of International Law. Problems caused by the Diversification and Expansion of International Law, Report of the Study Group of the International Law Commission*. Finalized by Martti Koskenniemi. A/CN4/L.682, 13 April 2006, esp. pp. 65–101.

[39] See, for instance, David Kennedy, 'Challenging Expert Rule: The Politics of Global Governance', *Sydney Journal of International Law* 27 (2005): p. 11.

Stability Mechanism and monetary penalties for non-compliance,[40] that its signatories should obey the principle of a balanced budget. This principle is certified, by invoking economic expertise, as a 'natural' solution, a common-sense approach for financial crisis prevention, despite the fact that while it is advanced by certain economic theories, it is contested by others. The behaviour of subjects of international law thus appears to be channelled in directions resulting from certainties that are cognitive, emerging from economic or technical facts, and not from normative ideas of transcendental, unquestionable, authority, but, nevertheless, with similar effects. In technocratic governance, 'the vocabularies of constraint are cognitive rather than normative'.[41] The intellectual roots of such hubristic knowledge claims, advanced in the name of self-presented 'apolitical' expertise, lead to theology.

Heidegger had already formulated the critique of the certainty of common sense, which appeals to the 'obviousness' of its 'truths' based on practical experience, and which resists all questioning.[42] He recognized the method of searching for the absolutely certain and secure in various instances of modern thought: in Enlightenment's reliance on human reason and its laws, in positivism's confidence in the real and the factual which is ordered and arranged by human reason, in the idea of progress in universal rationality.[43] He criticized this approach to truth as excessively rationalistic and foundational, producing intellectual 'idols'.[44] Heidegger argued that the priority of certainty became a stable feature of modern philosophy from Descartes' *cogito*, with philosophy itself having become a theory of knowledge and Plato and Aristotle reinterpreted as epistemologists. This turn, Heidegger notes, has metaphysical origins, traceable in the tradition of authoritative truth attributable only to the truth of the Church and faith, and in the priority of the certainty of salvation.[45]

Yannaras investigates closer the theological origins of the certainty of knowledge articulated by Heidegger. For him, the search for the absolute, unshakable ground for truth does not start with Duns Scotus as John Milbank proposes,[46] nor with Aquinas, as advanced at a certain point by Jean-Luc Marion,[47] but descends

[40] The Treaty on Stability, Coordination and Governance in the Economic and Monetary Union (TSCG or the Fiscal Compact) (Brussels, 2 March 2012), Preamble and art. 8 (2) respectively.

[41] Martti Koskenniemi, 'The Fate of International Law: Between Technique and Politics', in *The Politics of International Law* (Oxford: Hart Publishing, 2011), pp. 331–61, 338.

[42] Martin Heidegger, 'On the Essence of Truth' in *Basic Writings*, edited by David Farell Krell (San Francisco: Harper, 1992), pp. 111–39.

[43] Heidegger, *Nietzsche*, p. 101.

[44] Martin Heidegger, 'What is Metaphysics', in *Basic Writings*, edited by David Farell Krell (San Francisco: Harper San Francisco, 1992), pp. 89–110, at p. 110; Martin Heidegger, 'The Onto-Theo-Logical Constitution of Metaphysics' in *Identity and Difference*, translated by Joan Stambaugh (New York, Evanston and London: Harper & Row, Publishers, 1969), pp. 42–74.

[45] Martin Heidegger, 'Modern Science, Metaphysics, Mathematics', in *Basic Writings*, edited by David Farell Krell (San Francisco: Harper San Francisco, 1992), pp. 267–307, at pp. 295–8.

[46] John Milbank, *Theology and Social Theory: Beyond Secular Reason*, 2nd edn (Oxford: Blackwell Publishing, 2006).

[47] Jean-Luc Marion, *Dieu sans l'être* (Paris: PUF, 1982).

all the way back to Augustine. Thus Augustine's work, developed under Rome's cultural influence, shows unfamiliarity with the ethos of Greek philosophy, which was preserved, albeit transfigured by the specific experience of the God made flesh, in the theology of the primitive Church developed by Church fathers, contemporary to Augustine, living under the Hellenic cultural influence of Constantinople. Augustine's work, Yannaras contends, expressed a rationalist and instrumental ethos due to the influence of Roman legal thought of Cicero, Tertulian, or Ambroise of Milan. Yannaras contends further that it was precisely the influence of this Roman spirit that made Augustine an attractive figure for the Frankish Empire in its ambition to excise anything Greek from the new identity it wanted to give itself, starting in the ninth century.[48] This specific event of appropriation is also used by Yannaras to explain Augustine's tremendous impact on virtually all areas of Western culture and civilization.

Two aspects, I think, would be useful for an attempt to briefly conceptually explain this genealogy of cognitive certainty out of Western theology in Yannaras' revisionist reading of history: Augustine's intellectualism and his ensuing construction of the intelligibility of God. With respect to intellectualism, Yannaras shows that Augustine (like Descartes later), identifies knowledge (and existence) with intellection, which is believed to possess the certainty of knowledge.[49] For Augustine, the intellect is also the supreme part of the soul, and intelligence the part of it which makes the soul superior to the body:

> The rational soul stands out above all the things God has fashioned, ... cleaving to Him in charity the more it perceives these Reasons ... with that chief part of itself by which it is superior, that is, with its intelligence.[50]

As a corollary of the dominant place reserved to human intellectual capacity, Augustine is confident that the human mind can understand God: 'God is for the mind to understand, as body is for the eye to see'.[51] Although Augustine points to various limits of the human capacity to truly *comprehend* God, the central point for this discussion is that divine intelligibility is innately suited to the intellect.

Yannaras criticizes Augustine's intellectualism and Platonism from the perspective of his wish to advance apophaticism. The intellect, seeming to be the objection, needs to resort to objective criteria of confirmation and to authority. Apophaticism, as understood by the Greek fathers and as it will be discussed in the next section, proposes a very different attitude indeed on the question of the intelligibility of God, one that places the emphasis on indeterminacy, freedom, and relatedness, and testifies to the gulf separating the East from the West in terms of philosophical differences. Yannaras even ventures to suggest that the Latin Church had encouraged intellectualism out of a fear of the freedom entailed by the

[48] Yannaras, *The Schism*, p. 91. [49] Ibid., p. 92.

[50] As shown by David Bradshaw, *Aristotle East and West. Metaphysics and the Division of Christendom* (Cambridge: Cambridge University Press, 2004), p. 227.

[51] Sermon 117.5, cited by Phillip Cary, *Augustine's Invention of the Inner Self: The Legacy of a Christian Platonist* (New York: Oxford University Press, 2000), esp. at p. 58.

epistemological priority of personal relationships and experience[52] (instead giving priority to cognitive certainty).

Scholasticism perfected the idea of certainty of knowledge brought by reason, through the enthusiastic embrace, in the twelfth century, of Aristotelian logic (the *Organon* in arabic translation) in an absolutized way, unrelated to the context of Aristotle's other works, which came to be known in Western Europe only later.[53] Syllogistic thought and systematic thinking spoke, of course, of the possibility of man's emancipation from the 'totalitarian structures of Western medieval society', and restored his dignity. They inspired confidence in the 'thinking subject's mastery of the truth of natural, historical and metaphysical reality',[54] but they also led to the construction of an objective knowledge, and identified knowledge with intellectual conceptualization.[55] Thomas Aquinas perfected the tendency towards rationalization of faith by building a theory of God as a transcendent 'object' of metaphysics, and as the highest intelligible object (in contrast with the God beyond knowing of the Easterners, presented below). He inaugurated the Scholastic path to knowledge, *analogia entis*, the analogical relation between beings and Being (or essence): we may know God by attributing to Him the perfections of the qualities we observe in beings. This analogy between God and beings turns metaphysics from ontology into a supernatural version of physics, Yannaras notes. Scholastic epistemology exhausts the possibilities of cognition in the conventional categories of objective syllogisms in the sense that truth is understood as coincidence of the concept with the object of thought.[56]

As an effect, acquiring secular knowledge in this specific epistemology of certainty of knowledge presents the same absolutist, axiomatic character of metaphysical, transcendent axiology. The syllogistic/mathematical or experimental proof replaces in the secular realm, but mimics the given and impervious character of transcendent universals.[57] This transfer, Yannaras notices, prompted existentialists like Kierkegaard to deplore it as the replacement of a transcendent authority with an equally absolutized intellectual certainty, as it appears in Descartes' *cogito* or Hegel's dialectics.[58]

It appears from this specific account that the initial direction of the communication between the sacred and the worldly was initially from faith towards science: faith took, in the Latin West, a systematic rationalistic shape to express the sacred, inspired by Roman legal mind, and, from there, rationalism passed back into natural sciences.[59] Theological rationalism furnished inspiration for technology in the secular realm. It is gothic architecture, Yannaras contends, which first offered the visible form to the scholastic attempt to subject reality to the individual's intellect, will, and desire. The construction material of the cathedral is

[52] Yannaras, *The Schism*, p. 148. [53] Ibid., p. 91. [54] Ibid., p. 96.
[55] Ibid., p. 96. [56] Yannaras, *Person and Eros*, p. 210–12.
[57] Yannaras, *The Schism*, p. 231. [58] Ibid., p. 234.
[59] '… the rationalistic structuring and systematization of knowledge in the medieval West is drawn primarily from jurisprudence, and is first introduced into theology, and then from there into cosmology and the natural sciences'. Yannaras, *Person and Eros*, p. 99.

subjected to the *a priori* given forms aimed at by the 'ideological objective' of the builder, who is not interested, unlike the Byzantine builder, in entering into a relationship with the specific *logos* of the material of construction, to let the matter's potentialities participate in the moulding of the final architectonic shape. The builder's analytic spirit dominates the construction; technology tames matter. Similarly, the systematic logical inferences in *Summa Theologiae* discipline the truth of the world in a unity which is not organic, but mechanical.[60]

The construction of international law as a science to tame the unfolding of life into the legal form can also be treated as a reflection of this tendency towards scientific certainty. We recognize it in Hans Kelsen's building up of the edifice of norms of the discipline, and placing law at the foundation of a political community, with the result of submitting politics to law.[61] Equally, Lauterpacht's proposed technical language, aspiring to catch and control international law's inner morality, can be explained by the influence of such rationalistic metaphysics. Modern positivism also facilitates the 'constitutionalization' of international law by spreading the view that public law values, given their inherent rationality, are indeed universal, suitable in every context to discipline desires.

One long ranging consequence of this epistemological approach is that it does not leave room for alterity and freedom. Even God cannot choose to be other than the logical necessity of an impersonal principle and cause of the world.[62] Human existence too is compelled to submit to the authority of absolute reason, which becomes foundational.[63] The priority of certainty compels to ground truth (or the universal) on fixed and firm foundations within the limits of concepts with clearly defined boundaries and unchangeable properties. This foundational imagination does not allow for participation in truth formation: truth is objectively given, and

[60] 'Gothic architecture, following soon after scholasticism, is the first technological application of scholastic thought. It sets out in visible form the scholastic attempt to subject truth to the individual intellect, drawing on the new logical structures introduced by scholastic theology. In the thirteenth century, for the first time a truth is arranged and discussed systematically, under a number of sub-divisions. A complete work is divided into books, the books into chapters, the chapters into paragraphs, and the paragraphs into articles. Each assertion is established by the systematic refutation of objections, and phrase by phrase, the reader is gradually brought to a full intellectual clarification of a given truth.... In an analogous manner, the technique of Gothic architecture is based on a structure of small cut stones of uniform shape. The stones form columns, and the columns are sub-divided into ribbed composite piers, with the same number of ribs as those in the vaulting above them. The arrangement of the columns and the division of the ribs create a rigid skeleton which neutralizes the weight of the material by balancing the thrust of the walls. Here again, thesis is reinforced by the systematic refutation of antithesis, ... the weight of the material is neutralized by balances arranged on rational principles.... The structure manifests the intellectual conception and will of the craftsman rather than the potentialities of the material—the moral obedience of matter to spirit, not the "glory" of matter, the revelation of God's energies in the *logos* of material things.' Ibid., pp. 101–2.

[61] And see the link to rationalistic theology made by Carl Schmitt: 'At the foundation of his [Kelsen's] identification of state and legal order rests a metaphysics that identifies the lawfulness of nature and normative lawfulness'. *Political Theology—Four Chapters of the Concept of Sovereignty* (Chicago: Chicago University Press, 1996), p. 41.

[62] See David Bradshaw's explanation about Aquinas unsuccessful struggle to prove God's capacity of free choice, coming from his reliance on the Aristotelian idea of the prime mover in *Aristotle East and West* (2004), pp. 242–50.

[63] Yannaras, *The Schism*, p. 184.

follows the rigors of logics; it is not subject to the making of man. Subjects are free only to strive towards the given model; they cannot participate in the formation of the model.

The above discussion of the priority of cognitive certainty has the significance of approaching foundationalism from the perspective of epistemology. In the next section, I will discuss foundationalism form the perspective of existence; that is, of ontology.

Theological origins of foundational universalism

The theological location of foundational universality, of the kind encountered also in international law's universalistic aspirations, may be looked for, Yannaras suggests, in an understanding of the universal that derives from what he calls an 'ontic', exterior approach to existence. The ontic/ontological divide, which Yannaras takes from Heidegger, is an additional conceptual tool to perform his critique of the autonomous and absolutized reason, and contributes, in my opinion, to the deconstruction of the theoretical articulations of un-freedom in European thought.

An ontic approach, Yannaras explains, is one which is not concerned with existence itself, but is guided by the methodological question of 'what is the substance' of Being (or the universal). It supposes the existence of a specific bearer of the general *possibilities* of Being,[64] which is endowed with a definitive identity—a set of characteristics, amongst which is the feature of being considered as the cause of existence (and not as participant in existence, as in an ontological approach). God (or the universal) is itself defined in an ontic fashion, by a set of attributes—self-causation, cause of beings, pure act. *Transcendentalia,* God's predicates (*unum, verum, bonum, res, aliquid*), attributed to Thomas Aquinas and Albert the Great, are an illustration of such an ontic approach. They exhaustively describe the substance, or the essence, of God and are particularly suitable to an intellectual and rationalistic perspective. In contrast, an ontological version of Being (as shall be argued in the next part of this chapter) would deny a definitive character of Being (of the universal), or the possibility to exhaust it in the static nature of a final definition.[65]

The expression in theology of such an ontic approach to the universal is to be found, according to Yannaras, in the inversion of the metaphysical question by the Scholastics, from the problem of existence to God as an object of metaphysical inquiry: 'the object of our scientific knowledge is God'.[66] God became an object of knowledge, of the same substance as existents, but the most accomplished amongst them, and susceptible to be defined positively by applying an objective apodictic methodology.

Yannaras locates the origin of this mode of thinking again in Augustine, namely in his approach to *universalia*, which was allegedly taken over and stabilized in Scholasticism *via* Anselm, Abelard, Tomas Aquinas, and Duns Scotus.[67] Augustine,

[64] Ibid., p. 168. [65] Ibid., p. 184. [66] Ibid., p. 181. [67] Ibid., p. 228.

in Yannaras' interpretation, transferred Plato's autonomous world of ideas to the substance or essence of God, and contended that the ideas/ forms existed outside and independently of sensible things. Ideas had in themselves a given and essential perfection because they were encompassed within the essence of God. They pre-existed in God and were impressed in beings in the course of creation, and constituted the ontological principle of being, absolutely predetermining the form or mode and goal of existence for sensible things.[68] Yannaras reads this Augustinian interpretation as a schematization of ancient Greek philosophy, which wiped away elements of dynamic indeterminacy that Yannaras claims (contrary to Heidegger's interpretation) can be found in Plato's and Aristotle's thought (but which, on the contrary, were acknowledged and built upon in Eastern Christian thought).

Problematic about such an ontic approach to the universal is that it produces determinism and axiology. Determinism works to inhibit existential freedom and otherness, distinctiveness from the given model. Every possibility of existential differentiation is traced back to the given model, not to a capacity of existents to be self-determined, and any deviation from the ideal model must be banished. What is more, everyone must conform to and is measured against the model offered universally by means of international law, of justice, human rights or the like. The attributes of each living being (of each subject of the law) are axiologically evaluated by reference to the concept of the most accomplished of their version (*transcendentalia*). Hence, the oppressiveness of universal ideals on bare life.

From this, important consequences result for identity formation. The very identity of existing things is constituted by reference to the given rationale of existence. It presupposes the complete ontological self-sufficiency of universals, and a corresponding and polarizing ontological uncertainty of particular existences, because the ontological principle of existents is constantly referred back for confirmation to the realm of intellectual substances or realities.[69] Existence is axiologically depreciated as towards the given model:

> Then I thought upon those other things that are *less* than You, and I saw that they neither absolutely are nor yet totally are not: they are, in as much as they are from You: they are not, in as much they are not what You are. For that truly is, which abides unchangeably'.[70] [emphasis mine]

In this sense, beings must become something other than themselves, than that which they are; they must strive for conformity with the given model.

A moment in the history of international law very illustrative for such a problematic ontic approach to identity formation is the recognition of states during the nineteenth century. Non-European states (colonies) were basically required

[68] Ibid., p. 226. [69] Ibid., p. 226.

[70] Augustine, *Confessions* VII.11, cited in David Bradshaw, *Aristotle West and East* (2004), p. 223. For Thomas Aquinas, depreciation of existents appears, for instance from his approach to the question of substance/ *esse*: '... only God is his own *esse* ... ; hence all other beings are not their own *esse*, and so must possess *esse* by participation ... in God.... one can say that He [God] is that supreme *esse* in which other entities participate and thereby are'. David Bradshaw, *Aristotle West and East* (2004), p. 250.

to comply with authoritative standards in order to be recognized subjects of international law. But, as Anthony Anghie tells us, finally acquiring the desired identity by conforming to canons posed as natural or rational (and therefore universal) by European colonial powers did not lead to empowerment of the newly sovereign states,[71] but to painful self-alienation. Those external standards did not allow the non-European world to preserve its authentic identity, to stay that which it was, if it wanted to have its existence acknowledged and be allowed to participate in international law-making.

Similarly, logics of exclusion result from using ontic attributes, which define our humanity and distinguish amongst actors. For instance, David Harvey[72] powerfully shows how Kant's reliance on 'maturity' and capacity to reason as normative concepts for defining the humanity of a person introduces an exclusionary dynamic towards the 'immature' and the 'irrational', who do not qualify for political voice in 'rational' deliberations in public life. Access to general aspirations, like peace or political participation is not universal but conditioned upon fulfilling certain particular conditions of possibility, like cognitive faculties, feelings, and desires. Only those exhibiting certain traits, like rational behaviour, will be allowed to partake in humanity's shared destiny.[73] What happens when universal ethics is applied to issues of world governance, in a world in which some members are considered more 'civilized' than others, is aptly illustrated in how universal principles of law operated during the colonial encounter, and in how the ontic fashion of identity formation continues to perpetuate long into the twenty-first century international law.[74] For instance, one can detect a similar dynamic in the way membership to various international clubs (like the European Union) is currently conceived: 'lesser' states have to reform themselves to fit into the pre-set criteria, to correspond to some foundational optimal model, while levelling away all kinds of specific features, in order to be considered worthy of engagement with.

To sum up the critique formulated in this section, foundationalism as an obstacle to democratic participation in international law-making is explained by a rationalist epistemology which objectifies and absolutizes knowledge, and by a resulting ontic approach to the universal which produces determinism, axiology, and problematic identity formation.

Alternative Theology

Yannaras proposes to search for a solution to onto-theology (the problem of excessive rationalization and foundationalism in Western metaphysics) in a genuine biblical theology of revelation that advances relationality and participation as

[71] Anthony Anghie, *Imperialism, Sovereignty and the Making of International Law* (Cambridge: Cambridge University Press, 2004), p. 108.

[72] David Harvey, *Cosmopolitanism and the Geographies of Freedom*, pp. 17–36.

[73] Ibid., p. 27.

[74] Anthony Anghie, *Imperialism, Sovereignty and the Making of International Law*, pp. 58–60, 112.

ontological reality. He discloses an alternative mode of metaphysics, a post-modern one,[75] which is not based on immutable truths to which the living must adapt, a metaphysics whose content and form are fluid, inviting the living to participate to their transient determination and whose spirit is relational and referential, as opposed to autonomous. He presents this ethos as alternative to the totalitarianism of the absolute systems arrived at in modern European thought due to rationalism and foundationalism in Western metaphysics.

Yannaras suggests that this genuine biblical theology is to be found in the thought of the Greek fathers of the Church, from the second into the fifteenth century, covering the early and middle Christian periods and located historically in 'the Greek Empire of the Christian East', also known by the name *Byzantium*, a mocking term employed in dominant Western historiography to designate the entire Eastern Roman Empire by the name—*Byzantion*—of the tiny ancient Greek colony upon which Constantinople, the capital of an empire of millenarian existence, was built.[76] Yannaras points out that such authors perceived the fact of existence around different coordinates than eternal substances, hierarchical relationships, and axiological comparisons between imperative universals and imperfect particular existences.[77] This vision is presented as an exceptional synthesis between 'two utterly different and fundamentally incompatible epistemologies and ontologies',[78] those of Hellenism and of the Christian Church respectively, and which constituted a radical discontinuity with the history of Western philosophy. In what follows, I will briefly present this vision on epistemology and the ontological perspective over the universal in certain aspects I find relevant for the critique of foundational universalism in international law.

Apophaticism as alternative to cognitive certainty

Before the suspicion of grand narratives prompted thinkers like Derrida[79] and Jean-Luc Marion[80] to explore apophaticism as an alternative way of theological thinking, Yannaras resorts to Dionysios the Areopagite in his book *On the Absence and Unknowability of God*[81] to contest the self-assurance of positive reason. Unlike in the Latin tradition (Augustine's concept of the intelligibility of God sketched above), for Dionysios, God is beyond the power of comprehension of the human creature, and cannot be precisely grasped by positive predicates, because He is not of the order of beings. Hence, what Heidegger calls the void, the nothingness into which Western metaphysics ends up with the exposing of the absence of the God

[75] Christos Yannaras, *Postmodern Metaphysics*, translated by Norman Russell (Brookline, Mass.: Holy Cross Orthodox Press, 2004).

[76] Yannaras, *The Schism*, p. 198. [77] Ibid., p. 197. [78] Ibid., p. 197.

[79] J. Derrida, 'Comment ne pas parler: dénégations', in *Psyché: inventions de l'autre,* (Paris: Galilée, 1987).

[80] Jean-Luc Marion, *L'Idole et la distance*, (Paris: Grasset, 1977); *Dieux sans l'être* (1982).

[81] Christos Yannaras, *On the Absence and Unknowability of God. Heidegger and the Areopagite*, edited by Andrew Louth, translated by Haralambos Ventis (London: T&T Clark International, 2005), with the original Greek first published in 1967 as *The Theology of the Absence and Unknowability of God.*

of onto-theology, is in fact the unknowability of God beyond being. This contrasts with Augustine's and Aquinas'[82] concept of God as intrinsically intelligible: '... the essence of God, the pure and perfect act, is absolutely and perfectly in itself intelligible'.

Apophaticism[83] has two important components: indeterminacy—the 'refusal to exhaust truth in its formulation',[84] and the social verification of knowledge. I will present indeterminacy in this section in connection with its effect of destabilizing certainties (cognitive or normative) and explain the second component, the social verification of knowledge, in the last section of this chapter, in connection with the theme of the participatory character of law-making.

Indeterminacy is the initial presupposition of apophatic epistemology, and allows truth/ the universal not to be posited in definitive terms, as, Yannaras explains, language only signals it in a referential way. Language suggests reality, but it does not impose it by claiming to give a definitive and exhaustive representation of it precisely because, Yannaras contends, it leaves place to the dynamic indeterminacy of relationships that constantly shapes reality and destabilizes certainties. This contrasts with the ascertainment of the preciseness of objective reason, the precursor of Western positivism. Apophaticism aims at freedom from any conceptual predeterminations of knowledge.[85]

Apophaticism receives its confirmation, Yannaras notes, in the scientific discoveries of the twentieth century, which abandons the idea of certainty of knowledge and returns to confirm the epistemological presuppositions of Greek philosophy of the fifth century BCE concerning the relative character of what is signified, the dynamic character of substance, and to contest the ontic, foundational understanding of substance: Einstein's theory of relativity, quantum physics (Heisenberg's *uncertainty principle*, Niels Bohr's radical observations on the electron's property of appearing either as a particle or a wave without being in itself neither one nor the other but something that presupposes both), the assertion of the existence of anti-matter and the theory of the continuing genesis of matter.[86]

These findings are increasingly penetrating the fields of the humanities and social sciences, including law,[87] to shake both positivism and naturalism's certainties. Ideals to be reached, such as cosmic order and harmony, are shown in light of the most recent understandings of physics to be indeterminate dynamics of becoming rather than fixed states. Apophaticism indeed comes to contradict the Western political culture, supporting 'distrust rather than confidence in human

[82] *S.T.* I.87.1, cited in David Bradshaw, *Aristotle East and West* (2004), p. 254, fn. 96.

[83] For a discussion of apophaticism in a larger philosophical context, see my 'Re-thinking universalism: Post-Foundational Cosmopolitanism in a relational key', in *Re-grounding Cosmopolitanism. Towards a Post-Foundational Cosmopolitanism*, edited by T. Caraus and E. Paris (Routledge, 2016), pp. 64–85, esp. pp. 78–81.

[84] Christos Yannaras, *Postmodern Metaphysics* (2004), p. 85.

[85] Yannaras, *The Schism*, p. 75 . [86] Ibid., p. 76.

[87] Roberto Bin, 'Order and Disorder. Legal Adjudication and Quantum Epistemology', Straus Institute Working Paper no. 02 (2012).

reason'.[88] The aim would be to produce political institutions capable of symbolizing not the illusion of firm ground and absolute certainty but the ultimately ungrounded nature of all political claims.

Apophaticism mirrors the thesis of indeterminacy in international law. The source of indeterminacy is, in both cases, an inherent quality of the language, and both of them have made similar findings like the meaning of an expression being relational.[89] The effect is similarly to displace certitudes and expose the contingency and contestability of every act of grounding. But apophaticism goes beyond structuralism and polarizing concepts like naturalism/positivism with respect to the basis of obligation in international law, or normativity/concreteness (authority/convention as sources of ethics). Yannaras provides an ontological explanation for such binary opposites. These are coming from the Augustinian treatment of the universals, from the polarization between the transcendent, completely self-sufficient, and the immanent, in perpetual search for an identity eternally dependent on the degree of sameness with intellectual substances. Unable to overcome such contrasts, Yannaras notes, Western thought ended up with treating them as inherent. This can be recognized in the explanation given in international law of such polarizations as being structurally given, unavoidable.[90] Nominalism's denouncing of the universals as simply names, *flatus vocis*, was not enough to overcome the impasse.[91] This is because the metaphysically given objectivity of universals was transferred progressively into rationally (hence universally) obligatory truths with respect to empirical knowledge. Reference back to a given and transcendent character of the universal is preserved if only as an absolutized axiology: man in the quest for the most perfect form of the organization of life.[92] This tendency can be noticed in visions of *civitas maxima* which animated at various moments the projects of international law. In Yannaras' observation, such absolutized axiology breeds, in turn, exclusion and intolerance to the manifestations of life that do not fit the perfection of the model.

One specific contribution made by the Greek theologians of the Byzantine period to the apophatic epistemology of Platonist and Aristotelian tradition is the distinction between the essence and energies of God, which helps overcome the divide between relativism and absolutism. The theme appears explicitly in the hiesychast controversy that opposed in fourteenth-century Gregory Palamas and the Westerner Varlaam on the 'definition' of God (divine intelligibility). The Easterner objected the idea that we cannot have a positive knowledge of God through our rational faculties, and proposed the distinctions between the essence and energies of God, showing that God's essence/substance remains unknown

[88] Hélène Ahrweiler, *L'Idéologie Politique de l'Empire Byzantin* (1975), Marinos Diamantides, 'Constitutional Theory and its Limits—Reflections on Comparative Political Theologies', *Law, Culture and the Humanities* 11, no. 1 (2012): p. 27.

[89] Martti Koskenniemi, *From Apology to Utopia. The Structure of International Legal Argument* (Cambridge: Cambridge University Press, 2005), pp. 8–9.

[90] Martti Koskenniemi, *From Apology to Utopia* (2005), p. 62.

[91] Yannaras, *The Schism*, p. 229.

[92] Ibid., p. 231.

(no certain knowledge about it), but we are saved from agnosticism because God makes himself known to us through his activities, in His historical appearances. In a similar way we know the other persons—through their disclosing themselves to us and the acceptance by us of the revelation of such disclosure.[93] Knowledge is a fact of personal relationship freely entered into: a free self-revelation to the other and a free acceptance of such disclosure on the part of the recipient. That is the referentiality of knowledge. Knowledge as disclosure is a fact of participation, not a matter of acquiring information, and it is apophatic because it is inexhaustible.

Yannaras' apophaticism, in comparison to the theory of indeterminacy in international law, is accompanied by a distinctive, relational, ontology. It proposes intersubjectivity in the law-making process based on participation in knowledge formation and referentiality as alternatives to a Sartrean type[94] of self-definition of existence. What is more, essence itself is conceived as a dynamic becoming of relations, not as a set of given attributes or firm matter. In this version, ontology helps overcome the divide between transcendent and immanent and other pairs of opposites deriving from it. It confirms and further explains the relativity of concepts observed from an epistemological perspective, by exposing all grounds as being dependent on the dynamic indeterminacy of life itself. In addition, this relational ontology manages to drop off autonomous reason—any superior form of reason, the rational standard against which to evaluate the living: there is no *a priori* standard which is not subject to the contribution of all who interact with it.

This ontological side of the argument about indeterminacy, related to relationality, is exposed in the remainder of this chapter, where I mean to describe how it could open up new horizons for expressing the normative content of international law beyond natural law.

Alternative theology for universals

Before exposing elements of such relational ontology, it would be convenient to examine the ontological approach that Yannaras proposes against the 'ontic' interpretation of existence. An ontological perspective, in this author's understanding, denies the definitive character of Being, its identification with the cause of beings, and any comparative evaluation of beings against the universal as standard. The Scholastic approach to God as an object of knowledge is contrasted with the approach to God in the Christian East where God is not the logical necessity of a first mover derived from the observation of the world, a foundational essence, but appears as a specific historical intervention and action: He unexpectedly calls Abraham, 'and converses with him "face to face, as one speaks to a friend" (Exod 33:11)'.[95] It is a God of historical revelation and of personal relationship, which also requires trust in an inherited experience, a tradition—the 'God of our fathers'.

[93] Christos Yannaras, *Postmodern Metaphysics* (2004), p. 136.

[94] See Sahib Singh, 'Koskeniemi's images of the international lawyer', *Leiden Journal of International Law* 29 (2016): pp. 699–726.

[95] Yannaras, *The Schism*, p. 196.

The accent is placed on an experiential approach to truth, and not on the axiomatic character of the doctrine, deduced from the autonomous operation of logic, detached from the experience of the ecclesial body.

This vision offers a contrasting perspective on the issue of the substance of the universal and of its relationship with particular existents. With respect to the substance of the universal, Yannaras recapitulates that we can find in Plato and Aristotle, as understood in Byzantium, very differently than in Western thought, a relational and non-essentialist concept of substance. Essence (*ousia*) is the *fact* of participation in Being, and participation is realized as the *mode* and rational principle (*logos*) of the relations of every existent within the context of the totality of existents, as an organic insertion into the universal social realization of life as participation. Consequently, substance only exists as the dynamic fact of realizing unique relations. The substance corresponds not to the *what* (a matter, a form, their combination), but to the *how,* the mode or rational principle of the dynamic realization of relations that constitute the fact of participation of beings in Being. God describes Himself to Moses as 'I am he who is' (Exod 3:14), not 'I am the substance' (or the *transcendentalia*), explained Gregory of Nazianzus in the fourth century.[96] Meaning that God's personal identity is not dependent on the necessity of having certain characteristics like being immortal, infinite, almighty, and so forth, God is free to be who he is, his personal identity. And God identifies Himself with this hypostasis, with being a person, not with the Divine nature or substance. There is non-essentialism, indeterminacy, and dynamism in the 'model' itself, very much similar to Heidegger's 'groundless ground', and this might also radically transform man's relationship with the model.

Yannaras further notes that, in ancient Greek thought, although substance is conceived of as a dynamic process, there is a remnant of determinism: knowledge and life are subject to the laws of this relational reason (*cosmos*). Christianity's innovation in this respect was to promote an understanding of the world as a product of freedom. The Cappadocian fathers (fourth century—Basil of Caesarea, Gregory of Nazianzus, Gregory of Nissa) suggested this when they proposed that 'Person' meant the hypostasis of Being, the mode by which Being subsists as existential reality. They also emphasized that the fact of participation in Being did not have ontological priority in relation to the person, who continued to be a person irrespective of if she realized participation in Being or not (choses to live in an autonomous fashion and not in relation, for instance). In turn, Being does not exist outside its hypostatic realization in persons; it is the persons who make Being a reality. This means that Being itself is only a hypostasis of personal otherness, which means freedom from predeterminations of substance, cause, or rational principle.[97]

Furthermore, again echoing Aristotle's categories, 'substance' (*ousia*) for the Cappadocians simply meant the general, the community of attributes, the universal form of species (man-as-a-whole, horse-as-a-whole), whereas 'hypostasis' meant individual otherness, 'peculiarity of each existence', (that particular man or that

96 Ibid., p. 206–7.

97 Ibid., p. 205.

particular horse) that differs from the substance in the uniqueness and dissimilarities of its properties. Thus is explained the paradoxical experience of the *one* and triadic God, and more precisely how it was possible that the universal substance of the Godhead does not negate the real character of the particular existences and, simultaneously, how it is possible that no particular existence exhausts the reality of the one universal substance. This way, neither the universal exists in an absolute fashion, nor the particulars. They are united in interaction and communion.[98]

These explanations also show an understanding of alterity in its identity-constitutive role, contrasting to the constitution of identity described in the previous section, and which is based, contrastingly, on sameness with the given model. On the problem of identity formation, this perspective reinstitutes the ontological quality of existents by its rejection of *a priorism* and axiology. Identity is formed as otherness, is given by the uniqueness and distinctiveness of the relations with other beings, and not by semblance to an *a priori* given and abstract principle (*adequatio*).

It remains to be discussed how law can reflect such a vision of the universal which emphasizes the utter indeterminacy of every ground and refuses to submit life to any exterior, pre-existent model.

A Relational Approach to the Universal and International Law-making

I have been discussing so far an alternative vision to the formation and operation of the universal from within Christian thought of non-Western origin, after having first deconstructed the foundational approach to the *universalia* and the certainties of positive knowledge from the point of view of this particular perspective. I have contrasted this approach with an alternative theology developed in the Eastern Hellenic Christianity, which in its attitude to epistemology and the ontology of substance makes use of apophaticism and relationality to bring fluidity and dynamism into our thinking of the universal. I will elaborate in what follows on some possible practical implications for international law-making of this alternative metaphysical understanding of the world centred on endorsing the ultimate relativity of the possibilities of knowledge, and in so doing, explore the participatory, hence anti-authoritarian, potential of this approach.

This alternative ethos might meaningfully contribute to overcoming the divide with which international law is struggling between (state) consent and remaining normative, or between concreteness and normativity.[99] Problematic about these polarities is that they structure international law around a choice between

[98] Ibid., p. 205.

[99] Martti Koskenniemi, *From Apology to Utopia. The Structure of International Legal Argument* (2005), pp. 17–23; Jan Klabbers, 'Towards a Culture of Formalism? Martti Koskenniemi and the Virtues', *Temple International and Comparative Law Journal* 27, no. 2 (2013): pp. 415, 416.

stabilizing a certain ideal in rules and institutions and pure voluntarism, that is, allowing States to be involved in forging legal solutions that would reflect what takes place in the political and economic world. Consensualism has been treated as problematic, allowing for cynicism, whereas normativity is suspected of being potentially oppressive.

My suggestion is that an attitude to knowledge—formation which is apophatic in the sense explained appeases this polarity. Indeed, apophaticism seems to delegitimize claims about an imperative truth that has been obtained outside the participation of those on which that truth is made mandatory. It thus destabilizes the universal's normativity, any 'ought' pretending to be obtained beyond interaction. At the same time, apophaticism presupposes, besides the refusal to exhaust truth in its formulation, the social, communal verification of knowledge, truth as participation. This, in turn, enables participation in law-making. But subjective participation is true only as an event of communion, as common reason, according to the Greek legacy as transformed by the Fathers of the Church. This introduces a different grounding for consensualism, which is beyond instrumental reason, be it private interest or common good.

Yannaras traces the idea of relationality even in the epistemological argument, in the ancient Greek approach to the formation of *logos* as an event of relation. Thus, ancient Greeks thought, reason itself is not autonomous as in modernity, but relational, meaning a shared experience of rational contemplation. Heraclitus connects truth with the *common logos*: 'when we share something in common, we express the truth, and when we hold something in private we deceive ourselves'.[100] This characteristic of knowledge refers to the way truth is formed, that is, in communion. We are rational 'in the degree in which we participate in the common *logos*' of life, and not because we have the power to reason, private intelligence. The effort to become rational individually leads to error, according to Heraclitus.[101] Knowledge is rational, therefore, only as a result of participation in the common *logos* of the ordered/social realization of life.[102]

It is precisely this dynamic that is behind the embodiment of participation in the political realization of life that distinguishes the ethos that Yannaras wants to propose from modernity, and which, I think, is relevant for an attempt to 'put back the politics in international politics'. Truth as participation means that every member of the relevant community, has the capacity, that is, the political standing to participate in the forging of truth. There is no collective will or impersonal rationality which is imposed on the living, no *a priori* given and abstract model towards which existents must coincide, and the fact that recognition of the 'other' is not conditional upon fulfilment of various ontic attributes means that there is no further condition for participation in law-making than just being there. This account reveals a metaphysics whereby one cannot claim that law which reflects universal values, like *ius cogens*, or *erga omnes* obligations, is situated beyond experience of the life in common, independent of interaction of actors and of their contribution.

[100] Yannaras, *The Schism*, p. 45. [101] Ibid., p. 46. [102] Ibid., p. 47.

Such normative legislation is also formed in relation, just as positive law is. And positive law, in turn, should be nothing less than normative if the special dynamic towards truth was followed. The specificity of this dynamic lies in that it emphasizes that truth is not on the side of the many, as Augustine maintains, according to Yannaras.[103] It is not reached through a quantitative criterion. The criterion of truth is the fullness of the subject's participation in existence. The big question is, therefore, how fully do we participate in existence? According to Yannaras, only when we access reality through its relational dimension can we fully participate in existence. This means a realization of life according to a dynamically actualized common *logos*, a perpetual realization of relations, as indeterminate as the relations of which it is formed. Relationality means otherness and referentiality:[104] accepting that every particular participant takes her identity from the other beings, of which she distinguishes herself, amounts to an invitatory attitude to knowledge formation, which excludes domination of one actor by the other. It is this spirit that any consensual law-making should manifest in order to be normative. For Yannaras, it is the *polis*, best exemplified by Athens of the fifth century BCE, which represents a model of political organization that illustrates such a dynamic. The polis is organized around an ordering principle according to which citizens gather in order to constitute relations which 'aspire to the imitation and expression of cosmic harmony and order', and which is obtained by the coordination between the individual *logos* with the common *logos* of the citizens.[105] The common *logos* (the ordered event of life) is the only possibility for the expression and manifestation of the truth of life.

However, the ordering principle of the *polis* is not a finished solution, does not operate as a Kantian 'regulative principle' that might organize international interaction around ideals such as universality, perfectibility, pluralistic international world, or universal community.[106] With this distinction, Yannaras points to a different dynamic in the way 'being true' is used[107] and, at the same time, makes a distinction between participation in the formation of truth and participation in the fulfilment of a pre-set ideal.

With respect to the dynamics of truth formation, laws of the *polis* derive organically from the reality of life as social interaction, not from a metaphysical higher authority, or from the subjective perception of a hegemon, imposed on the political life. They rest on an anthropological premise according to which the reality of life is relationship and commonality, not individuality and autonomy. The 'principle of political symbiosis' is coordination between the individual rationality (*logos*) (of the individual subject) and the common *logos* of the citizens. This coordination is organic, expressed in the identity constitutive role of referentiality,

[103] Ibid., p. 93. [104] Ibid., p. 52. [105] Ibid., p. 44.

[106] For appeals to the function of a Kantian regulative principle in international law, see, for instance, Martti Koskenniemi, 'The Politics of International Law—Twenty Years Later', 'What Is International Law For?', 'The Fate of Public International Law: Between Technique and Politics', in *The Politics of International Law* (Oxford: Hart Publishing, 2011).

[107] Yannaras, *The Schism*, p. 47.

and not mechanical, as coordination with a view to fulfil an interest, be it the common good. The dangers for the *polis*, for the community, comes from autonomization, self-sufficiency. Participation is inhibited not only by the imposition of abstract universals or autonomous rational knowledge (constitutionalism), but also by claims of absolute validity of the subjectively asserted beliefs (pluralism).

Autonomization and self-sufficiency is noticeable in pluralism and fragmentation (and the way they are reflected in international law-making)—the desire to become autonomous and self-contained displayed by the various (functional or State) regimes into which international law is split, and the refusal of those autonomous regimes to come into coordination with the rationalities of the other participants in international interaction. Yannaras explains such cultivation of autonomy by pointing to the tendency towards an individualized absolute, which he analyses as employing the same mechanisms of building infallible truths as every oppressive ideology. He names this tendency 'monism of the subject', and interprets it as having come to replace the pre-Socratics' 'monism of the one substance' and owing its theoretical formulation to Kant. In Yannaras' view, Kant's 'Copernican revolution' merely sought to replace the Scholastic epistemology's foundations on the objective authority of natural theology and intellectualist metaphysics with the human subject's epistemic capacities. Subjectivism, thus, is not relativism, but an assertion of the absolute value of individual capacities. It explains the eternal antagonism pluralism leaves us with; it leads, ultimately, to the rejection of democratic principles in law-making. 'To realise the relative validity of one's convictions, and yet stand for them unflinchingly is what distinguishes a civilised man from a barbarian'.[108] This is where pluralism usually leaves us: in a permanent struggle between individual attempts to firmly ground their subjective versions of the universal, irrespective of whether they have consciousness of the ultimately un-groundable nature of their claim.[109]

The type of consensualism this produces is not one conducive to a plausible normativity of the kind Yannaras has in mind. Celebration of autonomy and individualism, private *logos*, is denial of truth, un-truth. The alternative that I discuss goes further than pluralistic antagonism or agony:[110] acknowledgement of the relativity and indeterminacy of all concepts (indeed reached in post-modern thought) does not lead to their bold self-assertion, but to circumspection in advancing them. It amounts to an aporetic and inviting attitude towards truth formation in common

[108] This is Joseph A. Schumpeter, *Capitalism, Socialism, and Democracy* (London, 1943). p. 243, admiratively cited by Isaiah Berlin in 'Two Concepts of Liberty', in *Liberty*, edited by Henry Hardy (Oxford: Oxford University Press, 2013), p. 217.

[109] In this respect see, for instance, Ernesto Laclau, 'Identity and Hegemony: The Role of Universality in the Constitution of Political Logics', in Judith Butler, Ernesto Laclau, and Slavoj Zizek, *Contingency, Hegemony, Universality: Contemporary Dialogues on the Left* (London: Verso, 2000), pp. 44–89; and in (international) law literature, Gunther Teubner, *Constitutional Fragments: Societal Constitutionalism and Globalization*, translated by Gareth Norbury (Oxford: Oxford University Press, 2012), esp. pp. 150–74; and, critically, Martti Koskenniemi, 'International Law and Hegemony: a Reconfiguration', *Cambridge Review of International Affairs* 17 (2004): p. 197.

[110] Chatal Mouffe, *Agonistics. Thinking the World Politically* (London and New York: Verso, 2013).

and its social verification, to rejection of certainties as vain, unrealistic. The political implications of such aporetic attitude might disturb, in fact, both pluralists and constitutionalists, because it destabilizes their common reflex of grounding their respective claims.

The specific metaphysics described above inspires the idea that conflict is solvable and order is achievable through relationality: not coming to terms with the hegemonic nature of politics, nor resorting to rational consensus or a process of juridification and constitutionalization à la Habermas. Conflict can be solved and consensus reached through overcoming the natural urge for individual self-affirmation, and through referentiality, that is, understanding alterity in its identity-constitutive role. Yannaras suggests that we should not fear the high dose of relationality of this perspective, because the alternatives available end up, indeed, in onticity and all its discontents discussed above.

This point about onticity brings us to discuss the different understandings of participation that further differentiate the operation of the ordering principle of the *polis* and of the Kantian regulative principle. Yannaras makes us notice that there is in Western thought a consistent reliance on rationalities that are independent from the dynamics of relations that form life, and which is the point of reference proposed by Yannaras. Thus, he explains that, when the existing thing's identity depends on its participation in Being as cosmic harmony (as with Plato), or in the primordial purity of its existence (Augustine's city of God), or in the reality of the being in itself (as with Kant),[111] the ideal becomes an objective and obligatory given, is turned into a law to which individual understanding must submit, becomes substantively hierarchical and force existents to identify with the model. Hence, no more otherness, but sameness with the model is accepted. An ethics of reason results—a body of rules and laws imposed on life compulsorily to ensure conformity to reason.

This type of participation (participation in an ideal model), conceptualized under the neo-platonist influence of Augustine and Aquinas, is not the kind of horizontal, participation-enabling for existents that Yannaras is searching for. Yannaras contests this Augustinian and Thomist 'metaphysics of participation' and *analogia entis* (analogical being) as conducive, in its reflections on the organization of political life, to hierarchical, subordinating relationships between the universal and the existents. For Yannaras, the proper conditions of possibility for participation in the formation of the universal is to stop thinking in ontic categories, eliminating axiology and apriorism.

From this perspective, if we are to search for a non-oppressive way of using the universal, for a language that would resist instrumental thinking in international law, and would also differ from natural law, allowing participation in freedom, the search for a 'regulative principle of action', in the Kantian manner, is not the answer. Here is Kant himself, attesting to the disciplinary vocation in the way regulative principles operate:

[111] Yannaras, *The Schism*, p. 68.

'The cosmopolitan society is in itself an unreachable idea ... It is only a *regulative principle*, demanding that we yield generously to the cosmopolitan society as the destiny of the human race.... achievement is difficult, because *we cannot expect to reach our goal by free consent of individuals*, but only through *progressive organization* of the citizens of the earth within and toward the species as a system which is united by cosmopolitical bonds'[112] (emphasis mine).

The critique of the regulative principle might be done through Yannaras' noticing of the strategy of the Enlightenment to 'turn away from the ontological problem altogether and focus attention exclusively on the functioning of regulative principles'.[113] This approach transposes the problem of truth from the level of existence to the level of conduct (utilitarian intentionality). Indifference to the ontological clarification of the givens of life attracts, in turn, an absence of interest to distinguish between the real and the imaginary: the contemporary temptation of using universality (of metaphysical, rational or natural origin) as an ideal, a grid against which to measure the current state of affairs.[114]

Hence, the alternative rationale is existential, not deontological: the 'ordering principle' structures the life of the *polis* around the coordination between the individual *logos* and the common *logos* of the citizens. It is an 'achievement' of the people who constitute the *polis*, of the citizens. This means, first, that common *logos* is a dynamically actualized truth, not an objective given to which the individual *logoi* must be subordinated. Second, since it is an achievement, it contains also the possibility of non-achievement, of the probable inability (or even unwillingness) of some of those who participate in the symbiosis to achieve those relations that form the *polis* as a unified and organic reality of life. Every *logos* so identified as universally valid is checked by reason (understood as relationship, communion) by socially verifying to what extent it is shared. Reason only functions to prevent truth from becoming un-truth, autonomous from the dynamics of relations, from being apprehended individually and alienated into an objective given that is only *possessed* individually and not shared in common. This way, truth remains free of any pre-determinations and can be identified with the universal becoming of relations.

This is not a vocabulary reducible to a specific model of governance (Yannaras is reluctant to propose ready-made recipes), but an attitude expressing an ethos. The *polis* invoked is not a finished model; it dynamically actualizes itself constantly. At the same time, the idea of the never finishing model forged in communion is an invitation for every human person to participate, to leave her mark on the constitution of the model/of the universal. Such features, I think, make this ethos relevant for the search in international law of a vocabulary, alternative to natural law, capable of expressing our ethical commitments without reducing them to various

[112] Kant, *Anthropology from a Pragmatic Point of View* (The Hague: Martinus Nijhoff, 1974), pp. 249–51, cited in David Harvey, *Cosmopolitanism and the Geographies of Freedom*, p. 23.

[113] Yannaras, *The Schism*, p. 155.

[114] See Martti Koskenniemi, 'The Fate of Public International Law: Between Technique and Politics', in *The Politics of International Law* (Oxford: Hart Publishing, 2011), pp. 360–1.

techniques of governance.[115] It also promptly politicizes international law against technicalization and neutralization by some anonymous logics because there is no irrefutable truth, but a common *logos*, which is relational and referential. Every individual participant is essential to the formation of the common *logos*, and this by the mere quality of being a citizen.

From this perspective, the empty form decided upon at Westphalia as the basis of the international community of states appropriately accommodates this spirit: every state (or actor) is an equal member of the society of states—that is, has political standing—and international law has no particular content outside the one decided upon by the members of this community. Hence, there is no polarity between consent (will) and the law's normative quality, and the danger of instrumentalism is cast aside, *so long as* the result of social interaction is checked by reason, understood as relationality, the relationship of communion. The ethical, then, is the way in which the person relates to the existential adventure of her freedom, translatable into a project of unconditional acceptance of the cultural and political self-identity of all participants to international life.

Bibliography

Ahrweiler, Hélène. *L'Idéologie Politique de l'Empire Byzantin* (Paris: Presses Universitaires de France, 1975).

Alford, William P. 'Exporting the Pursuit of Happiness'. *Harvard Law Review* 113 (2000): p. 1677.

Angie, Anthony. *Imperialism, Sovereignty and the Making of International Law* (Cambridge: Cambridge University Press, 2004).

Archibugi, Daniele. *Debating Cosmopolitics* (London: Verso, 2003).

Archibugi, Daniele and David Held. *Cosmopolitan Democracy: An Agenda for a New World Order* (Cambridge: Polity, 1995).

Berlin, Isaiah. 'Two Concepts of Liberty'. In *Liberty*, edited by Henry Hardy (Oxford: Oxford University Press, 2013).

von Bogdandy, Armin and Sergio Dellavalle. 'Universalism and Particularism as Paradigms of International Law'. IILJ Working Paper no. 3 (2008) (History and Theory of International Law Series).

Bradshaw, David. *Aristotle East and West. Metaphysics and the Division of Christendom* (Cambridge: Cambridge University Press, 2004).

Bin, Roberto, 'Order and Disorder. Legal Adjudication and Quantum Epistemology'. Straus Institute Working Paper no. 02 (2012).

Cary, Phillip. *Augustine's Invention of the Inner Self: The Legacy of a Christian Platonist* (New York: Oxford University Press, 2000).

[115] On the need to search for a better vocabulary in international law, see 'The Lauterpacht Tradition and its Successors: Towards Theory?: Discussion', in *The Function of Law in the International Community: An Anniversary Symposium*, edited by James Crawford and Margaret Young (2008), Proceedings of the 25th Anniversary Conference of the Lauterpacht Center for International Law. Available at http://www.lcil.cam.ac.uk/25th_anniversary/book.php.

Crawford, James and Margaret Young, eds. 'The Lauterpacht Tradition and its Successors: Towards Theory?: Discussion'. In *The Function of Law in the International Community: An Anniversary Symposium*. Proceedings of the 25th Anniversary Conference of the Lauterpacht Center for International Law (2008). Available at http://www.lcil.cam.ac.uk/25th_anniversary/book.php.

Derrida, Jacques. 'Comment ne pas Parler: Dénégations'. In *Psyché: Inventions de l'autre* (Paris: Galilée, 1987).

Diamantides, Marinos. 'Constitutional Theory and its Limits—Reflections on Comparative Political Theologies'. *Law, Culture and the Humanities* 11, no. 1 (2012): pp. 4, 27. doi: 10.1177/1743872112437683.

Dupuy, Pierre. 'L'Unité de l'ordre juridique international. Cours général de droit international public'. In *Recueil des Cours de l'Académie de Droit International* (Brill/Nijhoff, Leiden/Boston, 2002): p. 297.

Falk, Richard. *Law in an Emerging Global Village: A Post-Westphalian Perspective* (Ardsley: Transnational Publishers, 1998).

Fassbender, Bardo. 'The United Nations Charter as a Constitution of the International Community'. *Columbia Journal of Transnational Law* 36 (1998): p. 530.

Fischer-Lescano, Andreas and Gunter Teubner. 'Regime-Collisions: The Vain Search for Legal Unity in the Fragmentation of Global Law'. *Michigan Journal of International Law* 25 (2004): p. 999.

Foucault, Michel. *Lectures at the Collège de France 1975–1976* (London: Allen Lane/Penguin, 2003).

Habermas, Jürgen. 'The Crisis of the European Union in the Light of a Constitutionalisation of International Law'. *European Journal of International Law* 23, no. 2 (2012): p. 335.

Habermas, Jürgen. 'The Constitutionalization of International Law and the Legitimation Problems of a Constitution for World Society'. *Constellations* 15, no. 4 (2008): p. 444.

Habermas, Jürgen. *The Postnational Constellation: Political Essays* (Cambridge: Polity, 2001).

Hardt, Michael and Antonio Negri. *Empire* (Cambridge, MA: Harvard University Press, 2000).

Harvey, David. *Cosmopolitanism and the Geographies of Freedom* (New York: Columbia University Press, 2009).

Heidegger, Martin. *Nietzsche*, vol. 4 'Nihilism', translated by Frank A. Capuzzi, edited by David Farell Krell (San Francisco: Harper, 1996).

Heidegger, Martin. *Basic Writings*, edited by David Farell Krell (San Francisco: Harper, 1992).

Heidegger, Martin. *Identity and Difference*, translated by Joan Stambaugh (New York, Evanston and London: Harper & Row Publishers, 1969).

Kant, Immanuel. *Anthropology from a Pragmatic Point of View* (The Hague: Martinus Nijhoff, 1974).

Kant, Immanuel. *Groundwork for the Metaphysics of Morals*, edited and translated by Allen W. Wood (New Haven and London: Yale University Press, 2002).

Kennedy, David 'Challenging Expert Rule: The Politics of Global Governance'. Sydney Journal of International Law 27 (2005): p. 11.

Kennedy, David. 'Putting the Politics Back in International Politics'. *The Finnish Yearbook of International Law* IX (1998): p. 17.

Klabbers, Jan. 'Constitutionalism Lite?'. *International Organisations Law Review* 1 (2004): p. 31.

Klabbers, Jan. 'Towards a Culture of Formalism? Martti Koskenniemi and the Virtues'. *Temple International and Comparative Law Journal* 27, no. 2 (2013): p. 415.

Klabbers, Jan, Anne Peters, and Geir Ulfstein. *The Constitutionalization of International Law* (Oxford: Oxford University Press, 2009).

Koskenniemi, Martti. 'Constitutionalism as Mindset: Reflections on Kantian Themes About International Law and Globalization'. *Theoretical Inquiries In Law* 8 (2007): p. 9.

Koskenniemi, Martti. 'Declaratory Legislation. Towards a Genealogy of Neoliberal Legalism'. In *International Law-Making: Essays in Honor of Jan Klabbers*, edited by Rain Liivoja and Jarna Petman (New York: Routledge, 2014), ch. 2.

Koskenniemi, Martti. *Fragmentation of International Law. Problems caused by the Diversification and Expansion of International law, Report of the Study Group of the International Law Commission.* Finalized by Martti Koskenniemi. A/CN4/L.682, 13 April 2006.

Koskenniemi, Martti. *From Apology to Utopia. The Structure of International Legal Argument* (Cambridge: Cambridge University Press, 2005).

Koskenniemi, Martti. 'International Law and Hegemony: A Reconfiguration'. *Cambridge Review of International Affairs* 17 (2004): p. 197.

Koskenniemi, Martti. *The Politics of International Law* (Oxford: Hart Publishing, 2011).

Laclau, Ernesto. 'Identity and Hegemony: The Role of Universality in the Constitution of Political Logics'. In Judith Butler, Ernesto Laclau and Slavoj Zizek, *Contingency, Hegemony, Universality: Contemporary Dialogues on the Left* (London: Verso, 2000): p. 44.

Louth, Andrew. 'Some Recent Works by Christos Yannaras in Translation'. *Modern Theology* 25, no. 2 (2009): p. 329.

Maduro, Miguel Poiares. 'Courts and Pluralism: Essay on a Theory of Judicial Adjudication in the Context of Legal and Constitutional Pluralism'. In *Ruling the World? Constitutionalism, International Law and Global Governance*, edited by Jeffrey L. Dunoff and Joel P. Trachtman (Cambridge: Cambridge University Press, 2009), ch. 12.

Maduro, Miguel Poiares. 'In Search of a Meaning and not in Search of the Meaning: Judicial Review and the Constitution in Times of Pluralism'. *Wisconsin Law Review* 2 (2013): p. 541.

Marchart, Oliver. *Post-Foundational Political Thought: Political Difference in Nancy, Lefort, Badiou and Laclau* (Edinburgh: Edinburgh University Press, 2007).

Marion, Jean—Luc. *Dieu sans l'être* (Paris: PUF, 1982).

Marion, Jean—Luc. *L'Idole et la distance*, (Paris: Grasset, 1977).

Mehta, Uday Singh. *Liberalism and Empire: A Study in Nineteenth Century British Liberal Thought* (Chicago: University of Chicago Press, 1999).

Milbank, John. *Theology and Social Theory: Beyond Secular Reason*, 2nd edn (Oxford: Blackwell Publishing, 2006).

Mouffe, Chantal. *Agonistics: Thinking the World Politically* (London and New York: Verso, 2013).

Pabst, Adrian. 'Rival Modernities: Theological Theorisations of International Society'. In *Medieval Foundations of International Relations*, edited by William Bain (Routledge, 2017).

Paris, Elena. 'Re-thinking Universalism: Post-foundational Cosmopolitanism in a Relational Key'. In *Re/grounding Cosmopolitanism. Towards a Post-foundational Cosmopolitanism*, edited by Tamara Caraus and Elena Paris (New York: Routledge, 2016).

Schmitt, Carl. *Political Theology—Four Chapters of the Concept of Sovereingty* (Chicago: Chicago University Press, 1996).

Singh, Sahib. 'Koskenniemi's Images of the International Lawyer'. *Leiden Journal of International Law* 29 (2016): p. 699.

Sumares, Manuel. 'Post-Secularity, Orthodoxy and the *Theosis* Factor: Blondel and St. Gregory Palamas'. *Revista Portuguesa de Filosofia* 67 (2011): p. 81.

Teubner, Gunther. *Constitutional Fragments: Societal Constitutionalism and Globalization*, translated by Gareth Norbury (Oxford: Oxford University Press, 2012).

Walker, Neil. 'The Idea of Constitutional Pluralism'. *Modern Law Review* 65 (2002): p. 317.

de Wet, Erika. 'The Emergence of International and Regional Value Systems as a Manifestation of the Emerging International Constitutional Order'. *Leiden Journal of International Law* 19 (2006): p. 611.

de Wet, Erika and André Nollkaemper. 'Review of the Security Council by National Courts'. *German Yearbook of International Law* 45 (2002): p. 166.

Yannaras, Christos. *On the Absence and Unknowability of God: Heidegger and the Areopagite*, edited by Andrew Louth, translated by Haralambos Ventis (London: T&T Clark International, 2005).

Yannaras, Christos. *Postmodern Metaphysics*, translated by Norman Russell (Brookline, MA: Holy Cross Orthodox Press, 2004).

Yannaras, Christos. *Relational Ontology*, translated by Norman Russell (Brookline: Holy Cross Orthodox Press, 2011).

Yannaras, Christos. *The Schism in Philosophy*, translated by Norman Russell (Brookline: Holy Cross Orthodox Press, 2015).

17

The Law of Nations at the Origin of American Law

Paul W. Kahn

In 1815, the United States Supreme Court declared the law of nations to be 'part of the law of the land'.[1] That same year, the Court described the law of nations as resting upon 'the great principles of reason and justice'.[2] Yet, fifteen years later Chief Justice Marshall raised considerable doubt about the justice of the law of nations when he wrote, '[P]ower, war, conquest, give rights, which, after possession, are conceded by the world; and can never be controverted by those on whom they descend.'[3] These incontrovertible rights are a far cry from the self-evident truths of the Declaration of Independence. The self-evidence of the latter rests on justice and dignity for the individual; the self-evidence of the former rests on the use of violence among states. A law of nations grounded in violence and power is not a part of the project of democratic self-authorship expressed by American constitutionalism.

Already in the Marshall Court, then, the relationship of domestic to international law was something of a puzzle. The difficulty—then and now—emerges directly from the two faces of sovereignty: one, a *project* of law creation taken up by a self-governing community; the other, participation in a *system* of law among independent states. The 'reason and justice' of a project are not the same as that of a system. The norms of a project operate as final causes; those of a system as formal causes. A political project requires intentional action: it requires implementation of a design grounded in a theory of justice. In a project, practice follows from theory. A political system, on the other hand, emerges independently of the ends of any particular actors, whether within the system or outside of it. For a system, theory follows from practice. The role of the theorist is to bring to light the principles of order already operating in the system. The paradigm of a system is the market, the order of which is attributed to an 'invisible hand'. The paradigm of a project is the Constitution, the order of which is attributed to the Framers.

[1] *The Nereide*, 9 Cranch 388, 423 (1815).
[2] *Thirty Hogsheads of Sugar v. Boyle*, 9 Cranch 191 (1815).
[3] *Worcester v. Georgia*, 31 U.S. 515, 543 (1832).

Whether the social order should be approached as a project or a system is one way of describing the central debate of modern theory. On this turns the political place of revolution and reform. Similarly, on it turn the great economic debates over market intervention. In both the domains of law and economics, the project/system debate replicates itself at every level of analysis from the origins of order to particular interventions in policy and practice.

The history of American constitutional thought moves between these two models of order: contrast the Founders' *project* of constitutional construction with late nineteenth-century appeals to a *system* of common law constitutionalism.[4] In the nineteenth century, appeals to system were likely to be from conservatives. Today, the political valence of these terms has inverted with conservative constitutional theorists arguing for adherence to the exact terms of the Founders' project and their liberal opponents arguing for a system of organic growth of constitutional norms. The system/project distinction is more basic than the political purposes for which it can be used.

The law of nations moves through the same conceptual antithesis, although in a different time frame. International law cannot really be imagined as a project until the twentieth century, with the rise of transnational institutions capable of having a law-making project. The writers on international law in the seventeenth and eighteenth centuries thought they were describing a system.

The Marshall Court provides an early case study for considering how these competing ideas of law—project or system—were understood in relation to each other. In the post-Founding era, the American legal imaginary was shaped primarily by the idea of project. To ask how the Court understood the law of nations, then, is to ask how project related to system. What we find is not a series of compromises forced upon a democratic, law-making project by the reality of violence among states; rather, we find a sort of modern theodicy. The law of nations provides the ground for morally problematic hierarchies that domestic law perpetuates as if they were natural facts about the world. This should not be entirely surprising, since the idea of system had long served as a source for theodicy. There was a need for theodicy to explain the puzzling appearance of evil within God's project of creation.[5] The answer was that creation was system, as well as project. This same relationship reappears in the understanding of the modern state.

[4] See Paul W. Kahn, *Legitimacy and History: Self-Government in American Constitutional Theory* (New Haven: Yale University Press, 1992).

[5] Susan Neiman discusses various philosophical systems devised to advance the project of solving the problem of evil. See Susan Neiman, *Evil in Modern Thought: An Alternative History of Philosophy* (Princeton: Princeton University Press, 2002). For example, 'Enlightened theists like Leibniz and Pope had standard ways of coping with catastrophe. They argued that a world which works according to general natural law is far better than a world requiring God's intervention in special cases. The latter would be ad hoc and chaotic, unbefitting the dignity of a majestic and omnicompetent sovereign. Physical accidents that sometimes occur are the unfortunate side effects of those general laws which give the world order and allow us to orient ourselves in it. To rail against their Author because of occasional negative consequences would be as stupid, and ungrateful, as to rail against a monarch whose great system of law contains an occasional weakness.' Neiman, *Evil in Modern Thought*, p. 38.

Project and System

In his eloquent Second Inaugural Address, President Obama describes America as a journey that will remain incomplete until 'these words, these rights, these values—of Life, and Liberty, and the Pursuit of Happiness—[are] real for every American'.[6] The President is appealing to the earliest understanding of the meaning of the nation: America is a project. That politics can or should be a project is hardly self-evident.[7] Yet, on the opening page of the Federalist Papers, we find the idea of the political project posed as the question of modernity itself: 'it seems to have been reserved to the people of this country … to decide the important question, whether societies of men are really capable of establishing good government from reflection and choice … '.[8]

A modern political practice is one in which theory informs actions. Thus, revolutionaries don't want only to arouse a crowd; they want to write books. The Republic of Letters and the political republic are intersecting communities.[9] *The Federalist Papers* is itself an important work in political theory, published in newspapers as part of a democratic campaign of persuasion in support of the new Constitution. The theoretical ambition of the Founders remains startling. Adams and Madison studied classical political theory before attempting to draft a modern constitution; Hamilton studied economic theory while acting as Washington's aide during the Revolution; Jefferson's library formed the core of our national library.

Modern revolution and modern political theory were two sides of a single, Enlightenment project. Kant famously captured the leading thought of the era when he responded to the question, 'what is Enlightenment?' by arguing that it is to take responsibility for the self in thought and action.[10] Notably, Kant imagined morality as a kind of self-legislation, a project of giving law to the self. This idea of responsibility is no less true of the state: revolution is the moment of taking

[6] Barack Obama, 'Inaugural Address by President Barack Obama', 21 January 2013, http://www.whitehouse.gov/the-press-office/2013/01/21/inaugural-address-president-barack-obama.

[7] Compare Edmund Burke's anti-project views of politics in *Reflections on the Revolution in France* (London: Penguin Books, 1968), p. 152: 'It is with infinite caution that any man ought to venture upon pulling down an edifice which has answered in any tolerable degree for ages the common purposes of society, or on building it up again, without having models and patterns of approved utility before his eyes.'

[8] Alexander Hamilton, 'The Federalist No. 1', in Alexander Hamilton, James Madison, and John Jay, *The Federalist*, edited by J. R. Pole (Indianapolis: Hackett Publishing Company, 2005), p. 1.

[9] The connection between law and literature in the years from the Revolution to the Civil War is discussed by Robert A. Ferguson, *Law and Letters in American Culture* (Cambridge, Mass.: Harvard University Press, 1984). For a modern version of this connection, see Timothy Garton Ash, 'From the Lighthouse: The World and the NYR After Fifty Years', *The New York Review of Books*, 7 November 2013, http://www.nybooks.com/articles/archives/2013/nov/07/lighthouse-world-and-nyr-after-fifty-years/, describing the *New York Review* as a 'journal at the frontier between literature and politics' and 'a contemporary equivalent of the Enlightenment's "republic of letters"'.

[10] Immanuel Kant, 'An Answer to the Question: What is Enlightenment?', in *Perpetual Peace, and Other Essays on Political and Moral Practice*, edited and translated by Ted Humphrey (Indianapolis: Hackett Publishing Company, 1983), pp. 41–8.

responsibility—ending what Kant called 'superstitious belief'—while constitution is the moment of self-legislation directed by reason.[11] Social contract theories flourish precisely because they are efforts to imagine politics as a project in which choice is driven wholly by reflection.[12] Because politics is to be informed by theory, it gains a universal aspect. Thus, Thomas Paine can easily take his political theorizing from the American to the French Revolution—as can Thomas Jefferson. More importantly, a project always contains a perfectionist element: to take up political responsibility is to move towards more perfect realization of a theoretical ideal. Reform is built into a political project at its very foundation.[13]

The modernism of the Founders is remarkable given the prominent role of religious exiles in the colonial origins of the nation. If we mean by 'a project' a practice informed by a discipline of reason, these early religious exiles were not engaged in a project at all. They crossed the ocean to preserve a revealed truth, not to invent political order under the guidance of theory. The earliest statement of what they were up to, The Mayflower Compact, lists 'the Glory of God, Advancement of the Christian Faith, and the Honour of our King and Country' as their ends.[14] Their proof texts were not works of modern science—natural and political—but the Old and New Testaments. They do 'covenant and combine' to form a 'civil Body Politick', but do so as the ancient Israelites did, 'in the presence of God'.[15] They do not think they are solving a Hobbesian problem of social choice; they are not acting to save themselves from nature, but to save their souls for God.

America has always offered refuge to religious exiles who want nothing to do with a scientific modernity. They object to the very idea that the community can or should be the object of a project. For them, political perfectionism borders on sin. By the end of the eighteenth century, however, the political centre of gravity had moved decisively in the direction of science over faith, commerce over church. This is all the more remarkable given that the Second Great Awakening—a Protestant revival movement—starts to sweep the country around 1790 and continues through the first decades of the century. Yet, none of the leading Founders

[11] Immanuel Kant, *Critique of Judgment*, translated by Werner S. Pluhar (Indianapolis: Hackett Publishing Company, 1987), p. 161: 'Liberation from superstition is called *enlightenment*.'

[12] The relation of political theory to political projects is exemplified in Locke's writing of a charter for the Carolinas and Rousseau's writing of a Polish constitution: John Locke, 'The Fundamental Constitutions of Carolina: 1 March 1669,' (accessed 8 April 2014), http://avalon.law.yale.edu/17th_century/nc05.asp; Jean-Jacques Rousseau, 'Considerations on the Government of Poland', in *Rousseau: The Social Contract and Other Later Political Writings*, edited and translated by Victor Gourevitch (Cambridge: Cambridge University Press), pp. 177–260.

[13] Thus, not surprisingly one explicit goal of the Constitution is 'to form a more perfect Union'. This movement towards perfect realization of a theoretical ideal also underlies various arguments for judicial review. John Hart Ely noted that 'the prevailing academic line has held for some time that the Supreme Court should give content to the Constitution's open-ended provisions by identifying those values that are, by one formula or another, truly important or fundamental'. John Hart Ely, *Democracy and Distrust: A Theory of Judicial Review* (Cambridge, Mass.: Harvard University Press, 1980), p. 43.

[14] 'The Mayflower Compact', in *Documents of American History*, edited by Henry Steele Commager, 5th edn (New York: Appleton-Century-Crofts, 1958), p. 15.

[15] 'The Mayflower Compact', pp. 15–16.

is anchored in a traditional community of religious belief.[16] Religion has already become a sort of supplement to the modern project of politics and commerce. A project no longer for the honour of the king, no longer seems for the glory of God. Religion, of course, remains a vital presence, but politics and religion have, by the end of the eighteenth century, come to occupy separate spheres.

Many of the Founders are lawyers. Indeed, this is what makes them of special interest to us. The American project is uniquely bound up with law, but so too is modernity. Modern legal academics still labour under the idea of a project when they expect scholarship to speak to the reform of law.[17] Law is imagined as the point at which theory can inform practice. The centrality of the project to modernity creates the irony of democracies embodying a deep scepticism towards populist movements. The people always threaten to abandon reflection and thus the perfectionist character of the project.[18]

The project is a distinctive form of what Carl Schmitt described as the political-theological imagination. Of course, in some sense the idea of a project is as old as the classical idea of a *techné*. Only with modernity, however, does it become possible to imagine that an entire society could make itself a project directed by theory.[19] The democratic, political project of self-formation imagines the community as capable of constructing itself as a people under law. That project always calls for recommitment—it must continue to be *our* project—because it is set against a secularized idea of sin: the pursuit of private interests over the public good, the preference for factions over the collective whole. A failure to choose the order of reason does not leave us with the premodern idea of natural law, but rather with an unrealized ideal—a modern, political pathology.

The project is not just the dominant political idea of the era: Benjamin Franklin famously describes the way in which he made himself a project in his *Autobiography*. Yet, already the theoretical imagination of that era was beginning to move in the direction of a different archetypal form: the system. In the same year as the Declaration of Independence, Adam Smith publishes *The Wealth of Nations*, in which he theorizes the economy as a system. In this system, the pursuit of what might appear to be private vices from the point of view of a public project will

[16] Only one practising minister, John Witherspoon of New Jersey, signed the Declaration of Independence—and he is better known as the modernizing President of what was to become Princeton University. See Jeffry [sic] Hays Morrison, 'John Witherspoon and "The Public Interest of Religion"', *Journal of Church and State* 41 (1999): pp. 551–73.

[17] See Paul W. Kahn, *The Cultural Study of Law: Reconstructing Legal Scholarship* (Chicago: University of Chicago Press, 1999), pp. 7–18.

[18] The unreasonableness of the people is a trope of conservative politics. Such an argument, for example, animated the jurisprudence of the Fuller Court. See Owen M. Fiss, *Troubled Beginnings of the Modern State, 1888–1910*, vol. 8, Oliver Wendell Holmes Devise History of the Supreme Court of the United States (New York: Macmillan, 1993). Of course, this concern is much older than the Fuller Court; Thucydides emphasizes the short-sightedness and the failures of popular politics and popular leaders in his *Histories*.

[19] See Benedict Anderson, *Imagined Communities: Reflections on the Origin and Spread of Nationalism*, rev. and extended edn (London/New York: Verso, 1991). Compare Plato's idea of rule by a philosopher-king. Plato, *Republic*, translated by G. M. A. Grube, revised by C. D. C. Reeve, 2nd edn (Indianapolis: Hackett Publishing Company, 1992), I.342e, IV.428b–429a.

nevertheless produce public good.[20] A system creates order spontaneously, that is, independently of the deliberate decisions of those within the system. Order emerges from the reciprocal relationship between parts and whole. A market works as if by an 'invisible hand', in marked contrast to the visible hands of a political project. Accordingly, a system does not necessarily become more reasonable as the actors within it act on their own idea of the reason of the whole. The reasonable order of a market, for example, depends on each individual pursuing his or her own interests, not on their application of a theory.

System too is an ancient idea, present as soon as there was reflection on organic form.[21] Its modern genealogy, however, is in Christian theodicies. The idea of creation as a divine project could not easily explain the occurrence of evil. Theodicies turned to an idea of system in which no part could be understood independently of the others. Evil, accordingly, was a function of our limited vision: we could not see the systemic reason for that which appeared to us as evil. Absent a God's eye view of the whole, we could not see the true character of what was undoubtedly 'the best of all possible worlds'.[22]

When the Founders spoke of creating a political order of balanced powers in which ambition would be balanced against ambition, the two models were at a point of intersection: The *project* was to create a *system*. Political theory throughout the modern era moves endlessly between these poles of project and system. This tension continues in the Supreme Court's self-understanding. Does the Court exercise reason to advance the perfection of the project?[23] Or, is the Court a kind of outside regulator, intervening only to correct pathologies that keep the system from working on its own?[24]

[20] Adam Smith, *The Wealth of Nations, Books IV–V*, edited by Andrew Skinner (London: Penguin Books, 1999), p. 32: 'By pursuing his own interest [a private individual] frequently promotes that of the society more effectually than when he really intends to promote it. I have never known much good done by those who affected to trade for the public good.'

[21] See, for example, Aristotle, *On the Parts of Animals*, edited and translated by James G. Lennox (Oxford: Oxford University Press, 2002), I.645a20–25: '[O]ne should approach research about each of the animals without disgust, since in every one there is something natural and good. For what is not haphazard but rather for the sake of something is in fact present most of all in the works of nature; the end for the sake of which each animal has been constituted or comes to be takes the place of the good.' See also Immanuel Kant, *Critique of Judgment*, in which teleology of nature is linked to both systemic order and organic form.

[22] Gottfried Wilhelm Leibniz, 'The Principles of Nature and of Grace, Based on Reason (1714)', in *G.W. Leibniz: Philosophical Papers and Letters*, edited and translated by Leroy E. Loemker, 2nd edn (Dordrecht: Reidel, 1969), pp. 636–42, at 639: 'It follows from the supreme perfection of God that he has chosen the best possible plan in producing the universe, a plan which combines the greatest variety together with the greatest order; with situation, place, and time arranged in the best way possible; with the greatest effect produced by the simplest means; with the most power, the most knowledge, the greatest happiness and goodness in created things which the universe could allow. For as all possible things have a claim to existence in God's understanding in proportion to their perfections, the result of all these claims must be the most perfect actual world which is possible. Without this it would be impossible to give a reason why things have gone as they have rather than otherwise.' Voltaire would famously mock this line of argument in *Candide*, in the character of Pangloss.

[23] Things get even more confused when this continuation of the project idea is labelled 'living constitutionalism'—an organic, and thus systemic, reference.

[24] These views roughly correlate with substantive and procedural approaches to judicial review.

Project and system are both secularized theological concepts.[25] The *Old Testament* is largely an account of God's project of creation. The *New Testament* is largely an account of creation as a system.[26] Secularization continues to require negotiation of the dual perspectives of project and system in multiple domains, most importantly today in understanding the relationship of politics to markets. In early American legal practice, the site of tension is not yet politics versus economy, but rather that of domestic law versus the law of nations. The project is represented in constitution-making, while the law of nations is received as a system. Accordingly, to examine the relationship between the domestic and the international legal orders at the beginning of the nineteenth century is to ask how project relates to system. How does the political project of American constitutionalism relate to the system of the law of nations?

A Modern Theodicy

While the early constitutional period raised questions in both directions across the project–system divide, particularly interesting is the way in which the domestic project of law drew upon the resource of the systemic character of the law of nations. The law of nations that comes into view is not a space of Christian values (an anticipation of human rights) but of realist politics. For the Marshall Court, the law of nations offered the possibility of legitimation of moral failure in the national project of law-making. It offered a new form of theodicy. The global order of the law of nations became a site upon which to project the nation's sins, even as it offered a kind of legitimation.[27]

We can quickly get to the heart of the matter by looking to some shared beliefs of two great antagonists of the early Republic: Chief Justice John Marshall and President Thomas Jefferson. Their disagreement is usually framed as one between a nation-centred and a state-centred view of the constitutional order. Framed this way, their family dispute—they were cousins—becomes a precursor of the American civil war. There is certainly some truth in this: the origins of the Civil War do go all the way back. Yet, they did not think they were on the path to war. Rather, they saw themselves as equal participants in the same political project.

Both were men of the Enlightenment; both were lawyers; both were property owners and slave holders from Virginia. Neither believed in the divinity of Jesus Christ; neither was a member of any denomination. Marshall participated in the church as a social organization, invested in its architecture, and brought his family

[25] Their competition suggests that Schmitt was wrong in thinking that every era has one dominant archetype. See Carl Schmitt, *Political Theology: Four Chapters on the Concept of Sovereignty*, translated by George Schwab (Chicago: University of Chicago Press 1985), pp. 45–7.

[26] For example, the redemptive character of Christ's sacrifice, as well as the Church as the body of Christ, are ideas that only have meaning from a system point of view.

[27] Something similar will happen later with Social Darwinist accounts of system providing the legitimating 'facts' for normative difference.

there. Jefferson had even less involvement with any church. He went so far as to put together his own version of the Bible: one in which he redacted all the material about miracles and revelation, while keeping the ethical narratives. Ethics was serious business; faith in the divine was not.[28]

The Founders understood the usefulness of organized religion to their own project, but expected no help from a guiding Providence. They believed they were on their own. Excluding religion from politics, however, made the moral content of political practice more, not less, of an issue. A politics that escapes from the control of the church has constantly before itself questions of the public good. Conceiving of politics as a project, participants will judge themselves. Governments are made well or poorly as they achieve or fail to achieve those ends set out in the Constitution: justice, tranquillity, defence, and the general welfare.[29] A government judged to be performing poorly can be removed or restructured. To those who imagine politics as a project, constitution is always limited by the possibility of revolution.

Yet, the American political project hardly began in a state of innocence. Both Jefferson and Marshall owned slaves. That ownership interest rather notoriously survived a revolution proclaimed in the name of equality.[30] Both men knew perfectly well that slavery was deeply immoral. Jefferson famously said so in his *Notes on the State of Virginia*:

> Indeed I tremble for my country when I reflect that God is just: that his justice cannot sleep for ever: that considering numbers, nature and natural means only, a revolution of the

[28] See, for example, Thomas Jefferson, 'Letter to John Adams', 11 April 1823, in *Jefferson's Extracts from the Gospels: 'The Philosophy of Jesus'* and *'The Life and Morals of Jesus'*, edited by Dickinson W. Adams and Ruth W. Lester (Princeton: Princeton University Press, 1983), pp. 412–13: 'The truth is that the greatest enemies to the doctrines of Jesus are those calling themselves the expositors of them, who have perverted them for the structure of a system of fancy absolutely incomprehensible, and without any foundation in his genuine words. And the day will come when the mystical generation of Jesus, by the supreme being as his father in the womb of a virgin will be classed with the fable of the generation of Minerva in the brain of Jupiter. But we may hope that the dawn of reason and freedom of thought in these United States will do away all this artificial scaffolding, and restore to us the primitive and genuine doctrines of this the most venerated reformer of human errors.' Compare, however, 'Washington's Farewell Address', 17 September 1796, in *Documents of American History*, edited by Henry Steele Commager, 5th edn (New York: Appleton-Century-Crofts, 1958), pp. 169–75, at 173: '[L]et us with caution indulge the supposition that morality can be maintained without religion. Whatever may be conceded to the influence of refined education on minds of peculiar structure, reason and experience both forbid us to expect that national morality can prevail in exclusion of religious principle.'

[29] US Constitution, Preamble: 'We the People of the United States, in Order to form a more perfect Union, establish Justice, insure domestic Tranquility, provide for the common defence, promote the general Welfare, and secure the Blessings of Liberty to ourselves and our Posterity, do ordain and establish this Constitution for the United States of America.'

[30] In a 1775 pamphlet, for example, Samuel Johnson notes: 'We are told, that the subjection of Americans may tend to the diminution of our own liberties; an event, which none but very perspicacious politicians are able to foresee. If slavery be thus fatally contagious, how is it that we hear the loudest yelps for liberty among the drivers of negroes?' Samuel Johnson, 'Taxation No Tyranny: An Answer to the Resolutions and Address of the American Congress', in *Political Writings*, vol. 10, The Works of Samuel Johnson, edited by Donald J. Greene (New Haven: Yale University Press, 1977), p. 454.

> wheel of fortune, an exchange of situation, is among possible events ... The Almighty has no attribute which can take sides with us in such a contest.... I think a change already perceptible, since the origin of the present revolution. The spirit of the master is abating, that of the slave rising from the dust, his condition mollifying, the way I hope preparing, under the auspices of heaven, for a total emancipation, and that this is disposed, in the order of events, to be with the consent of the masters, rather than by their extirpation.[31]

We should take the references to the Almighty as merely rhetorical, but the claims of justice and the fear of violence are very real. Marshall said no less: '[E]very man has a natural right to the fruits of his own labour ... and no other person can rightfully deprive him of those fruits, and appropriate them against his will ...'[32] Still, neither Jefferson nor Marshall was able to use his public power to do anything other than to perpetuate slavery, although both believed that a state that relies on popular consent to establish unjust law is failing in the project of modernity.[33]

The dispute over slavery was so difficult because legally the slave was property. Marshall identified the legal conundrum of slavery as follows: 'claims in which the sacred rights of liberty and property come in conflict with each other'.[34] This was not an even match. While revolution may grant priority to liberty, law is a system for the protection of private property. This was not just a matter of interest, although the interests were very substantial. More fundamentally, to give up natural liberty was to recognize a legal right to property. They were two sides of a single act of coming out of the state of nature.

The Founders, however, had no theory of just entitlements, which would have required connecting claims of property to the conditions of liberty. Just the opposite: they believed the origins of property—and thus of law—lay in violence. Jefferson's imagined slave revolt would be the origin of a new regime of property—perhaps inversely related to the present regime. Property rights represented the end of liberty in the double sense of the word 'end'. Existing property rights blur the boundary between claims of liberty and accusations of injustice. Thus, the problem of the slave.[35] Judicial review had a critical role here: the courts will protect 'vested rights'—paradigmatically property.[36]

[31] Thomas Jefferson, *Notes on the State of Virginia*, edited by William Peden (Chapel Hill and London: University of North Carolina Press, 2006), p. 163.

[32] *The Antelope*, 23 U.S. (10 Wheaton) 66, 120 (1825).

[33] Lincoln's Second Inaugural is at the end of this line of thought. He urges us to see God's justice in the suffering of both sides in the Civil War: 'every drop of blood drawn with the lash shall be paid by another drawn by the sword.' Abraham Lincoln, 'Second Inaugural Address', in *Documents of American History*, edited by Henry Steele Commager, 5th edn (New York: Appleton-Century-Crofts, 1958), p. 443.

[34] *The Antelope*, 23 U.S. at 114. Of course, the sacred right of property does not make it into the Declaration of Independence.

[35] We still see this in arguments about inheritance tax.

[36] See *Marbury v. Madison*, 1 Cranch 137, 163 (1803) ('The government of the United States has been emphatically termed a government of laws, and not of men. It will certainly cease to deserve this high appellation, if the laws furnish no remedy for the violation of a vested legal right.'), 167 ('The question whether a right has vested or not, is, in its nature, judicial, and must be tried by the judicial authority.').

In this new secular project, the place of violence has moved from an imagined end of time—the problem of eschatology—to the beginning of history—the problem of the origin of property. A legal regime of property stands in opposition to Christian ideas of charity, poverty, and, more deeply still, the mystical corpus. Law represents the material corpus, which will have to seek a new reconciliation with faith. That reconciliation will occur later in the century as organized religion comes to have a prominent political presence. This will be a church thoroughly co-opted by the legal regime of property.

This constellation of ideas explains why property is missing from the Declaration of Independence. It speaks of the equality of all men, who are 'endowed by their creator with certain unalienable Rights ... among these are Life, Liberty and the pursuit of Happiness'. Where is property? Locke had included property in his trilogy of natural rights.[37] Property does appear at the very end of the document, where the signers pledge to each other their lives, fortunes, and honour. Property is put at risk in the revolutionary act. One cannot overthrow law without undermining property.[38]

Property has no place in a document that is essentially a declaration of war. As between those at war, property claims fail. In this respect, war is a return to a state of nature. This takes a quite literal form: enemy property—private and public—can be seized or destroyed. Similarly, domestic property can be taken for the war effort. Property is a legal relationship, requiring reciprocal recognition within a stable community. If property only begins with peace, it is nevertheless grounded in the violence of war. Property is inevitably victors' justice. This is true of the territorial claims of the sovereign—conceived as property won at war. It is true as well of private property claims that have their origins in those same acts of violence. This begins with a soldier's traditional legal right to booty, but extends to slavery. Thus, the Creator cannot endow men with property because we are created as individuals in a state of nature, not as citizens living under the rule of law.

This view of the origin of property in violence is distinctly not Lockean. Instead, it reflects something like Hobbes's views. Hobbes famously wrote that in the state of nature everyone has an equal right to everything—including the body of the other. Locke grounded property in the body proper, but Hobbes had seen that even the body fails as a barrier to violence.[39] Property must wait for law, and there is no law apart from the sovereign power to enforce duties. 'Propriety [property], being necessary to peace, depending on sovereign power, is the act of that power

[37] John Locke, *Second Treatise of Government*, edited by C. B. Macpherson (Indianapolis: Hackett Publishing Company, 1980), p. 46 (§ 86): 'Man being born, as has been proved, with a title to perfect freedom, and an uncontrouled enjoyment of all the rights and privileges of the law of nature, equally with any other man, or number of men in the world, hath by his nature a power, not only to preserve his property, that is, his life, liberty and estate, against the injuries and attempts of other men; but to judge of, and punish the breaches of that law in others, as he is persuaded the offence deserves.'

[38] Of course, state law remained even as the law of Britain was overturned.

[39] Thomas Hobbes, *Leviathan*, edited by Edwin Curley (Indianapolis: Hackett Publishing Company, 1994), p. 78 (in the state of nature, there is 'no propriety, no dominion, no *mine* and *thine* distinct; but only that to be every man's that he can get; and for so long as he can keep it'.).

…'[40] The Hobbesian sovereign does not act under the Lockean proviso that limits property claims for the sake of equal liberty. There is no property prior to the settlement of the Hobbesian sovereign. While in the abstract, the sovereign can settle however he wants; in fact, a community comes out of the state of nature with claims and expectations that are founded on the successful use of force. Actual sovereigns never begin from scratch.

This understanding of the origins of property gains considerable legal significance when coupled with the traditional view that sovereigns have the right under the law of nations to contest property claims through war.[41] Thus, Grotius wrote that:

> However, by the Law of Nations, not only he that makes War for a just Cause, but every Man in a solemn War acquires the Property of what he takes from the Enemy, and that without Rule or Measure: so that both he and his Assigns are to be defended in Possession of them by all Nations, which, as to the external Effects of it, may be called the Rights of Property.[42]

A century later, Vattel writes that 'a just war is a legitimate means of acquiring property according to natural law'.[43] Justice here is not acting as an objective limit on war, since each sovereign decides for itself the justice of its cause. Putting the theoretical and the legal points together, we can say that domestic law stands on the achievements of past violence, just as it is always threatened by future violence. The law of nations is the systemic order that emerges spontaneously from states in nature. Its function is to mediate between the violent chaos of the state of nature and the political project of domestic law.

The Revolution is hardly the first act of political violence upon which the colonies rely. These communities are the inheritors of a long tradition of violence against Native Americans, against slaves, and against competing European colonial claims. The Declaration of Independence stands in this tradition when it puts off property claims as long as war continues. Property is the result of, not the condition for, the 'natural right' to pursue happiness through violence. Law is the expression of public happiness obtained; property is its reified form. For Americans, the pursuit began not with the violent act of dispossession of the British from the colonies, but of the indigenous communities. It continued daily in the violent possession

[40] Ibid., p. 114. See also p. 80 ('[B]ecause the condition of man … is a condition of war of everyone against everyone … it followeth that in such a condition every man has a right to everything, even to one another's body.'); p. 89 ('Therefore before the names of just and unjust can have place, there must be some coercive power … to make good that propriety which by mutual contract men acquire, in recompense of the universal right they abandon; and such power there is none before the erection of a commonwealth.').

[41] See James Q. Whitman, *The Verdict of Battle: The Law of Victory and the Making of Modern War* (Cambridge, Mass.: Harvard University Press, 2012).

[42] Hugo Grotius, *The Rights of War and Peace*, edited by Richard Tuck, translated by Jean Barbeyrac (Indianapolis: Liberty Fund, 2005), pp. 1316–17 (Book III, Chapter VI.II).

[43] Emer de Vattel, *Le droit des gens, ou, Principes de la loi naturelle, appliqués à la conduit & aux affaires des nations & des souverains*, edited by Paul Pradier-Fodéré (Paris: Guillaumin, 1863), 3:74 (bk. III, chap. 13, §193). The translation quoted here is from Whitman, *Verdict of Battle*, p. 115.

of the slave. It was pursued episodically in wars against the French and then in the Revolution itself. Property is the material embodiment of victory and defeat. Furthermore, that which is obtained by violence must be defended against threats of violence, for the law of nations always permits recourse to violence. A title that cannot be defended is literally worthless. Thus, British predation on American shipping leads to the American declaration of war in 1812, but American predation on Spanish interests leads to the transfer of Florida to the United States.

There is promise as well as threat in this principle. Prior to the Civil War, abolition was associated with compensation precisely because the slave was property. Lincoln, however, can free the slaves under his wartime, emergency power to seize the property of the enemy. If slaves are property, they are subject to seizure without compensation.[44] The only question was what the Confederacy could do about it. The same principle of property as violence achieved is present in the Louisiana Purchase: a sovereign who can declare war in pursuit of territory can also sell his title to a potential adversary.

People have always puzzled about Jefferson's claim of a natural right to liberty in light of his ownership of slaves. He was not, however, forgetting the slave when he wrote of liberty. He was following the logic of the law of nations. Neither was Marshall blind to the moral travesty of slavery, when he ordered slaves returned to their Spanish owners.[45] Both men knew slavery to be immoral and both were sympathetic to the slave's position. They understood slavery to be a consequence of war. 'Slavery,' Marshall wrote, 'has its origin in force;' … 'the victor might enslave the vanquished.'[46] The slave prefers life to death, just as the victor prefers to enslave rather than to kill. While the Christian nations had abandoned this practice of war, Marshall thought that African nations had not. In Africa, 'it is still the law of nations that prisoners are slaves'.[47] The law of nations effectively recognizes this sovereign right to create property in the prisoner. That recognition includes protection of the third party purchaser, just as my earlier quotation from Grotius stated. There is nothing natural or just in this regime, although there is certainly a kind of reason realized in the reciprocal threats and acts of violence among states. Whatever the justice of a domestic legal regime, it does not attach to the origin of entitlements. They do not come from God, but from violence applied and resisted.

The oppressed, of course, have no responsibility to the law that perpetuates their defeat. Slaves have a 'natural right' to rebel, to declare war on their masters. Jefferson recognized this right, even as he feared it. Exactly that right provided the rhetoric of the American Revolution itself: Americans would not be slaves to the

[44] The pre-Civil War understanding of slaves' property status in wartime is discussed in John Fabian Witt, *Lincoln's Code: The Laws of War in American History* (New York: Free Press, 2012), ch. 2. Witt notes a divergence between the older view, according to which property, including slaves, can be seized in wartime without compensation; and a 'humane' and 'enlightened' view, according to which seized property requires compensation. These debates of course resurface during the Civil War. See James Oakes, *Freedom National: The Destruction of Slavery in the United States, 1861–1865* (New York: W.W. Norton, 2013).

[45] *The Antelope*, 23 US 66.

[46] Ibid., at 120–1.

[47] Ibid., at 120–1.

British.[48] Conversely, the British legal entitlements in the colonies were only as good as their capacity to defend them. Not surprisingly, the British offered freedom to any slave who would rebel and join the war on their side. The Americans thought this 'uncivilized,' meaning they worried that the slaves would kill their women and children—after all, slavery was hardly respectful of women and children, and slaves had not entered into any convention agreeing to restraint in what is otherwise a state of nature. The Americans thought British behaviour ground for serious complaint, but they did not think that generally slaves had any obligations to their oppressors.

Slavery—real and metaphoric—was not the only place at which a property claim rooted in the law of nations was asked to do what we would consider work beyond its station. Marshall tells a very similar story about American Indians in their relationship to what the law of nations called the rights of discovery and of conquest. In *Johnson v. M'Intosh*, we learn that Indians cannot convey title to their land. They have only a right of occupancy for themselves. There is nothing just or moral in this. Marshall is scornful of what he calls the 'apology' that the Indians received compensation in the form of 'civilization and Christianity'.[49] Indians cannot hold title because they lost their wars to the Europeans. Having been defeated, all that they can rely upon is charity from the victor. As Marshall explains, 'The title by conquest is acquired and maintained by force. The conqueror prescribes its limits.'[50] These are systemic values. The victor has extended to Indians only temporary rights of occupancy. If the Indians forget that they have been defeated, they will be defeated again.

Indian title would require Indian victory. That there has been no such victory is one way of understanding what Marshall means when he describes Indian tribes as 'domestic dependent nations'.[51] The defeated do not get to litigate their claims in court. Marshall knows there is no justice in this, for he knows the tribes to be significant and enduring political communities. Indians, he says, 'maintained their title with as much persevering courage as was ever manifested by any people'.[52] Law is not an abstract domain of natural rights, but only a local equilibrium of a world of violence. The restrictions imposed on Indians 'may be opposed to natural right ... yet, if it be indispensable to that *system* under which the country has been settled ... it may, perhaps, be supported by reason, and certainly cannot be rejected

[48] Numerous primary sources are quoted in Andrew Burstein, *Sentimental Democracy: The Evolution of America's Romantic Self-Image* (New York: Hill and Wang, 1999), pp. 52–82. To provide just a few examples: After the passage of the Stamp Act, colonists held mock funerals for Liberty across the country; one such funeral, in Rhode Island, featured a long oration ending with the moral 'Britannia's Sons despise Slavery, / And dare to be nobly free.' Similarly, following the passage of the Revenue Acts, colonial supporters of a boycott against imported goods argued that the fundamental question at stake in the boycott was 'whether, for the future, we shall have any Property at all, or not—whether we shall be Freemen or Slaves?' George Washington, after the British retreat to Concord, wrote that 'the once happy and peaceful plains of America are either to be drenched in Blood, or inhabited by slaves. Sad alternative! But can a virtuous Man hesitate in his choice?' Burstein, *Sentimental Democracy*, pp. 55–6, 61, 79.

[49] *Johnson v. M'Intosh*, 21 U.S. 543, at 573 (1823).

[50] Ibid., at 586.

[51] *Cherokee Nation v. Georgia*, 30 U.S. 1, 17 (1831).

[52] *Johnson*, 21 U.S. 543 at 586.

by Courts of justice'.[53] The business of the courts is not, or not yet, dignity, but administration of a system of order founded on victory and defeat.

We will be misled if we stick with the formalisms of law, where we frequently find references to land transfer from the Indians through treaties or government purchases.[54] These 'legal' acts operate much like the idea of consent after defeat in Hobbes.[55] Violence is a way of forcing the will. Law does not depend on some measure of a legitimate will as opposed to a coerced will. These Indian treaties occur under conditions of radical asymmetry; they are not opposed to violence, but the result of violence. A negotiated peace always represents the reality of the distribution of violence. That reality has its own order: that of a system.

That Indians have even a right of occupancy remains contingent on political decisions, for charity at war is ultimately a matter of sovereign decision. As we move from Africa, to America, to Europe those principles of charity become more pronounced. The fundamental point of the law of nations remains the same: the arrangement of property rights is a function of the system of sovereign power that rests ultimately on violence. International law extends recognition to the outcome of conflicts of power. For some other nation to have declined to recognize the loss of Indian title, for example, would have been a hostile act against the United States.

European nations at war with each other recognized some property claims of the enemy. They did so because they stood in a relationship of equal, reciprocal threat. Those who cannot subordinate the other are compelled to recognize a kind of equality among themselves. Thus, in the same opinions discussing the displacement of the Indians, Marshall expresses admiration for the European practice of recognizing a legal right of discovery in the New World. This was an agreement among European sovereigns to extend a reciprocal deference to whoever could establish the fact of discovery. The point of the rule was to avoid conflict among themselves. The rule, however, could last only as long as conflict avoidance remained a mutual goal. Often, that was not very long. This aspect of European

[53] Ibid., at 591–2 (emphasis added).

[54] Looking back on the international law of this era, Schmitt writes: 'One could not speak logically of a legal succession in an *imperium*, not even when a European land-appropriator had concluded treaties with indigenous princes or chieftains, and, for whatever motives, considered them to be binding. The land-appropriating state did not need to respect any rights to the soil existing within the appropriated land ...' Carl Schmitt, *Nomos of the Earth in the International Law of the Jus Publicum Europaeum*, translated by G.L. Ulmen (New York: Telos Press, 2003), p. 198.

[55] See Hobbes, *Leviathan*, pp. 130–1: 'Dominion acquired by conquest, or victory in war ... is the dominion of the master over his servant. And this dominion is then acquired to the victor when the vanquished, to avoid the present stroke of death, convenanteth either in express words, or by other sufficient signs of the will, that so long as his life and the liberty of his body is allowed him, the victor shall have the use thereof, at his pleasure. And after such covenant made, the vanquished is a SERVANT, and not before; for by the word *servant* ... is not meant a captive ... but one that, being taken, hath corporal liberty allowed him, and upon promise, not to run away, nor to do violence to his master, is trusted by him. It is not therefore the victory that giveth the right of dominion over the vanquished, but his own covenant. Nor is he obliged because he is conquered ... but because he cometh in, and submitteth to the victor; nor is the victor obliged by an enemy's rendering himself... to spare him for this his yielding to discretion, which obliges not the victor longer, than in his own discretion he shall think fit.'

international law, of course, had no legal claim upon the Indians. They had not agreed to be discovered any more than slaves had agreed to be oppressed.

A law of nations among civilized nations is an effort to prevent descent all the way into the state of nature that is otherwise the condition of nations at war. Without that law, all the world, in terms borrowed from Locke, would be America: a land of oppressed slaves and defeated natives. Civilized nations do agree to limit their reciprocal violence. This gives us one set of rules for war among Europeans and quite another for war against non-Europeans.[56] Americans wanted to be on the right side of this divide.

Where there is a relative equality in the capacity for violence, reciprocal restraint is likely. This is a good description of the sea, where it was traditionally difficult to marshal forces and where commercial shipping often found itself without protection. Trading nations were, for this reason, deeply invested in the law of prize throughout the eighteenth and nineteenth century. This was, from our perspective, a remarkable legal arrangement in which domestic courts regularly applied the law of nations against the violent acts of their own sovereigns. This is only another way of saying that they were giving effect to property claims grounded in violence legitimated by the law of nations. This is all that a 'prize' is. Again, the law of nations offers the means to move from violence to property.

We can read a similar account of the relationship of violence to property in the legal imagining of the pirate. The pirate represents violence without law. He treats the sea literally as if it were the state of nature, which it is always threatening to become. He recognizes no sovereign and, accordingly, no property claims. Unlike the sovereign, the pirate is chronically unable to convert his violence to property. His actions are not theft, but acts of war without settlement. He is the enemy of mankind. At war with everyone, he can be killed by anyone. He is a kind of pathogen in the system.

The move from slavery, to Indians, to trade is meant to suggest a common thread: all reflect a regime of property that rests upon violence. Civilized states might agree to limit their violence towards each other. They do so by extending reciprocal recognition to certain property claims. We should not, however, think that civilized in this usage corresponds to justice. High on the American list of property claims to be given reciprocal recognition was their interest in slaves. So high was it, that it dominated the post-war negotiations of reciprocal compensation right through the administration of John Quincy Adams in the 1820s.[57]

The law of nations gave effect to a fundamental idea: property begins with the power to seize; it continues with the power to hold. To recognize sovereignty is to recognize property claims achieved. This is an 'economy of violence' acting alongside the economy of peace realized in trade. Both economies are systems to which

[56] There is an extended discussion of this point in Schmitt, *Nomos of the Earth*. Schmitt notes the importance of 'amity lines' to 'the bracketing of war achieved by traditional European international law … Beyond the line was an "overseas" zone in which, for want of any legal limits to war, only the law of the stronger applied.' Schmitt, *Nomos of the Earth*, pp. 93–4.

[57] See Witt, *Lincoln's Code*, ch. 2.

the domestic political project must respond and upon which it relies. Domestic law could, in theory, right the injustices of the order of violence: it could free the slaves; it could recognize Native Americans as constituting their own polities. But domestic law is never writing on a clean slate. There are always countervailing claims based on propertied expectations.

Not surprisingly, both Marshall and Jefferson thought that ending slavery required compensation to the property holders. The alternative was civil war. The same problem arose with the Indians when Georgia notoriously refused to carry out even Marshall's limited effort to protect the Cherokee from violent persecution by the state.[58] In American mythology, Jackson is reported to have said 'Marshall made his decision, now let him carry it out.' That too is nothing less than an invitation to civil war.

Domestic law holds slaves and Indians in their place. More dramatically, it holds all of us in our place vis-a-vis the property of others. When we trace property title, we ultimately arrive at a history of injustice, of violence threatened and achieved. A court that administers the law is doing the work of violence by other means. It cannot claim a moral position superior to that of the violence it sustains. It cannot make gentlemen of slave holders. This, we might say, is the cost of civil peace. Victors get the peace they win through violence. Americans are, from the beginning, proud of their rule of law, but this does not relieve them of the fear of a slave revolt or of war with the Indians. These fears flow easily into a fear of a working class revolt one hundred years later. Behind the history of property is always a history of violence.

Conclusion

These early American attitudes suggest that the Founders did not understand the law of nations as part of a Christian, civilizing project either at home or abroad. For Americans, the law of nations is not yet figuring as a device to legitimate expansion abroad. Rather, the importance of this body of law is to address the legitimation problem that attaches to a democratic regime that cannot reconcile its simultaneous commitments to equality and liberty. Equality is an end of the legal project; liberty occupies a system. Later, this double will play itself out in the contrast between the egalitarian project of redistribution and the liberty of the marketplace.

The Founders had an Enlightenment optimism that made it possible for them to take up the modern project of state formation. This was connected to their faith in reason as well as in their own capacity to persuade the people to consent to reasonable governance. Yet, they also knew their project of state construction to be deeply immoral and unchristian in its foundations. The figure who will most exquisitely represent this double legacy of faith and sin is Lincoln, who will try to

58 *Worcester*, 31 US 515.

use violence to achieve a new beginning—a rebirth—with a better balance of liberty and equality.

The Founders do not fear a retributive God, because they don't believe in any sort of an active, intervening God. They do fear the just actions of oppressed peoples. By the latter part of the nineteenth century, Americans are much more likely to speak of themselves as a Christian nation—language adopted even by the Supreme Court.[59] This extends not only to their domestic law, but to their foreign policy which easily moves from a missionary project to a project of empire. By the end of the century, Americans can no longer easily tell the difference between republican ideas of empire, Christian civilization, and commercial interests in trade.[60] What all of these have in common is that they have taken up a systemic perspective. Constitutional law, too, has become a matter of system, not project, by the latter part of the nineteenth century.

The point at which international law enters the legal imagination shifts in response to this new political reality. It is no longer deployed to legitimate the violent origins of the American project, but to justify the extension of American power. This corresponds, I suspect, to a shift in where and how property enters into the ideology of law. As the problem of origins recedes into the deep past, property comes to be seen as a natural right. The state of nature no longer looks like a state of war; rather, it looks like an unregulated market—a natural system.

Property in the account I have given of the founding era is rooted in a narrative of violence. Property is not yet fully free of classical ideas of the private as a privative domain compared to a public life of reason and deliberation. The public pursuit of happiness is not yet aligned with success in commerce. With the development of modern economics—and capitalism—the locus of reason shifts from the internal perspective of the citizen pursuing a public project to the external perspective of the scholar observing a system. The property regime becomes the material face of reason in the market; it is no longer the residue of violence. Public life, in turn, is more likely to be seen as the space for expression of unreasonable interests, for it is viewed as a kind of market without competition. Businessmen become statesmen; politicians become leaders of factions.

These new statesmen tend to think that commerce is the path to perpetual peace, even as they use state violence to extend the reach of commerce. The model of system—the economy—comes to dominate that of the project. The end of law becomes to create the conditions for the success of markets, and otherwise to reject the false ideology of projects. By the end of the century, laissez faire—an idea of system—is dominating American political, economic, and legal thought. This mix of ideas grounds new deployments of international law that will advance the commercial interests of what is simultaneously a Christian nation and a project of civilization. A Christian, commercial republic has forgotten where it has come from. It has forgotten the violence of origins, and the role the law of nations played in legitimating those origins.

[59] *Worcester*, 31 US 515. [60] Consider the figure of Theodore Roosevelt.

Bibliography

Anderson, Benedict. *Imagined Communities: Reflections on the Origin and Spread of Nationalism*, rev. and extended ed. (London and New York: Verso, 1991).
Aristotle. *Metaphysics*, vol. 18. *Aristotle in 23 Volumes*, translated by Hugh Tredennick (Cambridge, Mass.: Harvard University Press, 1935).
Aristotle. *On the Parts of Animals*, edited and translated by James G. Lennox (Oxford: Oxford University Press, 2002).
Burke, Edmund. *Reflections on the Revolution in France* (London: Penguin Books, 1968).
Burstein, Andrew. *Sentimental Democracy: The Evolution of America's Romantic Self-Image* (New York: Hill and Wang, 1999).
Commager, Henry Steele, ed. *Documents of American History*, 5th edn (New York: Appleton-Century-Crofts, 1958).
Ely, John Hart. *Democracy and Distrust: A Theory of Judicial Review* (Cambridge, Mass.: Harvard University Press, 1980).
Ferguson, Robert A. *Law and Letters in American Culture* (Cambridge, Mass.: Harvard University Press, 1984).
Fiss, Owen M. *Troubled Beginnings of the Modern State, 1888–1910*, vol. 8. Oliver Wendell Holmes Devise History of the Supreme Court of the United States (New York: Macmillan, 1993).
Garton Ash, Timothy. 'From the Lighthouse: The World and the NYR After Fifty Years'. *The New York Review of Books*, 7 November 2013. http://www.nybooks.com/articles/archives/2013/nov/07/lighthouse-world-and-nyr-after-fifty-years/.
Grewal, David S. *The Invention of the Economy: The Origins of Economic Thought* (Cambridge, Mass.: Harvard University Press, forthcoming).
Grotius, Hugo. *The Rights of War and Peace*, edited by Richard Tuck, translated by Jean Barbeyrac (Indianapolis: Liberty Fund, 2005).
Hamilton, Alexander, James Madison, and John Jay. *The Federalist*, edited by J. R. Pole (Indianapolis: Hackett Publishing Company, 2005).
Hobbes, Thomas. *Leviathan*, edited by Edwin Curley (Indianapolis: Hackett Publishing Company, 1994).
Jefferson, Thomas. *Jefferson's Extracts from the Gospels: 'The Philosophy of Jesus' and 'The Life and Morals of Jesus'*, edited by Dickinson W. Adams and Ruth W. Lester (Princeton: Princeton University Press, 1983).
Jefferson, Thomas. *Notes on the State of Virginia*, edited by William Peden (Chapel Hill and London: University of North Carolina Press 2006).
Jefferson, Thomas. *The Writings of Thomas Jefferson*, edited by Andrew A. Lipscomb and Albert E. Bergh (Washington, D.C.: Thomas Jefferson Memorial Association of the United States, 1903–1904).
Johnson, Samuel. 'Taxation No Tyranny: An Answer to the Resolutions and Address of the American Congress'. In *Political Writings*, vol. 10. The Works of Samuel Johnson, edited by Donald J. Greene (New Haven: Yale University Press, 1977).
Kahn, Paul W. *The Cultural Study of Law: Reconstructing Legal Scholarship* (Chicago: University of Chicago Press, 1999).
Kahn, Paul W. *Legitimacy and History: Self-Government in American Constitutional Theory* (New Haven: Yale University Press, 1992).
Kahn, Paul W. *Putting Liberalism in Its Place* (Princeton: Princeton University Press, 2008).

Kant, Immanuel. 'An Answer to the Question: What is Enlightenment?'. In *Perpetual Peace, and Other Essays on Political and Moral Practice*, edited and translated by Ted Humphrey (Indianapolis: Hackett Publishing Company, 1983), pp. 41–8.

Kant, Immanuel. *Critique of Judgment*, translated by Werner Pluhar (Indianapolis: Hackett Publishing Company, 1987).

Leibniz, Gottfried Wilhelm. 'The Principles of Nature and of Grace, Based on Reason (1714)'. In *G. W. Leibniz: Philosophical Papers and Letters*, edited and translated by Leroy E. Loemker, 2nd edn (Dordrecht: Reidel, 1969).

Locke, John. *Second Treatise of Government*, edited by C. B. Macpherson (Indianapolis: Hackett Publishing Company, 1980).

Locke, John. 'The Fundamental Constitutions of Carolina: March 1, 1669'. Accessed 8 April 2014. http://avalon.law.yale.edu/17th_century/nc05.asp.

Morrison, Jeffry [sic] Hays. 'John Witherspoon and "The Public Interest of Religion"'. *Journal of Church and State* 41 (1999).

Neiman, Susan. *Evil in Modern Thought: An Alternative History of Philosophy* (Princeton: Princeton University Press, 2002).

Obama, Barack. 'Inaugural Address by President Barack Obama'. January 21 2013. http://www.whitehouse.gov/the-press-office/2013/01/21/inaugural-address-president-barack-obama.

Plato. *Republic*, translated by G. M. A. Grube, revised by C. D. C. Reeve, 2nd edn (Indianapolis: Hackett Publishing Company, 1992).

Rousseau, Jean-Jacques. 'Considerations on the Government of Poland'. In *Rousseau: The Social Contract and Other Later Political Writings*, edited and translated by Victor Gourevitch (Cambridge: Cambridge University Press, 1997).

Schmitt, Carl. *The* Nomos *of the Earth in the International Law of the Jus Publicum Europaeum*, translated by G. L. Ulmen (New York: Telos Press, 2003).

Smith, Adam. *The Wealth of Nations*, Books IV–V, edited by Andrew Skinner (London: Penguin Books, 1999).

Vattel, Emer de. *Le droit des gens, ou, Principes de la loi naturelle, appliqués à la conduit & aux affaires des nations & des souverains*, edited by Paul Pradier-Fodéré (Paris: Guillaumin, 1863).

Whitman, James Q. *The Verdict of Battle: The Law of Victory and the Making of Modern War* (Cambridge, Mass.: Harvard University Press, 2012).

Witt, John Fabian. *Lincoln's Code: The Laws of War in American History* (New York: Free Press, 2012).

Cases and Statutory Instruments

The Antelope, 23 U.S. (10 Wheaton) 66 (1825).

Cherokee Nation v. Georgia, 30 U.S. 1 (1831).

Johnson v. M'Intosh, 21 U.S. 543 (1823).

Marbury v. Madison, 1 Cranch 137 (1803).

The Nereide, 9 Cranch 388 (1815).

Thirty Hogsheads of Sugar v. Boyle, 9 Cranch 191 (1815).

U.S. Constitution.

Worcester v. Georgia, 31 U.S. 515 (1832).

18

Messianic Visions of the United States

International Law, Religion, and the Cuban Intervention, 1898–1917

Paolo Amorosa

On 17 December 2014, Presidents Obama and Raúl Castro spoke to announce a new course in the relationship between Cuba and the United States, re-establishing diplomatic relations after fifty-three years of severance. In his statement,[1] Obama acknowledged the serious differences that would still divide the two countries, especially on human rights issues. Yet, he depicted the harsh Cuban policy conducted by his predecessors as the counterproductive relic of a global war against communism the United States had already won. Obama, indeed, did not look further back than the 1959 Castrist revolution, focusing on Cold War events and themes.

In his speech,[2] Raúl Castro instead opened up to a different frame of reference. He made a brief remark commending the loyalty of the Cuban people to its principles since the beginning of independence wars in 1868. Castro was referring to the various attempts by Cubans to topple Spanish colonial power in the island. When in 1898 Spain was finally forced to leave, Cuba was formally independent but occupied by the United States army. Historians have often pointed out that recovering events and the related narratives from the turn of the century is crucial to understanding how the United States and Cuba have mutually contributed to shape each other's political identity long before their Cold War confrontations.[3] I contribute to that enterprise with a related claim. The narrative of 1898, depicting North Americans as selfless helpers of the Cuban people, has contributed to the articulation of international law as a professional discipline in the United States and its ties to religious discourse. That narrative had its most powerful and popular expounding in the theological terms used by preachers across the country when

[1] Available at http://www.whitehouse.gov/the-press-office/2014/12/17/statement-president-cuba-policy-changes (last accessed 22 January 2015).

[2] Available at http://www.voltairenet.org/article186231.html (last accessed 22 January 2015).

[3] See for instance Louis A. Pérez, *Cuba in the American Imagination: Metaphor and the Imperial Ethos* (Chapel Hill: University of North Carolina Press, 2008), especially pp. 1–23.

commenting on the Cuban intervention. The grip of this narrative was not only in the influence it had in framing the 1898 war and its immediate aftermath. It persisted in the exceptionalist understanding of the role of the United States in the international legal system maintained by the founders of the American Society of International Law (ASIL)[4] up to the end of the First World War and beyond.

Recognizing the religious matrix of this narrative helps make sense of the rhetoric of this early generation of American international lawyers. They insisted on understanding law as science, proposing a specific kind of legal formalism as the guarantee of justice and equality. At the same time, their faith in the United States and international law as messianic forces helped them to dismiss anxieties and unfavourable events as momentary setbacks in an inevitable providential plan. In this chapter I set out to show how, through faith, these international lawyers reconciled imperial ambitions and democratic values. This composite mindset presented international law as a political theology: metaphysically founded but with clear pragmatic implications for the direction of international relations.

James Brown Scott in Havana: International Law and the Selfless Empire

On the evening of 22 January 1917, James Brown Scott (1866–1943), President of the American Institute of International Law, took the floor at the Institute's Second Annual Meeting in Havana, in the presence of Cuban President Mario García Menocal. Scott remarked at the outset that he had waited nineteen years to be there in Cuba, but the moment had finally come. He was referring to the 1898 Spanish–American War. At the time a volunteer private in the United States Army, Scott was about to leave for the island. His regiment was instead finally attached to the forces on the Pacific front, tasked with the operations in the other Spanish colony of the Philippines. Yet the United States won the war faster than anyone could have expected. 'A splendid little war', John Hay, the soon-to-be Secretary of State, called it. Scott's regiment would never leave California.

The year before he finally reached Havana, Scott had published a volume entitled 'Military and Colonial Policy of the United States'. The book was part of a series, edited by Scott and his colleague Robert Bacon, collecting the speeches and writings of their mentor Elihu Root (1845–1937). In the book's foreword, Scott remarked how the texts therein addressed issues to be seen 'as consequence

[4] The most prominent among the founders were arguably Elihu Root and James Brown Scott. Elihu Root had been the Secretary of War who first set up the United States administration of overseas territories. He later became Secretary of State and first President of the ASIL. Root's legal advisor at the State Department, James Brown Scott, an academic by profession, not a legal practitioner like Root, was the driving force behind the foundation of the ASIL. On the foundation of the American Society of International Law see Frederic L. Kirgis, Jr., *The American Society of International Law's First Century: 1906–2006* (Leiden: Martinus Nijhoff Publishers, 2006), pp. 1–49.

or aftermath of the war with Spain in 1898'[5] and told the story of how Root was involved in colonial administration and the spirit with which he carried out his task. It all started in July 1899 with an unexpected phone call. The President's office was calling to tell Root he had been chosen to be the new Secretary of War. Root had been involved in Republican Party politics for a long time. He was especially known as an anti-corruption reformer in his home state of New York, where his thriving corporate law practice was based. He had never held office before;[6] neither did he believe he was suited for the position. 'Thank the President for me, but say it is quite absurd, I know nothing about war', Root replied. But President McKinley did not want an army man. He wanted a lawyer to set up administration in the newly acquired territories and the lawyer he wanted was Root. At that point, for Root, 'there was but one answer to make'. He 'went to perform a lawyer's duty upon the call of the greatest of all our clients, the Government of' the United States. None other than Root himself painted this neat recollection of the conversation in a public speech almost seventeen years after it happened.[7] One might doubt if Root had 'adjusted' the exchange for storytelling purposes and an audience of lawyers. Yet, the message he wanted to relay was clear. It was not about war. It was about law, justice, and efficient administration. That was Root's task: to export and spread American freedom through law.

Scott in Havana was still carrying out the American world-civilizing mission Root had undertaken when he accepted McKinley's cabinet position offer. This mission had a broad scope, not restricted to the American imperial enterprises that followed the Spanish–American War. International lawyers had been at the forefront of a revolution. A country that had understood since its independence its foreign relations as being aimed at maintaining isolation and avoid entanglements, felt now ready to assume an active role of primary importance in international politics. Of course, such a momentous change came with anxieties and ambiguities. It was the entire identity of the United States as a nation that was under discussion. On that evening of 1917 in Cuba, Scott was giving his take on that change. It was

[5] Elihu Root, *The Military and Colonial Policy of the United States: Speeches and Reports*, collected and edited by Robert Bacon and James Brown Scott (Cambridge, Mass.: Harvard University Press, 1916), p. XI.

[6] Root had been a delegate-at-large, designated by the Republican caucus, at the 1894 New York Constitutional Convention, where he was the major force behind the reform of the state judicial system (see Philip C. Jessup, *Elihu Root:* vol. 1 (New York: Dodd, Mead & Company, 1938), pp. 175–7. Yet, he saw this task and other institutional tasks he would perform as technical and professional rather than political. Root, notwithstanding continued party pressures to run for various positions including President of the United States, would seek office only once and late in his life. In 1909, he was elected United States Senator for the state of New York, a position he would hold until 1915.

[7] Root held the speech before the New York County Lawyers' Association on 13 March 1915. Scott had published the text of the entire address in another volume of the series ('The Lawyer of Today', in Elihu Root, *Addresses on Government and Citizenship*, collected and edited by Robert Bacon and James Brown Scott (Cambridge, Mass.: Harvard University Press, 1916), pp. 503–9.) as he noted when referring to it in the preface to *The Military and Colonial Policy*. For a political background and an account of the reactions to Root's nomination as Secretary of War see Jessup, *Elihu Root*: vol. 1: pp. 215–19.

the view of an idealist international lawyer who believed that the values on which the United States was founded could and would redeem the whole world.

Scott began his address reminding the audience how the United States became the occupying power in Cuba in 1898. The Spanish–American War was one of humanitarian intervention on behalf of the Cuban people to stop the barbarities perpetrated by the Spanish Government. Indeed the United States Congress, in declaring war, had affirmed through the Teller Amendment that there was no intention to exercise any control beyond the temporary one necessary to pacify the island. 'That was', according to Scott, 'the intention of the United States':[8] to keep Cuba free from foreign intervention and under a republican government that would truly represent the Cuban people. Scott points to the Platt Amendment, drafted by Root, as the primary means with which the United States pursued the goal of a free and independent Cuba. This statement exposes the depth of the contradictions international lawyers in the United States faced in order to recreate a viable national identity for their country as a world power. The Platt amendment, indeed, represented the American legislative step towards insertion in the Cuban Constitution of a right of intervention for the United States in Cuban affairs.

Scott, in his speech, recounted the details of the amendment's legislative history. After being adopted by Congress on 2 March 1901 as an amendment to the Army Appropriation Bill, the text of the Platt Amendment also became part of the then draft Cuban Constitution on the following 12 June. In 1903, Cuba and the United States entered into a bilateral treaty that reproduced the text of the amendment. Scott made sure to underline that the amendment originated in the instructions given by Root on 9 February 1901 to the military governor of the island, Major General Leonard Wood, as preparation for the withdrawal of the United States' troops. The instructions contained a series of measures that would be replicated, with slight modifications, in the text of the amendment. Such measures would greatly restrict the room for manoeuver for the future Cuban government, ranging from constitutional limitations on treaty-making with countries other than the United States to restrictions on the assumption of public debt. Yet the key provision 'the people of Cuba should desire', according to Root, was indeed the constitutional recognition of the right of intervention of the United States in Cuban affairs. In the discursive part of the instructions, Root switched often in considering Cuban independence as desirable because of United States' interests or because of democratic values, as it would give the chance to Cubans to rule themselves with a republican form of government. However, when formulating the draft provisions that would end up in the Platt Amendment, Root made use only of a language of selflessness and duty. The American right of intervention would serve the 'preservation of Cuban

[8] James Brown Scott, 'The Platt Amendment—Recommendations of Habana Concerning International Organization', in American Institute of International Law, *The Recommendations of Habana Concerning International Organization*, address and commentary by James Brown Scott (New York: Oxford University Press, 1917), p. 3.

independence and the maintenance of a stable government, adequately protecting life, property and individual liberty'.[9]

This second line of reasoning, the one focused on American selflessness, was the one followed by Scott in his Havana speech. Scott explained the American-Cuban relationship as regulated by the Platt Amendment as an anti-imperialist model of equal relations. Yet an occupying power had dictated into the Constitution of the occupied a right of intervention in its own favour. How that could be called equality and serve the achievement of self-government for the Cuban people?

This seemingly specific question is an inspiring starting point to reflect on a key moment for the study of international law in the United States. The Spanish–American War and the unexpected ease of its victory led to a renewed attention to international law, partly in order to reconcile the new leading global role of the country with its democratic tradition. Scott, Root, and the other founders of the ASIL recast even the formal colonialism in the Philippines and the tutelage of the newly independent Cuba as an expression of egalitarian values, American and universal at the same time. This ambiguous nationalist/cosmopolitan identity was based on a narrative of progress: the peak of civilization reached by the United States would gradually expand world-wide through example and benevolent assimilation. In the eyes of these international lawyers, if this was to be called imperialism it had nothing to do with the predatory attitude of European mould. The American civilizing mission was geared towards the selfless goal of creating 'a new imperialism—the imperialism of liberty'.[10] The natural American adherence to international law and its underlying liberal values was considered as the *trait d'union* between the colonial policy of the United States and its global promotion of international institutions and adjudication.

International Law as Science and the Social Context: The Platt Amendment as Equality

There are aspects of the interaction between American identity and the development of international law that are insufficiently studied.[11] For instance, historians acknowledge the close ideological connection between Christianity and Western values underwriting international law and its imperial aspirations in the second half of the nineteenth century and the early twentieth century. Most scholarship seems, however, to assume that the international lawyers of the age, cosmopolitans

[9] This formula is used by Root in the Instructions (cfr. Scott, 'The Platt Amendment', p. 6) and then replicated in the Platt Amendment (cfr. Scott, 'The Platt Amendment', p. 10).

[10] Congregationalist theologian Lyman Abbott (1835–1922), quoted in Andrew Preston, *Sword of the Spirit, Shield of Faith: Religion in American War and Diplomacy* (New York: Alfred A. Knopf, 2012), p. 225.

[11] For a deeper exploration of this paragraph's themes see Paolo Amorosa, 'James Brown Scott's International Adjudication between Tradition and Progress in the United States', *Journal of the History of International Law* 17(1) (2015): pp. 15–46.

often on the liberal side of the political spectrum, were not people living intense religious experiences but rather were shallow cultural Christians sharing a secularized rationalist identity. Such an assumption would definitely be incorrect in relation to many key founders of the ASIL. James Brown Scott, for instance, was a fervent religious believer. A Presbyterian of Scottish strain, he would base his career work on the American exceptionalism with an internationalist flavour that emerged primarily in the mainstream religious discourse in the key year of 1898.[12] While he insisted on the scientific nature of international law, Scott also underlined the importance of its egalitarian moral foundations and found its origin in the theology of the Salamanca school. In this aspect Scott seems to represent a tension that has been present throughout the various expressions of American national identity over the course of history. To this day, the Enlightenment roots of the Revolution keep clashing and melting with the messianic visions of American civil religion.[13]

The Havana speech represented a telling example of Scott's composite sensibility and of the way it shaped his international legal scholarship and activism. Moreover, it established a direct link between the Spanish–American War and the new egalitarian era of international relations that Scott envisioned as emerging under the influence of the United States. The 'splendid little war', its preparation, and its aftermath has received more and more attention by scholars as a catalyst for fundamental changes in the political imagination and the foreign policy of the United States. Yet its implications for the development and professionalization of international law have been largely ignored.[14]

James Brown Scott was at the forefront of international lawyers striving to provide the discipline with scientific status and professional dignity. The mindset linked to this enterprise would be crucial in shaping Scott's understanding of the Platt Amendment. International lawyers, pressured by the Austinian challenge, felt even more than other legal scholars the necessity to establish law as a science. This led them, at least in rhetorical terms, to relegate religious values to the foundations of international law and exclude them from its operation. However, this hardly meant that they perceived a problematic tension between science and Christian faith. Indeed, one distinctive trope in the intellectual milieu in the United States at the time, accepted by most theologians, was the theorized harmony (or at least non-contradiction) of science, including Darwinism, and religion.[15]

[12] Cf. Matthew McCullough, *The Cross of War: Christian Nationalism and U.S. Expansion in the Spanish–American War* (Madison: The University of Wisconsin Press, 2014).

[13] See for instance Paul T. McCartney, *Power and Progress: American National Identity, the War of 1898, and the Rise of American Imperialism (* Baton Rouge: Louisiana State University Press, 2006), pp. 27–43.

[14] One notable exception is Carl Landauer, 'The Ambivalences of Power: Launching the American Journal of International Law in an Era of Empire and Globalization', *Leiden Journal of International Law* 20 (2007): pp. 325–58.

[15] For a description of the debates that led to the adoption of the harmony position in the Presbyterian denomination see Bradley J. Longfield, *Presbyterians and American Culture: A History* (Louisville, Kentucky: Westminster John Knox Press, 2013), pp. 120–7.

In the academic milieu of the turn of the century, social sciences' main aspiration was to achieve a level of objectivism comparable to the one of natural sciences. In law schools, the drive for scientific systematization took the shape of Langdellian formalism. Christopher Columbus Langdell (1826–1906), Dean of Harvard Law School, is known to have revolutionized the teaching of law in the United States through the use of the case method. For Langdell, judicial decisions were the raw material that lawyers should empirically study. From them, lawyers would be able to induce principles and systematize them. In turn, solutions for further legal questions could be deducted from these principles. Such a rationalist and formalist understanding of law was strongly connected with the idea of the United States as a messianic project. The constant evolution towards systematization meant the removal of arbitrariness in court decisions, so realizing the ideal of 'a government of laws, not of men'. Leading at the peak of civilization, the American legal system had realized equality before the law for everyone.

Scott was a self-professed follower of Langdellian scientism.[16] In 1902 he published the first of three editions of his international law casebook.[17] Yet, as the introduction to the casebook made clear, his goal was not only to provide law students with material, but also to sustain his nationalist and, at the same time, internationalist project. Scott underlined how the status of international law as a legal discipline could not be denied because of a basic observation: international law was applied in courts. Therefore, it could be studied and developed in scientific terms. Crucially for Scott, it had been 'English and American courts of justice' acting to 'enforce international law ... repeatedly ... for the past two centuries'. This seemingly technical point underwrote a whole series of implications. International law was of Anglo-Saxon origin, in itself a valid pedigree of civilization for a discipline in the turn of the century United States. It was also American, part of the United States' municipal law and developed within its judicial system with the Supreme Court at its top. For that reason international law was universal as well, as the Supreme Court, with its effective jurisdiction over sovereign states, was the only tested and viable model for a future international court. Alongside this procedural point ran the substantial one: formalist law as developed by American courts meant the realization of freedom and equality. If the Old World wanted progress and the peace that came along with it, it just had to learn from the United States. The tables had turned.

Freedom and equality within the Langdellian strain of formalism concretely meant absolute freedom of contract. The rejection of any form of constraint on

[16] See James Brown Scott, 'The Study of the Law', *The American Law School Review* 2, no. 2 (1906): pp. 3–4, and John Hepp, 'James Brown Scott and the Rise of Public International Law', *Journal of the Gilded Age and Progressive Era* 7 (2008): pp. 162–4.

[17] James Brown Scott, *Cases on International Law: Selected from Decisions of English and American Courts, edited, with Syllabus, and Annotation by James Brown Scott* (Boston: Boston Book Company, 1902. Reissued by West Publishing Company, 1906). The second edition was released in 1922 (*Cases on International Law: Principally Selected from Decisions of English and American Courts* (St. Paul: West Publishing) and the third and last (*Cases on International Law*, co-edited with Walter H. E. Jaeger (St. Paul: West Publishing) in 1937, three years before Scott's retirement from public life.

freedom of contract as a progressive affirmation of individualism would be for decades a cornerstone of the United States' legal system. American courts, especially the Supreme Court of the Lochner era, systematically intervened to void, for instance, legislation for the protection of workers,[18] using freedom of contract in the interest of employers. As union leader John L. Mitchell put it, workers seemed to be 'guaranteed the liberties they do not want and denied the liberty that is of real value to them'.[19] Law and freedom were construed as blind to insuperable disproportions in bargaining power. This individualist and formalist stance of the Langdellian mould was shared by the majority of the American legal elite of the time.[20] Progress for the elite did not entail redistribution. Freedom was political, not social or economic. The equality to be guaranteed was formal, not substantial.

It is easy to read a similar formalist understanding of equality in Root and Scott's theorization of the Platt Amendment.[21] The representatives of the Cuban people had agreed to it and that manifestation of will was all that mattered in order to create a legal obligation. Equality meant absolute freedom of contract. Therefore, the circumstance that the contracting parties were in a relation of occupying and occupied, and the importance of the object, the constitutional document of a party, could be deemed irrelevant. With a legal theory that considered a legal obligation as neutral and just by definition, it was possible to mask the contradiction between democratic ideals and imperial uses of American power.

Before the War: Public Opinion, Humanitarianism, and Religious Discourse

The intrinsic 'diversity' of American imperialism was an article of faith in more than one sense. It was often assumed and only thinly argued. American actors in public discourse did not feel the need to support the dogma of the selfless empire, but rather preferred to continue expounding it with slight variations. The progressive credentials of the New World and the evident success of the United States as a country, especially after the triumphant war, sufficed. But more pointedly the exceptional moral nature of the American empire was constructed in explicitly religious terms because the narrative of the 1898 war came largely from the pulpits. Historians underline the role of the 'yellow press' in exciting the public opinion towards war. But what is too often forgotten is that at the time texts of popular diffusion were hardly limited to the secular press, which itself made use of religious

[18] For the discussion of an example of stricken-down social legislation under the described ideology see Jonathan Zasloff, 'Law and the Shaping of American Foreign Policy: From the Gilded Age to the New Era', *New York University Law Review* 78 (2003), pp. 269–70.

[19] John L. Mitchell, 'The Workingman's Conception of Industrial Liberty', *American Federationist* 17 (May 1910): pp. 406–7, quoted in Eric Foner, *The Story of American Freedom* (New York: W. W. Norton, 1998), p. 123.

[20] The critique of scholars like Oliver Wendell Holmes Jr. (1841–1935), aimed at keeping law opened to social considerations, would remain a minority voice for a few more decades.

[21] Cf. for instance, Scott, 'The Platt Amendment', pp. 14–16.

imagery and printed sermons. The religious press was widespread and influential at both national and local level. In 1898 it featured sermons and editorials that framed a comprehensive and quite uniform Christian understanding of the war.

The 1890s represented a period of unprecedented interest and involvement of the American people in foreign policy debates. Information travelled much faster between continents thanks to the recently laid-out web of transatlantic telegraphic cables. The 'sensationalist "yellow press", seeking to increase daily circulation, found foreign affairs to be an ideal source of provocative headlines'.[22] American public opinion had already been inflamed about international crises before the Cuban rebellion that led to the 1898 war took the stage. Some of those crises particularly resonated with the American public, anticipating the themes of humanitarianism and exceptionalism that would come together in the narrative of 1898.

Humanitarian demands first took the form of requests for governmental support of international relief actions. In 1892, the American people, informed of a famine in Russia that threatened the life of millions of peasants, pressured for institutional action. After much infighting and indecisiveness, both Congress and President Grover Cleveland refused to get directly involved, even refusing to ship privately collected relief goods to Russia. Yet press campaigns led the Iowa governor Horace Boies to create the Iowa Famine Relief Commission. With the refusal of Congress, the Red Cross took charge of delivering the Iowan aid to Russia. The American Red Cross had been founded in 1881, thanks to the lobbying of Clara Barton, still at the helm during the Russian famine relief effort. A veteran nurse and relief organizer of the American Civil War and the Franco-Prussian War, Barton had eventually convinced President Chester Arthur to support the creation of an American branch of the organization, which since then had already dealt with domestic crises.[23] '[T]he entire Russian famine relief effort raised Barton's and the American Red Cross's visibility further convincing humanitarian activists of their ability to mobilize voters and move government to ameliorate the world's ills.'[24] The pattern repeated itself a couple of years later when newspapers and magazines started reporting Turkish persecution of Armenians. Cleveland claimed not to have the constitutional authority to act and it was once again Barton and the Red Cross who travelled to provide the help offered by American private relief organizations.

In 1895, a diplomatic crisis of a more traditional kind brought strong public support for the Cleveland administration's reassertion of the Monroe Doctrine. A slow-burning dispute over the boundary between Venezuela and the colony of British Guyana escalated to the point that the United Kingdom seemed on the verge of military intervention. The United States did not show much interest in intervening until the Venezuelan government put William Scruggs on its payroll. A former United States minister to Venezuela turned lobbyist, Scruggs published

[22] Frank Ninkovich, *The United States and Imperialism* (Malden: Blackwell Publishers, 2001), p. 14.

[23] Cf. Jeffrey Bloodworth, 'For Love or for Money?: William McKinley and the Spanish-American War', *White House Studies* 9 (2009): p. 140.

[24] Bloodworth, 'For Love or for Money?', p. 141.

a pamphlet titled *British Aggressions in Venezuela or the Monroe Doctrine on Trial* in October 1894 and ensured its wide distribution. The point he made was simple: the United States had both a moral duty and interest to protect self-government in the continent against the despotic greediness of European empires.[25] While the controversy dragged on, the Royal Navy occupied a Nicaraguan port in April 1895 to protect British nationals over an unrelated matter. The American 'public opinion was violently outraged. The Cleveland Administration was vigorously attacked for its supineness in the face of British brutality and aggression; and Scruggs, in his campaign on behalf of Venezuela, found a powerful if unexpected ally in the Royal Navy'.[26] In July, the new Secretary of State Richard Olney sent a provocative diplomatic note to London. It contained a sentence that would go down in history as the Olney corollary to the Monroe Doctrine. While crafted in language 'undoubtedly of the bumptious order',[27] as Olney himself would later admit, it represented the growing self-confidence and self-righteousness of the United States in international matters. According to the note, 'today the United States is practically sovereign on this continent and its fiat is law'.[28] Eventually the British government accepted to solve the dispute through arbitration. American public opinion rejoiced in what was perceived as a historic victory against European imperialism and recognition of the United States' leadership in the New World.

The religious press was very active in reporting and taking position on these crises, as it would be in the context of the 1898 war. Moreover, the interest of American religious denominations and their clergy in international issues predated by decades the one of the yellow press. Indeed, the idea to substitute force with law in international relations, by resorting to international adjudication rather than war, had been advocated by American religiously inspired organizations much before it became a project of lawyers and of the United States government. The early American peace societies grew out of the idea that war is incompatible with Christian religion.[29] Following the foundation of the New York Peace Society in 1815, other local ones quickly appeared in the rest of the United States, even if the centre of the movement would remain in the Northeast.[30] David Low Dodge (1774–1852), the force behind the creation of the New York Society, ascribed even this organizational success to divine intervention. He suggested that the independent way in which societies were 'formed, without any correspondence or knowledge of each other' was due to 'providence having paved the way'. For him, it was 'the spirit of God' that 'had moved on the hearts of many of his children to consider the

[25] Cf. Robert Arthur Humphreys, 'Presidential Address: Anglo-American Rivalries and the Venezuela Crisis of 1895', *Transactions of the Royal Historical Society* 17 (1967): pp. 142–6.

[26] Humphrey, 'Anglo-American Rivalries', p. 148.

[27] Richard Olney to Philander Knox, 29 January 1912, no. 16, *Knox Papers*, Manuscript Division, Library of Congress, Washington, DC, quoted in Ninkovich, *The United States and Imperialism*, p. 13.

[28] Quoted in Ninkovich, *The United States and Imperialism*, p. 13.

[29] Cf. James Brown Scott, 'Introduction' in William Ladd, *An Essay on a Congress of Nations* (New York: Oxford University Press—American Branch, 1916), pp. v–vii.

[30] Cfr. Mark Janis, *The American Tradition of International Law: Great Expectations, 1789–1914* (Oxford: Oxford University Press, 2004), p. 98.

subject' of peace.[31] The man who more decidedly led the pacifist effort towards the promotion of international institutions was William Ladd (1778–1841), a Maine landowner turned preacher and activist. He succeeded in his effort to unite the local peace societies under one banner, founding the American Peace Society in 1828. Ladd's leadership was also connected to a shift in the movement from the radical pacifism of Dodge to a more gradualist approach and the refusal to condemn all wars in the present. Gradualism brought with it pragmatism, a connection of peace with concrete plans rather than simply high-minded religious claims. Ladd published *An Essay on a Congress of Nations* in 1840. His proposal envisioned a Congress made of 'Christian and civilized nations', enjoying equal voting rights and a permanent Court of Nations modelled on the American Supreme Court. Indeed, James Brown Scott would advertise those early American efforts by republishing in 1916 the *Essay* in the Classics of International Law series he edited. Ladd figured well in Scott's international law pedigree as he claimed that the originality of his institutional proposal lay in the Langdellian theme of the separation between political (the Congress) and judicial functions (the Court). Moreover, the publication reinforced Scott's strong ties with the American Peace Society. Indeed, by the time of the foundation of the American Society of International Law in 1906, the Peace Society had become moderate enough to ally on a steady basis with pragmatist, establishment international lawyers.[32]

The pre-1890s international activism of religious leaders that inspired the narrative of 1898 hardly stopped at the peace movement however. Shaping the world through direct action rather than only by American example was crucial in the mindset that led to the impressive growth of foreign missionary work in the nineteenth century. Missionaries spearheaded expansionism outside the American continent. Indeed, they exported American values long before Frederick Jackson Turner's theory of the frontier in 1893 would certify that expansion now could and would only happen beyond the United States' boundaries. It is important to note that American missionary enterprises went beyond evangelization. For instance, missionaries built and managed schools and hospitals. This focus on good works was in line with the growing influence of Darwinism and biblical criticism. Progressive Protestant ministers argued for the compatibility of Christian faith and science. This modernist turn resonated with many secular intellectuals who, like Scott, strove to combine their enthusiasm for evolutionary theories and

[31] David Low Dodge and others, *Memorial of Mr. David L. Dodge* (Boston: S. K. Whipple & Co., 1854), p. 99.

[32] International lawyers of Scott's generation still strove to distinguish themselves from radical groups in the peace movement. For lawyers peace was a worthy objective obtainable in the long run through scientifically based institutional plans and the education of the public opinion. That is why they deemed plain appeals to abolish war on the basis of its immorality as irrational and counterproductive. Scott found a precious ally for his gradualist and judicialist project in the American Peace Society. With the progress of the First World War, Scott's ideas came to be challenged by the growing popularity of collective security as the cornerstone of the post-war world order. The American Peace Society was one of the few institutions to remain on Scott's side when, while still influential, he was firmly on the losing side of international legal debates in the United States.

scientific progress with providential and millennialist Christian beliefs. The success of the missionary movement also meant that missionaries were one of the primary sources of information for Americans about the rest of the world. The United States' diplomatic missions were few and scarcely staffed: a comprehensive reform and strengthening of the State Department structure would come only under the tenure of Elihu Root as Secretary, starting in 1905. Missionary presence abroad prevailed not only through sheer numbers: missions were often placed in remote areas where no American diplomat had the chance to set foot. While the coexistence of diplomats and missionaries often led to turf frictions, in many cases diplomats too, like Americans at home, had to rely on missionaries as their only source of information.

No wonder, then, that religious leaders felt so well placed to tell Americans the true meaning of a Cuban intervention. Their organizations had been aiming at shaping the world in the United States' image and told back home about it long before the rest of the country also became ready to cross the oceans. In the initial phases of the Cuban crisis, the largest part of religious leaders stood by President McKinley, praising him for his restraint and opposing intervention. Indeed, before 1898, calls by religious leaders for American full-blown foreign military intervention had been rare and isolated. Social Gospeler Josiah Strong's invocation of intervention in response to the Armenian crisis had been a notable exception to the general trend. It was in 1895, while the Armenian atrocities were garnering attention, rebellion in Cuba broke out again. Indignation in the United States rose up when the Spanish military governor Valeriano Weyler enacted a reconcentration policy on the island. To deprive the rebel guerrilla of support, Weyler ordered concentrating the inhabitants of rural areas in guarded camps. The lack of adequate provisions and sanitation in the camps led to the eventual deaths of approximately one hundred thousand Cubans by early 1898.[33] The yellow press reports stirred indignation in the United States' public opinion. The Christian press joined the condemnation of Weyler's policies, depicting them as an expression of the barbaric rule of Catholic Spain. Yet the support for the Cuban rebellion did not turn in a call for intervention. 'Even as ministers, editors, and denominational resolutions called for an end to Spanish rule on the island, they also continued to insist on American neutrality in the conflict.'[34]

Even after the sinking of the USS *Maine* in the Havana harbour on 15 February 1898, the opinion of the religious establishment stood firmly against intervention. McKinley had sent the battleship, with the reluctant permission of the Spanish government, to monitor the situation and ensure the safety of United States citizens. When the *Maine* suddenly sank because of an explosion, causing the death of two hundred and sixty-six American sailors, the already inflamed public opinion immediately blamed the Spanish government. Restraint was once again the watchword of religious leaders. Support for the President was coupled with accusations against the sensationalist press, blamed by a sermon preached

[33] McCullough, *The Cross of War*, p. 15. [34] Ibid.

on 27 February on 'the strain and the nervousness and nation-wide exasperation of the past two weeks'. In that same sermon, Charles Parkhurst of the Madison Square Presbyterian Church went on to explain how the press and its 'lying' was exploiting the 'vast population' and compromising its 'moral marrow'. It did so by impressing 'hundreds of thousands of inconsiderate ones who are not necessarily without conscience, but who are childishly fascinated by its flamboyancy and who become in time so debilitated, intellectually and morally debilitated, by its stimulated piquancy as to come in time really to love a lie well sell seasoned better than the truth'.[35]

This paternalistic view of public opinion points to another point of contact between religious leaders and secular intellectuals of the time. They considered the universal project of modernity, in which the United States, providence, reason, and democracy had become one and the same, endangered by the unreflective nature of the people. As Paul Kahn notes, this type of 'argument ... animated the jurisprudence of the [Supreme] Court' at the time, under Melvin Fuller as Chief Justice between 1898 and 1910. The 'deep skepticism of populist movements' is a constant contradiction of modern democracies.[36] This is reflected in the idea of Langdellian international lawyers that progress is a process of education. It is not by chance that the article opening the very first issue of the *American Journal of International Law*,[37] authored by Root, is titled 'The Need of Popular Understanding of International Law'. Education, though, meant primarily learning from and listening to the ones who knew better, the establishment. This ambiguity is well reflected in the expression Root used when he first penned the provisions that would become the Platt Amendment: those were the provisions that 'the Cubans should desire' in their Constitution. In the same way as the domestic public opinion was reasonable only within the parameters set by the establishment, the Platt Amendment was conceived not as what the United States government or the Cuban people desired, but as what Root believed the Cubans should desire.

International Law as Civilization and the Religious Discourse: the Platt Amendment as Selflessness

How, then, did the religious leadership come to support the intervention and give it its meaning?

[35] Charles Parkhurst, 'The State of the Country', printed in the Presbyterian *Evangelist* (10 March 1898): pp. 11–12, quoted in McCullough, *The Cross of War*, pp. 17–18. McCullough also notes that on 3 March 'the Nation, a prominent secular periodical highly critical of rampant jingoism, confirmed that the tone' of moderation 'was typical of the ministerial response' to the sinking of the *Maine* 'nationwide' (p. 18).

[36] See in this volume, Chapter 17, Paul W. Kahn, 'Law of Nations at the Origins'.

[37] Elihu Root, 'The Need of Popular Understanding of International Law', *American Journal of International Law* 1 (1907): pp. 1–3.

In the weeks immediately following the sinking of the *Maine*, Congress was pushing for war. The representatives of big business instead in this phase still believed that their economic interests in Cuba would be further prejudiced by an American military intervention. The President strove to keep his options as open as possible while several powerful forces required him to take a stance. On 21 March, the inquiry ordered by McKinley in the immediate aftermath of the sinking did not assign blame, but concluded that the explosion was external to the ship.[38] The belief that there had been Spanish foul play grew stronger in the United States. The vengeful slogan 'Remember the *Maine*' quickly spread in the yellow press and on the streets.

The sinking of the *Maine* is one of the most remembered events of the Spanish-American War and it is often assumed to have been the last drop that pushed the United States to intervene. Yet several historians point at a different event that might have swayed the sceptical voices in American society to support intervention. A few days before the release of the *Maine* enquiry, on 17 March, Senator Redfield Proctor of Vermont delivered a speech in Congress about his recent trip to Cuba. Proctor was known as a cool-headed pro-business conservative, sceptical of the reports of the yellow press. However his direct experience convinced him that reality was even worse than how it was described in the newspapers:

> Reporters noted that Proctor read his speech describing the starvation of tens of thousands without any trace of dramatic flourish. The calm, deliberate manner in which he offered his testimony to Congress made for a striking contrast with the sensational claims of the 'yellow' journalists. In short, when this man described what he had seen in this way, conditions of mass starvation and widespread Spanish brutality, people believed him.[39]

The Proctor speech swayed Wall Street, now convinced by one they saw as their own that the situation was too dire, also in relation to their business interest, for the United States not to act.[40] Finally, on 11 April, McKinley asked Congress for the authorization to intervene. On 25 April, Congress declared the existence of a state of war with Spain. Matthew McCullough, author of the most complete study to date of 1898 sermons and religious editorials on the war,[41] argues that the Proctor speech coincides with what he calls 'the great reversal' for religious leadership too. He claims that '[i]n the religious press, in the wake of this report, focus shifted over resistance to jingoes over possible retaliation for the *Maine* to wholehearted support for intervention'.[42] With this swift reversal, ministers took up the responsibility to frame the intervention as Christian, motivated only by selfless and

[38] Later investigations would prove the explosion to be accidental, due to the ignition of powder charges stored in the ship.

[39] McCullough, *The Cross of War*, p. 19.

[40] Cf. Mike Sewell, 'Humanitarian Intervention, Democracy, and Imperialism: The American War with Spain, 1898, and After', in *Humanitarian Intervention: A History*, edited by Brendan Simms and David J. B. Trim (Cambridge: Cambridge University Press, 2011), pp. 310–11.

[41] McCullough, *The Cross of War*.

[42] Ibid., pp.19–20.

humanitarian considerations. The United States would sacrifice lives and resources to help the Cubans in their struggle for freedom without any desire of territorial or financial gain. According to McCullough, two main biblical *topoi* were used to explain the intervention in Christian terms: the parable of the Good Samaritan[43] and the sacrificial death of Jesus Christ.[44]

The biblical parable exemplified the love of neighbour the United States was showing in intervening in favour of Cubans. The Samaritan intervened to help a robbed and wounded Israelite, with whom he shared no other bond than the common humanity. Before him two religious leaders had passed and left their fellow Israelite in his misery. In the same way as the Samaritan, ministers argued, the United States were ready to change course from the previous fear of entanglements and intervene, fulfilling its role of a chosen Christian nation. The passers-by would be made to symbolize the isolationist voices within the United States or the selfish European nations that would not help those in need.

Even more powerful was the evoking of the sacrificial death of Christ. Sacrifice for national values had been the most recurring characterization of the Civil War, a still open wound Americans hoped to finally heal through the unity inspired by the 1898 war. Ministers would use for the first time the category of sacrifice not to understand purely national events but as made in favour of another people. To those who protested that Cuban lives were not as worthy as American ones, New York Presbyterian David Gregg pointed out, in a sermon delivered on 24 April, that Christ had sacrificed himself for sinful human beings. Gregg did not challenge the notion of the Cubans' lesser value: social Darwinism and racist theories had a strong hold on liberal Protestants then. But he argued that sacrifice for them was still the Christian thing to do. Fellow New York Presbyterian Henry Van Dyke would add, in his 1 May sermon, that intervention was a providential necessity, an act of submission to God. Resorting to war to fulfil God's will was the cross that the nation was called to bear. On the same day, modernist minister Thomas Dixon argued that only from now on could there be a new Christian understanding of international relations. The 'old law of nations' was based on self-interest as the 'supreme standard of life'. The United States intervention on behalf of the Cubans represented 'the first time in modern history' that 'a great nation ha[d] accepted the Spirit of Jesus Christ as the motive power of life' and 'the law of Christ' as 'sacrificial and redemptive love'.[45] The ministers made a strong case to convince American society and the world at large that the United States was truly the 'Good Samaritan among nations', as Texas Baptist B. H. Carroll put it.[46]

[43] Ibid., pp. 28–31. [44] Ibid., pp. 31–6.

[45] Thomas Dixon, 'The Battle Cry of Freedom', *Dixon's Sermons: A Monthly Magazine* (June 1898): pp. 4–6, quoted in McCullough, *The Cross of War*, p. 35.

[46] B. H. Carroll, 'Sermon on John 15:13', quoted in McCullough, *The Cross of War*, p. 28.

Messianism and Ingratitude

The rhetoric of Scott's Havana speech of 1917 came straight from 1898. To frame the Platt Amendment as just, as I argued above, he resorted to Langdellian legal themes, widespread in the establishment thought of his generation. But the speech and Scott's scholarship in general went further, evoking eschatological themes. Through his numerous works, Scott wove together events like the discovery of the Americas, the Mayflower Compact, the adoption of the United States Constitution, and the Second Hague Peace Conference. Such linear narrative did not only merge science and religion, progress and providence. It also identified international law with the United States: the United States was the chosen nation, the Messiah and the new egalitarian international law was its Word of Salvation.

In the Havana speech, Scott evoked the Christ-like nature of the United States by referring to the self-sacrifice of both the Cuban intervention and the Platt Amendment. The right to intervention was a burden the United States accepted to keep Cuba free. The relations between the two countries ('friendly, confidential and without a trace of suspicion as to the motives of either')[47] set an example towards the global achievement of peace. If all powerful nations, the argument went, would interact through law with the less powerful, like the United States had done with Cuba, rather than exploiting their power to gain advantage, all international controversies would eventually be solved peacefully through adjudication. To reinforce the point Scott resorted to biblical imagery and quoting Christ: 'If we are not our brothers' keeper, we are, or at least we should be, the conservators of the law.... "Inasmuch as ye have done it unto one of the least of these, my brethren, ye have done it unto Me."'[48] For Scott, it was not a question of 'if', but a question of 'when'. Progress was moving from politics to law and the United States was the providential force that would make sure to drive history and civilization further.

Scott's speech refers to events later than 1898 and the adoption of the Platt Amendment, yet it fails to acknowledge the anxieties lived by the American society in consequence of the Spanish–American War. The bloody repression of the rebellion that broke out in 1899 in the Philippines against the United States as colonial power would leave scars. The rebellion was officially quashed in 1902 but hostilities continued for close to a decade in many areas of the archipelago. Congressional hearings and investigative press informed Americans that their army had been using the so-called water cure to extract information on the rebel forces from Filipinos. Important public figures who had reluctantly supported intervention turned into vocal anti-imperialists.[49] The triumphalism did not disappear from American political discourse, but the claim of purity of the motives of the

[47] Scott, 'The Platt Amendment', p. 14. [48] Ibid., p. 39.

[49] One of them was magnate Andrew Carnegie, the man who would generously fund the Carnegie Endowment for International Peace, the powerhouse through which Scott and Root kept their international legal theories influential for a long time after they had been overcome in academia and the American Society of International Law.

American colonial enterprise receded as the new President, Theodore Roosevelt, insisted on his country's military power more than his predecessor did. The succession in the White House and its tragic circumstances[50] marked another symbolic change: McKinley would be the last Civil War veteran to hold the presidential office. The restraint caused by the trauma of the Civil War would leave place to more confident muscular politics.

In this political climate, the United States would occupy Cuba for a second time in 1906, the same year in which Scott and Root would be at the forefront of the foundation of the American Society of International Law. By this time, Cuba had become a nuisance more than a place of world redemption. The United States reluctantly heeded the call of Cuba's political factions, both of which hoped to gain advantages by the American presence. Both President Estrada Palma and the rebelling Liberals forced the hand of the United States,[51] voluntarily creating conditions under which Roosevelt had to intervene. This time the objectives of the intervention were much less ambitious. The main goal was to protect United States investments, primarily in sugar estates and sugar mills, and do so without firing a shot. Roosevelt dispatched to Cuba as provisional governor Secretary of War William Howard Taft. Taft had clear in his mind that a Cuban question would hurt his presidential ambitions. When it was time to find a longer-term solution the choice fell, under the suggestion of Root, now Secretary of State, on Nebraska lawyer Charles E. Magoon, former governor of the Panama Canal Zone. Magoon did what he had to to keep Cuba stable, thereby setting a precedent for future United States policy. He heavily resorted to patronage and gave in to the requests of the Liberals in order to keep them from resorting to arms again, thus creating the conditions for an unfair electoral process. Yet the goal of a quick normalization was achieved and Magoon could leave Cuba in the hands of newly elected President Gomez in January 1909. Cuban political leaders learned their lesson: as long as enough order was maintained they could continue with personalist politics, rigging elections and make large use of public money for patronage purposes. Until the rise of Fulgencio Batista and the military in the early thirties, Cuban politics maintained a semblance of democratic process. Anytime investors felt threatened, the United States government would send to Cuba a reminder in the form of battleships or marines. The bottom line set by the 1906–1909 occupation was that reform and democratic values did not matter to the United States as long as Cuba kept quiet.

Scott not only failed to acknowledge the complications brought to the 1898 narrative by the post-war reality in the United States' discourse: he also ignored the Cuban resistance to it and the subsequent North American accusations of ingratitude. Cuban rebels had been suspicious of the United States' possible motives since before intervention became a concrete possibility. Their fears came true when they

[50] McKinley was shot by an anarchist on 6 September 1901 and would die eight days later. Roosevelt would succeed him being his vice-president, before being elected in his own right in 1904.

[51] Cf. José M. Hernández, *Cuba and the United States: Intervention and Militarism, 1868–1933* (Austin: University of Texas Press, 1993), p. 150.

realized that the United States wanted to keep tight control over the post-war political arrangements. Contrary to the United States' narrative, Cuban rebels believed they would have won the war even without external intervention. Seeing their powerful neighbour sweeping in to reap the fruits of their three-years long fight and then ignore them created resentment. Yet the United States, convinced of its sole merit for ousting Spain and its selfless motives, required gratitude.[52] Lack of appreciation for the United States' sacrifice of lives and resources became entangled with racial themes. 'The realization that the armed ranks of *Cuba Libre* included large numbers of Cubans of color immediately had a sobering effect on American enthusiasm for independence'[53] and dissolved the early parallels between the revolutionary struggles of Cuba and the United States.

Gratitude became the measure of Cuban readiness for self-government. Cubans appeared to North Americans less civilized than initially thought and the ingratitude they showed towards their self-appointed liberators was construed as definite proof that they did not deserve full independence. The New York Times feared 'an irresponsible government of half-breeds'. Governor General Leonard Wood claimed that '[t]he only people who are howling for [self-government] are those whose antecedents and actions demonstrate the impossibility of self-government at present'.[54] When the United States posed the enshrining of the Platt Amendment into the Cuban Constitution as the condition for self-government, Cubans protested that both their war efforts and the official American promise of independence for Cuba in the Teller Amendment had been betrayed. In June 1901, the Cuban Constitutional Convention would accept the Platt Amendment by one vote. Even Tomás Estrada Palma, soon to become the first President of the Cuban Republic and widely considered pro-American, would harshly protest the 'brusque and precipitous manner in which the Platt resolution was imposed'[55] while also remarking the necessity to accept it to express gratitude to the United States.

Once the occupation ended in 1902, commentators in the United States jumped at the chance to present their country as faithful to its promise of Cuban independence and a civilizational mission achieved. Yet, as Leonard Wood had admitted in a letter to Roosevelt, '[t]here is of course, little or no independence left in Cuba under the Platt Amendment'.[56]

[52] For an exploration of this theme see Louis A. Pérez Jr., 'Incurring in a Debt of Gratitude: 1898 and the Moral Sources of United States Hegemony in Cuba', *American Historical Review* 104 (1999): pp. 356–98.

[53] Ibid., p. 365.

[54] The *New York Times*, 1 August 1898: p. 6; Leonard Wood to William McKinley, 6 February 1900, *Elihu Root Papers, Special Correspondence*, Manuscript Division, Library of Congress, Washington, DC, quoted in Pérez, 'Incurring in a Debt of Gratitude', p. 365.

[55] Tomás Estrada Palma to Gonzalo de Quesada, in Gonzalo de Quesada, *Archivo de Gonzalo de Quesada*, vol. 1 (14 March 1901); Havana: Gonzalo de Quesada y Miranda, 1948, pp. 151–2, quoted in Pérez. 'Incurring in a Debt of Gratitude', p. 374.

[56] Leonard Wood to Theodore Roosevelt, 28 October 1901, *Leonard Wood Papers*, Manuscript Division, Library of Congress, Washington, DC, quoted in Pérez, 'Incurring in a Debt of Gratitude', p. 375.

Scott could dismiss events countering his narrative and internal contradictions exactly because he was a man of faith. He believed in the saving power of international law and science, that they were tools of God to bring about the millennium. In front of the workings of providence through history, certified by the evident progress of mankind, embodied by the United States, even major conflicts and contradictions could be considered as bumps on a road to peace otherwise well traced. For Scott the 1906 Second Occupation was a bump in the road of progress; even the still raging First World War was one. Indeed, Scott in Havana was not speaking only about United States–Cuban relationships but also about the post-world war order.

Scott was a Wilsonian in the vague meanings we give to the word today: one who aimed at reforming the world by exporting American values and a believer in international institutions. This does not, however, tell us much about the stakes involved in the United States foreign policy at the end of the First World War. Scott was also, arguably, the staunchest opponent of Wilson's plans on collective security. In that January of 1917, the idea of collective security had already gained traction in foreign policy discourse and overcame the dominance Scott's judicialist plans had previously enjoyed. A few months later, in April, Scott would be challenged for the first time within the ASIL on this point. From then on, Scott would be honoured and remembered as a noble father, but a younger generation would take control of the Society's academic directions. Yet Scott's religious-like belief in American values would prove to be a long-standing feature of subsequent international legal scholarship in the United States even through the years in which the realist critique was at its peak.

Conclusions

The Cuban intervention and the Spanish–American War were crucial to the eventual self-understanding of the United States as the main global player. Now it seems that that role for the United States is coming to an end. Joseph Weiler has called the phenomenon 'the end of the Pax Americana'.[57] As the formula suggests, Weiler has a primarily positive outlook towards the century of American hegemony. While acknowledging the shortcomings and contradictions of the United States' policies over this period, he argues that 'the decline of American global authoritativeness' would necessarily bring about an increased global instability. For Weiler, that means that we risk falling, without even knowing how, into the destructive patterns in place before the American leadership came about. '[S]uddenly one finds oneself in a situation where … a meaningless assassination of a meaningless Archduke, is sufficient to ignite a conflagration serving the values and interests of none.' Even if one does not agree with Weiler's analysis, his final suggestion is to

[57] Joseph H. Weiler, 'Editorial—Sleepwalking Again: The End of the Pax Americana 1914–2014', *European Journal of International Law* 25 (2013): pp. 635–41.

be shared. The fact that the global role of the United States is declining and that it will bring consequences in international relations can hardly be disputed in these general terms. Weiler wants the world not to sleepwalk into this situation, like it did into the First World War, but rather to have a "robust debate" about it.

Weiler suggests it is time to realize, especially for Europeans, that assuming that our security would necessarily be guaranteed by the United States has turned into a self-delusion. Interestingly Weiler, to make this point, compares the United States to a father figure. The world is growing up realizing that the father 'is just not so strong, not so rich, not so right and not so determined. And critically, in a variety of subtle ways, America has discovered that too'. Also the father is growing up, not only the children. One way to address 'the end of the Pax Americana' could be for the father to give up its own self-delusions about its exceptionality and moral standing. This does not necessarily mean giving up belief in certain values and action in their support. It means creating the condition for the 'robust debate'[58] Weiler is calling for. In the aftermath of the Cuban intervention, Root decided what Cubans should desire. Has the father learned yet to ask what the growing children desire first? On the one hand, the newly inaugurated course in the relationship with Cuba could be a sign that the United States is opening up to a new, more complex understanding of itself, more open to different views and dialogue. On the other hand, it could simply be seen as part of the retrenchment of a declining global power.

Bibliography

Amorosa, Paolo. 'James Brown Scott's International Adjudication between Tradition and Progress in the United States'. *Journal of the History of International Law* 17(1) (2015): pp. 15–46.

Bloodworth, Jeffrey. 'For Love or for Money?: William McKinley and the Spanish-American War'. *White House Studies* 9 (2009): pp. 135–57.

Dodge, David Low, and others. *Memorial of Mr. David L. Dodge* (Boston: S. K. Whipple & Co., 1854).

Foner, Eric. *The Story of American Freedom* (New York: W. W. Norton, 1998).

Hernández, José M. *Cuba and the United States: Intervention and Militarism, 1868–1933* (Austin: University of Texas Press, 1993).

Humphreys, Robert Arthur. 'Presidential Address: Anglo-American Rivalries and the Venezuela Crisis of 1895'. *Transactions of the Royal Historical Society* 17 (1967): pp. 131–64.

Janis, Mark. *The American Tradition of International Law: Great Expectations, 1789–1914* (Oxford: Oxford University Press, 2004).

Jessup, Philip C. *Elihu Root*, 2 vols (New York: Dodd, Mead & Company, 1938).

Kahn, Paul W. 'Law of Nations at the Origins', in this volume.

[58] Weiler, 'Sleepwalking Again', pp. 640–1.

Kirgis, Frederic L. Jr. *The American Society of International Law's First Century: 1906–2006* (Leiden: Martinus Nijhoff Publishers, 2006).

Ladd, William. *An Essay on a Congress of Nations* (New York: Oxford University Press—American Branch, 1916 [1840]).

Landauer, Carl. 'The Ambivalences of Power: Launching the American Journal of International Law in an Era of Empire and Globalization'. *Leiden Journal of International Law* 20 (2007): pp. 325–58.

Longfield, Bradley J. *Presbyterians and American Culture: A History* (Louisville: Westminster John Knox Press, 2013).

McCartney, Paul T. *Power and Progress: American National Identity, the War of 1898, and the Rise of American Imperialism* (Baton Rouge: Louisiana State University Press, 2006).

McCullough, Matthew. *The Cross of War: Christian Nationalism and U.S. Expansion in the Spanish–American War* (Madison: The University of Wisconsin Press, 2014).

Ninkovich, Frank. *The United States and Imperialism* (Malden: Blackwell Publishers, 2001)

Pérez, Louis A. Jr. *Cuba in the American Imagination: Metaphor and the Imperial Ethos* (Chapel Hill: University of North Carolina Press, 2008).

Pérez, Louis A. Jr. 'Incurring in a Debt of Gratitude: 1898 and the Moral Sources of United States Hegemony in Cuba'. *American Historical Review* 104 (1999): pp. 356–98.

Preston, Andrew. *Sword of the Spirit, Shield of Faith. Religion in American War and Diplomacy* (New York: Alfred A. Knopf, 2012).

Root, Elihu. 'The Lawyer of Today'. In *Addresses on Government and Citizenship*, collected and edited by Robert Bacon and James Brown Scott (Cambridge: Harvard University Press, 1916), pp. 503–9.

Root, Elihu. *The Military and Colonial Policy of the United States: Speeches and Reports*, collected and edited by Robert Bacon and James Brown Scott (Cambridge: Harvard University Press, 1916).

Root, Elihu. 'The Need of Popular Understanding of International Law'. *American Journal of International Law* 1 (1907): pp. 1–3.

Scott, James Brown. 'The Platt Amendment—Recommendations of Habana Concerning International Organization'. In American Institute of International Law, *The Recommendations of Habana Concerning International Organization. Address and Commentary by James Brown Scott* (New York: Oxford University Press, 1917), pp. 1–79.

Scott, James Brown. 'The Study of the Law'. *The American Law School Review* 2, no. 1 (1906): pp. 1–10.

Scott, James Brown. ed., *Cases on International Law Selected from Decisions of English and American Courts with Syllabus and Annotations* (Boston: Boston Book Company, 1902).

Sewell, Mike. 'Humanitarian Intervention, Democracy, and Imperialism: The American War with Spain, 1898, and After'. In *Humanitarian Intervention: A History*, edited by Brendan Simms and David J. B. Trim (Cambridge: Cambridge University Press, 2011), pp. 303–22.

Weiler, Joseph H. 'Editorial—Sleepwalking Again: The End of the Pax Americana 1914–2014'. *European Journal of International Law* 25 (2013): pp. 635–41.

Zasloff, Jonathan. 'Law and the Shaping of American Foreign Policy: From the Gilded Age to the New Era'. *New York University Law Review* 78 (2003): pp. 239–373.

Index